SO-EKM-726

Here's What the Experts Have to Say About
CALIFORNIA GOLF

For golfers who wonder if the grasses are greener on the other side of the state, (CALIFORNIA GOLF) fits you to a tee.
Escondido Times-Advocate

(These) insightful descriptions of California courses are a must-read for any avid golfer.
Roger Maltbie, Five-time PGA Tour Winner

An excellent reference guide for golf enthusiasts.
Sacramento Bee

An excellent resource book for any golfer who's looking to test his or her skills at a new course.
Golf Today

It's the perfect book not only for the good golfer but the average player as well. It's something every golfer should have.
Julie Inkster,
Three-time U.S. Women's Amateur Champion and LPGA Touring Pro

---

Here's What Readers Have to Say About
CALIFORNIA GOLF

Our typical weekend includes camping, exploring back roads, and trying different golf courses. This book is our bible!
Bob Summers, Walnut Creek

Great book—a wealth of well-researched data!
Pat Falcaro, La Crescenta

Appreciate your women's yardages and slopes.
Mary Jobson, Sonoma

A great book. Will keep in my car for use as I travel around the state.
Bill Page, Coalinga

51695

ISBN 0-935701-16-8

9 780935 701166

To my wife Barbara

CALIFORNIA GOLF

1992-93 Edition

Ray A. March

Foghorn Press Inc.

TABLE OF CONTENTS

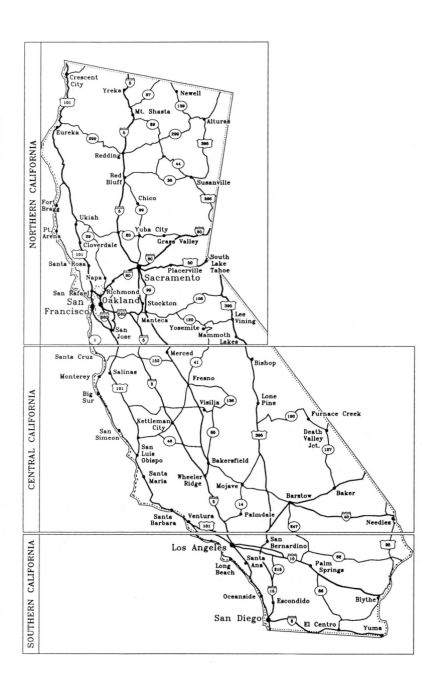

AUTHOR'S FOREWORD
State of Golf in California

AFTER checking out more than 700 golf courses for this book, one thing is apparent: Golf is certainly in good health, but how long does it have to live?

The golf industry in California was running so hard when the 1990-91 recession hit that it barely felt the impact of the collision. Sure, there were courses that saw some golfers brown bagging it or skipping the clubhouse lunch break, or playing nine instead of 18 holes, but for most courses statewide this last summer saw golf as usual.

Which poses the question, Golf may be crazy, but why all the insanity? Consider a few points:

> **—It's typical, especially in the impacted metropolitan areas, that golfers are getting up earlier on weekends than during the work week.**

Why the insanity? The answer, quite simply, is that there are far more golfers than there are golf courses—or as they say in the trade, "The ratio of holes to golfers sucks." That's why so many golfers are driven to sunrise tee times. Given the present supply and demand problem, it only makes sense to beat the rush hour on the first tee.

> **—Membership fees in private clubs are on the increase and more than one semi–private club has closed its doors to the public in the last year.**

It's also common sense that potential club members, unwilling to pay the higher fees, are taking their business to the public courses, which in turn adds playing pressure to an already overloaded system.

—Some so-called public courses have green fees that stretch way beyond the capacity of the average wallet.

As a result, golfers looking for deals tend to drift over to the less expensive courses, which in turn puts additional pressure on the little guy.

—Some courses have eliminated bunkers to speed up play. (Why not just put magnets in the holes and metal cores in golf balls?)

The counter theory is that there still remain some heavy grass undulations that players must navigate, requiring the same skills that it takes to escape a heavily entrenched sand trap.

OK, so, "Golf is going berserk," as one staff member of a large golf association said. The point is that golf, with all its traditions, is too important a sport and a business to let slide into an anarchy of quick-fix solutions. More golf courses would help. The 146,000-member Southern California Golf Association, for instance, would like to build two courses at Diamond Bar. But that project has been in the planning stage for more than five years. Most recently, negotiations were over an access road. Then, of course, there is a lengthy permitting process for the course still ahead. And for better or worse, scenarios such as this are common throughout the state.

The Links at Spanish Bay was on the drawing boards for 20 years—including the permit procedure—before it opened to a long waiting list five years ago.

The Northern California Golf Association, luckily, owns Poppy Hills and that's a recruitment enticement for an association that already numbers an estimated 140,000. It's now looking at purchasing Mather Golf Course as something of a smart investment, if not a band-aid cure. If the deal goes through, the NCGA plans to expand the AFB layout to 36 holes.

Other possible solutions to reducing the pressure on overcrowded courses are more severe. When rounds take five to six hours to play they leave the lingering but logical questions of how to speed up play. Unfortunately, the questions are there; it's the answers golfers are looking for.

—Should there be a verified handicap system or a similar method for establishing an ability to play a given course on a busy weekend?

—Will there be more nine-hole play?

—How about playing the back nine first, perhaps at sunrise?

—Should future golf courses be designed to make play easier, and therefore faster?

Granted, no one is willing to suggest, for the time being, that restrictive measures be taken to answer the problem of supply and demand, but everyone in the sport knows that eventually the answers must come.

Indeed, this is a predicament other sports would just love to be in. Got any answers?

--Ray A. March
September, 1991

PEBBLE BEACH
The Crown Jewel

S INCE it opened to rave reviews on Washington's Birthday in 1919, Pebble Beach Golf Links has always been the talk of the golfing world, but at no period in its history has there been more discussion—and speculation—about this great course than currently.

The reason for the attention is logical: Pebble Beach, mecca to the golfing public for more than 70 years, may soon become a private club with limited public play.

The controversy over a public vs. private Pebble Beach is now deeply entrenched in the public agency process, and as of late 1991, settlement talks between the new owners of the Pebble Beach Company, the Monterey County Board of Supervisors and the California Coastal Commission seem to assure that tee times for the public will be guaranteed, at least for the time being.

A quick primer on what has transpired at Pebble Beach:

In September, 1990, the Chicago-based real estate partnership of Miller, Klutznick, Davis & Gray sold all its interests in the Pebble Beach Company to Minoru Isutani of Japan for an estimated $835 million. The package included not only the Pebble Beach Golf Links, but also The Links at Spanish Bay, Spyglass Hill Golf Course and Old Del Monte. And that's only the golf side of the purchase.

Isutani already owned two golf-related affiliates, Cosmo World and Ben Hogan Property Companies I and II. The Ben Hogan subsidiary became the management overseer. In order to finance the purchase, it was rumored that memberships in a "Pebble Beach

National Club" ranging anywhere from US$150,000 to US$740,000 would be sold in Japan.

Under an extremely complex re-financing plan, the Isutani's purchase was re–structured and in March, 1991, the Mitsubishi Trust and Banking Company of Tokyo gained a majority owner-ship. Isutani became a minority holder.

For now the center of attention is Pebble Beach Golf Links, but if the Pebble Beach National Club is realized, and a compromise is reached between the owners of Pebble Beach and the public agen-cies, membership will include the Spyglass Hill Golf Course, the Links at Spanish Bay, and Old Del Monte—courses that now are either semi-private or public. There is no indication, however, that public play will be restricted at those courses.

If you have never played Pebble Beach, or even if you have, it's a good idea to have a feeling for the course. Pebble Beach Golf Links was the idea of S.F.B. Morse, founder of Del Monte Proper-ties Company back in 1919. His dream was to create a course on land fronting Carmel Bay and the ocean. For his architect, he hired Jack Neville, an amateur golfer with considerable credentials as a player. He had, however, never designed a golf course.

At the time, Neville had won the coveted California State Ama-teur Championship three times, and he was to go on to win it a total of five times, plus playing on the winning 1923 U.S. Walker Cup team. With the help of Douglas Grant—who did the bunkering—Neville designed what became known as one of the world's most distinguished tests of championship golf.

Jack Nicklaus, winner of the U.S. Amateur and the U.S. Open at Pebble Beach, once said, "If I had only one more round of golf to play, I would choose to play it at Pebble Beach. My hat is off to the two men who designed Pebble—they did everything right. After all these years with no major revisions Pebble Beach still stands up. It's a superb championship test."

Deceptive in its early holes, Pebble Beach gives the impression that it's easily conquered, but any golfer who believes that is in for a long day. This design of the course runs so closely to the Pacific

Ocean that during the winter months the waves at the 18th crash over the sea wall and onto the fairway.

You need long, accurate shots and unwavering concentration to succeed at Pebble. Eight holes run beside the ocean, which is directly or indirectly in play at all times. With the ocean at your elbow, it's easy to be intimidated into a slice or hook (the ocean is present coming and going), but most importantly the greens slope toward the ocean. Bluffs and cliffs dominate the right side going out, and they reappear at the finish for the 17th and 18th. To stray on either of these final holes is to be severely punished.

The inland holes are considered the siren's enticement, giving no hint of the terrors to follow. After the fifth, the course only gets tougher and over the years it has drawn varying comments from those who have challenged it.

Lee Trevino once quipped with the gallery as he stood on the forbidding sixth tee, "If you're five over when you hit this tee it's the best place in the world to commit suicide." Trevino knew that ahead of him lay the toughest four-hole sequence in golf.

Pebble has become a regular tournament venue, and has hosted various major championships. In addition to the 1992 U.S. Open, both the 1972 and 1982 U.S. Opens were held here. Three U.S. Men's Amateurs (1929, 1947 and 1961) and two U.S. Women's Amateurs (1940 and 1948) were staged at Pebble. The 1977 PGA Championship was played at Pebble, and of course, the Bing Crosby National Pro-Am (now the AT&T Pebble Beach National Pro-Am) has been at home here since 1947.

Dave Marr, the former PGA champion and now ABC's color commentator, first played Pebble Beach back in 1957. His first impressions of Pebble Beach speak for all golfers.

"I was stunned," he said. "There is nothing like it. As a golfer, my career wouldn't be complete without knowing the beauty and the grandeur of Pebble Beach."

Hopefully, Marr's is a sentiment that many will be able to share via a public Pebble Beach for many, many years to come.

PREPPING PEBBLE for the U.S. Open
by Jack Nicklaus

Editor's note: Now under new ownership, Pebble Beach Company has made a considerable investment and commitment to assuring that Pebble Beach Golf Links will be in prime condition—not only for the 1992 U.S. Open which will be played there, but for the future as well. In this light, they hired Jack Nicklaus to take stock of the course and restore it to its original condition. We asked Nicklaus to share his thoughts on this prestigious undertaking with us.

AS Pebble Beach readies for the 1992 U.S. Open, I've been asked to make my recommendations on how the course can be efficiently returned to its original design.

The layout of the course has easily survived the test of time, and after more than 70 years of tournament and pleasure play, it remains one of the great golf courses of the world. Without question, Jack Neville and Douglas Grant, the two men responsible for Pebble back in 1919, are to be praised for creating such an exciting and endurable golf course.

It would seem then, that Pebble has escaped the normal aging process that takes place with the passage of time. Unfortunately that isn't the case. In fact, golf course design goes far beyond the configuration of the hole-by-hole layout, and in some important ways Pebble Beach *has* seen some evolution.

Greens and bunkers, two extremely important design elements at Pebble, gradually changed their shape and their precise location. Over the years, little particles of sand, blasted onto the greens, eventually build up, changing the size of the greens and the bunkers. On a day to day basis, the sand built-up is imperceptible, but by comparing a green's current size to what it was in an earlier period, the difference can be surprisingly significant.

For accurate information on the greens, two forms of research have been used: one new and one old.

Thanks to modern technology, we have determined the shapes of earlier greens by taking soil probes from the perimeter of the greens. An analysis of these soil mixes revealed the exact location, shape and size of the earlier greens. These findings were supported by observing *poa annua* and creeping bentgrass that would typically be in the greens rather than in the current collars or immediate rough.

We also relied on traditional detective tricks: We looked at old photographs from the Pebble Beach archives. By studying early pictures of the course we were able to compare what the photographer saw then to what we see now.

Based on our research, the following restorative changes will have been made well in advance of the U.S. Open. Hole-by-hole:

—The greens at one, four, five, six, seven, eight, nine, 10, 11 and 12 have been completely rebuilt or restored to their original size and shape, including an innovative soil heating system for number five because it's in shade much of the time. All greens are poa annua. (It's interesting to note that Jack Neville designed the greens even smaller than was the fashion back in 1919 because he wanted to reward the long iron hitter. It was his opinion that long irons took the most skill and a golfer who could hit a tight target should be rewarded).

—Because most of the greens have been returned to their original size, there is now a greater choice of pin placement. This means less wear on the green and more options for increasing the difficulty of the hole.

—Number three hole has been lengthened 15 yards by repositioning the championship tee.

—A total of 12 tees (one through five, seven through 12, and 17) were either rebuilt, reseeded or resurfaced. Sometimes there were combinations of changes at the tees, including enlarging some.

—Kikuyu grass was eradicated from virtually every fairway. All fairways and tees were reseeded in perennial rye grass.

—All bunkers now conform to a links style and appearance that is expected of an oceanside golf course. Over time they had become too formal.

The overall result has not been "change," but rather a polishing of a rare and valuable gem. There is nothing at Pebble Beach that wasn't there originally. After nearly two years of research and restoration, Pebble Beach is in prime condition, and when the first round of the 1992 U.S. Open is played on June 15 it will be its old self—tough, rugged and unforgiving.

DESIGNING SPANISH BAY
A Walk with the Masters

I N 1986, when plans for a new course within the golf-sacred confines of Pebble Beach were finally approved, after decades of discussion and argument at the state, county and community levels, the golf world was elated. One of the most revered locations in the world was now poised to deliver yet another gem to which golfers would flock, drawn by the mystique of Pebble Beach, yet also ready to witness and take on what may very well be the last course built along the embattled California coastline—The Links at Spanish Bay.

Similarly, the choice of the design team was eagerly awaited, and when it was announced that Robert Trent Jones, Jr.—along with Tom Watson and Frank "Sandy" Tatum—had been awarded the honor of designing Spanish Bay, they found themselves in the golf world's spotlight: What would they do with the 195 acres of prime Pebble Beach real estate which had been entrusted to their creativity?

They are men of letters in the science of golf, to be sure. They come from distinctly different backgrounds and experiences, but they bring with them an extraordinary repository of golfing knowledge. To summarize their credentials:

Watson: 1982 U.S. Open champion, five-time British Open winner, twice U.S. Masters champion, 1977 and 1978 Pebble Beach National Pro-Am victor. A four-time Ryder Cup representative, in 1988 Watson was elected to the PGA World Golf Hall of Fame.

Jones: Golf course architect, designer of more than 100 courses on five continents, including Poppy Hills, also at Pebble Beach.

Tatum: The consummate amateur golfer, past president of the United States Golf Association.

It was a threesome united for the first time when Jones put in his six million dollar bid for designing and building the course at Spanish Bay. It was his theory that with Watson's obvious success on windy British courses and Tatum's guardianship approach to pure and challenging golf that the three could create an incomparable linksland course in the golfing tradition of England, Scotland and Ireland.

Historically, when golf took hold in the United States, it became a hitter's game in which obstacles were conquered by clearing them in the air, rather than on the ground. Linksland golf—a practical concept of using rolling, windswept land—became a rarity.

With the 6,870-yard-long Links at Spanish Bay, Jones, Watson and Tatum took it upon themselves to resurrect the "aulde worlde" linksland golfing concept. During the design process, the three men periodically toured their emerging links together, taking a "committee" approach to evaluating its progress. The following tour took place on November 25, 1986, when portions of the course were still being graded or seeded, while other holes were actually playable. All three men had arrived the previous day, with Jones coming in from Australia, Watson from Japan and Tatum from his law offices in San Francisco.

12th Tee Box

We meet up with Jones, Watson and Tatum at the 12th, a par-4 hole that was to play 410 yards from the championship tee. They have just started walking the course. With them is Al Tikkanten of Greenscape, the course contractor. For 14 years he has been Jones' right-hand man at job sites.

Watson is holding a white sketch pad and waving a pencil over it from time to time. Jones and Tatum are standing on a mound that will become the back tee. They're looking down a stretch of dirt and tractor tracks that will soon be transformed into a long, left-sloping fairway with a bunker at its left midriff. They're dressed casually in slacks and polo shirts. Watson is wearing a yellow sweater and white jogging-type shoes. He has that boy-next-door look. Jones, a roundish man, sports a new blue visor. Tatum, with solid silver hair, is erect and thin, the taller and older of the three. To the unsuspecting, they could pass for three guys looking to fill out a foursome at the local country club. Watson hands the sketch pad to Jones.

> **WATSON: "This is the way I see it."**
>
> **JONES: "I see it just the reverse."**
>
> **WATSON: "I don't think it's necessary to tell a person he has to hit it here (pointing)."**
>
> **TATUM: "Either one is fine with me."**

Watson explains his sketch to Jones and Tatum, stressing his concern that the left side of the fairway will be built up too much. Jones makes his own additions to Watson's drawing as Tatum looks on.

> **TATUM: "We should make sure the player knows there's a bunker there. He doesn't have to see it all."**
>
> **JONES: I want to see him hit a straight shot. I'm not sure a long fade will hit the bunker."**

The three debate the virtues of a blind bunker versus a visible one. Jones agrees with Tatum that the bunker should not be blind. Watson says it should be below the level of the fairway. Jones suggests "setting it up from the tee" so it can be seen. Watson agrees and the three compromise on the placement of the bunker.

12th Fairway about 270 Yards Out

Watson goes directly to the spot on the fairway that he had sketched for Jones and Tatum. He stands looking at the placement of the green in the distance.

> **WATSON: "You can knock it right onto it."**
>
> **JONES: (laughing) "You would, but what about the rest of us mere mortals?"**

Jones turns back to look at the tee behind him, then up to the green and says he likes Watson's concept of the fairway layout better after a closer look. Tatum remains firm.

TATUM: "You don't need to make the hole that severe."

WATSON: "I think you do."

They discuss the merits of the bunker further and eventually compromise. There will be a partial view of the bunker from the tee. The fairway debate seems an exercise in choice of words, rather than views, and the conversation, between holes, switches to speculation on whether any members of then-President Ronald Reagan's cabinet will resign over the secret sale of arms to Iran. No one ventures a guess.

13th Hole

The course makes a turn at the 12th green, coming out of the woods and facing a downhill view of Spanish Bay and the Pacific Ocean in the distance. The 14th fairway, already in the fescue grass native to Scotland and Ireland, casts a lush green against the blues of the water beyond. The contrast is unexpected and the view is riveting.

WATSON: "Whoa!"

JONES: "Fabulous!"

TATUM: "It's something! The whole scene is so sensational."

Immediately in front is the target hole 13th, an inviting landing zone merely 100 yards out from the regular tee. But like the seventh at Pebble Beach, its postage stamp size green will play tougher than it looks. There are a couple of scrawny, juvenile pine trees just above an elongated green that runs away from the hitter. The three share concern over the trees eventually blocking the view, but they rationalize they also may screen a set of condos to be built in the background. Tatum suggests that a gallery mound could replace the trees and Watson recommends more natural sand dunes. They defer to Tikkanten, asking him to check out the exact condo location.

Tikkanten seems to be the mediator, or sounding board for the threesome. Jones, in particular, asks him frequent questions about earth moving, re-shaping greens and grading fairways. Once, in a side comment, Tikkanten quoted Jones on the subject of building a golf course: "You take all the theory and put it on the ground."

They leave the 13th and head for the 14th fairway, but not without a last salute to the shortest par-3 on the course.

JONES: "Great little hole."

WATSON: "Yep."

Watson is not overly chatty, but when he talks he loses the "aw shucks" look about him and comes to the point. Both he and Tatum are thoughtful and perceptive in their observations. It is apparent they have a feeling for what they want and they are, in their ways, adamant about their ideas. Still, it is Jones who supplies the technical knowledge that answers the overriding question, "Will it work?"

The 14th at Mid-fairway

TATUM: "I think it's sensational."

JONES: "Fabulous."

TATUM: "Makes you want to play."

WATSON: "Let's go get our clubs."

The 18th Green

They short-cut to the 18th green, skipping numbers 15, 16 and 17, which are already playable and not part of this inspection tour. The green of the 18th is a deceitful expanse of 7,500 square feet, forming an irregular circle that encompasses an uphill climb to a protecting dune in the back. It has recently been seeded and a sprinkler system is fanning a mist over it and little green sprouts are showing. Watson is by himself, walking around the edges of the green and looking at it from all angles.

JONES: "We call this 'Watson's Wonder.' This is a great hole—a great finishing hole."

Tatum has momentarily left to get a sweater. He'll catch up with the group at the 10th green. Watson is alone at the green he masterminded. Lost in thought, he lingers, steps away from the green, then stops and looks back at it again. He's asked if he can relate to this course the way he did in winning five British Open championships at a record five different courses.

> WATSON: "Yep. I sure can. That's what we wanted."

Until now, Watson has been rationing his words, saving his opinions and thoughts for Jones and Tatum, but now, instead of reminiscing about his British Open triumphs, Watson talks about the months and years spent getting approvals for the construction of Spanish Bay and of the concept of the course's design—a linksland layout where a long roll of the ball is better than an astronautical shot. When he relaxes, he's engaging and inquisitive and the boy-next-door charm that goes with his looks emerges again. But he's soon back to business at the 10th green.

10th Green

Watson sizes up the 10th green like he was going for all the money at the 1982 U.S. Open. In fact, during the entire tour he does not walk the course—he stalks it. While Jones and Tatum stroll, Watson attacks. Now, at the 10th green, he squats down, tournament style and eyeballs the undulating slopes and runs in front of him. Then he suggests carrying the right hand slope into the green. Tatum is back with a dark blue sweater draped over his lean shoulders, covering the back of his neck and the green windbreaker he's been wearing.

> WATSON: "That's what looks natural to me. The toughest putt of all is the one that has to go up and over and then down."
>
> JONES: "Yes."

Tatum is like the college professor who is willing to help instead of dragging the student painfully to some obvious conclusions. He enjoys seeing the entire concept of the course like a huge painting and he can easily relate the parts to the whole.

> TATUM: "This hole tells you a lot about the course. There's reward and risk. One feature is that from the tee you will be able to understand the hole. This hole demonstrates the basic philosophical approach to carrying out the design of the course."

Jones is much like a genial host. Since the tour began, he's everywhere; simultaneously listening to Watson and Tatum, talking with Tikkanten and tending to details. He's worried about some drainage and he wants to see a mound of dirt reduced in size.

> **JONES: "From a purely aesthetic point of view that big lump of dirt should go way down. It should look like the sand blew up and then fell down like a wave."**

At the Sixth Green and Fairway

The green has recently been seeded and everybody gingerly skirts the apron. Jones admits to Watson and Tatum that initially he didn't like their ideas for this par-4 hole, but now that he sees it in a more finished condition he's changed his mind. From the regular tees it runs 345 yards with a dogleg right down the stretch.

> **JONES: "This is a hard golf hole. It will play longer than it looks."**

Jones jokes about what he calls "Tatum's Trap" in the middle of the fairway, and says Tatum hasn't "signed off" on this hole yet. Watson picks up on Jones' ribbing Tatum. Seems that on a previous tour of the course Watson hit some tee shots off the sixth to test the distance of the bunker and its effectiveness.

> **WATSON: "We put a bunker out there thinking somebody could reach it, but nobody can. I couldn't carry it, but I got to it."**
>
> **TATUM: "He was using a graphite shaft, aluminum head and wearing tennis shoes!"**
>
> **JONES: "That should have made the ball go farther!"**

In an aside, Jones explains that the bunkers give a littered look to the course like in Scotland and that's the purpose of the design. Tikkanten laughs, "It gives me fits sometimes trying to figure out what's going on."

As we walk toward the fifth, Jones talks about his method of veneering white sand on the natural mounds, saying "it's man's vision of what nature would do." Then the subject changes to a magazine article that quoted his interest in the French existential author Albert Camus. Jones pronounces *The Stranger* in French as he stops on a small rise and looks back at the sixth fairway littered with bunkers.

> **JONES: "This is existential. You know your ball is going to die somewhere so you might as well keep living and playing."**

Off in the northern distance, around the curve of Monterey Bay, you can hear big guns firing at the Fort Ord army center. Jones pauses to listen then he continues discussing the principles and theme of replicating nature. Existentialism, for Jones, need not be restricted to literature; it's here on the golf course as well. He points to a marsh nestled near the eighth tee across Spanish Bay Road that will be a natural hazard. With its resting birds and swaying reeds, the marsh looks like its been there forever and the golf course had passed around it instead of being constructed from a previous low, wet drainage area. The doctrine of emphasizing man's responsibility for making his own nature as well as the importance of personal freedom comes to life at the marsh.

> **JONES: "It's wild, not refined."**

The Fifth

At about 470 yards this is considered the strongest par-4 on the course. Jones points out it plays into prevailing winds and there's a slope leading into a funnel bunker. Drawing a comparison to the 17th at Saint Andrews, he calls it a "road hole."

> **JONES: "You're in a road if you attack it."**
>
> **WATSON: "I'm not crazy about the narrowness of the fairway. The bunkers should be put farther left."**
>
> **JONES: "It's a tough hole."**
>
> **WATSON: "Damn right it is."**

At the Third Green

Jones is concerned about the drainage around the green and Watson wonders about the design of the contour. Tatum wants to know how difficult any changes might be. Tikkanten, somehow, files it all away. By now the sun is dropping close to the horizon, keeping well south at this time of year, and the threesome begins to pick up the pace, limiting their time at each stop.

WATSON: "I don't think the green is big enough. It needs a stronger contour (otherwise) you'd have a bowl effect here and a bowl effect there. I'd like to see a definite demarcation."

Fourth Tee

JONES: "The dunes in front block the majestic dunes in back."

Second Hole Landing Area

WATSON: "You're going to have five million divots here. Flatten the son-of-a-bitch out. You can't ask a guy to hit over there."

JONES: "We're running out of light."

TIKKANTEN: "Yeah, we missed the sunset on number one; it's fantastic."

First Hole and Fairway

This hole is obviously a favorite of Tatum's and Jones good-naturedly jokes about the inclusion of a yet-to-be constructed marsh in the fairway fronting the green.

JONES: "That's 'Tatum's Marsh."

TATUM: "I'll take credit for that. A big hitter has to carry the marsh, otherwise he has to go to the left. But the farther left he goes, the tougher it gets. There's drama. The hole unfolds with each shot. It's certainly unusual in its drama and its beauty. It's a perfect introduction to the golf course."

JONES: "There's a lot of work to be done, it's not finished. There's a slight slope and crown to get rid of."

The sun is down by now, just to the south of the first hole, but there was a hint of what Tikkanten had said—it must have been fantastic. Briefly, talk turns to the future of the course, a course almost surely destined to be rated higher than its par 72. Will it some day be added to the list of great courses like Pebble Beach and Spyglass Hill? Will the strength of the course be tested in tournaments such as the AT&T Pebble Beach Pro-Am or a USGA championship? Watson said he preferred to reserve his opinion until after the course was finished, but Jones, and particularly Tatum, were optimistic.

> **TATUM: "Our objective is to create a *great* golf course. We've given it everything we can in an effort to produce the best we can. If we succeed, you bet it would be a very substantial addition to the AT&T, and I would hope to see a USGA championship here. It's going to be a very distinctive course—without question."**
>
> **JONES: "It's my hope that it will hold championships so the best players can be tested by one of the best courses in the nation. Certainly it's different. It's unique in its own way, but it's in a setting with other great golf courses and therefore it should attract championships—as it will attract players who want to be challenged in a new way."**

In January, 1988, The Links at Spanish Bay opened with great public fanfare and an enthusiastic critical response. Later that same year, it was voted as the best new resort course of the year by *Golf Digest*. For now, though, Spanish Bay will go untested by the level of golf that a major tournament would bring. The course is undergoing a maturation process that is expected to continue for another two years. Because of this, Pebble Beach Company has no foreseeable plans to host a galleried tournament at its newest course.

Still, there is no question that Spanish Bay, along the magnificent Pebble Beach coastline, is among California's top courses—and in the minds of many, it will become one of the top resort courses in the country as it matures.

PGA WEST

Southern California's Diabolical Best
by Mark Soltau

WHAT'S it like to play golf on the moon? It's simple to find out. Just pack up the clubs and head to the Stadium Course at PGA West in La Quinta. It will cost less—only slightly—but the ride could be just as bumpy.

Difficulty-wise, PGA West is the highest-rated course in the state (77.1). In 1986, the PGA Tour used the course for the Bob Hope Classic. Unfortunately for the players, the weather was unseasonably cold and rainy, resulting in scores that looked like they belonged more to the senior ladies 18-hole group.

Naturally, players weren't amused. Although spectators loved seeing the pros struggle like weekend hackers, the players complained so much that the course was removed from the rotation and hasn't been used since.

This unique creation was designed by Florida architect Pete Dye, who is noted for his originality. His forte is stadium (amphitheater) courses and he built the diabolical Tournament Players Club in Ponte Vedra, Florida, site of the PGA Tour's Players Championship.

PGA West has many of the same characteristics as the Tournament Players Club, including an island green, railroad ties and enough rocks to make Fred Flintstone envious. The greens are roughly the size of Texas and have enough undulations to bury several elephants. Golfers have been known to disappear. It's loaded with crater-sized grass and sand bunkers, the kind that require ladders to get out of them. This is not to suggest the course is unfair, although you'll probably need a stiff drink or a psychiatric appointment upon completion of your round.

Like any difficult tract, home-course knowledge helps tremendously. Until you learn the course, play smart and save yourself time and golf balls. There are places you simply cannot hit the ball. and if you do hit there, simply reload and save yourself the aggravation. You can thank me later.

Most holes offer two alternatives: the safe route and the gamblers route. As Clint Eastwood said: "Do you feel lucky?" Sure, you can save yardage by taking shortcuts. But if you fail, deep bunkers, boulders, sand and water await. Three of the four par-3s require lengthy carries over water. Plan on making several deposits (golf balls) during the round.

My personal favorite is the par-5 16th hole, which features a cavernous bunker down the entire left side. Miss the green to the left and you'll need a chair lift to get back up the hill. A 19-foot-deep greenside bunker has walls that are taller than a double-decker bus and not nearly as friendly.

Having survived that, turn your attention to the par-3 17th, a truly horrifying experience. It's a downhill shot to an island green. Depending on which tees you use, the hole calls for anything from a 6-iron to a wedge. No matter where you play from, the shot will get your adrenalin flowing. Hit the green and your round has been a success. Lee Trevino scored a hole-in-one here during the annual Skins Game and earned megabucks. Most players are happy just to stay dry.

In case I've given you the idea PGA West should be renamed "Masochist Country Club," think again. Yes, it will drive you crazy. It will also titillate your socks off. Patience, a sense of humor and extra golf balls are the key to an enjoyable round. Yes, it's an unforgiving course. It's also imaginative, exhilarating and fun. Frankly, there is nothing else like it. Just remember to keep smiling. After all, you could be doing this for a living.

Northern California Golf Courses

NORTHERN CALIFORNIA COURSES

The golf courses of Northern California are remarkable for the sheer diversity of their landscape. In the upper reaches of the state, near Crescent City and the border with Oregon, are courses which play through huge stands of ancient redwoods, subject to eerie winter mists and rain—a most unusual atmosphere for golf!

Then, over near Klamath River, you can play golf and then cast off into one of the best fly-fishing rivers in the West.

You can play a relaxed game of golf in a place you've probably never heard of—like Weaverville, Montague, and Fall River Mills—and then tell all your friends about one of the best-kept golfing secrets in the state.

On the other hand, as you enter the more heavily-traveled resort areas, such as Napa, you can find courses of unexcelled manicure and hotels with decided panache.

Of course the San Francisco Bay area boasts the prestigious Presidio, Olympic, San Francisco, and Burlingame golf clubs, tracts with more than an abundance of history, who count the movers and shakers of Northern California among their members today as they have for generations.

That's not to say that public golf is not popular or good—it is. In our reader's ballots for the best courses in the state (see Populist Poll, page 588), public access layouts such as Arbuckle, Graeagle, Edgewood (Tahoe), and Ancil Hoffman (near Sacramento) received abundant and enthusiastic support.

Sierra courses, though not open year-round because of weather, are among the most scenic courses in the world—and they can challenge you severely with their slopes and lies.

In all, it is fair to say that the courses of Northern California operate at a far more relaxed pace than many of the more impacted courses you'll find in other parts of the state. Combine that with the fact that many Northern California courses offer entirely affordable tee times, as well, and a golf excursion through the north becomes quite an attractive proposition.

NOR-CAL BY AREA
(MAP, COURSES, PAGES)

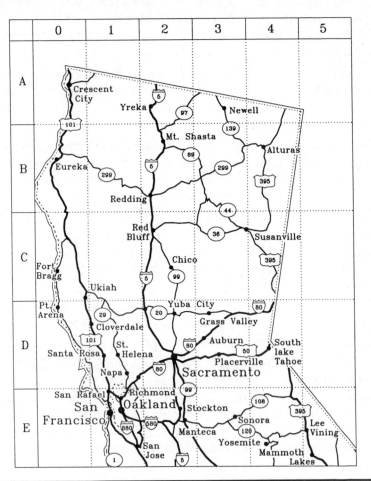

NOR-CAL BY CITY
(CITY and MAP PAGE)

NORTHERN

MAP AO
(2 COURSES)

PAGES.......36-37

NOR-3CAL MAP ..see page 34
adjoining maps
NORTH ....no map
EAST ....no map
SOUTH (B0) ....see page 44
WEST ....no map

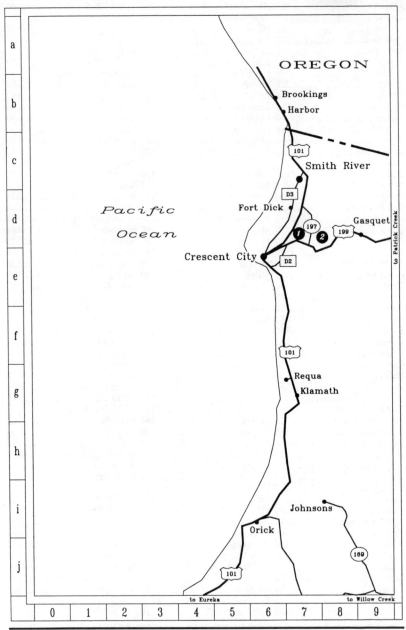

KINGS VALLEY GOLF COURSE

1965

Course information: This public course has nine holes. Par is 56 for 18 holes. The course is 2,564 yards and rated 51.8 from the regular tees. The slope rating is 70. Women's tees are 2,564 yards and rated 54.1 from the forward tees. The slope rating is 77.

Play policy and fees: Green fees are $7 on weekdays and $8 on weekends. There are no power carts.

Location: From Highway 101 in Crescent City, drive east on Highway 199 to Kings Valley Road North. Turn left on Lesina Road and follow it to the course. The course is 18 miles south of the Oregon line.

Course description: Situated in a country setting, this short course is flat with only two par-4. It's a good course for the average player. Redwoods abound and it's walkable. The men's course record is 49, held by Jim Bantrup and the women's record is 58, held by Phyllis Hall.

3030 Lesina Road
Crescent City, CA 95531
Pro shop   (707) 464-2886

- ■ driving range
- ■ practice greens
- □ power carts
- ■ pull carts
- ■ golf club rental
- □ locker rooms
- □ showers
- □ executive course
- □ accommodations
- ■ food and beverages
- ■ clubhouse

Keith Fields
Owner/Manager
Scott Fields
Superintendent

DEL NORTE GOLF COURSE

Course information: This semi-private course has nine holes. Par is 71 for 18 holes. The course is 5,849 yards and rated 66.5 from the regular tees. The slope rating is 106. Women's tees are 5,849 yards and rated 74.0 from the forward tees. The slope rating is 124.

Play policy and fees: Outside play is accepted. Green fees are $13 weekdays and $15 weekends. Carts are $15. Reservations are recommended one day in advance.

Location: From Highway 101 in Crescent City, drive east across the Smith River on Highway 199. Turn right on Club Drive and head north to the course.

Course description: This course is mostly flat with trees and ditches coming into play. The par-4, 420-yard fourth hole has a blind tee shot over a hill onto a narrow fairway that doglegs right.

130 Club Drive
Crescent City, CA 95531
Pro shop   (707) 458-3214

- ■ driving range
- ■ practice greens
- ■ power carts
- ■ pull carts
- ■ golf club rental
- □ locker rooms
- □ showers
- □ executive course
- □ accommodations
- ■ food and beverages
- ■ clubhouse

Owen Westbrook
Manager

MAP A2
(4 COURSES)

PAGES.......38-41

NOR-CAL MAP....................34
adjoining maps
NORTH ....no map
EAST (A3)............see page 42
SOUTH (B2) ....see page 52
WEST ....no map

EAGLES NEST GOLF COURSE

1971

Course information: This public course has nine holes. Par is 64 for 18 holes. The course is 3,724 yards and rated 58.7 from the regular tees. The slope rating is 96. Women's tees are 3,634 yards and rated 61.1. The slope rating is 99.

Play policy and fees: Green fees are $7.50 weekdays and $10 weekends.

Location: From Yreka, drive eight miles north on Interstate 5. Take Highway 96 west to the city of Klamath River. On the east side of town, take the Lockhaven exit south across the Klamath River to Klamath River Road. The course is on the right.

Course description: This course has lots of trees and is flat except for one big hill. Players must keep the ball on the fairway to score well.

22112 Klamath River Road
Klamath River, CA 96050

Pro shop (916) 465-2424

- ☐ driving range
- ■ practice greens
- ☐ power carts
- ■ pull carts
- ☐ golf club rental
- ☐ locker rooms
- ☐ showers
- ☐ executive course
- ☐ accommodations
- ☐ food and beverages
- ☐ clubhouse

NORTHERN A2

Nuno Bonnano
Manager

Melven Rocco
Superintendent

SHASTA VALLEY GOLF COURSE

Course information: This public course has nine holes. Par is 36 for nine holes. The course is 6,280 yards for 18 holes and rated 67.7 from the regular tees. The slope rating is 110. Women's tees are 5,468 yards and rated 69.4 from the regular tees. The slope rating is 105.

Play policy and fees: Green fees are $6 for nine holes and $10 for 18 holes weekdays, and $7 for nine holes and $12 for 18 holes weekends. Carts are $8 for nine holes and $16 for 18 holes. Shirts and shoes must be worn in the clubhouse.

Location: From Interstate 5 in Yreka, drive east on Highway 3 to Montague. Exit south onto Golf Course Road.

Course description: There's a lot of water to contend with on this short course, so there's a premium on accuracy. The course is the home of the Yreka City Golf Tournament, which takes place in September. The men's course record is 68, set in 1979 by host pro Paul Kirchen and tied by Darien Tucker in 1991, and the women's record is 72.

500 Golf Course Road
Montague, CA 96064

Pro shop (916) 842-2302

- ■ driving range
- ■ practice greens
- ■ power carts
- ■ pull carts
- ■ golf club rental
- ☐ locker rooms
- ☐ showers
- ☐ executive course
- ☐ accommodations
- ■ food and beverages
- ■ clubhouse

Paul Kirchen
Professional

John Howe
Manager

WEED GOLF COURSE

1929

Course information: This semi-private course has nine holes. Par is 70 for 18 holes. The course is 5,469 yards for 18 holes and rated 66.5 from the regular tees. The slope rating is 105. Women's tees are 4,812 yards and rated 68.0. The slope rating is 113.

Play policy and fees: Outside play is accepted. Summer green fees are $12 for nine holes and $15 for 18 holes on weekdays, and $14 for nine holes and $17 for 18 holes weekends. After 3 p.m. green fees are $8 for unlimited play. Carts are $10 for nine holes and $15 for 18 holes. Shoes and shirts must be worn. The course is open year-round depending on weather conditions.

Location: From Weed, drive one half mile north on Interstate 5. Take the North Weed exit. You will run right into the golf course.

Course description: This rolling course, bordered by trees and a creek, has magnificent views of Mount Shasta and the Eddy Mountains. The greens are fast and water comes into play on four of the nine holes. The first hole, a tricky, 327-yard par-4, doglegs left and tests players from the very start. The course is the site of the Siskiyou Open Invitational each August. The men's course record is 62.

PO Box 204
Weed, CA 96094

27730 Old Edgewood Road
Weed, CA 96094

Pro shop   (916) 938-9971
Clubhouse (916) 235-2640

□ driving range
■ practice greens
■ power carts
■ pull carts
■ golf club rental
□ locker rooms
□ showers
□ executive course
□ accommodations
■ food and beverages
■ clubhouse

Dixie Nehring
Manager

Donald Nehring
Superintendent

LAKE SHASTINA
GOLF COURSE

1 9 7 3
Robert Trent Jones, Jr.

Course information: This resort course has 27 holes. Par is 72 for 18 holes. There are two courses. One is a short, nine-hole Scottish links course.

The 18-hole layout is 6,609 yards and rated 70.8 from the championship tees, and 6,042 yards and rated 69.5 from the regular tees. The slope ratings are: 122 championship and 119 regular. Women's tees are 5,560 yards and rated 70.4, with a slope rating of 110.

The Scottish links course is 3,009 yards and rated 34.7 from the regular tees. The slope rating is 52.

Play policy and fees: Green fees are $36 for 18 holes and $9 for the Scottish links course. Carts are $12 per person. Reservations are accepted 30 days in advance. Summer rules are played here year-round.

Location: From Interstate 5, take the exit for Weed. Drive four miles east on Highway 97 and turn left on Big Springs Road.

5925 Country Club Drive
Weed, CA 96094

Pro shop   (916) 938-3201

- ■ driving range
- ■ practice greens
- ■ power carts
- ☐ pull carts
- ■ golf club rental
- ☐ locker rooms
- ☐ showers
- ■ executive course
- ■ accommodations
- ■ food and beverages
- ■ clubhouse

Dave Schoenmann
Professional

Ed Irwin
Superintendent

NORTHERN A2

Course description: These courses, designed by Robert Trent Jones, Jr., are located at the base of Mount Shasta. There are spectacular views from both courses. The large course is sprawling and long with five lakes. It's challenging and requires proficiency with irons. The 16th hole is one of the toughest par-3s in Northern California. PGA Tour pro Peter Jacobsen earned his first pro win here at the 1976 Northern California Open.

MAP ON PAGE 38   41

MAP A3
(1 COURSE)

PAGES.......42-43

NOR-CAL MAP.....see page 34
adjoining maps
NORTH ....no map
EAST ....no map
SOUTH (B3) ....see page 58
WEST (A2).............see page 38

INDIAN CAMP GOLF COURSE

1982
Malcolm Crawford

Box 46-A
Tulelake, CA 96134

Route 1
Tulelake, CA 96134

Pro shop   (916) 667-2922

□ driving range
■ practice greens
□ power carts
■ pull carts
■ golf club rental
□ locker rooms
□ showers
■ executive course
□ accommodations
□ food and beverages
□ clubhouse

Dan Crawford
Owner

Jim Walker
Manager

Course information: This public course has nine holes. Par is 56 for 18 holes. The course is 1,512 yards. Women's tees are 1,350 yards.

Play policy and fees: Green fees are $5 for nine holes and $4 for the second nine holes. There is a special $15 all-day fee.

Location: From Tulelake, take Highway 139 north to Highway 161 (State Line Road). Turn west onto Highway 161 and drive to Hill Road. Turn south (left) on Hill Road and drive to the course.

Course description: Indian Camp is the northern most golf course in California. As a matter of fact, it's less than 300 yards from the Oregon border. According to archaeologists, the course is on the site of an age-old hunting and fishing camp. It is said that Captain Jack of the Modoc Indian tribe fished and hunted here in the 1870s when he wasn't skirmishing with the U.S. Army. The course is mostly flat with scenic views and eight par-3 holes. The only par-4 is the 255-yard second hole.

NORTHERN A3

MAP BO
(4 COURSES)

PAGES.......44-47

NOR-CAL MAP.....see page 34
adjoining maps
NORTH (A0) ....see page 36
EAST (B1).............see page 48
SOUTH (C0) ....see page 62
WEST ....no map

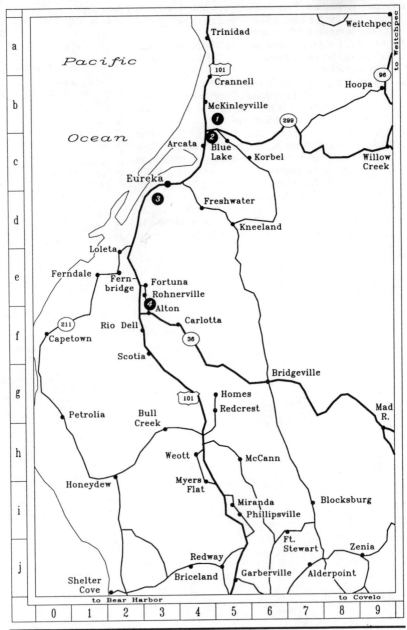

BEAU PRE GOLF COURSE

1967
Don Harling

Course information: This semi-private course has 18 holes and par is 71. The course is 5,890 yards and rated 68.1 from the championship tees, and 5,448 yards and rated 66.2 from the regular tees. The slope ratings are 116 championship and 112 regular. Women's tees are 4,882 yards and rated 67.6. The slope rating is: 116.

Play policy and fees: Outside guests are welcome. Green fees are $12 on weekdays and $16 on weekends. Twilight rates are $7 after 3 p.m. any day. Carts are $14. Reservations are recommended, especially on the weekends.

Location: From Highway 101 in McKinleyville, take the Murray Road exit to Central Avenue. Turn north on Central Avenue to Norton Road. Turn right on Norton Road and drive to the course.

Course description: Over the years this scenic course has gradually expanded from a nine-hole layout into 18 holes. It has lush fairways and ocean views. Pine and spruce trees line most of the fairways on each side; sometimes too many of them. Water comes into play on nine holes and the bunkers are strategically placed. The men's course record is 64, set by Fred Schreiber in 1989.

PO Box 2278
McKinleyville, CA 95221

1777 Norton Road
McKinleyville, CA 95221

Pro shop   (707) 839-3412
Clubhouse   (707) 839-2342

- ■ driving range
- ■ practice greens
- ■ power carts
- ■ pull carts
- ■ golf club rental
- ■ locker rooms
- □ showers
- □ executive course
- □ accommodations
- ■ food and beverages
- ■ clubhouse

Don Harling
Manager/Professional

Ted Mattila
Assistant Professional

Ken Frost
Superintendent

BAYWOOD GOLF
AND COUNTRY CLUB

1956
R.E. Baldock

3600 Buttermilk Lane
Arcata, CA 95521

Pro shop   (707) 822-3688
Clubhouse (707) 822-3686

Course information: This private course has 18 holes and par is 72. The course is 6,356 yards and rated 70.8 from the championship tees, and 6,097 yards and rated 69.6 from the regular tees. The slope ratings are 124 championship and 122 regular. Women's tees are tees, 5,739 yards and rated 74.0. The slope rating is 125.

Play policy and fees: Reciprocal play is accepted with members of other private clubs. Guest fees are $15 when accompanied by a member, $25 when sponsored by a member and $35 for reciprocal players. Carts are $16. Reservations are recommended. No blue jeans or T-shirts may be worn.

Location: From Highway 101 in Arcata, take the Sunny Brae exit east. Pass the California Highway Patrol station. Turn left on Buttermilk Lane and drive to the course.

Course description: Situated in the midst of towering redwoods, this scenic course offers a challenging, tree-guarded layout. It's often foggy or misty. Hole number 11 is a par-4, 440-yard challenge not to forget. It's fairly long with a downhill green surrounded by bunkers. Count on a good drive to get there in two, and the green's not easy to stick. The men's course record is 63, set in 1984 by host pro Jim Hosley, and the women's record is 72.

- ■ driving range
- ■ practice greens
- ■ power carts
- ■ pull carts
- ■ golf club rental
- ☐ locker rooms
- ■ showers
- ☐ executive course
- ☐ accommodations
- ■ food and beverages
- ■ clubhouse

Jim Hosley
Professional

Pete Williams
Superintendent

EUREKA GOLF COURSE

1958
Robert Dean Putman

4750 Fairway Drive
Eureka, CA 95501

Pro shop   (707) 443-4808

- ■ driving range
- ■ practice greens
- ■ power carts
- ■ pull carts
- ■ golf club rental
- □ locker rooms
- □ showers
- □ executive course
- □ accommodations
- ■ food and beverages
- ■ clubhouse

NORTHERN B0

Course information: This public course has 18 holes and par is 70. The course is 5,667 yards and rated 66.8 from the regular tees. The slope rating is 109. Women's tees are 5,391 yards and rated 70.6. The slope rating is 118.

Play policy and fees: Green fees are $8 weekdays and $11 weekends. Twilight rates are $4 weekdays and $6 weekends. Senior rates are $5.50 weekdays and $8 weekends. Carts are $9 for nine holes and $14 for 18 holes. Reservations recommended during the summer.

Location: From Highway 101 in Eureka, take the Herrick exit east. Drive one–quarter mile to the golf course.

Course description: This mostly flat, open course has some trees and lots of water hazards in the form of canals. Bring lots of golf balls when you play this layout.

Don Roller, Jr.
Superintendent

Rob Kagay
Professional

REDWOOD EMPIRE GOLF AND COUNTRY CLUB

Country Club Drive
Fortuna, CA 95540

Pro shop   (707) 725-5194
Clubhouse   (707) 725-5195

- ■ driving range
- ■ practice greens
- ■ power carts
- ■ pull carts
- ■ golf club rental
- ■ locker rooms
- ■ showers
- □ executive course
- □ accommodations
- ■ food and beverages
- ■ clubhouse

Course information: This private course has nine holes. Par is 72 for 18 holes. The course is 6,000 yards and rated 68.2 from the regular tees (18 holes). The slope rating is 109. Women's tees are 5,352 yards and rated 70.7 from the regular tees. The slope rating is 115.

Play policy and fees: Reciprocal play is accepted with members of other private clubs. Fees are $20 for reciprocal players. Guest fees are $10 weekdays and $16 weekends when accompanied by a member. Carts are $13.

Location: From Highway 101 in Fortuna, take the Kenmar Road exit to Fortuna Boulevard. Drive east past Rhonerville Road to Mill Street and turn right on Mill Street. Then turn right on Country Club Drive.

Course description: This course plays much longer than the yardage indicates. Situated on a ridge, it's tight and hilly with lots of trees, sidehill lies, prevailing winds and not much roll. It's a great test of the short game. The greens are fast, but they hold well.

Tom Mathena
Professional

Mark Van Lienden
Superintendent

MAP B1
(2 COURSES)

PAGES.......48-51

NOR-CAL MAP.....see page 34
adjoining maps
NORTH ....no map
EAST (B2)............see page 52
SOUTH.........................no map
WEST (B0)...........see page 44

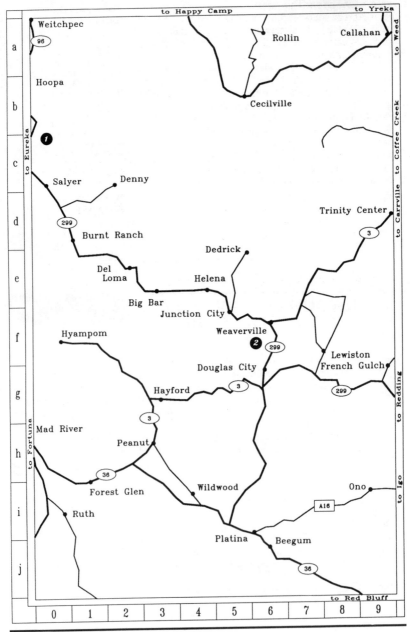

BIGFOOT GOLF AND COUNTRY CLUB

Course information: This semi-private course has nine holes. Par is 70 for 18 holes. The course is 5,007 yards and rated 63.9 from the regular tees. The slope rating is 103. Women's tees are 5,007 yards and rated 67.9 from the regular tees. The slope rating is 112.

Play policy and fees: Outside play is accepted. Green fees are $8 for nine holes and $12 for 18 holes weekdays, and $10 for nine holes and $14 for 18 holes weekends. Carts are $7 per nine holes. No spectators are allowed.

Location: From Highway 101 in Arcata, take Highway 299 east to Willow Creek. Turn left on Country Club Road and cross the Trinity River. Turn left on Patterson at the "T." Turn right on Bigfoot Avenue.

Course description: This short course is situated in a scenic valley frequented by geese and deer. Trees line the fairways, and water comes into play on eight holes. Greens are typically small, and host pro Bob Newell likes to call his layout "the course with a bite." An example of a tough hole is the 477-yard, par-5 fourth. It may be short for a par-5, but the green looks like an island because it's almost completely surrounded by water. Also, watch for the breaks on the first and fifth greens. If you misread them, you're off to a bad start.

PO Box 836
Willow Creek, CA 95573

Patterson Road
Willow Creek, CA 95573

Pro shop   (916) 629-2977
Clubhouse (916) 629-2193

- ■ driving range
- ☐ practice greens
- ■ power carts
- ■ pull carts
- ■ golf club rental
- ☐ locker rooms
- ☐ showers
- ☐ executive course
- ☐ accommodations
- ■ food and beverages
- ■ clubhouse

Bob Newell
Professional

Cappy Kramer
Superintendent

TRINITY ALPS GOLF AND COUNTRY CLUB

Course information: This semi-private course has nine holes. Par is 62 for 18 holes. The course is 3,512 yards and rated 59.0 from the regular tees. The slope rating is 87. Women's tees are 3,474 yards and rated 59.0 from the regular tees. The slope rating is 96.

Play policy and fees: Outside play is accepted. Green fees are $8 for nine holes and $10 for 18 holes. Pull carts are 50 cents per nine holes. Power carts are $5 per nine holes.

Location: From Redding, drive 49 miles west on Highway 299 to Weaverville. Exit south onto Glen Road, travel to Golf Course Drive to the course.

Course description: There are two water hazards on this rolling, short and walkable course. It's picturesque, with lots of trees and views of the Trinity Alps. When you're not looking at the views, watch for hole number seven. This par-3, 140-yard hole has two water hazards coming into play. You must hit over water to the green. There's more water to the left of the green and bunkers to the right. Watch for the tree in front of the green. You won't miss it because you have to hit over it. Then again you *may* miss it, if you're lucky.

PO Box 582
Weaverville, CA 96093

111 Golf Course Drive
Weaverville, CA 96093

Pro shop   (916) 623-5411

- ■ driving range
- ■ practice greens
- ■ power carts
- ■ pull carts
- ■ golf club rental
- ■ locker rooms
- □ showers
- ■ executive course
- □ accommodations
- ■ food and beverages
- ■ clubhouse

Felix Claveran
Professional

Bobby Tyler
Superintendent

MAP B2
(8 COURSES)

PAGES.......52-57

NOR-CAL MAP.....see page 34
adjoining maps
NORTH (A2) ....see page 38
EAST (B3)............see page 58
SOUTH (C2) ....see page 66
WEST (B1)...........see page 48

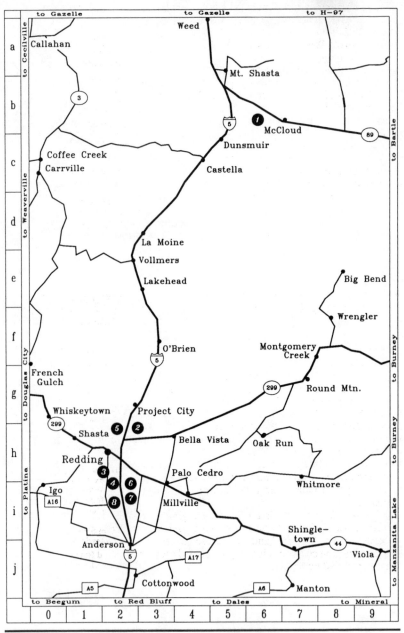

McCLOUD GOLF COURSE

NORTHERN B2

Course information: This public course has nine holes. Par is 72 for 18 holes. The course is 6,020 yards and rated 67.5 from the regular tees (18 holes). The slope rating is 109. Women's tees are 5,262 yards and rated 69.1. The slope rating is 114.

Play policy and fees: Green fees are $8 for nine holes and $10 for 18 holes weekdays, and $10 for nine holes and $12 for 18 holes weekends and holidays. Carts are $10 per nine holes and $15 for 18 holes. The course is open April through November.

Location: From Interstate 5 north of Redding and Dunsmuir, take the Highway 89 exit. Drive east to McCloud. In McCloud, turn right on to Squaw Valley Road south and follow it to the course.

Course description: Nestled in the mountains, this course is mostly flat with a few creeks. Many bunkers come into play.

PO Box 728
McCloud, CA 96057

1001 Squaw Valley Road
McCloud, CA 96057

Pro shop   (916) 964-2535

- ■ driving range
- ■ practice greens
- ■ power carts
- ■ pull carts
- ■ golf club rental
- □ locker rooms
- □ showers
- □ executive course
- □ accommodations
- ■ food and beverages
- ■ clubhouse

Charles Nutt
Manager

Earl Martin
Superintendent

GOLD HILLS COUNTRY CLUB

1979
R.E. Baldock

Course information: This public course has 18 holes and par is 72. The course is 6,495 yards and rated 71.0 from the championship tees, and 6,131 yards and rated 69.4 from the regular tees. The slope ratings are 127 championship and 123 regular. Women's tees are 5,556 yards and rated 71.7. The slope rating is 124.

Play policy and fees: Green fees are $13 weekdays and $16 weekends. Carts are $16.

Location: From Interstate 5 on the north side of Redding, take the Oasis Road exit east and drive one–half mile. Turn right on Gold Hills Drive and follow it to the course.

Course description: This is a hilly, challenging course with views of Mount Shasta and Mount Lassen. Rocks border many fairways and can cause all sorts of problems. The course has lots of pine and oak trees and is surrounded by homes.

1950 Gold Hills Drive
Redding, CA 96003

Pro shop   (916) 246-7867

- ■ driving range
- ■ practice greens
- ■ power carts
- ■ pull carts
- ■ golf club rental
- □ locker rooms
- ■ showers
- □ executive course
- □ accommodations
- ■ food and beverages
- ■ clubhouse

Tom Schenke
Professional

Fred Burns
Superintendent

RIVERVIEW GOLF AND COUNTRY CLUB

Course information: This private course has 18 holes and par is 72. The course is 6,474 yards and rated 70.3 from the regular tees. The slope rating is 117. Women's tees are 5,850 yards and rated 73.0. The slope rating is 122.

Play policy and fees: Reciprocal play is accepted with members of other private clubs. Guest fees are $15 when accompanied by a member and $30 unaccompanied. Carts are $12 with a member and $15 without. Closed Mondays.

Location: From Interstate 5 in Redding, take the Bonneyview Road/Churn Creek exit. Go over the overpass and turn right on Bechelli Lane. Follow it to the course on the left.

Course description: This mature course is tight and twisty with a lot of trees and small, tricky greens. The Sacramento River comes into play on four holes. At the first hole, some golfers toss their first ball into the water right away, trying to appease the river gods.

4200 Bechelli Lane
Redding, CA 96002

Pro shop   (916) 223-1617
Clubhouse (916) 223-1551

- ■ driving range
- ■ practice greens
- ■ power carts
- ■ pull carts
- ☐ golf club rental
- ■ locker rooms
- ■ showers
- ☐ executive course
- ☐ accommodations
- ■ food and beverages
- ■ clubhouse

Kim Thurman
Professional

Dick Howe
Superintendent

ALLEN'S GOLF COURSE

Course information: This public course has nine holes. Par is 62 for 18 holes. The course is 3,412 yards and rated 56.9 from the regular tees. The slope rating is 92. Women's tees are 3,370 yards and rated 58.2. The slope rating is 89.

Play policy and fees: Green fees are $5 for nine holes and $9.50 for 18 holes weekdays, and $5.50 for nine holes and $10.50 for 18 holes weekends. Senior and junior rates are $4 for nine holes and $7.25 for 18 holes on weekdays. Wednesday specials for seniors are $3.50 for nine holes and $6.50 for 18 holes.

Location: From Interstate 5 in Redding, take the Bonneyview Road/Churn Creek exit. Turn left on Bonneyview Road and left on East Side Road. Turn left on Star Drive, which becomes Sacramento Drive. The course is on the left, just past Olney Creek.

Course description: This short, tricky course is tight, with out-of-bounds on every hole. If that sounds like the course is tough, it is.

2780 Sacramento Drive
Redding, CA 96001

Pro shop   (916) 241-5055

- ☐ driving range
- ■ practice greens
- ☐ power carts
- ■ pull carts
- ☐ golf club rental
- ☐ locker rooms
- ☐ showers
- ■ executive course
- ☐ accommodations
- ☐ food and beverages
- ■ clubhouse

Patsy Allen
Manager

Bob Allen
Superintendent

LAKE REDDING GOLF COURSE

Course 5
MAP B2 grid h2

1959

1795 Benton Drive
Redding, CA 96003

Pro shop   (916) 243-5531

□ driving range
■ practice greens
■ power carts
■ pull carts
■ golf club rental
□ locker rooms
□ showers
■ executive course
□ accommodations
■ food and beverages
■ clubhouse

Daryl and Peggy Sutterfield
Owner/Manager

Dan Ross
Superintendent

NORTHERN B2

Course information: This public course has nine holes. Par is 62 for 18 holes. The course is 3,757 yards and rated 57.3 from the regular tees. The slope rating is 84. Women's tees are 3,757 yards and rated 60.5 from the regular tees. The slope rating is 88.

Play policy and fees: Green fees are $5.50 for nine holes and $10.50 for 18 holes. Green fees for seniors are $3.50 Monday through Friday before noon, and $5 for nine holes and $9.50 for 18 holes after noon and on Saturdays and Sundays. After 4 p.m., seasonal green fees are $4 for unlimited play. Carts are $8 for nine holes and $15 for 18 holes.

Location: Heading north on Interstate 5 in Redding, take the Highway 299 East exit. Turn left and drive to the second stop light and turn left again. At the bottom of the hill take the first right, which is Benton Drive. Take Benton Drive to the course.

Course description: This short executive course is known as requiring accuracy because of its narrow fairways lined with trees. There are four lakes that come into play. Bunkers have been added for more challenge. There are new tee boxes, the fairways are double cut and some of the greens have been rebuilt.

CHURN CREEK GOLF COURSE

Course 6
MAP B2 grid I2

8550 Churn Creek Road
Redding, CA 96002

Pro shop   (916) 222-6353

■ driving range
■ practice greens
■ power carts
■ pull carts
■ golf club rental
□ locker rooms
□ showers
□ executive course
□ accommodations
■ food and beverages
□ clubhouse

Chuck Sherman
Professional

Art Saldana
Superintendent

Course information: This public course has nine holes. Par is 72 for 18 holes. The course is 6,203 yards and rated 68.6 from the regular tees. The slope rating is 108. Women's tees are 5,516 yards and rated 71.4 with a slope rating of 117.

Play policy and fees: Green fees are $6 for nine holes and $12 for 18 holes. Carts are $7 for nine holes and $14 for 18 holes.

Location: From Interstate 5 in Redding, take the Knighton Road exit east. Knighton Road turns into Churn Creek Road, which leads to the course.

Course description: This flat course is characterized by out-of-bounds on every hole but two, and there are hazard stakes on those two. It has two small lakes and narrow, tree-lined fairways. Greens are small and hold up well through the summer heat.

MAP ON PAGE 52

ANDERSON-TUCKER OAKS GOLF COURSE

Course information: This public course has nine holes. Par is 72 for 18 holes. The course is 6,371 yards and rated 67.2 from the regular tees (18 holes). The slope rating is 98. Women's tees are 5,899 yards and rated 71.6. The slope rating is 109.

Play policy and fees: Green fees are $6 for nine holes and $12 for 18 holes any day. Carts are $7 for nine holes and $14 for 18 holes. Closed the third Monday of each month during the summer.

Location: From Interstate 5 in Anderson, take the Riverside exit to Airport Road north. Drive across the Sacramento River and turn left on Churn Creek Road. Continue to the course.

Course description: This flat course has lots of trees, including giant oaks, and bunkers on every hole. It's a pleasant golf course to play.

PO Box 654
Anderson, CA 96007

11411 Churn Creek Road
Redding, CA 96001

Pro shop   (916) 365-3350

■ driving range
■ practice greens
■ power carts
■ pull carts
■ golf club rental
□ locker rooms
□ showers
□ executive course
□ accommodations
■ food and beverages
■ clubhouse

Chuck Sherman
Professional

Mike Ervin
Superintendent

RIVER BEND GOLF AND COUNTRY CLUB

1991
Bill Ralston

Course information: This semi-private course has nine holes. Par is 64 for 18 holes. The course is 4,150 yards for 18 holes and rated 59. The slope rating is 90. Women's tees are currently unrated.

Play policy and fees: Members and guests only. Only players with NCGA, SCGA or out-of-state golf association handicaps or guests of members are allowed to play the course. Green fees are $6 for nine holes and $10 for 18 holes daily. Reservations are recommended.

Location: From Interstate 5, take the Churn Creek/Bechelli exit and turn west. Cross over the Sacramento River and turn right onto Indianwood Drive, which leads to the River Bend Estate. Drive through the subdivision. The course is at the rear of the residential area.

Course description: This course was designed and built by Bill Ralston with the assistance of retired pro Eric Batten. With its tight layout, two ponds and the Sacramento River slough coming into play on five holes, consider this a target course of the most demanding dimensions. And don't forget the huge oak trees that come into play on seven of the holes. Thankfully, this course boasts large greens for the distance.

1863 Keystone Court
Redding, CA 96003

5369 Indianwood Drive
Redding, CA 96001

Pro shop   (916) 246-9077
Office   (916) 222-8101

□ driving range
■ practice greens
■ power carts
■ pull carts
■ golf club rental
■ locker rooms
□ showers
■ executive course
□ accommodations
■ food and beverages
□ clubhouse

MAP B3
(1 COURSE)

PAGES.......58-59

NOR-CAL MAP.....see page 34
adjoining maps
NORTH (A3).........see page 42
EAST (B4)...........see page 60
SOUTH (C3).........see page 74
WEST (B2)...........see page 52

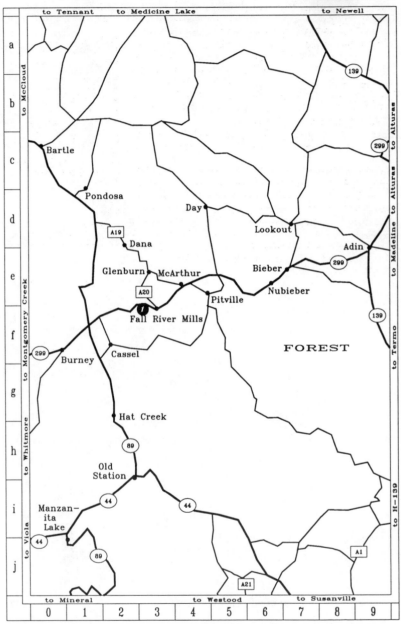

FALL RIVER GOLF AND COUNTRY CLUB

1980
Clark Glasson

PO Box PAR
Fall River Mills, CA 96028

Highway 299 East
Fall River Mills, CA 96028

Pro shop   (916) 336-5555

- driving range
- practice greens
- power carts
- pull carts
- golf club rental
- □ locker rooms
- □ showers
- □ executive course
- □ accommodations
- food and beverages
- clubhouse

Karen Estes
Manager

Mike Glasson
Superintendent

NORHTERN B3

Course information: This public course has 18 holes and par is 72. The course is 7,367 yards and rated 75.2 from the championship tees, and 6,835 yards and rated 72.5 from the regular tees. The slope ratings are: 131 championship and 126 regular. Women's tees are 6,129 and rated 73.5 from the regular tees. The slope rating is 120.

Play policy and fees: Green fees are $15 on weekdays and $19 on weekends. Senior rates are $10 on Fridays. The Monday fee is $13. Carts are $18.

Location: From Interstate 5 in Redding, drive east on Highway 299 to Fall River Mills. The course is on the right.

Course description: This course is located in the intermountain area with views of Mount Shasta and Mount Lassen. The long, rolling course with three lakes and some trees is one of longest, toughest-rated courses in the state. The greens are large, and ball placement is a must to score. This course is right in the middle of some of the best fly fishing in the country, so pack your rods and your clubs for a super combo.

MAP ON PAGE 58

NOR-CAL MAP.....see page 34
adjoining maps
NORTH ....no map
EAST ....no map
SOUTH (C4).........see page 80
WEST (B3)...........see page 58

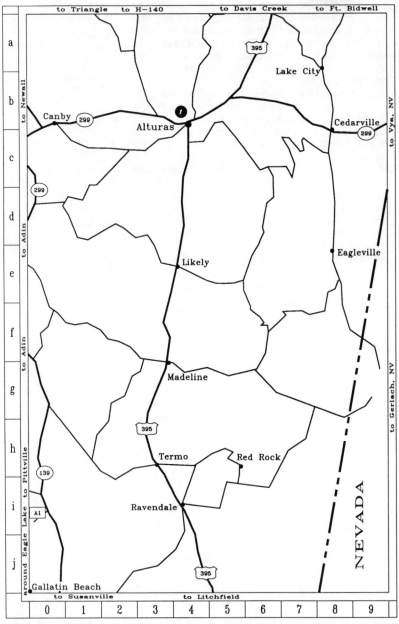

ARROWHEAD GOLF COURSE

1949
William Park Bell

1901 North Warner Street
Alturas, CA 96101

Pro shop   (916) 233-3404

- ■ driving range
- ■ practice greens
- ■ power carts
- ■ pull carts
- ■ golf club rental
- □ locker rooms
- □ showers
- □ executive course
- □ accommodations
- ■ food and beverages
- ■ clubhouse

Bud Porter
Professional

Gary McClellan
Manager/Superintendent

NORTHERN B4

Course information: This public course has nine holes. Par is 70 for 18 holes. The course is 6,136 yards for 18 holes and rated 67.9 from the regular tees. The slope rating is 109. Women's tees are 5,494 yards and rated 71.0 from the regular tees. The slope rating is 112.

Play policy and fees: Green fees are $5 for nine holes and $8 for 18 holes weekdays, and $6 and $10 weekends. Memberships are available. Carts are $6 for nine holes and $10 for 18 holes. The clubhouse is closed November through February, but there is a drop box for collecting fees.

Location: From Interstate 5 in Redding, drive east on Highway 299 to Alturas. Take the Warner Street exit, and drive north to the course.

Course description: This course has wide fairways and elevated greens. Irrigation ditches come into play on every hole, but there are no bunkers. There is a long par-4 from the men's tees and two par-5 holes from the women's tees.

MAP C0
(4 COURSES)

PAGES.......62-65

NOR-CAL MAP.....see page 34
adjoining maps
NORTH (B0).........see page 44
EAST.............................no map
SOUTH (D0).........see page 82
WEST............................no map

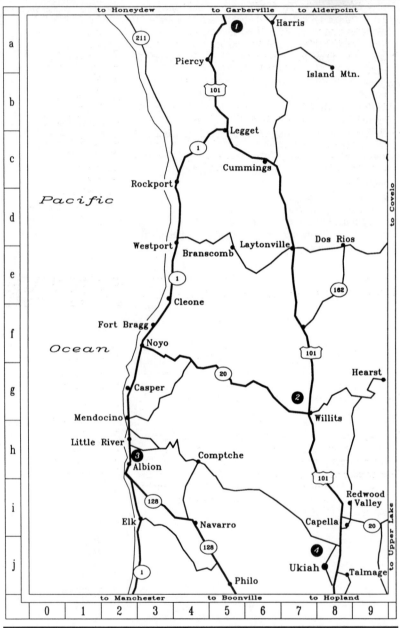

to Honeydew   to Garberville   to Alderpoint

a

211

Harris

Piercy

Island Mtn.

b

101

Legget

c

1

Cummings

Rockport

Pacific

d

to Covelo

Westport

Laytonville Dos Rios

Branscomb

e

1

162

Cleone

Fort Bragg

f

Ocean

Noyo

101

20

Hearst

g

Casper

2

Mendocino

Willits

Little River

h

Comptche

101

3

Albion

i

128

Redwood Valley

Elk

Navarro

Capella

20

128

j

1

4

Ukiah Talmage

Philo

to Manchester   to Boonville   to Hopland

to Upper Lake

| 0 | 1 | 2 | 3 | 4 | 5 | 6 | 7 | 8 | 9 |

BENBOW GOLF COURSE

Course information: This resort course has 18 holes. Par is 70. The course is 5,074 yards and rated 64.8 from the regular tees. The slope rating is 101. Women's tees are 5,077 and rated 69.1 with a slope rating of 114.

Play policy and fees: Green fees are $9 for nine holes and $12 for 18 holes weekdays, and $11 for nine holes and $14 for 18 holes weekends. Carts are a dollar a hole.

Location: On Highway 101 two miles south of Garberville take the Benbow exit directly to the course.

Course description: This mountainous course is short with narrow, redwood-lined fairways. It's a spooky course to play because it's like a bowling alley, so take a lot of balls. It's a gradually climbing course, but walkable.

7000 Benbow Drive
Garberville, CA 95440

Pro shop   (707) 923-2777

☐ driving range
■ practice greens
■ power carts
■ pull carts
■ golf club rental
☐ locker rooms
☐ showers
☐ executive course
☐ accommodations
■ food and beverages
☐ clubhouse

Don Hunt
Manager

John Wheeler
Superintendent

BROOKTRAILS GOLF COURSE

Course information: This public course has nine holes. Par is 56 for 18 holes. The course is 2,653 yards and rated 53.0 from the regular tees. The slope rating is 80. Women's tees are 2,653 yards and unrated.

Play policy and fees: Green fees are $4.50 for nine holes and $6.50 for 18 holes weekdays, and $5.50 for nine holes and $9 for 18 holes weekends.

Location: Drive north on Highway 101 through Willits, take the Sherwood exit northwest. Drive 2.5 miles to Birch Street. The course is on the right.

Course description: A creek meanders through four fairways on this fun, short course. The course is tight and flanked by redwoods. It's mostly flat with small, fast greens.

PO Box 1003
Willits, CA 95490

24860 Birch Street
Willits, CA 95490

Pro shop   (707) 459-6761

☐ driving range
■ practice greens
☐ power carts
■ pull carts
■ golf club rental
☐ locker rooms
☐ showers
■ executive course
☐ accommodations
■ food and beverages
■ clubhouse

Ron Runberg
Co-Owner

Curt Reese
Co-Owner

Doug Poulson
Superintendent

MAP ON PAGE 62

LITTLE RIVER INN GOLF AND TENNIS RESORT

Course information: This resort course has nine holes. Par is 71 for 18 holes. The course is 5,458 yards and rated 66.6 from the regular tees (18 holes). The slope rating is 115. Women's tees are 4,995 yards and rated 68.6 from the regular tees. The slope rating is 111.

Play policy and fees: Outside play is accepted. Green fees are $12 for nine holes and $15 for 18 holes on weekdays, and $15 for nine holes and $20 for 18 holes on weekends and holidays. Carts are $13 for nine holes and $20 for 18 holes.

Location: The course is located on Highway 1, south of Mendocino, in the town of Little River.

Course description: This oceanside course is hilly and tight with lots of trees. Deer, quail and squirrels abound.

PO Box Drawer B
Little River, CA 95456

7750 North Highway 1
Little River, CA 95456

Pro shop   (707) 937-5667

■ driving range
■ practice greens
■ power carts
■ pull carts
■ golf club rental
□ locker rooms
□ showers
□ executive course
■ accommodations
■ food and beverages
■ clubhouse

Doug Howe
Pro/Superintendent

Tim Finn
Manager

UKIAH MUNICIPAL GOLF COURSE

Course information: This public course has 18 holes and par is 70. The course is 5,850 yards and rated 67.4 from the championship tees, and 5,657 yards and rated 66.2 from the regular tees. The slope ratings are 108 championship and 105 regular. Women's tees are 5,657 yards and rated 71.4 from the championship tees, and 5,312 yards and rated 69.5 from the regular tees. The slope ratings are 125 championship and 120 regular.

Play policy and fees: Green fees are $6 for nine holes and $10 for 18 holes weekdays, and $7 for nine holes and $12 for 18 holes weekends. Carts are $9 for nine holes and $18 for 18 holes. Reservations are recommended and accepted daily.

Location: From Highway 101 in Ukiah, take the Perkins Street exit west to North State Street. Turn left on Scott Street and follow it two blocks to Walnut Street. Walnut Street turns into Park Boulevard.

Course description: Situated in the foothills, this short course is tight and especially hilly on the first few holes. There are lots of sidehill lies to small, elevated greens. The Mendocino County Men's Amateur is held here each spring, and the Ukiah Junior Open is held here each summer. Summer clinics are held.

PO Box 364
Ukiah, CA 95482

599 Park Boulevard
Ukiah, CA 95482

Pro shop   (707) 462-8857

□ driving range
■ practice greens
■ power carts
■ pull carts
■ golf club rental
□ locker rooms
□ showers
□ executive course
□ accommodations
■ food and beverages
■ clubhouse

Jeff McMillen
Professional

Ken Woods
Assistant Professional

MAP C2
(10 COURSES)

PAGES.......66-73

NOR-CAL MAP.....see page 34
adjoining maps
NORTH (B2).........see page 52
EAST (C3) ....see page 74
SOUTH (D2) ....see page 112
WEST ....no map

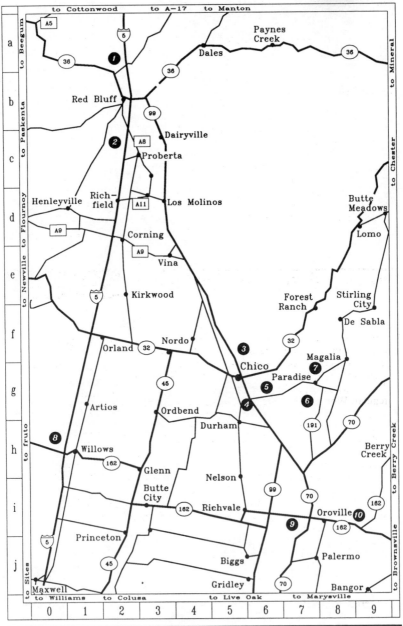

WILCOX OAKS GOLF COURSE

NORTHERN C2

Course information: This private course has 18 holes and par is 72. The course is 6,143 yards and rated 68.5 from the regular tees. The slope rating is 114. Women's tees are 6,102 yards and rated 74.5 from the championship tees, and 5,777 yards and rated 72.7 from the regular tees. The women's slope ratings are 127 championship and 122 regular.

Play policy and fees: Reciprocal play is accepted with members of other private clubs. Outside play is accepted. General green fees are $40. Green fees are $30 for reciprocators, and guest fees are $15 when accompanied by a member. Carts are $12.

Location: From Interstate 5 just north of Red Bluff, take the Wilcox Oaks Golf Road exit. The course is on the west side of Interstate 5.

Course description: Wild turkeys and deer frequent this flat, open course. There are lots of trees and water comes into play on the 18th hole.

PO Box 127
Red Bluff, CA 96080

Wilcox Oaks Golf Road
Red Bluff, CA 96080

Pro shop   (916) 527-7087
Clubhouse   (916) 527-6680

- ■ driving range
- ■ practice greens
- ■ power carts
- ■ pull carts
- ■ golf club rental
- ■ locker rooms
- ■ showers
- □ executive course
- □ accommodations
- ■ food and beverages
- ■ clubhouse

Bill DeWildt
Professional

Lin Westmoreland
Superintendent

OAK CREEK GOLF COURSE

Course information: This public layout has nine holes. Par is 70 for 18 holes. The course is 5,350 yards and rated 64.4 from the championship tees, and 5,140 yards and rated 63.2 from the regular tees (18 holes). The slope ratings are 105 championship and 103 regular. Women's tees are 5,062 yards and rated 66.2 from the regular tees. The slope rating is 106.

Play policy and fees: Green fees are $7 for nine holes and $13 for 18 holes. Senior rates are $6 for nine and $11 for 18 holes. Twilight rates are $6. Reservations are recommended.

Location: From Interstate 5 in Red Bluff traveling north, take the Main Street exit (first exit in Red Bluff). At the end of the exit ramp, turn north onto Main Street. When you reach Montgomery Road, turn left and follow it to the course.

Course description: Mount Shasta and Mount Lassen are visible from this flat course. Annual tournaments include the Red Bluff Junior Golf Championship, Cinco De Mayo Tournament, Polar Bear, Oak Creek Challenge Cup (two-man low net) and the Project Santa Invitational. The course is undergoing major improvements, but it remains fully operational. A restaurant is expected to open in 1992.

2620 Montgomery Road
Red Bluff, CA 96080

Pro shop   (916) 529-0674

- ■ driving range
- ■ practice greens
- ■ power carts
- ■ pull carts
- ■ golf club rental
- □ locker rooms
- □ showers
- □ executive course
- □ accommodations
- ■ food and beverages
- ■ clubhouse

Paul Goddard
Owner

Chris Goddard
Manager

Don Moore
Superintendent

BIDWELL PARK GOLF COURSE

1929

Course information: This public course has 18 holes and par is 70. The course is 6,178 yards and rated 68.6 from the regular tees. The slope rating is 115. Women's tees are 6,178 yards and rated 74.9 from the championship tees, and 5,860 yards and rated 73.1 from the regular tees. The slope ratings are 126 championship and 123 regular.

Play policy and fees: Green fees are $11 weekdays and $15 weekends. This is an all day rate; you can play as much or as little as you want. Carts are $9 for nine holes and $16 for 18 holes.

Location: From Highway 99 in Chico, take the East Avenue exit and drive east to Wildwood Avenue north.

Course description: Situated in a beautiful part of upper Bidwell Park, this tight course is flanked by trees and water. The front nine is set in the foothills, and the back nine is flat and longer. Accuracy is important.

PO Box 1341
Chico, CA 95927

Wildwood Avenue
Chico, CA 95927

Pro shop (916) 891-8417
Clubhouse (916) 894-2667

- ■ driving range
- ■ practice greens
- ■ power carts
- ■ pull carts
- ■ golf club rental
- ▢ locker rooms
- ▢ showers
- ▢ executive course
- ▢ accommodations
- ■ food and beverages
- ■ clubhouse

John Pease, Jr.
Professional

John Farley
Superintendent

BUTTE CREEK COUNTRY CLUB

1965
R.E. Baldock

Course information: This private course has 18 holes and par is 72. The course is 6,897 yards and rated 72.8 from the tournament tees, and 6,663 yards and rated 71.7 from the championship tees, and 6,103 yards and rated 69.3 from the regular tees. The slope ratings are: 125 tournament, 122 championship and 117 regular. Women's tees are 6,086 yards and rated 74.8 from the regular tees. The slope rating is 126.

Play policy and fees: Members and guests only. Reciprocal play is accepted with members of other private clubs. Guest fees are $15 when accompanied by a member and $25 without. Carts are $12 with a member and $20 without.

Location: From Highway 99 in Chico, take the Estates Drive exit. Drive one mile west to the course.

Course description: This underrated valley course is long, open and lined with mature oak trees. The greens are undulating, large and well maintained. Water comes into play on seven holes. The course will lull you to sleep, but that's when you're in trouble. Stay alert on this layout.

175 Estates Drive
Chico, CA 95928

Pro shop (916) 343-8292
Clubhouse (916) 343-7979

- ■ driving range
- ■ practice greens
- ■ power carts
- ■ pull carts
- ■ golf club rental
- ■ locker rooms
- ■ showers
- ▢ executive course
- ▢ accommodations
- ■ food and beverages
- ■ clubhouse

Ed Hester
Professional

Curtis Carrico
Superintendent

CANYON OAKS
COUNTRY CLUB

NORTHERN C2

Course information: This public course has 18 holes and par is 72. The course is 6,779 yards and rated 72.9 from the tournament tees, 6,221 yards and rated 70.5 from the championship tees, and 5,701 yards and rated 68.1 from the regular tees. The slope ratings are: 133 tournament, 128 championship and 123 regular. Women's tees are 5,701 and rated 73.6 from the championship tees, and 5,030 yards and rated 70.4 from the regular tees. The slope ratings are: 137 championship and 127 regular.

Play policy and fees: Green fees are $17 weekdays and $22 weekends. Carts are $16. Reservations recommended one week in advance. This course is available for outside tournaments. There is a dress code.

Location: From Highway 99 in Chico, take Highway 32 east. Turn left on Bruce Road and drive past the California Park Pavilion to the course.

Course description: On the site of a former driving range, this hilly course has narrow fairways and greens of varying size and contour. The course is tree-lined and a creek bed runs throughout. Water is everywhere but actually comes into play on three holes. The hot hole is number six. It's 180 yards and par-3, and it looks like it plays longer than it is. That's because it plays over water to a narrow green. Bring lots of balls, and play this course while you can. There are plans to go private.

PO Box 7790
Chico, CA 95927

Yosemite Drive
Chico, CA 95927

Pro shop   (916) 345-1622

- ■ driving range
- ■ practice greens
- ■ power carts
- ■ pull carts
- ■ golf club rental
- ◻ locker rooms
- ◻ showers
- ◻ executive course
- ◻ accommodations
- ■ food and beverages
- ◻ clubhouse

Paul Bullock
Professional

Bill Fosnot
Superintendent

MAP ON PAGE 66

69

TALL PINES GOLF COURSE

1 9 6 5
Joe Balch

5325 Clark Road
Paradise, CA 95969

Pro shop   (916) 877-5816

■ driving range
■ practice greens
■ power carts
■ pull carts
■ golf club rental
□ locker rooms
□ showers
□ executive course
□ accommodations
■ food and beverages
■ clubhouse

Joe Balch
Owner/Professional

Course information: This public course has nine holes. Par is 68 for 18 holes. The course is 4,267 yards and rated 60.1 from the regular tees. The slope rating is 84. Women's tees are 4,267 yards and rated 64.1 from the regular tees. The slope rating is 98.

Play policy and fees: Green fees are $7 for nine holes and $9 for 18 holes weekdays, and $8 for nine holes and $10 for 18 holes weekends. Carts are $8 for nine holes and $14 for 18 holes weekdays and $9 for nine holes and $18 for 18 holes weekends and holidays. Pull carts are $1.50. Seniors are $5 weekdays only.

Location: Drive north on Highway 70, through Oroville. Take the Highway 191/Clark Road exit toward Paradise. Drive 11 miles north on Highway 191 (Clark Road) to Paradise. The course is on the left.

Course description: This a tough course layout: it's tight and hilly with lots of trees and elevated greens. Water comes into play on three holes. No two holes are alike. Players must keep the ball in the air. The men's record is 60, held by Randy Garth.

PARADISE PINES GOLF COURSE

PO Box 1367
Magalia, CA 95954

13917 South Park Drive
Magalia, CA 95954

Pro shop   (916) 873-1111

■ driving range
■ practice greens
■ power carts
■ pull carts
■ golf club rental
□ locker rooms
□ showers
□ executive course
□ accommodations
■ food and beverages
□ clubhouse

Chuck Overmyer
Professional

Dave Roberts
Superintendent

Course information: This public course has nine holes. Par is 68 for 18 holes. The course is 4,990 yards and rated 64.9 for 18 holes. The slope rating is 113. Women's tees are 4,962 yards and rated 69.3 from the championship tees, and 4,782 yards and rated 68.3 from the regular tees. The slope ratings are 115 championship and 113 regular.

Play policy and fees: Green fees are $8 for nine holes and $9 for 18 holes on weekdays, and $9 for nine holes and $10 for 18 holes weekends. Carts are $8 for nine holes and $13 for 18 holes. Reservations are recommended. Tee time reservations are accepted two days in advance. Shirts are required.

Location: From Highway 99 in Chico, take the Skyway exit and drive to Magalia. In Magalia, turn left on South Park Drive.

Course description: This short course has tight, tree-lined fairways and offers diversity from hole to hole. The seventh hole is a tough par-5 that doglegs left and climbs uphill between two bunkers.

GLENN GOLF AND COUNTRY CLUB

C o u r s e   8
MAP C2 grid h0

Route 2, Box 172F
Willows, CA 95988

Bayliss Blue Gum Road
Willows, CA 95988

Pro shop   (916) 934-9918

■ driving range
■ practice greens
■ power carts
■ pull carts
■ golf club rental
□ locker rooms
□ showers
□ executive course
□ accommodations
■ food and beverages
■ clubhouse

Tony De Napoli
Professional

David Delay
Superintendent

NORTHERN C2

Course information: This semi-private course has nine holes. Par is 72 for 18 holes. The course is 6,516 yards and rated 69.6 from the regular tees. The slope rating is 111. Women's tees are 5,917 yards and rated 72.4. The slope rating is 114.

Play policy and fees: Outside play is accepted. Green fees are $10 on weekdays and $15 weekends. Senior rates are $5 during the week. Carts are $15.

Location: The course is five miles north of Willows on Bayliss Blue Gum Road. From Interstate 5, take the Bayliss Blue Gum Road exit west.

Course description: This long course is lined with weeping willows and eucalyptus. It has some of the best greens in the northern Sacramento Valley and a great view of the Sierra. There are four par-5 holes. The number-one handicap hole is the fourth, at 215 yards and par-3. This is an exceedingly tough hole. There is out-of-bounds to the left and in the back of the green, which is guarded by bunkers in the front. If you hit on the back of the green you are out-of-bounds. Just for good measure, the green is the smallest on the course and, of course, small for the distance. There are willow trees on the right side, so stay away because you won't have a recovery shot. The average score on this par-3 is 4.3. The men's course record is 63, set by Ken Dunn in 1988.

TABLE MOUNTAIN GOLF COURSE

C o u r s e   9
MAP C2 grid i7

1 9 5 6
R.E. Baldock

PO Box 2767
Oroville, CA 95965

2700 West Oro Dam Blvd.
Oroville, CA 95965

Pro shop   (916) 533-3922
Clubhouse (916) 533-3924

■ driving range
■ practice greens
■ power carts
■ pull carts
■ golf club rental
□ locker rooms
□ showers
□ executive course
□ accommodations
■ food and beverages
■ clubhouse

Ron Anderson
Professional

Course information: This public course has 18 holes and par is 72. The course is 6,505 yards and rated 70.1 from the regular tees. The slope rating is 116. Women's tees are 5,916 yards and rated 72.1 from the regular tees. The slope rating is 112.

Play policy and fees: Green fees are $8 for nine holes and $11 for 18 holes weekdays, and $9 for nine holes and $13 for 18 holes weekends. Senior and junior rate is $8 weekdays. Twilight rate is $7.50 after 4 p.m. weekdays. Carts are $10 for nine holes and $16 for 18 holes with a $2 deposit.

Location: This course is located in Oroville on Highway 162 (West Oro Dam Boulevard) between Highway 99 and Highway 70.

Course description: This sprawling course has wide fairways that are lined with evergreens. It's mostly flat with large greens and water on eight holes. Accuracy is important.

MAP ON PAGE 66

71

KELLY RIDGE GOLF LINKS

1974
Homer Flint

Course information: This semi-private course has nine holes. Par is 66 for 18 holes. The course is 4,160 yards and rated 62.5 at 18 holes. The slope rating is 106. Women's tees are also 4,160 yards, with a rating of 64.6. The slope rating is 120.

Play policy and fees: Reciprocal play is accepted with members of other private clubs. Just show your NCGA card. Outside play is accepted. Green fees are $7 for nine holes and $9 for 18 holes weekdays; $9 and $11 weekends and holidays. On Tuesdays and Wednesdays after 2 p.m., nine holes and a cart costs $17 for two people, $27 for 18 holes. Carts are $8 for nine holes and $14 for 18 holes weekdays, and $10 for nine holes and $14 for 18 holes weekends and holidays. Reservations are recommended at least 24 hours in advance weekends. Shirts are required.

Location: From Highway 70 in Oroville, take the Oro Dam Boulevard exit east 1.5 miles to Olive Highway. Turn right and drive 5.5 miles to Kelly Ridge Road. Turn left and go left again at Royal Oaks Drive.

Course description: Situated in the Sierra Alton foothills on the Oro Dam, this short course is hilly and tight with narrow fairways and well bunkered greens. Balls tend to roll to the right. Many players are intimidated by the 135-yard, par-3 third hole, which requires a carry over a deep ravine; however, the yardage doesn't make play that difficult. There are six par-4 and three par-3 holes.

5131 Royal Oaks Drive
Oroville, CA 95966

Pro shop   (916) 589-0777

- ☐ driving range
- ■ practice greens
- ■ power carts
- ■ pull carts
- ■ golf club rental
- ☐ locker rooms
- ☐ showers
- ☐ executive course
- ☐ accommodations
- ■ food and beverages
- ■ clubhouse

Paul Mares
Manager/Professional

Berry Roderick
Superintendent

MAP C3
(7 COURSES)

PAGES.......74-79

NOR-CAL MAP.....see page 34
adjoining maps
NORTH (B3).........see page 58
EAST (C4) ....see page 80
SOUTH (D3).......see page 134
WEST (C2) ....see page 66

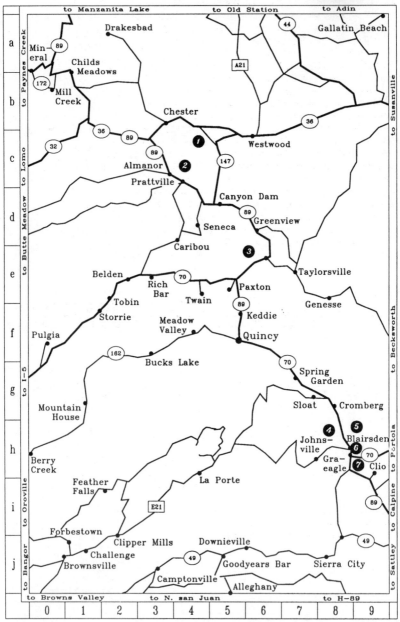

LAKE ALMANOR
COUNTRY CLUB

Course information: This private course has nine holes. Par is 70 for 18 holes. The course is 5,913 yards and rated 67.0 from the regular tees (18 holes). The slope rating is 110. Women's tees are 5,630 yards and rated 71.0 from the regular tees. The slope rating is 116.

Play policy and fees: Public play is accepted after 3 p.m. Green fees are $12 for nine holes and $20 for 18 holes for non-members. Carts are $8.50 per nine holes. Outside players will not be permitted through the gate without a pre-arranged tee time. Reservations should be made on the day of play.

Location: From Interstate 5 in Red Bluff, take Highway 36 through Chester. Turn on County Road A13 and drive about one mile. Turn right on Walker Road and drive to the gate.

Course description: This rolling, scenic mountain course has big trees and undulating greens. The par-4 second hole provides a breathtaking view of Mount Lassen. Wildlife abounds. Deer roam many of the fairways. The men's record is 63, held by Mark Soltau.

PO Box 3323
Lake Almanor, CA 96137

951 Clifford Drive
Lake Almanor, CA 96137

Pro shop   (916) 259-2868
Clubhouse (916) 259-2141

- ■ driving range
- ■ practice greens
- ■ power carts
- ■ pull carts
- ☐ golf club rental
- ☐ locker rooms
- ☐ showers
- ☐ executive course
- ☐ accommodations
- ■ food and beverages
- ■ clubhouse

Mike Stoltz
Professional

Dale Larrabee
Manager

ALMANOR WEST
GOLF COURSE

Course information: This public course has nine holes. Par is 72 for 18 holes. The course is 6,318 yards and rated 69.6 from the regular tees (18 holes). The slope rating is 114. Women's tees are 5,361 yards and rated 69.6. The slope rating is 117.

Play policy and fees: Green fees are $13 for nine holes and $19 for 18 holes. Carts are $16.

Location: From Interstate 5 in Red Bluff, take Highway 36 to Highway 89. Drive south on Highway 89 to Lake Almanor west. Turn left on Slim Drive and you'll find the course.

Course description: This picturesque mountain layout offers a dramatic view of Mount Lassen. It has towering pines and large, undulating greens.

PO Box 1040
Chester, CA 96020

111 Slim Drive
Chester, CA 96020

Pro shop   (916) 259-4555

- ■ driving range
- ■ practice greens
- ■ power carts
- ■ pull carts
- ☐ golf club rental
- ☐ locker rooms
- ☐ showers
- ☐ executive course
- ☐ accommodations
- ■ food and beverages
- ■ clubhouse

June Szody
Manager/Professional

Gary Boatwright
Superintendent

MAP ON PAGE 74   **75**

MOUNT HUFF

Course information: This public course has nine holes. Par is 66 for 18 holes. The course is 4,375 yards and rated 60.2 from the regular tees. The slope rating is 92. Women's tees are 3,782 yards and rated 61.1 from the regular tees. The slope rating is 93.

Play policy and fees: Green fees are $6 for nine holes and $10 for 18 holes weekdays, and $7 and $12 weekends and holidays. Carts are $7 for nine holes and $12 for 18 holes.

Location: From Interstate 5 in Red Bluff, take Highway 36 to Highway 89. Follow Highway 89 to Crescent Mills (between Greenville and Quincy). The course is located on Highway 89 at the Taylorsville "T"' Coming from Oroville take Highway 70 east to Highway 89. Turn left on Highway 89 and drive six miles to the course.

Course description: Don't be confused by the change in the spelling in this course's name. It was formerly known as Mount Hough (pronounced "huff"), after a nearby mountain by the same name. The course originated as a six-hole layout about 25 years ago, and was designated nine holes in 1981. Many seniors enjoy this course because it isn't too hilly. However, flat doesn't mean easy. There is a pond just before the third hole that eats balls, and the ninth hole is no picnic either.

PO Box 569
Greenville, CA 95947

Highway 89 at the
Taylorsville "T"
Crescent Mills, CA 95934

Pro shop   (916) 284-6204

- ■ driving range
- ☐ practice greens
- ■ power carts
- ■ pull carts
- ■ golf club rental
- ☐ locker rooms
- ☐ showers
- ■ executive course
- ☐ accommodations
- ■ food and beverages
- ■ clubhouse

Loren Lindner
Manager

Todd Posch
Superintendent

Clyde Alexander
Professional

GRAEAGLE MEADOWS GOLF COURSE

Course information: This public course has 18 holes and par is 72. The course is 6,639 yards and rated 70.7 from the regular tees. The slope rating is 118. Women's tees are 6,632 yards and rated 76.7 from the championship tees, and 5,639 yards and rated 71.3 from the regular tees. The slope ratings are 132 championship and 118 regular.

Play policy and fees: Green fees are $20 weekdays and $25 weekends. Carts are $20. Reservations are recommended. This course is available for outside tournaments. The course is open from April until about mid-November.

Location: From Truckee, drive 50 miles north on Highway 89. The course is on Highway 89 in Graeagle, three miles south of Highway 70.

Course description: The Feather River runs through this picturesque mountain course dotted by pine trees. The course is tight and well maintained.

PO Box 68
Graeagle, CA 96103

Highway 89
Graeagle, CA 96103

Pro shop   (916) 836-2323
Clubhouse (916) 836-2348

- ■ driving range
- ■ practice greens
- ■ power carts
- ■ pull carts
- ■ golf club rental
- ☐ locker rooms
- ☐ showers
- ☐ executive course
- ☐ accommodations
- ■ food and beverages
- ■ clubhouse

Bob Klein Jr.
Professional

Ross Ripple
Superintendent

PLUMAS PINES
COUNTRY CLUB

1980
Homer Flint

402 Poplar Valley Road
Blairsden, CA 96103

Pro shop   (916) 836-1420
Clubhouse (916) 836-1305

■ driving range
■ practice greens
■ power carts
□ pull carts
■ golf club rental
■ locker rooms
■ showers
□ executive course
■ accommodations
■ food and beverages
■ clubhouse

Gregory Katerba
Professional

Ben Keechler II
Superintendent

Course information: This public course has 18 holes and par is 72. The course is 6,538 yards and rated 71.6 from the championship tees, and 5,953 yards and rated 69.0 from the regular tees. The slope ratings are 127 championship and 120 regular. Women's tees are 5,824 yards and rated 74.1 from the championship tees, and 4,966 yards and rated 68.5 from the regular tees. The slope ratings are 136 championship and 122 regular.

Play policy and fees: Green fees are $50, including cart. There is a $45 mid-week and $55 weekend golfers' special that includes dinner for tee times after 2 p.m. Twilight rates begin at 3:30 p.m. and are $30. Reservations are recommended and should be made three weeks in advance. Shirts and shoes must be worn at all times. The course is open from April to November.

Location: The course is located in Blairsden just off Highway 70.

Course description: This busy course boasts a pro shop that is considered one of the top 100 in the country. This scenic, hilly course is situated in the midst of Plumas National Forest and is bordered by the Middle Fork of the Feather River. The fairways are tight with lots of trees. One notable hole is the second, a 419-yard par-4 with the river to the left and trees to the right. Another tough hole is the 201-yard, par-3 third over water. This is a regular qualifying site of the USGA Women's Mid-Amateur Championship Tournament. The course record is rumored to be 67.

NORTHERN C3

FEATHER RIVER
GOLF COURSE

Course information: This public course has nine holes. Par is 68 for 18 holes. The course is 5,760 yards and rated 66.2 from the regular tees (18 holes). The slope rating is 98.

Play policy and fees: Green fees are $11 weekdays and $13 weekends. Senior rates are $9 weekdays and $11 weekends. Carts are $8 for nine holes and $12 for 18 holes weekdays, and $10 for nine holes and $15 for 18 holes weekends. The course is open from April to about mid-October.

Location: The course is located on Highway 70 in Blairsden.

Course description: This scenic, flat course is tight with lots of trees.

PO Box 67
Blairsden, CA 96103

Highway 70
Blairsden, CA 96103

Pro shop   (916) 836-2722

☐ driving range
■ practice greens
■ power carts
■ pull carts
■ golf club rental
☐ locker rooms
☐ showers
☐ executive course
☐ accommodations
■ food and beverages
☐ clubhouse

Hal Janney
Professional

Barry White
Manager

Bob Ruff
Superintendent

FEATHER RIVER
PARK RESORT

Course information: This public course has nine holes. Par is 70 for 18 holes. The course is 5,164 yards at 18 holes and unrated.

Play policy and fees: Green fees are $11 weekdays and $13 weekends and holidays. Carts are $10 for nine holes and $14 for 18 holes. No reservations necessary. The course is open from April to mid-October.

Location: From Interstate 80 in Truckee, drive north on Highway 89. The course is a one-hour drive from Truckee and is past the town of Graeagle. The course is right on Highway 89.

Course description: This scenic course is flat, open and walkable. There are two par-5s, both reachable in two; there are three par-3s, the 179-yard third hole being the longer one.

PO Box 37
Blairsden, CA 96103

8339 Highway 89
Blairsden, CA 96103

Pro shop   (916) 836-2328

☐ driving range
☐ practice greens
■ power carts
■ pull carts
■ golf club rental
☐ locker rooms
☐ showers
☐ executive course
☐ accommodations
■ food and beverages
■ clubhouse

Don Whedon
Manager

Dave Bishop
Superintendent

MAP C4
(1 COURSE)

PAGES.......80-81

NOR-CAL MAP.....see page 34
adjoining maps
NORTH (B4) 60
EAST ....no map
SOUTH (D4) ....see page 144
WEST (C3) ....see page 74

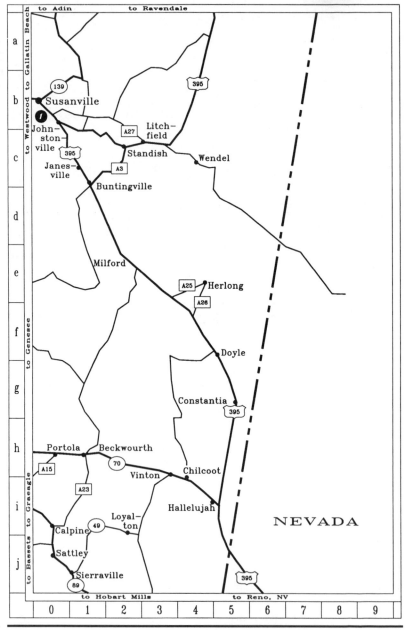

EMERSON LAKE
GOLF COURSE

NORTHERN C4

Course information: This public course has nine holes. Par is 72 for 18 holes. The course is 6,348 yards and rated 68.8 from the regular tees (18 holes). The slope rating is 107. Women's tees are 5,398 yards and rated 68.9 from the regular tees. The slope rating is 103.

Play policy and fees: Green fees are $7 for nine holes and $12 for 18 holes. Carts are $8 for nine holes and $14 for 18 holes. Reservations recommended one week in advance. This course is available for outside tournaments.

Location: From Interstate 5 in Red Bluff, take Highway 36 to Susanville. Take the Wingfield Road exit and drive to the course. From Reno, take Highway 395 to Susanville. Turn left on Richmond Road at Mount Lassen Motors Drive and drive about three miles. Turn left on Wingfield Road and drive one-quarter mile to the club house.

Course description: This rolling course is well maintained and walkable. It has two creeks, one lake, which is frequently dry, and some hills. Evergreens flank the entire course. The men's record is 64, set by Tom Swickard. Expect to see this course grow to 18 holes in the next three years, as an additional nine holes, designed by Jack Bridges, are on the drawing board.

470-835 Wingfield Rd. N.
Susanville, CA 96130

Pro shop   (916) 257-6303

- ■ driving range
- ■ practice greens
- ■ power carts
- ■ pull carts
- ■ golf club rental
- □ locker rooms
- ■ showers
- □ executive course
- □ accommodations
- ■ food and beverages
- ■ clubhouse

Bob Genasci
Professional

Dan Dailey
Superintendent

NOR-CAL MAP.....see page 34
adjoining maps
NORTH (C0).........see page 62
EAST (D1) ....see page 86
SOUTH..........................no map
WEST ....no map

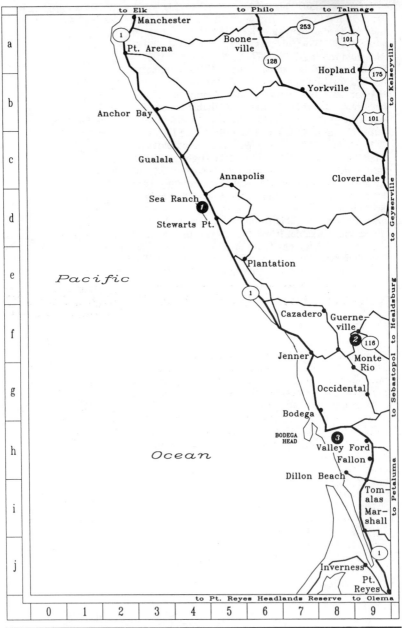

SEA RANCH GOLF LINKS

Course 1
MAP D0 grid d4

1973
Robert Muir Graves

PO Box 10
Sea Ranch, CA 95497

49300 Highway 1
Sea Ranch, CA 95497

Pro shop   (707) 785-2468

- ■ driving range
- ■ practice greens
- ■ power carts
- □ pull carts
- ■ golf club rental
- □ locker rooms
- □ showers
- □ executive course
- ■ accommodations
- ■ food and beverages
- ■ clubhouse

Rich Bland
Professional

Greg Sherwood
Superintendent

Course information: This resort course has nine holes. Par is 72 for 18 holes. The course is 6,712 yards and rated 73.5 from the championship tees, and 6,238 yards and rated 71.4 from the regular tees (18 holes). The slope ratings are 133 championship and 128 regular. Women's tees are 5,544 yards and rated 72.4 from the regular tees. The slope rating is 128.

Play policy and fees: Green fees are $15 for nine holes and $20 for 18 holes weekdays, and $20 for nine holes and $30 for 18 holes weekends. Carts are $12 for nine holes and $20 for 18 holes.

Location: From Jenner, drive 30 miles northwest on Highway 1 to Sea Ranch.

Course description: This is a scenic, seaside links with a traditional Scottish layout. It's mostly open. Plans for a lodge and a back nine are on the drawing board.

NORTHWOOD GOLF COURSE

Course 2
MAP D0 grid f9

1929
Alister MacKenzie

19400 Highway 116
Monte Rio, CA 95462

Pro shop   (707) 865-1116

- ■ driving range
- ■ practice greens
- ■ power carts
- ■ pull carts
- ■ golf club rental
- □ locker rooms
- □ showers
- □ executive course
- ■ accommodations
- ■ food and beverages
- ■ clubhouse

John Moore
Professional

Gaylord R. Schaap
Manager

Edwin Bale
Superintendent

Course information: This public course has nine holes. Par is 72 for 18 holes. The course is 5,746 yards and rated 68.8 from the regular tees (18 holes). The slope rating is 115. Women's tees are 5,596 yards and rated 71.6 with a slope rating of 116.

Play policy and fees: Green fees are $12 for nine holes and $18 for 18 holes weekdays, and $15 for nine holes and $23 for 18 holes weekends. There is a twilight rate of $9 after 3 p.m. any day. Carts are $10 on weekdays and $16 on weekends. Reservations are recommended two weeks in advance.

Location: From Guerneville, drive three miles west on Highway 116. The course is on the left.

Course description: Situated in the Russian River resort area near the Bohemian Grove, this course was designed in 1928 by Alister MacKenzie. It's flat and narrow with lots of redwood trees. The 525-yard ninth hole has been voted the toughest par-5 in Sonoma County. Numerous doglegs make play longer than the yardage suggests.

NORTHERN D0

BODEGA HARBOUR
GOLF LINKS

1977
Robert Trent Jones, Jr.

PO Box 368
Bodega Bay, CA 94923

21301 Heron Drive
Bodega Bay, CA 94923

Pro shop   (707) 875-3538

Course information: This semi-private course has 18
holes and par is 70. The course is 6,211 yards and rated
71.9 from the championship tees, and 5,630 yards and
rated 69.2 from the regular tees. The slope ratings are
130 championship and 125 regular. Women's tees are
4,741 yards and rated 68.9. The slope rating is 121.

Play policy and fees: Outside play is accepted. Property
owners on the golf course are eligible for membership.
Green fees are $35 on weekdays and $53 on weekends.
Carts are $12 per person. Reservations are required.
Reservations are accepted 60 days in advance. There
is a dress code.

Location: From Bodega Bay, drive south on Highway 1.
Take the South Harbour Way exit to the right and drive
150 yards to Heron Drive. Turn right on Heron Drive
and drive one-half mile to the course.

Course description: This course originated as a nine-
hole layout and was expanded to 18 holes in 1988. It
is a challenging, oceanside links course. The fairways
are narrow with scenic views. The front nine is hilly
and the back nine is flat. There are 58 pot bunkers (count 'em) on the front nine
and 36 on the back. The par-4 16th, par-3 17th and par-4 18th all border the ocean
and cross a fresh water marsh. This three-hole sequence makes for an excellent
finish. The course record for men is 68, set by Charlie Gibson in 1988 and tied
by Bob Borowicz in 1991. The women's record is 71, held by Lois Hodge.

- ☐ driving range
- ■ practice greens
- ■ power carts
- ■ pull carts
- ■ golf club rental
- ■ locker rooms
- ■ showers
- ☐ executive course
- ■ accommodations
- ■ food and beverages
- ■ clubhouse

Dennis Kalkowski
Professional

Chester Manni
Superintendent

MAP D1
(33 COURSES)

PAGES.... 86-111

NOR-CAL MAP.....see page 34
adjoining maps
NORTH ....no map
EAST (D2) ....see page 112
SOUTH (E1) ....see page 150
WEST (D0) ....see page 82

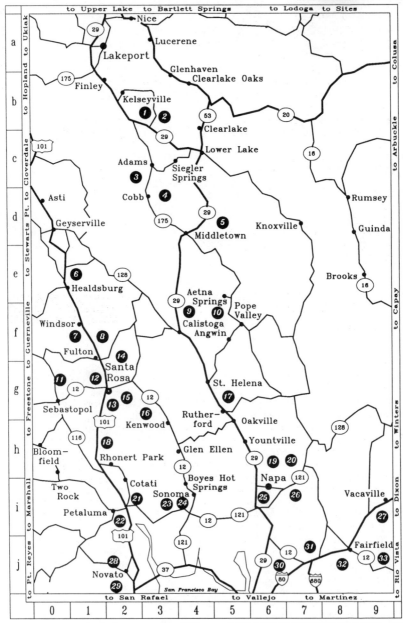

BUCKINGHAM GOLF AND COUNTRY CLUB

Course information: This private course has nine holes. Par is 72 for 18 holes. The course is 5,958 yards and rated 68.4 from the regular tees (18 holes). The slope rating is 114. Women's tees are 5,616 yards and rated 71.9. The slope rating is 124.

Play policy and fees: Reciprocal play is accepted with members of other private clubs, otherwise members and guests only. Guests of guests of the Konocti Harbor Inn are also welcome. Green fees are $12 without a cart and $18 with a cart for nine holes, and $17 without a cart and $29 with a cart for 18 holes any day.

Location: Drive north on Highway 101 past Cloverdale to Hopland and take the Highway 175/Hopland Road exit east to Lakeport. Take Soda Bay Road east across Highway 29 one mile to Eastlake Drive.

Course description: This flat course circles a 25-acre lake called Little Borax. There are some large boulders in the fairways. It has lots of pine and oak trees and is one of the better maintained courses in Northern California.

2855 Eastlake Drive
Kelseyville, CA 95451

Pro shop   (707) 279-4863

☐ driving range
■ practice greens
■ power carts
■ pull carts
■ golf club rental
■ locker rooms
■ showers
☐ executive course
■ accommodations
■ food and beverages
■ clubhouse

Marlene Swanson
Manager
Bill Dykstra
Superintendent

NORTHERN D1

CLEAR LAKE RIVIERA YACHT AND GOLF CLUB

1965
Ed DeFelice

Course information: This semi-private course has nine holes. Par is 72 for 18 holes. There is also a six-hole pitch-and-putt course. The course is 5,638 yards and rated 67.5 from the regular tees (18 holes). The slope rating is 112. Women's tees are 5,105 yards and rated 68.7 from the regular tees. The slope rating is 119.

Play policy and fees: Outside play is accepted. Memberships are available. Green fees are $10 for nine holes and $12 for 18 holes on weekdays, and $11 for nine holes and $18 for 18 holes on weekends. Carts are $9 for nine holes and $13 for 18 holes weekdays. $11 and $18 weekends. Reservations are recommended.

Location: From Napa on Highway 29 drive to Lower Lake, turn left and drive to Soda Bay Road. Turn right and drive to Fairway Drive. From Ukiah take Highway 20 to Lakeport and Kelseyville. Turn left on Soda Bay Road and travel to Fairway Drive.

Course description: This hilly, picturesque course offers views of Clear Lake. It has sidehill lies, big greens and elevated tees. This is a panoramic course, but tough. Brings lots of golf balls.

10200 Fairway Drive
Kelseyville, CA 95451

Pro shop   (707) 277-7129
Restaurant   (707) 277-9126

☐ driving range
■ practice greens
■ power carts
■ pull carts
■ golf club rental
☐ locker rooms
☐ showers
■ executive course
☐ accommodations
■ food and beverages
■ clubhouse

Dusty Millar
General Manager
Rex Thrasher
Superintendent

ADAMS SPRINGS GOLF COURSE

Course 3
MAP D1 grid c3

1962
Jack Fleming

PO Box 2088
Loch Lomond, CA 95426

14347 Snead Court
Loch Lomond, CA 95426

Pro shop   (707) 928-9992

□ driving range
■ practice greens
■ power carts
■ pull carts
■ golf club rental
□ locker rooms
□ showers
□ executive course
□ accommodations
■ food and beverages
■ clubhouse

V.S. Doucette
Manager

F.H. Doucette
Superintendent

Course information: This public course has nine holes. Par is 68 for 18 holes. The course is 5,280 yards and rated 64.6 from the regular tees (18 holes). The slope rating is 111. Women's tees are 4,998 yards and rated 68.1. The slope rating is 119.

Play policy and fees: Green fees are $7 for nine holes and $10 for 18 holes weekdays, and $9 for nine holes and $12 for 18 holes weekends. Carts are $15.

Location: From Highway 29 in Middletown, take Highway 175 west. Drive 11 miles to the course (one mile past Hoberg and one mile south of Loch Lomond). There are signs on the road to direct you.

Course description: One thing this course has going for it are the green fees: they haven't increased in the last three years. Better yet, this mountain-setting course has a rolling terrain with generous fairways and is walkable. Three lakes come into play on five holes. You'll see lots of wildlife. Plans call for overnight lodging.

HOBERG'S FOREST LAKE GOLF AND COUNTRY CLUB

Course 4
MAP D1 grid d3

PO Box 2325
Cobb, CA 95436

10200 Golf Road
Cobb, CA 95436

Pro shop   (707) 928-5276

□ driving range
■ practice greens
■ power carts
■ pull carts
■ golf club rental
□ locker rooms
□ showers
□ executive course
□ accommodations
■ food and beverages
□ clubhouse

Les Russo
Professional

Helmut Knorn
Superintendent

Course information: This public course has nine holes. Par is 66 for 18 holes. The course is 4,482 yards and rated 61.5 from the regular tees. The slope rating is 107. Women's tees are 4,482 yards and rated 64.6. The slope rating is 107.

Play policy and fees: Green fees are $8 for nine holes and $11 for 18 holes weekdays, and $10 for nine holes and $13 for 18 holes weekends. Carts are $8 for nine holes and $15 for 18 holes.

Location: Drive north on Highway 29 to Highway 175. Take Highway 175 to the town of Cobb. The course is set at Highway 175 and Golf Road.

Course description: A creek meanders through this pretty mountain course located 3,600 feet above sea level. There are bunkers on every hole and many pine trees come into play. This course is open for play year-round, weather permitting.

HIDDEN VALLEY LAKE GOLF AND COUNTRY CLUB

Course 5
MAP D1 grid d4

1970
William Francis Bell

PO Box 5130
Middletown, CA 95461

1 Hartman Road
Middletown, CA 95461

Pro shop   (707) 987-3035
Restaurant (707) 987-3147

- driving range
- practice greens
- power carts
- pull carts
- golf club rental
- locker rooms
- showers
- ☐ executive course
- ☐ accommodations
- food and beverages
- clubhouse

Rob Kenny
Professional

Robert Leas
Superintendent

NORTHERN D1

Course information: This semi-private course has 18 holes and par is 72. The course is 6,603 yards and rated 71.6 from the championship tees, and 6,278 yards and rated 70.1 from the regular tees. The slope ratings are 118 championship and 115 regular. Women's tees are 6,195 yards and rated 74.8 from the championship tees, and 5,613 yards and rated 71.5 from the regular tees. The slope ratings are 133 championship and 123 regular.

Play policy and fees: Green fees are $10 for nine holes and $15 for 18 holes on weekdays, and $15 for nine holes and $22 for 18 holes on weekends. Property owners are eligible for special rates. Carts are $18 on weekdays and $20 on weekends. Reservations are recommended. Shirts must be worn at all times. No tank tops, halter tops, short shorts or street shoes may be worn.

Location: From Middletown, drive five miles north on Highway 29. The course is on the right.

Course description: This sprawling course is scenic and hilly. The front nine is long and flat. The back nine is shorter with elevated tees. Water comes into play on 10 of the holes mostly, during the winter months. The most dramatic hole is the 377-yard, par-4 15th, where golfers tee off several hundred feet above the fairway and are afforded spectacular views. It looks like you have to hit it a country mile, but you don't. If you over hit, you're likely to land in the trees on the right, which just proves that going for the green will get you in trouble. Insiders suggest aiming for the swimming pool and you're safe. You'll understand when you see it.

MAP ON PAGE 86

89

Course information: This public course has nine holes. Par is 70 for 18 holes. The course is 5,304 yards and rated 65.6 from the regular tees (18 holes). The slope rating is 112. Women's tees are 4,884 yards and rated 68.4. The slope rating is 113.

Play policy and fees: Green fees are $9 for nine holes and $11 for 18 holes weekdays, and $11 for nine holes and $13 for 18 holes weekends. There is a $7 senior rate for nine holes. Carts are $9 for nine holes and $16 for 18 holes.

Location: Driving north on Highway 101 into Healdsburg, take the Central Healdsburg exit onto Healdsburg Avenue. Drive on Healdsburg Avenue through two lights before turning right on Matheson Street. You'll see the course on the left.

Course description: This is a hilly, tree-lined course with small greens. It's walkable.

PO Box 1193
Healdsburg, CA 95448

927 S. Fitch Mountain Road
Healdsburg, CA 95448

Pro shop   (707) 433-4275

- ☐ driving range
- ■ practice greens
- ■ power carts
- ■ pull carts
- ■ golf club rental
- ☐ locker rooms
- ☐ showers
- ☐ executive course
- ☐ accommodations
- ■ food and beverages
- ■ clubhouse

Mike Ash
Manager/Professional

WINDSOR GOLF CLUB

1989
Fred Bliss

6555 Skylane Boulevard
Windsor, CA 95492

Pro shop   (707) 838-7888

■ driving range
■ practice greens
■ power carts
■ pull carts
■ golf club rental
□ locker rooms
□ showers
□ executive course
□ accommodations
■ food and beverages
□ clubhouse

Charlie Gibson
Professional

Rick Hansen
Superintendent

Course information: This public course has 18 holes and par is 72. The course is 6,650 yards and rated 72.3 from the tournament tees, 6,169 yards and rated 70.1 from the championship tees, and 5,628 yards and rated 67.0 from the regular tees. The slope ratings are 126 tournament, 121 championship and 118 regular. Women's tees are 5,628 yards and rated 72.5 from the championship tees, and 5,116 yards and rated 69.3 from the regular tees. The slope ratings are 136 championship and 125 regular.

Play policy and fees: Green fees are $19 on weekdays, and $29 on weekends. Twilight rates are $12 on weekdays and $18 on weekends. Senior rates are $12 weekdays. Junior rates are $7 weekdays. Carts are $10 per person for 18 holes and $15 for a single rider. Twilighters get the carts for $15. Pull carts are $2. Reserve a tee time seven days in advance.

Location: From Highway 101 in Santa Rosa, take the Shiloh Road exit. Drive one-half of a mile west of the freeway. The course is on the right.

Course description: This course boasts a winding creek, four lakes and many mature oaks. Hole four is the pride of the course: It's 194 yards over a lake to a rock-banked green. The best way to shoot this hole, of course, is over the lake. As the clubhouse tale goes, a hole-in-one was once sunk like this: the ball bounced off a rock in the lake, rebounded up onto the green and found the hole! Hole 17 is also notable. It's 368 yards from an elevated tee, with bunkers to the left and a lake to the right. The second shot is over a lake to a small green (par is four). It's a beauty. Former PGA Tour player Charlie Gibson is both the pro and director of golf operations. The course is host to a Ben Hogan Tour event annually, and holes 11 and 16 are rated in the top 15 toughest holes on the tour.

WIKIUP GOLF COURSE

1963

Course information: This public course has nine holes. Par is 58 for 18 holes. The course is 3,223 yards and rated 54.0 from the regular tees (18 holes). The slope rating is 80. Women's yardage and ratings were unavailable.

Play policy and fees: Green fees are $7 for nine holes and $10 for 18 holes on weekdays, and $9 for nine holes and $12 for 18 holes on weekends and holidays. Student and senior rates are $7 for 18 holes. Carts are $9 for nine holes and $12 for 18 holes.

Location: From Santa Rosa, drive four miles north on Highway 101 to River Road. Turn east on River Road. Turn north on Old Redwood Highway and drive one-half mile. Turn east on Wikiup Drive and drive one-half mile to the course.

Course description: This is a challenging, short course with no adjacent holes. It is scenic and well bunkered with two par-4s. The short 268-yard, par-4 second hole is a temptation. It makes players choose between laying up or carrying a water hazard. The gentle slopes make the course easily walkable.

5001 Carriage Lane
Santa Rosa, CA 95401

Pro shop   (707) 546-8787

☐ driving range
■ practice greens
■ power carts
■ pull carts
■ golf club rental
☐ locker rooms
☐ showers
☐ executive course
☐ accommodations
■ food and beverages
☐ clubhouse

Pete Perilli
Professional

Thomas Langbein
Superintendent

MOUNT SAINT HELENA GOLF COURSE

Course information: This public course has nine holes. Par is 68 for 18 holes. The course is 5,496 yards and rated 65.9 from the regular tees (18 holes). The slope rating is 105. Women's tees are 5,294 yards and rated 69.1. The slope rating is 113.

Play policy and fees: Green fees are $9 on weekdays and $12 on weekends. Senior rates are $7 on weekdays and $9 weekends. Carts are $8 for nine holes and $14 for 18 holes. Shirts must be worn at all times. No rubber spikes are allowed.

Location: Driving north toward Calistoga on Highway 29, take the Lincoln exit north to Grant Street. Turn left and follow the road to the course at the fairgrounds on the left.

Course description: This course is located in the middle of the Napa County Fairgrounds. It's short and flat with narrow fairways. Accuracy is important. There are no par-5s. The sixth hole, formerly a par-5, is now a 435-yard par-4. Water comes into play on two holes.

PO Box 344
Calistoga, CA 94515

Grant Street,
Napa Co. Fairgrounds.
Calistoga, CA 94515

Pro shop   (707) 942-9966

☐ driving range
☐ practice greens
■ power carts
■ pull carts
■ golf club rental
☐ locker rooms
☐ showers
☐ executive course
☐ accommodations
■ food and beverages
☐ clubhouse

Roy Wells
Manager

Dick Hall
Superintendent

AETNA SPRINGS
GOLF COURSE

NORTHERN D1

Course information: This public course has nine holes. Par is 70 for 18 holes. The course is 5,372 yards and rated 64.7 from the regular tees. The slope rating is 102. Women's tees are 5,054 and rated 69.2. The slope rating is 113.

Play policy and fees: Green fees are $8 weekdays and $10 for nine holes or $12 for 18 holes weekends. Seniors and juniors are $5 weekends. All day play is permitted for the same price on weekdays. Twilight green fee is $4 after 4 p.m. weekdays. Carts are $8 for nine holes and $15 for 18 holes. This course is available for tournaments.

Location: From Highway 29 heading north toward Calistoga, drive one mile past Saint Helena. Turn right on Deer Park Road North. Stay on this road and drive through Angwin. The road turns into Howell Mountain Road. Once in Pope Valley veer to the left where the road branches at the service station. Drive to Pope Valley Road and go left. Drive four miles to Aetna Springs Road (just past the Hub Cap Ranch). Turn onto Aetna and drive one mile to the course.

Course description: Built around the turn of the century, this is one of the oldest courses in California. It's nestled in the mountains with gentle hills and two creeks running through it. It has six par-4s, two par-3s and one par-5. Bring the family, picnic tables border the course. There is also a barbecue area.

1600 Aetna Springs Road
Pope Valley, CA 94567

Pro shop   (707) 965-2115

- ■ driving range
- ■ practice greens
- ■ power carts
- ■ pull carts
- ■ golf club rental
- □ locker rooms
- □ showers
- □ executive course
- □ accommodations
- ■ food and beverages
- ■ clubhouse

Kent Stuth
Professional/Manager

Daniel Hicks
Superintendent

MAP ON PAGE 86   93

SEBASTOPOL GOLF COURSE

Course information: This public course has nine holes. Par is 62 for 18 holes. The course is 3,242 yards and rated 55.0 from the regular tees. The slope rating is 86. Women's yardage and ratings were unavailable.

Play policy and fees: Green fees are $7 for nine holes and $9 for 18 holes weekdays, and $8 for nine holes and $10 for 18 holes weekends. Senior and student rates are $6 on weekdays. Carts are $7 for nine holes and $10 for 18 holes.

Location: From Sebastopol, drive three miles north on Highway 116 to Scotts Right-of-Way to the course.

Course description: This short course is all par-3s and par-4s, with the longest hole measuring 240 yards. The most notable is the 190-yard, par-3 second hole, which requires an uphill shot to a two-tiered green. Water comes into play on the 195-yard, par-4 eighth hole.

2881 Scotts Right-of-Way
Sebastopol, CA 95472

Pro shop   (707) 823-9852
Clubhouse (707) 823-2003

☐ driving range
■ practice greens
■ power carts
■ pull carts
■ golf club rental
☐ locker rooms
☐ showers
■ executive course
☐ accommodations
■ food and beverages
■ clubhouse

Gene Phillips
Professional

Lee Farris
Manager

Wade Farris
Superintendent

SANTA ROSA GOLF AND COUNTRY CLUB

1958
Jack Fleming

Course information: This private course has 18 holes and par is 72. The course is 6,730 yards and rated 71.3 from the tournament tees, 6,418 yards and rated 69.9 from the championship tees, and 5,425 yards and rated 67.7, the regular tees. The slope ratings are 119 tournament, 117 championship and 112 regular. Women's tees are 6,412 yards and rated 76.6 from the championship tees, and 5,912 yards and rated 73.7 from the regular tees. The slope ratings are 131 championship and 127 regular.

Play policy and fees: Members and guests only. Reciprocal play is accepted with members of other private clubs. Reciprocal fees are $40 on weekdays and $50 on weekends. Guest fees are $25 when accompanied by a club member. Carts are $10 and are mandatory. Reservations recommended. Shirts must have a collar and shorts must have a six-inch inseam. No blue jeans, halter tops or tank tops may be worn.

Location: From Highway 101, take the Highway 12 west toward Sebastopol. Turn right on Fulton Road and left on Hall Road. Turn left on Country Club road. Turn right on Oak Meadow Drive and drive to the course.

Course description: This sprawling course is lined with beautiful oak trees and is tougher than it looks. The course record for men is 63.

5110 Oak Meadow Drive
Santa Rosa, CA 95401

Pro shop   (707) 546-6617
Clubhouse (707) 546-3485

■ driving range
■ practice greens
■ power carts
■ pull carts
■ golf club rental
■ locker rooms
■ showers
☐ executive course
☐ accommodations
■ food and beverages
■ clubhouse

Val Verhunce
Professional

Ed Stocke
Superintendent

BENNETT VALLEY GOLF COURSE

Course information: This public course has 18 holes and par is 72. The course is 6,583 yards and rated 70.6 from the championship tees, and 6,221 yards and rated 69.0 from the regular tees. The slope ratings are 112 championship and 109 regular. Women's tees are 5,958 yards and rated 72.5. The slope rating is 116.

Play policy and fees: Green fees are $6 for nine holes and $9 for 18 holes weekdays, and $8 and $12 weekends. Senior rates are $5 for nine holes and $6 for 18 holes and available on weekdays only. Carts are $16 for 18 holes. Reservations are recommended.

Location: Take Highway 12 east off Highway 101. At the fairgrounds veer right onto Bennett Valley Road, which will take you to Yulupa Avenue.

Course description: This is a flat, well conditioned course with lots of trees. The greens are fast and the course is walkable. A creek wanders through the course, and provides some water hazard encounters. Bennett Valley Golf Course hosts the first leg of the Santa Rosa City Championship.

3330 Yulupa Avenue
Santa Rosa, CA 95405
Pro shop   (707) 528-3673

- driving range
- practice greens
- power carts
- pull carts
- golf club rental
- locker rooms
- showers
- executive course
- accommodations
- food and beverages
- clubhouse

Bob Borowicz
Professional

Steve Tiedeman
Superintendent

John Flachman
Superintendent

NORTHERN D1

FOUNTAINGROVE RESORT AND COUNTRY CLUB

1985
Ted Robinson

Course information: This semi-private course has 18 holes and par is 72. The course is 6,759 yards and rated 72.8 from the championship tees, and 6,332 yards and rated 70.9 from the regular tees. The slope ratings are 132 championship and 128 regular. Women's tees are 5,619 yards and rated 72.1. The slope rating is 128.

Play policy and fees: Outside play is accepted. Green fees are $45 on weekdays, $55 on Fridays, and $65 on weekends. Carts are mandatory and included in the green fees. Reservations are recommended up to a week in advance. Carts are allowed on paths only.

Location: In Santa Rosa on Highway 101, take the Mendocino Avenue/Old Redwood Highway exit. Drive east and turn left on Fountaingrove Parkway. Continue up the hill to the course, which is on the left.

Course description: This Ted Robinson design is a tight, hilly layout with lots of trees and good greens. The 17th hole is picturesque. It is a par-3 that requires a 218-yard shot over water. The course records are 67 for men and 73 for women.

1525 Fountaingrove Parkway
Santa Rosa, CA 95403
Pro shop   (707) 579-4653
Clubhouse (707) 544-1330

- driving range
- practice greens
- power carts
- pull carts
- golf club rental
- locker rooms
- showers
- executive course
- accommodations
- food and beverages
- clubhouse

Mike Jonas
Professional

Robert Tyler
Superintendent

FAIRGROUNDS GOLF COURSE AND DRIVING RANGE

Course information: This public course has nine holes. Par is 58 for 18 holes. The course is 3,296 yards and rated 54.6 (18 holes). The slope rating is 73. Women's yardage and ratings were unavailable.

Play policy and fees: Green fees are $6 for nine holes and $7 for 18 holes weekdays, and $7 and $8 weekends. Senior and junior rates are $5 for nine holes and $6 for 18 holes weekdays, and $6 and $7 for weekends. Twilight rates are $4.50 for nine holes and $5.50 for 18 holes (after 5 p.m.). Pull carts are $2.

Location: In Santa Rosa on Highway 101 north, take the Santa Rosa Fairgrounds exit which will take you to the fairgrounds and the course on your right.

Course description: This course, situated in the center of the Santa Rosa Fairgrounds race track, is a good practice course. There are two water hazards and some sand traps. The course is flat and the greens are fairly small. A night driving range is open to 9 p.m.

1350 Bennett Valley Road
Santa Rosa, CA 95404

Pro shop   (707) 546-2469

- ■ driving range
- ■ practice greens
- ■ power carts
- ■ pull carts
- ■ golf club rental
- ☐ locker rooms
- ☐ showers
- ☐ executive course
- ☐ accommodations
- ■ food and beverages
- ■ clubhouse

Gene Phillips
Professional

Nate DeJung
Manager/Superintendent

OAKMONT GOLF COURSE

1963
Ted Robinson

7025 Oakmont Drive
Santa Rosa, CA 95409

West course(707) 539-0415
East course (707) 538-2454

- ■ driving range
- ■ practice greens
- ■ power carts
- ■ pull carts
- ■ golf club rental
- ■ locker rooms
- ■ showers
- ■ executive course
- □ accommodations
- ■ food and beverages
- ■ clubhouse

Dean F. James
Professional

Mike Clark
Superintendent

Course information: This semi-private facility has 36 holes. Par is 72 for the West Course and 63 for the East Course.

The West Course is 6,379 yards and rated 70.4 from the championship tees, and 6,059 yards and rated 69.0 from the regular tees. The slope ratings are 115 championship and 112 regular. Women's tees are 5,573 yards and rated 71.9. The slope rating is 128..

The East Course is 4,293 yards and rated 59.8 from the regular tees. The slope rating is 94. Women's tees are 4,067 yards and rated 62.2. The slope rating is 94.

Play policy and fees: Outside play is accepted. West Course green fees are $20 on weekdays and $28 on weekends. East Course green fees are $15 on weekdays and $20 on weekends. Carts are $20. Reservations are recommended. Shirts must have collars. No tank tops may be worn.

Location: From Santa Rosa, drive east on Highway 12 toward Sonoma. Turn right on Oakmont Drive into the community of Oakmont. The course is on the right, eight miles east of Highway 101.

Course description: The West Course is short with lots of trees. There is water on 14 holes. The pride of the West Course is the 381-yard, par-4 eighth hole, which boasts two lakes and out-of-bounds on both sides. The East Course is a short, executive course with some challenging par-3s. The 171-yard, par-3 14th hole, for example, requires a longish carry over a creek. Oakmont co-hosts the Santa Rosa City Championship.

MEADOWOOD RESORT HOTEL GOLF COURSE

1963

Course information: This private resort course has nine holes. Par is 62 for 18 holes. The course is 4,106 yards and rated 59.5 from the regular tees (18 holes). The slope rating is 92. Women's tees are 3,982 yards and rated 61.9. The slope rating is 94.

Play policy and fees: Reciprocal play is accepted with members of other private clubs. Hotel guests are welcome. Green fees are $25 for hotel guests, and $40 for reciprocators every day. Shirts with collars must be worn.

Location: From Napa, drive north on Highway 29. Turn right on Pope Street and take Pope Street to Silverado Trail. Jog left then right on Silverado Trial to Howell Mountain Road. Follow Howell Mountain road to Meadowood Lane.

Course description: This is a short, tight and tricky course with lots of trees. There are some hills and undulating greens. It's an excellent course for beginners and intermediates.

900 Meadowood Lane
Saint Helena, CA 94574

Pro shop   (707) 963-3646

- ☐ driving range
- ■ practice greens
- ☐ power carts
- ■ pull carts
- ■ golf club rental
- ☐ locker rooms
- ☐ showers
- ■ executive course
- ■ accommodations
- ■ food and beverages
- ☐ clubhouse

Joe Roberts
Professional

Dana Waldor
Superintendent

MOUNTAIN SHADOWS GOLF COURSE

1 9 6 3
R.E. Baldock

100 Golf Course Drive
Rohnert Park, CA 94928

Pro shop   (707) 584-7766

- ■ driving range
- ■ practice greens
- ■ power carts
- ■ pull carts
- ■ golf club rental
- □ locker rooms
- □ showers
- □ executive course
- □ accommodations
- ■ food and beverages
- ■ clubhouse

Greg Anderson
Professional

Mike Nauroth
Superintendent

NORTHERN D1

Course information: This public facility has two 18-hole courses. Par is 72 for each.

The North Course is 6,392 yards and rated 69.2 from the championship tees, and 5,867 yards and rated 67.5 from the regular tees. The slope ratings are 112 championship and 108 regular. Women's tees are 5,543 yards and rated 70.5 from the regular tees. The slope rating is 117.

The South Course is 6,490 yards and rated 70.1 from the championship tees, and 6,086 yards and rated 68.0 from the regular tees. The slope ratings are 115 championship and 111 regular. Women's tees are 5,806 yards and rated 71.4 from the regular tees. The slope rating is 117.

Play policy and fees: The North Course weekday green fees are $29 before 2 p.m., $20 from 2 p.m. to 4 p.m., $15 from 4 p.m. to 6 p.m., and $10 after 6 p.m. Green fees for Fridays, weekends and holidays are $35 before 3 p.m., $25 from 3 p.m. to 5 p.m., $15 from 5 p.m. to 7 p.m., and $10 after 7 p.m.

South Course weekday green fees are $16 without cart or $27 with cart before 2 p.m., $13 without cart or $18 with cart from 2 p.m. to 4 p.m., $8 without cart or $15 with cart from 4 p.m. to 6 p.m., and $5 without cart and $8 with cart after 6 p.m. Weekend and holiday green fees are $25 until 3 p.m., $13 without cart or $20 with cart from 3 p.m. to 5 p.m., $8 without cart and $15 with cart from 5 p.m. to 7 p.m., and $5 without cart or $8 with cart after 7 p.m. Call for mandatory cart policy.

Location: From Santa Rosa, drive seven miles south on Highway 101. Take the Wilfred exit east to Golf Course Drive.

Course description: Both courses are tight with a rolling terrain and large, undulating greens. Notable is the seventh hole on the North Course. It was rated one of the most difficult holes in Northern California with out-of-bounds to the left and a lake running down the entire right side. The green sits on a well bunkered peninsula. It's a beauty. The Redwood Empire Championship-Golden State Tour and the Sonoma County Men's Amateur Championship tournaments are held here annually.

CHIMNEY ROCK
GOLF COURSE

1966
R.E. Baldock

5320 Silverado Trail
Napa, CA 94559

Pro shop   (707) 255-3363

☐ driving range
■ practice greens
■ power carts
■ pull carts
■ golf club rental
☐ locker rooms
☐ showers
☐ executive course
☐ accommodations
■ food and beverages
■ clubhouse

Harrie Thomas
Manager

Course information: This public course has nine holes. Par is 72 for 18 holes. The course is 6,836 yards and rated 71.0 from the championship tees, and 6,618 yards and rated 70.0 from the regular tees (18 holes). The slope ratings are 110 championship and 108 regular. Women's tees are 5,884 yards and rated 72.9. The slope rating is 124.

Play policy and fees: Green fees are $12 for nine holes and $16 for 18 holes weekdays, and $15 and $20 weekends. Senior rates are $7.50 for unlimited play weekdays only. Carts are $13 for nine holes and $18 for 18 holes.

Location: From Napa heading north on Highway 29, go right on Trancos Road. Follow Trancos Street to Silverado Trail and turn left and travel 4.5 miles to the course.

Course description: This course is set in the vineyards and three lakes come into play. It's flat andeasily walkable.

SILVERADO COUNTRY CLUB

1955
Johnny Dawson

1600 Atlas Peak Road
Napa, CA 94558

Pro shop (707) 257-5460
Clubhouse (707) 257-0200

■ driving range
■ practice greens
■ power carts
□ pull carts
■ golf club rental
■ locker rooms
■ showers
□ executive course
■ accommodations
■ food and beverages
■ clubhouse

Jeff Goodwin
Professional
Brian Morris
Superintendent

NORTHERN D1

Course information: This private resort facility has two 18-hole courses. Par is 72 for each.

The North Course is 6,896 yards and rated 73.4 from the championship tees, and 6,351 yards and rated 70.9 from the regular tees. The slope ratings are: 131 championship and 126 regular. Women's tees are 5,857 yards and rated 73.9. The slope rating is 124.

The South Course is 6,670 yards and rated 72.4 from the championship tees, and 6,253 yards and rated 70.5 from the regular tees. The slope ratings are 129 championship and 124 regular. Women's tees are 5,782 yards and rated 71.8. The slope rating is 123.

Play policy and fees: Reciprocal play is accepted with members of other private clubs. Hotel guests are welcome. Green fees are $80 for hotel guests and $90 for reciprocal players. Carts are mandatory and included in the green fees. Reservations are recommended two days in advance unless you are a hotel guest.

Location: From Napa, drive north on Highway 121. Take the Atlas Peak Road exit north. Drive less than a mile to the course.

Course description: The North Course is a longer, championship course, while the South Course is shorter and requires more finesse shots. Both have sprawling layouts with large, undulating greens. Water and large oak trees guard the courses. Remodeled by Robert Trent Jones, Jr. in 1966, the North Course was formerly used for the PGA Tour's Kaiser International and Anheuser-Busch Classic. The South Course is the site of the Senior PGA Tour's Transamerica Open.

ADOBE CREEK GOLF COURSE

1990
Robert Trent Jones, Jr.

1901 Frates Road
Petaluma, CA 94954

Pro shop   (707) 765-3000

- ■ driving range
- ■ practice greens
- ■ power carts
- □ pull carts
- ■ golf club rental
- □ locker rooms
- □ showers
- □ executive course
- □ accommodations
- ■ food and beverages
- ■ clubhouse

Dana Banke
Professional

Peter Dempsey
Superintendent

Course information: This public course has 18 holes and par is 72. The course is 6,825 yards and rated 72.6 from the tournament tees, 6,221 yards and rated 70.0 from the championship tees, and 5,668 yards and rated 67.5 from the regular tees. The slope ratings are 126 tournament, 120 championship and 115 regular. Women's tees are 5,027 yards and rated 68.3. The slope rating is 115.

Play policy and fees: Green fees are $45 weekdays and $55 weekends, carts included. Reservations are accepted two weeks in advance.

Location: From Highway 101 in Petaluma, take the Highway 116 exit east and drive 1.25 miles. Turn left on Frates Road and drive three-fourths of a mile to the course on the left.

Course description: This sprawling course, situated in the Sonoma County countryside, has many mounds. Five lakes, a stream and 70 bunkers make accuracy a must. Beware of the seventh hole: It's a par-4, 405-yard challenge with a creek on the right and a creek fronting the large green. Two creeks equal trouble.

PETALUMA GOLF AND COUNTRY CLUB

PO Box 26
Petaluma, CA 94953

1100 Country Club Drive
Petaluma, CA 94953

Pro shop   (707) 762-7041

- ■ driving range
- ■ practice greens
- ■ power carts
- ■ pull carts
- ■ golf club rental
- □ locker rooms
- □ showers
- □ executive course
- □ accommodations
- ■ food and beverages
- ■ clubhouse

Terry Cline
Manager

Bill Maeder
Superintendent

Course information: This private course has nine holes. Par is 70 for 18 holes. The course is 5,574 yards and rated 66.0 from the regular tees (18 holes). The slope rating is 107. Women's tees are 5,426 yards and rated 70.5 from the regular tees. The slope rating is 119.

Play policy and fees: Reciprocal play is accepted with members of other private clubs. Call to make arrangements.

Location: Heading north on Highway 101 toward Petaluma, take the Petaluma Boulevard South exit northwest into town. Take McNear Avenue south to Country Club Drive to the course.

Course description: This short, hilly course is called "Goat Hill." It has lots of bunkers, no water and is walkable if you have one leg shorter than the other.

SONOMA GOLF CLUB

Course 23
MAP D1 grid i4

1926
Sam Whiting

1991
Robert Muir Graves Re-Design

NORTHERN D1

17700 Arnold Drive
Sonoma, CA 95416

Pro shop (707) 996-0300
Clubhouse (707) 996-2625

■ driving range
■ practice greens
■ power carts
□ pull carts
■ golf club rental
■ locker rooms
■ showers
□ executive course
□ accommodations
■ food and beverages
■ clubhouse

Ron Blum
Professional

Joyce Currie
Manager

Larry Norman
Superintendent

Course information: This public course has 18 holes and par is 72. The course is 7,069 yards and rated 73.5 from the championship tees, and 6,583 yards and rated 71.3 from the regular tees. The slope ratings are 127 championship and 123 regular. Women's tees are 5,519 yards and rated 71.5. The slope ratings is 128.

Play policy and fees: Green fees include cart and are $60 weekdays, and $80 weekends. Twilight green fees are half price after 2 p.m.

Location: North on Highway 101 take Highway 37 east to Highway 121. Travel north on Highway 121 to the Arnold Drive exit. Drive about seven miles on Arnold Drive to the golf course.

Course description: This course has undergone a major renovation under the design guidance of Robert Muir Graves. It reopened in March, 1991 to rave reviews, and is considered one of the top public courses in the country. A driving range was added, causing some realignment, but the hole sequence remains the same. It's mostly flat but there is a lot of mounding and subtle elevation changes. The greens were totally rebuilt and enlarged during the 15-month, $10 million renovation period, but are well established. They are also very subtle and maintain a traditional flavor. There is nothing tricky about the greens. Because it is an old, mature course, there are lots of oaks and redwoods guarding several tight doglegs. Two new lakes were added, but they don't come noticeably into play unless your shot is particularly errant. The rough has just been stripped and redone. This is definitely the new course to play in Northern California.

MAP ON PAGE 86   103

LOS ARROYOS GOLF CLUB

Course information: This public course has nine holes and par is 58 for 18 holes. The course is 3,078 yards and not rated.

Play policy and fees: Green fees are $5 weekdays and $8 weekends. This is an all-day rate. Pull carts are $2.

Location: From San Francisco heading north on Highway 101, take the Highway 116 exit east to Sonoma. The course is at the intersection of Highway 116 and Highway 121.

Course description: This tree-lined executive course is fairly flat and makes a good iron course. There are two par-4s.

5000 Stage Gulch Road
Sonoma, CA 95476

Pro shop   (707) 938-8835

- ■ driving range
- □ practice greens
- □ power carts
- ■ pull carts
- ■ golf club rental
- □ locker rooms
- □ showers
- ■ executive course
- □ accommodations
- ■ food and beverages
- ■ clubhouse

Karen Sequeria
Manager

NAPA GOLF COURSE

1958
Jack Fleming

Course information: This public course has 18 holes and par is 72. The course is 6,730 yards and rated 71.7 from the championship tees, and 6,506 yards and rated 70.7 from the regular tees. The slope ratings are 118 championship and 115 regular. Women's tees are 4,958 yards and rated 68.5. The slope rating is are 120.

Play policy and fees: The city of Napa now has a resident/non-resident green fee policy for this course. Green fees for non-residents are $17 weekdays, $23 weekends and holidays, and $12 after 3 p.m. any day. Resident green fees are $13 weekdays, $17 weekends and holidays, and $10 after 3 p.m. any day. Carts are $17 for 18 holes and $10 for nine holes. Reservations are recommended seven days or less in advance. No single play is allowed. No spectators.

Location: From Highway 12 in Napa, take Highway 29 north. Take the Lake Berryessa exit at the fork. Drive two miles to Streblow Drive and turn left to get to the course.

Kennedy Parkway,
2295 Streblow Drive
Napa, CA 94558

Pro shop   (707) 255-4333

- ■ driving range
- ■ practice greens
- ■ power carts
- ■ pull carts
- ■ golf club rental
- □ locker rooms
- □ showers
- □ executive course
- □ accommodations
- ■ food and beverages
- ■ clubhouse

Bob Swan
Manager/Professional
Steve Good
Superintendent

Course description: This underrated course is long, tough and tight. It has many trees and water occurs on 14 holes. Nicknamed Kennedy Park because the course is situated in Napa's John F. Kennedy Park, this course was used for U.S. Open qualifying in 1972 and formerly for PGA Tour events at Silverado Country Club.

NAPA VALLEY
COUNTRY CLUB

1 9 9 0
Ron Fream

Course information: This private course has 18 holes and par is 71. The course is 6,051 yards and rated 70.1 from the championship tees, and 5,718 yards and rated 68.5 from the regular tees. The slope ratings are 123 championship and 119 regular. Women's tees are 5,230 yards and rated 69.8. The slope rating is 123.

Play policy and fees: Reciprocal play is accepted with members of other private clubs. Green fees for reciprocators are $60, including cart. Guest fees are $22 when accompanied by a member weekdays, and $27 weekends. Call to make arrangements. Carts are $8 per rider.

Location: From Highway 121 in Napa, drive 1.5 miles on Hagen Road to the course.

Course description: This scenic course has tight fairways and small, undulating greens. There are many oak trees. The course was expanded in the spring of 1990 to 18 holes under the design guidance of Ron Fream, and the new nine is beautiful. From it you can see the entire Bay Area and Napa Valley. From the 11th tee you can see the Golden Gate Bridge. When you're not looking at the view, check out this par-3. It's 135 yards to an island green. If you miss the green you're not in water, but you are in a mean barranca.

PO Box 3177
Napa, CA 94558

3385 Hagen Road
Napa, CA 94558

Pro shop   (707) 252-1114
Clubhouse (707) 252-1111

- ■ driving range
- ■ practice greens
- ■ power carts
- ■ pull carts
- ■ golf club rental
- ■ locker rooms
- ■ showers
- ☐ executive course
- ☐ accommodations
- ■ food and beverages
- ■ clubhouse

Mitch Johnson
Professional

Ron Forsythe
Superintendent

NORTHERN D1

MAP ON PAGE 86

105

Course information: This public facility has 27 holes and par is 72. The course is 6,368 yards and rated 69.1 from the championship tees, and 5,906 yards and rated 67.0 from the regular tees. The slope ratings are 109 championship and 105 regular. Women's tees are 5,396 yards and rated 68.3. The slope rating is 112. The Executive Course is 3,120 yards and par is 29.

Play policy and fees: Green fees are $10 on weekdays and $15 on weekends. Senior green fees are discounted 50 cents. Carts are $13 on weekdays and $15 on weekends and holidays. Reservations are recommended one week in advance.

Location: From Vacaville, drive east on Interstate 80, past the Nut Tree restaurant. Take the Leisure Town Road exit to the course.

Course description: The course is picturesque and well maintained. The tee shot on the unusual par-3 first hole must carry over a lake. The men's course record is 62.

PO Box 1056
Vacaville, CA 95688

999 Leisure Town Road
Vacaville, CA 95688

Pro shop   (707) 448-1420

■ driving range
■ practice greens
■ power carts
■ pull carts
□ golf club rental
□ locker rooms
□ showers
■ executive course
□ accommodations
■ food and beverages
■ clubhouse

Kelly Adams
Professional

Al Bandrowsky
Manager

Mike Scollaro
Superintendent

INDIAN VALLEY GOLF CLUB

Course 28
MAP D1 grid J2

1957

PO Box 351
Novato, CA 94948

3035 Novato Boulevard
Novato, CA 94947

Pro shop   (415) 897-1118

Course information: This public course has 18 holes and par is 72. The course is 6,023 yards and rated 68.6 from the championship tees, and 5,759 yards and rated 67.4 from the regular tees. The slope ratings are 118 championship and 114 regular. Women's tees are 5,411 yards and rated 70.9. The slope rating is 128.

Play policy and fees: Green fees are $20 on weekdays and $30 on weekends. Carts are $20. Reservations are recommended. This course is available for tournaments.

Location: From Highway 101 in Novato, take the San Marin Drive exit west to Novato Boulevard. Turn right on Novato Boulevard to the course.

Course description: This scenic course is challenging and diverse. There are rolling hills and many trees. Water comes into play on 10 holes. A premium is placed on chipping and putting. One of the best holes is the 16th. It's a par-5 and drops 250 feet from the tee. There is an elevator from the 13th to the 14th hole. The Hills Brothers Pro-Am is held here annually.

- ■ driving range
- ■ practice greens
- ■ power carts
- ■ pull carts
- ■ golf club rental
- ■ locker rooms
- ■ showers
- □ executive course
- □ accommodations
- ■ food and beverages
- ■ clubhouse

Ron Hoyt
Professional

Jeff McAndrew
Director

Terry Leach
Superintendent

MARIN COUNTRY CLUB

Course 29
MAP D1 grid J2

1959

500 Country Club Drive
Novato, CA 94949

Pro shop   (415) 382-6707
Clubhouse   (415) 382-6700

Course information: This private course has 18 holes and par is 72. The course is 6,595 yards and rated 71.9 from the championship tees, and 6,341 yards and rated 70.7 from the regular tees. The slope ratings are 126 championship and 124 regular. Women's tees are 5,804 yards and rated 73.7. The slope rating is 133.

Play policy and fees: Reciprocal play is accepted with members of other private clubs. Guest fees are $50. Carts are $18.

Location: From Highway 101 in Novato, take the Ignacio Boulevard exit west. Drive 1.5 miles. Turn left on Country Club Drive to the course.

Course description: This sprawling, hilly course has numerous trees andquite a bit of water. The fairways are tight, and the greens are undulating.

- ■ driving range
- ■ practice greens
- ■ power carts
- ■ pull carts
- □ golf club rental
- ■ locker rooms
- ■ showers
- □ executive course
- □ accommodations
- ■ food and beverages
- ■ clubhouse

Gil Bennett
Professional

Stanley Burgess
Superintendent

NORTHERN D1

CHARDONNAY GOLF CLUB

1987
Algie M. Pulley, Jr.

PO Box 3779
Napa, CA 94558

2555 Jameson Canyon Road
Napa, CA 94559

Pro shop   (707) 257-8950

Course information: This semi-private course has 27 holes and par is 72 for any 18-hole combination.

The Meadows-Lakes Course is 6,796 yards and rated 73.7 from the tournament tees, and 6,394 yards and rated 71.7 from the championship tees, and 5,974 yards and rated 69.8 from the regular tees. The slope ratings are 133 tournament, 127 championship and 122 regular. Women's tees are 5,162 yards and rated 70.1. The slope rating is 126.

The Lakes-Vineyards Course is 7,058 yards and rated 74.8 from the tournament tees, and 6,657 yards and rated 72.8 from the championship tees, and 6,247 yards and rated 70.7 from the regular tees. The slope ratings are 137 tournament, 130 championship and 126 regular. Women's tees are 5,892 yards and rated 74.2 from the championship tees, and 5,447 yards and rated 71.6 from the regular tees. The slope ratings are 137 championship and 130 regular.

- ■ driving range
- ■ practice greens
- ■ power carts
- ☐ pull carts
- ■ golf club rental
- ■ locker rooms
- ■ showers
- ☐ executive course
- ☐ accommodations
- ■ food and beverages
- ■ clubhouse

Mike Cook
Professional

Roger Billings
Director

Dick McAllister
Superintendent

The Vineyards-Meadows Course is 6,945 yards and rated 74.3 from the tournament tees, and 6,607 yards and rated 72.6 from the championship tees, and 6,177 yards and rated 70.6 from the regular tees. The slope ratings are 137 tournament, 130 championship and 127 regular. Women's tees are 5,698 yards and rated 72.9 from the championship tees, and 5,239 yards and rated 70.3 from the regular tees. The slope ratings are 131 championship and 124 regular.

Play policy and fees: Outside play is accepted. Green fees are $50. Carts and range balls are included. Reservations may be made seven days in advance.

Location: From Highway 29 south of Napa, take Highway 12 east. The entrance to the course is 1.3 miles from the intersection.

Course description: This unique Scottish design championship course is situated on 368 acres of natural rolling hills interlaced with 120 acres of vineyards, lakes, streams and rock outcroppings. It plays host to the Northern California Open and the Napa Valley Open.

GREEN VALLEY COUNTRY CLUB

Course information: This private course has 18 holes and par is 72. The course is 6,490 yards and rated 70.1 from the championship tees, and 6,284 yards and rated 69.2 from the regular tees. The slope ratings are 119 championship and 115 regular. Women's tees are 6,292 yards and rated 76.2 from the championship tees, and 5,881 yards and rated 73.7 from the regular tees. The slope ratings are 134 championship and 131 regular.

Play policy and fees: Reciprocal play is accepted with members of other private clubs. Guest fees are $20 with a member any day, and $50 without a member weekdays, and $60 without a member weekends. Carts are $18 with a member and $22 without.

Location: From Vallejo, take Interstate 80 to Green Valley Road. Head north to Country Club Drive and turn left to the course.

Course description: This well maintained course has a rolling, tree-lined layout with good greens. There are lots of short doglegs and undulating greens. It plays narrow. A creek runs through four of the holes. The course is picturesque and challenging but can get fairly windy.

35 Country Club Drive
Suisun City, CA 94585

Pro shop   (707) 864-0473
Clubhouse   (707) 864-1101

- ■ driving range
- ■ practice greens
- ■ power carts
- ■ pull carts
- ☐ golf club rental
- ■ locker rooms
- ■ showers
- ☐ executive course
- ☐ accommodations
- ■ food and beverages
- ■ clubhouse

Fred Covey
Professional
Ray Story
Superintendent

RANCHO SOLANO GOLF COURSE

1990
Gary Roger Baird

Course information: This public course has 18 holes and par is 72. The course is 6,705 yards and rated 72.9 from the tournament tees, and 6,210 yards and rated 70.7 from the championship tees, and 5,738 yards and rated 68.5 from the regular tees. The slope ratings are 125 tournament, 121 championship and 117 regular. Women's tees are 5,260 yards and rated 69.6. The slope ratings are 117.

Play policy and fees: Green fees are $11 weekdays and $15 weekends for residents of Fairfield, $17 and $22 for non-residents. Half price rates are available after 4 p.m. Carts are $18 for residents and $21 for non-residents.

Location: On Interstate 80 in Fairfield, exit on Waterman Boulevard west and follow it two miles. Go right on Rancho Solano Parkway to the course.

Course description: This new course is undulating with lots of sand. The greens are very large and tricky and still a little hard. Still, it's an enjoyable course.

3250 Rancho Solano
Parkway
Fairfield, CA 94533

Pro shop   (707) 429-4653

- ■ driving range
- ■ practice greens
- ■ power carts
- ■ pull carts
- ■ golf club rental
- ☐ locker rooms
- ☐ showers
- ☐ executive course
- ☐ accommodations
- ■ food and beverages
- ■ clubhouse

Dale Bradley
Manager/Professional
Tim McCoy
Superintendent

CYPRESS LAKES
GOLF COURSE

Course information: This military course has 18 holes and par is 72. The course is 6,816 yards and rated 72.6 from the championship tees, and 6,464 yards and rated 71.0 from the regular tees. The slope ratings are 122 championship and 119 regular. Women's tees are 5,794 yards and rated 72.9. The slope rating is 120.

Play policy and fees: Military personnel and their guests only. There is reciprocity with other Air Force courses. Green fees for guests are $12 on weekdays and $15 on weekends. Carts are $12 on weekdays and $14 on weekends. Reservations are recommended. Golf attire must be worn.

Location: From Vallejo, drive east on Interstate 80. Take the Elmira exit east. Turn right on Meridian to the course.

Course description: This course boasts big greens, seven lakes and lots of trees. It's flat and easily walkable. Plan to play the in wind.

5601 Meridian Road
Bldg 2012, Travis AFB,
CA 94535

Pro shop   (707) 448-7186

- driving range
- practice greens
- power carts
- pull carts
- golf club rental
- locker rooms
- showers
- executive course
- accommodations
- food and beverages
- clubhouse

Kenneth W. Cochran
Manager/Professional

Joe Goldbronn
Superintendent

NOR-CAL MAP.....see page 34
adjoining maps
NORTH (C2).........see page 66
EAST (D3) ....see page 134
SOUTH (E3) ....see page 238
WEST (D1) ....see page 86

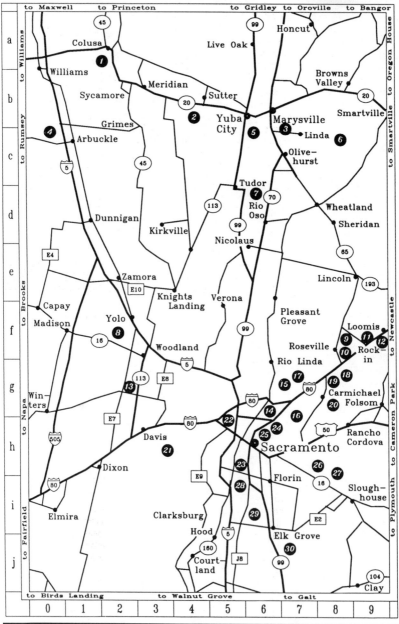

COLUSA COUNTRY CLUB

1 9 4 9

Course information: This private course has nine holes. Par is 72 for 18 holes. The course is 6,617 yards and rated 71.1 from the regular tees (18 holes). The slope rating is 118. Women's tees are 6,584 yards and rated 72.1 from the forward tees. The slope rating is 116.

Play policy and fees: Outside play is accepted. Green fees are $10 for nine holes and $14 for 18 holes weekdays, and $20 for nine or 18 holes weekends and holidays. Carts are $10 for nine holes and $20 for 18 holes.

Location: From Interstate 5 in Williams, drive east on Highway 20 to Colusa. The course is on Highway 20 on the right.

Course description: This flat, tree-lined course is tight and walkable. It's more challenging than meets the eye. A new sprinkler system has improved fairway conditions.

PO Box 686
Colusa, CA 95932

Highway 20 East
Colusa, CA 95932

Pro shop   (916) 458-5577

- ■ driving range
- ■ practice greens
- ■ power carts
- ■ pull carts
- ■ golf club rental
- ■ locker rooms
- ■ showers
- □ executive course
- □ accommodations
- ■ food and beverages
- ■ clubhouse

Randy Scott
Professional

Larry Colvin
Superintendent

NORTHERN D2

SOUTHRIDGE GOLF COURSE

1 9 9 1
Cal Olson

Course information: This semi-private course has 18 holes. Par 72 is for 18 holes. The course is 6,470 yards for 18 holes from the regular tees. The course is in the process of being rated. Women's yardage was unavailable.

Play policy and fees: Outside play is accepted. Green fees are $10 for nine holes and $16 for 18 holes weekdays, and $12 for nine holes and $20 for 18 holes weekends. Carts are $12 for nine holes and $20 for 18 holes. Reservations are recommended seven days in advance. This course is available for outside tournaments.

Location: From Yuba City drive west on Highway 20. The course is seven miles west of Yuba City and can be seen from the highway.

Course description: This layout is being developed in stages. The first nine holes opened for play September 1991, and the second nine holes are scheduled to open in the spring of 1992. For the player looking for extreme variety in terrain, this is the course to tackle. The first nine holes sit at the foot of Sutter Butte, and climbs the mountain. The second nine holes will be links-style. There are five large ponds coming into play on six holes (eight holes with the second nine).

9413 South Butte Road
Sutter, CA 95982

Pro shop   (916) 755-4653
                   (916) 755-4685

- ■ driving range
- ■ practice greens
- ■ power carts
- ■ pull carts
- ■ golf club rental
- □ locker rooms
- □ showers
- □ executive course
- □ accommodations
- ■ food and beverages
- □ clubhouse

Bob Anderson
Manager

Bill Malone
Professional

Mike McGee
Superintendent

PEACH TREE GOLF AND COUNTRY CLUB

1960
R.E. Baldock

PO Box 231
Marysville, CA 95901

2043 Simpson-Dantoni Road
Marysville, CA 95901

Pro shop   (916) 743-2039
Clubhouse   (916) 743-1897

- ■ driving range
- ■ practice greens
- ■ power carts
- ■ pull carts
- ■ golf club rental
- ■ locker rooms
- ■ showers
- □ executive course
- □ accommodations
- ■ food and beverages
- ■ clubhouse

Ed Lewis
Professional

Tim Philo
Superintendent

Course information: This private course has 18 holes and par is 72. The layout is 6,811 yards and rated 72.7 from the championship tees, and 6,506 yards and rated 71.2 from the regular tees. The slope ratings are 125 championship and 121 regular. Women's tees are 6,203 yards and rated 76.0 from the championship tees, and 5,865 yards and rated 74.0 from the regular tees. The slope ratings are 131.

Play policy and fees: Reciprocal play is accepted with members of other private clubs. Guest fees are $25 weekdays and $30 weekends when accompanied by a member. The fee for reciprocal players is $50. Carts are $18.

Location: From Sacramento, take Highway 70 through Marysville to Highway 20. Turn right on Ramirez Road and drive to Simpson-Dantoni Road. Turn left and drive to the course.

Course description: This long, challenging valley course is flanked by a variety of trees and several lakes. It boasts excellent greens. Many of the bunkers have been redesigned in the last year.

ARBUCKLE GOLF COURSE

1924

PO Box 975
Arbuckle, CA 95912

Hillgate Road
Arbuckle, CA 95912

Pro shop   (916) 476-2470

- ■ driving range
- ■ practice greens
- ■ power carts
- ■ pull carts
- ■ golf club rental
- □ locker rooms
- □ showers
- □ executive course
- □ accommodations
- ■ food and beverages
- ■ clubhouse

Carl Funk
Manager/Professional

Abel Gomez
Superintendent

Course information: This semi-private course has nine holes. Par is 72 for 18 holes. The course is 6,460 yards and rated 69.9 from the regular tees (18 holes). The slope rating is 111. Women's tees are 5,922 and rated 72.7 from the forward tees. The slope rating is 120.

Play policy and fees: Outside play is accepted. Green fees are $14 weekdays and $20 weekends. Carts are $18. Reservations recommended.

Location: From Interstate 5 in Arbuckle, exit on Arbuckle College City and drive to Hillgate Road west. Drive 4.5 miles on Hillgate Road to the course.

Course description: This challenging course has a rolling layout with a few tight doglegs. The greens are true, smooth and fast. The club has been in existence since 1924, but the greens weren't changed from sand to grass until 1960.

MALLARD LAKE
GOLF COURSE

NORTHERN D2

Course information: This public course has nine holes. Par is 68 for 18 holes. The course is 5,298 yards and rated 64.2 from the regular tees. The slope rating is 103. Women's tees are 5,190 yards and rated 68.4. The slope rating is 115.

Play policy and fees: Green fees are $7 for nine holes and $12 for 18 holes weekdays, and $9 for nine holes and $14 for 18 holes on weekends. Carts are $9 for nine holes and $13 for 18 holes.

Location: From Yuba City, drive south on Highway 99. The course is a quarter mile south of Oswald Road on Sawtelle Avenue (Highway 99).

Course description: This mostly flat course has water on all nine holes. It's short and tough with small, well maintained greens.

4238 South Highway 99
Yuba City, CA 95991

Pro shop   (916) 674-0475

- ■ driving range
- ■ practice greens
- ■ power carts
- ■ pull carts
- ■ golf club rental
- ☐ locker rooms
- ☐ showers
- ☐ executive course
- ☐ accommodations
- ■ food and beverages
- ■ clubhouse

Pete Tor
Co–Manager

Dirk Ekey
Co–Manager

Bill Hardin
Professional

Ernest Carranza
Superintendent

BEALE AIR FORCE BASE
GOLF COURSE

Course information: This military course has nine holes. Par is 70 for 18 holes. The course is 6,287 yards and rated 69.6 from the regular tees (18 holes). The slope rating is 118. Women's tees are 5,326 yards and rated 69.7. The slope rating is 119.

Play policy and fees: Outside play is accepted with prior arrangement. Guest fees are $11 weekdays and $13 weekends for civilians. Green fees are $7 weekdays and $10 weekends for military ranked E-5 and above and Department of Defense personnel. Carts are $13.

Location: From Highway 70 in Marysville, take the North Beale Road east exit. Drive to the main gate of Beale Air Force Base.

Course description: This flat, tree-lined course offers some of the best greens in Northern California. It has two lakes.

SSRG Building 2241
Beale AFB, CA 95903

Pro shop   (916) 634-2124
Clubhouse (916) 634-2127

- ■ driving range
- ■ practice greens
- ■ power carts
- ■ pull carts
- ■ golf club rental
- ■ locker rooms
- ■ showers
- ☐ executive course
- ☐ accommodations
- ■ food and beverages
- ■ clubhouse

PLUMAS LAKE GOLF AND COUNTRY CLUB

Course 7
MAP D2 grid d6

1929

Course information: This semi-private layout has 18 holes and par is 71. The course is 6,400 yards and rated 70.5 from the championship tees, and 6,153 yards and rated 69.3 from the regular tees. The slope ratings are 122 championship and 120 regular. Women's tees are 5,759 and rated 73.2 from the regular tees. The slope rating is 126.

Play policy and fees: Outside play is accepted. Green fees are $12 weekdays and $15 weekends. Carts are $16. Closed Mondays during the winter.

Location: From Marysville, drive south on Highway 70. Take the Feather River Boulevard exit and drive about 6.5 miles. Turn left on Country Club Avenue.

Course description: A creek runs through this mostly flat, tight but sprawling course. It's an oldie, but a goodie.

1551 Country Club Ave.
Marysville, CA 95901

Pro shop   (916) 742-3201
Clubhouse (916) 742-3202

- ■ driving range
- ■ practice greens
- ■ power carts
- ■ pull carts
- ■ golf club rental
- ■ locker rooms
- ■ showers
- □ executive course
- □ accommodations
- ■ food and beverages
- ■ clubhouse

Pat Gould
Professional

Foy "Cotton" Triplett
Superintendent

YOLO FLIERS COUNTRY CLUB

Course 8
MAP D2 grid f2

1919

Course information: This private course has 18 holes and par is 72. The course is 6,546 yards and rated 70.1 from the regular tees. The slope rating is 119. Women's yardage is 6,081 and rated 74.2. The slope rating is 122.

Play policy and fees: Reciprocal play is accepted with members of other private clubs. Guest fees are $18 with a member and $40 unaccompanied. Carts are $14 for members and $20 for non-members.

Location: From Interstate 505 in Woodland, take Highway 16 East. Drive four miles and turn north on Road 94B. The course is located by the Woodland Municipal Airport.

Course description: This flat course is flanked with trees. The fairways are tight with some doglegs, and the greens are well maintained. Temperatures soar in the summer. If you're curious, the name of the course originated with the tradition many years ago of flying in for a day of golf. That tradition still exists, but it's not heavily publicized.

PO Box 1366
Woodland, CA 95695

Off Highway 16, Rd. 94–B
Woodland, CA 95695

Pro shop   (916) 662-8050
Clubhouse (916) 662-0281

- ■ driving range
- ■ practice greens
- ■ power carts
- ■ pull carts
- ■ golf club rental
- ■ locker rooms
- ■ showers
- □ executive course
- □ accommodations
- ■ food and beverages
- ■ clubhouse

Bob Badger
Professional

Donald Baker
Superintendent

DIAMOND OAKS
GOLF COURSE

NORTHERN D2

Course information: This public course has 18 holes and par is 72. The course is 6,193 yards and rated 68.2 from the regular tees. The slope rating is 110. Women's tees are 5,608 yards and rated 70.5. The slope rating is 112.

Play policy and fees: Green fees are $5.50 for nine holes and $9 for 18 holes weekdays, and $6.25 and $10 weekends. Carts are $8 for nine holes and $14 for 18 holes. The twilight rate is $4.50 after 5:30 p.m. during the summer. Reservations are recommended one week in advance for weekdays and the Monday before for weekend tee times. There is an unusual $1 reservation fee.

Location: From Interstate 80 in Roseville, take the Atlantic Street exit to Yosemite Street. Turn right and drive to Diamond Oaks Road. Turn left and drive 400 yards to the course.

Course description: Mature oaks line the fairways of this rolling course. It has some hills, water and doglegs. The uphill, 430-yard, par-4 18th is a great finishing hole. Tee shots must contend with a large oak tree in the right center at 250 yards. Annual tournaments include the Roseville City Championships in April, the Sacramento Valley Best Ball in July, and the Father-Son Championship in September.

PO Box 248
Roseville, CA 95662

349 Diamon Oaks Road
Roseville, CA 95661

Pro shop   (916 783-4847
Clubhouse   916 782-3513

- ■ driving range
- ■ practice greens
- ■ power carts
- ■ pull carts
- ■ golf club rental
- □ locker rooms
- □ showers
- □ executive course
- □ accommodations
- ■ food and beverages
- ■ clubhouse

Ed Vasconcellos
Professional

Henry Singh
Superintendent

MAP ON PAGE 112

117

SIERRA VIEW COUNTRY CLUB

1956
Jack Fleming

105 Alta Vista
Roseville, CA 95661

Pro shop (916) 783-4600
Clubhouse (916) 782-3741

Course information: This private layout has 18 holes and par is 72. The course is 6,481 yards and rated 70.6 from the regular tees. The slope rating is 121. Women's tees are 5,936 yards and rated 74.5 from the forward tees. The slope rating is 129.

Play policy and fees: Reciprocal play is accepted with members of other private clubs, otherwise members and guests only. Guest fees are $20 weekdays and $25 weekends when accompanied by a member. Carts are $16. Reciprocal players should have their golf pro arrange a tee time in advance. Green fees for reciprocators are the same as their home course fees.

Location: Off Interstate 80 in Roseville, exit at Atlantic Street and take the second right onto Yosemite Street. Drive a few blocks until the road bends. Look for Alta Vista and go left to the course.

Course description: This course has a rolling terrain with lots of oak trees and two lakes. Distance and accuracy are both rewarded on this long course. The hole to remember is the par-4, 463-yard third. It has a dogleg to the left with fairway bunkers bordering the landing zone. Be ready for a sidehill lie or for hitting out of the rough. Bunkers are waiting at the green. The length makes this hole tough. San Francisco 49er quarterbacks seem to have the most time and money for golf, so look for Joe and Steve to play this course. Retired 49ers receiver Dwight Clark makes up the threesome when they're not working out at summer training camp.

- driving range
- practice greens
- power carts
- pull carts
- golf club rental
- locker rooms
- showers
- ☐ executive course
- ☐ accommodations
- food and beverages
- clubhouse

Bill Wompler
Manager

James Salazar
Professional

Ben Hartley
Superintendent

SUNSET WHITNEY
COUNTRY CLUB

NORTHERN D2

Course information: This private course has 18 holes and par is 72. The course is 6,618 yards and rated 71.8 from the championship tees, and 6,222 yards and rated 70.0 from the regular tees. The slope ratings are 124 championship and 120 regular. Women's tees are 6,218 yards and rated 75.8 from the championship tees, and 5,507 yards and rated 72.0 from the forward tees. The slope ratings are 134 championship and 128 forward.

Play policy and fees: Reciprocal play is accepted with members of other private clubs. Guest fees are $20 weekdays and $30 weekends with a member. Green fees for reciprocal players are $50 weekdays and $60 weekends, carts included. Carts are $18. Reservations are recommended seven days in advance. This course is available for outside tournaments.

Location: From Interstate 80 in Rocklin, take the Taylor Road North exit. Turn left on Midas Avenue and drive to the course.

Course description: Situated in the Sierra Nevada foothills, this tight, twisting course has water, bunkers and undulating greens. It's tricky. The front nine is tree-lined, and the back nine is wide open. Joe Montana and Steve Young, of the San Francisco 49ers, have been known to play this course during summer training camp breaks. The club has a new golf and tennis pro shop, restaurant and bar. In addition to the golf, there are eight tennis courts.

PO Box 788
Rocklin, CA 95677

4201 Midas Avenue
Rocklin, CA 95677

Pro shop   (916) 624-2610
Clubhouse (916) 624-2402

- ■ driving range
- ■ practice greens
- ■ power carts
- ■ pull carts
- ■ golf club rental
- ☐ locker rooms
- ☐ showers
- ☐ executive course
- ☐ accommodations
- ■ food and beverages
- ■ clubhouse

Eric Pohl
Professional

Mike Kaveney
Superintendent

INDIAN CREEK COUNTRY CLUB

Course 12
MAP D2 grid f9

1966

Course information: This public course has nine holes. Par is 64 for 18 holes. The course is 4,164 yards and rated 59.2 from the regular tees. The slope rating is 98. Women's tees are 4,164 yards and rated 63.1. The slope rating is 97.

Play policy and fees: Green fees are $6 for nine holes and $8.50 for 18 holes weekdays, and $7 for nine holes and $10.50 for 18 holes weekends. Senior (65 and over) rates are $5.50 for nine holes and $7.50 for 18 holes weekdays, and $6.50 for nine holes and $9.50 for 18 holes weekends. Carts are $6 per nine holes.

Location: From Interstate 80 east in Rocklin, take the Rocklin Road exit (not the exit for the town of Rocklin). Turn right on Rocklin Road and drive about two miles to the end. Turn left on Barton Road and drive one mile to the course.

Course description: This short course boasts five par-4s. The greens are elevated. There are lots of oak trees and water on two holes. During summer training camp look for some of the San Francisco 49ers coaches to play this course.

PO Box 303
Loomis, CA 95650

4487 Barton Road
Loomis, CA 95650

Pro shop   (916) 652-5546
Clubhouse   (916) 652-3147

- ■ driving range
- ■ practice greens
- ■ power carts
- ■ pull carts
- ■ golf club rental
- ☐ locker rooms
- ☐ showers
- ■ executive course
- ☐ accommodations
- ■ food and beverages
- ■ clubhouse

Paul Lukavic
Professional

Dave Cogdell
Professional

Peter Nash
Manager

Paul Booterbaugh
Superintendent

DAVIS GOLF COURSE

Course 13
MAP D2 grid g2

1964

Course information: This public course has 18 holes and par is 66. The course is 4,998 yards and rated 63.4 from the championship tees, and 4,445 yards and rated 60.9 from the regular tees. The slope ratings are 98 championship and 93 regular. Women's tees are 4,484 yards and rated 64.3. The slope rating is 96.

Play policy and fees: Green fees are $9 for all day play. Seniors and juniors during the weekday pay $6 and $5 respectively. Twilight rates are $6 after 4 p.m. Carts are $8 for nine holes and $15 for 18 holes. Reservations are recommended one week in advance.

Location: From Interstate 80 in Davis, take the Highway 113 exit. Drive five miles north to County Road 29. The course is on the left.

Course description: This short, flat course has strategically placed trees, lots of out-of-bounds and requires accuracy. Undulating greens make it difficult to shoot for the pins.

PO Box 928
Davis, CA 95617

Highway 113 and Road 29
Davis, CA 95616

Pro shop   (916) 756-4010

- ■ driving range
- ■ practice greens
- ■ power carts
- ■ pull carts
- ■ golf club rental
- ☐ locker rooms
- ☐ showers
- ☐ executive course
- ☐ accommodations
- ■ food and beverages
- ☐ clubhouse

Jerry Lilliedoll
Professional

Tim Conner
Superintendent

HAGGIN OAKS GOLF COURSE

1932
Alister MacKenzie

3645 Fulton Avenue
Sacramento, CA 95821

Pro shop   (916) 481-4507
Clubhouse (916) 965-5970

- driving range
- practice greens
- power carts
- pull carts
- golf club rental
- ☐ locker rooms
- ☐ showers
- ☐ executive course
- ☐ accommodations
- food and beverages
- clubhouse

Terry Daubert
Manager

Ken Morton
Professional

Joe Andrade
Superintendent

Course information: This public facility has 36 holes and par is 72 on both.

The South Course is 6,633 yards and rated 70.6 from the championship tees, and 6,344 yards and rated 69.3 from the regular tees. The slope ratings are 113 championship and 110 regular. Women's tees are 5,784 yards and rated 71.4 from the forward tees. The slope rating is 113.

The North Course is 6,985 yards and rated 71.4 from the championship tees, and 6,660 yards and rated 69.9 from the regular tees. The slope ratings are: 115 championship and 112 regular. Women's tees are 5,853 yards and rated 70.6 from the forward tees. The slope rating is 107.

Play policy and fees: Green fees are $11.50 weekdays and $14 weekends. Carts are $18. Reservations are recommended. Reserve a tee time one week in advance.

Location: Take the Fulton Road exit north off Business 80 in Sacramento and follow it to the course.

Course description: Both courses are wide open, flat and tree-lined with some water. The South Course has large greens and a lot of doglegs. The California State Fair Championship is played here annually. This course hosted the men's National USGA Publinx in 1983 and the women's National USGA Publinx will be played here in 1992. On the South Course, the men's record is 63 and the women's is 69. On the North Course the men's record is 65 and the women's is 72.

NORTHERN D2

LAWRENCE LINKS
GOLF COURSE

Course information: This military course has nine holes. Par is 72 for 18 holes. The course is 6,063 yards and rated 69.7 from the regular tees (18 holes). The slope rating is 123. Women's tees are 5,232 yards and rated 70.2 from the forward tees. The slope rating is 120.

Play policy and fees: Reciprocal play is accepted with members of other military clubs. Green fees for military personnel are $6 for nine holes and $9 for 18 holes weekdays, and $7 nine holes and $11 for 18 holes weekends. Guest fees for civilians are $7 for nine holes and $12 for 18 holes weekdays, and $8 for nine holes and $12 for 18 holes weekends. Carts are $6 per nine holes.

Location: From Interstate 80 in Sacramento, take the Watt Avenue exit north and drive past the entrance to McClellan Air Force Base. Turn right on Blackfoot Way and drive to the end. The course is about 5.5 miles from Interstate 80.

Course description: This tough, demanding course has four lakes that provide water hazards on every hole. Bring lots of balls.

McClellan AFB, 7823
Blackfoot Way
North Highlands, CA 95660

Pro shop   (916) 643-3313

☐ driving range
■ practice greens
■ power carts
■ pull carts
■ golf club rental
■ locker rooms
■ showers
☐ executive course
☐ accommodations
■ food and beverages
■ clubhouse

Wes Cline
Manager

ANCIL HOFFMAN
GOLF COURSE

1 9 6 8
William Francis Bell

PO Box 790
Carmichael, CA 95608

6700 Tarshes Drive
Carmichael, CA 95608

Pro shop   (916) 482-5660

NORTHERN D2

Course information: This public course has 18 holes and par is 72. The course is 6,794 yards and rated 72.5 from the championship tees, and 6,434 yards and rated 71.0 from the regular tees. The slope ratings are 123 championship and 119 regular. Women's tees are 5,954 yards and rated 73.4. The slope rating is 123.

Play policy and fees: Green fees are $13 weekdays and $15 weekends. Carts are $16.

Location: From Business 80 in Sacramento, take the Marconi Avenue exit east. Drive five miles to Fair Oaks Boulevard and turn right. Turn left on Kenneth Avenue. Turn right on California Avenue and left on Ancil Hoffman Park Road (Tarshes Drive) and follow to the course.

- ■ driving range
- ■ practice greens
- ■ power carts
- □ pull carts
- ■ golf club rental
- □ locker rooms
- □ showers
- □ executive course
- □ accommodations
- ■ food and beverages
- ■ clubhouse

Steve Price
Professional

Rich Sizelove
Superintendent

Course description: This demanding course rates as one of the top public courses in the state. In fact, *Golf Digest* ranks it among the top 75 public courses in the country. Situated in Ancil Hoffman Park on the American River, ominous oak and pine trees come into play on nearly every hole. The fairways are tight and the greens are contoured. For difficulty check out the par-4, 449-yard 16th. There is a monster oak tree 200 yards out which has must be cleared to stay in the fairway. The green is good-sized for the distance. The American River runs the side of the hole, and as the locals say, "It's just a wedge away." This heavily played course is most often in great shape.

CHERRY ISLAND GOLF COURSE

1990
Robert Muir Graves

Course information: This public course has 18 holes and par is 72. The course is 6,562 yards and rated 71.1 from the tournament tees, and 6,201 and rated 69.5 from the championship tees, and 5,556 yards and rated 69.9 from the regular tees. The slope ratings are 124 tournament, 121 championship and 117 regular. Women's tees are 5,137 yards and rated 69.9 from the forward tees. The slope rating is 117.

Play policy and fees: Green fees are $13 weekdays and $15 weekends. Carts are $16. Reservations accepted one week in advance. Call on Monday for weekend starting times. There is a reservation fee of $2.

Location: From Interstate 80 in Sacramento, take the Watt Avenue exit north. Drive five miles to Elverta Road and turn left. Drive one mile to the course on the left.

Course description: This tough layout requires pinpoint accuracy to narrow fairways and small greens. There are five lakes and water comes into play on 10 holes. Watch out for the 544-yard, par-5 15th hole that features water on the right, out-of-bounds on the left and a well bunkered green. Aside from that, it's easy!

2360 Elverta Road
Elverta, CA 95626

Pro shop   (916) 991-7293
Starter   (916) 991-0770
Clubhouse (916) 991-0655

- ■ driving range
- ■ practice greens
- ■ power carts
- ■ pull carts
- ■ golf club rental
- □ locker rooms
- □ showers
- □ executive course
- □ accommodations
- ■ food and beverages
- ■ clubhouse

Blair Kline
Professional

Steve Smith
Superintendent

ROSEVILLE ROLLING GREENS GOLF COURSE

1952

Course information: This public course has nine holes. Par is 54 for 18 holes. The course is 3,000 yards and rated 53.9 from the regular tees. The slope rating is 79. Women's tees are also 3,000 yards and rated 56.5. The slope rating is 92.

Play policy and fees: Green fees are $7 for nine holes and $11 for 18 holes weekdays, and $8 for nine holes and $13 for 18 holes weekends. Play is on a first come, first served basis.

Location: From Interstate 80 in Roseville, take the Douglas Street exit east. Turn right on Sierra College Boulevard and left on Eureka Road.

Course description: This short, par-3 course has rolling terrain and can be tough, especially the 225-yard par sixth, which has only been aced once. The course record is 50 for 18 holes.

5572 Eureka Road
Roseville, CA 95661

Pro shop   (916) 797-9986

- □ driving range
- ■ practice greens
- □ power carts
- ■ pull carts
- □ golf club rental
- □ locker rooms
- □ showers
- ■ executive course
- □ accommodations
- ■ food and beverages
- □ clubhouse

Bob Peterson
Manager/Professional

George Angus
Superintendent

SUNRISE GOLF COURSE

NORTHERN D2

Course information: This private facility has nine holes. Par is 64 for 18 holes. The course is 4,080 yards and rated 59.7 from the regular tees. The slope rating is 95. Women's tees are 4,080 and rated 64.2. The slope rating is 96.

Play policy and fees: Reciprocal play is accepted with members of other private clubs. Green fees are $5 for nine holes when accompanied by a member.

Location: From Interstate 80 in Citrus Heights (northeast of Sacramento), take the Greenback Lane exit east. Drive four miles to Sunrise Boulevard and turn left. The course is located on your right.

Course description: This short, flat course has five holes over water. It has one par-5, three par-4s and five par-3s. It is a good layout for beginning and intermediate players. While the course is private, the driving range is open to the public until 10 p.m. nightly.

6412 Sunrise Boulevard
Citrus Heights, CA 95610

Pro shop   (916) 723-8854

- driving range
- practice greens
- power carts
- pull carts
- golf club rental
- ☐ locker rooms
- ☐ showers
- ☐ executive course
- ☐ accommodations
- food and beverages
- clubhouse

Marge Jones
Professional

Gary Leonard
Manager/Superintendent

NORTH RIDGE COUNTRY CLUB

1952
Robert Muir Graves

Course information: This private course has 18 holes and par is 72. The course is 6,552 yards and rated 71.9 from the championship tees, and 6,258 yards and rated 70.6 from the regular tees. The slope ratings are 125 championship and 122 regular. Women's tees are 5,895 yards and rated 74.1 from the forward tees. The slope rating is 129.

Play policy and fees: Reciprocal play is accepted with members of other private clubs. Guest fees are $25 with a member and $70 without. Carts are $16. Carts are included in the guest fee.

Location: From Sacramento, drive east on Interstate 80. Take the Madison Avenue exit east. Follow Madison Avenue for five miles to Mariposa.

Course description: This tree-lined course has Bermuda grass fairways and lots of long par-4s. Relax on the front nine, because the back nine has tighter fairways, lots of doglegs and undulating greens.

PO Box 326
Fair Oaks, CA 95628

7600 Madison Avenue
Fair Oaks, CA 95628

Pro shop   (916) 967-5716
Clubhouse (916) 967-5717

- driving range
- practice greens
- power carts
- pull carts
- golf club rental
- locker rooms
- showers
- ☐ executive course
- ☐ accommodations
- food and beverages
- clubhouse

Nate Pomeroy
Professional

Fritz Howell
Superintendent

MAP ON PAGE 112

125

EL MACERO COUNTRY CLUB

1961
R.E. Baldock

PO Box 2005
El Macero, CA 95618

1 Clubhouse Road
El Macero, CA 95618

Pro shop   (916) 753-5621

- ■ driving range
- ■ practice greens
- ■ power carts
- ■ pull carts
- ☐ golf club rental
- ■ locker rooms
- ■ showers
- ☐ executive course
- ☐ accommodations
- ■ food and beverages
- ■ clubhouse

Dick Madsack
Professional

Jack Calvera
Assistant Professional

Course information: This private course has 18 holes and par is 72. The course is 6,836 yards and rated 72.5 from the championship tees, and 6,480 yards and rated 70.6 from the regular tees. The slope ratings are 126 championship and 121 regular. Women's tees are 6,087 yards and rated 74.0 from the championship tees, and 5,585 yards and rated 71.0 from the forward tees. The slope ratings are 124 championship and 116 regular.

Play policy and fees: Reciprocal play is accepted with members of other private clubs. Guest fees are $20 with a member and $45 without. Carts are $9 for nine holes and $18 for 18 holes.

Location: From Davis, drive two miles east on Interstate 80. Take the Mace Boulevard exit south in El Macero. Drive south to Clubhouse Road.

Course description: This long, narrow course has lots of out-of-bounds and challenging fairway bunkers. There are three lakes. The talk of this course is hole number 15. It is 512 yards and par-5. There are two fairway bunkers in the right landing zone and if you survive those the undulating green is surrounded by more bunkers. Trees are everywhere. Out-of-bounds mark both sides of the wide fairway. If you stray, you have to hit out of the trees.

LIGHTHOUSE GOLF COURSE

1990
Bert Stamps

NORTHERN D2

Course information: This public course has 18 holes and par is 64. The course is 4,729 yards and rated 63.7 from the championship tees, and 4,463 yards and rated 62.6 from the regular tees. The slope ratings are 107 championship and 104 regular. Women's tees are 4,057 yards and rated 62.5 from the forward tees. The slope ratings is 103.

Play policy and fees: Green fees are $18 weekdays and $20 weekends. Carts are $8 per person.

Location: From the Interstate 80 Business Loop in West Sacramento, take the Jefferson exit north. Turn right on Sacramento Avenue. Drive 1.5 blocks to Douglas Street and turn left. The course is at the end of Douglas.

Course description: This course is young, but growing. The old course, formerly the Riverbend Golf and Country Club, was plowed up and redesigned. There is now water on 15 holes. Mature trees were retained as part of the new course, and others have been planted. Surfacing as a spectacularly tough hole is the par-4, 418-yard 15th. There is water left and right. The elevated green is narrow in the front and deep in the back. Pin position often makes this a particularly difficult hole. This course is shaping up as a real challenge.

500 Douglas Street
West Sacramento, CA 95605

Pro shop   (916) 372-4949
Clubhouse (916) 372-0800

- ■ driving range
- ■ practice greens
- ■ power carts
- ■ pull carts
- ■ golf club rental
- □ locker rooms
- □ showers
- □ executive course
- □ accommodations
- ■ food and beverages
- ■ clubhouse

Robert Halpenny
Professional

Don Howton
General Manager

Pargan Singh
Superintendent

WILLIAM LAND PARK
GOLF COURSE

Course information: This public course has nine holes. Par is 68 for 18 holes. The course is 5,168 yards and rated 63.0 for 18 holes. The slope rating is 96. Women's tees are 4,716 yards and rated 65.3. The slope rating is 100.

Play policy and fees: Green fees are $5.75 for nine holes and $11.50 for 18 holes weekdays, and $7 and $14 weekends and holidays. Senior (65 and over) rates are $4.50 for nine holes and $9 for 18 holes weekdays. Juniors are $3.25 for nine holes weekdays. Pull carts only.

Location: From Business 80 in Sacramento, exit on 16th Street and drive south. 16th Street turns into Land Park Drive. At the Sacramento Zoo entrance take a left turn to the clubhouse.

Course description: This older, mature course has open fairways and well bunkered, small greens. It has a variety of trees, including eucalyptus, oak, elm and pine. The course is in the middle of a park and is a gorgeous walk. Unfortunately, the third hole can be a spoiler. It is 152 yards and par-3, but don't count on scoring well here. There are two huge cottonwood trees about 20 yards in front of the green. The tee shot must either go over, between or under the trees. If you navigate the trees, which incidentally are growing together, there are bunkers to the left and right of the green. One consolation: The green is uphill and receives the shot well if you can get it past the trees. Oh, yes. There is also a wall of trees on the left and a ravine on the right. This is a brutal hole that is regularly rated one of the most difficult in Northern California.

1701 Sutterville Road
Sacramento, CA 95822

Pro shop   (916) 455-5014

□ driving range
■ practice greens
□ power carts
■ pull carts
■ golf club rental
□ locker rooms
□ showers
□ executive course
□ accommodations
■ food and beverages
■ clubhouse

Steve Feliciano
Professional

Frank Acosta
Superintendent

DEL PASO COUNTRY CLUB

1916
Herbert Fowler

Course information: This private course has 18 holes and par is 72. The course is 6,320 yards and rated 70.0 from the regular tees. The slope is 119. Women's tees are 5,931 yards and rated 74.4 from the forward tees. The slope rating is 128.

Play policy and fees: Reciprocal play is accepted only with specific private clubs. Call for specifics. Guest fees are $20 with a member and $50 without. Carts are $7.50 per person with a member and $10 per person without. Reservations are recommended.

Location: From Business 80 in Sacramento, take the Marconi Avenue exit east. Drive 1.5 miles to the course, which is on the left. From Interstate 80 take the Watt Avenue exit. Travel on Watt Avenue to Marconi Avenue, turn right on Marconi and follow it to the course.

Course description: This rolling, tree-lined layout is narrow with small, undulating greens. The fairways and greens are well bunkered. The men's course record is 63. Del Paso has hosted several USGA events: the 1957 and 1976 U.S. Women's Amateur and the 1964 Senior Women's Amateur. The 1982 U.S. Women's Open was held here.

3333 Marconi Avenue
Sacramento, CA 95821

Pro shop   (916) 483-0401
Clubhouse (916) 489-3681

- ■ driving range
- ■ practice greens
- ■ power carts
- ■ pull carts
- □ golf club rental
- ■ locker rooms
- ■ showers
- □ executive course
- □ accommodations
- ■ food and beverages
- ■ clubhouse

Les Streeper
Professional

Richard Forney
Manager

Tom Unruh
Superintendent

NORTHERN D2

MAP ON PAGE 112

CAMPUS COMMONS GOLF COURSE

1973
Bill McDowell

Course information: This private course has nine holes. Par is 58 for 18 holes. The course is 3,146 yards and rated 54.3 from the regular tees. The slope rating is 83. Women's tees are 3,080 yards. The ratings were unavailable.

Play policy and fees: Outside play is accepted. Green fees are $6 for nine holes and $10 for 18 holes weekdays, and $6.50 for nine holes and $10.50 for 18 holes weekends. Carts are $8 per nine holes. Pull carts are $1.50. Club rental is $5. Reservations are required one week in advance.

Location: From Highway 50 in Sacramento, take the Howe Avenue North exit. Turn left on Cadillac Drive and drive to the course.

Course description: This rolling executive course is bordered by the American River. The greens are elevated and there is a lot of roll to the fairways. The river comes into play on the fifth, seventh and eighth holes. The fifth hole is the most unforgiving of the three. The river borders the fairway on the right and there is OB to that side. The river is only 25 yards from the center of the fairway, so hold your slice down to a minimum. Look for a new clubhouse with snack bar and pro shop to open in the spring of '92.

2 Cadillac Drive
Sacramento, CA 95825

Pro shop   (916) 922-5861

- ☐ driving range
- ■ practice greens
- ■ power carts
- ■ pull carts
- ■ golf club rental
- ☐ locker rooms
- ☐ showers
- ■ executive course
- ☐ accommodations
- ■ food and beverages
- ☐ clubhouse

Ray Arrino
Manager/Professional

Dale Arrino
Superintendent

MATHER GOLF COURSE

1963

Course information: This military course has 18 holes and par is 72. The course is 6,771 yards and rated 70.6 from the championship tees, and 6,447 yards and rated 69.2 from the regular tees. The slope ratings are 115 championship and 111 regular. Women's tees are 5,976 yards and rated 72.4. The slope rating is 119.

Play policy and fees: Military personnel and invited guests only. Guest fees are $18. Carts are $14.

Location: From Sacramento, drive east on Highway 50. Take the Mather Air Force Base exit.

Course description: This long course is lined with mature trees and a creek runs through the third hole. It demands length off the tee. There are six par-4s that are 420 yards or longer. The final two holes are a tough finish. Number 17 is 458 yards and par-4. It is straight away and long with trees left and right. The front of the relatively large green is open but there is a bunker to the left. Hit it long and straight. Number 18 is 420 yards and par-4. It features a dogleg left and trees down both sides. The hole is especially difficult if you stay left. So, go right for a shot to the receptive and undulating green.

Building 8855, Mather AFB
CA 95655–5000

Pro shop   (916) 364-4462

- ■ driving range
- ■ practice greens
- ■ power carts
- ■ pull carts
- ■ golf club rental
- ☐ locker rooms
- ☐ showers
- ☐ executive course
- ☐ accommodations
- ■ food and beverages
- ■ clubhouse

Jack Emmons
Professional

Les Wright
Manager

Larry Johnson
Superintendent

CORDOVA GOLF COURSE

Course information: This public course has 18 holes and par is 63. The course is 4,755 yards and rated 61.0 from the regular tees. The slope rating is 90. Women's tees are 4,728 yards and rated 64.9. The slope rating is 96.

Play policy and fees: Green fees are $5 weekdays and $6 weekends. Carts are $6 for nine holes and $12 for 18 holes. Reservations are recommended 24 to 48 hours in advance. This course is available for tournaments. Arrangements must be made through the Cordova Park District.

Location: From Highway 50 in Sacramento, take the Highway 16/Jackson Road exit. Drive five miles to the course. It is between Bradshaw Road and South Watt Avenue.

Course description: This is a sneaky, short course that plays long because of the challenging bunkers and doglegs. There are three lakes and an abundance of trees.

9425 Jackson Road
Sacramento, CA 95826

Pro shop   (916) 362-1196

- ■ driving range
- ■ practice greens
- ■ power carts
- ■ pull carts
- ■ golf club rental
- □ locker rooms
- □ showers
- □ executive course
- □ accommodations
- ■ food and beverages
- ■ clubhouse

Jim Marta
Professional

Stanley Flood
Superintendent

NORTHERN D2

BING MALONEY GOLF COURSE

Course information: This public course has 18 holes and par is 72. The course is 6,281 yards and rated 69.4 from the regular tees. The slope rating is 108. Women's tees are 5,972 yards and rated 72.6. The slope rating is 119. There is also a short executive course that is 1,330 yards and rated 58.0.

Play policy and fees: Green fees are $11.50 weekdays and $14 weekends. Twilight rates are $7 weekdays and $8 weekends after 5 p.m. during the summer season. Carts are $16. Reservations are recommended and there is a $2 reservation fee. This course is available for outside tournaments.

Location: From Sacramento, drive six miles south on Highway 80. Take the Florin Road exit east. Turn left on Freeport Road and drive toward the Sacramento International Airport. The course is on the right.

Course description: This course is surrounded by trees. The greens are extremely large and well bunkered. Accuracy is a must. The men's course record is 62, held by Tom Doris.

PO Box 23031
Sacramento, CA 95823

6801 Freeport Boulevard
Sacramento, CA 95822

Pro shop   (916) 428-9401

- ■ driving range
- ■ practice greens
- ■ power carts
- ■ pull carts
- ■ golf club rental
- □ locker rooms
- □ showers
- ■ executive course
- □ accommodations
- ■ food and beverages
- □ clubhouse

Tom Doris
Professional

Dale Achondo
Superintendent

VALLEY HI COUNTRY CLUB

Course information: This private course has 18 holes and par is 72. The course is 6,765 yards and rated 71.6 from the championship tees, and 6,543 yards and rated 70.5 from the regular tees. The slope ratings are 120 championship and 117 regular. Women's yardage is 5,953 yards and rated 73.9 from the forward tees. The slope rating is 126.

Play policy and fees: Reciprocal play is accepted with members of other private clubs. Guest fees are $20 with a member and $40 without. Carts are $17 per cart.

Location: From Sacramento, drive south on Highway 99, take the Elk Grove Boulevard exit west. Drive 3.5 miles until it deadends at Franklin Boulevard. Turn right. The course is on the right.

Course description: This long, flat course has three lakes, which spell trouble for the sliced ball. The greens are large and contoured, making it difficult to get approach shots close to the hole. The pride of the course is the 424-yard, par-4 11th hole. A prevailing south wind and small green conspire against the golfer.

PO Box 850
Elk Grove, CA 95624

9595 Franklin Boulevard
Elk Grove, CA 95624

Pro shop   (916) 423-2170
Clubhouse   (916) 423-2093

- ■ driving range
- ■ practice greens
- ■ power carts
- ▢ pull carts
- ■ golf club rental
- ■ locker rooms
- ■ showers
- ▢ executive course
- ▢ accommodations
- ■ food and beverages
- ■ clubhouse

Nick West
Manager

Jim Collart
Professional

Mike Jones
Superintendent

EMERALD LAKES
GOLF CENTRE

1991
Rick Yount

10651 East Stockton
Boulevard
Elk Grove, CA 95624

Pro shop   (916) 685-4653

■ driving range
■ practice greens
■ power carts
■ pull carts
■ golf club rental
□ locker rooms
□ showers
□ executive course
□ accommodations
■ food and beverages
□ clubhouse

John Hoag
Professional

Larry Feliciano
Superintendent

NORTHERN D2

Course information: This public course has nine holes. Par is 66 for 18 holes. The course is 4,832 yards and rated 62.7 for 18 holes from the regular tees. The slope rating is 98. Women's tees are 4,034 yards from the regular tees and are currently unrated.

Play policy and fees: Green fees are $6 for nine holes and $12 for 18 holes weekdays, and $7 for nine holes and $14 for 18 holes weekends. The senior rate is $4 for nine holes weekdays. The rate for juniors holding an etiquette card is $3 for nine holes weekdays. Carts are $8 for nine holes. Reservations are recommended weekday evenings and weekends. There is a $1 reservation fee. This course is available for outside tournaments. The driving range is open summer months until 10 p.m.

Location: From Highway 99 in Elk Grove take the Grant Line Road exit east. Drive south on Stockton Boulevard (frontage road). Stockton Boulevard dead ends in the parking lot of the course.

Course description: This course opened in May, 1991. The layout consists of one par-5, four par-4s and four par-3s. The fairways are relatively narrow, with few trees. There are three lakes which come into play on six holes. The greens, which are the best part of this young course, are undulating and fast. Two of the greens are two-tiered.

MAP D3
(14 COURSES)

PAGES.. 134-143

NOR-CAL MAP.....see page 34
adjoining maps
NORTH (C3)..........see page74
EAST (D4) ....see page 144
SOUTH (E4) ......see page 248
WEST (D2) ....see page 112

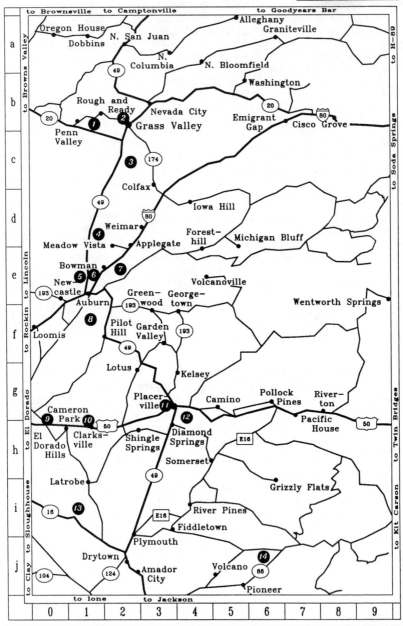

LAKE WILDWOOD COUNTRY CLUB

Course information: This private course has 18 holes and par is 72. The course is 6,508 yards and rated 71.0 from the championship tees, and 6,268 yards and rated 69.7 from the regular tees. The slope ratings are 125 championship and 123 regular. Women's tees are 5,743 yards and rated 73.0 from the forward tees. The slope rating is 130.

Play policy and fees: Reciprocal play is accepted with members of other private clubs. Guest fees are $15 for nine holes and $25 for 18 holes when accompanied by a member and $30 without. Carts are $10 for nine holes and $15 for 18.

Location: From Marysville, drive 30 miles east on Highway 20 to Pleasant Valley Road. Turn left and drive one mile to the four-way stop. Turn right onto Cottontail Way.

Course description: This rolling course is lined with mature oaks. Water comes into play on five holes and the back nine is hilly.

11255 Cottontail Way
Penn Valley, CA 95946

Pro shop   (916) 432-1163
Clubhouse   (916) 432-1152

- ■ driving range
- ■ practice greens
- ■ power carts
- ■ pull carts
- ■ golf club rental
- ■ locker rooms
- ■ showers
- ☐ executive course
- ☐ accommodations
- ■ food and beverages
- ■ clubhouse

John Klein
Professional

Dave Wilber
Superintendent

NEVADA COUNTY COUNTRY CLUB

Course information: This semi-private course has nine holes. Par is 68 for 18 holes. The course is 5,463 yards and rated 65.6 from the regular tees (18 holes). The slope rating is 110. Women's tees are 5,153 and rated 68.1 from the forward tees. The slope rating is 112.

Play policy and fees: Outside play is accepted Monday through Friday after 2 p.m. Green fees are $10 for nine holes and $18 for 18 holes weekdays. Carts are $10 for nine holes and $18 for 18 holes.

Location: From Highway 49 in Grass Valley, take the Idaho Maryland exit. At the end of the ramp turn left and drive to East Main Street. Turn right and drive to the course on the left.

Course description: This short, hilly course has tricky greens, a good test for beginning and intermediate players.

1040 East Main Street
Grass Valley, CA 95945

Pro shop   (916) 273-6436

- ■ driving range
- ■ practice greens
- ■ power carts
- ■ pull carts
- ■ golf club rental
- ☐ locker rooms
- ☐ showers
- ☐ executive course
- ☐ accommodations
- ☐ food and beverages
- ■ clubhouse

Jeff Fish
Manager/Professional

Tim Schobert
Superintendent

ALTA SIERRA GOLF AND COUNTRY CLUB

1965
R.E. Baldock

Course information: This semi-private course has 18 holes and par is 72. The course is 6,537 yards and rated 71.6 from the championship tees, and 6,342 yards and rated 70.5 from the regular tees. The slope ratings are 124 championship and 122 regular. Women's tees are 5,988 yards and rated of 73.9. The slope rating is 127.

Play policy and fees: Outside play is accepted after 11:30 a.m. Green fees are $25 for 18 holes weekdays and $30 for 18 holes weekends. Green fees for nine holes are $15 weekdays and $20 weekends. Carts are $18. Reservations are recommended. Reserve tee times one to four weeks in advance. Proper golf attire required.

Location: From Highway 49 between Grass Valley and Auburn, take the Alta Sierra Drive East exit. Drive two miles to the course on Tammy Way. Follow the signs.

Course description: This hilly, scenic course has a links-style layout with big greens. There are no parallel fairways. Deer and other wildlife are plentiful. Hole 15 offers a nice view of the Sierra. The Club Championship, Spring Invitational and Ladies Invitational play here annually. The course record is 64.

144 Tammy Way
Grass Valley, CA 95949

Pro shop   (916) 273-2010
Clubhouse   (916) 273-2041

- ■ driving range
- ■ practice greens
- ■ power carts
- □ pull carts
- ■ golf club rental
- □ locker rooms
- □ showers
- □ executive course
- □ accommodations
- ■ food and beverages
- ■ clubhouse

Willie Hall
Assistant Professional

Jeff Chleboun
Professional

Sean O'Brien
Superintendent

LAKE OF THE PINES
COUNTRY CLUB

NORTHERN D3

Course information: This private course has 18 holes and par is 71.The course is 6,069 yards and rated 69.3 from the championship tees, and 5,839 yards and rated 68.2 from the regular tees. The slope ratings are 119 championship and 117 regular. Women's tees are 5,530 yards and rated 72.1. The slope rating is 124.

Play policy and fees: Reciprocal play is accepted with members of other private clubs, otherwise members and guests only. Green fees for reciprocators are $20 for nine holes weekdays and $15 for 18 holes weekdays, and $25 for nine holes weekends and $30 for 18 holes weekends. Guest fees are $12 for nine holes and $20 for 18 holes weekdays, and $15 for nine and $25 for 18 holes weekends. Mandatory carts are $15 for nine holes and $20 for 18 holes.

Location: In Auburn, drive north on Highway 49 to Combie Road East. Turn right and drive to Lakeshore North. Turn right and drive to the course.

Course description: This hilly course is about 25 years old. It's narrow with lots of out-of-bounds. Water comes into play on seven holes. The number eight hole can be a headache. At 505 yards, it's a tough par-5. There are hazards everywhere on this hole. Your drive must clear a creek. The fairway doglegs to the left and there are OB stakes on both sides. The green is small but thankfully holds well.

11665 Lakeshore North
Auburn, CA 95603

Pro shop   (916) 269-1544
Clubhouse   (916) 269-1133

■ driving range
■ practice greens
■ power carts
□ pull carts
■ golf club rental
□ locker rooms
□ showers
□ executive course
□ accommodations
■ food and beverages
■ clubhouse

Richard Conroy
Director

Mike Henry
Professional

Herman Proctor
Superintendent

AUBURN VALLEY GOLF AND
COUNTRY CLUB

Course information: This private course has 18 holes and par is 72. The course is 6,852 yards and rated 72.8 from the championship tees, and 6,509 yards and rated 71.1 from the regular tees. The slope ratings are 128 championship and 124 regular. Women's tees are 5,849 yards and rated 73.6 from the forward tees. The slope rating is 131.

Play policy and fees: Reciprocal play is accepted with members of other private clubs. Guest fees are $20 weekdays and $30 weekends. Carts are $16. Reciprocator green fees are $30 weekdays and $50 weekends.

Location: From Auburn, drive 10 miles north on Highway 49. Take the Lone Star Road exit west to Auburn Valley Road.

Course description: This is a long, hilly, challenging course with fast greens and 11 lakes that come into play. Of note: course superintendent Mike Phillips put Pebble Beach in shape for the 1982 U.S. Open.

8800 Auburn Valley Road
Auburn, CA 95603

Pro shop   (916) 269-1837
Clubhouse   (916) 269-2775

■ driving range
■ practice greens
■ power carts
■ pull carts
■ golf club rental
■ locker rooms
■ showers
□ executive course
□ accommodations
■ food and beverages
■ clubhouse

Greg French
Professional

Mike Phillips
Superintendent

MAP ON PAGE 134

BLACK OAK GOLF COURSE

1984
John Walker

2455 Black Oak Road
Auburn, CA 95603

Pro shop   (916) 878-1900
Clubhouse (916) 878-8568

Course information: This public course has nine holes. Par is 72 for 18 holes. The course is 6,226 yards and rated 71.0 from the tournament tees, and 6,061 yards and rated 70.1 from the championship tees, and 5,896 yards and rated 69.2 from the regular tees (18 holes). The slope ratings are 123 tournament, 119 championship and 117 regular. Women's tees are 6,008 yards and rated 70.6. The slope rating is 122.

Play policy and fees: Green fees are $8 for nine holes and $14 for 18 holes weekdays, and $9 for nine holes and $16 for 18 holes weekends. Senior and junior rates are $6 for nine holes and $11 for 18 holes weekdays. Reservations are recommended one week in advance. Carts $8 per nine holes.

Location: From Interstate 80, take the Dry Creek Road exit west and drive two miles. Turn right on Black Oak Road and follow it to the course.

Course description: This challenging, nine-hole course is one of the toughest of its kind in Northern California. It has an up and down, wide-open terrain with mature oaks, water and sand. The greens are fast and undulating. Every hole is a killer, but a standout is the par-4, 376-yard number two. It plays uphill and is longer than it looks. The green is guarded by a bunker on the right and everything slopes to the left. You can three- or four-putt this hole easily if you're careless. The course is open year-round unless it's rained out or there is snow.

- ■ driving range
- ■ practice greens
- ■ power carts
- ■ pull carts
- ■ golf club rental
- □ locker rooms
- □ showers
- □ executive course
- □ accommodations
- ■ food and beverages
- ■ clubhouse

Norman Morrice
General Manager

Vic Kulik
Professional

Gordon Morrice
Owner

Matt Dillon
Superintendent

ANGUS HILLS GOLF COURSE

14520 Musso Road
Auburn, CA 95603

Pro shop   (916) 878-7818

- ■ driving range
- ■ practice greens
- ☐ power carts
- ■ pull carts
- ■ golf club rental
- ☐ locker rooms
- ☐ showers
- ☐ executive course
- ☐ accommodations
- ■ food and beverages
- ■ clubhouse

Fred Strong
Professional/Superintendent
Brandy Jones
Manager

Course information: This public course has nine holes. Par is 58 for 18 holes. The course is 3,000 yards and rated 53.3 from the regular tees. The slope rating is 78. Women's yardage and ratings are the same as the men's yardage and ratings.

Play policy and fees: Green fees are $4 weekdays and $4.75 weekends. Reserve a tee time two to three days in advance. Shoes and shirts are required.

Location: From Interstate 80 in Auburn, take the Bell Road exit. Drive to Musso Road and continue to the course.

Course description: This short course has several water hazards and is tougher than it looks. There are twilight tournaments every other Friday from April to November. The Columbus Weekend Tournament is held here in October. The Saint Paddy's Tournament is also held here annually. The men's course record is 24 (9 holes), set by Fred Strong in 1989; and the women's course record is 27 (9 holes), set by Aileen Purdy in 1982.

AUBURN LAKE TRAILS GOLF COURSE

PO Box 728
Auburn, CA 95614

2277 Westville Trail
Auburn, CA 95614

Pro shop   (916) 885-6526

- ☐ driving range
- ■ practice greens
- ☐ power carts
- ■ pull carts
- ☐ golf club rental
- ☐ locker rooms
- ☐ showers
- ■ executive course
- ☐ accommodations
- ☐ food and beverages
- ☐ clubhouse

Edwin Vitrano
Manager
William Nigh
Superintendent

Course information: This private course has nine holes. Par is 58 for 18 holes. The course is 2,745 yards and rated 52.5 from the regular tees. The slope rating is 77. Women's tees are also 2,745 yards but rated 54.8. The slope rating is 80.

Play policy and fees: Members and guests only. Guest fees are $7 per nine holes when accompanied by a property owner.

Location: From Auburn, drive six miles south on Highway 49.

Course description: This course is an executive-type course that is maintained for and by the local property owners. The course is short and hilly with lots of out-of-bounds.

EL DORADO HILLS
GOLF COURSE

Course 9
MAP D3 grid g0

Robert Trent Jones, Sr.

3775 El Dorado Hills Blvd.
El Dorado Hills, CA 95630

Pro shop   (916) 933-6552

- ■ driving range
- ■ practice greens
- ■ power carts
- ■ pull carts
- ■ golf club rental
- ☐ locker rooms
- ☐ showers
- ☐ executive course
- ☐ accommodations
- ■ food and beverages
- ☐ clubhouse

Ted R. Fitzpatrick
Professional

Ram Bali
Superintendent

Course information: This public course has 18 holes and par is 61. The course is only 3,920 yards and rated 58.3 from the regular tees. The slope rating is 93. Woman's tees are 3,875 yards but rated 60.9. The slope rating is 91.

Play policy and fees: Green fees are $16 weekdays and $20 weekends. Twilight rates are available. Carts are $16 weekdays and $18 weekends.

Location: From Sacramento, drive 25 miles east on Highway 50. Take the El Dorado Hills Boulevard exit north and drive to the course, which is on the right.

Course description: Although primarily a test for irons, this course does have five par-4s and one par-5. The front nine is hilly. The course is well maintained and has lots of trees and water.

CAMERON PARK
COUNTRY CLUB

Course 10
MAP D3 grid g0

1963
Bert Stamps

3201 Royal Drive
Cameron Park, CA 95682

Pro shop   (916) 677-4573
Clubhouse (916) 933-0270

- ■ driving range
- ■ practice greens
- ■ power carts
- ■ pull carts
- ■ golf club rental
- ■ locker rooms
- ■ showers
- ☐ executive course
- ☐ accommodations
- ■ food and beverages
- ■ clubhouse

Steve Frye
Professional

Ambrose Mrozek
Superintendent

Course information: This private course has 18 holes and par is 72. The course is 6,463 yards and rated 71.0 from the championship tees, and 6,289 yards and rated 70.2 from the regular tees. The slope ratings are 127 championship and 125 regular. Women's tees are 5,883 yards and rated 74.1. The slope rating is 134.

Play policy and fees: Reciprocal play is accepted with members of other private clubs. Green fees for reciprocal players are $50. Guest fees are $25 weekdays and $30 weekends. Carts are $16.

Location: From Sacramento, drive 30 miles east on Highway 50. Take the Cameron Park Drive exit. Turn left and drive under the overpass. Make the first left (don't get back on the freeway) onto Country Club Drive. Drive about one-half mile, just past the driving range. Make the first right past the driving range (Royal Drive) and drive to the course entrance.

Course description: This position course has fast, undulating greens and water hazards on 14 holes. It's hilly and demands a variety of shots. The 210-yard, par-3 17th hole may be the toughest on the course. You must hit over a water hazard. It's OB to the left and the green is guarded by a bunker in front and to the left. Hitting this flat green is the difficult part.

COLD SPRINGS GOLF AND COUNTRY CLUB

1960/1979

Course information: This private course has 18 holes and par is 72. The course is 6,160 yards and rated 69.2 from the regular tees. The slope rating is 116. Women's tees are 5,597 and rated 73.2. The slope rating is 125.

Play policy and fees: Reciprocal play is accepted with members of other private clubs, otherwise members and guests only. The green fees for reciprocal players are $35. Guest fees are $20 weekdays and $25 weekends. Carts are $16.

Location: From Highway 50 in Placerville, take the Placerville Drive/Forni Road exit. Drive over the overpass to the second stop sign. Turn left on Cole Springs Road. Drive three miles and turn left on Richard Avenue, which turns into Clubhouse Drive.

Course description: Weber Creek winds through this course. The ninth hole is tough. At 545 yards, this par-5 requires a shot from an elevated tee over a lake. The back nine has newer, elevated greens and is long and narrow. The original nine holes opened in 1960 and the second nine opened in 1979.

6500 Clubhouse Drive
Placerville, CA 95667

Pro shop   (916) 622-4567
Clubhouse   (916) 622-9948

- ■ driving range
- ■ practice greens
- ■ power carts
- ■ pull carts
- ■ golf club rental
- ■ locker rooms
- ■ showers
- □ executive course
- □ accommodations
- ■ food and beverages
- ■ clubhouse

NORTHERN D3

Randy Thomas
Professional

Jose Lua
Superintendent

SIERRA GOLF COURSE

1959

Course information: This public course has nine holes. Par is 62 for 18 holes. The course is 3,368 yards and rated 55.4 from the regular tees. The slope rating is 82. Women's tees are 3,368 and rated 58.1. The slope rating is 92.

Play policy and fees: Green fees are $7 for nine holes and $10 for 18 holes on weekdays, and $8 for nine holes and $12 for 18 holes weekends. Junior rate is $5 for nine holes and $6 for 18 holes. Reservations are not required.

Location: From Highway 50 in Placerville, take the Main Street exit. Take Cedar Ravine to Country Club Drive and the course. Watch for the airport sign and you'll find the course.

Course description: This short course is flat with tricky, hard-to-read greens. Oak, pine and cedar trees line the fairways.

1822 Country Club Drive
Placerville, CA 95667

Pro shop   (916) 622-0760

- □ driving range
- ■ practice greens
- □ power carts
- ■ pull carts
- □ golf club rental
- □ locker rooms
- □ showers
- □ executive course
- □ accommodations
- ■ food and beverages
- ■ clubhouse

Dean Peterson,
Manager/Professional

Frank Herrer
Superintendent

RANCHO MURIETA
COUNTRY CLUB

1971
Bert Stamps
(North)

1971
Ted Robinson
(South)

14813 Jackson Road
Rancho Murieta, CA 95683

Pro shop   (916) 354-2400
Clubhouse (916) 354-3400

- ■ driving range
- ■ practice greens
- ■ power carts
- □ pull carts
- ■ golf club rental
- ■ locker rooms
- ■ showers
- □ executive course
- ■ accommodations
- ■ food and beverages
- ■ clubhouse

David Hall
Professional

Rich Scholes
Superintendent

Course information: This private facility has two 18 hole championship golf courses. Par is 72 on both.

The North Course is 6,839 yards and rated 72.8 from the championship tees, and 6,335 yards and rated 70.6 from the regular tees. The slope ratings are 131 championship and 126 regular. Women's tees are 5,607 yards and rated 74.2. The slope rating is 136.

The South Course is 6,885 yards and rated 72.6 from the championship tees, and 6,285 yards and rated 70.0 from the regular tees. The slope ratings are 127 championship and 121 regular. Women's tees are 5,583 yards and rated 71.6. The slope rating is 122.

Play policy and fees: Reciprocal play is accepted with members of other private clubs. Guests must be invited by a member. Guest fees are $30 with a member. Reciprocator green fees are $75, including cart. Carts are $22 and mandatory. Reservations are required. Reciprocal guests should have their golf pro call three days in advance. Shirts must have collars and shorts must have a five-inch inseam.

Location: From Sacramento drive 18 miles east on Highway 50. Take the Highway 16/Jackson Road exit and follow Jackson Road to Rancho Murieta and the course.

Course description: The North Course opened for play in 1971 and the South Course, designed by Ted Robinson, followed in 1980. Arnold Palmer redesigned both courses in 1987. These are long, sprawling, tree-lined courses with large, undulating greens. There is out-of-bounds on both sides of the tight fairways. The North Course's third hole is an extremely difficult par-5, and the 455-yard fourth is a difficult driving hole. Water and rocks come into play. This is one of the best tests in the area. The course is used for the Rancho Murieta Senior Gold Rush, an annual Senior PGA Tour event.

MACE MEADOW GOLF AND COUNTRY CLUB

1966
Jack Fleming

26570 Fairway Drive
Pioneer, CA 95666

Pro shop   (209) 295-7020
Clubhouse   (209) 295-4443

- ■ driving range
- □ practice greens
- ■ power carts
- ■ pull carts
- ■ golf club rental
- □ locker rooms
- □ showers
- □ executive course
- □ accommodations
- ■ food and beverages
- ■ clubhouse

Jack Fox
Professional

Larry Anderson
President

Jed Noonkester
Superintendent

NORTHERN D3

Course information: This semi-private course has 18 holes and par is 72. The course is 6,285 yards and rated 70.1 from the championship tees, and 6,010 yards and rated 70.1 from the regular tees. The slope ratings are 122 championship and 120 regular. Women's tees are 5,387 yards and rated 70.1 from the forward tees. The slope rating is 112.

Play policy and fees: Outside play is accepted. Green fees are $7 for nine holes and $12 for 18 weekdays, and $10 for nine holes and $17 for 18 holes weekends. Carts are $16.

Location: From Highway 99, drive 60 mile northeast on Highway 88. Stay on Highway 88 through Clements, Jackson and Pine Grove. The course is located 18 miles east of Jackson on Highway 88, and five miles east of Pioneer in Buckhorn. In Buckhorn, look for Meadow Drive at the parking lot. Fairway Drive is right there.

Course description: This tight course has lots of trees and eight lakes. It's mostly flat and walkable. Water comes into play on nine holes.

MAP ON PAGE 134

NOR-CAL MAP.....see page 34
adjoining maps
NORTH (C4).........see page 80
EAST.............................no map
SOUTH (E4).......see page 248
WEST (D3).........see page 134

TAHOE DONNER GOLF AND COUNTRY CLUB

Course information: This resort course has 18 holes and par is 72. The course is 6,942 yards and rated 73.1 from the championship tees, and 6,595 yards and rated 71.5 from the regular tees. The slope ratings are 130 championship and 127 regular. Women's tees are 6,012 yards and rated 73.4. The slope rating is 127.

Play policy and fees: Outside play is accepted. Green fees for 1991 were $70, including cart; 1992 rates were unavailable. Twilight rates are $30, cart not included. Reservations are required. Call 14 days in advance to reserve a tee time. No rubber spikes may be worn, and only shirts with collars are acceptable. The course is open from May to October, and is available for outside tournaments.

Location: From Interstate 80 east, take the first Truckee exit (Donner Pass Road). Turn left on Donner Pass Road and drive to the blinking red light. Turn left on Northwoods Boulevard. The course is located three miles from Interstate 80.

Course description: This long, narrow, tree-lined course offers great mountain views. The greens are large and undulating. Water comes into play on eight holes. There are woods on both sides of the 18 holes and no out-of-bounds. There are three par-5s that measure more than 500 yards, but the ball carries farther in the thin mountain air. It takes about five hours to play.

PO Box 11049
Truckee, CA 95737

12850 Northwoods Boulevard
Truckee, CA 95737

Pro shop   (916) 587-9440
Clubhouse (916) 587-9400

- ■ driving range
- ■ practice greens
- ■ power carts
- ■ pull carts
- ■ golf club rental
- ■ locker rooms
- ■ showers
- □ executive course
- □ accommodations
- ■ food and beverages
- ■ clubhouse

Bruce Towle
Professional

James Schumann
Manager

Joel Blaker
Superintendent

NORTHERN D4

PONDEROSA GOLF CLUB

Course information: This public course has nine holes. Par is 72 for 18 holes. The course is 6,036 yards and rated 67.0 from the championship tees, and 5,792 yards and rated 65.8 from the regular tees (18 holes). The slope ratings are 109 championship and 106 regular. Women's tees are 5,792 yards and rated 71.8 from the championship tees, and 5,112 yards and rated 68.2 from the regular tees. The slope ratings are 113 championship and 108 regular.

Play policy and fees: Green fees for 1991 were $20 for nine holes and $27 for 18 holes. Carts are $10 for nine holes and $18 for 18 holes. Green fees for 1992 were unavailable. Non-playing children or adult spectators are not permitted on the course. It is open from April to October.

Location: From Interstate 80 in Truckee, take the Northshore Boulevard (Highway 267) exit south and drive to the course. The course is a 12 minute drive from Lake Tahoe.

Course description: Baseball great Jackie Jensen was one of the original owners of this course when it was sold by the city of Truckee. This course is mostly flat and is well guarded by towering ponderosa pines. It's a hidden little utopia where both the low handicapper or the "Sunday duffer" can find a good game of golf. The pride of the course is the 492-yard, 5-par ninth, the number one handicap hole. It takes about two hours and 15 minutes to play nine holes and about four and a half hours for 18 holes.

PO Box 729
Truckee, CA 95734

Hwy. 267 & Reynold Way
Truckee, CA 95734

Pro shop   (916) 587-3501

☐ driving range
■ practice greens
■ power carts
■ pull carts
■ golf club rental
☐ locker rooms
☐ showers
☐ executive course
☐ accommodations
■ food and beverages
☐ clubhouse

Greg Carter
Professional

Don Colton
Superintendent

WOODVISTA GOLF COURSE

1924

NORTHERN D4

PO Box 1269
Kings Beach, CA 95719

7900 North Lake Boulevard
Kings Beach, CA 95719

Pro shop   (916) 546-9909

- ■ driving range
- ■ practice greens
- ■ power carts
- ■ pull carts
- ■ golf club rental
- □ locker rooms
- □ showers
- □ executive course
- □ accommodations
- ■ food and beverages
- □ clubhouse

Dave Lewis
Professional

Nancy Lewis
Professional

Dave Laurie
Superintendent

Course information: This resort course has nine holes. Par is 70 for 18 holes. The course is 6,474 yards and rated 71.1 from the championship tees, and 6,076 yards and rated 69.8 from the regular tees (18 holes). The slope ratings are 116 championship and 113 regular. Women's tees are 5,596 yards and rated 66.9. The slope rating is 113.

Play policy and fees: Green fees are $20 for nine holes and $30 for 18 holes. The twilight rate is $15 after 4 p.m. Call for off-season rates. Carts are $12 for nine holes and $20 for 18 holes. Reservations are taken any time. The course is open from about April 15 to November 1.

Location: This course is located on the north shore of Lake Tahoe where Highway 28 (North Lake Boulevard) and Highway 267 intersect.

Course description: This scenic mountain course, flanked by trees, is tight with narrow fairways and small greens. The most notable hole is the seventh, a 555-yard par-5, bordering a creek. Accuracy is important. In the off-season this is a snowmobile track.

NORTHSTAR-AT-TAHOE GOLF COURSE

1975
Robert Muir Graves

PO Box 129
Truckee, CA 95374

Basque Drive
Truckee, CA 95734

Pro shop   (916) 587-0290

- ■ driving range
- ■ practice greens
- ■ power carts
- □ pull carts
- ■ golf club rental
- ■ locker rooms
- ■ showers
- □ executive course
- ■ accommodations
- ■ food and beverages
- ■ clubhouse

Jim Anderson
Professional

Kevin Ely
Superintendent

Course information: This resort course has 18 holes and par is 72. The course is 6,776 yards and rated 72.0 from the tournament tees, and 6,294 yards and rated 69.3 from the championship tees, and 5,929 yards and rated 67.4 from the regular tees. The slope ratings are 135 tournament, 130 championship and 125 regular. Women's tees are 5,491 yards and rated 71.2 from the forward tees. The slope rating is 134 regular.

Play policy and fees: Green fees are $53, cart included. Carts are mandatory until after 12:30 p.m. After 12:30 p.m. green fees are $42 without cart. Reservations are recommended up to 21 days in advance. This course is open from May 1 to October 30.

Location: In Truckee, drive six miles south on Highway 267. Exit at Northstar Drive. Turn left on Basque Drive and follow it to the clubhouse.

Course description: This challenging course has nine holes in the trees and nine holes in the valley. Water comes into play on almost every hole, especially on the par-5 seventh and the par-4 eighth. It takes about five hours to play this course.

MAP ON PAGE 144

147

TAHOE CITY GOLF AND COUNTRY CLUB

May Dunn

PO Box 226
Tahoe City, CA 95730

251 North Lake Boulevard
Tahoe City, CA 95730

Pro shop   (916) 583-1516

Course information: This public course has nine holes. Par is 66 for 18 holes. The course is 5,261 yards and rated 63.4 from the regular tees (18 holes). The slope rating is 108. Women's tees are 4,806 yards and rated 65.7 from the regular tees. The slope rating is 105.

Play policy and fees: Green fees are $20 for nine holes and $30 for 18 holes. Carts are $13 for nine holes and $20 for 18 holes. Reservations recommended up to two weeks in advance. The course is open from April to November, depending on the weather.

Location: This course is located near the intersection of Highway 89 and Highway 28 in Tahoe City. At the junction, turn onto Highway 28 (North Lake Boulevard) and follow it to the course.

Course description: This layout has the rare distinction of being designed by a woman. It is the second oldest course on Lake Tahoe. (The oldest course at Lake Tahoe is Glenbrook, which opened in 1924 and is located nine miles from Stateline on the Nevada side.) Offering great views of Lake Tahoe, Tahoe City Golf and Country Club is a scenic mountain course lined with pine, fir and cedar. The greens are well maintained and the fairways are tight.

- ■ driving range
- ■ practice greens
- ■ power carts
- ■ pull carts
- ■ golf club rental
- ☐ locker rooms
- ☐ showers
- ☐ executive course
- ☐ accommodations
- ■ food and beverages
- ■ clubhouse

Don Hay
Professional

Bobby Bonino
Manager/Superintendent

EDGEWOOD TAHOE GOLF COURSE

Lake Parkway Drive
and Hwy 50
Stateline, NV 89449

Pro shop   (702) 588-3566

Course information: This long public course has 18 holes and par is 72. The course is 7,725 yards and rated 76.0 from the tournament tees, 7,030 yards and rated 72.7 from the championship tees, and 6,444 yards and rated 70.8 from the regular tees. The slope ratings are 139 tournament, 133 championship and 128 regular. Women's tees are 5,610 yards and rated 71.6. The slope rating is 125.

Play policy and fees: Green fees are $100, including cart.

Location: From Highway 50 in South Lake Tahoe, take the Lake Parkway Drive exit north and drive to the course.

Course description: The course is actually in Nevada, but it's so close, we've included it in this year's listing. (Some players have sworn their tee shot at the ninth hole landed in California.) Situated at 6,200 feet, this scenic mountain course overlooks Lake Tahoe. There are lots of trees and water. The fairways are tight with undulating greens. The course is long, demanding, and ranked in the top 100 courses in the nation. It was the site of the 1985 U.S. Senior Open.

- ■ driving range
- ■ practice greens
- ■ power carts
- ☐ pull carts
- ■ golf club rental
- ■ locker rooms
- ■ showers
- ☐ executive course
- ☐ accommodations
- ■ food and beverages
- ■ clubhouse

Lou Eiguren
Professional

Steve Seibel
Superintendent

LAKE TAHOE COUNTRY CLUB

NORTHERN D4

Course information: This public course has 18 holes and par is 71. The course is 6,718 yards and rated 70.6 from the championship tees, and 6,244 yards and rated 67.9 from the regular tees. The slope ratings are 117 championship and 110 regular. Women's tees are 5,675 yards and rated 70.1 from the forward tees. The slope rating is 115. The course is open from mid-April to mid-October. It is available for outside tournaments.

Play policy and fees: Green fees are $27. Carts are $20.

Location: This course is located on Highway 50 between South Lake Tahoe and Meyers. Reservations are recommended up to 30 days with a major credit card.

Course description: The Truckee River runs through this scenic course. With the river and five ponds, water comes into play on 16 holes. The greens are smooth, true and among the best in Northern California. The 447-yard, par-4 13th is the hole dealing trouble on this course. It's like working your way through a minefield with the wind in your face. There is a slight dogleg left and the landing area is guarded by a pond on the right and a bunker to the left. The undulating green is surrounded by bunkers. Bring your best irons. The only salvation here is the elevation. At 6,200 feet, the ball will fly.

PO Box 10406
S. Lake Tahoe, CA 95702

Highway 50 West
S. Lake Tahoe, CA 95731

Pro shop   (916) 577-0788

- ■ driving range
- ■ practice greens
- ■ power carts
- ■ pull carts
- ■ golf club rental
- ☐ locker rooms
- ☐ showers
- ☐ executive course
- ☐ accommodations
- ■ food and beverages
- ■ clubhouse

Russell Lee
Professional

John Stanowski
Superintendent

TAHOE PARADISE GOLF COURSE

Course information: This public course has 18 holes and par is 66. The course is 4,021 yards and rated 59.9 from the regular tees. The slope rating is 94. Women's tees are 3,886 and rated 61.7. The slope rating is 96.

Play policy and fees: Green fees are $13.50 for nine holes and $21 for 18 holes any day of the week. Senior rates are $11 for nine holes and $17 for 18 holes. Twilight rates are available. Carts are $11 for nine holes and $17 for 18 holes. Reservations recommended two to three days in advance. This course is available for tournaments.

Location: This course is located in Meyers on Highway 50, three miles south of the Lake Tahoe Airport.

Course description: This valley course has hilly, rolling terrain with narrow, tree-lined fairways. The greens are small and well maintained. There are very few bunkers on this short course.

PO Box 11074
Tahoe Paradise, CA 95708

1031 Highway 50
Meyers, CA 95708

Pro shop   (916) 577-2121
Clubhouse (916) 577-2233

- ■ driving range
- ■ practice greens
- ■ power carts
- ■ pull carts
- ■ golf club rental
- ☐ locker rooms
- ☐ showers
- ■ executive course
- ☐ accommodations
- ■ food and beverages
- ■ clubhouse

Dave Beeman
Manager/Professional

NOR-CAL MAP.....see page 34
adjoining maps
NORTH (D1).........see page 86
EAST (E2)...........see page 220
SOUTH (F1) ....see page 258
WEST ....no map

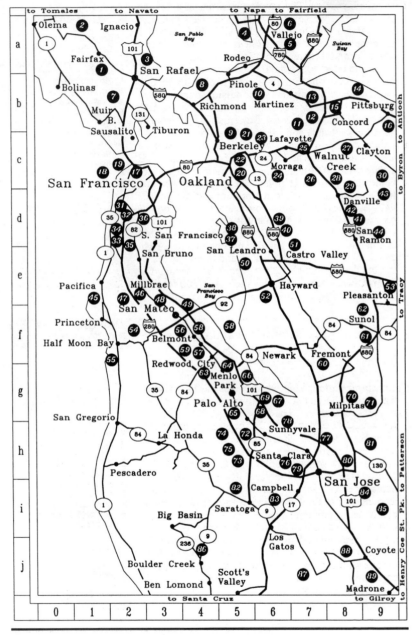

MEADOW CLUB

1926
Alister MacKenzie

1001 Bolinas Road
Fairfax, CA 94930

Pro shop (415) 456-9393
Clubhouse (415) 453-3274

- driving range
- practice greens
- power carts
- pull carts
- golf club rental
- locker rooms
- showers
□ executive course
□ accommodations
- food and beverages
- clubhouse

Steven Snyder
Professional

Dave Sexton
Superintendent

Course information: This private course has 18 holes and par is 71. The course is 6,574 yards and rated 71.2 from the championship tees, and 6,257 yards and rated 70.1 from the regular tees. The slope ratings are 125 championship and 122 regular. Women's tees are 5,942 yards and rated 74.9. The slope rating is 137.

Play policy and fees: Limited reciprocal play is accepted with members of other private clubs. Reciprocal fees are $75 with a mandatory $30 cart fee. Guest fees are $35 on weekdays and $40 on weekends when accompanied by a member. Carts are $20.

Location: From Highway 101, take the Sir Francis Drake Boulevard exit west (toward Fairfax). Turn left on Bolinas Road and follow it to the course.

Course description: This is an austere, tight course nestled in the foothills of Mount Tamalpais. It's not long, but it requires keen shot placement to the greens.

SAN GERONIMO VALLEY GOLF COURSE

1965
A. Vernon Macan

PO Box 130
San Geronimo, CA 94963

5800 Sir Francis Drake Blvd.
San Geronimo, CA 94963

Pro shop (415) 488-4030
Clubhouse (415) 488-9849

□ driving range
- practice greens
- power carts
□ pull carts
- golf club rental
□ locker rooms
□ showers
□ executive course
□ accommodations
- food and beverages
- clubhouse

Doug Talley
Professional

Tony Perino
Manager

David Michael
Superintendent

Course information: This public course has 18 holes and par is 72. The course is 6,707 yards and rated 72.0 from the championship tees, and 6,376 yards and rated 70.7 from the regular tees. The slope ratings are 125 championship and 122 regular. Women's tees are 5,688 yards and rated 73.4. The slope rating is 126.

Play policy and fees: Green fees before 2 p.m. are $35 for weekdays and $45 weekends. Call for twilight hour rates. Carts are $20. Reservations are recommended one week in advance.

Location: Driving on Highway 101 south of San Rafael, take the San Anselmo exit to Sir Francis Drake Boulevard and drive 15 miles west to the course.

Course description: Memberships are being sold in this course and it could go private. A lot of work was put into the course three years ago. Renovations include a new irrigation system, re-contoured greens, and the addition of 50 bunkers and seven lakes. The greens are tough and there are a few blind holes. Overall, it can be difficult.

PEACOCK GAP GOLF
AND COUNTRY CLUB

1959

Course information: This semi-private course has 18 holes and par is 71. The course is 6,354 yards and rated 69.7 from the championship tees, and 5,997 yards and rated 67.9 from the regular tees. The slope ratings are 121 championship and 118 regular. Women's tees are 5,994 yards and rated 73.6 from the championship tees, and 5,629 yards and rated 71.2 from the forward tees. The slope ratings are 128 championship and 123 forward.

Play policy and fees: Outside play is accepted. Memberships are available. Green fees are $24 on weekdays and $29 on weekends. Twilight rate is $17 weekdays and $22 weekends. Carts are $20. Reservations are recommended seven days in advance for weekdays and by Thursday at noon for the following weekend. Men must wear shirts and golf shoes are required. No tank tops may be worn.

Location: From Highway 101 in San Rafael, take the Central San Rafael exit. Turn east onto Second Street and drive five miles. Turn left on Biscayne Drive to the course.

Course description: This sprawling, tree-lined course is mostly flat with water on 12 holes. A creek meanders through the course. On the 16th hole, there's a 157-yard shot over a water inlet of the San Pablo Bay. There are bunkers on the fairways and the greens. The course is well maintained and very forgiving. PGA Tour standout Raymond Floyd holds the course record at 63.

333 Biscayne Drive
San Rafael, CA 94901

Pro shop   (415) 453-4940

- ■ driving range
- ■ practice greens
- ■ power carts
- ■ pull carts
- ■ golf club rental
- □ locker rooms
- □ showers
- □ executive course
- □ accommodations
- ■ food and beverages
- ■ clubhouse

Al Hand
Professional

Richard Levine
Superintendent

MARE ISLAND GOLF COURSE

Course information: This military course has nine holes. Par is 71 for 18 holes. The course is 6,207 yards and rated 69.1 from the regular tees. The slope rating is 114. Women's tees are 5,299 and rated 69.6 from the forward tees. The slope rating is 116.

Play policy and fees: Outside play is encouraged. Call the pro to make arrangements. Guest fees are $6 for active duty servicemen, $7 for retirees, $7.50 for Department of Defense personnel, and $9 for guests. Add $1 to all of above for weekend rates. Carts are $12 for active duty personnel and $14 for civilians.

Location: From Highway 29, take the Tennessee exit and head west to the main entrance and to the course.

Course description: On this course, water comes into play on four holes and it's very hilly. Look out for the 10th hole. This 434-yard, par-4 doglegs slightly right.

1800 Club Drive,
Mare Is;amd
Vallejo, CA 94592

Pro shop   (707) 644-3888

☐ driving range
■ practice greens
■ power carts
■ pull carts
■ golf club rental
■ locker rooms
■ showers
☐ executive course
☐ accommodations
■ food and beverages
■ clubhouse

Jim Johnson
Manager/Professional

Frank Moore
Superintendent

JOE MORTARA GOLF COURSE

1 9 8 1
Joe Mortara, Sr.
Jack Flemming

Course information: This public course has nine holes. Par is 56 for 18 holes. The course is 3,182 yards and rated 54.4 from the regular tees.

Play policy and fees: Green fees are $2.50 for nine holes weekdays with $1.75 for each additional nine holes, and $3 for nine holes weekends with $2 for each additional nine holes. Pull carts are $1 for the day.

Location: From Interstate 80 on the north end of Vallejo, take the Redwood exit. Turn right on Fairgrounds Drive. The course is located at the Solano County Fairgrounds.

Course description: This short course is flat and a good test for beginners and brushing up on your iron game. There is only one par-4. The course is situated in the middle of the track of the Solano Country Fairgrounds.

900 Fairgrounds Drive
Vallejo, CA 94590

Pro shop   (707) 642-5146

☐ driving range
■ practice greens
☐ power carts
■ pull carts
■ golf club rental
☐ locker rooms
☐ showers
☐ executive course
☐ accommodations
■ food and beverages
■ clubhouse

Joe Mortara, Jr.
Professional

Bob Wagner
Superintendent

MAP ON PAGE 150

BLUE ROCK SPRINGS GOLF COURSE

Course 6
MAP E1 grid a6

1941
Jack Flemming
Joe Mortara, Sr.

PO Box 5207
Vallejo, CA 94591

Columbus Parkway
Vallejo, CA 94591

Pro shop   (707) 643-8476

☐ driving range
☐ practice greens
■ power carts
■ pull carts
■ golf club rental
■ locker rooms
■ showers
☐ executive course
☐ accommodations
■ food and beverages
■ clubhouse

Ralph Harris
Professional

Bob Ludwig
Club Secretary

Bob Wagner
Superintendent

Course information: This public course has 18 holes and par is 72. The course is 6,091 yards and rated 68.2 from the regular tees. Women's tees are 5,879 yards and rated 72.9. The slope rating is 114.

Play policy and fees: Green fees are $8 on weekdays and $11 on weekends. The twilight rates are $4 weekdays and $5 weekends. Carts are $8 for nine holes and $14 for 18 holes. Spiked shoes and shirts with collars must be worn.

Location: From Interstate 80 in Vallejo, take the Columbus Parkway exit and drive three miles east to the course on the right.

Course description: This is a sprawling, hilly course with lots of trees. Short and fun, it has four par-5s. The front nine is hilly, while the back is flat with many doglegs. Four holes are up and down. There are no water hazards. The men's course record is 63 and the women's is 72. It's also known as the Vallejo Golf Course and is the site the annual Vallejo City Open. This course was designed by Joe Mortara, Sr. and Jack Flemming in 1938. Look for this course to expand in the future.

MILL VALLEY GOLF COURSE

Course 7
MAP E1 grid b2

1919

280 Buena Vista Avenue
Mill Valley, CA 94941

Pro shop   (415) 388-9982

☐ driving range
■ practice greens
■ power carts
■ pull carts
■ golf club rental
☐ locker rooms
☐ showers
☐ executive course
☐ accommodations
■ food and beverages
☐ clubhouse

Stephen Yuhas
Manager/Professional

William Osborn
Superintendent

Course information: This public course has nine holes. Par is 65 for 18 holes. The course is 4,216 yards and rated 60.6 from the regular tees. The slope rating is 100. Women's tees are 4,251 yards and rated 64.4 from the championship tees, and 4,124 yards and rated 63.7 from the forward tees. The slope ratings are 105 championship and 103 forward.

Play policy and fees: Green fees are $7 for nine holes and $10 for 18 holes on weekdays, and $9 for nine holes and $12 for 18 holes on weekends. Senior rates are $5 for nine holes and $7 for 18 holes on weekdays only. Power carts are $8 for nine holes and $14 for 18 holes.

Location: From Highway 101 in Mill Valley, take the East Blithdale Avenue exit west. Turn right on Carmelita Avenue and then right again on Buena Vista Avenue to the course.

Course description: A creek comes into play on half the holes. This short, hilly course is walkable, but golf spikes are mandatory. The men's course record is 56 by Malcolm Brown and the women's is 64 by Karen Zielenski.

RICHMOND COUNTRY CLUB

1924

Course information: This private course has 18 holes and par is 72. The course is 6,499 yards and rated 71.5 from the tournament tees, 6,316 yards and rated 70.7 from the championship tees, and 5,023 yards and rated 64.8 from the regular tees. The slope ratings are 122 tournament, 121 championship and 109 regular. Women's tees are 6,316 yards and rated 76.6 from the tournament tees, 6,066 yards and rated 75.0 from the championship tees, and 5,023 yards and rated 69.0 from the forward tees. The slope ratings are 132 tournament, 128 championship and 116 forward.

Play policy and fees: Reciprocal play is accepted with members of other private clubs. Have your club pro call ahead. Green fees for guests accompanied by a member are $30 on weekdays and $50 on weekends. For unaccompanied guests, the fees are $50 on weekdays and $60 on weekends. Carts are $16. Make reservations one week in advance. Wear suitable golf attire. No tank tops, blue jeans or shorts of inappropriate length may be worn.

Location: From Interstate 80 in Richmond, take the El Portal Drive exit west. El Portal turns into Broadway. Take Broadway to 11th Street. Turn right on 11th Street and go to the first stop sign, which is Stanton. Turn left and drive to Giant Road. Turn right to the course.

Course description: This mature course is short and very secluded. The fairways are tight and tree lined. The terrain is gentle and rolling, and there are very tall and broad pine and eucalyptus trees. In the late 1940s and 50s, men's and women's pro tournaments were held here featuring such players as Patty Berg, Babe Zaharias, Ben Hogan and Sam Snead. The men's course record is 63, the women's is 64. Playing time is roughly four hours for 18 holes.

3900 Giant Road
Richmond, CA 94086

Pro shop   (510) 232-7815
Clubhouse (510) 232-1080

- driving range
- practice greens
- power carts
- pull carts
- golf club rental
- locker rooms
- showers
- □ executive course
- □ accommodations
- food and beverages
- clubhouse

Tom Zahradka
Professional

George Bartholomeu
Superintendent

NORTHERN E1

MIRA VISTA COUNTRY CLUB

Course 9
MAP E1 grid b5

1924
William "Willie" Watson

PO Box 600
El Cerrito, CA 94530

7901 Cutting Boulevard
El Cerrito, CA 94530

Pro shop   (510) 237-7045
Clubhouse   (510) 233-7550

- ■ driving range
- ■ practice greens
- ■ power carts
- ■ pull carts
- ■ golf club rental
- ■ locker rooms
- ■ showers
- □ executive course
- □ accommodations
- ■ food and beverages
- ■ clubhouse

Carol Pence
Professional

Victor Loustalot
Director of Golf

Frank Barberio
Superintendent

Course information: This private course has 18 holes and par is 71. The course is 6,157 yards and rated 70.2 from the regular tees. The slope rating is 122. Women's tees are 5,938 yards and rated 73.8. The slope rating 125.

Play policy and fees: Reciprocal play is accepted with members of other private clubs. Have the golf pro from your club call in advance to arrange tee times. For guests accompanied by a member, green fees are $18 on weekdays and $25 on weekends. For unaccompanied guests, the fees are $30 on weekdays and $35 on weekends. Carts are $8 per person.

Location: From Interstate 80 in El Cerrito, take the Cutting Boulevard exit east. Drive to the end of Cutting Boulevard.

Course description: This sprawling course has small, severe greens. There are great views of San Francisco. It often gets windy. The course is undulating with lots of trees. Water comes into play on one hole.

FRANKLIN CANYON GOLF COURSE

Course 10
MAP E1 grid b6

1968
Robert Muir Graves

Highway 4
Rodeo, CA 94572

Pro shop   (510) 799-6191

- ■ driving range
- ■ practice greens
- ■ power carts
- ■ pull carts
- ■ golf club rental
- □ locker rooms
- □ showers
- □ executive course
- □ accommodations
- ■ food and beverages
- ■ clubhouse

Brett Smithers
Professional

Abelardo Pacheco
Superintendent

Course information: This public course has 18 holes and par is 72. The course 6,637 and rated 70.9 from the championship tees, and 6,193 yards and rated 68.9 from the regular tees. The slope ratings are 118 championship and 114 regular. Women's tees are 5,551 yards and rated 71.2. The slope rating is 123.

Play policy and fees: Green fees are $16 weekdays and $28 weekends. Carts are $20.

Location: Located on Highway 4 in Rodeo, three miles east of Interstate 80.

Course description: This hilly, sprawling course has two ponds that come into play on four holes. Several tight doglegs require accurate positioning. The wind often affects play, and the large undulating greens are difficult to read. Not to be ignored are the canyons running throughout this course. There are lateral hazards on three holes on the front nine and five holes on the back nine.

PLEASANT HILL GOLF AND COUNTRY CLUB

Course information: This semi-private course has been closed for redevelopment and remodeling into a short nine hole course. The course will reopen in 1992.

Play policy and fees: Current information is unavailable. The 1991 edition of *California Golf* contained the following: Outside play is accepted. Green fees were $8 weekdays and $10 weekends. Carts were $5 for nine holes and $10 for 18 holes.

Location: From Interstate 680 in Pleasant Hill, take the Contra Costa Boulevard exit north over the overpass. Go two blocks and turn left at Gregory Lane and follow it to the hill.

Course description: This short course has only four par-4s, the rest are par-3s. Information on its future configuration was unavailable.

1093 Grayson Road
Pleasant Hill, CA 94523

Pro shop   (510) 947-0237

☐ driving range
☐ practice greens
■ power carts
■ pull carts
☐ golf club rental
☐ locker rooms
☐ showers
☐ executive course
☐ accommodations
■ food and beverages
■ clubhouse

Keith Boam
Professional

NORTHERN E1

PINE MEADOWS GOLF COURSE

Course information: This public course has nine holes. Par is 54 for 18 holes. The course is 2,774 yards. No rating is available.

Play policy and fees: Green fees are $6 for the first nine holes and $4 for the second nine holes weekdays. Weekday senior rates are $5 for the first nine holes and $3 for the second nine holes. Weekend green fees are $8 for the first nine holes and $6 for second nine holes.

Location: From Interstate 80, take Highway 4 to the Morrelo exit in Martinez. Drive past two stop signs and turn left on Center. Turn left at Vine Hill Way. The course is on the left.

Course description: There are plans to improve the irrigation system for this course and to open a bar and restaurant in the spring of 1992. There is also the possibility of its being lengthened to qualify for NCGA ratings. This all-par-3 course has rolling hills and lots of trees. The longest hole is the 200-yard ninth. This is not an easy course. In fact, it's been rumored that in one recent 18-month stretch no one shot par.

451 Vine Hill Way
Martinez, CA 94553

Pro shop   (510) 228-2881

☐ driving range
■ practice greens
■ power carts
■ pull carts
■ golf club rental
☐ locker rooms
☐ showers
☐ executive course
☐ accommodations
■ food and beverages
■ clubhouse

John Dodson
Manager

CONTRA COSTA COUNTRY CLUB

Course information: This private course has 18 holes and par is 72. The course is 6,473 yards and rated 70.7 from the championship tees, and 6,189 yards and rated 69.7 from the regular tees. The slope ratings are 125 championship and 123 regular. Women's tees are 5,598 and rated 71.9. The slope rating is 124.

Play policy and fees: Reciprocal play is accepted with members of other private clubs. Have your club pro call for arrangements. Guest fees are $23.50 weekdays and $29.50 weekends when accompanied by a member, and $39 weekdays and $51 weekends without a member. Carts are $10.75 for nine holes and $19.50 for 18 holes. Carts for reciprocators are $26.

Location: From Interstate 680 in Pleasant Hill, take either the Willow Pass or Concord Avenue exits, turning onto Contra Costa Boulevard and winding around Diablo Valley College. The course is a one-half mile behind the college.

Course description: This course dates back to the 1920s and was designed and built by members. It offers scenic views of Mount Diablo. The greens are large with lots of undulation. Almost every green is bunkered, and there are barrancas on the 13th and 17th holes.

801 Golf Club Road
Pleasant Hill, CA 94523

Pro shop (510) 685-8288
Clubhouse (510) 798-7135

- ■ driving range
- ■ practice greens
- ■ power carts
- ■ pull carts
- ☐ golf club rental
- ■ locker rooms
- ■ showers
- ☐ executive course
- ☐ accommodations
- ■ food and beverages
- ■ clubhouse

Ray Goddard
Professional

Mike Roberts
Assistant Professional

Tony Steers
Superintendent

DIABLO CREEK GOLF COURSE

Course information: This public course has 18 holes and par is 72. The course is 6,763 yards and rated 70.9 from the championship tees, and 6,344 yard and rated 69.3 from the regular tees. The slope ratings are 111 championship and 107 regular. Women's tees are a long 6,000 yards and rated 73.2 from the forward tees. The slope rating is 118.

Play policy and fees: Green fees are $14 weekdays and $17 weekends. Carts are $16. Reservations are strongly recommended.

Location: From Highway 4 in Concord, exit on Port Chicago exit and drive to the course.

Course description: This is one of the best-kept municipal courses in Northern California. There are five lakes on the front nine. The back nine is tight and narrow. The third hole is tough. At 660 yards from the back, this par-5 requires a shot into the wind around two ponds. The course is flat. The Concord City Championships are held here each October.

PO Box 129
Concord, CA 94522

4050 Port Chicago Hwy.
Concord, CA 94522

Pro shop (510) 686-6262
Clubhouse (510) 686-6266

- ■ driving range
- ■ practice greens
- ■ power carts
- ■ pull carts
- ■ golf club rental
- ☐ locker rooms
- ☐ showers
- ☐ executive course
- ☐ accommodations
- ■ food and beverages
- ■ clubhouse

John Oderda
Professional

Rod Kilcoyne
Superintendent

BUCHANAN FIELDS
GOLF COURSE

1960
Robert Muir Graves

Course information: This public course has nine holes. Par is 66 for 18 holes. The course is 5,164 yards and is rated 63.0 from the regular tees. The slope rating is 98. Women's tees are 5,142 yards and rated 66.5. The slope rating is 105.

Play policy and fees: Green fees are $7.50 for nine holes and $11.50 for 18 holes on weekdays, $9 for nine holes and $14 for 18 holes on weekends. Senior rates are $6 for nine holes and $10 for 18 holes on weekdays only. Carts are $9 per nine holes. Reservations are recommended three days in advance. Shirts and shoes must be worn.

Location: From Interstate 80 in Concord, take the Concord Avenue exit east. Follow Concord Avenue to the course. Turn left just before reaching the Sheraton Inn.

Course description: This course is relatively short and flat. There is a creek and a large lake. The greens are undulating. This is a great practice course for any golfer, but is an excellent test for seniors and women.

3330 Concord Avenue
Concord, CA 94520

Pro shop   (510) 682-1846

- ■ driving range
- ■ practice greens
- ■ power carts
- ■ pull carts
- ■ golf club rental
- ☐ locker rooms
- ☐ showers
- ☐ executive course
- ☐ accommodations
- ■ food and beverages
- ■ clubhouse

Tim Sullivan
Owner/Professional

Ram Pal
Superintendent

Resham Singh
Manager

NORTHERN E1

DELTA VIEWS GOLF COURSE

1947
Alister MacKenzie

1991
Robert Muir Graves

2222 Golf Club Road
Pittsburg, CA 94565

Pro shop   (510) 427-4940
Clubhouse (510) 427-5852

- ■ driving range
- ■ practice greens
- ■ power carts
- ■ pull carts
- ■ golf club rental
- ☐ locker rooms
- ☐ showers
- ☐ executive course
- ■ accommodations
- ■ food and beverages
- ■ clubhouse

Mike Jordan
Professional

Carl King
Superintendent

Course information: This public course has 18 holes. Par is 72 for 18 holes. The course is 6,359 yards from the championship tees, and 5,992 yards from the regular tees. Women's tees are 5,405 yards from the forward tees. The course is in the process of being rated by the NCGA.

Play policy and fees: Green fees for Pittsburg residents are $7 for nine holes and $9 for 18 holes weekdays, and $9.50 for nine holes and $11.50 for 18 holes weekends. Non-resident green fees are $9.50 for nine holes and $11.50 for 18 holes weekdays, and $11.50 for nine holes and $13.50 for 18 holes weekends. Carts are $9 for nine holes and $15 for 18 holes. The twilight rate for residents is $4 for nine holes and $6.50 for 18 holes, and $6 for nine holes and $9 for 18 holes for non-residents after 3:30 p.m. You must wear a shirt and shoes in and around the clubhouse and on the course.

Location: From Concord, drive east on Highway 4. Take the Bailey Road exit south. Turn left on West Leland Road and drive to Golf Club Road.

Course description: Formerly the Pittsburg Golf and Country Club, and now called Delta Views Golf Course, this layout expanded to a full 18 holes in June, 1991. The architect for the second nine was Robert Muir Graves. This sporty course gets windy, but it rewards the accurate driver. Hills abound as do an assortment of trees. The course plays harder than the yardage would indicate. It's murder for the slicer and gives you trouble on every hole to the right, particularly on the new nine. Every October 6th and 7th the Pittsburg City Championships are held here.

PRESIDIO GOLF CLUB

1895

NORTHERN E1

Course information: This private course has 18 holes and par is 72. This is both a military course and a private civilian course. The course is 6,589 yards and rated 71.8 from the championship tees, and 6,225 yards and rated 70.2 from the regular tees. The slope ratings are 129 championship and 126 regular. Women's tees are 5,808 yards and rated 73.5. The slope rating is 128.

Play policy and fees: Limited reciprocal play is accepted with members of other private clubs. Contact the golf professional for more information. Guest fees are $30 weekdays and $50 weekends. Carts are $16. Reservations are recommended one week in advance. Proper golf attire required. Closed Mondays.

Location: Driving into San Francisco over the Golden Gate Bridge on Highway 101, take the 19th Avenue exit south. At the first light after passing through the tunnel (Lake Street), turn right. Flip a U-turn and head east on Lake. Follow Lake Street up to Arguello Boulevard and turn left. The course is at the top of the hill.

Course description: As the second oldest golf course west of the Mississippi, this course originated as a member-built, nine-hole layout in 1895 and expanded to 18 holes in 1910. It was first known as the San Francisco Golf Club. The military has been the operator of the course since the 1950s. This hilly course meanders through the San Francisco Presidio and commands spectacular views of the city. Challenging and steep, it's heavily wooded with cypress and eucalyptus. Beware of the 533-yard, par-5 11th hole. It has a blind elevated green that is completely lined with traps. The course record of 64, probably dating back to the late 1920s, is held by the late Lawson Little, who grew up playing this course. The course annually hosts major charity golf events, including Project Open Hand.

PO Box 29103
San Francisco, CA 94129

8 Presidio Terrace
San Francisco, CA 94118

Pro shop   (415) 751-4063
Clubhouse   (415) 751-1322

- ■ driving range
- ■ practice greens
- ■ power carts
- ■ pull carts
- ■ golf club rental
- ■ locker rooms
- ■ showers
- □ executive course
- □ accommodations
- ■ food and beverages
- ■ clubhouse

John Murray
Professional

Jeff Yee
Manager

Louise Gibson
Manager

John Buckley
Superintendent

MAP ON PAGE 150

161

GOLDEN GATE PARK GOLF COURSE

1950
Jack Fleming

Course information: This public course has nine holes. Par is 54 for 18 holes. The course is 2,714 yards for 18 holes. This course is unrated.

Play policy and fees: Green fees are $6 weekdays and $9 weekends. Carts are $8 for nine holes. Pull carts are $3.50. Club rental is $6 per bag.

Location: Located at the far west end of Golden Gate Park on Fulton Street off 47th Avenue. Take the 19th Avenue exit off Highway 101 into San Francisco. Follow 19th Avenue (Park Presidio) until you reach Fulton Street. Turn right and follow it along the park until 47th Avenue. Turn into the park and the course.

Course description: Situated at the end of Golden Gate Park by the ocean, this short course is tight and twisty with lots of trees. The longest hole is the 193-yard fifth and the shortest is the 109-yard eighth. It offers good practice for your irons game. The course hosts the annual San Francisco Family Championship.

McLaren Lodge
Golden Gate Park
San Francisco, CA 94117

47th Avenue & Fulton Street
San Francisco, CA 94117

Pro shop   (415) 751-8987

☐ driving range
■ practice greens
■ power carts
■ pull carts
■ golf club rental
☐ locker rooms
☐ showers
☐ executive course
☐ accommodations
■ food and beverages
☐ clubhouse

Jim Thigpin
Manager

LINCOLN PARK GOLF COURSE

Jack Fleming

Course information: This public course has 18 holes and par is 68. The course is 5,131 yards and rated 64.4 from the regular tees. The slope rating is 106. Women's tees are 4,989 yards and rated 68.6 from the regular tees. The slope rating is 111.

Play policy and fees: Green fees are $15 weekdays and $19 weekends. Carts are $18.

Location: Crossing over the Golden Gate Bridge on Highway 101 into San Francisco, take the 19th Avenue exit south, follow it through the tunnel and then turn right onto Clement Street. Follow Clement a few miles to the entrance of the course on the right.

Course description: Nestled around the Legion of Honor with views of San Francisco below, this extremely scenic course is tight and twisty. Part of the course runs along steep cliffs above the ocean. The 17th hole in particular offers a spectacular view of the Golden Gate Bridge. There are lots of trees and good placement shots are vital. It's hilly, but walkable. Pro golfers Johnny Miller and George Archer grew up playing here.

3139 Clement Street
San Francisco, CA 94121

Pro shop   (415) 221-9911
Clubhouse (415) 221-8727

driving range
■ practice greens
■ power carts
■ pull carts
■ golf club rental
☐ locker rooms
☐ showers
☐ executive course
☐ accommodations
■ food and beverages
■ clubhouse

John Constantine
Manager/Professional
Jim Mannion
Superintendent

MONTCLAIR GOLF COURSE

Course 20
MAP E1 grid c5

1973

Course information: This public course has nine holes. Par is 27. The course is 567 yards.

Play policy and fees: Green fees are $2.50 weekdays and $3 weekends.

Location: From Highway 13 in Oakland, take the Park Boulevard exit west. Follow it to Monterey Boulevard and drive one-quarter mile to the course.

Course description: This short, par-3 course is situated in the Oakland Hills and is mostly flat. It's a good beginner's course. There is a two-deck driving range.

2477 Monterey Boulevard
Oakland, CA 94611

Pro shop   (510) 482-0422
Clubhouse (510) 482-4444

- ■ driving range
- □ practice greens
- □ power carts
- □ pull carts
- ■ golf club rental
- □ locker rooms
- □ showers
- □ executive course
- □ accommodations
- ■ food and beverages
- ■ clubhouse

Pillim Lee
Owner

NORTHERN E1

TILDEN PARK GOLF COURSE

Course 21
MAP E1 grid c5

1935
William Park Bell

Course information: This public course has 18 holes and par is 70. The course is 6,294 and rated 69.9 from the championship tees, and 5,823 and rated 67.8 from the regular tees. The slope ratings are 118 championship and 114 regular. Women's tees are 5,399 and rated 69.7. The slope rating is 115.

Play policy and fees: Green fees are $13 on weekdays and $18 on weekends. Carts are $12 for nine holes and $20 for 18 holes. The recommended lead time for tee time reservations is one week.

Location: From Highway 24 in Berkeley, take the Fish Ranch Road exit (on the east side of the Caldecott Tunnel) and drive one mile north. Turn on Grizzly Peak Boulevard and follow it to the course.

Course description: Situated in the Berkeley Hills, this course has squirrels, raccoons and deer. Overall, it's a tight, hilly course that allows little margin for error. There are lots of trees and the greens are tricky. The 411-yard, par-4 first hole is straight uphill and plays like a par-5. The Bay Regional Tournament and the 72-Hole event are held the last weekend in July and the first weekend in August. The men's record is 65 and is held jointly by Al Norris and Greg Anderson.

8 Shasta Road
Berkeley, CA 94708

Pro shop   (510) 848-7373

- ■ driving range
- ■ practice greens
- ■ power carts
- ■ pull carts
- ■ golf club rental
- □ locker rooms
- □ showers
- □ executive course
- □ accommodations
- ■ food and beverages
- ■ clubhouse

Paul Wyrybkowski
Professional

Dave Smith
Superintendent

CLAREMONT COUNTRY CLUB

1904

Course information: This private course has 18 holes and par is 68. The course is 5,449 yards and rated 67.0 from the regular tees. The slope rating is 119. Women's tees are 5,372 yards and rated 71.4. The slope rating is 127.

Play policy and fees: Members and guests only. Guests must be accompanied by a member. Green fees are $25 when accompanied by a member. Carts are $20.

Location: From Highway 24 in Oakland, exit onto Broadway southwest. Turn right on Broadway Terrace. The course is one-half mile on the right. Or as an alternative, take Highway 13 and exit on Broadway Terrace west.

Course description: Alister MacKenzie is credited with re-working this course. This is a tight, rolling course in the Oakland hills. It is one of the oldest courses in Northern California. It's very exclusive and formerly hosted PGA tour events in the 1940s. Play the number 12 hole as smart as you can. It's 400 yards even and a par-4 with an uphill tee shot through a narrow fairway. There is OB right and a drop-off to the left. The green is sloped and well trapped. Sam Snead won the Oakland Open here in 1937.

5295 Broadway Terrace
Oakland, CA 94618

Pro shop   (510) 655-2431
Clubhouse (510) 653-6789

☐ driving range
■ practice greens
■ power carts
■ pull carts
■ golf club rental
■ locker rooms
■ showers
☐ executive course
■ accommodations
■ food and beverages
■ clubhouse

John Fite
Professional

Randy Gai
Superintendent

ORINDA COUNTRY CLUB

Course 23
MAP E1 grid c6

1925
William "Willie" Watson

315 Camino Sobrante
Orinda, CA 94563

Pro shop   (510) 254-0811
Clubhouse (510) 254-4313

□ driving range
■ practice greens
■ power carts
■ pull carts
■ golf club rental
■ locker rooms
■ showers
□ executive course
□ accommodations
■ food and beverages
■ clubhouse

Ray Orr
Professional

David Rosenstraugh
Superintendent

NORTHERN E1

Course information: This private course has 18 holes and par is 72. The course is 6,339 yards and rated 71.0 from the tournament tees, 6,127 yards and rated 70.1 from the championship tees, and 5,859 yards and rated 68.5 from the regular tees. The slope ratings are 125 tournament, 123 championship and 116 regular. Women's tees are 6,097 yards and rated 75.3 from the championship tees, and 5,718 and rated 73.0 from the forward tees. The slope ratings are 135 championship and 129 forward.

Play policy and fees: Reciprocal play is accepted with members of other private clubs. Guest fees vary, call ahead.

Location: From Highway 24, take the Orinda-Moraga exit. Turn left on San Pablo Dam Road. Turn right at the second stop light at Camino Sobrante. Go through the stop sign and drive one mile up the winding road to the course on the left. Turn left at the lake.

Course description: This tight, rolling course was built in 1924 and opened in 1925. It has traditional small greens and a creek winds through it. Two long par-4s, the ninth and 11th holes, create the most trouble. The ninth is a rolling 432-yard demon. You can see the green from the tee box, but you're driving over two mounds to a blind fairway. There is a slope from left to right. Long hitters can fly both hills on the fairway, but most will land in the second bank, requiring a long iron or wood for the second shot. It's considered the best hole on the course because everybody has a chance to par it if they play it smart and look for some roll. The 11th hole is 442 yards from the back and doglegs 220 yards out to the left. Trees border the right fairway and there is OB on the left. There is a creek 75 yards short of the green you have to carry if you're going for it. But beware: The green has very interesting natural mounds all around it and there is OB to the left.

MAP ON PAGE 150   **165**

MORAGA COUNTRY CLUB

1974
Robert Muir Graves

Course information: This private course has nine holes and is expanding to 18 holes. Par is 70 for 18 holes. The course is 5,718 yards and rated 68.8 from the championship tees, and 5,632 yards and rated 67.5 from the regular tees (18 holes). The slope ratings are 124 championship and 118 regular. Women's tees are 4,831 and rated 68.4. The slope rating is 124.

Play policy and fees: Reciprocal play is accepted with members of other private clubs in the area. Guest fees are $10 for nine holes and $18 for 18 holes weekdays, and $15 for nine holes and $35 for 18 holes weekends. Carts are $8 for nine holes and $16 for 18 holes.

Location: From Highway 24 in Moraga, take the Moraga Way exit south four miles to Saint Andrews Drive.

Course description: This course demands a good short game. It's tight and hilly with bunkers and slick greens. The course is expanding to 18 holes by the fall of 1992 under the design expertise of Algie Pulley. In the meantime, 13 holes are open and various combinations are used for a full 18.

1600 Saint Andrews Drive
Moraga, CA 94556

Pro shop   (510) 376-2253
Clubhouse   (510) 376-2200

- ■ driving range
- ■ practice greens
- ■ power carts
- ■ pull carts
- ■ golf club rental
- ■ locker rooms
- ■ showers
- □ executive course
- □ accommodations
- ■ food and beverages
- ■ clubhouse

John Lundahl
Manager/Professional

Gary Ingram
Superintendent

DIABLO HILLS GOLF COURSE

1975
Robert Muir Graves

Course information: This public course has nine holes. Par is 68 for 18 holes. The course is 4,604 yards and is rated 62.5 from the regular tees. The slope rating is 100. Women's tees are 4,475 yards and rated 65.7. The slope rating is 104.

Play policy and fees: Green fees are $10 for nine holes and $14 for 18 holes on weekdays, and $13 for nine holes and $26 for 18 holes on weekends and holidays. A junior monthly card is $35. Carts are $12 for nine holes and $24 for 18 holes. Shirts with collars must be worn.

Location: From Interstate 680 in Walnut Creek, take the Ygnacio Valley Road exit to Marchbanks Drive. Drive two miles to the course.

Course description: This flat course winds through condominiums, but is wide open. There are slightly rolling, yet walkable, hills with many sand traps. This is the ideal course for beginning and junior golfers, and there is a junior tournament every Tuesday for $6. The Singh Invitational takes place every September. Host pro Nick Andrakin holds the course record with 60 for 18 holes and 29 for nine holes.

1551 Marchbanks Drive
Walnut Creek, CA 94598

Pro shop   (510) 939-7372
Clubhouse   (510) 937-1270

- □ driving range
- ■ practice greens
- ■ power carts
- ■ pull carts
- ■ golf club rental
- □ locker rooms
- □ showers
- □ executive course
- □ accommodations
- ■ food and beverages
- ■ clubhouse

Nick Andrakin
Professional

Hardev Singh
Owner

ROSSMOOR GOLF COURSE

Course 26
MAP E1 grid c7

1965
Desmond Muirhead

1010 Stanley Dollar Drive
Walnut Creek, CA 94595

Pro shop   (510) 933-2607

- ■ driving range
- ■ practice greens
- ■ power carts
- ■ pull carts
- ■ golf club rental
- □ locker rooms
- □ showers
- □ executive course
- □ accommodations
- ■ food and beverages
- ■ clubhouse

Norm Oliver
Professional

Joe Rodriquez
Superintendent

NORTHERN E1

Course information: This private course has 27 holes and par is 72 on both combinations of 18.

The South Course is 6,048 yards and rated 68.8 from the championship tees, and 5,856 yards and rated 67.6 from the regular tees. The slope ratings are 118 championship and 115 regular. Women's tees are 5,508 yards and rated 70.3. The slope rating is 120.

The North Course is 5,950 yards and rated 67.3 from the regular tees. The slope rating is 115. Women's tees are 5,608 yards and rated 70.6. The slope rating is 117.

Play policy and fees: Members and guests only. Guest fees are $9 for nine holes and $15 for 18 holes weekdays, and $15 for nine holes and $25 for 18 holes weekends and holidays. Carts are $18.

Location: From Highway 24 east of Lafayette, take the Pleasant Hill Road exit south to Olympic Boulevard east. Then turn right on the Tice Valley Boulevard and right again on Rossmoor Parkway. Turn right onto Stanley Dollar Drive to the course.

Course description: These are retirement community courses. They are mostly flat and walkable although the South Course has some hills. Both layouts are a good test of irons and short game strategy. The greens are very tricky. The North Course may be short, but it can be tough.

BOUNDRY OAK GOLF COURSE

Course 27
MAP E1 grid c8

1969
Robert Muir Graves

PO Box 4759
Walnut Creek, CA 94596

3800 Valley Vista Road
Walnut Creek, CA 94598

Pro shop   (510) 934-6211
Clubhouse   (510) 935-8121

- ■ driving range
- ■ practice greens
- ■ power carts
- ■ pull carts
- ■ golf club rental
- □ locker rooms
- □ showers
- □ executive course
- □ accommodations
- ■ food and beverages
- ■ clubhouse

Bob Boldt
Manager/Pro/Superintendent

Course information: This public course has 18 holes and par is 72. The course is 6,788 yards and rated 72.2 from the championship tees, and 6,406 yards and rated 70.4 from the regular tees. The slope ratings are 120 championship and 116 regular. Women's tees are 5,705 yards and rated 72.1. The slope rating is 123.

Play policy and fees: Green fees are $12 weekdays and $17 weekends. Carts are $20.

Location: From Interstate 680, Take the Ygnacio Valley Road exit east. Drive three miles into Walnut Creek. Turn right on Oak Grove Road, then left on Valley Vista Road.

Course description: This course has a sprawling, demanding layout with both trees and water coming into play. It's a good driving course. Coincidentally, head pro Bob Boldt led the senior PGA Tour in driving distance in 1988.

MAP ON PAGE 150   167

ROUND HILL GOLF AND COUNTRY CLUB

Course 28
MAP E1 grid c8

1978
William Francis Bell

3169 Round Hill Road
Alamo, CA 94507

Pro shop   (510) 837-7424
Clubhouse (510) 934-8211

Course information: This private course has 18 holes and par is 72. The course is 6,440 yards and rated 71.2 from the championship tees, and 6,227 yards and rated 70.3 from the regular tees. The slope ratings are 127 championship and 125 regular. Women's tees are 5,929 yards and rated 74.1. The slope rating is 134.

Play policy and fees: Reciprocal play is accepted with members of other private clubs. Have your club pro call to make arrangements. Guest fees are $25 when accompanied by a member and $50 unaccompanied. Carts are $30 for guests. This course is available for outside tournaments on Mondays only.

Location: From Interstate 680 in Alamo, take the Stone Valley Road exit east to Round Hill Road north. The course is one mile from Interstate 680.

Course description: This tight, rolling course is located in San Ramon Valley. It has undulating greens, many trees, lots of side-hill lies, and narrow approach shots. In the past, LPGA events have taken place here. The Northern California Junior Championships were held here in 1991.

- ■ driving range
- ■ practice greens
- ■ power carts
- ☐ pull carts
- ■ golf club rental
- ■ locker rooms
- ■ showers
- ☐ executive course
- ☐ accommodations
- ■ food and beverages
- ■ clubhouse

Al Krueger
Professional

George Cherolis
Superintendent

DIABLO COUNTRY CLUB

Course 29
MAP E1 grid c8

PO Box 777
Diablo, CA 94528

1 Clubhouse Road
Diablo, CA 94528

Pro shop   (510) 837-9233
Clubhouse (510) 837-4221

Course information: This private course has 18 holes and par is 71. The course is 6,640 yards and rated 71.5 from the championship tees, and 6,277 yards and rated 70.1 from the regular tees. The slope ratings are 123 championship and 120 regular. Women's tees are 6,211 yards and rated 76.2 from the championship tees, and 5,752 yards and rated 73.2 from the forward tees. The slope ratings are 136 championship and 129 forward.

Play policy and fees: Reciprocal play is accepted with members of other private clubs. Have your club pro call for arrangements. Guest fees are $30 weekdays and $40 weekends with a member. Reciprocal fees are $55. Carts are $10 per person.

Location: From Interstate 680 in Danville, take the Diablo Road exit to the course.

Course description: This course has a hilly, tree-lined layout with small, demanding greens. It's an old course with tough par-3s.

- ☐ driving range
- ■ practice greens
- ■ power carts
- ☐ pull carts
- ☐ golf club rental
- ■ locker rooms
- ■ showers
- ☐ executive course
- ☐ accommodations
- ■ food and beverages
- ■ clubhouse

Paul Wilcox, Jr.
Professional

Sohan Singh
Superintendent

OAKHURST COUNTRY CLUB

1990
Ron Fream

Course information: This semi-private course has 18 holes. Par is 72. The course is 6,739 yards and rated 73.1 from the tournament tees, 6,275 yards and rated 70.9 from the championship tees, and 5,843 yards and rated 69.1 from the regular tees. The slope ratings are 132 tournament, 127 championship and 122 regular. Women's tees are 5,285 yards and rated 70.3. The slope rating is 123.

Play policy and fees: Outside play is accepted. Green fees are $50 weekdays and $60 weekends. Carts are included. Reservations are recommended three days in advance. This course is available for outside tournaments.

Location: From Highway 680, take Ignacio Valley exit east to Clayton Road. Turn right on Clayton Road and drive two miles to the course.

Course description: Just a year old, this course has quickly become a solid test of any player's game. It's a highly rated semi-private layout, with lots of lateral hazards and out-of-bounds. The fairways are undulating with few even lies. The greens, although still maturing, are quick and true. You can count on reliable putting, considering their youth.

PO Box 358
Clayton, CA 94517

8000 Clayton Road
Clayton, CA 94517

Pro shop   (510) 672-9737

- ■ driving range
- ■ practice greens
- ■ power carts
- □ pull carts
- ■ golf club rental
- □ locker rooms
- □ showers
- □ executive course
- □ accommodations
- ■ food and beverages
- ■ clubhouse

Dick Huff
Director of Golf

Dennis Simon
Professional

NORTHERN E1

HARDING PARK GOLF COURSE

Course 31
MAP E1 grid d2

1925
William "Willie" Watson

15 Morton Drive
Daly City, CA 94015

Pro shop   (415) 664-4690
Clubhouse (415) 878-4427

■ driving range
■ practice greens
■ power carts
■ pull carts
■ golf club rental
□ locker rooms
□ showers
■ executive course
□ accommodations
■ food and beverages
■ clubhouse

Dave Mutton
Professional

Jeff Wilson
Director of Golf

Raul Hernandez
Superintendent

Course information: This public course has 27 holes and par is 72.

The Harding Course is 6,586 yards and rated 71.3 from the regular tees. The slope rating is 119. Women's tees are 6,178 yards and rated 74.1. The slope rating is 120.

The Fleming Course, a nine-hole, par-3, beginner layout, is 2,700 yards and par is 31.

Play policy and fees: Green fees are $17 weekdays and $22 weekends at the Harding Course. Senior resident of San Francisco rates are available for $8 weekdays and $13 weekends. The Fleming Course fees are $9 weekdays and $10 weekends. A resident discount is available for $20 for both courses. It's good for one year. With a card, fees at the Harding Course drop to $12 weekdays and $15 weekends, and $5 and $6 at Fleming. Senior rates are also available. Carts are $10 for nine holes and $18 for 18 holes with a $5 deposit.

Location: Heading north into San Francisco on Interstate 280 onto 19th Avenue, make a left on Skyline Boulevard. Follow Skyline to Morton Drive and turn left to the course.

Course description: This underrated, sprawling course is surrounded by Lake Merced and is mostly flat but well guarded by trees. The latest nine was designed by Jack Fleming. The back nine is one of the best in Northern California. The course was formerly used for the PGA Tour's Lucky International Open and a Senior PGA Tour event. It is the annual site for Publinx Qualifying, and is used for the San Francisco City Golf Championship, the biggest and oldest city tournament in the country.

SAN FRANCISCO GOLF CLUB

1915
A.W. Tillinghast

Junipero Serra Boulevard
and Brotherhood Way
San Francisco, CA 94132

Pro shop (415) 469-4122
Clubhouse (415) 469-4103

- driving range
- practice greens
- power carts
□ pull carts
- golf club rental
- locker rooms
- showers
□ executive course
□ accommodations
- food and beverages
- clubhouse

Roberta Foster
Manager

Rick Rhoads
Professional

Robert Klinesteker
Superintendent

NORTHERN E1

Course information: This private course has 18 holes and par is 71. The course is 6,627 yards and rated 72.9 from the championship tees, and 6,316 yards and rated 71.5 from the regular tees. The slope ratings are 133 championship and 130 regular. Women's tees are 6,015 and rated 76.3. The slope rating is 140.

Play policy and fees: Reciprocal play is not accepted. Members and guests only. Guest fees when accompanied by a member are $35 and $100 unaccompanied. Carts are allowed only with a medical excuse and the fee is $20 with a member and $25 without.

Location: From the Golden Gate Bridge into San Francisco, take the 19th Avenue exit and follow it through town until it turns into Junipero Serra Boulevard (past San Francisco State University). Turn right on Brotherhood Way and then take the first left onto Saint Thomas Moore Way to the course on the left.

Course description: This serene, immaculate course is rated among the top in the state. It's a medium-length, sprawling course with fast, undulating greens and lots of bunkers. Designed in 1915 by A.W. Tillinghast, the course has strategically placed pine trees that make accuracy essential. It played host to the 1974 Curtis Cup Match and is a regular site of the U.S. Open sectional qualifying.

LAKE MERCED GOLF AND COUNTRY CLUB

1922
Will Lock

Course information: This private course has 18 holes and par is 72. The course is 6,786 yards and rated 72.8 from the championship tees, and 6,499 yards and rated 71.5 from the regular tees. The slope ratings are 128 championship and 125 regular. Women's tees are 5,968 and rated 75.1. The slope rating is 135.

Play policy and fees: Reciprocal play is accepted with members of other private clubs only on Tuesdays and Thursdays at the discretion of the pro. Guest fees when accompanied by a member are $30 weekdays and $35 weekends. Green fees for reciprocators are $75 with a member and $85 without a member. Carts are $10 with a member and $15 without.

Location: On 19th Avenue in San Francisco or Highway 1, merge onto Junipero Serra Boulevard toward Daly City and follow to the course.

Course description: This is a long, challenging course with big, undulating greens, huge pines and San Francisco weather. There are some difficult par-3s, especially the 15th hole. It's long at 200 yards and narrow. Designed by Will Lock in 1922 and remodeled in 1964 by Robert Muir Graves, this course is well maintained and walkable. It was the 1990 site of the USGA Boys' National Championship. It was the site of the Western Open and the Northern California Junior Championship.

2300 Junipero Serra Blvd.
Daly City, CA 94015

Pro shop   (415) 755-2239
Clubhouse (415) 755-2233

- ■ driving range
- ■ practice greens
- ■ power carts
- ☐ pull carts
- ☐ golf club rental
- ■ locker rooms
- ■ showers
- ☐ executive course
- ☐ accommodations
- ■ food and beverages
- ■ clubhouse

Adair B. Chew
Manager

Woody Wright
Professional

Lou Tonelli
Superintendent

THE OLYMPIC CLUB

1924
Wilfred Reid

PO Box 3216
Daly City, CA 94015

Off Skyline Boulevard
Daly City, CA 94105

Pro shop   (415) 587-8338
Clubhouse (415) 587-4800

■ driving range
■ practice greens
■ power carts
□ pull carts
■ golf club rental
■ locker rooms
■ showers
□ executive course
■ accommodations
■ food and beverages
■ clubhouse

David Nightingale
Manager

Jim Lucius
Professional

John Fleming
Superintendent

NORTHERN E1

Course information: This private facility has 36 holes. Par on the Lake Course is 71. Par on the Ocean Course is 72.

The Lake Course is 6,808 yards and rated 74.1 from the championship tees, and 6,464 yards and rated 72.3 from the regular tees. The slope ratings are 135 championship and 133 regular. Women's tees are 6,134 yards and rated 75.4. The slope rating is 135.

The Ocean course is 6,359 yards and rated 71.0 from the championship tees, and 6,024 yards and rated 69.5 from the regular tees. The slope ratings are 126 championship and 123 regular. Women's tees are 5,631 yards and rated 72.8. The slope rating is 128.

Play policy and fees: Reciprocal play is not accepted. Members and guests only. All guests must be accompanied by a member. Guest fees are $50 for the Lake Course and $40 for the Ocean Course. Carts are $10 per rider.

Location: Driving south on 19th Avenue through San Francisco, turn right on Sloat Boulevard. Follow it until it splits into a "Y" (before the San Francisco Zoo). Turn left onto Skyline Boulevard. The course is at the top of the hill, obscured by a fence.

Course description: Add William "Willie" Watson's designer influence to the Ocean Course. History also links him to the Lake Course. The Lake Course has been the site of three U.S. Opens (1955, 1966 and 1987) and ranks among the top 10 courses in the country. It is long, tight and has lots of trees. The greens are small and undulating. The Lake Course was designed by Wilfred Reid and Sam Whiting in 1924. Two of the biggest upsets in U.S. Open history happened on this course. In 1955, Jack Fleck shocked Ben Hogan in a playoff. In 1966, Billy Casper made up a seven-stroke deficit with nine holes to play to tie Arnold Palmer, then defeated him in a playoff. The course was also the site of the 1981 U.S. Amateur, where Nathaniel Crosby pulled off an upset victory. The Ocean Course is shorter and tighter, but equally challenging. Wind and fog come into play.

CYPRESS HILLS
GOLF COURSE

1961
Jack Fleming

Course information: This public course has nine holes. Par is 74 for 18 holes. The course is 6,886 yards from the regular tees (18 holes). Women's yardage was not available. The course is unrated.

Play policy and fees: Green fees are $10 weekdays and $15 weekends and holidays. Senior rates are $7 before 9 a.m. Monday through Friday. Carts are $10 for nine holes.

Location: From Interstate 280 in South San Francisco, take the Serramonte Boulevard exit. Cross over to the east side of the freeway and drive south on Hillside Boulevard. Continue down about 500 yards to the course entrance on the left.

Course description: This course is tight and well guarded by trees. It has a lake, two par-5s and only one par-3.

2001 Hillside Boulevard
Colma, CA 94014

Pro shop   (415) 992-5155

- ■ driving range
- ■ practice greens
- ■ power carts
- ■ pull carts
- □ golf club rental
- □ locker rooms
- □ showers
- □ executive course
- □ accommodations
- ■ food and beverages
- ■ clubhouse

David G. Newman
Director of Golf

Don Giovannini
Professional

Mike Castillo
Superintendent

GLENEAGLES
INTERNATIONAL
GOLF COURSE

1963
Jack Fleming

NORTHERN E1

Course information: This semi-private course has nine holes. Par is 72 for 18 holes. The course is 6,642 yards and rated 73.6 from the championship tees, and 6,421 yards and rated 71.0 from the regular tees. The slope ratings are 136 championship and 116 regular. Women's yardage and ratings were unavailable.

Play policy and fees: Outside play is accepted. Green fees are $9 for nine holes and $15 for 18 holes weekdays, and $20 for 18 holes weekends. There is no nine-hole play on weekends or holidays. Carts are $10 for nine holes and $20 for 18 holes.

Location: Driving south on Highway 101 on the way out of San Francisco, take the Paul Avenue exit. At the stop sign, proceed up the hill on Manzell and over the top to Sunnydale Avenue and turn left. The course is located 400 yards at the first driveway on the left. It's unmarked. Driving north on Highway 101 into San Francisco, take the Cow Palace/Brisbane exit to Old Bayshore and go left at Geneva Street. In 1.5 miles, turn right on Moscow and then right again on Persia. It's three blocks to Sunnydale Avenue.

2100 Sunnydale Avenue
San Francisco, CA 94134

Pro shop   (415) 587-2425

☐ driving range
■ practice greens
■ power carts
☐ pull carts
☐ golf club rental
☐ locker rooms
☐ showers
☐ executive course
☐ accommodations
■ food and beverages
■ clubhouse

Erik DeLambert
Owner/Manager

Mick Soli
Professional

Ben DeLambert
Superintendent

Course description: This sleeper course is patterned after a Scottish links-type course with a rolling terrain. You'll find tight, tree-lined fairways and tricky greens. Good target shots are required. It's well maintained and often foggy and windy. In spite of the five-year drought, the greens and tee boxes are in great shape. The course record is 66, set by former PGA Tour player and host pro Mick Soli. An eight-stool, Scottish-style pub with ales and beers will soothe your frayed nerves after you finish.

MAP ON PAGE 150

LEW F. GALBRAITH
GOLF COURSE

1966
R.E. Baldock

Course information: This public course has 18 holes and par is 72. The course is 6,777 yards and rated 71.0 from the championship tees, and 6,298 yards and rated 69.7 from the regular tees. The slope ratings are 118 championship and 117 regular. Women's tees are 5,732 yards and rated 71.7. The slope rating is 111.

Play policy and fees: Green fees are $11 weekdays and $15 weekends. Call for special senior, junior and twilight rates. Carts are $16.

Location: From Interstate 880 in Oakland, exit at Hegenberger Road southwest. Drive one mile to Doolittle Drive. Turn left and drive to the course on the right.

Course description: This flat course plays long. The fifth and 18th holes are two beautiful, challenging par-4s.

10505 Doolittle Drive
Oakland, CA 94603

Pro shop   (510) 569-9411
Clubhouse (510) 562-7474

- ■ driving range
- ■ practice greens
- ■ power carts
- ■ pull carts
- ■ golf club rental
- ■ locker rooms
- □ showers
- □ executive course
- □ accommodations
- ■ food and beverages
- ■ clubhouse

Dan Osterberg
Professional

Jeff Livacich
Superintendent

ALAMEDA GOLF COURSE

1927
William Park Bell
William Francis Bell

1 Memorial Drive
Alameda, CA 94501

Pro shop   (510) 522-4321

■ driving range
■ practice greens
■ power carts
■ pull carts
■ golf club rental
■ locker rooms
□ showers
□ executive course
□ accommodations
■ food and beverages
■ clubhouse

Steve Videtta
Professional

Dennis Plato
Superintendent

NORTHERN E1

Course information: This public facility has 36 holes and par is 71 for both. There is an adjacent par-3 course.

The Earl Fry Course is 6,160 yards and rated 68.8 from the championship tees, and 5,830 and rated 67.3 from the regular tees. The slope ratings are 115 championship and 111 regular. Women's tees are 5,553 yards and rated 71.0. The slope rating is 114.

The Jack Clark Course is 6,503 yards and rated 70.1 from the championship tees, and 5,947 yards and rated 68.0 from the regular tees. The slope ratings are 114 championship and 110 regular. Women's tees are 6,055 yards and rated 73.8 from the championship tees, and 5,421 yards and rated 70.0 from the forward tees. The slope ratings are 118 championship and 110 forward.

Play policy and fees: Green fees are $10 weekdays and $13 weekends. Carts are $16.

Location: From Interstate 880 (Nimitz Freeway) south of the Oakland Coliseum, take the Hegenberger Road exit west one mile. Turn right on Doolittle Road and follow it to Island Drive and turn left. Turn left again on Memorial Drive to the course.

Course description: These are flat, challenging courses. The Jack Clark Course is longer and more difficult. It was designed by William Francis Bell. The Earl Fry Course was designed by William ''Billy'' Park Bell. Both are well-maintained and walkable courses with lots of trees and some water. This is the site of the annual Alameda Commuters Tournament each April, one of Northern California's oldest and best-run amateur events.

SEQUOYAH COUNTRY CLUB

1913

Course information: This private course has 18 holes and par is 70. The course is 6,056 yards and rated 69.8 from the championship tees, and 5,901 yards and rated 69.1 from the regular tees. The slope ratings are 126 championship and 124 regular. Women's tees are 5,617 yard. The slope rating is 131.

Play policy and fees: Reciprocal play is accepted with members of other private clubs weekdays only. Have your club pro call to make arrangements. Guest green fees are $55 weekdays and $65 weekends, including mandatory cart. The golf dress code is in effect.

Location: From Interstate 580 in southern Oakland, take the 98th Avenue exit. Cross to the east side of the freeway. Turn left onto Mountain Boulevard. Turn right on Sequoyah Road and follow it for three-fourths of a mile. Turn right on Heafey Road and drive to the course.

Course description: This mature course is short, hilly and tight. The elevated tees and fast greens make for exciting par-3s. It's very exclusive. This course was the site of the PGA Tour's Oakland Open in the 1930s, featuring players such as Ben Hogan and Sam Snead.

4550 Heafey Road
Oakland, CA 94605

Pro shop   (510) 632-4069
Clubhouse (510) 632-2900

- ■ driving range
- ■ practice greens
- ■ power carts
- □ pull carts
- □ golf club rental
- ■ locker rooms
- ■ showers
- □ executive course
- □ accommodations
- ■ food and beverages
- ■ clubhouse

John R. Bearden
Professional

Mike Meillon
Manager

Blake Swint
Superintendent

LAKE CHABOT GOLF COURSE

1923

Course information: This public course has 18 holes and par is 71. The course is 5,933 yards and rated 65.9 from the regular tees. The slope rating is 114. Women's tees are 5,268 yards and rated 68.5. The slope rating is 116. A par-3 executive course is also available, measuring 1,040 yards.

Play policy and fees: Green fees are $11 weekdays and $15 weekends. Twilight rates are $6 weekdays and $9 weekends. The recommended lead time for tee time reservations is one week. Carts are $16 weekdays and $18 weekends.

Location: From Interstate 580 in Oakland, take the Golf Links Road exit and follow the road to the end.

Course description: This course is hilly but walkable. The 18th hole is a unique 690-yard par-5, down (or is it up) from its former par of 6 at 665 yards. The hole starts off level and slopes down and then up. Out-of-bounds is to the left and trees are on the right. Take your complaints to course manager Raymond Chester, former All-Pro tight end with the Oakland Raiders. The course is one of the oldest in Northern California. Tony Lema, 1964 British Open champion, grew up near Lake Chabot. The course record of 60 is shared by John Fry and Gary Vanier.

Golf Links Road
Oakland, CA 94605

Pro shop   (510) 351-5812

- ■ driving range
- ■ practice greens
- ■ power carts
- ☐ pull carts
- ■ golf club rental
- ☐ locker rooms
- ☐ showers
- ■ executive course
- ☐ accommodations
- ■ food and beverages
- ■ clubhouse

Jeff Dennis
Professional

Raymond Chester
Manager

Bill Menear
Superintendent

CANYON LAKES COUNTRY CLUB

1987
Ted Robinson

Course information: This public course has 18 holes and par is 71. The course is 6,379 yards and rated 70.1 from the championship tees, and 5,975 yards and rated 68.2 from the regular tees. The slope ratings are 116 championship and 113 regular. Women's tees are 5,230 yards and rated 69.9. The slope rating is 121.

Play policy and fees: Green fees are $50 weekdays and $55 weekends, mandatory carts included. Reserve starting times a week in advance. This course is available for tournaments. Closed Mondays.

Location: From Interstate 680 in San Ramon, take the Bollinger Canyon exit east over the freeway. Turn left on Canyon Lakes Drive, and left again on Bollinger Canyon Way to the course.

Course description: Situated in the foothills of San Ramon, this course opened as a nine-hole layout in 1987 and expanded to 18 holes in the fall of 1989. It has lots of water, trees and bunkers. The fairways are contoured, and the greens undulate.

640 Bollinger Canyon Way
San Ramon, CA 94583

Pro shop   (510) 735-6511
Clubhouse   (510) 735-6224

- ☐ driving range
- ■ practice greens
- ■ power carts
- ☐ pull carts
- ■ golf club rental
- ■ locker rooms
- ■ showers
- ☐ executive course
- ☐ accommodations
- ■ food and beverages
- ■ clubhouse

Russ Dicks
Manager/Professional

Bobby Cox
Superintendent

MAP ON PAGE 150

CROW CANYON COUNTRY CLUB

1977
Ted Robinson

711 Silver Lake Drive
Danville, CA 94526

Pro shop   (510) 735-8300
Clubhouse (510) 735-8200

■ driving range
■ practice greens
■ power carts
□ pull carts
■ golf club rental
■ locker rooms
■ showers
□ executive course
□ accommodations
■ food and beverages
■ clubhouse

Dave Anderson
Professional

Ernie Martin
Superintendent

Course information: This private course has 18 holes and par is 69. The course is 5,909 yards and rated 68.6 from the regular tees. The slope rating is 118. Women's tees are 5,554 yards and rated 72.3. The slope rating is 126.

Play policy and fees: Reciprocal play is accepted with members of other private clubs. Have your club pro call for arrangements. Guest fees are $30 weekdays and $40 weekends. Reservations are recommended one week in advance. Golf shoes and shirts with collars are required. No jeans, tank tops, T-shirts, short shorts, gym shorts or tennis shorts may be worn. Closed Mondays.

Location: From Interstate 680 in San Ramon, take the Crow Canyon exit east. Turn left on El Capitan and right on Silver Lake Drive.

Course description: This is a hilly, rolling course. The sixth hole is a notable par-3. It's 200 yards against the wind to an elevated green. This course is known for being very well manicured with great drainage during the rainy season. The course is well bunkered with water coming into play on nine holes. The Diablo Advocates Pro-Am initially started at Crow Canyon, with such great golfers as Johnny Miller, George Archer, Larry Nelson, Bill Russell, Joe Morgan and Jim Rice. Watch out for the 400-yard, par-4 18th hole, which features an elevated tee and water along the left side of the hole. The men's and women's course records are held by Sean Clark (63) and Jane Crafter (64), respectively.

BLACKHAWK COUNTRY CLUB

1 9 8 1
Bruce Devlin
Robert Von Hagge
(Lakeside Course)

Ted Robinson
(Falls Course)

599 Blackhawk Club Drive
Danville, CA 94526

Pro shop   (510) 736-6565
Clubhouse (510) 736-6500

NORTHERN E1

Course information: This private club has 36 holes and par is 72 on both courses.

The Lakeside Course is 6,845 yards and rated 74.2 from the championship tees, and 6,407 yards and rated 71.8 from the regular tees. The slope ratings are 135 championship and 132 regular. Women's tees are 5,424 and rated 71.2. The slope rating is 132.

The Falls Course is 6,731 yards and rated 72.8 from the championship tees, and 6,155 yards and rated 70.2 from the regular tees. The slope ratings are: 128 championship and 122 regular. Women's tees are 5,374 yards and rated 70.5. The slope rating is 128.

Play policy and fees: Members and guests only. No reciprocal play. Guests must be accompanied by a member at time of play. Guest fees are $35 weekdays and $50 weekends. Carts are $20 and mandatory on both courses.

Location: From Interstate 680 in Danville, take the Sycamore Valley Road exit. Turn right on Camino Tassajara and left on Blackhawk Road. Drive to Blackhawk Club Drive and turn right.

■ driving range
■ practice greens
■ power carts
□ pull carts
■ golf club rental
■ locker rooms
■ showers
□ executive course
□ accommodations
■ food and beverages
■ clubhouse

Rob Frederick
Professional

Charlie Johnson
Superintendent

Course description: The Lakeside Course is rolling and imaginative. Designed by Bruce Devlin and Robert Von Hagge, it has large, undulating greens, lots of water, and tight fairways. There are many up and down holes threading through oak trees. It's a traditional, non-gimmicky course and requires shot making. It is the tougher of the two courses. The Falls Course, designed by Ted Robinson, is a shorter version with emphasis on placement. It is rolling and hilly between holes. The first hole is a straight drop, but after that it flattens out. It's a fun course to play. Each course has a clubhouse and pro shop.

MAP ON PAGE 150   181

SAN RAMON ROYAL VISTA GOLF COURSE

Course 44
MAP E1 grid d9

1962
Clark Glasson

9430 Fircrest Lane
San Ramon, CA 94583

Pro shop   (510) 828-6100

■ driving range
■ practice greens
■ power carts
■ pull carts
■ golf club rental
■ locker rooms
■ showers
□ executive course
□ accommodations
■ food and beverages
■ clubhouse

Mark Fleshman
Professional

Edward Ferreira
Superintendent

Course information: This semi-private course has 18 holes and par is 72. The course is 6,564 yards and rated 70.9 from the championship tees, and 6,350 yards and rated 69.8 from the regular tees. The slope ratings are 115 championship and 113 regular. Women's tees are 5,870 yards and rated 72.7. The slope rating is 119.

Play policy and fees: This course is open to the public. Green fees are $15 weekdays and $25 weekends. There is a $10 rate for nine holes before 8 a.m. Twilight rate is $10 weekdays and $14 weekends. Carts are $12 for nine holes and $18 for 18 holes. Reservations are recommended one week in advance. Shirts with collars are required. No T-shirts or tank tops on the course or at the driving range. This course is available for outside tournaments.

Location: Driving south on Interstate 680 in San Ramon, take the Alcosta Boulevard exit. Cross back over the freeway and drive one mile. Turn on Fircrest Lane to the course.

Course description: This is a flat course with large greens. Homes line almost every fairway. More than 300 new trees have been planted. The course is in beautiful condition, thanks to on-site well water.

SHARP PARK GOLF COURSE

1929
Alister MacKenzie

Course information: This public course has 18 holes and par is 72. The course is 6,289 yards and rated 69.6 from regular the tees. The slope rating is 114. Women's tees are 6,095 yards and rated 73.0. The slope rating is 120.

Play policy and fees: Green fees are $15 weekdays and $19 weekends. Half-price twilight rates are available. Carts are $18. Reservations are required one week in advance for weekday play, the prior Wednesday for Saturday play and the prior Thursday for Sunday play. This course is available for outside tournaments.

Location: Heading south on Interstate 280 from San Francisco, take the second exit toward the town of Pacifica. Continue on to Pacifica on Highway 1. Turn to the course at Fairway Drive.

Course description: This is a flat, tree-lined course located at sea level. The front nine is set inland, and the back nine runs along the ocean. The fairways are tight with large greens. This could be considered the poor man's option to Pebble Beach. There's sand, water, views and golf. The 13th hole is a par-5, 525-yard dogleg left over water and it's a doozie.

PO Box 1275
Pacifica, CA 94044

Sharp Park Road and Hwy. 1
Pacifica, CA 94044

Pro shop   (415) 359-3380
Clubhouse (415) 355-7900

NORTHERN E1

☐ driving range
■ practice greens
■ power carts
■ pull carts
■ golf club rental
☐ locker rooms
☐ showers
☐ executive course
☐ accommodations
■ food and beverages
■ clubhouse

Jack Gage
Professional

Joan W. Lantz
Manager

Sean Sweeney
Superintendent

GREEN HILLS COUNTRY CLUB

1932
Alister MacKenzie

Course information: This private course has 18 holes and par is 71. The course is 6,278 yards and rated 71.0 from the championship tees, and 6,056 yards and rated 70.0 from the regular tees. The slope ratings are 126 championship and 124 regular. Women's tees are 6,001 yards and rated 76.2 from the championship tees, and 5,752 yards and rated 74.7 from the forward tees. The slope ratings are 142 championship and 138 forward.

Play policy and fees: Reciprocal play is accepted with members of other private clubs. Guest fees are $40 weekdays and $50 weekends when accompanied by a member, and $85 unaccompanied. Fees for reciprocators are $85. Carts are $10 per rider. Four-bagger prices are available if you'd like a cart to tow your bag while you walk.

Location: Located between Interstate 280 and Highway 101 in Millbrae. Exit on Millbrae Avenue off Highway 101 and drive north on El Camino Real. Turn left on Ludeman Lane and drive up the hill to the course.

Course description: This short, but tricky Alister Mac-Kenzie course is situated in the foothills among the pine and cypress. It has small, undulating greens and is well bunkered. The pride of the course is the uphill 180-yard, par-3 15th hole, which crosses a ravine. You must hit to a two-level green with severe undulation between the levels. The green is slick and difficult. Count on the back level to be the toughest. Two lakes have been added to the par-5 16th, so it's no longer a gimmie birdie hole for long hitters. There is a 120-yard practice area for 8- and 9-iron play. It's hilly, but walkable.

End of Ludeman Lane
Millbrae, CA 94030

Pro shop   (415) 583-0882
Clubhouse (415) 588-4616

□ driving range
■ practice greens
■ power carts
□ pull carts
■ golf club rental
■ locker rooms
■ showers
□ executive course
□ accommodations
■ food and beverages
■ clubhouse

Jack Mahoney
Manager

John Joseph
Professional

Walt Barrett
Superintendent

CALIFORNIA GOLF CLUB

1920
Vernon Macan

844 West Orange Avenue
South San Francisco
CA 94080

Pro shop   (415) 589-0144
Clubhouse (415) 761-0210

- ■ driving range
- ■ practice greens
- ■ power carts
- □ pull carts
- □ golf club rental
- ■ locker rooms
- ■ showers
- □ executive course
- □ accommodations
- ■ food and beverages
- ■ clubhouse

Dennis Mahoney
Manager

Al Vaccaro
Professional

Charles Pratt
Superintendent

Course information: This private course has 18 holes and par is 72. The course is 6,677 yards and rated 72.9 from the championship tees, and 6,474 yards and rated 72.0 from the regular tees. The slope ratings are 134 championship and 132 regular. Women's tees are 5,969 yards and rated 75.4. The slope rating is 134.

Play policy and fees: Members and guests only. Guest fees are $50 with a member and $100 without. Carts are $10.

Location: From San Francisco, take Interstate 280 South to the Westborough Avenue exit east. At the bottom of the hill, turn right on Orange Avenue and follow it to the course.

Course description: This sprawling, challenging course is situated above San Francisco International Airport and is often windy. It's loaded with 185 bunkers and is hilly. Once you play here you'll understand why the San Francisco Giants want to move out of Candlestick Park. The par-5s and par-3s are especially challenging.

BURLINGAME COUNTRY CLUB

1893
Tom Nicoll

80 New Place Road
Hillsborough, CA 94010

Pro shop   (415) 342-0750
Clubhouse (415) 343-1843

- ■ driving range
- ■ practice greens
- ■ power carts
- ■ pull carts
- ■ golf club rental
- ■ locker rooms
- ■ showers
- □ executive course
- □ accommodations
- ■ food and beverages
- ■ clubhouse

Maurice Ver Brugge
Professional

Arthur Frey
Manager

Terry Grasso
Superintendent

Course information: This private course has 18 holes and par is 70. The course is 6,394 yards and rated 70.3 from the regular tees. The slope rating is 126. Women's tees are 5,731 yards and rated 73.0. The slope rating is 130.

Play policy and fees: Members and guests only. Guest fees are $25 when accompanied by a member and $75 unaccompanied. Carts are $25.

Location: Driving on Highway 101 in Burlingame, take the Broadway exit southwest to El Camino Real. Go left and, in less than one mile, turn right on Floribunda Avenue. When it dead ends, turn left on Eucalyptus and then right on New Place Road. The course is on the right.

Course description: This course is the oldest west of the Mississippi, dating back to 1893. It has a sprawling, tree-lined layout and the narrow fairways require precise shots off the tee. It's largely flat and walkable. Bing Crosby was one of the many prominent members of this highly exclusive club.

SAN MATEO GOLF COURSE

1934

Course information: This public course has 18 holes and par is 70. The course is 5,917 yards and rated 67.0 from the championship tees, and 5,598 yards and rated 65.5 from the regular tees. The slope ratings are 104 championship and 101 regular. Women's tees are 5,498 and rated 70.4. The slope rating is 117.

Play policy and fees: Green fees are $14 weekdays and $18 weekends and holidays. After 3 p.m., twilight rates are available for $9.50 weekdays and $11 weekends and holidays. There are special rates for seniors and high school students within the city of San Mateo. Carts are $14. Pull carts are available for $1 plus a $1 handle deposit.

Location: This course is located on the east side of Highway 101 in San Mateo and visible from the freeway. From the north, take the Poplar Avenue exit. From the south, take the Dore exit. Follow the signs marked Coyote Point Drive from both exits to the course.

Course description: This course is short and flat with tight eucalyptus-lined fairways. The greens are in the traditional style: very small, elevated, well bunkered and well contoured. Because of this, there is a premium on approach shots and putting. The course is usually windy and has several water hazards. It's walkable.

Box 634
San Mateo, CA 94401

1700 Coyote Point Drive
San Mateo, CA 94401

Pro shop   (415) 347-1461

- ☐ driving range
- ■ practice greens
- ■ power carts
- ■ pull carts
- ■ golf club rental
- ☐ locker rooms
- ☐ showers
- ☐ executive course
- ☐ accommodations
- ■ food and beverages
- ■ clubhouse

Jake Montes
Manager/Professional

John Grant
Superintendent

TONY LEMA GOLF COURSE

1982
William Francis Bell

13800 Neptune Drive
San Leandro, CA 94577

Pro shop   (510) 895-2162

■ driving range
■ practice greens
■ power carts
■ pull carts
■ golf club rental
■ locker rooms
■ showers
■ executive course
□ accommodations
■ food and beverages
■ clubhouse

Steve Elbe
Professional

John Lloyd
Superintendent

Course information: This public course has 27 holes. Par is 71 on the Tony Lema Course. Par is 58 for 18 holes on the nine-hole Marina Course.

The Tony Lema Course is 6,633 yards and rated 70.7 from the championship tees, and 6,175 yards and rated 68.6 from the regular tees. The slope ratings are 115 championship and 107 regular. Women's tees are 5,718 yards and rated 71.3. The slope rating is 113.

The Marina Course is 3,316 yards and rated 53.8 from the regular tees. The slope rating is 73. Women's yardage and ratings were unavailable.

Play policy and fees: Green fees are $9.50 weekdays and $13.50 weekends for the Tony Lema course, $4 for nine holes weekdays and $5 for nine holes weekends for the Marina Course. Call for discount rates. Carts are $18.

Location: From Interstate 880 in San Leandro, take the Marina Boulevard exit west, which curves left into Neptune Drive to the course.

Course description: Named for the late Tony Lema, the 1964 British Open champion, this course and facilities were remodeled about 18 months ago. The course is mostly flat and windy. Play early to miss the prevailing southeast wind off the bay. One of the more difficult holes is the number six, par-4 and 420 yards dead into the wind with a lake on the left. The hole plays like a par-5 because of the wind. Keep the ball low if you can, but there is no sure way to conquer this hole. On good days, there are great views of San Francisco Bay.

MAP ON PAGE 150

WILLOW PARK GOLF COURSE

Course 51
MAP E1 grid e6

1 9 6 7

Course information: This public course has 18 holes and par is 71. The course is 6,201 yards and rated 69.7 from the championship tees, and 5,783 yards and rated 67.4 from the regular tees. The slope ratings are 115 championship and 110 regular. Women's tees are 5,783 yards and rated 72.4 from the championship tees, and 5,227 yards and rated 69.2 from the forward tees. The slope ratings are 124 championship and 117 forward.

Play policy and fees: Green fees are $9 for nine holes and $13 for 18 holes weekdays, and $11 for nine holes and $17 for 18 holes weekends. Carts are $12 for nine holes and $18 for 18 holes.

Location: Located in Castro Valley, two miles north of Interstate 580 on Redwood Road.

Course description: This course is mostly flat with narrow fairways. A creek borders the front nine holes. There are deer in the outlying areas. The driving range has an unusual feature: You hit into a lake about 175 yards out. Floater balls are provided.

PO Box 2407
Castro Valley, CA 94546

17007 Redwood Road
Castro Valley, CA 94546

Pro shop   (510) 537-2521
Clubhouse (510) 886-4810

- ■ driving range
- ■ practice greens
- ■ power carts
- ■ pull carts
- □ golf club rental
- ■ locker rooms
- □ showers
- □ executive course
- □ accommodations
- ■ food and beverages
- ■ clubhouse

Robert Bruce
Professional

Rene S. Viviani
Superintendent

SKYWEST GOLF COURSE

Course 52
MAP E1 grid e6

1 9 6 4
R.E. Baldock

Course information: This public course has 18 holes and par is 72. The course 6,930 yards and par is 72.8 from the championship tees, and 6,550 yards and rated 70.9 from the regular tees. The slope ratings are 121 championship and 116 regular. Women's tees are 6,171 yards and rated 74.3. The slope rating is 123.

Play policy and fees: Green fees are $8 for nine holes and $12 for 18 holes weekdays, and $10 for nine holes and $15 for 18 holes weekends. Carts are $10 for nine holes and $17 for 18 holes weekdays, and $11 and $18 weekends.

Location: From Interstate 880 in Hayward, take the A Street exit west to Skywest Drive North. Turn left at Golf Course Road to the course (next to the Hayward air terminal.)

Course description: This flat course has lush, well maintained, wide fairways with lots of trees. It tests every club in the bag. The talked about hole on this course is number 16. It's 192 yards and par-3, playing especially difficult against the wind. There is a lake on the right and OB on the left. The green slopes back to front, but fortunately it holds well.

1401 Golf Course Road
Hayward, CA 94541

Pro shop   (510) 278-6188

- ■ driving range
- ■ practice greens
- ■ power carts
- ■ pull carts
- □ golf club rental
- □ locker rooms
- □ showers
- □ executive course
- □ accommodations
- ■ food and beverages
- ■ clubhouse

Cheryl Pastore
Professional

Gale Wilson
Manager

Wes Sakamot
Superintendent

PLEASANTON FAIRWAYS GOLF COURSE

1974
Ron Curtola

Course information: This public course has nine holes. Par is 60 for 18 holes. Irons only on the driving range. The course is 3,428 yards and rated 55.9 for 18 holes from the regular tees. The slope rating is 82. Women's tees are 3,172 yards. The ratings were unavailable.

Play policy and fees: Green fees are $7 for nine holes and $13.50 for 18 holes weekdays, and $8 for nine holes and $15.50 for 18 holes weekends. Reservations are recommended. Closed Christmas and during the Alameda County Fair (late June to early July).

Location: From Interstate 680 in Pleasanton driving south, take the Bernal exit to the right, make a loop and head east on Bernal. Turn left on Pleasanton Avenue and left at the fairgrounds entrance. Once in the fairgrounds, drive slowly to the tunnel to the track.

Course description: This short, flat course is located in the middle of the racetrack at the Alameda County Fairgrounds. This is not a course for beginners. The greens are all elevated and a driver is needed on three holes. You must be accurate to stick the par-3 greens. Be of serious mind when you approach this course.

PO Box 123
Pleasanton, CA 94566

Alameda Fairgrounds
Pleasanton, CA 94566

Pro shop   (510) 462-4653

NORTHERN E1

- ■ driving range
- ■ practice greens
- □ power carts
- ■ pull carts
- ■ golf club rental
- □ locker rooms
- □ showers
- ■ executive course
- □ accommodations
- ■ food and beverages
- ■ clubhouse

Ron Curtola
Owner/Manager

Paul H. Marty
Superintendent

CRYSTAL SPRINGS GOLF COURSE

1924
Herbert Fowler

Course information: This public course has 18 holes and par is 72. The course is 6,677 yards and rated 72.1 from the championship tees, and 6,362 yards and rated 70.7 from the regular tees. The slope ratings are: 125 championship and 122 regular. Women's tees are 5,920 yards and rated 74.0. The slope rating is 130.

Play policy and fees: Green fees are $35 weekdays plus cart, and $51 weekends including cart. Carts are $11 per person and are mandatory on weekends and holidays from 7:30 a.m. to 2:30 p.m. Twilight rates after 2:30 p.m. are $28 weekdays plus cart, and $34 weekends plus cart. Carts are not mandatory for twilight play. Memberships are available.

Location: On Interstate 280 heading south in Burlingame, take the Hayne and Black Mountain Road exit. Make a right on Skyline Boulevard and follow it to Golf Course Drive. The course is visible from the highway.

Course description: This hilly, meandering course has sidehill lies and requires decent placement shots. Situated in the midst of a California State Game Preserve, wildlife abounds. The weather ranges from San Francisco fog to peninsula sun. It has some steep holes, but is walkable.

6650 Golf Course Drive
Burlingame, CA 94010

Pro shop   (415) 342-0603
Clubhouse (415) 342-4188

- driving range
- practice greens
- power carts
- pull carts
- golf club rental
- locker rooms
- showers
- executive course
- accommodations
- food and beverages
- clubhouse

Roger Graves
Professional

Charles Leider
Director of Golf

Michael Collins
Manager

Pete Galea
Superintendent

HALF MOON BAY GOLF LINKS

1973
Francis Duane

PO Box 871
Half Moon Bay, CA 94019

2000 Fairway Drive
Half Moon Bay, CA 94019

Pro shop   (415) 726-4438
Clubhouse   (415) 726-6384

NORTHERN E1

☐ driving range
■ practice greens
■ power carts
☐ pull carts
■ golf club rental
☐ locker rooms
☐ showers
☐ executive course
☐ accommodations
■ food and beverages
■ clubhouse

Jim Wagner
Manager/Director

Moon Mullins
Professional

Dan Miller
Superintendent

Course information: This public course has 18 holes and par is 72. The course is 7,050 yards and rated 74.5 from the championship tees, and 6,402 yards and rated 71.0 from the regular tees. The slope ratings are 136 championship and 130 regular. Women's tees are 6,360 yards and rated 76.7 from the championship tees, and 5,694 yards and rated 72.6 from the forward tees. The slope ratings are 135 championship and 126 forward.

Play policy and fees: Green fees are $65 weekdays and $85 weekends. The twilight fee is $42. Fees include a mandatory cart. Reservations are recommended one week in advance.

Location: Heading toward Half Moon Bay via Highway 1 or Highway 92, the course is located three miles south of the highway junction, south of Half Moon Bay on the oceanside.

Course description: This oceanside course is long and demanding. The 18th hole spans 428 yards along an ocean cliff and has been rated one of the top 100 holes in the country. Check out the pin placement on this hole. If the pin is on top of the green, the landing area will be very tight. Fog and wind often come into play. Big, undulating greens and long par-3s add to the challenge. Arnold Palmer was a consultant on the design of this course.

MAP ON PAGE 150

PENINSULA GOLF AND COUNTRY CLUB

1911
Donald Ross

Course information: This private course has 18 holes and par is 71. The course is 6,559 yards and rated 71.7 from the championship tees, and 6,357 yards and rated 70.5 from the regular tees. The slope ratings are 128 championship and 126 regular. Women's tees are 5,782 and rated 73.0. The slope rating is 126.

Play policy and fees: Reciprocal play is accepted with members of other private clubs. Have your club pro call to make arrangements. Guest fees are $30 when accompanied by a member. The green fee for reciprocators is $70 and includes a cart. Carts are $6 per person for nine holes and $10 per person for 18 holes.

Location: Located between Highway 101 and Interstate 280, take Highway 92 to Alameda De Las Pulgas south. Turn right on Madera Drive.

Course description: This mature course offers undulating greens and tight fairways lined with manzanita and eucalyptus trees. The par-4 10th hole measures 447 yards and is especially challenging. You hit from an elevated tee box to a fairly wide open fairway with trees on both sides and OB on the left. The green is sizeable, but is surrounded by bunkers. Play center left off the tee and go for the center of the slightly undulating green. Stay below the hole if possible. The course overlooks the peninsula.

701 Madera Drive
San Mateo, CA 94403

Pro shop   (415) 345-9521
Clubhouse   (415) 573-5511

- ■ driving range
- ■ practice greens
- ■ power carts
- □ pull carts
- ■ golf club rental
- ■ locker rooms
- ■ showers
- □ executive course
- □ accommodations
- ■ food and beverages
- ■ clubhouse

Henry Johns
Manager

Tom Toschi
Professional

Marvin King
Superintendent

MENLO COUNTRY CLUB

1900
Tom Nicoll

2300 Woodside Road
Woodside, CA 94062

Pro shop   (415) 366-9910
Clubhouse   (415) 366-5751

- ■ driving range
- ■ practice greens
- ■ power carts
- ▢ pull carts
- ▢ golf club rental
- ■ locker rooms
- ■ showers
- ▢ executive course
- ▢ accommodations
- ■ food and beverages
- ■ clubhouse

NORTHERN E1

Michel Dubes
Manager

Mark Smithwick
Professional

Scott Lewis
Superintendent

Course information: This private course has 18 holes and par is 70. The course is 6,250 yards and rated 70.1 from the championship tees, and 6,004 yards and rated 69.0 from the regular tees. The slope ratings are 126 championship and 123 regular. Women's tees are 5,641 yards and rated 72.6. The slope rating is 128.

Play policy and fees: Reciprocal play is not accepted. Guest fees are $25 weekdays and $30 weekends when accompanied by a member. Guests must be accompanied by a member. Carts are $20.

Location: Located between Interstate 280 and Highway 101 in Redwood City, take either freeway, exiting on Woodside Road or Highway 84. The course is on the north side of the street, seven-tenths of a mile from Interstate 280.

Course description: This is a short but sneaky course. Overhanging old oaks add character and line the fairways. Beware of the 16th hole where there's a massive oak in the middle of the fairway. The course mixes the old-style, traditional, small greens with recent innovations by Robert Trent Jones, Jr. It's mostly flat and walkable.

BAY MEADOWS GOLF COURSE

PO Box 5050
San Mateo, CA 94402

Delaware Street
San Mateo, CA

Pro shop   (415) 341-7204

- ▢ driving range
- ■ practice greens
- ▢ power carts
- ■ pull carts
- ■ golf club rental
- ▢ locker rooms
- ▢ showers
- ▢ executive course
- ▢ accommodations
- ■ food and beverages
- ■ clubhouse

Bill Finlay
Professional

R. Roberts
Superintendent

Course information: This public course has nine holes. Par is 56 for 18 holes. The course is 2,730 yards for 18 holes. No rating is available.

Play policy and fees: Green fees are $5 for nine holes and $10 for 18 holes. Special 10-play books are available for $40. Carts are $2 and club rental is $3. During racing season, the course is only open Mondays and Tuesdays from 7 a.m. to 6 p.m., and Fridays from 7 a.m. to 1 p.m.

Location: From Highway 101 in San Mateo, take the Delaware Street exit, which will lead you to the fairgrounds and the race track. Just follow the signs. Park in the race track parking lot and walk to the center of the track.

Course description: This course is situated in the middle of Bay Meadows race track. It's in good condition and a nice course for beginners with eight par-3s and one par-4.

EMERALD HILLS
GOLF CLUB

Course information: This public course has nine holes. Par is 54 for 18 holes. The course is 2,326 yards for 18 holes and rated 50.9 from the regular tees. The slope rating is 67. Women's tees are 2,276 yards and unrated.

Play policy and fees: Green fees are $6 for nine holes and $10 for 18 holes weekdays, and $7 for nine holes and $12 for 18 holes weekends. Senior rates are $4 for nine holes weekdays only.

Location: From Interstate 280 in Redwood City, exit on Edgewood Road southwest. Turn left on Canada Road. Drive 1.5 miles to Jefferson Avenue and turn left again, following it to Wilmington Way. Turn right to the course.

Course description: This is a short, starter course composed of par-3s. It's hilly but walkable and has a perfect layout for juniors, seniors and beginners. The course is owned by the Redwood City Elks Lodge.

1059 Wilmington Way
Redwood City, CA 94062

Pro shop   (415) 368-7820

- ■ driving range
- ■ practice greens
- ☐ power carts
- ■ pull carts
- ■ golf club rental
- ☐ locker rooms
- ☐ showers
- ☐ executive course
- ☐ accommodations
- ☐ food and beverages
- ☐ clubhouse

Ed Granados
Manager

Joe Ramos
Superintendent

PARKWAY GOLF COURSE

1971

Course information: This public course has nine holes and par is 27. The course is 2,048 yards and rated 49.0 for 18 holes from the regular tees. The slope rating is 67. Women's tees are 2,048 yards and rated 50.3. The slope rating is 70.

Play policy and fees: Green fees are $5.50 for nine holes and $7.50 for 18 holes on weekdays, $7.50 for nine holes and $11.00 for 18 holes on weekends. Senior rates are $4.50 for nine holes and $6.50 for 18 holes on weekdays. Reserve tee times one week in advance. Proper golf etiquette must be followed.

Location: From Interstate 880 in Fremont, take the Stevenson Boulevard exit east. Drive 1.5 miles east to the course.

Course description: Condo development took over nine holes of this formerly 18-hole course in 1991. This is a short course with only par-3s. There are several water hazards and an abundance of trees, which demand accuracy and make the course a challenge for any level of player. Don't underestimate the dinky 67-yard number six. This is a hole that requires finesse. You must hit over water, which always means trouble. Typically, players either fly the hole or dump it in the lake, although golf humor at the course has it that someone actually skipped the ball over the water and into the hole for an ace. But you can't believe everything you read—or hear—at a golf course. In any event, keep it low and under the wind. Annual tournaments include the TAK Ladies Invitational (May), the St. Patrick's Day Tournament (March), Christmas Tournament (December) and the Thanksgiving Tournament (November). Host pro Mike Pope holds the men's course record at 49. There is no women's course record.

3400 Stevenson Road
Fremont, CA 94538

Pro shop   (510) 656-6862

☐ driving range
■ practice greens
☐ power carts
■ pull carts
■ golf club rental
☐ locker rooms
☐ showers
☐ executive course
☐ accommodations
■ food and beverages
■ clubhouse

Mike Pope
Manager/Professional

Paul Fudenna
Superintendent

NORTHERN E1

SUNOL VALLEY GOLF COURSE

Clark Glason
PO Box 609
Sunol, CA 94586

Interstate 680
at Andrade Road
Sunol, CA 94586

Pro shop   (510) 862-2404

Course information: This public facility has 36 holes. Par is 72 on both courses.

The Palm Course is 6,895 yards and rated 72.2 from the championship tees, and 6,464 yards and rated 70.3 from the regular tees. The slope ratings are 118 championship and 114 regular. Women's tees are 5,954 and rated 73.7 from the championship tees, and 5,765 yards and rated 72.0 from the forward tees. The slope ratings are 122 championship and 119 forward

The Cypress Course is 6,185 yards and rated 69.1 from the championship tees, and 5,806 yards and rated 67.2 from the regular tees. The slope ratings are 115 championship and 112 regular. Women's tees are 6,083 yards and rated 74.4 from the championship tees, and 5,479 yards and rated 70.1 from the forward tees. The slope ratings are 124 championship and 115 forward.

Play policy and fees: Green fees are $25 weekdays and $40 weekends. Carts are included. Reserve tee times seven days in advance. This course is available for outside tournaments.

Location: From Interstate 680 in Sunol, exit on Andrade Road North. The course is located adjacent to the freeway.

Course description: Nestled in the Mission Hills, the Palm Course is aptly named, with palm trees lining the wide fairways. There's plenty to worry about on both courses: tight, rolling hills, lots of trees, water hazards and bunkers. An estimated 500 tournaments were played on these two courses last year.

☐ driving range
■ practice greens
■ power carts
☐ pull carts
■ golf club rental
■ locker rooms
■ showers
☐ executive course
☐ accommodations
■ food and beverages
■ clubhouse

Jerry Thormann
Professional

Bill Andrade
Superintendent

CASTLEWOOD
COUNTRY CLUB

1923
William Park Bell

707 Country Club Circle
Pleasanton, CA 94566

Pro shop   (415) 846-5151
Clubhouse   (415) 846-2871

- driving range
- practice greens
- power carts
- pull carts
- golf club rental
- locker rooms
- showers
- □ executive course
- □ accommodations
- food and beverages
- clubhouse

Ernie Barbour
Professional

Larry O'Leary
Director of Golf

Bob Dalton
Superintendent

Course information: This private club has 36 holes. Par is 72 for the Valley Course and 70 for the Hill Course.

The Valley Course is 6,642 yards and rated 72.0 from the championship tees, and 6,361 yards and rated 70.7 from the regular tees. The slope ratings are 126 championship and 123 regular. Women's tees are 6,366 yards and rated 76.5 from the championship tees, and 5,900 yards and rated 73.8 from the forward tees. The slope ratings are 136 championship and 129 forward.

The Hill Course is 6,248 yards and rated 70.8 from the championship tees, and 6,003 yards and rated 69.8 from the regular tees. The slope ratings are 124 championship and 123 regular. Women's tees are 5,984 yards and rated 74.5 from the championship tees, and 5,523 yards and rated 72.0 from the forward tees. The slope ratings are 133 championship and 129 forward.

Play policy and fees: Reciprocal play is accepted with members of other private clubs. Have your club pro call for arrangements. Green fees are $35 plus $10 for a cart when accompanied by a member, and $50 plus $12 for a cart when unaccompanied. Shirts with collars and golf shoes are required. Shorts must have a five-inch inseam. No jeans may be worn. Closed Mondays.

Location: From Interstate 680 in Pleasanton, take the Sunol-Castlewood Drive exit. Drive straight for one block. The Valley Course is on the right side of the road and the Hill Course is further up the hill.

Course description: The meandering Valley Course is long with narrow fairways. The Hill Course is tight with sidehill lies and more trees. Phoebe Atherton Hearst originally owned all of the property here. Luther Burbank planted exotic trees and palms. The 1981 Sectional U.S. Open Qualifying was held at Castlewood. This club is host each August to the Wilson Pro-Junior Golf Tournament. Hole 18 affords a spectacular view of the valley. The men's course record is held by former PGA Tour winner Ron Cerrudo, who scored 62 on both courses in 1962. Don't expect to see anyone break that record; the course has changed considerably in the last 30 years. It's five shots tougher now because the trees are taller and the fairways aren't hard rock like they were in '62.

SHARON HEIGHTS GOLF AND COUNTRY CLUB

Course information: This private course has 18 holes and par is 72. The course is 6,872 yards and rated 73.5 from the championship tees, and 6,520 yards and rated 71.8 from the regular tees. The slope ratings are 132 championship and 129 regular. Women's tees are a long 6,185 yards and rated 76.4 from the forward tees. The slope rating is 141.

Play policy and fees: Reciprocal play is accepted with members of other private clubs upon approval of the head pro. Guests must be sponsored by a member. Guest fees are $35 weekdays and $50 weekends when accompanied by a member, and $75 if unaccompanied on weekdays, and $100 if unaccompanied on weekends. Carts are $18.

Location: From Interstate 280 in Menlo Park, take Sand Hill Road exit toward Stanford University. The course is located on the left, less than a quarter mile off Sand Hill Road.

Course description: This course is long and challenging. Redwoods, ranging in height from 40 to 80 feet, often come into play. They seemingly just jump right out into the fairway at times. The course boasts some of the best greens between San Francisco and Monterey. They're large, smooth and fast. The course is hilly, but walkable. Members include 49er greats Randy Cross and Bill Walsh and baseball superstar Willie Mays.

Course 63
MAP E1 grid g4

1962
Jack Fleming

2900 Sand Hill Road
Menlo Park, CA 94025

Pro shop   (415) 854-6429
Clubhouse (415) 854-6422

- ■ driving range
- ■ practice greens
- ■ power carts
- ■ pull carts
- ■ golf club rental
- ■ locker rooms
- ■ showers
- □ executive course
- □ accommodations
- ■ food and beverages
- ■ clubhouse

Robert E. Lee
Manager

James Knipp
Professional

Ross Brownlie
Superintendent

PALO ALTO AND MENLO PARK VETERANS GOLF COURSES

Course information: This private facility has two courses. They are reportedly short, but no yardage or rating information was available.

Play policy and fees: Free to patients of Palo Alto or Menlo Park VA Hospitals. Must have a doctor's order. Course has special hours and requirements. It is not open to the public.

Location: From Highway 101 in Palo Alto/Menlo Park, take the Menlo Park or Willow Road exit. Follow it to the hospital. The courses are on hospital grounds.

Course description: These short, short courses are essentially open to all patients of the Veterans Administration Hospitals in Palo Alto and Menlo Park. There are two small courses at either site, so call first to see which is open. Good luck!

Course 64
MAP E1 grid f9

1923
William Park Bell

707 Country Club Circle
Pleasanton, CA 94566

Pro shop   (510) 846-5151
Clubhouse (510) 846-2871

- ■ driving range
- ■ practice greens
- ■ power carts
- ■ pull carts
- ■ golf club rental
- ■ locker rooms
- ■ showers
- □ executive course
- □ accommodations
- ■ food and beverages
- ■ clubhouse

Ernie Barbour
Professional

Larry O'Leary
Director

STANFORD GOLF COURSE

3801 Miranda Avenue
Palo Alto, CA 94303

Pro shop   (415) 493-5000
Extension 2348

□ driving range
■ practice greens
□ power carts
■ pull carts
□ golf club rental
□ locker rooms
□ showers
□ executive course
□ accommodations
□ food and beverages
□ clubhouse

NORTHERN E1

Course information: This private course has 18 holes and par is 71. The course is 6,770 yards and rated 72.9 from the tournament tees, 6,438 yards and rated 70.4 from the championship tees, and 6,095 yards and rated 69.1 from the regular tees. The slope ratings are 126 tournament, 121 championship and 116 regular. Women's tees are 6,094 yards and rated 74.8 from the championship tees, and 5,539 yards and rated 71.8 from the forward tees. The slope ratings are 130 championship and 124 forward.

Play policy and fees: Members and guests only. Guests must be accompanied by a member. Guest fees are $33 weekdays and $38 weekends. Carts are $21.

Location: From Interstate 280, take the Sand Hill Road exit in Menlo Park. Drive east toward Stanford University. Turn right on Junipero Serra Boulevard and continue to the course. From Highway 101, take the University Avenue exit, which turns into Palm Drive. Turn right on West Campus Drive, right again on Junipero Serra Boulevard and continue to the course.

Course description: This sprawling layout is dotted with towering eucalyptus and oak trees and is characterized by large, contoured greens and lots of bunkers. There are no breathers, especially on the nerve-wracking, infamous, par-4 12th hole. It's extremely long with one big oak positioned in the middle of the fairway. Rated among the top courses in the state, it was host to the 1946, 1966, 1981 and 1989 NCAA Men's Championships; the 1981 and 1988 NCAA Women's Championships; the 1959 USGA Junior Championship and the Western Amateur. It offers far-reaching views of San Francisco and, weather permitting, the entire bay.

PALO ALTO GOLF COURSE

1956
William Francis Bell

1875 Embarcadero Road
Palo Alto, CA 94303

Pro shop   (415) 856-0881

- ■ driving range
- ■ practice greens
- ■ power carts
- ■ pull carts
- ■ golf club rental
- □ locker rooms
- □ showers
- □ executive course
- □ accommodations
- ■ food and beverages
- □ clubhouse

Brad Lozares
Professional
Paul Dias
Superintendent

Course information: This public course has 18 holes and par is 72. The course is 6,861 yards and rated 72.1 from the tournament tees, and 6,496 yards and rated 70.4 from the championship tees, and 5,981 yards and rated 68.0 from the regular tees. The slope ratings are 116 tournament, 113 championship and 108 regular. Women's tees are 6,488 yards and rated 77.0 from the championship tees, and 5,975 yards and rated 74.0 from the forward tees. The slope ratings are: 130 championship and 122 forward.

Play policy and fees: Green fees are $14 weekdays and $18 weekends. Twilight rates are $9 weekdays and $12 weekends. Carts are $17. Call for reservations. On weekdays a seven-day lead time is recommended and on weekends by the Tuesday preceding. Shirts must be worn at all times.

Location: From Highway 101 in Palo Alto, take the Embarcadero Road exit east. The course is located on the left about a half mile from the highway. It's just before the airport.

Course description: This is a long and often windy course. The greens are large. Trees and straight fairways are characteristic. Hole four is the most difficult. It's a 435-yard par-4, usually into the wind. Hole 14, a 235-yard par-3, also plays into the wind and is a good test for the driver. Annual tournaments include: Palo Alto City Women's Amateur (April), Santa Clara Valley Best-Ball (May), Palo Alto City Men's Amateur (September), Palo Alto City Seniors Amateur (October), Times-Tribune Junior Tournament, and Town & Country Women's Golf Tournament. The course record of 64 is held by Brad Henninger. The women's course record was not available.

MOFFETT FIELD GOLF COURSE

Course 67
MAP E1 grid g6

1968
Robert Muir Graves

MWR Fund, Building 25
NAS Moffett Field,
CA 94035

Pro shop   (415) 404-4702
Clubhouse (415) 404-4705

- driving range
- practice greens
- power carts
- pull carts
- golf club rental
- locker rooms
- showers
- ☐ executive course
- ☐ accommodations
- food and beverages
- clubhouse

Lee Henderson
Manager
Bobby Bihl
Professional
Jeff Hardy
Superintendent

NORTHERN E1

Course information: This military course has 18 holes and par is 72. The course is 6,491 yards and rated 70.0 from the championship tees, and 6,329 yards and rated 69.3 from the regular tees. The slope ratings are 111 championship and 109 regular. Women's tees are 6,003 yards and rated 72.9 from the championship tees, and 5,976 yards and rated 72.7 from the forward tees. The slope ratings are 116 championship and 116 forward.

Play policy and fees: Active and retired military personnel and guests only. Guest fees are $10 for nine holes and $15 for 18 holes. Carts are $9 for nine holes and $13 for 18 holes. Weekdays play is on a first-come first-served basis. Reservations are required for weekends and holidays.

Location: From Highway 101 in Mountain View, take the Moffett Boulevard exit. Drive north to the main gate of Moffett Field Naval Air Station for instructions.

Course description: This course is mostly flat and open with more than 7,000 pine, poplar and cedar trees. Three lakes come into play, and it is easily walkable.

SUNNYVALE GOLF COURSE

Clark Glasson

605 Macara Lane
Sunnyvale, CA 94086

Pro shop   (408) 738-3666
Clubhouse (408) 739-8900

Course information: This public course has 18 holes and par is 70. The course is 6,227 yards and rated 69.7 from the championship tees, and 5,751 yards and rated 67.6 from the regular tees. The slope ratings are 199 championship and 114 regular. Women's tees are 5,292 yards and rated 70.2. The slope rating is 120.

Play policy and fees: Sunnyvalle resident green fees are $14 weekdays and $18 weekends. Non-resident green fees are $16 weekdays and $21 weekends. Twilight rates for residents are $10 weekdays and $12 weekends. Non-residents twilight rates are $11 weekdays and $14 weekends. Carts are $19. Play is first-come first-served weekdays, and the Monday prior for residents reserving weekend play, and the Tuesday prior for non-residents reserving weekend play.

Location: From Highway 101 in northern Sunnyvale, exit onto Mathilda Avenue south. Turn right on Maude Avenue and right again on Macara Avenue.

Course description: The short, flat course boasts several long par-3s. Conspiring trees, wind, lakes and doglegs all demand good positioning. Beware of the 18th hole, a par-4 over water with a three-tiered green guarded by bunkers. Extensive remodeling of the course was completed in early 1991.

- ☐ driving range
- ■ practice greens
- ■ power carts
- ■ pull carts
- ■ golf club rental
- ☐ locker rooms
- ☐ showers
- ☐ executive course
- ☐ accommodations
- ■ food and beverages
- ■ clubhouse

Art Wilson
Professional

Mark Petersen
Manager

Ken Sakai
Superintendent

SHORELINE GOLF LINKS

1973
Robert Trent Jones, Jr.

PO Box 1206
Mountain View, CA 94043

2600 North Shoreline Blvd.
Mountain View, CA 94043

Pro shop   (415) 969-2041

NORTHERN E1

Course information: This public course has 18 holes and par is 72. The course is 6,720 yards and rated 72.5 from the championship tees, and 6,124 yards and rated 70.1 from the regular tees. The slope ratings are 125 championship and 121 regular. Women's tees are 5,421 yards and rated 70.8. The slope rating is 115.

Play policy and fees: Green fees are $29 weekdays and $38 weekends. Twilight rates are $17 every day. Carts are $20. Reservations are recommended. You may reserve a tee time six days in advance.

Location: From Highway 101 in Mountain View, take the Shoreline Boulevard exit north. Follow it to the 2600 block.

Course description: This sprawling, flat, links-style course demands accuracy with the long irons. The greens are large and undulating, the fairways are narrow and there are more than 80 bunkers. It's very easy to land a ball in the long grass or the water (and there's plenty of water). Hole four is a short par, but look out because it's over water and between bunkers. You're also shooting across water on the 11th and 17th holes. The wind can blow here, but it's a fun course. The course record is 64. The city approved a new clubhouse and soil samples have been taken, but there has been no formal ground breaking yet. The grass driving range is one of the busiest on the peninsula.

- ■ driving range
- ■ practice greens
- ■ power carts
- ■ pull carts
- ■ golf club rental
- □ locker rooms
- □ showers
- □ executive course
- □ accommodations
- ■ food and beverages
- □ clubhouse

Jack Guio
Manager/Professional

Al Rafalski
Superintendent

SUMMITPOINTE
GOLF COURSE

1978

Course information: This public course has 18 holes and par is 72. The course is 6,329 yards and rated 70.3 from the championship tees, and 6,062 yards and rated 68.7 from the regular tees. The slope ratings are 121 championship and 117 regular. Women's tees are 5,519 yards and rated 71.1. The slope rating is 119.

Play policy and fees: Green fees are $20 weekdays and $31 weekends. Carts are $20. Twilight rates after 3 p.m. are $15 weekdays and $20 weekends. Twilight rates after 5 p.m. are $10 weekdays. Reservations are recommended one week in advance. This course is available for outside tournaments.

Location: From Interstate 680 in Milpitas, take the Jacklin Road exit east to Evans Road. Turn left and then right on Country Club Drive.

Course description: The front nine is mostly open and hilly, while the back nine is flat and tight. Almost every hole on the back nine has water. The greens are tough and fast with tricky breaks. Hole 16, a par-3, is 180 yards over water, and was once described as one of the best holes in Northern California. Annual tournaments include the Milpitas/Berryessa YMCA (April), 100 Club (May), and the Chamber of Commerce (August). The course record of 65 is held jointly by Estaban Toledo and Skip McCaslin. McCaslin tied the record on September 5, 1991.

1500 Country Club Drive
Milpitas, CA 95035

Pro shop   (408) 262-8813
Clubhouse   (408) 262-2500

☐ driving range
■ practice greens
■ power carts
■ pull carts
■ golf club rental
☐ locker rooms
☐ showers
☐ executive course
☐ accommodations
■ food and beverages
■ clubhouse

Kimberly Sandmann
Manager

Mark Dorcak
Professional

Paul Gillis
Superintendent

SPRING VALLEY
GOLF COURSE

NORTHERN E1

Course information: This public course has 18 holes and par is 70. The course is 6,099 yards and rated 68.8 from the championship tees, and 5,866 yards and rated 67.8 from the regular tees. The slope ratings are 114 championship and 111 regular. Women's tees are 5,513 yards and rated 69.2. The slope rating is 109.

Play policy and fees: Green fees are $17 weekdays and $25 weekends. Twilight rates are $12 weekdays and $14 weekends. Carts are $20. Reservations recommended.

Location: From Interstate 880 or Interstate 680 in Milpitas, Drive about 2.5 miles east to 3441 Calaveras Boulevard.

Course description: Three holes are being remodeled so look for a possible change in par and ratings. This rolling course is set in the foothills outside Milpitas. It's a gambler's paradise. Doglegs and water, plus cypress, pine and elm trees all come into play. There aren't many bunkers, but as a consolation they made the bunkers extra tricky. Stay below the pin.

PO Box 360050
Milpitas, CA 95035

3441 East Calaveras Boulevard
Milpitas, CA 95035

Pro shop   (408) 262-1722

- driving range
- practice greens
- power carts
- pull carts
- golf club rental
- ☐ locker rooms
- ☐ showers
- ☐ executive course
- ☐ accommodations
- food and beverages
- clubhouse

Richard Stewart
Professional

Rick Jetter
Director of Golf

Greg Jetter
Superintendent

MAP ON PAGE 150

205

LOS ALTOS GOLF AND COUNTRY CLUB

1923
Tom Nicoll

1560 Country Club Drive
Los Altos, CA 94022

Pro shop   (415) 948-2146
Clubhouse (415) 948-1024

□ driving range
■ practice greens
■ power carts
■ pull carts
■ golf club rental
□ locker rooms
□ showers
□ executive course
□ accommodations
■ food and beverages
□ clubhouse

Brian Inkster
Professional

Jerry Hecht
Manager

Mike Simpson
Superintendent

Course information: This private course has 18 holes and par is 71. The course is 6,473 yards and rated 71.4 from the championship tees, and 6,273 yards and rated 70.5 from the regular tees. The slope ratings are 126 championship and 123 regular. Women's tees are 5,911 yards and rated 74.9. The slope rating is 129.

Play policy and fees: Reciprocal play is accepted with members of other selected private clubs. Have your club pro call for arrangements. Members and guests only. Green fees for reciprcators are $60, plus $20 for a cart. Guests fees are $30 when accompanied by a member and $60 unaccompanied. Carts are $16. Reservations required two weeks in advance.

Location: From Interstate 280 in Los Altos, take the Magdelena Avenue exit northeast. Turn right on the Foothill Expressway and continue to Loyola Drive. Flip a right and another right onto Country Club Drive.

Course description: It's pretty out here. The course is tight, tree-lined and has undulating greens. The par-3 third hole requires a 200-yard carry over a barranca from an elevated tee. It'll test you. Three-time U.S. Amateur Champion and LPGA standout Julie Inkster holds the women's record of 68. The men's course record is 64, set by Jeff Brehaut in 1989. Dan Forsman, three-time PGA tour winner, is also from here. The clubhouse is currently undergoing renovation and is expected to open in late summer of 1992. Come enjoy the scenery.

DEEP CLIFF GOLF COURSE

Course information: This public course has 18 holes and par is 60. The course is 3,164 yards and rated 55.2 for 18 holes from the weekend tees, and 3,260 yards and rated 55.6 from the regular tees. The slope ratings are 84 weekend and 85 regular. Women's yardage and ratings were unavailable.

Play policy and fees: Green fees are $13 weekdays and $17 weekends. Reservations are recommended one week in advance. This course is available for tournaments.

Location: From Interstate 280 in Sunnyvale, take the Foothill Expressway exit south to McClellan Road. Turn left and then turn right onto Clubhouse Lane.

Course description: This executive course has three par-4s on the front nine and three par-4s on the back nine. It requires good placement shots because of the narrow corridor-type fairways. A creek feeding into Saratoga Creek bisects the course and comes into play on several holes.

1965
Clark Glasson

PO Box 60302
Cupertino, CA 95014

10700 Clubhouse Lane
Cupertino, CA 95014

Pro shop   (408) 253-5357
Clubhouse (408) 253-5359

☐ driving range
■ practice greens
☐ power carts
■ pull carts
■ golf club rental
☐ locker rooms
☐ showers
■ executive course
☐ accommodations
■ food and beverages
■ clubhouse

L. Scott Cline
Professional

Mark Francetic
Superintendent

NORTHERN E1

PALO ALTO HILLS GOLF AND COUNTRY CLUB

1962
Clark Glasson

3000 Alexis Drive
Palo Alto, CA 94304

Pro shop   (415) 948-2320
Clubhouse (415) 948-1800

- ■ driving range
- ■ practice greens
- ■ power carts
- ■ pull carts
- ■ golf club rental
- ■ locker rooms
- ■ showers
- □ executive course
- □ accommodations
- ■ food and beverages
- ■ clubhouse

Lyn Nelson
Manager

Mike Garvale
Superintendent

Course information: This private course has 18 holes and par is 71. The course is 6,249 yards and rated 71.2 from the championship tees, and 6,036 yards and rated 70.2 from the regular tees. The slope ratings are 130 championship and 128 regular. Women's tees are 6,044 yards and rated 75.7 from the championship tees, and 5,703 yards and rated 73.7 from the forward tees. The slope ratings are 138 championship and 135 forward.

Play policy and fees: Reciprocal play is accepted with members of other private clubs. Have your pro call to set up a time. Green fees for reciprocators are $55 weekdays and $75 weekends. Carts are additional. Guest fees are $35 weekdays and $45 weekends when accompanied by a member. Carts are $18. Reservations are recommended. Proper golf attire required.

Location: From Interstate 280 or Highway 101, take the Page Mill Expressway exit south. Drive one mile to Alexis Drive and continue a half mile to the course.

Course description: Although this sporty course is short, it plays considerably longer than the yardage indicates. It's a defensive course, tight with undulating fairways and elevated greens. Water comes into play on five holes. Low-handicappers shouldn't be overly confident (unless you're naturally that way) and first-timers should beware. Watch out for the par-4 third hole, a nasty, downhill tester. Situated in the hills, the course offers picturesque views of the bay, so don't forget to look up. The Tall Tree Invitational Tournament plays here at the end of May. Course records are owned by John Test with a 62 and Shirley Cerrudo who shot a 72.

BLACKBERRY FARM
GOLF COURSE

Course information: This public course has nine holes. Par is 58 for 18 holes. The course is 3,182 yards and rated 55.9 for 18 holes from the regular tees. The slope rating is 78. Women's tees are 3,182 and rated 58.5 for 18 holes. The slope rating is 83.

Play policy and fees: Green fees for residents of Cupertino are $5.75 weekdays and $7.50 weekends. Nonresident green fees are $6.75 weekdays and $8.50 weekends. Reservations are accepted one week in advance. This course is available for outside tournaments.

Location: From Interstate 280 in Cupertino, take the Foothill Expressway exit south. Continue to Stevens Creek Boulevard, turn left and drive one-half mile up to the course on the left.

Course description: This flat, narrow course has lots of water and trees. It's relatively short with dome shaped greens. The 120-yard, par-3 eighth hole is over water. Short and sweet, but you can work on the putting.

1962
Robert Muir Graves

22100 Stevens Creek Blvd.
Cupertino, CA 95014

Pro shop   (408) 253-9200
Clubhouse   (408) 255-3300

NORTHERN E1

☐ driving range
■ practice greens
☐ power carts
■ pull carts
■ golf club rental
☐ locker rooms
☐ showers
☐ executive course
☐ accommodations
■ food and beverages
■ clubhouse

Jeff Piserchio
Manager/Professional

Ernie Alvarez
Superintendent

SUNKEN GARDENS
GOLF COURSE

Course information: This public course has nine holes. Par is 58 for 18 holes. The course is 2,876 yards. It is not rated.

Play policy and fees: Green fees are $7 weekdays and $9 weekends. To reserve a tee time you must pre-pay each day for a tee time that day. Weekend reservations are made the Tuesday prior to the weekend. This course is available for outside tournaments.

Location: This course is located between Highway 101 and Interstate 280 in Sunnyvale. Exit off on Wolfe Road toward El Camino Real. The course is on the east side of the street.

Course description: This mostly flat course borders a former quarry and is somewhat tight. There are two par-4s and the rest are par-3s. The course is an excellent layout for beginners, juniors and seniors.

1959
Robert Dean Putman

1010 South Wolfe Road
Sunnyvale, CA 94086

Pro shop   (408) 739-6588
Clubhouse   (408) 732-4980

■ driving range
■ practice greens
■ power carts
■ pull carts
■ golf club rental
☐ locker rooms
☐ showers
■ executive course
☐ accommodations
■ food and beverages
■ clubhouse

Mike Grant
Professional

SAN JOSE MUNICIPAL
GOLF COURSE

1968
Robert Muir Graves

1560 Oakland Road
San Jose, CA 95131

Pro shop   (408) 441-4653

- ■ driving range
- ■ practice greens
- ■ power carts
- ■ pull carts
- ■ golf club rental
- ☐ locker rooms
- ☐ showers
- ☐ executive course
- ☐ accommodations
- ■ food and beverages
- ■ clubhouse

Mike Rawitser
Director of Golf

Bob McGrath
Professional

John Martin
Superintendent

Course information: This public course has 18 holes and par is 72. The course is 6,659 yards and rated 70.1 from the championship tees, and 6,362 yards and rated 68.7 from the regular tees. The slope ratings are 108 championship and 105 regular. Women's tees are 5,504 yards and rated 69.7. The slope rating is 112.

Play policy and fees: Green fees are $18 weekdays and $25 weekends. Twilight rates are $12 weekdays and $15 weekends. There is a special $12 rate for the first 40 players each day for the first hour the course is open. You play the back nine. Carts are $11 for nine holes and $20 for 18 holes. Reservations are recommended one week in advance and there is a standby list each day.

Location: From Highway 101 heading south in San Jose, take the 13th Street exit and cross back over the freeway on Oakland Road. Follow it for one mile to the course on your right.

Course description: This course averages from 400 to 450 players a day, depending on the season. The course is relatively flat and undemanding, and makes a good intermediate test of golf. There are a few long par-4s. The fairways are wide and the water hazards have lost some of their zip due to the drought. Watch for lots of doglegs and large, undulating greens. The course itself is in excellent condition.

SANTA CLARA GOLF AND TENNIS CLUB

NORTHERN E1

5155 Stars & Stripes
Santa Clara, CA 95054

Pro shop   (408) 980-9515
Clubhouse (408) 986-1666

- driving range
- practice greens
- power carts
- pull carts
- golf club rental
- locker rooms
- showers
□ executive course
- accommodations
- food and beverages
- clubhouse

Tim Walsh
Manager

Tom Hale
Professional

Allan Schlothauer
Superintendent

Course information: This public course has 18 holes and par is 72. The course is 6,853 yards and rated 72.2 from the tournament tees, 6,474 yards and rated 70.5 from the championship tees, and 6,078 yards and rated 68.6 from the regular tees. The slope ratings are 121 tournament, 118 championship and 114 regular. Women's tees are 5,672 yards and rated 71.8. The slope rating is 116.

Play policy and fees: Green fees for residents of the city of Santa Clara are $11 weekdays and $16 weekends. Non-resident green fees are $16 weekdays and $22 weekends. Twilight rates for residents are $6 weekdays and $10 weekends. Twilight rates for non-residents are $10 weekdays and $14 weekends. Carts are $9 for nine holes and $18 for 18 holes. A single-rider cart is $12. Residents must reserve tee times eight days in advance at 7 a.m., and non-residents must reserve tee times seven days in advance at 7 a.m. Residents must have an ID card issued by the pro shop. This course is available for outside tournaments.

Location: From Highway 101 north in Sunnyvale or Highway 237 south, take the Great America Parkway exit. Go east on Tasman Drive to Centennial Boulevard. Turn left and drive to Stars & Stripes Avenue.

Course description: This course has rolling hills and is long and open with a links-style rough on the fairway. There are a few blind holes, which make approach shots important. It's usually windy. It is walkable. It's situated across the street from the San Francisco 49ers' training facilities.

PRUNERIDGE GOLF COURSE

Jack Fleming

400 North Saratoga Avenue
Santa Clara, CA 95050

Pro shop   (408) 248-4424

Course information: This public course has nine holes. Par is 62 for 18 holes. The course is 3,720 yards and rated 56.3 for 18 holes from the regular tees. The slope rating is 73. Women's tees are 3,408 yards and rated 60.0. The slope rating is 75.

Play policy and fees: Green fees are $7 weekdays and $8 weekends.

Location: The course is located between Highway 101 and Interstate 280 in Santa Clara on Saratoga Avenue, which is off the San Tomas Expressway. From Interstate 280, take the Saratoga Avenue exit north.

Course description: This course is short, flat and walkable was redesigned in 1977 by Robert Trent Jones, Jr. Watch out for ducks on the lake at the ninth hole. They can get aggressive if they aren't fed on the spot. Just kidding.

- ■ driving range
- ■ practice greens
- □ power carts
- ■ pull carts
- ■ golf club rental
- □ locker rooms
- □ showers
- ■ executive course
- □ accommodations
- ■ food and beverages
- ■ clubhouse

Kevin McKay
Professional

Wayne Wallick
Director of Golf

Tom Wallick
Superintendent

THUNDERBIRD GOLF COURSE

221 South King Road
San Jose, CA 95116

Pro shop   (408) 259-3355

Course information: This public course has 18 holes and par is 64. The course is 4,700 yards and rated 56.6 from the regular tees. The slope rating is 81. Women's tees are 4,700 yards and unrated.

Play policy and fees: Green fees are $12 weekdays and $14 weekends. Twilight rates are $8 after 3 p.m. weekdays and $10 weekends and holidays. Seniors (over 65) rate is $9 weekdays. Carts are $15. Play is on a first-come first-served basis.

Location: The course is located on King Road in San Jose where Interstate 680, Interstate 280 and Highway 101 meet. From Interstate 680, take the King Road exit and head north to the course.

Course description: This mostly flat course is short with lots of trees and mostly par-3s. There's one par-5 on each end of the course.

- ■ driving range
- ■ practice greens
- ■ power carts
- ■ pull carts
- ■ golf club rental
- □ locker rooms
- □ showers
- □ executive course
- □ accommodations
- □ food and beverages
- □ clubhouse

Brigid Moreton
Professional

Paul Lopez
Manager/Superintendent

SAN JOSE COUNTRY CLUB

1912
Tom Nicoll

15571 Alum Rock Avenue
San Jose, CA 95127

Pro shop   (408) 258-3636
Clubhouse (408) 258-4901

- ■ driving range
- ■ practice greens
- ■ power carts
- ■ pull carts
- ■ golf club rental
- ■ locker rooms
- ■ showers
- □ executive course
- □ accommodations
- ■ food and beverages
- ■ clubhouse

Howard Blethen
Manager

Barry Brumfield
Professional

Robert Dauterman
Superintendent

Course information: This private course has 18 holes and par is 70. The course is 6,179 yards and rated 69.9 from the championship tees, and 5,923 yards and rated 68.6 from the regular tees. The slope ratings are 118 championship and 115 regular. Women's tees are 5,474 yards and rated 71.2. The slope rating is 125.

Play policy and fees: Reciprocal play is accepted with members of other private clubs. Have your professional call in advance for arrangements. Guest fees are $30 everyday when accompanied by a member and $75 without a member. Carts are mandatory and included in the fees. The dress code is strictly enforced.

Location: From Interstate 680 in San Jose, take the Alum Rock Avenue exit east. Drive 2.5 miles to 15571 Alum Rock Avenue.

Course description: Situated in the foothills overlooking the Santa Clara Valley, this course is one of the oldest in California with a history that extends back to 1896. The course is short, hilly and tight. The small greens require accurate iron play and a deft short game. From the tee on the fourth hole, you can see all 18 holes. Keep perspective. The Santa Clara County Championship has been held here for 64 years. The men's record is 59 and the women's is 69.

MAP ON PAGE 150

213

Course information: This private course has nine holes. Par is 68 for 18 holes. The course is 4,286 yards and rated 62.4 for 18 holes from the regular tees. The slope rating is 111. Women's tees are 3,956 yards and rated 63.7 from the regular tees. The slope rating is 113.

Play policy and fees: Reciprocal play is accepted with members of other private clubs. Guest fees are $10 for nine holes and $15 for 18 holes weekdays, and $18 for nine holes and $25 for 18 holes weekends. Carts are $7 for nine holes and $14 for 18 holes.

Location: From Interstate 280 in Cupertino, take the Highway 85/Sunnyvale Road exit south to the Saratoga city line. Turn right on Prospect Road to the course.

Course description: Two holes on this course are being lengthened, so look for the yardage and ratings to change. A driving range is expected to be ready in the spring of 1992. This hilly course has extremely narrow fairways lined with poplar and pine trees. The par-4 ninth will permit an easy enough birdie.

PO Box 2759
Saratoga, CA 95070

21990 Prospect Road
Saratoga, CA 95070

Pro shop   (408) 253-5494
Clubhouse (408) 253-0340

☐ driving range
■ practice greens
■ power carts
■ pull carts
■ golf club rental
■ locker rooms
■ showers
■ executive course
☐ accommodations
■ food and beverages
■ clubhouse

Mike Fish
Professional

Leon Snethen
Superintendent

LA RINCONADA
COUNTRY CLUB

NORTHERN E1

Course information: This private course has 18 holes and par is 70. The course is 6,028 yards and rated 69.5 from the regular tees. The slope rating is 120. Women's tees are 6,028 yards and rated 75.9 from the championship tees, and 5,708 yards and rated 73.7 from the forward tees. The slope ratings are 133 championship and 130 forward.

Play policy and fees: Reciprocal play is accepted with members of other private clubs Tuesdays, Thursdays and Fridays. Advance arrangements are required. Green fees for reciprocators are $50 when unaccompanied by a member, plus cart. Guest fees are $40. Carts are $10 for nine holes and $18 for 18 holes.

Location: From Highway 17 in San Jose, take the Lark Avenue exit. Turn left on Winchester Boulevard. Turn right on La Rinconada Drive and follow it to Clearview Drive. Turn left to the course.

Course description: Robert Dean Putman redesigned this course in 1960. Club records credit pro Phil Jefferson with grooming this course during its youth. The course is on the site of the former Puccinelli vineyard. This mature layout is short and narrow with tree-lined fairways and undulating greens. There is a lake that comes into play on the 14th and 15th holes. Located in the foothills of Los Gatos, this course offers a scenic view of the southern Santa Clara Valley. It is walkable. In case you're wondering about the club's logo: It's shaped like a cat, which seems logical for a Los Gatos golf course.

14597 Clearview Drive
Los Gatos, CA 95030

Pro shop   (408) 395-4220
Clubhouse   (408) 395-4181

- ■ driving range
- ■ practice greens
- ■ power carts
- ■ pull carts
- ■ golf club rental
- ■ locker rooms
- ■ showers
- □ executive course
- □ accommodations
- ■ food and beverages
- ■ clubhouse

Charlie Eddie
Professional

Don Boyd, Jr.
Superintendent

PLEASANT HILLS
GOLF COURSE

Course information: This public course has 18 holes and par is 72. There is also an 18-hole, par-3 course. The course is 6,478 yards and rated 71.0 from the championship tees, and 6,125 yards and rated 69.5 from the regular tees. The slope ratings are: 122 championship and 119 regular. Women's tees are 5,754 yards and rated 70.9. The slope rating is 114.

Play policy and fees: Green fees are $17 weekdays and $22 weekends. Twilight rates are $11 weekdays and $13 weekends. Carts are $11 for nine holes and $19 for 18 holes. Green fees for the executive course are $7 weekdays and $9 weekends. Reservations are recommended one week in advance for the regulation course, and first-come first-served for the executive course.

Location: From Highway 101 in San Jose, take the Tully Road East exit. Drive northeast past Capitol Expressway and turn left on South White Road to the course.

Course description: Situated at the base of the foothills, this course has a half-million trees (or so it seems), including fig, apple and eucalyptus, that all come into play. It is mostly flat and walkable.

2050 South White Road
San Jose, CA 95152-1386

Pro shop   (408) 238-3485
Clubhouse (408) 243-7533

□ driving range
■ practice greens
■ power carts
■ pull carts
■ golf club rental
□ locker rooms
□ showers
■ executive course
□ accommodations
■ food and beverages
■ clubhouse

Francis Duino
Manager
Henry Duino, Jr.
Superintendent

THE VILLAGES GOLF AND
COUNTRY CLUB

1970
Robert Muir Graves

Course information: This private course has 27 holes and par is 72. The Villages Course is 6,707 yards and rated 71.5 from the tournament tees, 6,338 yards and rated 69.8 from the championship tees, and 5,851 yards and rated 67.4 from the regular tees. The slope ratings are 119 tournament, 115 championship and 108 regular. Women's tees are 5,851 yards and rated 72.4. The slope rating is 123. The executive nine is 730 yards and par is 27.

Play policy and fees: Reciprocal play is accepted with members of other private clubs. Green fees for reciprocators are $36. Guest fees are $20 weekdays and $25 weekends. Carts are $12 for nine holes and $18 for 18 holes.

Location: From Highway 101 in eastern San Jose, take the Capitol Expressway northeast. Turn right on Aborn Road and drive one mile. Turn right on San Felipe Road and drive 2.5 miles to the Villages Parkway. Turn left and drive to Cribari Lane and the course.

Course description: This flat, bumpy course has lots of trees and some water. The fairways are wide open, and the greens are tricky to read.

5000 Cribari Lane
San Jose, CA 95135

Pro shop   (408) 274-3220
Clubhouse (408) 272-4400

■ driving range
■ practice greens
■ power carts
□ pull carts
□ golf club rental
□ locker rooms
□ showers
■ executive course
□ accommodations
■ food and beverages
■ clubhouse

Al Braga
Professional
Brian Bagley
Superintendent

BOULDER CREEK GOLF AND COUNTRY CLUB

1963
Jack Fleming

16901 Big Basin Highway
Boulder Creek, CA

Pro shop   (408) 338-2121
Clubhouse   (408) 338-2111

Course information: This resort course has 18 holes and par is 65. The course is 4,279 yards and rated 61.5 from the regular tees. The slope rating is 98. Women's tees are 3,970 yards and rated 63.3. The slope rating is 98.

Play policy and fees: Green fees are $16 weekdays and $26 weekends. Special discount rates are available. Carts are $16.

Location: From Santa Cruz, drive 12 miles north on Highway 9 to Boulder Creek. In Boulder Creek, take Highway 236 three miles northwest to the course on the right.

Course description: This scenic course is situated in the midst of the redwoods and is well maintained. It's short, slightly rolling and tight. The course is the home of the Boulder Creek Pro Am, and the Northern California Junior 13-And-Under Championships (August).

- ☐ driving range
- ■ practice greens
- ■ power carts
- ☐ pull carts
- ■ golf club rental
- ☐ locker rooms
- ☐ showers
- ■ executive course
- ■ accommodations
- ■ food and beverages
- ■ clubhouse

Hal Wells
Professional

Leonard A. Walsh
Superintendent

NORTHERN E1

ALMADEN GOLF AND COUNTRY CLUB

1955
Jack Fleming

Course information: This private course has 18 holes and par is 72. The course is 6,831 yards and rated 72.5 from the championship tees, and 6,501 yards and rated 71.0 from the regular tees. The slope ratings are 128 championship and 125 regular. Women's tees are 6,501 yards and rated 76.8 from the championship tees, and 6,069 yards and rated 74.3 from the forward tees. The slope ratings are 133 championship and 130 forward.

Play policy and fees: Reciprocal play is accepted with members of other private clubs Tuesdays, Thursdays and Fridays. Green fees for reciprocators are $40 with a member and $75 unaccompanied. Carts are $10 for nine holes and $20 for 18 holes.

Location: From Highway 101 in San Jose, exit on Capitol Expressway west to the Almaden Expressway. Turn left and drive 4.5 miles to Crown Boulevard. Turn right and continue to Hampton Drive.

Course description: This scenic, demanding course set in the Silicon Valley has a tree-lined, rolling terrain. The greens are large and undulating. It was the site of the annual San Jose LPGA Classic. The women's course record is 62, set by Palo Alto native Vicki Fergon during the 1984 San Jose Classic. (As a result, she entered the LPGA all-time record books by tying Mickey Wright's 18-hole scoring record of 62, posting another all-time record of 11 birdies in one round.) The men's course record is unknown.

6663 Hampton Drive
San Jose, CA 95120

Pro shop   (408) 268-3959
Clubhouse (408) 268-4653

- ■ driving range
- ■ practice greens
- ■ power carts
- ■ pull carts
- ■ golf club rental
- ■ locker rooms
- ■ showers
- □ executive course
- □ accommodations
- ■ food and beverages
- ■ clubhouse

D. Scott Hoyt
Professional

Mike Basile
Superintendent

SANTA TERESA GOLF CLUB

Course 88
MAP E1 grid j8

1963
George Santana

260 Bernal Road
San Jose, CA 95119

Pro shop   (408) 225-2650
Restaurant (408) 226-3170

- ■ driving range
- ■ practice greens
- ■ power carts
- ■ pull carts
- ■ golf club rental
- □ locker rooms
- □ showers
- □ executive course
- □ accommodations
- ■ food and beverages
- ■ clubhouse

Bob Mejias
Professional

John Snopkowski
Assistant Professional

Jim Ross
Superintendent

NORTHERN E1

Course information: This public course has 18 holes and par is 71. The course is 6,742 yards and rated 71.1 from the championship tees, and 6,430 yards and rated 70.0 from the regular tees. The slope ratings are 121 championship and 119 regular. Women's tees are 6,207 yards and rated 72.7. The slope rating is 120.

Play policy and fees: Green fees are $20 weekdays and $28 weekends. Twilight rates are $13 weekdays and $16 weekends and holidays. Carts are $11 for nine holes and $20 for 18 holes. Reserve a tee time one week in advance.

Location: From Highway 101 in San Jose, take the Bernal Road exit west. Drive two miles to the course.

Course description: This challenging course is long with tree-lined fairways. The front nine is flat, and the back nine is hilly. This course was voted the best municipal course in Santa Clara Valley. The testy 16th hole is one reason why: It's a tough par-3. Assistant Pro John Snopkowski holds the men's course record at 65, set in mid-1991. The women's course record was unavailable.

RIVERSIDE GOLF COURSE

Course 89
MAP E1 grid j9

1967
Jack Fleming

PO Box 13128
Coyote, CA 95013

Monterey Road
at Palm Avenue
Coyote, CA 95013-1328

Pro shop   (408) 463-0622

- ■ driving range
- ■ practice greens
- ■ power carts
- ■ pull carts
- ■ golf club rental
- □ locker rooms
- ■ showers
- □ executive course
- □ accommodations
- ■ food and beverages
- ■ clubhouse

Tom Smith
Professional

Cliff Rourke
Superintendent

Course information: This public course has 18 holes and par is 72. The course is 6,825 yards and rated 70.8 from the championship tees, and 6,504 yards and rated 69.6 from the regular tees. The slope ratings are 116 championship and 113 regular. Women's tees are 5,969 yards and rated 72.3. The slope rating is 118.

Play policy and fees: Green fees are $17 weekdays and $22 weekends. Carts are $23. Reservations are recommended one week in advance. Shirts and shoes are required at all times. This course is available for outside tournaments.

Location: From Highway 101 in Morgan Hill, take the Cochrane Road exit. From Highway 101 Coyote, exit at Bernal Road. Turn onto the Monterey Road heading south toward Morgan Hill. Turn at Palm Avenue and look for the signs.

Course description: This long, rolling course rewards good positioning. There are a lot of small, but wily trees. The greens are fast and among the best in the Santa Clara Valley. Knowing how to putt can't hurt, but then again learning how to putt can.

NOR-CAL MAP.....see page 34
adjoining maps
NORTH (D2).......see page 112
EAST (E3)..........see page 238
SOUTH (F2) ....see page 282
WEST (E1)..........see page 150

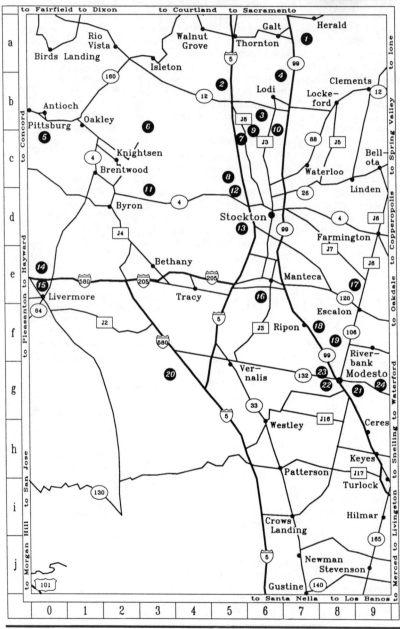

DRY CREEK RANCH GOLF COURSE

Course 1
MAP E2 grid a7

1962
Jack Fleming

809 Crystal Way
Galt, CA 95632

Pro shop   (209) 745-2330
Clubhouse   (209) 745-4653

NORTHERN E2

■ driving range
■ practice greens
■ power carts
■ pull carts
■ golf club rental
■ locker rooms
■ showers
□ executive course
□ accommodations
■ food and beverages
■ clubhouse

Rod Sims
Professional

Dave Davies
Superintendent

Course information: This public course has 18 holes and par is 72. The course is 6,707 yards and rated 71.6 from the championship tees, and 6,464 yards and rated 70.0 from the regular tees. The slope ratings are 119 championship and 116 regular. Women's tees are 5,952 yards and rated of 73.6. The slope rating is 126.

Play policy and fees: Green fees are $14 on weekdays and $24 on weekends and holidays. Make tee time reservations two weeks in advance. This course is available for outside tournaments.

Location: From Sacramento, drive 24 miles south on Highway 99 to Galt. Take the Central Galt exit onto ''C'' Street and drive east. Turn right on Crystal Way and drive to the course.

Course description: Tour professional Bob Eastwood assisted in the design-construction of the second nine in 1963. This challenging, tree-lined course has been rated among the top public courses in the state. It has a difficult combination of first and last holes. The first hole tees off into a narrow chute with a grove of oaks as out-of-bounds. The 18th hole doglegs to the left with oak trees and a creek bed that provide headaches. Rounds are made or ruined on either hole. Tommy Smothers, Bill Russell and Bill Cartwright are regular players on the course. The California Police Olympics, Boy Scouts of America, and the Muscular Dystrophy benefits are just a few of the tournaments that take place here every year. The women's course record is 70, and the men's course record is 63.

MAP ON PAGE 220

221

WOODBRIDGE GOLF AND COUNTRY CLUB

1923

Course information: This private course has 27 holes and par is 71. The three nine-hole course combinations are Lake Middle, River Lake and Middle River. Play any combination of two for an 18-hole round.

The Lake Middle Course is 6,494 yards for 18 holes from the regular tees. The slope rating is 120. Women's tees are 6,168 yards and rated 76.2. The slope rating is 134.

The River Lake Course is 6,394 yards and rated 69.5 from the regular tees. The slope rating is 118. Women's tees are 6,009 yards and rated 75.0. The slope rating is 127.

The Middle River Course is 6,314 yards for 18 holes and rated 69.2 from the regular tees. The slope rating is 117. Women's tees are 6,031 yards and rated 75.4. The slope rating is 131.

Play policy and fees: No outside play accepted. Reciprocal play is accepted on a limited basis with members of other private clubs. Green fee for reciprocators is $35. Members and guests only. Carts are $14. Reservations are required one week in advance. Closed Mondays.

Location: Located between Interstate 5 and Highway 99 in Woodbridge on Woodbridge Road.

Course description: Built in 1923, the greens are small and traditional. Of the three nines, the River Course is the oldest. The Middle Course has rolling terrain, and the Lake Course is the youngest and boasts lots of water. All three reward accuracy over distance.

PO Box 806
Woodbridge, CA 95258

800 East Woodbridge Road
Woodbridge, CA 95258

Pro shop   (209) 369-2371
Clubhouse (209) 334-5454

- ■ driving range
- ■ practice greens
- ■ power carts
- ■ pull carts
- ■ golf club rental
- ■ locker rooms
- ■ showers
- ☐ executive course
- ☐ accommodations
- ■ food and beverages
- ■ clubhouse

Robert E. Vocker
Professional

Jim Husting
Superintendent

VENETIAN GARDENS GOLF COURSE

Course information: This private course has 18 holes and par is 54. The yards and ratings were unavailable.

Play policy and fees: The course is private. No outside or reciprocal play is accepted.

Location: From Interstate 5 in Stockton, turn onto March Lane and drive one mile east to Venetian Drive North. Turn right on Mosaic Way to the Venetian Gardens Community golf course.

Course description: This course is located in Venetian Gardens, a private residential community.

1555 Mosaic Way
Stockton, CA 95207

Pro shop   (209) 447-3871

■ driving range
■ practice greens
□ power carts
□ pull carts
□ golf club rental
□ locker rooms
□ showers
□ executive course
□ accommodations
□ food and beverages
□ clubhouse

NORTHERN E2

FOREST LAKE GOLF COURSE

1957

Course information: This public course has 18 holes and par is 60 on Mondays, Tuesday and Thursdays, and 66 on Fridays, Saturdays and Sundays.

The course is 3,743 yards and rated 57.1 from the alternate regular tees, and 3,517 yards and rated 56.0 from the regular tees. The slope ratings are 85 alternate and 83 regular. Women's tees are 3,491 yards and rated 58.2 from the alternate forward tees, and 3,488 yards and rated 58.2 from the forward tees. The slope ratings are 83 alternate and 82 regular.

Play policy and fees: Green fees are $5 for nine holes and $7 for 18 holes weekdays, and $7 for nine holes and $10 for 18 holes weekends and holidays. Carts are $7 for nine holes and $12 for 18 holes. Reservations required one week in advance. This course is available for outside tournaments.

Location: From Highway 99 in Acampo (just north of Lodi), take the Jahant Road exit west, which turns into Woodson Road. Take Woodson Road one mile to the course on the left.

Course description: This short course offers tight fairways and a variety of mature trees and some water. The new front nine, with some elevated greens and tees, is slightly tougher than the back nine. The men's par-60 course record is 52, held by Mitch Harrison, and women's par-60 course record is 61. The men's par-66 course record is 64, held by Ray Madrid. Information on women's course records is not posted at the club.

2450 East Woodson Road
Acampo, CA 95220

Pro shop   (209) 369-5451

■ driving range
■ practice greens
■ power carts
■ pull carts
■ golf club rental
□ locker rooms
□ showers
□ executive course
□ accommodations
■ food and beverages
■ clubhouse

David Ring
Manager

Jerry Bodenhorn
Superintendent

LONE TREE GOLF COURSE

Course information: This public course has 18 holes and par is 73. The course is 6,260 yards and rated 69.8 from the championship tees, and 5,946 yards and rated 67.8 from the regular tees. The slope ratings are 116 championship and 112 regular. Women's tees are 5,769 yards and rated 71.8. The slope rating is 119.

Play policy and fees: Green fees for residents of the city of Antioch are $8 for nine holes weekdays, $9.50 for 18 holes weekdays and $12 for 18 holes weekends. Non-resident green fees are $10 for nine holes weekdays, $11.50 for 18 holes weekdays and $14 for 18 holes weekends. Carts are $10 for nine holes and $16 for 18 holes.

Location: From Highway 4 in Antioch, take the Lone Tree Way exit south.

Course description: This hilly yet open course has a unique par of 73. In spite of its name, there are lots of trees and it's walkable.

PO Box 986
Antioch, CA 94509

4400 Lone Tree Way
Antioch, CA 94509

Pro shop   (510) 757-5200

- ■ driving range
- ■ practice greens
- ■ power carts
- ■ pull carts
- ■ golf club rental
- ❏ locker rooms
- ❏ showers
- ❏ executive course
- ❏ accommodations
- ■ food and beverages
- ■ clubhouse

Pat Cain
Manager/Professional

Wayne Lindelof
Superintendent

THE ISLAND GOLF CLUB

1 9 6 6
R.E. Baldock

Course information: This public course has 18 holes and par is 72. The course is 6,480 yards and rated 69.2 from the regular tees. The slope rating is 114. Women's tees are 5,814 and rated 71.9. The slope rating is 113.

Play policy and fees: Green fees are $8.50 for nine holes, and $11 for 18 holes weekdays and $15 for 18 holes weekends. There is no weekend rate for nine-holes. Carts are $11 for nine holes and $18 for 18 holes.

Location: Take Highway 4 toward Oakley and exit at Cypress Road east. Turn left at Bethel Island Road and then right at Gateway Road to the course.

Course description: Formerly known as the Bethel Island Golf Course, this links-style layout has been around for more than 25 years. It is flat and windy with lots of trees, water and bunkers. The average golfer will be at home. It's a challenging, but fair test. The course is being renovated by Robert Muir Graves.

PO Box 27
Bethel Island, CA 94511

3303 Gateway Road
Bethel Island, CA 94511

Pro shop   (510) 684-2654
Clubhouse (510) 684-2775

- ■ driving range
- ■ practice greens
- ■ power carts
- ■ pull carts
- ■ golf club rental
- ❏ locker rooms
- ❏ showers
- ❏ executive course
- ❏ accommodations
- ■ food and beverages
- ■ clubhouse

Ron Parsons
Professional

Dan Nordell
Superintendent

Lou Scott
Manager

SWENSON PARK
GOLF COURSE

1952
Jack Fleming

6803 Alexandria Place
Stockton, CA 95207

Pro shop   (209)477-0774

■ driving range
■ practice greens
■ power carts
■ pull carts
■ golf club rental
□ locker rooms
□ showers
■ executive course
□ accommodations
■ food and beverages
■ clubhouse

Ernie George
Professional

Tom Nowak
Superintendent

Course information: This public course has 18 holes and par is 72. A par-3 executive course is also available. The course is 6,407 yards and rated 69.0 from the regular tees. The slope rating is 110. Women's tees are 6,266 yards and rated 73.8 from the forward tees. The slope rating is 117.

Play policy and fees: Weekday green fees are $8 until 2 p.m., and $7 after 2 p.m. Weekday junior and senior green fees are $5.50 after 11 a.m. Weekend and holiday green fees are $9 until 2 p.m., and $8 for twilight play. Weekend and holiday junior and senior green fees are $7 after 11 a.m. Green fees for the par-3 course are $5.50 for adults and $5 for juniors and seniors weekdays, and $6 weekends and holidays. Replays are $2.25. Carts are $9 for nine holes and $16 for 18 holes any day. Pull carts are $1.50. Reservations are recommended one week in advance. There is a $1 reservation fee. This course is open for outside tournaments. Make tournament reservations early.

Location: Heading north on Interstate 5 on the north side of Stockton, take the Benjamin Holt Drive exit east. Turn left on Alexandria Place and drive to the course on the left.

Course description: This mostly flat course has lots of big oak trees. The tee shot on the 16th hole shoots through a 250 yard long tunnel of oak trees no more than 25 yards wide. The greens are elevated. Accuracy with the long-to-middle irons is essential for good scoring, especially on holes 15 and 16 (known locally as the "Enchanted Forest" Don't ask why).

STOCKTON GOLF AND COUNTRY CLUB

1914
Alister MacKenzie

Course information: This private course has 18 holes and par is 71. The course is 6,426 yards and rated 70.8 from the championship tees, and 6,270 yards and rated 70.1 from the regular tees. The slope ratings are 120 championship and 118 regular. Women's tees are 6,023 yards and rated 74.8. The slope rating is 126.

Play policy and fees: Reciprocal play is accepted with members of other private clubs. Guest fees are $20 when accompanied by a member and $50 without. Carts are $8 for nine holes and $15 for 18 holes. Closed Mondays.

Location: From Interstate 5 in Stockton, take the Country Club Boulevard exit west and drive 1.5 miles to the course.

Course description: Set on the deep water channel cutting through the valley, this course has narrow fairways and is heavily guarded by cottonwood and eucalyptus trees. Nine holes have water. The greens are traditionally small and are known for their excellent condition. There are 63 bunkers.

PO Box 336
Stockton, CA 95204

West End of Country
Club Boulevard
Stockton, CA 95204

Pro shop   (209) 466-6221
Clubhouse (209) 466-4313

- ■ driving range
- ■ practice greens
- ■ power carts
- ■ pull carts
- ■ golf club rental
- ■ locker rooms
- ■ showers
- □ executive course
- □ accommodations
- ■ food and beverages
- ■ clubhouse

Alan Reed
Manager

Hal Ingram
Professional

Bill Fountain
Superintendent

ELKHORN COUNTRY CLUB

Bert Stamps

1050 Elkhorn Drive
Stockton, CA 95209

Pro shop   (209) 477-0252
Clubhouse (209) 477-8896

- ■ driving range
- ■ practice greens
- ■ power carts
- ■ pull carts
- □ golf club rental
- ■ locker rooms
- ■ showers
- □ executive course
- □ accommodations
- ■ food and beverages
- ■ clubhouse

Bob Young
Professional

Ty Caplin
Director

Del Burgess
Superintendent

Course information: This private course has 18 holes and par is 71. The course is 6,554 yards and rated 70.9 from the championship tees, and 6,084 yards and rated 69.0 from the regular tees. The slope ratings are 124 championship and 120 regular. Women's tees are 5,975 yards and rated 74.1 from the championship tees, and 5,642 yards and rated 72.0 from the forward egular tees. The slope ratings are 129 championship and 122 forward.

Play policy and fees: Reciprocal play is accepted with members of other private clubs. Bring your credentials. Members and guests only. Guest fees are $20 on weekdays and $30 on weekends. Guest fees after 2 p.m. are $10. Fees for reciprocal players are $29 on weekdays and $39 on weekends. Carts are $20. Reservations are recommended one week in advance. This course is available for outside tournaments.

Location: From Interstate 5, take the Eight Mile Road exit and drive three miles east. Turn right on Davis Road and drive one-quarter mile. Turn left on Elkhorn drive.

Course description: This tough course rewards accuracy over distance. It has mostly short par-4s. Over 63 bunkers guard the fairways and the elevated greens. Trees abound. Every year the Oldsmobile Scramble Sectionals and the NCPGA Junior Championships are held here. Don Blake, Jeff Wilson and Rod Souza share the men's course record of 63. The women's mark is 69 by Dana Arnold.

OAKMOORE GOLF COURSE

3737 North Wilson Way
Stockton, CA 95205

Pro shop   (209) 462-6712
Reservations (209) 943-1981

- □ driving range
- ■ practice greens
- ■ power carts
- □ pull carts
- □ golf club rental
- ■ locker rooms
- ■ showers
- □ executive course
- □ accommodations
- □ food and beverages
- ■ clubhouse

Tony Garcia
Superintendent

Course information: This private course has nine holes. Par is 72 for 18 holes. The course is 6,517 yards. Women's yardage and other ratings were unavailable.

Play policy and fees: This course is reserved exclusively for tournament groups. Call for reservations.

Location: From Highway 99 in Stockton, exit at Business 99/Wilson Way south and follow to the course.

Course description: This short, tight course has lots of trees and is well guarded by bunkers.

DISCOVERY BAY

Course 11
MAP E2 grid d3

1986
Ted Robinson

1475 Clubhouse Drive
Byron, CA 94514

Pro shop   (510) 634-0705

■ driving range
■ practice greens
■ power carts
■ pull carts
■ golf club rental
■ locker rooms
■ showers
□ executive course
□ accommodations
■ food and beverages
■ clubhouse

Leroy Silva
Professional

Rich Eichner
Superintendent

Course information: This private course has 18 holes and par is 71. The course is 6,517 yards and rated 72.1 from the championship tees, and 6,030 yards and rated 69.8 from the regular tees. The slope ratings are 128 championship and 123 regular. Women's tees are 6,173 yards and rated 75.4 from the championship tees, and 5,262 yards and rated 70.2 from the forward tees. The slope ratings are 132 championship and 123 forward.

Play policy and fees: Reciprocal play is accepted with members of other private clubs. Have your club pro call to make arrangements. Members and guests only. Green fees for reciprocators are $38 weekdays and $55 weekends. Guest fees are $28 weekdays and $32 weekends. Guests must be accompanied by a member. Carts are $20.

Location: From Highway 4, take the Discovery Bay Boulevard exit. Take the second right onto Clubhouse Drive.

Course description: This challenging, short course boasts water on 16 holes. The first hole has an island green. Four to five bunkers are found on every hole. It's often windy. Good positioning is a must.

LYONS GOLF COURSE

Course 12
MAP E2 grid d5

Rough and Ready Island
Stockton, CA 95203

Pro shop   (209) 944-0442

□ driving range
■ practice greens
□ power carts
■ pull carts
■ golf club rental
□ locker rooms
□ showers
□ executive course
□ accommodations
□ food and beverages
□ clubhouse

Kermit Hagan
Professional

Fred Fitzgerald
Superintendent

Course information: This military course has nine holes. Par is 64 for 18 holes. The course is 4,143 yards and rated 58.7 from the regular tees. The slope rating is 86. Women's yardage and ratings were unavailable.

Play policy and fees: Public play is not accepted: federal government employees, military and guests only. Green fees vary according to military status. Senior rates (over 62) are $6.

Location: From Interstate 5 in Stockton, take the Highway 4/Charter Way exit west. Turn right on Navy Drive and drive to Washington Street. Cross the bridge over the river onto Rough and Ready Island and onto the course.

Course description: This course has ponds that come into play on five of the nine holes. The greens are well bunkered.

VAN BUSKIRK GOLF COURSE

1969

Course information: This public course has 18 holes and par is 72. The course is 6,572 yards and rated 69.2 from the regular tees. The slope rating is 110. Women's tees are 6,541 yards and rated 75.7 from the championship tees, and 6,210 yards and rated 73.7 from the regular tees. The slope ratings are 120 championship and 117 regular.

Play policy and fees: Green fees are $8 weekdays and $9 weekends. Carts are $9 for nine holes and $16 for 18 holes.

Location: From Interstate 5 in Stockton, exit at Eighth Street West. Drive along the freeway south on Manthey Road to Houston Avenue and drive to the course.

Course description: This flat, open course has three ponds with water coming into play on nearly every hole in the front nine. Notable is the seventh hole, a long par-5 with out-of-bounds on the left and water on the right. On the back nine, the greens are somewhat elevated.

1740 Houston Avenue
Stockton, CA 95206

Pro shop   (209) 464-5629
Clubhouse (209) 463-0653

- ■ driving range
- ■ practice greens
- ■ power carts
- □ pull carts
- ■ golf club rental
- □ locker rooms
- ■ showers
- □ executive course
- □ accommodations
- ■ food and beverages
- ■ clubhouse

Jose Santiago
Manager/Professional

Tom Nowak
Superintendent

SPRINGTOWN GOLF COURSE

1961

Course information: This public course has nine holes. Par is 70 for 18 holes. The course is 5,710 yards rated 65.9 from the regular tees (18 holes). The slope rating is 104. Women's tees are 5,338 yards and rated 70.4 from the championship tees, and 5,126 yards and rated 67.9 from the forward tees. The slope ratings are 111 championship and 106 forward.

Play policy and fees: Green fees are $10 for nine holes and $15 for 18 holes on weekdays, $12 for nine holes and $18 for 18 holes on weekends. Carts are $20 for each nine holes. Reservations are recommended seven days in advance. This course is available for outside tournaments.

Location: From Interstate 580 in Livermore, take the Springtown Boulevard exit north. Turn right on Bluebell, which turns into Larkspur Drive.

Course description: This short course is well maintained with water on two holes, undulating greens, and two long par-3s of 190 and 202 yards. This is a test for golfers of all abilities.

939 Larkspur Drive
Livermore, CA 94550

Pro shop   (510) 455-5695

- ■ driving range
- ■ practice greens
- ■ power carts
- ■ pull carts
- ■ golf club rental
- □ locker rooms
- □ showers
- □ executive course
- □ accommodations
- ■ food and beverages
- ■ clubhouse

Mike Orlando
Robert Erler
Professionals

Keith Boam
Martha Boam
Managers

Mulkh Raj
Superintendent

MAP ON PAGE 220

229

LAS POSITAS GOLF COURSE

Course information: This public course has 18 holes and par is 72. There is also a nine-hole executive course. The course is 6,678 yards and rated 72.0 from the tournament tees, 6,347 yards and rated 70.5 from the championship tees, and 5,719 yards and rated 67.8 from the regular tees. The slope ratings are 126 tournament, 122 championship and 117 regular. Women's tees are 5,270 yards and rated 70.1. The slope rating is 120.

Play policy and fees: Green fees for residents of Livermore are $11 for nine holes and $16 for 18 holes weekdays, and $14 for nine holes and $21 for 18 holes weekends. Non-resident green fees are $12 for nine holes and $17 for 18 holes weekdays, and $15 for nine holes and $25 for 18 holes weekends. Carts are $18 weekdays and $20 weekends for two people. This course is available for outside tournaments. Closed Christmas.

Location: From Interstate 580 East, exit on Airway Boulevard. This course is located near the Livermore Airport on the south side.

Course description: This flat, tree-lined course has four lakes and a creek that come into play on seven holes. The greens are large and some are elevated. The fairways are wide and lush. This is a fly-in course with overnight accommodations nearby.

PO Box 1048
Livermore, CA 94550

909 Clubhouse Drive
Livermore, CA 94550

Pro shop   (510) 443-3122

- ■ driving range
- ■ practice greens
- ■ power carts
- ■ pull carts
- ■ golf club rental
- □ locker rooms
- □ showers
- ■ executive course
- □ accommodations
- ■ food and beverages
- ■ clubhouse

Dan Lippstreu
Professional

Mulkh Raj
Superintendent

MANTECA GOLF COURSE

1967

Course information: This public course has 18 holes and par is 72. The course is 6,447 yards and rated 70.2 from the championship tees, and 6,281 yards and rated 69.2 from the regular tees. The slope ratings are 119 championship and 115 regular. Women's tees are 6,271 yards and rated 74.7 from the championship tees, and 5,748 yards and rated 72.1 from the forward tees. The slope ratings are 121 championship and 115 regular.

Play policy and fees: Green fees are $10.75 weekdays and $14.25 weekends. Carts are $16 weekdays and $18 weekends.

Location: Located in Manteca off Highway 120 between Interstate 5 and Highway 99. From Highway 120, take the Union Road exit heading north. The course is on the left, past Center Street.

Course description: This challenging layout is a well maintained and tight. It opened as a nine-hole course in 1967 and went to 18 holes in 1976. Lakes come into play on nine holes and out-of-bounds on seven holes. The greens are small, flat and smooth. There are lots of trees, and accuracy is required. The course underwent some reconfiguration mid-1991, so watch out for hole number two (formerly number 11). It's a par-4, 433-yard tightrope all the way. Out-of-bounds marks the entire left side to the green, and there is a fairway bunker at 230 yards. A bunker shot makes this hole particularly tough. The green is fairly flat with some undulation and it's guarded by bunkers left and right. There is OB a mere five yards to the left of the green, so if you hit left count on a bunker landing or going OB. This is one of those memorable holes where you either score a four or a seven.

PO Box 611
Manteca, CA 95336

305 North Union Road
Manteca, CA 95336

Pro shop   (209) 823-5945
Clubhouse (209) 239-2868

■ driving range
■ practice greens
■ power carts
■ pull carts
■ golf club rental
■ locker rooms
□ showers
□ executive course
□ accommodations
■ food and beverages
■ clubhouse

Alan Thomas
Professional

Allen Mooser
Manager/Superintendent

NORTHERN E2

ESCALON GOLF COURSE

1985
Ken Roberts

17051 South Escalon
Bellota Road
Escalon, CA 95320

Pro shop   (209) 838-1277

- ■ driving range
- ■ practice greens
- ☐ power carts
- ■ pull carts
- ■ golf club rental
- ☐ locker rooms
- ☐ showers
- ■ executive course
- ☐ accommodations
- ■ food and beverages
- ■ clubhouse

Course information: This public course has nine holes. Par is 62 for 18 holes. The course is 3,060 yards and rated 52.6 for 18 holes from the regular tees. The slope rating is 67. Women's tees are 3,060 yards and rated 55.1. The slope rating is 70.

Play policy and fees: Green fees are $4.50 for nine holes and $8 for 18 holes weekdays, and $5 for nine holes and $9 for 18 holes weekends. Reservations are taken anytime.

Location: Driving south on Highway 99, take the Manteca exit heading toward Escalon. Turn left on Escalon Bellota Road and drive to the course.

Course description: This short course is flat with one pond with four par-4s and five par-3s. There are lots of trees.

Tom Hagan,
Owner/Manager/
Superintendent

Tony Hall
Professional

SPRING CREEK GOLF AND COUNTRY CLUB

Course 18
MAP E2 grid f7

1976
Jack Fleming

PO Box 535
Ripon, CA 95366

16436 East Spring Creek
Drive
Ripon, CA 95366

Pro shop   (209) 599-3630
Clubhouse (209) 599-3258

NORTHERN E2

Course information: This private course has 18 holes and par is 72. The course is 6,380 yards and rated 70.7 from the championship tees, and 6,144 yards and rated 69.6 from the regular tees. The slope ratings are 124 championship and 121 regular. Women's tees are 6,160 yards and rated 75.3 from the championship tees, and 5,626 yards and rated 72.1 from the forward tees. The slope ratings are 128 championship and 119 forward.

Play policy and fees: Reciprocal play is accepted with members of other private clubs. Have your club pro call for arrangements after 2 p.m. Guest fees are $20 when accompanied by a member and $35 when unaccompanied. Mandatory carts are $16. Appropriate dress is required.

Location: From Highway 99 in Ripon (north of Modesto), take the Ripon exit to the east side of the freeway. Drive two miles to Spring Creek Drive and the course.

Course description: This flat course is tight with lots of oak trees, two of which are stationed in the middle of narrow fairways. The ninth hole is a notable par-4 that crosses water. At 432 yards, it places a premium on accuracy. Annual tournaments include the JGANC Spring Creek Classic, Seniors Invitational, Men's Invitational, Ladies Invitational, and Couples Invitational. The NCGA Qualifying and CGA Qualifying have been held here. The men's course record is 64, held jointly by Ron Brown and Robert Warren. The women's course record is 68, held by Keri Arnold-Cusenza.

- ■ driving range
- ■ practice greens
- ■ power carts
- □ pull carts
- □ golf club rental
- ■ locker rooms
- ■ showers
- □ executive course
- □ accommodations
- ■ food and beverages
- ■ clubhouse

Steve Brown
Professional

Peter Hand
General Manager

Cal Shipman
Superintendent

DEL RIO COUNTRY CLUB

1926
William Park Bell

801 Stewart Road
Modesto, CA 95356

Pro shop   (209) 545-0013
Clubhouse (209) 545-0723

- ■ driving range
- ■ practice greens
- ■ power carts
- ■ pull carts
- ■ golf club rental
- ■ locker rooms
- ■ showers
- ☐ executive course
- ☐ accommodations
- ■ food and beverages
- ■ clubhouse

Dick Wiseman
Manager

Bill Womeldorf
Professional

Scott Jorgenson
Superintendent

Course information: This private course has 18 holes and par is 72. The course is 6,875 yards and rated 72.8 from the championship tees, and 6,650 yards and rated 71.7 from the regular tees. The slope ratings are 126 championship and 122 regular. Women's tees are 6,345 yards and rated 76.2 from the championship tees, and 5,986 yards and rated 75.0 from the forward tees. The slope ratings are 131 championship and 130 forward.

Play policy and fees: Reciprocal play with members of other private clubs is accepted on Tuesdays, Thursdays and Fridays. Guest fees are $25 with a member and $50 without weekdays, and $35 with a member weekends. No play is allowed without a member on weekends. Carts are $16. This course is available for limited outside tournaments. Closed Mondays.

Location: From Highway 99 in Modesto, take the Salida exit onto Kerinin Avenue North. Turn left at Dale Road and follow it to the "T." Turn right on Ladd and drive one mile to Saint John and go left up to the club.

Course description: This course was designed in 1926 by William Park Bell. It's a challenging, rolling country course that demands good shot placement. The greens are fast, undulating, and have subtle breaks. Nine additional holes are on the design boards. It hosted the 1990 U.S. Senior Women's Amateur Championship, and annually hosts the Bumgartner Junior Championships in July.

TRACY GOLF AND COUNTRY CLUB

Course information: This private course has 18 holes and par is 72. The course is 6,506 yards and rated 70.7 from the championship tees, and 6,227 yards and rated 69.5 from the regular tees. The slope ratings are 118 championship and 115 regular. Women's tees are 5,776 yards and rated 73.4. The slope rating is 128.

Play policy and fees: Reciprocal play is accepted with members of other private clubs. Have your club pro call ahead for arrangements. Guest fees are $18 on weekdays and $25 on weekends when accompanied by a member, $25 weekdays and $32 on weekends without a member. Carts are $14.

Location: From Interstate 580, take the Chrisman Road exit. The course is located next to the highway.

Course description: This flat course has rolling terrain, fast, elevated greens, four ponds and numerous bunkers. The original nine holes were designed by Robert Trent Jones, Sr. Host pro Steve Moreland holds the men's course record with a 63.

C o u r s e   2 0
MAP E2 grid g4

1956
Robert Trent Jones, Sr.

35200 South Chrisman Road
Tracy, CA 95376

Pro shop   (209) 835-9463

- ■ driving range
- ■ practice greens
- ■ power carts
- ■ pull carts
- ■ golf club rental
- ■ locker rooms
- ■ showers
- ☐ executive course
- ☐ accommodations
- ■ food and beverages
- ■ clubhouse

Steve Moreland
Manager/Professional

George Murakami
Superintendent

NORTHERN E2

RIVER OAKS GOLF COURSE

Course information: This public course has 18 holes and par is 58. The course is 2,886 yards and rated 52.7 from the regular tees. The slope rating is 74. Women's tees are 2,640 yards with a rating of 54.3. The slope rating is 75.

Play policy and fees: Green fees are $8 weekdays and $10 weekends and holidays. Reservations are recommended one week in advance. All players must wear proper golf attire. Only golf or tennis shoes may be worn on the course.

Location: From Modesto, drive south on Highway 99. Take the Hatch Road exit east. The course is located on the left past Mitchell Road.

Course description: This tree-lined course runs along the Tuolumne River. It has some ponds and no bunkers. It doesn't take much time to get through this course. You can whip through the first nine in an hour. The men's record, 56, is held by Rob Phipps and Evelyn Phillips holds the record for women at 65.

C o u r s e   2 1
MAP E2 grid g8

1979
Jim D. Phipps

PO Box 97
Ceres, CA 95307

3441 East Hatch Road
Hughson, CA 95362

Pro shop   (209) 537-4653

- ■ driving range
- ■ practice greens
- ☐ power carts
- ■ pull carts
- ■ golf club rental
- ☐ locker rooms
- ☐ showers
- ■ executive course
- ☐ accommodations
- ■ food and beverages
- ☐ clubhouse

Robert Phipps
Manager

Linda Collins–Maurer
Professional

Gregory F. Ritschy
Professional

Mike Phipps
Superintendent

DRYDEN PARK GOLF COURSE

1959

Course information: This public course has 27 holes. Par is 72 for the Dryden Course and 70 for the Modesto Municipal Course at 18 holes.

The Dryden Course is 6,531 yards and rated 69.3 from the championship tees, and 6,238 yards and rated 67.9 from the regular tees. The slope ratings are 119 championship and 116 regular. Women's tees are 6,031 yards and rated 73.3. The slope rating is 115.

The Modesto Municipal Course is 6,074 yards and rated 68.2 for 18 holes from the regular tees (18 holes). The slope rating is 113. Women's tees are 5,868 yards and rated 72.0 for 18 holes. The slope rating is 112.

Play policy and fees: Green fees are $13 weekdays and $15 weekends. Twilight rate is $11. Carts are $16. Reservations are recommended one week in advance. This course is available for outside tournaments.

Location: This course is located right off Highway 99 in Modesto. Take the Tuolumne Boulevard/B Street exit and make a right on Tuolumne.

Course description: The Tuolumne River runs along side this course. The front nine is flat, and the back nine is somewhat hilly. There are lots of trees. Accuracy is more important than distance. (See the listing for Modesto Municipal Course for additional information.)

920 South Sunset Boulevard
Modesto, CA 95351

Pro shop   (209) 577-5359
Muni Course (209) 577-5360
Clubhouse   (209) 529-5530

- ■ driving range
- ■ practice greens
- ■ power carts
- ■ pull carts
- ■ golf club rental
- □ locker rooms
- □ showers
- □ executive course
- □ accommodations
- ■ food and beverages
- ■ clubhouse

Sue Fiscoe
Professional

Leonard Theis
Superintendent

MODESTO MUNICIPAL GOLF COURSE

Course 23
MAP E2 grid g8

NORTHERN E2

921 Sunset
Modesto, CA 95351

Pro shop   (209) 577-5360

☐ driving range
■ practice greens
■ power carts
■ pull carts
■ golf club rental
☐ locker rooms
☐ showers
☐ executive course
☐ accommodations
■ food and beverages
■ clubhouse

Sue Fiscoe
Professional
Leonard Theis
Superintendent

Course information: This public course has nine holes and par is 70 for 18 holes. The course is 6,074 yards and rated 68.2 for 18 holes from the regular tees. The slope rating is 113. Women's tees are 5,868 yards and rated 72.0 for 18 holes. The slope rating is 112.

Play policy and fees: Green fees are $9 for nine holes and $13 for 18 holes weekdays, and $11 for nine holes and $15 for 18 holes weekends and holidays. The weekday late-play green fee after 3 p.m. during the summer season is $7. The weekend late-play green fee after 3 p.m. is $9. Wednesdays are senior (65 and over) days and the green fee is $5 for nine holes between 9 a.m. and 3 p.m. Carts are $8 for nine holes and $16 for 18 holes. Reservations are recommended.

Location: On Highway 99 off Toulumne Boulevard, take the "B" Street off-ramp and make a right at the stop sign. Drive one-half block on Neece Drive, and stay left along the river to the course.

Course description: This course is walkable and fairly flat. The greens are relatively undulating, the fairways are narrow and the trees are mature. The ninth is considered one of the top 18 holes in the area. At 424 yards, it's a par-4 dogleg right with OB on the right and trees on both sides. You can't see the green from the tee, but there is a bunker to the left front and a cart path to the right. The green holds if the shot is well executed. It's a fun little course to play. (See the Dryden Park Golf Course listing for additional information.)

MODESTO CREEKSIDE GOLF COURSE

Course 24
MAP E2 grid g9

1991
Steve Halsey

701 Lincoln
Modesto, CA 95353

Pro shop   (209) 571-5123

■ driving range
■ practice greens
■ power carts
■ pull carts
■ golf club rental
☐ locker rooms
☐ showers
☐ executive course
☐ accommodations
■ food and beverages
■ clubhouse

Sue Fiscoe
Manager/Professional

Course information: This public course has 18 holes. Par is 72. The course is 6,021 yards and rated 68.5 from the regular tees. The slope rating is 112. Women's tees are 5,496 yards and are in process of being rated.

Play policy and fees: Green fees are $13 weekdays and $15 weekends. Carts are $16. This course is available for outside tournaments. Weekday reservations are recommended one week in advance, and weekend reservations are taken the prior Monday.

Location: From Highway 99 in Modesto, take Highway 132 to Lincoln. Turn left on Lincoln and follow it to the deadline at the course.

Course description: This course opened for play September 13, 1991. It is relatively flat with two holes playing into the creekside. There are three ponds which come into play on six holes. There are some two-tiered greens, but they're large. The course is wide open for now, but wait for the trees to grow in and they will spell trouble.

MAP ON PAGE 220   237

MAP E3

(14 COURSES)

PAGES.. 238-247

NOR-CAL MAP.....see page 34
adjoining maps
NORTH (D3).......see page 134
EAST (E4)..........see page 248
SOUTH (F3) ....see page 288
WEST (E2).........see page 220

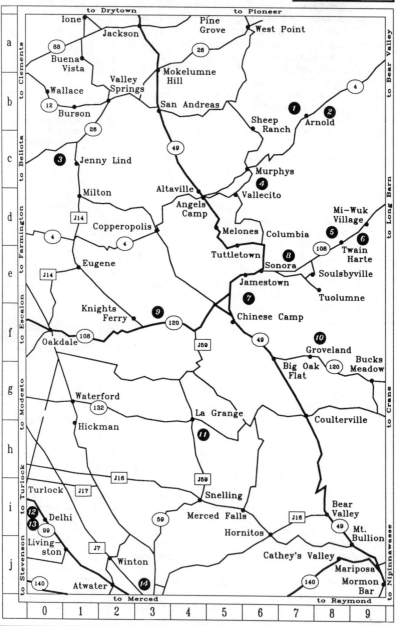

238   NORTHERN CALIFORNIA

MEADOWMOUNT GOLF COURSE

Course information: This public course has nine holes. Par is 72 for 18 holes. The course is 5,748 yards and rated 67.6 for 18 holes from the regular tees. The slope rating is 113. Women's tees are 5,482 yards and rated 71.0. The slope rating is 114.

Play policy and fees: Green fees are $8.50 for nine holes and $13.25 for 18 holes weekdays, and $10 for nine holes and $14.50 for 18 holes weekends. Carts are $9.75 for nine holes and $18 for 18 holes.

Location: From Highway 99, drive 70 miles east on Highway 4, past Murphys to Arnold. The course is on the left.

Course description: Raes Creek crisscrosses this gently sloping course and comes into play on every hole. Poplar trees divide the narrow fairways. The greens are small.

PO Box 586
Arnold, CA 95223

Highway 4 and
Country Club Drive
Arnold, CA 95223

Pro shop   (209) 795-1313
Clubhouse (209) 795-3585

■ driving range
■ practice greens
■ power carts
■ pull carts
■ golf club rental
□ locker rooms
□ showers
□ executive course
□ accommodations
■ food and beverages
■ clubhouse

Jeff Christensen
Manager/Pro/Superintendent

SEQUOIA WOODS COUNTRY CLUB

1976

Course information: This private course has 18 holes and par is 70. The course 5,494 yards and rated 66.3 from the championship tees, and 5,312 yards and rated 65.5 from the regular tees. The slope ratings are 109 championship and 107 regular. Women's tees are 5,295 yards and rated 70.0 from the championship tees, and 5,068 yards and rated 68.9 from the forward tees. The slope ratings are 112 championship 110 forward.

Play policy and fees: Reciprocal play is accepted with members of other private clubs. Guest fees are $20 when accompanied by a member and $30 without. Carts are $18 when accompanied by a member and $20 without. Reservations are recommended two weeks in advance. This course is available for outside tournaments.

Location: From Highway 99, drive east on Highway 4 to Arnold. Exit right on Blue Lake Springs and follow the signs to the club. The course is a 90-minute drive from Stockton.

Course description: This sprawling, mountain course is tougher than the rating indicates. The front nine is situated in a spacious meadow. Trade in the woods for irons on the back nine, because it gets narrow and steep. Out-of-bounds run along both sides of the fairways.

PO Box 748
Arnold, CA 95223

1000 Cypress Point Drive
Arnold, CA 95223

Pro shop   (209) 795-2141
Clubhouse (209) 795-1378

□ driving range
■ practice greens
■ power carts
■ pull carts
■ golf club rental
■ locker rooms
■ showers
□ executive course
□ accommodations
■ food and beverages
■ clubhouse

Larry Babica
Professional

John Castillou
Superintendent

MAP ON PAGE 238

239

LA CONTENTA GOLF CLUB

1974

Course information: This semi-private course has 18 holes and par is 72. The course is 6,412 yards and rated 71.3 from the championship tees, and 5,976 yards and rated 69.4 from the regular tees. The slope ratings are 127 championship and 124 regular. Women's tees are 5,272 yards and rated 70.8. The slope rating is 120.

Play policy and fees: Green fees are $15 on weekdays and $26 on weekends. The rate after 3 p.m. is $7 on weekdays and $13 on weekends. Carts are $18. Reservations are recommended two weeks in advance. This course is available for outside tournaments.

Location: From Highway 99 in Stockton, take the Fremont (Highway 26) exit east. Drive 28 miles on Highway 26 to the course.

Course description: Set in the rolling foothills 35 miles east of Stockton, this tight, hilly course challenges you with out-of-bounds on 14 holes and water on nine holes. The trademark hole is the 13th, a par-3 that drops 100 feet from the tee to an "L" shaped green almost completely surrounded by water.

1653 Highway 26
Valley Springs, CA 95252

Pro shop   (209) 772-1081
Clubhouse   (209) 772-1082

☐ driving range
■ practice greens
■ power carts
■ pull carts
■ golf club rental
☐ locker rooms
☐ showers
☐ executive course
☐ accommodations
■ food and beverages
■ clubhouse

Bob Laugenour
Manager

John DeFilippi
Professional

Rod Metzler
Director of Golf

Curt Hammond
Director of Golf

Rod Butler
Superintendent

FOREST MEADOWS
GOLF COURSE

1974
Robert Trent Jones, Jr.

Highway 4 Box 70
Murphys, CA 95247

Pro shop   (209) 728-3439
Clubhouse   (209) 728-3440

☐ driving range
☐ practice greens
■ power carts
■ pull carts
■ golf club rental
☐ locker rooms
☐ showers
■ executive course
■ accommodations
■ food and beverages
■ clubhouse

Norbert A. Wilson
Professional

Ward Souza
Superintendent

Course information: This public course has 18 holes and par is 60. The course is 3,886 yards and rated 57.5 from the regular tees. The slope rating is 97. Women's tees are 3,221 yards and rated 57.0. The slope rating is 86.

Play policy and fees: From October 1 through April 30, green fees are $8 on weekdays and $9 on weekends for nine holes, and $14 on weekends and $16 on weekends for 18 holes. From May 1 through September 30, green fees are $12 for nine holes and $20 for 18 holes. Carts are $9 for nine holes and $16 for 18 holes. Reservations are recommended two weeks in advance. Shirts and shoes are required. No short shorts may be worn. This course is available for outside tournaments. Winter play is subject to weather conditions.

Location: From Highway 99, drive east on Highway 4 to Murphys. The course is about 3.5 miles east of Murphys on Highway 4.

Course description: This is a beautiful Sierra Nevada course traversed by the Stanislaus Canyon. Situated at 3,500 feet, its panoramic layout mixes aesthetics and serious play and offers a challenge to low- and high-handicappers alike. Known for its excellent, fast greens, the course places a premium on putting.

NORTHERN E3

TWAIN HARTE GOLF AND COUNTRY CLUB

1961
R.E. Baldock
Robert Dean Putman

PO Box 333
Twain Harte, CA 95383

22909 Meadow Lane
Twain Harte, CA 95383

Pro shop   (209) 586-3131

□ driving range
■ practice greens
□ power carts
■ pull carts
■ golf club rental
□ locker rooms
□ showers
□ executive course
□ accommodations
■ food and beverages
■ clubhouse

Course information: This short semi-private course has nine holes. Par is 58 for 18 holes. The course is 3,436 yards and rated 57.1 for 18 holes from the championship tees, and 3,326 yards and rated 56.4 from the regular tees. The slope ratings are 88 championship and 87 regular. Women's tees are 3,515 yards and rated 61.0 for 18 holes from the championship tees, and 3,433 yards and rated 59.7 from the forward tees. The slope ratings are 98 championship and 92 forward.

Play policy and fees: Green fees are $10 for nine holes and $15 for 18 holes. Senior rates are $6 for nine holes and $10 for 18 holes Mondays only, and junior rates (under 16) are $5 and $8.

Location: From Highway 108 in Twain Harte (10 miles east of Sonora), turn left on Meadow Lane.

Course description: This short course has narrow fairways, a few ponds, many towering trees and gorgeous scenery. It's flat and good for beginners.

Tim Huber
Manager/Professional

Curtis Johnson
Superintendent

SIERRA PINES GOLF COURSE

1967

PO Box 1013
Twain Harte, CA 95383

23736 South Fork Road
Twain Harte, CA 95383

Pro shop   (209) 586-2118

■ driving range
■ practice greens
■ power carts
■ pull carts
■ golf club rental
□ locker rooms
□ showers
□ executive course
□ accommodations
■ food and beverages
■ clubhouse

MaryBeth Ryan
Manager

Course information: This public course has nine holes. Par is 62 for 18 holes. The course is 4,373 yards and rated 61.2 for 18 holes from the regular tees. The slope rating is 94. Women's tees are 4,194 yards and rated 63.9. The slope rating is 104.

Play policy and fees: Green fees are $9 for nine holes and $12 for 18 holes weekdays, and $10 for nine holes and $14 for 18 holes weekends. Carts are $12 for nine holes and $16 for 18 holes. Reservations are recommended. This course is available for outside tournaments.

Location: From Highway 108, take the Twain Harte Drive exit and drive into Twain Harte. Drive one mile, making sure you pass under the arch. Drive straight through town and take the left fork in the road, which is South Fork Road. Follow South Fork to the course.

Course description: This is a challenging, but friendly course with a barbecue picnic area. Some of the greens are sloped, so study the course carefully. This hilly, mountain course is nestled in a valley with lots of trees. It's cool in the summer months. This is a family course, bring the grandparents. There is no charge for non-players.

MOUNTAIN SPRINGS GOLF COURSE

Course 7
MAP E3 grid e6

1990
Robert Muir Graves

1000 Championship Drive
Sonora, CA 95370

Pro shop   (209) 532-1000

- ■ driving range
- ■ practice greens
- ■ power carts
- □ pull carts
- ■ golf club rental
- ■ locker rooms
- ■ showers
- □ executive course
- □ accommodations
- ■ food and beverages
- ■ clubhouse

Douglas Wayne
Professional

Al Huber
Director of Golf

Jim Smith
Superintendent

NORTHERN E3

Course information: This semi-private course has 18 holes and par is 72. The course is 6,568 yards and rated 71.9 from the tournament tees, 6,198 yards and rated 70.2 from the championship tees, and 5,614 yards and rated 67.7 from the regular tees. The slope ratings are 128 tournament, 124 championship and 119 regular. Women's tees are 5,644 yards and rated 72.0 from the championship tees, and 5,146 yards and rated 68.8 from the forward tees. The slope ratings are: 122 championship and 112 forward.

Play policy and fees: Outside play is accepted. Green fees are $14 weekdays and $22 weekends. Carts are $16. Reservations are accepted one week in advance. This course is available for outside tournaments.

Location: From Highway 108 in Sonora, turn right on Lime Kiln Road. Drive two miles to the course entrance on the right.

Course description: This rolling layout is located in the heart of the Gold Country and offers sweeping views. Six lakes and 70 bunkers come into play. Scenic vistas are afforded on the first, fifth, 10th, 15th and 17th holes. The pride of the course is the 200-yard, par-3 eighth hole across water, hitting to a narrow green with bunkers in the back with water up to the apron. This new course is maturing well.

PHOENIX LAKE GOLF COURSE

Course 8
MAP E3 grid e7

1968
Bert Stamps

21448 Paseo de Los Portales
Sonora, CA 95370

Pro shop   (209) 532-0111

- ■ driving range
- ■ practice greens
- ■ power carts
- ■ pull carts
- ■ golf club rental
- □ locker rooms
- □ showers
- □ executive course
- □ accommodations
- ■ food and beverages
- ■ clubhouse

Chris Bitticks
Professional

George Graul
Superintendent

Course information: This public facility has nine holes. Par is 70 for 18 holes. The course is 5,358 yards and rated 66.4 from the regular tees (18 holes). The slope rating is 115. Women's tees are 4,830 yards and rated 67.8. The slope rating is 114.

Play policy and fees: Green fees are $7 for nine holes and $10 for 18 holes weekdays, and $8 for nine holes and $11 for 18 holes weekends. Carts are $9 for nine holes and $16 for 18 holes.

Location: From Highway 108 in Sonora, take the Phoenix Lake Road exit left. The course is on the left on Paseo de Los Portales. The course is about three miles from Highway 108.

Course description: This short course is mostly flat with narrow fairways. It's lined with some cedars and numerous oak trees.

OAKDALE GOLF AND COUNTRY CLUB

1957
Robert Dean Putman

Course information: This private course has 18 holes and par is 72. The course is 6,717 yards and rated 71.8 from the championship tees, and 6,445 yards and rated 70.6 from the regular tees. The slope ratings are: 122 championship and 120 regular. Women's tees are 5,765 yards and rated 73.7. The slope rating is 125.

Play policy and fees: Reciprocal play is accepted with members of other private clubs. Have your club pro call in advance for arrangements. Guest fees are $20 weekdays and $25 weekends when accompanied by a member. Guests must be accompanied by a member. Green fee for reciprocators is $40. Carts are $9 for nine holes and $16 for 18 holes.

Location: Driving east on Highway 108, turn left on Stearns Road. The course is located north of Oakdale.

Course description: This is a long and hilly course with elevated tees and greens. It is mostly wide open. Notable is the ninth hole. At 230 yards, this par-3 has a great view with a lake on the right.

243 North Stearns Road
Oakdale, CA 95361

Pro shop   (209) 847-2924
Clubhouse (209) 847-2984

- ■ driving range
- ■ practice greens
- ■ power carts
- ■ pull carts
- ■ golf club rental
- ■ locker rooms
- ■ showers
- □ executive course
- □ accommodations
- ■ food and beverages
- ■ clubhouse

Joe Comella
Manager

Jay D. Ward
Professional

Fred Northcutt
Superintendent

PINE MOUNTAIN LAKE GOLF COURSE

1969
William Francis Bell

Course information: This private course has 18 holes and par is 70. The course is 6,358 yards and rated 70.6 from the tournament tees, 6,146 yards and rated 69.5 from the championship tees, and 5,770 yards and rated 67.9 from the regular tees. The slope ratings are 125 tournament, 122 championship and 118 regular. Women's tees are 5,355 yards and rated 70.8. The slope rating is 128.

Play policy and fees: Reciprocal play is accepted with members of other private clubs. Property owners and their guests only. Green fees for reciprocators is $50. Guest green fees are $30. Carts are $22. Reservations should be made two weeks in advance.

Location: From Interstate 5 in Manteca, take Highway 120 east to Groveland. The course is located north of Groveland on Mueller Drive.

Course description: Formerly a semi-private course, this course went private in January, 1991. At an elevation of 3,500 feet, this mountain course has narrow fairways with lots of trees and some hills. Driving accuracy is vital. The fourth hole is a standout. At 466 yards, the par-5 fourth has a blind second shot that doglegs right.

PO Box PMLA
Groveland, CA 95321

Mueller Drive
Groveland, CA 95321

Pro shop   (209) 962-7471
Clubhouse (209) 962-7866

- ■ driving range
- ■ practice greens
- ■ power carts
- □ pull carts
- ■ golf club rental
- ■ locker rooms
- □ showers
- □ executive course
- ■ accommodations
- ■ food and beverages
- ■ clubhouse

Steve Caulkins
Professional

Kirk Golden
Superintendent

LAKE DON PEDRO GOLF AND COUNTRY CLUB

Course information: This semi-private course has 18 holes and par is 70. The course is 6,244 yards and rated 68.5 from the championship tees, and 6,017 yards and rated 67.4 from the regular tees. The slope ratings are 112 championship and 110 regular. Women's tees are 5,561 yards and rated 70.8. The slope rating is 112.

Play policy and fees: Outside play is accepted. Green fees are $10 weekdays and $12 weekends. Carts are $16 weekdays and $18 weekends. Reservations are recommended one week in advance. This course is available for outside tournaments.

Location: From Highway 99 in Modesto, drive 30 miles east on Highway 132 to La Grange. In six miles, exit on Hayward Road south and follow to the course to Fachada/Ranchito.

Course description: There are three water hazards on this short, hilly course. It is not a walkable course.

Course 11
MAP E3 grid h4

1970
William Francis Bell

PO Box 193
La Grange, CA 95329

Ranchito Drive at Fachada
La Grange, CA 95329

Pro shop   (209) 852-2242

NORTHERN E3

☐ driving range
■ practice greens
■ power carts
☐ pull carts
☐ golf club rental
■ locker rooms
■ showers
☐ executive course
☐ accommodations
■ food and beverages
■ clubhouse

Ray Claveran
Manager/Professional

John Michaels
Superintendent

TURLOCK GOLF AND COUNTRY CLUB

Course information: This private course has 18 holes and par is 72. The course is 6,632 yards and rated 71.9 from the championship tees, and 6,368 yards and rated 70.6 from the regular tees. The slope ratings are 123 championship and 121 regular. Women's tees are 5,822 yards and rated 73.4. The slope rating is 129.

Play policy and fees: Reciprocal play is accepted with members of other private clubs. Reciprocal fees are $30. Guest fees are $30. Carts are $20.

Location: From Highway 99 south in Turlock, exit on Lander Avenue south and turn left on Bradbury. Turn right onto Golf Links Road and drive to the course.

Course description: This flat course is deceiving. It's tight, and the rough is difficult. The 14th hole is a stickler. At 374 yards, this par-4 requires a carry over water and then doglegs 90 degrees. It's primarily a placement course with tricky greens. The California State Amateur Qualifying was held here in 1991.

Course 12
MAP E3 grid i0

1959
Robert Dean Putman

PO Box X
Turlock, CA 95381

10532 North Golf Links Road
Turlock, CA 95380

Pro shop   (209) 634-4976
Clubhouse   (209) 634-5471

■ driving range
■ practice greens
■ power carts
■ pull carts
☐ golf club rental
■ locker rooms
■ showers
☐ executive course
☐ accommodations
■ food and beverages
■ clubhouse

Shane Balfour
Professional

Dave Rodriguez
Superintendent

POQUITO LAKE GOLF AND COUNTRY CLUB

Course information: This public course has nine holes. Par is 58 for 18 holes. The course is 5,426 yards for 18 holes from the regular tees. It is in the process of being rated.

Play policy and fees: Green fees are $6 for nine holes and $11 for 18 holes weekdays, and $7 for nine holes and $12 for 18 holes weekends. Green fees for seniors and juniors are $5 for nine holes and $9 for 18 holes weekdays, and $6 for nine holes and $11 for 18 holes weekends. Reservations are recommended. This course is available for tournaments.

Location: From Highway 99 south of Turlock, take the Lander Avenue exit. Turn on First Street and drive to the course. It's right next door to the Hilmar Post Office.

Course description: There is cause of celebration in Hilmar. This course reopened August 15, 1991 after a two-year closure. It is the former Golden Valley Golf Course. It has undergone a complete rejuvenation of greens and fairways. New bunkers have been added. There are 12 different species of mature trees, including coast redwoods, Italian stonepine, Canary Island pine and, of course, Monterey pine. This course is flat, tight and narrow. There are two par-4s and lots of water. It's tough to shoot par here. The course records of 25 for nine holes and 54 for 18 holes are held by George Buzzini. Several local tournaments are held at this course annually. This course is considered one of best maintained courses in the San Joaquin Valley.

PO Box 268
Hilmar, CA 95324

19920 West First Street
Hilmar, CA 95324

Pro shop   (209) 668-2255
Lounge   (209) 668-3825

□ driving range
■ practice greens
■ power carts
■ pull carts
■ golf club rental
□ locker rooms
□ showers
■ executive course
□ accommodations
■ food and beverages
■ clubhouse

Bill Garcia
Owner/Manager

Cindy Garcia
Owner/Manager

Ralph Garcia
Superintendent

RANCHO DEL REY GOLF COURSE

1963

Course information: This public course has 18 holes and par is 72. The course is 6,760 yards and rated 71.8 from the championship tees, and 6,290 yards and rated 69.7 from the regular tees. The slope ratings are 119 championship and 115 regular. Women's tees are 6,237 yards and rated 76.0 from the championship tees, and 5,874 yards and rated 73.6 from the forward tees. The slope ratings are 128 championship and 126 forward.

Play policy and fees: Green fees are $9 for nine holes and $16 for 18 holes weekdays, and $11 for nine holes and $20 for 18 holes weekends. Twilight rates begin at noon and are $7 for nine holes and $11 for 18 holes weekdays, and $8 nine holes and $13 for 18 holes weekends. Carts are $10 for nine holes and $18 for 18 holes. Tee times are made Monday to Monday. Shirts must be worn at all times. This course is available for outside tournaments.

Location: From Highway 99 in Atwater, exit north onto Bucharch Road. Then turn left on Green Sands Avenue and follow it to the course.

Course description: This course is mostly flat with sand and water. You'll need every club in your bag. It's open every day of the year.

5250 Green Sands Avenue
Atwater, CA 95301

Pro shop   (209) 358-7131
Clubhouse (209) 358-0024

- ■ driving range
- ■ practice greens
- ■ power carts
- ■ pull carts
- ■ golf club rental
- □ locker rooms
- □ showers
- □ executive course
- □ accommodations
- ■ food and beverages
- ■ clubhouse

Bob Riechel
Manager/Professional

Jack Brink
Superintendent

NORTHERN E3

NOR-CAL MAP.....see page 34
adjoining maps
NORTH (D4).......see page 144
EAST (E5)..........see page 250
SOUTH (F4).......see page 294
WEST (E3)..........see page 238

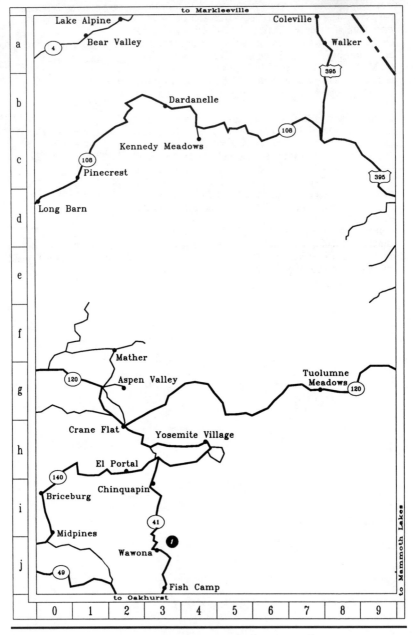

to Markleeville

Lake Alpine

Coleville

Bear Valley

Walker

4

395

a

Dardanelle

b

108

Kennedy Meadows

c

108

395

Pinecrest

Long Barn

d

e

f

Mather

Aspen Valley

Tuolumne Meadows

g

120

120

Crane Flat

Yosemite Village

h

El Portal

140

Chinquapin

Briceburg

i

41

1

Midpines

Wawona

j

49

Fish Camp

to Oakhurst

to Mammoth Lakes

0   1   2   3   4   5   6   7   8   9

WAWONA HOTEL
GOLF COURSE

1918
Alister MacKenzie

Course information: This public course has nine holes. Par is 70 for 18 holes. The course is 6,015 yards and rated 69.1 for 18 holes from the regular tees. The slope rating is 117. Women's tees are 5,506 and rated 70.9. The slope rating is 119.

Play policy and fees: Green fees are $10.25 for nine holes and $15 for 18 holes. Carts are $10 for nine holes and $15 for 18 holes. Reservations are recommended during the entire season. Guests of the Wawona Hotel should make golf reservations at the same time they make room reservations. The course is open April 1 to November 1.

Location: This course is located between Oakhurst and Yosemite on Highway 41 on the south end of the park.

Course description: This is a short, scenic course in Yosemite National Park. There are lots of redwood trees, and the course is well maintained. Deer and other wildlife abound. The adjacent Wawona Hotel is a wonderful place to stay and dine.

PO Box 2005
Yosemite National Park
CA 95389

Highway 41
Yosemite National Park
CA 95389

Pro shop   (209) 375-6572

□ driving range
■ practice greens
■ power carts
■ pull carts
■ golf club rental
■ locker rooms
■ showers
□ executive course
■ accommodations
■ food and beverages
□ clubhouse

Sam Winstead
Manager

Kim Porter
Superintendent

NORTHERN E4

NOR-CAL MAP.....see page 34
adjoining maps
NORTH ....no map
EAST ....no map
SOUTH (F5) ....see page 304
WEST (E4).........see page 248

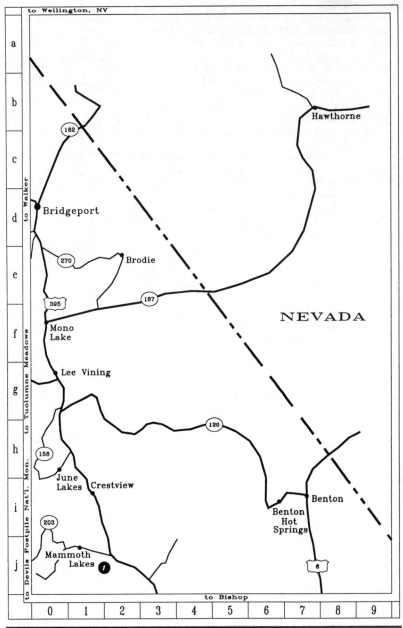

SNOWCREEK GOLF COURSE

1991
Ted Robinson

PO Box 569
Mammoth Lakes, CA 93546

Snowcreek Golf Course/
Old Mammoth Road
Mammoth Lakes, CA 93546

Pro shop   (619) 934-6633

NORTHERN E5

- ■ driving range
- ■ practice greens
- ■ power carts
- ■ pull carts
- ■ golf club rental
- ☐ locker rooms
- ☐ showers
- ☐ executive course
- ☐ accommodations
- ■ food and beverages
- ■ clubhouse

Kristine McCue
Head Professional

Tim Standifer
General Manager

Carol Lozito
Superintendent

Course information: This public facility is nine holes. Par is 70 for 18 holes. The course is 6,310 yards and rated 70.5 for 18 holes from the tournament tees, 6,196 yards and rated 69.1 from championship, and 5,850 yards and rated 67.5 from the regular tees. The slope ratings are 118 tournament, 115 championship and 112 regular. Women's tees are 5,244 yards and rated 69.2. The slope rating is 114.

Play policy and fees: Green fees are $20 for nine holes and $30 for 18 holes weekdays, and $25 for nine holes and $35 for 18 holes weekends. Carts are $7 per person for nine holes and $10 per person for 18 holes. Reservations are recommended one week in advance. This course is available for outside tournaments. The course is open from Memorial Day Weekend through mid-October.

Location: From Highway 395, take Highway 203 west to Old Mammoth Road. Turn left on Old Mammoth Road and drive about one mile to the course. The course is on the left side.

Course description: The course appears to be wide open because of its setting against the majestic eastern Sierra range, but don't be fooled by the scenery. This is a target course all the way, and it pays to keep your eye on the ball and not on the mountains. The fairways are narrow and water comes into play on nearly every hole. The greens are relatively large for a course of this distance, which is a plus factor. Play the course while it's still a nine-hole layout because it's only going to get tougher. There are plans to expand the course to 18 holes in the spring of 1992, and with the expansion the course will balloon to over 7,000 yards from the back tees. At an elevation of 7,800 feet, oit promises to be one incredible challenge. Of course, at that elevation there is a one to one and one-half club difference over the typical Greater Los Angeles course. There are condos aplenty at Mammonth Lakes, including some which overlook the course. Take your pick of lodgings.

Central
California
Golf Courses

CENTRAL CALIFORNIA

CENTRAL CALIFORNIA COURSES

As soon as you declare that within the boundaries of Central California is Monterey Bay, it immediately becomes tempting to lump the entire region under one big golf heading: Pebble Beach.

True, Pebble Beach and her golf courses are the best-known of the region. And it's hard to argue against the supremacy of her tracts. Between Pebble Beach, Cypress Point, Spanish Bay and Poppy Hills, you get just about everything you could ask for: magnificent, challenging, well-maintained courses which fall into everybody's playing category—public, private and resort.

You want diversity of style? From the slick thumbnails that Pebble Beach has for greens to the rolling Scottish links of Spanish Bay, to the more open, free swinging American styling of Poppy Hills (which is still rated at 71.7 from the regular men's tees), you get extreme diversity. And all in top-notch condition.

But by no means is Pebble all that Central California has to offer. Because as you look inland, at the burgeoning Fresno area—and in fact much of the San Joaquin Valley—new courses are beginning to sprout up. This growth spurt in the central valley of the state can be fairly easily attributed to the favorable climate, availability of land at reasonable prices, and relative ease of permitting.

If crowds don't scare you away, try Morro Bay Golf Course. Called "the Poor Man's Pebble Beach," this delightful tract features ocean views on almost every hole—for only $13 per round! No wonder it's also one of the busiest course in the state.

Santa Barbara offers classic courses such as the private 1929 Alister MacKenzie layout at The Valley Club of Montecito, as well as an abundance of public courses such as the scenic and popular La Purisima Golf Course, a 1986 Robert Muir Graves design, which was named as one of the best courses in the state in our Populist Poll (see page 588).

Add to the mix the unusual Furnace Creek Golf Course in Death Valley—one of the lowest courses in the world at 214 feet below sea level, and it becomes abundantly clear that Central California provides golf courses of all ilk and trial.

CEN-CAL BY AREA
(MAP, COURSES, PAGE)

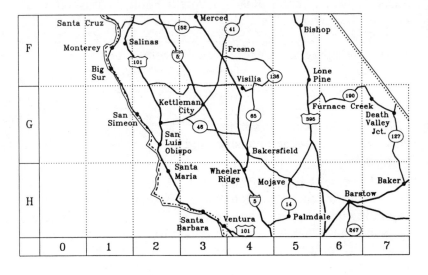

CEN-CAL BY CITY
(CITY and MAP PAGE)

CENTRAL

257

MAP F1
(28 COURSES)

PAGES.. 258-281

CEN-CAL MAP...see page 256
adjoining maps
NORTH (E1) ....see page 150
EAST (F2)..........see page 282
SOUTH..........................no map
WEST ....no map

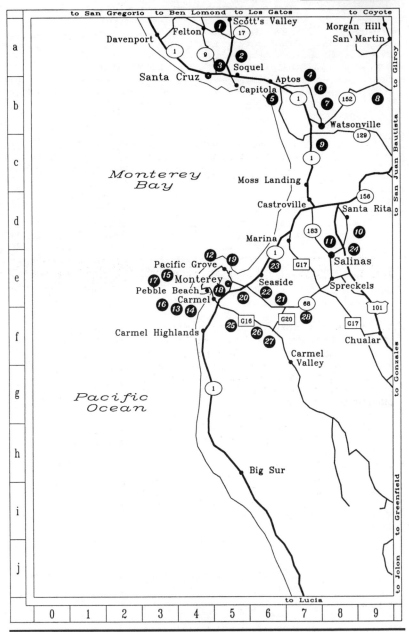

VALLEY GARDENS
GOLF COURSE

1971
R.E. Baldock

Course information: This public course has nine holes. Par is 62 for 18 holes. The course is 3,530 yards and rated 54.1 for 18 holes from the regular tees. The slope rating is 82. Women's tees are 3,114 yards and rated 57.4 for 18 holes. The slope rating is 85.

Play policy and fees: Green fees are $8 weekdays and $9 weekends for nine holes. Reservations are recommended one week in advance.

Location: From Highway 17 in Scotts Valley, drive one mile west on Mount Hermon Road.

Course description: This course is short, tight and flat. There are 27 different varieties of trees that come into play, which adds up to a lot of trees. Beginners, juniors and seniors will find it an excellent layout. The layout is in super shape.

263 Mount Hermon Road
Scotts Valley, CA 95066

Pro shop   (408) 438-3058

- ☐ driving range
- ■ practice greens
- ☐ power carts
- ■ pull carts
- ■ golf club rental
- ☐ locker rooms
- ☐ showers
- ■ executive course
- ☐ accommodations
- ■ food and beverages
- ■ clubhouse

Jerry Imel
Director of Golf

Sandy Woodruff
Owner

Pat Voeks
Superintendent

DE LAVEAGA GOLF COURSE

Course information: This public layout has 18 holes and par is 72. The course is 6,010 yards and rated 70.1 from the regular tees. The slope rating is 130. Women's tees are 5,979 yards and rated 74.3 from the championship tees, and 5,346 yards and rated 70.7 from the forward tees. The slope ratings are 134 championship and 126 forward.

Play policy and fees: Green fees are $18.50 weekdays and $25 weekends. Twilight rates are $12 weekdays and $16.50 weekends. Carts are $22 with a $3 returnable deposit.

Location: From San Francisco, take Interstate 280 to Highway 17 toward Santa Cruz. Take Highway 1 south to the Morrisey exit. Turn right on Fairmount and right on Branciforte Drive. Turn right again on Upper Park Road and proceed to the course.

Course description: This tight, rolling course in the Santa Cruz mountains has lateral hazards on nearly every hole. Staying on the fairways off the tee is vital. The course may give the appearance of birdie opportunities, but they don't come easily. The Santa Cruz City Championships were held here in 1991. The men's course record of 64 is held jointly by brothers Tim and Michael Loustalot, sons of host pro, Gary. Women's course record information was not available.

PO Box 1358
Soquel, CA 95073

401 Upper Park Road, Box A
Santa Cruz, CA 95065

Pro shop   (408) 423-7214
Clubhouse (408) 423-7212

- ■ driving range
- ■ practice greens
- ■ power carts
- ■ pull carts
- ■ golf club rental
- ☐ locker rooms
- ☐ showers
- ☐ executive course
- ☐ accommodations
- ■ food and beverages
- ■ clubhouse

Gary Loustalot
Professional

Campbell Turner
Superintendent

CENTRAL F1

PASATIEMPO GOLF COURSE

1929
Alister MacKenzie

PO Box 535
Santa Cruz, CA 95060

18 Clubhouse Road
Santa Cruz, CA 95060

Pro shop   (408) 426-3622

- ■ driving range
- ■ practice greens
- ■ power carts
- ■ pull carts
- ■ golf club rental
- □ locker rooms
- □ showers
- □ executive course
- □ accommodations
- ■ food and beverages
- ■ clubhouse

Shawn McEntee
Professional

Dean Gump
Superintendent

Course information: This semi-private course has 18 holes and par is 71. The course is 6,483 yards and rated 72.9 from the tournament tees, 6,154 yards and rated 71.4 from the championship tees, and 5,647 yards and rated 68.7 from the regular tees. The slope ratings are 138 tournament, 134 championship and 124 regular. Women's tees are 5,647 yards and rated 72.9. The slope rating is 133.

Play policy and fees: Outside play is accepted. Green fees are $70 Monday through Thursday, and $80 Friday through Sunday and holidays. Optional carts are $27. Reservations are recommended. To reserve a weekday tee time call one week before, and call on Monday at 10 a.m. for the coming weekend. Appropriate golf attire required. Rubber studded shoes are not allowed. This course is available for outside tournaments.

Location: From San Francisco, drive south on Interstate 280. Take Highway 17 toward Santa Cruz. Exit on Pasatiempo and follow the signs to the course.

Course description: This course was designed by Alister MacKenzie, creator of Cypress Point and Augusta National. It opened in 1929 and still ranks as one of the best in the nation. The par-4, 395-yard number 16 was Alister Mackenzie's "favorite hole in golf." It's a blind driving hole, hitting across a creek to a three-tiered green. There are hazards and OB on both sides of the fairway, which doglegs to the left. There's not much choice of route on this hole. Play it right-center on the drive to take advantage of a fairway that breaks back to the left. This was the site of the 1986 U.S. Women's Amateur and the annual Western Intercollegiate. The course overlooks the Pacific Ocean and Monterey Bay.

APTOS PAR-3 GOLF COURSE

1962

Course information: This public course has nine holes. Par is 27. The course is 1,044 yards for nine holes. All play is from the same tees. The course is unrated.
Play policy and fees: Green fees are $5 for nine holes. Reservations are recommended one day in advance.
Location: This course is located off Highway 1 in Aptos. Take the Park Avenue exit and drive under the freeway toward the hills. Turn right at the first stop sign at Soquel Drive. Drive past the fire station and proceed to the telephone pole which is handily marked "golf." Turn right and continue to the course.
Course description: This short, par-3 course is flat and open. It's excellent for beginners or players trying to sharpen their iron play. It takes about an hour and a half to get nine holes in. The men's record is 22.

2600 Mar Vista Drive
Aptos, CA 95003

Pro shop   (408) 688-5000

- ■ driving range
- ■ practice greens
- □ power carts
- □ pull carts
- ■ golf club rental
- □ locker rooms
- □ showers
- □ executive course
- □ accommodations
- ■ food and beverages
- □ clubhouse

Howard Menge
Professional

APTOS SEASCAPE GOLF COURSE

1927

Course information: This public course has 18 holes and par is 72. The course is 6,123 yards and rated 69.6 from the regular tees. The slope rating is 124. Women's tees are 5,576 yards and rated 71.8. The slope rating is 120.
Play policy and fees: Green fees May through September are $30 weekdays and $47 weekends and holidays. Twilight rates after 3 p.m. are $22 weekdays and $33 weekends and holidays. Super twilight rates after 5 p.m. are $14 weekdays and $20 weekends. Green fees October through April are $25 weekdays and $42 weekends and holidays. Twilight rates after 3 p.m. are $20 weekdays and $30 weekends and holidays. Super twilight rates after 5 p.m. are $12 weekdays and $17 weekends and holidays. Rates are subject to change March 1, 1992. Carts are $14 for nine holes and $22 for 18 holes. Reservations are recommended one week in advance for weekday play and the Monday prior at 10 a.m. for weekend and holiday play. This course is available for outside tournaments.
Location: From Santa Cruz, drive seven miles south on Highway 1. Exit on Rio Del Mar and go right. Turn left on Clubhouse Drive.
Course description: This scenic course has rolling, oceanside character, although you can't actually see the ocean. Cypress trees and bunkers border every hole. The course is tight and accuracy is vital. Par-3s are the key to success here. The 180-yard driving range is for iron practice only.

610 Clubhouse Drive
Aptos, CA 95003

Pro shop   (408) 688-3214
Clubhouse   (408) 688-3254

- ■ driving range
- ■ practice greens
- ■ power carts
- ■ pull carts
- ■ golf club rental
- ■ locker rooms
- ■ showers
- □ executive course
- □ accommodations
- ■ food and beverages
- ■ clubhouse

Bruce Pluim
General Manager

Don Elser
Professional

Mike McCraw
Superintendent

CENTRAL F1

CASSERLY PAR-3 GOLF COURSE

Course 6
MAP F1 grid b7

1966
Robert Sanford

626 Casserly Road
Watsonville, CA 95076

Pro shop   (408) 724-1654

Course information: This public course has nine holes. Par is 54 for 18 holes. The course is 2,316 yards for 18 holes. All play is from the same tees. The course is unrated.

Play policy and fees: Green fees are $4 for nine holes. Pull carts only. Play is on a first-come first-served basis.

Location: This course is located between Highway 101 and Highway 1. From Highway 1 heading east toward Watsonville, take the Airport Boulevard exit and follow it to Green Valley Road. Turn left and follow Green Valley Road 1.5 miles to Casserly Road.

Course description: This all par-3 course has two water hazards as well as hills that come into play. It's a good beginner course. You can play nine holes in an hour during your lunch break.

- ☐ driving range
- ■ practice greens
- ☐ power carts
- ■ pull carts
- ■ golf club rental
- ☐ locker rooms
- ☐ showers
- ☐ executive course
- ☐ accommodations
- ☐ food and beverages
- ☐ clubhouse

Robert Sanford
Manager

Jean Sanford
Manager

George Sanford
Superintendent

SPRING HILLS GOLF COURSE

Course 7
MAP F1 grid b8

1965
Hank Schimpeler

31 Smith Road
Watsonville, CA 95076

Pro shop   (408) 724-1404

Course information: This public course has 18 holes and par is 71. The course is 5,891 yards and rated 68.4 from the regular tees. The slope rating is 114. Women's tees are 5,784 yards and rated 73.3 from the championship tees, and 5,428 yards and rated 71.1 from the forward tees. The slope ratings are 121 championship and 117 forward.

Play policy and fees: Green fees are $15 weekdays and $20 weekends. Carts are $10 for nine holes and $20 for 18 holes. Reservations are recommended one week in advance. This course is available for outside tournaments.

Location: From Highway 1 in Watsonville, take Green Valley Road north to Casserly Road. Turn right and then left on Smith Road to the course. From Highway 152, take Carlton Road north to Casserly and then Smith Road.

Course description: The back nine opened for play in 1965 and the front nine opened for play in 1969. Situated in the foothills, this short course is tight with lots of trees. The many doglegs make placement important. The back nine is rolling and scenic.

- ■ driving range
- ■ practice greens
- ■ power carts
- ■ pull carts
- ☐ golf club rental
- ☐ locker rooms
- ☐ showers
- ☐ executive course
- ☐ accommodations
- ■ food and beverages
- ■ clubhouse

Hank Schimpeler
Owner

GAVILAN GOLF COURSE

Course information: This public course has nine holes. Par is 62 for 18 holes. The course is 3,613 yards and rated 55.6 for 18 holes from the regular tees. The slope rating is 73. Women's tees are 3,613 yards and rated 57.9 for 18 holes. The slope rating is 85.

Play policy and fees: Green fees are $8 weekdays and $10 weekends for all-day play. Senior rates are $6 on weekdays. Carts are $6 for nine holes and $10 for 18 holes. Play is on a first-come, first-served basis.

Location: From Highway 101 in Gilroy, take the Castro Valley exit and follow it until it dead ends. Turn right on Santa Teresa Boulevard. Go to the south gate at the Gavilan Community College Campus.

Course description: This course dates back to the 1960s. It is short, mostly flat course and excellent for beginners. The greens are small and tricky and offer a challenge.

5055 Santa Teresa Boulevard
Gilroy, CA 95020

Pro shop   (408) 848-1363

- ■ driving range
- ■ practice greens
- ■ power carts
- ■ pull carts
- ■ golf club rental
- □ locker rooms
- □ showers
- ■ executive course
- □ accommodations
- □ food and beverages
- □ clubhouse

Frank Pryor
Manager

Dene Pryor
Manager

Ted Hernandez
Superintendent

CENTRAL F1

PAJARO VALLEY GOLF COURSE

Course information: This public course has 18 holes and par is 72. The course is 6,234 yards and rated 69.0 from the championship tees, and 6,065 yards and rated 68.2 from the regular tees. The slope ratings are: 116 championship and 114 regular. Women's tees are 5,701 yards and rated 72.1. The slope rating is 121.

Play policy and fees: Green fees are $32 weekdays and $40 weekends and holidays. Twilight rates after 3 p.m. are $19. Carts are $22 and optional. Reservations recommended the last Friday of each month at 7 a.m. for weekdays, and the Monday prior at 12:30 p.m. for weekends and holidays. This course is available for outside tournaments.

Location: Take Highway 1 south past Watsonville. After the Riverside Drive exit, head to the top of the hill where the lanes merge. Turn left at the flashing yellow lights on Salinas Road and proceed three-fourths of a mile to the course on the right.

Course description: Dating back to the late 1920s, this course is short and wide with rolling fairways. The 12th hole, a long par-4, features a three-tiered green surrounded by bunkers. The Little Helpers Golf Tournament is held here annually.

PO Box 133
Watsonville, CA 95076

967 Salinas Road
Watsonville, CA 95076

Pro shop   (408) 724-3851

- ■ driving range
- ■ practice greens
- ■ power carts
- ■ pull carts
- ■ golf club rental
- ■ locker rooms
- ■ showers
- □ executive course
- □ accommodations
- ■ food and beverages
- ■ clubhouse

Gary Cursio
Manager

Nick Lombardo
Professional

Gary Feliciano
Superintendent

SHERWOOD GREENS GOLF COURSE

Course information: This public course has nine holes and par is 56 for 18 holes. The course is 2,673 yards and rated 53.7 from the regular tees. The slope rating is 73. Women's tees are rated the same.

Play policy and fees: Green fees are $4.25 for nine holes and $6.75 for 18 holes for Salinas residents, and $4.75 for nine holes and $7.55 for 18 holes for non-residents. Special discount rates are available for juniors 17 years and under. Pull carts are available for $1 for nine holes.

Location: From Highway 101 in Salinas driving south, take the Boronda Road exit. Driving north exit on Laurel Drive. Both Boronda and Laurel lead to North Main Street and the course, which is located next to the Salinas Rodeo stadium.

Course description: This short, flat course is tight and is a good test for beginners. It places a premium on iron play. Some trees will keep you honest off the tee.

1050 North Main Street
Salinas, CA 93906

Pro shop   (408) 758-7333

- ■ driving range
- ■ practice greens
- ■ power carts
- ■ pull carts
- ■ golf club rental
- ☐ locker rooms
- ☐ showers
- ☐ executive course
- ☐ accommodations
- ☐ food and beverages
- ☐ clubhouse

Glen Stubblefield
Professional

E.L. "Cotton" Kaiser
Professional

Tony Silvera
Superintendent

SALINAS GOLF AND COUNTRY CLUB

Course information: This private course has 18 holes and par is 72. The course is 5,887 yards and rated 68.6 from the regular tees. The slope rating is 116. Women's tees are 5,620 yards and rated 72.8. The slope rating is 125.

Play policy and fees: Reciprocal play is accepted with members of other private clubs. Guest fees are $25 when accompanied by a member and $35 when unaccompanied. Carts are $15. Tee times should be reserved one week in advance. Proper golf attire required. Closed Mondays.

Location: From Highway 101 in Salinas, take the Boronda Road exit. Turn right on Main Street (the first stoplight) and follow it to San Juan Grade Road. Turn right on San Juan Grade Road and drive 2.5 miles to the course.

Course description: This short course is tight and hilly with small, tricky greens. It has lots of trees. Many up and down holes require finesse shots from the sidehill lies. It's a good test for the irons and the short game. This course was the site of a battle fought by General Fremont during the Mexican-American War. The men's course record of 60 is held by Kurt Dillard, and the women's by Pat Cornett, at 67.

PO Box 4277
Salinas, CA 93912

475 San Juan Grade Road
Salinas, CA 93906

Pro shop   (408) 449-1526
Clubhouse (408) 449-1527
Office   (408) 449-6617

- ■ driving range
- ■ practice greens
- ■ power carts
- ■ pull carts
- ■ golf club rental
- ■ locker rooms
- ■ showers
- ☐ executive course
- ☐ accommodations
- ■ food and beverages
- ■ clubhouse

Gregg St. Germain
Professional

Bill Kissick
Superintendent

THE LINKS AT SPANISH BAY

1987
Robert Trent Jones, Jr.
Tom Watson
Frank "Sandy" Tatum

Course information: This resort course has 18 holes and par is 72. The course is 6,820 yards and rated 74.6 from the championship tees, and 6,078 yards and rated 72.1 from the regular tees. The slope ratings are 142 championship and 133 regular. Women's tees are 5,287 yards and rated 70.8. The slope rating is 120.

Play policy and fees: Green fees are $100 for Pebble Beach Resort guests, and $125 for the public. Carts are included. Caddies are $35 per bag. Players may carry their own bag. Golf club rental is $35. Resort guests may make tee time reservations with their room reservations 18 months ahead. Outside players (two or more) may make reservations 60 days in advance.

Location: From Highway 1 in Monterey, exit at Highway 68/W.R. Holman (Pacific Grove Carmel Highway) north. The highway becomes Forest Avenue. Turn left at Sunset Drive and take it to 17 Mile Drive in Pacific Grove. Turn left onto 17 Mile Drive and drive a one-quarter mile to the entrance gate of the 17 Mile Drive. The course is 500 yards past the gate.

PO Box 658
Pebble Beach, CA 93953

2700 17 Mile Drive
Pebble Beach, CA 93953

Pro shop   (408) 647-7500

☐ driving range
■ practice greens
■ power carts
☐ pull carts
■ golf club rental
☐ locker rooms
☐ showers
☐ executive course
■ accommodations
■ food and beverages
■ clubhouse

Rich Cosand
Manager/Professional

Jess Pifferinni
Superintendent

CENTRAL F1

Course description: This fast-rolling course, designed by Robert Trent Jones, Jr., Tom Watson and Frank "Sandy" Tatum in 1987, is tailored in the pure Scottish fashion, complete with fescue grass fairways and greens, pot bunkers and mounds. Unlike traditional layouts, the architects want golfers to hit run-up shots and keep the ball low. Considering that all but four holes flank the ocean, this strategy is especially advantageous when the wind kicks up, which it often does. Most of the holes are flanked by sand and natural vegetation indigenous to the area, making accuracy a must. Large expanses of sand dunes, up to 24 feet in height, covered with native grasses and plants characterize the course. The back nine is particularly enjoyable. It features a par-4 12th, a short par-3 13th and a difficult par-4 17th. (See the article on The Links At Spanish Bay on page 19.)

MAP ON PAGE 258   265

PETER HAY GOLF COURSE

1957
Peter Hay

Course information: This public layout has nine holes and par is 54 for 18 holes. The course is 1,570 yards at 18 holes.

Play policy and fees: Green fees are $7 for all day, and juniors under 16 are free when accompanied by an adult. No reservations are taken.

Location: From Highway 1, take the Pebble Beach gate. The guard will give you instructions and a map. The course is next to Pebble Beach Golf Links.

Course description: This par-3 course provides an excellent opportunity to tune-up your short game. It was closed for three months while being renovated, and reopened August 30, 1991. The course has been re-planted with rye grass to replace Kikuyu grass. Prior to renovation, the course had just one bunker; it now has 11. Additional tees were built to allow playing the holes from a different location on a second round. This par-3 course is short and tight, with some hills and lots of trees, the longest hole is 110 yards. It is named for the late Peter Hay, who was a longtime pro at Pebble Beach.

PO Box 658
Pebble Beach, CA 93953

17 Mile Drive
Pebble Beach, CA 93953

Pro shop   (408) 625-8518

- ■ driving range
- ■ practice greens
- ☐ power carts
- ■ pull carts
- ■ golf club rental
- ☐ locker rooms
- ☐ showers
- ■ executive course
- ☐ accommodations
- ■ food and beverages
- ☐ clubhouse

R.J. Harper
Professional

Brad Hines
Superintendent

PEBBLE BEACH GOLF LINKS

1919
Jack Neville

PO Box 658
Pebble Beach, CA 93953

17 Mile Drive
Pebble Beach, CA 93953

Pro shop   (408) 624-3811
Reservation (408) 624-6611

- driving range
- practice greens
- power carts
- pull carts
- golf club rental
- locker rooms
- showers
- executive course
- accommodations
- food and beverages
- clubhouse

R. J. Harper
Professional

Ed Miller
Director of Golf Operations

Brad Hines
Superintendent

CENTRAL F1

Course information: This resort course has 18 holes and par is 72. The course is 6,791 yards and rated 75.0 from the championship tees, and 6,345 yards and rated 72.7 from the regular tees. The slope ratings are 144 championship and 139 regular. Women's tees are 5,197 yards and rated 70.3. The slope rating is 130.

Play policy and fees: Green fees for Pebble Beach Resort guests are $150. For other players, the fee is $200, including carts. Carts are $18 per rider for spectators. Players now have the option of carrying their own bag. Caddies are available.

Location: From Highway 1, take the Pebble Beach exit and drive to the Pebble Beach Resort gate for instructions and a map.

Course description: Designed by Jack Neville in 1919, this is one of the most scenic and demanding courses in the world. Eight holes flank the ocean, placing the entire course under the influence of fog, mist and wind. The par-5 18th hole is considered by many to be the finest finishing hole in golf. Used regularly for the AT&T Pebble Beach Pro-Am (formerly the Bing Crosby Pro-Am), the course was the site of the 1972, and 1982 U.S. Opens, and will be again in 1992; the 1977 PGA Championship; and the 1929, 1947 and 1961 U.S. Amateur. The course is best remembered for Tom Watson's dramatic victory in the 1982 Open. Tied with Jack Nicklaus, Watson holed a chip shot for a birdie at the par-3 17th hole ("the shot that was heard around the world"), then birdied the picturesque but demanding 18th. (See related stories on pages 13 and 16.)

MONTEREY PENINSULA COUNTRY CLUB

Course 15
MAP F1 grid e4

1926
R.E. Baldock

PO Box 2090
Pebble Beach, CA 93953

3000 Club Road
Pebble Beach, CA 93953

Pro shop   (408) 372-8141

■ driving range
■ practice greens
■ power carts
■ pull carts
■ golf club rental
■ locker rooms
■ showers
□ executive course
□ accommodations
■ food and beverages
■ clubhouse

Mike Chapman
Professional

Bob Holmes
Operations Manager

Bob Zoller
Superintendent

Course information: This private facility has 36 holes. Par is 72 on the Dunes Course. Par is 71 on the Shore Course.

The Dunes Course is 6,505 yards and rated 70.9 from the championship tees, and 6,161 yards and rated 69.4 from the regular tees. The slope ratings are: 123 championship and 120 regular. Women's tees are 5,966 yards and rated 74.7. The slope rating is 129.

The Shore Course is 6,343 yards and rated 70.6 from the championship tees, and 6,155 yards and rated 69.7 from the regular tees. The slope ratings are: 125 championship and 123 regular. Women's tees are 5,935 yards and rated 74.4. The slope rating is 130.

Play policy and fees: Reciprocal play is not accepted. To play you must be sponsored or accompanied by a member. Guest fees are $30 when accompanied by a member and $115 without a member. Carts are $15 per player. Reservations are recommended 24 hours in advance. The dress code includes: no denims, no shorts, and skirts must be at least mid-knee in length.

Location: From Highway 1 in Monterey, take Highway 68/W.R. Holman (Pacific Grove exit). Take Highway 68/W.R. Holman to David Avenue. Turn left on David Avenue and drive less than a one-quarter of a mile. Turn right on Congress Avenue. Turn left at Forest Lodge Road and drive to the entrance gate of the 17 Mile Drive. Head south on Sloat Road and turn right on Club Road.

Course description: These meandering, scenic courses are flanked by pine trees and sand dunes. The greens are tricky and immaculate with a lot of undulation. Keep the ball below the hole. The picturesque Dunes Course is longer and situated farther inland. It was used for the Bing Crosby Pro-Am for 18 years. The Shore Course is shorter and tighter. Designed by R. E. Baldock, it flanks the ocean and is more exposed to the elements. The short par-5s are reachable in two for the long hitters.

CYPRESS POINT CLUB

1928
Alister MacKenzie

Course information: This private course has 18 holes and par is 72. The course is 6,536 yards and rated 72.3 from the championship tees, and 6,332 yards and rated 71.2 from the regular tees. The slope ratings are 134 championship and 130 regular. Women's tees are 5,816 yards and rated 73.9. The slope rating is 130.

Play policy and fees: Reciprocal play is not accepted. Members and guests only. Guest fees are $35 when accompanied by a member and $100 unaccompanied. Carts are $25.

Location: From Highway 1, take the Pacific Grove exit. At the first stop sign, drive to the Carmel Hill gate leading into Pebble Beach. Instructions and a map are given at the gate.

Course description: This spectacular course is the best-known work of the Scottish architect Alister Mac-Kenzie, who designed it in 1928. Flanked by sand and sea, the course makes the most of its natural resources. The greens are fast and undulating. The famous par-3 16th hole requires a 200-yard carry over the ocean and usually produces the highest per-hole stroke average on the PGA Tour. The shorter par-3 15th hole flanks the ocean and is one of the prettiest in the world. The club is exclusive. Members include Clint Eastwood and George Schultz. The course was used for the AT&T Pebble Beach National Pro-Am (formerly the Bing Crosby National Pro-Am) from 1947 to 1990.

PO Box 466
Pebble Beach, CA 93953

17 Mile Drive
Pebble Beach, CA 93953

Pro shop   (408) 624-2223

- ■ driving range
- ■ practice greens
- ■ power carts
- ■ pull carts
- ■ golf club rental
- ☐ locker rooms
- ☐ showers
- ☐ executive course
- ☐ accommodations
- ■ food and beverages
- ■ clubhouse

Jim Langley
Professional

Manuel Cardoza
Superintendent

CENTRAL F1

SPYGLASS HILL
GOLF COURSE

1966
Robert Trent Jones, Sr.

Course information: This semi-private course has 18 holes and par is 72. The course is 6,810 yards and rated 76.1 from the championship tees, and 6,277 yards and rated 73.1 from the regular tees. The slope ratings are: 141 championship and 135 regular. Women's tees are 5,556 yards and rated 72.8. The slope rating is 131.

Play policy and fees: Outside play is accepted. Green fees are $120 for NCGA members, $125 for non-members and $100 for Pebble Beach Resort guests (The Inn at Spanish Bay Inn or the Lodge at Pebble Beach). Carts are included in the fees. Resort guests may book 18 months ahead with the room reservations, and non-guests 60 days ahead.

Location: From Highway 1, take the Pebble Beach exit and drive to the Pebble Beach gate for instructions and a map.

Course description: This long, demanding course, designed by Robert Trent Jones, Sr. in 1966, can be unforgiving. Used annually for the AT&T Pebble Beach National Pro-Am, it almost always produces the highest scoring average. The first five holes wind through sand dunes and offer magnificent ocean views. It's surrounded by Monterey pines. The large, undulating greens are protected by ponds on three par-5s. The names given to each of the holes were derived from Robert Louis Stevenson's classic, *Treasure Island.* You'll find Treasure Island on the first hole (it's actually an island in the sand), Long John Silver on the 14th (a double dogleg par-5) and Black Dog on the 16th (an infamous par-4).

PO Box 658
Pebble Beach, CA 93953

Stevenson Drive and
Spyglass Hill
Pebble Beach, CA 93953

Pro shop   (408) 624-3811
Reservation (408) 624-6611
Golf Shop   (408) 625-8563

- ■ driving range
- ■ practice greens
- ■ power carts
- ☐ pull carts
- ■ golf club rental
- ☐ locker rooms
- ☐ showers
- ☐ executive course
- ■ accommodations
- ■ food and beverages
- ☐ clubhouse

Laird Small
Professional
Bill Davis
Superintendent

POPPY HILLS GOLF COURSE

1986
Robert Trent Jones, Jr.

Course information: This public course has 18 holes and par is 72. The course is 6,865 yards and rated 74.6 from the championship tees, and 6,288 yards and rated 71.7 from the regular tees. The slope ratings are: 141 championship and 134 regular. Women's tees are 5,433 yards and rated 71.8. The slope rating is 125.

Play policy and fees: Green fees are $35 for NCGA members and $60 for NCGA guests (limited to three per day), and $85 for nonmembers. Carts are $26. Reservations are recommended one month in advance on the corresponding date.

Location: From Highway 1, take the Pebble Beach exit and proceed to the Pebble Beach gate for instructions and a map.

Course description: Designed by Robert Trent Jones, Jr. in 1986, this course is long and tight with lots of trees, water and sand. The large, undulating greens are well guarded by bunkers and pot bunkers. Many of the greens are flanked by chipping areas, which give the player an option to chip or putt. On most holes, the option also exists to either play it safe or go for broke, especially on the par-5 ninth and 18th holes. This is the home of the Northern California Golf Association. There are numerous NCGA events held here throughout the year. This course became one of three in rotation for the annual AT&T Pebble Beach National Pro-Am in 1991. The other two courses are Pebble Beach Golf Links and Spyglass Hill Golf Course. The Men's NCAA Division I Championships were held here in 1991. It was also the site of the 1990 Spalding Invitation Pro-Am. The men's record of 66 is held jointly by John Cook and Larry Mize. Julie Inkster holds the women's course record of 67, set during the 1990 Spadling Invitational Pro-Am.

PO Box 1157
Pebble Beach, CA 93953

3200 Lopez on 17 Mile Drive
Pebble Beach, CA 93953

Pro shop   (408) 625-2154
Reservation (408) 625-2035

- ■ driving range
- ■ practice greens
- ■ power carts
- ■ pull carts
- ■ golf club rental
- ■ locker rooms
- ■ showers
- □ executive course
- □ accommodations
- ■ food and beverages
- ■ clubhouse

John Geertsen, Jr.
Professional

Kevin Orona
Manager

Manuel Sousa
Superintendent

CENTRAL F1

PACIFIC GROVE GOLF COURSE

Course information: This public course has 18 holes and par is 70. The course is 5,547 yards and rated 66.3 from the regular tees. The slope rating is 114. Women's tees are 5,553 yards and rated 71.8 from the championship tees, and 5,324 yards and rated 70.5 from the forward tees. The slope ratings are 117 championship and 114 forward.

Play policy and fees: Green fees are $17 Monday through Thursday, and $20 Friday through Sundays and holidays. Twilight rates after 4 p.m. are $10. Carts are $12. Reservations are recommended seven days in advance.

Location: From Highway 1 in Monterey, take Highway 68/W.R. Holman (Pacific Grove Highway) west. Turn right at Asilomar Avenue and follow it to the cemetery and lighthouse.

Course description: This tight, scenic oceanside course has a Scottish links-style flavor and is fun to play. The front nine weaves through the forest and is flanked by trees, while the back nine is bordered by sand dunes and ice plants. An old lighthouse stands guard over the course. Pacific Grove Golf Course used to be one of Monterey Peninsula's best kept secrets, but with an estimated 160,000 rounds nowadays played each year, you may want to make reservations.

77 Asilomar Boulevard
Pacific Grove, CA 93950

Pro shop   (408) 648-3177
Clubhouse (408) 648-3175

- ■ driving range
- ■ practice greens
- ■ power carts
- ■ pull carts
- ■ golf club rental
- □ locker rooms
- □ showers
- □ executive course
- □ accommodations
- ■ food and beverages
- ■ clubhouse

Peter Vitarisi
Professional

Dave Griffiths
Superintendent

OLD DEL MONTE
GOLF COURSE

1897
Charles Maud

Course information: This public course has 18 holes and par is 72. The course is 6,261 yards and rated 70.8 from the championship tees, and 6,007 yards and rated 69.5 from the regular tees. The slope ratings are 122 championship and 119 regular. Women's tees are 5,537 yards and rated 71.1. The slope rating is 118.

Play policy and fees: Hotel guest green fees are $37. Outside green fees are $40 Monday through Thursday and $45 Friday through Saturday. The course has special arrangements with hotels in the area and guests of those hotels (such as the adjacent Hyatt) get courtesy discount rates. Special discounts are available for residents also. Carts are $10 per rider Monday through Thursday, and $12 per rider Friday through Saturday.

Location: In Monterey heading south on Highway 1, take the central Monterey exit. At the first stoplight, go left on Camino Aguajito Road and go back under the highway. Turn left at Mark Thomas Drive which runs parallel to Highway 1 and turn right at Sylvan Road to the course. It's next to the Hyatt.

Course description: Considered the third oldest course west of the Mississippi, this course was built in 1897 as a nine-hole layout and expanded to 18 holes in 1901. It was reported in those early days of golf to be the first course in the world to have green fairways throughout the seasons. For this reason, perhaps, the course has been commonly thought of as the oldest course in the West. This inland course offers a meandering, hilly layout with lots of trees and tight doglegs. The short, but infuriating par-4, 18th hole looks simple to birdie, but will drive you crazy. This course plays host to the California State Amateur.

1300 Sylvan Road
Monterey, CA 93940

Pro shop   (408) 373-2436

☐ driving range
■ practice greens
■ power carts
■ pull carts
■ golf club rental
☐ locker rooms
☐ showers
☐ executive course
■ accommodations
■ food and beverages
■ clubhouse

Joe Holdridge
Professional

Pete Bibber
Superintendent

CENTRAL F1

LAGUNA SECA GOLF COURSE

1970
Robert Trent Jones, Sr.

Course information: This public course has 18 holes and par is 71. The course is 6,110 yards and rated 70.4 from the championship tees, and 5,711 yards and rated 68.5 from the regular tees. The slope ratings are 123 championship and 119 regular. Women's tees are 5,186 yards and rated 70.2. The slope rating is 119.

Play policy and fees: Green fees are $40 everyday. Twilight rates are $199 after 2 p.m. Carts are arts are $22. Reservations are recommended.

Location: On the east side of Monterey on Highway 68, exit north on York Road and drive to the end.

Course description: Designed by Robert Trent Jones, Sr., this challenging course has a number of elevated tees and greens. It's a sprawling course bordered by oak trees. There are lots of bunkers. It's known as "The Sunshine Golf Course" because it has some of the best weather in the area. Johnny Miller holds the course record with a 64.

10520 York Road
Monterey, CA 93940

Pro shop   (408) 373-3701

☐ driving range
■ practice greens
■ power carts
■ pull carts
■ golf club rental
■ locker rooms
■ showers
☐ executive course
☐ accommodations
■ food and beverages
■ clubhouse

Dian Murphy
Professional

Bob Costa
Executive Superintendent

John Kukawsky
Superintendent

U.S. NAVY GOLF COURSE

1962
Robert Muir Graves

Course information: This military course has 18 holes and par is 69. The course 5,574 yards and rated 67.4 from the regular tees. The slope rating is 116. Women's tees are 5,449 yards and rated 70.7 from the championship tees, and 5,195 yards and rated 69.3 from the forward tees. The slope ratings are 117 championship and 115 forward.

Play policy and fees: You must be accompanied by a member of the military to play. Green fees are $7 weekdays and $9 weekends. Guest green fees are $12 weekdays and $15 weekends. Carts are $6.50 for nine holes and $12.50 for 18 holes. Reservations are recommended 48 hours in advance for play on Fridays, Saturdays and Sundays. There is a dress code. No children under 8 years of age are permitted.

Location: From Highway 1 in Monterey, take the Casa Verde Way exit south to Fairgrounds Road.

Course description: This short, flat course has narrow fairways and lots of trees. Four lakes come into play. It has some of the best greens on the Monterey Peninsula. The men's course record here is 63, held by assistant professional Peter Niles. The women's course record is 70.

MWR Dept., Code 452
NPS Monterey, CA 93943

Mark Thomas Drive
and Garden Road
Monterey, CA 93943

Pro shop   (408) 646-2167
Clubhouse (408) 373-8118

■ driving range
■ practice greens
■ power carts
■ pull carts
■ golf club rental
☐ locker rooms
☐ showers
☐ executive course
☐ accommodations
■ food and beverages
■ clubhouse

Gene Newton
Manager/Professional

Daniel R. Tracy
Superintendent

FORT ORD GOLF COURSE

1953
Gen. Robert McClure

Box 40, McClure Way
Fort Ord, CA 93941

McClure Way
Fort Ord, CA

Pro shop   (408) 242-3268

Course information: This military facility has 36 holes. Par is 72 for both courses.

The Bayonet Course is 6,950 yards and rated 74.0 from the championship tees, and 6,577 yards and rated 72.1 from the regular tees. The slope ratings are 132 championship and 127 regular. Women's tees are 5,719 yards and rated 73.7. The slope rating is 134.

The Black Horse Course is 6,309 yards and rated 69.8 from the championship tees, and 6,040 yards and rated 68.4 from the regular tees. The slope ratings are 120 championship and 116 regular. Women's tees are 5,604 yards and rated 72.5. The slope rating is 129.

Play policy and fees: Guest fees are $25 weekdays and $30 weekends and holidays if sponsored by retired or active duty military personnel. Guest fees for non-sponsored guests are $50 weekdays and $60 weekends and holidays. The club is reciprocal with other Army facilities. Carts are $12 for military and $20 for civilians. Reservations are recommended seven days in advance for active duty personnel, six days in advance for retirees, and five days in advance for Department of Defense employees. Other guests may make reservations 48 hours in advance. No short shorts, rubber cleats or tank tops for men allowed.

- driving range
- practice greens
- power carts
- pull carts
- golf club rental
- locker rooms
- showers
- ☐ executive course
- ☐ accommodations
- food and beverages
- clubhouse

Doug Parker
Manager/Professional

Donald Frazier
Superintendent

Location: The main gate of Fort Ord is located on Highway 1 at Light Fighter Drive. Ask for directions at the gate. The course is located on McClure Way off North-South Road. You must show current vehicle insurance, license and registration to be admitted through the gate.

Course description: The Bayonet Course is long and difficult. The front nine is longer and more open and the back nine has several tight doglegs and tricky greens. It's used regularly for the PGA Tour qualifying school. The Black Horse Course is shorter and more forgiving. It has a meandering layout bordered by tall trees and bunkers. Both courses are located near the ocean and offer scenic views. They also can be foggy and windy. Nathaniel Crosby holds the Bayonet Course record for men with 66 and Julie Inkster holds the women's with 68. It's the site of the annual Patty Sheehan Invitational, hosted by San Jose State. The Women's NCAA Division I Championships were held here in 1991. Note: The clubhouse is being renovated and dinners will be served three nights a week.

CENTRAL F1

SALINAS FAIRWAYS
GOLF COURSE

Course information: This public links has 18 holes and par is 72. The course is 6,578 yards and rated 69.9 from the championship tees, and 6,347 yards and rated 68.8 from the regular tees. The slope ratings are 115 championship and 111 regular. Women's tees are 5,674 yards and rated 71.0. The slope rating is 115.

Play policy and fees: Green fees are $9 weekdays and $11.50 weekends for Salinas residents, and $10 weekdays and $12.50 weekends for non-residents. Twilight rates after 2:30 p.m. in the summer and 3:30 p.m. in the winter are $6.75 for residents and $7.50 for non-residents any day. Carts are $15. Reservations are recommended. This course has limited availability for tournaments.

Location: From Highway 101 in Salinas, exit on Airport Boulevard east and follow it until it dead ends at the airport. Turn left on Skyway Boulevard to the course.

Course description: This flat, tight course is well maintained, has lots of trees and is often windy. You can salvage par on this course because the greens are large and fair. The course is located next to the Salinas Airport.

PO Box 1201
Salinas, CA 93902

45 Skyway Boulevard
Salinas, CA 93905

Pro shop   (408) 758-7300

- ■ driving range
- ■ practice greens
- ■ power carts
- ■ pull carts
- ■ golf club rental
- ☐ locker rooms
- ☐ showers
- ☐ executive course
- ☐ accommodations
- ■ food and beverages
- ■ clubhouse

E.L. "Cotton" Kaiser
Professional

Glen Stubblefield
Professional

Roger Martinez
Superintendent

RANCHO CANADA
GOLF COURSE

1971
Robert Dean Putman

Course information: This public facility has 36 holes. Par is 71 on the East Course and 72 on the West Course.

The East Course is 6,118 yards and rated 69.2 from the championship tees, and 5,772 yards and rated 67.3 from the regular tees. The slope ratings are 114 championship and 111 regular. Women's tees are 5,279 yards and rated 69.5. The slope rating is 118.

The West Course is 6,306 yards and rated 70.6 from the championship tees, and 6,078 yards and rated 69.6 from the regular tees. The slope ratings are 122 championship and 120 regular. Women's tees are 5,574 yards and rated 71.6. The slope rating is 121.

Play policy and fees: Green fees are $48 until 3 p.m. and $24 after 3 p.m. There is a late twilight green fee of $10 after 5 p.m. during the summer season. Carts are $22. Reservations are recommended seven days in advance weekends and holidays, and up to 30 days in advance for weekdays. This course is available for outside tournaments.

Location: From Highway 1 in Carmel, take the Carmel Valley Road exit. Drive 1.5 miles east to the course.

Course description: These courses are short and tight with lots of trees. They offer excellent par-3 holes. The West Course is tougher with lots of mature pine trees. The Carmel River, although it does not always have water in it in dry years, comes into play on both courses. There are four lakes on the East Course. The 15th hole on the West Course may be the tightest par-4 you'll ever play. There's no shortage of conversation about this hole. This course hosted the 1991 Western Intercollegiate Championships, and annually hosts the Herman Edwards Benefit Tournament.

PO Box 22590
Carmel, CA 93922

Carmel Valley Road
Carmel, CA 93922

Pro shop   (408) 624-0111

- ■ driving range
- ■ practice greens
- ■ power carts
- ■ pull carts
- ■ golf club rental
- □ locker rooms
- □ showers
- □ executive course
- □ accommodations
- ■ food and beverages
- ■ clubhouse

Paul "Shim" LaGoy
Professional

Tim Greenwald
Superintendent

CENTRAL F1

THE GOLF CLUB AT QUAIL LODGE

1964
Robert Muir Graves

8000 Valley Greens Drive
Carmel, CA 93923

Pro shop   (408) 624-2770
Clubhouse   (408) 624-1581

- ■ driving range
- ■ practice greens
- ■ power carts
- □ pull carts
- ■ golf club rental
- ■ locker rooms
- ■ showers
- □ executive course
- ■ accommodations
- ■ food and beverages
- ■ clubhouse

Dan Weiss
Director of Golf

Denis Kerr
Superintendent

Course information: This private course has 18 holes and par is 71. The course is 6,515 yards and rated 71.9 from the championship tees, and 6,141 yards and rated 70.2 from the regular tees. The slope ratings are 126 championship and 122 regular. Women's tees are 5,572 yards and rated 72.0. The slope rating is 124.

Play policy and fees: Reciprocal play is accepted with members of other private clubs. Have your club pro call for arrangements. Guest fees are $95. Carts are included. Tee time reservations should be made six weeks in advance. Shirts with collars are required. Walking shorts are permitted, but no jeans, tank tops or hard rubber golf shoes may be worn.

Location: From Highway 1 in Carmel, take the Carmel Valley Road exit. Drive three miles to Valley Greens Drive. Turn right on Valley Greens Road and follow it to the course.

Course description: This is a five-star resort located in the beautiful Carmel Valley and flanked by ragged mountain vistas. Doris Day has a home overlooking this course. This scenic, hilly layout is notable for its fast greens, bunkers and water. A premium is placed on accuracy and shot placement. This course hosted the U.S. Golf Association Senior Amateur Championship in 1975, and the California Golf Association's 75th Amateur Championship in 1986. The men's course record is held by Lennie Clements, who shot 62 in the Spalding Pro-Am in 1988.

CARMEL VALLEY RANCH RESORT

1981
Pete Dye

1 Old Ranch Road
Carmel, CA 93923

Pro shop   (408) 626-2510

- ■ driving range
- ■ practice greens
- ■ power carts
- □ pull carts
- ■ golf club rental
- ■ locker rooms
- ■ showers
- □ executive course
- ■ accommodations
- ■ food and beverages
- ■ clubhouse

Ted Goin
Director of Golf

Mike Higuera
Superintendent

CENTRAL F1

Course information: This resort course has 18 holes and par is 70. The course is 6,088 yards and rated 70.1 from the championship tees, and 5,590 yards and rated 67.8 from the regular tees. The slope ratings are 124 championship and 119 regular. Women's tees are 5,542 yards and rated 72.6 from the championship tees, and 5,109 yards and rated 69.6 from the forward tees. The slope ratings are 143 championship and 135 forward.

Play policy and fees: Reciprocal play is accepted with members of other private clubs. The golf professional from the reciprocal course must call to make arrangements. Guest fees are $50 when accompanied by a member, $80 for hotel guests and $95 for unaccompanied guests (includes carts and range balls). Carts are mandatory. Golf attire is the only acceptable dress on the golf course. No blue jeans, tank tops or short shorts may be worn.

Location: From Highway 1 in Carmel, take the Carmel Valley Road exit and drive seven miles. Turn right on Robinson Canyon Road and left on Old Ranch Road.

Course description: This imaginative Pete Dye design features large greens, railroad ties and deep bunkers. Most holes are tight and unforgiving. The back nine is especially hilly and creative. The 14th hole is 90 yards wide with five distinct levels and an elevation change of at least 150 feet from top to bottom. Other elevation differences of up to 350 feet create interesting golf shots and spectacular views. The men's course record is 62.

MAP ON PAGE 258

CORRAL DE TIERRA COUNTRY CLUB

1959
R. E. Baldock

81 Corral de Tierra Road
Salinas, CA 93908

Pro shop   (408) 484-1325
Clubhouse (408) 484-1112

- ■ driving range
- ■ practice greens
- ■ power carts
- ■ pull carts
- ■ golf club rental
- ■ locker rooms
- ■ showers
- □ executive course
- □ accommodations
- ■ food and beverages
- ■ clubhouse

Gerry Greenfield
Professional

Grant Thompson
Superintendent

Course information: This private course has 18 holes and par is 72. The course is 6,537 yards and rated 71.4 from the tournament tees, 6,263 yards and rated 70.2 from the championship tees, and 6,072 yards and rated 68.7 from the regular tees. The slope ratings are 123 tournament, 120 championship and 115 regular. Women's tees are 6,263 yards and rated 75.5 from the championship tees, and 6,072 yards and rated 74.3 from the forward tees. The slope ratings are: 129 championship and 127 forward.

Play policy and fees: Reciprocal play is accepted with members of other private clubs on Thursdays and Fridays only. Guest fees are $30 when accompanied by a member and $60 when unaccompanied. Carts are $20. Reservations recommended one week in advance. No blue jeans may be worn. Closed Mondays.

Location: From Highway 68 between Salinas and Monterey, take the Corral de Tierra Road exit south. Drive three-fourths of a mile to the course.

Course description: This rolling, tree-lined course has undulating greens. Water comes into play on several holes. The par-4 first hole starts from a scenic, elevated tee. The par-5s are tight, but reachable in two for long hitters. The men's course record is 63 and the women's is 70.

CENTRAL F1

MAP F2
(6 COURSES)

PAGES.. 282-287

CEN-CAL MAP...see page 256
adjoining maps
NORTH (E2).......see page 220
EAST (F3)..........see page 288
SOUTH (G2)......see page 306
WEST (F1)..........see page 258

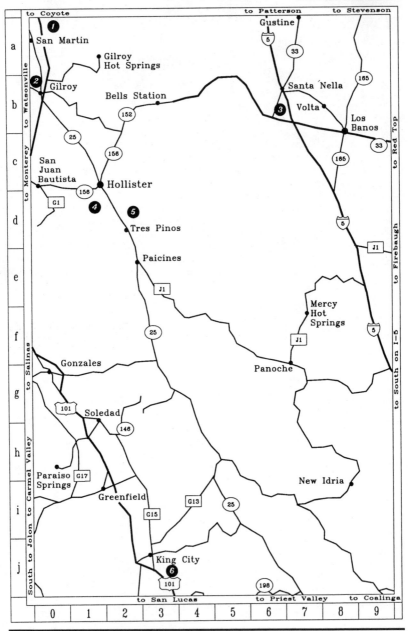

HILL COUNTRY GOLF COURSE

Course information: This public course has 18 holes and par is 58. The course is 3,110 yards and rated 52.0 from the regular tees. The slope rating is 81. Women's tees are 2,753 yards and rated 55.8. The slope rating is 81.

Play policy and fees: Green fees are $9 weekdays and $12 weekends and holidays. The seniors rate is $7 weekdays. Carts are $12. The pro shop closes daily at 2:30 p.m. weekdays, but the course is open. Check in at the restaurant bar. Play is first come, first-served. Reservations are recommended one week in advance for weekend play. This course is available for outside tournaments.

Location: From Highway 101 in Morgan Hill, exit at Tennant Avenue east. Drive to Foothill Avenue and turn right. The course is on the left.

Course description: Home of the "Flying Lady," this hilly course is mostly par-3s and a good test of the short game. The longest hole is the first one, a 368-yard par-4. This course can be played in under four hours. Water comes into play on half the holes at the green. There are two steep hills too, so stretch it out and enjoy yourself. Players only on the course.

PO Box 999
Morgan Hill, CA 95037

15060 Foothill Avenue
Morgan Hill, CA 95037

Pro shop (408) 779-4136
(408) 227-4607

☐ driving range
■ practice greens
■ power carts
■ pull carts
☐ golf club rental
☐ locker rooms
☐ showers
■ executive course
☐ accommodations
■ food and beverages
■ clubhouse

Jeannine Parshall
Manager

Irv Perch
Owner

Nick Altermirano
Superintendent

CENTRAL F2

GILROY GOLF COURSE

Course information: This public course has nine holes and par is 69 for 18 holes. The course is 5,947 yards and rated 67.8 from the regular tees. The slope rating is 109. Women's tees are 5,621 yards and rated 70.5. The slope rating is 112.

Play policy and fees: Green fees are $10 weekdays and $16 weekends and holidays. Twilight senior and junior rates are available. Reservations may be made seven days in advance. This course is available for outside tournaments.

Location: From Highway 101, drive two miles west on Hecker Pass Highway (Highway 152) in Gilroy. The course is on the right.

Course description: There are actually 11 holes on this course, changing the back nine into a different layout. This mature course is situated in oak-studded foothills. The terrain is rolling and hilly with tricky small greens. Panoramic views of the valley are available on the eighth and 17th holes.

2695 Hecker Pass Highway
Gilroy, CA 95020

Pro shop (408) 842-2501

■ driving range
■ practice greens
■ power carts
■ pull carts
■ golf club rental
☐ locker rooms
☐ showers
☐ executive course
☐ accommodations
■ food and beverages
■ clubhouse

Don DeLorenzo
Manager/Professional

Darren Marcus
Superintendent

FOREBAY GOLF COURSE

1964

Course information: This public course has nine holes. Par is 72 for 18 holes. The course is 6,519 yards and rated 69.7 for 18 holes from the regular tees. The slope rating is 105. Women's tees are 5,278 yards and rated 68.7 for 18 holes. The slope rating is 109.

Play policy and fees: Green fees are $7.50 for nine holes and $12 for 18 holes weekdays, and $9 for nine holes and $14 for 18 holes weekends. The senior rate is $6.50 for nine holes and $9 for 18 holes. Each Thursday is senior day and there is a special rate of $5.50 for nine holes and $7 for 18 holes. Carts are $8 for nine holes and $14 for 18 holes. Reservations are recommended one week in advance. This course is available for outside tournaments.

Location: In Santa Nella on Interstate 5, exit onto Highway 33 south. Turn right on Bayview Road and follow to the course.

Course description: This is a flat course with new trees and a creek. The testy, 424-yard, par-4 ninth hole requires a second shot carry over the creek.

PO Box 703
Santa Nella, CA 95322

29500 Bayview Road
Santa Nella, CA 95322

Pro shop   (209) 826-3637

- ■ driving range
- ■ practice greens
- ■ power carts
- ■ pull carts
- ■ golf club rental
- ☐ locker rooms
- ☐ showers
- ☐ executive course
- ☐ accommodations
- ■ food and beverages
- ☐ clubhouse

Greg Arnaudo
Owner

"Titi" Willington
Manager

RIDGEMARK GOLF AND COUNTRY CLUB

1972
Richard Bigler

3800 Airline Highway
Hollister, CA 95023

Pro shop   (408) 637-1010
Clubhouse (408) 637-8151

- ■ driving range
- ■ practice greens
- ■ power carts
- ■ pull carts
- ■ golf club rental
- ☐ locker rooms
- ☐ showers
- ☐ executive course
- ■ accommodations
- ■ food and beverages
- ■ clubhouse

Jim Prusa
General Manager

Kathy Wake
Professional

Rick Key
Superintendent

CENTRAL F2

Course information: This semi-private facility has 36 holes. Par is 72 on both courses.

The Diablo Course is 6,603 yards and rated 72.4 from the championship tees, and 6,032 yards and rated 69.8 from the regular tees. The slope ratings are 127 championship and 121 regular. Women's tees are 5,427 yards and rated 70.5. The slope rating is 110.

The Gabilan Course is 6,771 yards and rated 70.9 from the championship tees, and 6,271 yards and rated 68.6 from the regular tees. The slope ratings are 114 championship and 109 regular. Women's tees are 5,670 yards and rated 70.8. The slope rating is 110.

Play policy and fees: Outside play is accepted. Green fees are $25 Monday through Thursday, and $30 Fridays, weekends and holidays. Twilight rates are available. Carts are $20 and mandatory until 3 p.m. Tee time reservations should be made one week in advance. Every other day one of the two courses is open to public play. These courses are available for outside tournaments.

Location: From Highway 101 south, take the Highway 25 exit south of Gilroy and drive 13 miles on Highway 25 to Hollister. The course is located five miles south of Hollister.

Course description: These rolling, hilly courses have large, contoured greens. The Diablo Course is steeper and requires more placement. It's slightly shorter than the Gabilan Course and also has many more water hazards. The Gabilan Course is flatter and less deceptive. Wind is often a factor, as is frequent out-of-bounds.

MAP ON PAGE 282

285

BOLADO PARK GOLF COURSE

Course information: This public course has nine holes and par is 70 for 18 holes. The course is 5,986 yards and rated 67.6 for 18 holes from the regular tees. The slope rating is 110. Women's tees are 5,636 yards and rated 70.7. The slope rating is 114.

Play policy and fees: Green fees are $8 weekdays and $12 weekends. Carts are $9 for nine holes and $18 for $18 holes. Play is on a first-come first-served basis.

Location: This course is located five miles south of Hollister on Highway 25/Airline Highway in Tres Pinos.

Course description: This flat course has well-maintained greens. In fact, Senior PGA Tour pro George Archer uses these greens for practice.

PO Box 419
Tres Pinos, CA 95075

7777 Airline Highway 25
Tres Pinos, CA 95075

Pro shop   (408) 628-9995

■ driving range
■ practice greens
■ power carts
■ pull carts
□ golf club rental
■ locker rooms
□ showers
□ executive course
□ accommodations
■ food and beverages
■ clubhouse

Bob Trevino
Manager

Sal Hernandez
Superintendent

KING CITY GOLF COURSE

Course information: This public course has nine holes. Par is 70 for 18 holes. The course is 5,664 yards and rated 66.4 for 18 holes from the regular tees. The slope rating is 107. Women's tees are 5,192 yards and rated 68.3. The slope rating is 110.

Play policy and fees: Green fees are $8 for nine holes and $12 for 18 holes on weekdays, and $9 for nine holes and $14 for 18 holes on weekends and holidays. Twilight rates are $5 for nine holes and $8 for 18 holes after 2 p.m. Tee time reservations should be made one week in advance. This course is available for outside tournaments.

Location: From Highway 101 in King City, take the Canal Street exit. Turn right on Division Street. At the second stop sign, turn right on South Vanderhurst and drive to the course.

Course description: Robert Dean Putman redesigned this course in 1976. This flat, short course has small, tricky greens and tree-lined fairways. A creek meanders through the terrain and comes into play on four holes. It's well-conditioned. The men's course record is 62, set in 1984 by then-amateur Mark Pumphrey. The women's course record is 72.

613 South Vanderhurst
King City, CA 93930

Pro shop   (408) 385-4546

■ driving range
■ practice greens
■ power carts
■ pull carts
■ golf club rental
□ locker rooms
□ showers
□ executive course
□ accommodations
■ food and beverages
■ clubhouse

Jon Olson
Professional/Superintendent

Mark Pumphrey
Professional

MAP F3
(6 COURSES)

PAGES.. 288-293

CEN-CAL MAP ...see page 256
adjoining maps
NORTH (E3) ....see page 238
EAST (F4) ....see page 294
SOUTH (G3) ....see page 312
WEST (F2) ....see page 282

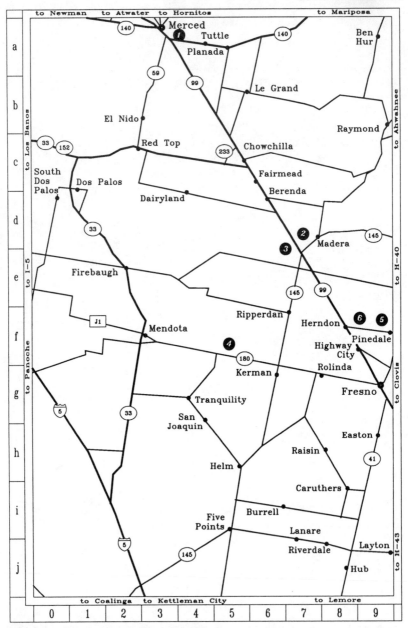

MERCED GOLF AND COUNTRY CLUB

Course 1
MAP F3 grid a3

1961
R.E. Baldock

6333 North Golf Road
Merced, CA 95340

Pro shop   (209) 722-3357
Clubhouse   (209) 722-6268

■ driving range
■ practice greens
■ power carts
■ pull carts
■ golf club rental
■ locker rooms
■ showers
□ executive course
□ accommodations
■ food and beverages
■ clubhouse

Ed Leinenkugel
Professional

Harold Stone
Superintendent

Course information: This private club has 18 holes and par is 72. The course is 6,433 yards and rated 70.4 from the championship tees, and 6,156 yards and rated 69.1 from the regular tees. The slope ratings are 119 championship and 117 regular. Women's tees are 6,139 yards and rated 75.7 from the championship tees, and 5,722 yards and rated 73.0 from the forward tees. The slope ratings are 132 championship and 124 forward.

Play policy and fees: Reciprocal play is accepted with members of other private clubs. Green fees for reciprocators are $35. Guest fees are $25 accompanied by a member and $35 unaccompanied. Carts are $7 for nine holes and $14 for 18 holes.

Location: From Highway 99 in Merced, take "G" Street north. Follow it to Bellevue Road, turn right and then turn left onto North Golf Road.

Course description: Redesigned by Robert Dean Putman, this quiet valley course is short with rolling hills and lots of trees.

MADERA GOLF AND COUNTRY CLUB

Course 2
MAP F3 grid d7

1955
R.E. Baldock

Road 26 at Avenue 19
Madera, CA 93638

Pro shop   (209) 674-2682
Clubhouse   (209) 674-9132

■ driving range
■ practice greens
■ power carts
■ pull carts
■ golf club rental
■ locker rooms
■ showers
□ executive course
□ accommodations
■ food and beverages
■ clubhouse

Howard Roseen
Professional

Bob Stucky
Superintendent

Course information: This private course has 18 holes and par is 72. The course is 6,659 yards and rated 70.8 from the championship tees, and 6,460 yards and rated 69.9 from the regular tees. The slope ratings are 119 championship and 117 regular. Women's tees are 5,900 yards and rated 74.3. The slope rating is 128.

Play policy and fees: Reciprocal play is accepted with members of other private clubs. Green fees for reciprocators are $30. Guest fees are $15 accompanied by a member and $30 unaccompanied. Carts are $14.

Location: From Highway 99 in Madera, north of downtown, take the Avenue 17 exit east. Turn left onto County Road 26. The course is at Avenue 19.

Course description: This sporty course has lots of rolling hills. Tall eucalyptus trees come into play on the front nine, and maturing pine trees on the back nine. It's easily walkable.

CENTRAL F3

MADERA MUNICIPAL GOLF COURSE

1991
Robert Dean Putman

Course information: This public course has 18 holes. Par is 72. The course is 6,816 yards and rated 71.3 from the championship tees, and 6,350 yards and rated 69.1 from the regular tees. The slope ratings are 119 championship and 115 regular. Women's tees are 5,471 yards and rated 70.3. The slope rating is 112.

Play policy and fees: Green fees are $4.50 for nine holes and $9 for 18 holes weekdays, and $6 for nine holes and $12 for 18 holes weekends. The twilight rate is $6 weekdays and $8 weekends. Senior green fees are $6 and carts are reduced $3 weekdays only with the purchase of an annual discount card. Carts are $16. Reservations are recommended seven days in advance.

Location: From Highway 99 north of Madera, take the Avenue 17 exit and follow it west one mile to the course.

Course description: Robert Dean Putman tested his course on opening day, June 8, 1991, and shot a 68. Graciously, Putman has designed a course with wide appeal. Both low and high handicappers will enjoy this course. The greens are large and undulating, and well bunkered. "Getting down in two on some holes will be a major accomplishment and three or four putt greens may not be that rare for some," reported Paul Bittick, *Madera Tribune* sports editor. The fairways are bunkered, too, and four lakes come into play on eight holes.

23200 Avenue 17
Madera, CA 93637

Pro shop   (209) 675-3504
Clubhouse (209) 675-3533

- ■ driving range
- ■ practice greens
- ■ power carts
- ■ pull carts
- ■ golf club rental
- □ locker rooms
- □ showers
- □ executive course
- □ accommodations
- ■ food and beverages
- ■ clubhouse

Robert Fernandez
Professional

Mark Goodmanson
Superintendent

FRESNO WEST GOLF COURSE

Course 4
MAP F3 grid f5

1966
R.E. Baldock

23986 West Whitesbridge Road
Kerman, CA 93630

Pro shop   (209) 846-8655

Course information: This public course has 18 holes and par is 72. The course is 6,959 yards and rated 72.4 from the championship tees, and 6,607 yards and rated 70.6 from the regular tees. The slope ratings are 118 championship and 114 regular. Women's tees are 6,000 yards and rated 74.1. The slope rating is 122.

Play policy and fees: Green fees are $12 weekdays and $14 weekends. Carts are $10 for nine holes and $20 for 18 holes. Reservations are recommended one week in advance. This course is available for outside tournaments.

Location: From Highway 99 in Fresno, take the Highway 180/Whitesbridge Road exit. Drive past Kerman to the course.

Course description: This is a very quiet, championship golf course. It's long, flat and often windy. There's water on eight holes. If you want to prove yourself a golfer make par on the eighth. It's a 174-yard par-3 with water to the left and behind the green.

■ driving range
■ practice greens
■ power carts
■ pull carts
■ golf club rental
□ locker rooms
□ showers
□ executive course
□ accommodations
■ food and beverages
■ clubhouse

Ron Goering
Manager/Professional

Carlos Rodriguez
Superintendent

CENTRAL F3

FIG GARDEN GOLF COURSE

Course 5
MAP F3 grid f9

1958
Nick Lombardo

7700 North Van Ness Boulevard
Fresno, CA 93711

Pro shop   (209) 439-2928

Course information: This semi-private course has 18 holes and par is 72. The course is 6,596 yards and rated 70.6 from the championship tees, and 6,205 yards and rated 68.7 from the regular tees. The slope rating are 117 championship and 113 regular. Women's tees are 5,753 yards and rated 72.2. The slope rating is 127.

Play policy and fees: Outside play is accepted. Green fees are $23 every day. Twilight rates after 3 p.m. summer season and 1 p.m. winter season are $10. Carts are $22 for 18 holes. Reservations are recommended. This course is available for outside tournaments. Call a year ahead.

Location: Heading south toward Fresno on Highway 99, take the Herndon exit east. Turn left on North Van Ness Boulevard and drive to the course.

Course description: Robert Dean Putman redesigned this course in 1973. It's a tight course and has two lakes and a river for a bonus. The greens are small and fast. The 465-yard, par-4 16th hole is a monster with the river flanking the left side.

■ driving range
■ practice greens
■ power carts
□ pull carts
■ golf club rental
■ locker rooms
□ showers
□ executive course
□ accommodations
■ food and beverages
■ clubhouse

Gary Bauer
Professional

Dave Knott
Superintendent

SAN JOAQUIN VALLEY COUNTRY CLUB

1961
Robert Dean Putman

Course information: This private course has 18 holes and par is 72. The course is 6,879 yards and rated 73.3 from the tournament tees, 6,504 yards and rated 71.6 from the championship tees, and 6,214 yards and rated 70.0 from the regular tees. The slope ratings are 128 tournament, 125 championship and 120 regular. Women's tees are 5,810 yards and rated 73.4. The slope rating is 128.

Play policy and fees: Reciprocal play is accepted with members of other private clubs. Guest fees are $25 with a member and $50 for reciprocal players. Carts are $9 per person.

Location: From Highway 99 in Herndon, take the West Herndon Avenue exit. Drive East to North Marks Avenue and turn left. Then turn right on West Bluff and continue to the course.

Course description: This is a long, rolling course with lots of trees. The San Joaquin River comes into play on the north side on three holes. The highlight here is the well-maintained greens, which are fast and tricky. The men's course record is 63, held by Mike Barr, and the women's course record is 67, held by Kathleen Scrivner.

3484 West Bluff Avenue
Fresno, CA 93711

Pro shop   (209) 439-3359
Clubhouse (209) 439-3483

■ driving range
■ practice greens
■ power carts
■ pull carts
□ golf club rental
■ locker rooms
■ showers
□ executive course
□ accommodations
■ food and beverages
■ clubhouse

Terry Treece
Professional

Mike Paniccia
Director of Golf

Owen Stone
Superintendent

MAP F4
(15 COURSES)

PAGES.. 294-303

CEN-CAL MAP ...see page 256
adjoining maps
NORTH (E4) ....see page 248
EAST (F5) ....see page 304
SOUTH (G4) ......see page 316
WEST (F3) ....see page 288

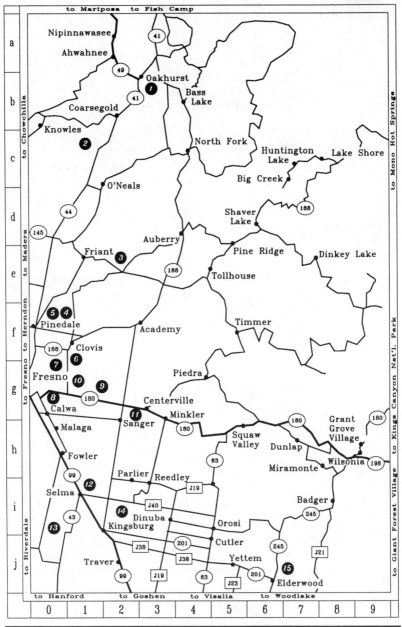

SIERRA SKY RANCH GOLF COURSE

Course information: This resort course has nine holes. Par is 70 for 18 holes. The course is 5,944 yards and rated 68.0 for 18 holes from the regular tees. The slope rating is 113. Women's tees are 5,552 yards and rated 69.4. Slope rating is 113.

Play policy and fees: Green fees are $6 for nine holes and $10 for 18 holes. Carts are $7 weekdays and $14 weekends. Reservations are recommended one day in advance. This course is available for outside tournaments.

Location: Driving north on Highway 41 to Oakhurst, take County Road 632 to the course.

Course description: This course dates back about 70 years, and was redesigned in 1951 by R.E. Baldock. A short course, it was built on a ranch and winds around Lewis Creek. The 3,000-foot elevation provides the golfer with a little extra yardage.

50556 Road 632
Oakhurst, CA 93644

Pro shop (209) 683-7433

- ■ driving range
- ■ practice greens
- ■ power carts
- ■ pull carts
- ■ golf club rental
- □ locker rooms
- □ showers
- □ executive course
- □ accommodations
- □ food and beverages
- □ clubhouse

Tom Godman
Professional/Manager/
Superintendent

CENTRAL F4

YOSEMITE LAKES PARK GOLF COURSE

Buck Noonkester

Course information: This private course has nine holes. Par is 62 for 18 holes. The course is 3,534 yards and rated 56.6 from the regular tees. The slope rating is 90. Women's tees are 3,009 yards and rated 57.1. The slope rating is 85.

Play policy and fees: Reciprocal play is accepted with members of other private clubs. Guest fees are $8. Carts are $9. Play is on a first-come first-served basis.

Location: Driving toward Yosemite National Park on Highway 41 before Coarsegold, turn left on Yosemite Springs Parkway. Drive four miles to the course.

Course description: This is a fun, short course. Hills and water come into play on five holes. The fairways are narrow and the course can be unforgiving unless the ball is kept in the air. Don't expect this to be an easy stroll in the park.

30250 Yosemite Springs Parkway
Coarsegold, CA 93614

Pro shop (209) 658-7468
Clubhouse (209) 658-7466

- □ driving range
- ■ practice greens
- ■ power carts
- ■ pull carts
- ■ golf club rental
- □ locker rooms
- □ showers
- ■ executive course
- □ accommodations
- ■ food and beverages
- ■ clubhouse

Karen Swagger
Manager
Buck Noonkester
Superintendent

MAP ON PAGE 294

BRIGHTON CREST
COUNTRY CLUB

1990
Johnny Miller

Course information: This private course has 18 holes. Par is 72. The course is 6,831 yards and rated 73.5 from the tournament tees, and 6,363 yards and rated 71.4 from the championship tees, and 5,917 yards and rated 69.4 from the regular tees. The slope ratings are 135 tournament, 131 championship and 126 regular. Women's tees are 5,195 yards and are in the process of being rated.

Play policy and fees: Outside play is accepted. Members and guests only. Reciprocal play is accepted with members of other private clubs at a reduced rate. Have your club pro call for arrangements. Outside green fees are $60. Green fees for guests accompanied by a member are $35 and $50 when unaccompanied. Carts are $10 per person for 18 holes. Reservations are recommended. This course is available for outside tournaments.

Location: From Fresno take Highway 41 north to the Friant Road/Millerton Lake exit. Drive east on Friant Road for 15 miles to Friant and the course.

PO Box 25281
Fresno, CA 93729-5281

21722 Fairway Oaks Lane
Friant, CA 93626

Pro shop   (209) 299-8586
Clubhouse (209) 323-8076

- ■ driving range
- ■ practice greens
- ■ power carts
- □ pull carts
- □ golf club rental
- □ locker rooms
- □ showers
- □ executive course
- □ accommodations
- ■ food and beverages
- ■ clubhouse

Ron Winsell
Professional

Mike Leach
Superintendent

Course description: This is the first Johnny Miller-designed course in California. It opened for play in September, 1990. The course features bent grass tees and greens. The fairways are rye and the roughs are fescue. At the 800-foot elevation the course is normally above the winter fog level and is also somewhat cooler during the summer months. The terrain is rolling and the course is dotted with native blue and valley oaks. *Golf Digest* has rated this course one of top 25 new courses in the country. The greens, which Miller has sized to fit the difficulty of the hole, are subtle but undulating. Miller has humanely left ample room for pin placement. When you reach the green you should still be able to survive the hole. One of Miller's favorite holes is the par-5, 505-yard number three. There is a slight dogleg right and the second shot must go between two oaks. There is a lateral hazard the entire left side, but until homes are built, the right side is clear. Water runs in front of the two-tiered small green. Watch out for native grasses off the fairway and the fescue rough. At 18 months old, the course looked like it had already been there for 50 years because of the terrain and large oaks. The unofficial men's course record is 66, held jointly by host pro Ron Winsell and former PGA Tour pro Forrest Fezler.

RIVERSIDE OF FRESNO GOLF COURSE

Course 4
MAP F4 grid f0

1939

Course information: This public course has 18 holes and par is 72. The course is 6,621 yards and rated 70.3 from the championship tees, and 6,395 yards and rated 68.9 from the regular tees. The slope ratings are 116 championship and 114 regular. Women's tees are 6,167 yards and rated 74.1. The slope rating is 124.

Play policy and fees: Green fees are $8.75 weekdays and $9.75 weekends and holidays. Carts are $10 for nine holes and $18 for 16 holes. Reservations are recommended one week in advance. This course is available for outside tournaments.

Location: From Highway 99 in Fresno, exit onto Herndon Avenue east. Cross the railroad tracks and turn left on Van Buren, then turn right on Josephine and follow it to the course.

Course description: This rolling course is long and well guarded by trees. It's testy with a number of sidehill lies to medium-sized greens. Bring every club. Notable is the 10th hole, which tees off from a bluff, hitting to a green guarded on the right by an overhanging tree. The hole is 425 yards and par-4.

7672 N. Josephine Avenue
Fresno, CA 93711

Pro shop   (209) 275-5900
Clubhouse   (209) 275-6515

■ driving range
■ practice greens
■ power carts
■ pull carts
■ golf club rental
□ locker rooms
□ showers
□ executive course
□ accommodations
■ food and beverages
■ clubhouse

Mike Catanesi
Professional

Gary Rogers
Superintendent

CENTRAL F4

FORT WASHINGTON GOLF AND COUNTRY CLUB

Course 5
MAP F4 grid f0

1925
William "Willie" Watson

Course information: This private course has 18 holes and par is 72. The course is 6,635 yards and rated 71.6 from the championship tees, and 6,446 yards and rated 70.4 from the regular tees. The slope ratings are 124 championship and 121 regular. Women's tees are 6,091 yards and 74.7. The slope rating is 129.

Play policy and fees: Reciprocal play is accepted with members of other private clubs. Guest fees are $20 with a member and $35 without, and $75 if you are from out of the area. Carts are $8.

Location: From Highway 99 in Fresno, take the Herndon Avenue exit east. Turn left on Blackstone Avenue. Turn right on Friant Road and then turn right again on Fort Washington which leads to the course.

Course description: This is a classic valley course. It was rated among the top 20 courses in Northern California in 1989. There are rolling hills, tree-lined fairways and fast, undulating greens. It's walkable. The Pro-Scratch is played here annually in May.

10272 North Millbrook Avenue
Fresno, CA 93720

Pro shop   (209) 434-9120
Clubhouse   (209) 434-1702

■ driving range
■ practice greens
■ power carts
□ pull carts
□ golf club rental
■ locker rooms
■ showers
□ executive course
□ accommodations
■ food and beverages
■ clubhouse

Michael S. Mattingly
Professional

Paul Ludington
Superintendent

VILLAGE GREEN GOLF COURSE

1 9 5 9
Robert Dean Putman

222 South Clovis Avenue
Fresno, CA 93727

Pro shop   (209) 255-2786
Clubhouse   (209) 255-9030

Course information: This public course has nine holes and par is 60 for 18 holes. The course is 3,429 yards and rated 56.8 from the regular tees. The slope rating is 87. All play is from the same tees.

Play policy and fees: Green fees are $5 for nine holes and $7 for 18 holes weekdays, and $6 for nine holes and $8 for 18 holes weekends. Carts are $7 for nine holes and $12 for 18 holes. Reservations are recommended. This course is available for outside tournaments.

Location: From Highway 99 in Fresno, take the Tulare Avenue exit east to Clovis Avenue. The course is in the Village Green Country Club apartment complex.

Course description: There are three par-4s and six par-3s on this course. All holes are well bunkered from tee to green and well maintained, with lots of trees. On hole seven, the ball carries over trees and a duck pond to the green. You can barely see the green. Try a five iron on this 157-yard, par-3 hole.

□ driving range
■ practice greens
■ power carts
■ pull carts
■ golf club rental
□ locker rooms
□ showers
□ executive course
■ accommodations
■ food and beverages
■ clubhouse

Gordon Israelsky, Jr.
Professional

Gerald Stone
Superintendent

PALM LAKES GOLF COURSE

5025 East Dakota
Fresno, CA 93727

Pro shop   (209) 292-1144

Course information: This public course has 18 holes and par is 62. The course is 4,150 yards and rated 60.7 from the regular tees. The slope rating is 100. Women's tees are 4,205 yards and rated 64.0. The slope rating is 97.

Play policy and fees: Green fees are $8 weekdays and $9 weekends and holidays. The rate for seniors $5.50 and students are $4.50. Carts are $7.50 for nine holes and $15 for 18 holes. Reservations are recommended. This course is available for outside tournaments.

Location: Driving south on Highway 99 from Madera, take the Shaw exit east past California State University Fresno. Turn right on Willow and then left at Dakota Avenue. The course is located across from the airport.

Course description: This short executive course has one large lake which comes into play on four holes. The course is about 20 years old, but was remodeled six years ago. It is walkable.

□ driving range
■ practice greens
■ power carts
■ pull carts
■ golf club rental
□ locker rooms
□ showers
■ executive course
□ accommodations
■ food and beverages
■ clubhouse

Jim Moore
Manager/Professional

Joe Woods
Superintendent

SUNNYSIDE COUNTRY CLUB

1906

Course information: This private club has 18 holes and par is 72. The course is 6,774 yards and rated 72.3 from the tournament tees, 6,438 yards and rated 70.4 from the championship tees, and 6,095 yards and rated 69.1 from the regular tees. The slope ratings are 126 tournament, 121 championship and 116 regular. Women's tees are 6,094 yards and rated 74.8 from the championship tees, and 5,539 yards and rated 71.8 from the forward tees. The slope ratings are 130 championship and 124 forward.

Play policy and fees: Reciprocal play is accepted with members of other private clubs. Have your club pro call for arrangements. Guest fees are $25 when accompanied by a member, and $50 when unaccompanied. Carts are $8 per person. No denim of any kind may be worn. Shorts must have a six-inch seam, and shirts must have collars.

Location: From Highway 99 in Fresno, take the Ventura Avenue/Kings Canyon Road exit east for seven miles to Clovis Avenue and turn left on East Butler to the course.

Course description: This long, demanding course has tight fairways and lots of sand and trees. Be careful of the greens: they look innocent enough, but they're small, fast and quite tricky. Originally built in 1906, William Park Bell redesigned the course in the 1940s. Kevin Sutherland holds the course record at 61. The women's record is owned by LPGA golfer Shelley Hamlin at 67. The USGA Junior Championship was played here in 1981. The United Express Pro-Scratch is the annual tournament played in early May.

5704 East Butler
Fresno, CA 93727

Pro shop   (209) 255-6871
Clubhouse   (209) 251-6011

- ■ driving range
- ■ practice greens
- ■ power carts
- ■ pull carts
- ■ golf club rental
- ■ locker rooms
- ■ showers
- □ executive course
- □ accommodations
- ■ food and beverages
- ■ clubhouse

Steve Menchinella
Professional

Al Korpak
Manager

Joe Tompkins
Superintendent

CENTRAL F4

BELMONT COUNTRY CLUB

Course information: This private course has 18 holes and par is 72. The course is 6,397 yards and rated 70.7 from the championship tees, and 6,234 yards and rated 69.7 from the regular tees. The slope ratings are 119 championship and 117 regular. Women's tees are 6,248 yards and rated 75.3 from the championship tees, and 5,989 yards and rated 73.8 from the forward tees. The slope ratings are 131 tournament, 130 championship and 127 forward.

Play policy and fees: Reciprocal play is accepted with members of other private clubs. Have your club pro call for arrangements. Guest fees are $20 when accompanied by a member and $30 unaccompanied weekdays, and $35 when accompanied by a member and $45 unaccompanied weekends. Carts are $8 for one person and $16 for two people. This course has limited availability for outside tournaments.

Location: In Fresno on Highway 99, take the Belmont Avenue exit east. Drive 13.5 miles to the course on the right.

Course description: This course was redesigned by Robert Dean Putman in 1985. It is a well-maintained course, short and tight with big greens and lots of trees. It's a good test of irons and short game.

8253 East Belmont
Fresno, CA 93727

Pro shop   (209) 251-5076
Clubhouse   (209) 251-5078

- ■ driving range
- ■ practice greens
- ■ power carts
- ■ pull carts
- ■ golf club rental
- ■ locker rooms
- ■ showers
- ☐ executive course
- ☐ accommodations
- ■ food and beverages
- ■ clubhouse

Mike Schy
Professional
Bill Griffith
Superintendent

FRESNO AIRWAYS GOLF COURSE

Course information: This public course has 18 holes and par is 68. The course is 5,194 yards and rated 63.7 from the regular tees. The slope rating is 104. Women's tees are 5,740 yards and rated 67.9. The slope rating is 110.

Play policy and fees: Green fees are $9 weekdays and $10 weekends. Carts are $17. Reservations are recommended. This course is available for outside tournaments.

Location: From Highway 99 in Fresno, exit on Belmont Avenue east and turn right on Clovis Avenue. Drive to East Shields Avenue and the course.

Course description: This flat, tree-lined course is short and sporty. It's a mature course and excellent for beginners and intermediate players.

5440 East Shields Avenue
Fresno, CA 93727

Pro shop   (209) 291-6254
Clubhouse   (209) 291-3162

- ■ driving range
- ■ practice greens
- ■ power carts
- ■ pull carts
- ■ golf club rental
- ☐ locker rooms
- ☐ showers
- ☐ executive course
- ☐ accommodations
- ■ food and beverages
- ■ clubhouse

Eric Thurston
Professional

SHERWOOD FOREST GOLF COURSE

Course 11
MAP F4 grid g3

1968
R.E. Baldock

79 North Frankwood Avenue
Sanger, CA 93657

Pro shop   (209) 787-2611

- ■ driving range
- ■ practice greens
- ■ power carts
- ■ pull carts
- ■ golf club rental
- □ locker rooms
- ■ showers
- □ executive course
- □ accommodations
- ■ food and beverages
- ■ clubhouse

Randy Hansen
Professional

Robert Tillema
Superintendent

Course information: This public course has 18 holes and par is 71. The course is 6,205 yards and rated 67.5 from the regular tees. The slope rating is 110. Women's tees are 5,605 yards and rated 70.5. The slope rating is 114.

Play policy and fees: Green fees are $12 Monday through Thursday, and $15 Fridays, weekends and holidays. Carts are $18. Reservations are recommended one week in advance. This course is available for outside tournaments.

Location: In Fresno on Highway 99, take Highway 180/Kings Canyon Road east 19 miles. Turn left on Frankwood Avenue. The course is on the left.

Course description: This scenic course runs along the Kings River and offers a view of the mountains on every hole. The course has trees on every hole. Only five holes are fairly open.

CENTRAL F4

SELMA VALLEY GOLF

Course 12
MAP F4 grid i1

1956
Robert Dean Putman

12389 East Rose Avenue
Selma, CA 93662

Pro shop   (209) 896-2424

- ■ driving range
- ■ practice greens
- ■ power carts
- ■ pull carts
- ■ golf club rental
- □ locker rooms
- □ showers
- □ executive course
- □ accommodations
- ■ food and beverages
- ■ clubhouse

Jerry Nikkel
Professional

Walt Short
Manager

Jack Lopez
Superintendent

Course information: This public course has 18 holes and par is 69. The course is 5,332 yards and rated 64.6 from the regular tees. The slope rating is 107. Women's tees are 5,280 yards and rated 69.6 from the championship tees, and 5,170 yards and rated 68.9 from the forward tees. The slope ratings are 119 championship and 117 forward.

Play policy and fees: Green fees are $9 weekdays and $12 weekends. Carts are $8 for nine holes and $14 for 18 holes. Reservations are recommended one week in advance. This course is available for outside tournaments. Dates are booked the second week in January for 1992.

Location: From Highway 99 in Selma (20 miles south of Fresno), exit onto Rose Avenue east. The course is 2.5 miles on the right.

Course description: This mostly flat course is short with many doglegs. Particularly good for beginning and intermediate players. It's a fast course to play. A round can be played in less than four hours on a weekend.

MAP ON PAGE 294

KINGS COUNTRY CLUB

Course information: This private course has 18 holes and par is 72. The course is 6,715 yards and rated 71.5 from the championship tees, and 6,423 yards and rated 70.1 from the regular tees. The slope ratings are 115 championship and 112 regular. Women's tees are 5,983 yards and rated 74.2. The slope rating is 126.

Play policy and fees: Reciprocal play is accepted with members of other private clubs. Green fees for reciprocators are $35 any day. Guest fees are $15 when accompanied by a member weekdays and $25 unaccompanied weekends. Carts are $14.

Location: Driving south on Highway 99 from Fresno, take the Highway 43 exit south and turn right at Dover Avenue. Drive two miles to 12th Avenue and turn right and follow it to the end.

Course description: This tough course plays longer than the yardage suggests. Towering oak trees and two lakes conspire against the golfer. Don't take the 628-yard, par-5 15th for granted. It may appear to be a dull straight-away stretch, but figure on using all the wood in your bag to eventually arrive at the green. Fortunately, it's a welcoming green. For those familiar with Fort Ord's Bayonet Course, this hole is reported to be reminiscent of the 13th there.

3529 12th Avenue
Hanford, CA 93230

Pro shop   (209) 582-0740
Clubhouse   (209) 582-2264

■ driving range
■ practice greens
■ power carts
■ pull carts
■ golf club rental
■ locker rooms
■ showers
□ executive course
□ accommodations
■ food and beverages
■ clubhouse

John Echols
Professional

Bob Dalton
Superintendent

KINGS RIVER GOLF AND COUNTRY CLUB

Course information: This private course has 18 holes and par is 72. The course is 6,678 yards and rated 71.5 from the championship tees, and 6,396 yards and rated 70.2 from the regular tees. The slope ratings are 122 championship and 119 regular. Women's tees are 6,431 yards and rated 76.4 from the championship tees, and 6,022 yards and rated 74.3 from the forward tees. The slope ratings are 135 championship and 130 forward.

Play policy and fees: Reciprocal play is accepted with members of other private clubs. Guest fees are $20 with a member and whatever your club charges guests without. Carts are $12. Closed Mondays.

Location: Located between Fresno and Visalia on Highway 99, take the Highway 201/Avenue 400 exit east over the Kings River to the course on the left.

Course description: This course is mostly flat and walkable. The Kings River borders the course. Robert Dean Putman redesigned the back nine of this course in 1957.

3100 Avenue 400
Kingsburg, CA 93631

Pro shop   (209) 897-2077
Clubhouse   (209) 897-5661

■ driving range
■ practice greens
■ power carts
■ pull carts
■ golf club rental
□ locker rooms
□ showers
□ executive course
□ accommodations
■ food and beverages
■ clubhouse

Charles Blanks
Professional

David Stone
Superintendent

OAK PATCH GOLF COURSE

Course information: This public course has nine holes and par is 56 for 18 holes. The course is 5,200 yards for 18 holes.

Play policy and fees: Green fees are $3.50 for nine holes and $7 for 18 holes, and $4 for nine holes and $8 for 18 holes weekends. Carts are $1.50

Location: From Visalia, drive seven miles east on Highway 198 to Ivanhoe. Turn off on County Road 156. Follow signs under the bridge, turning right after the bridge, and continue on to the course.

Course description: This is course has one par-4, the "toughest hole in the Valley," according to pro Harry Harrison, who gets the Nicest Pro Award. This hole is 240 yards and runs along the Kaweah River.

30400 Road 158
Visalia, CA 93291

Pro shop   (209) 733-5000

☐ driving range
■ practice greens
☐ power carts
■ pull carts
■ golf club rental
☐ locker rooms
☐ showers
■ executive course
☐ accommodations
■ food and beverages
■ clubhouse

Harry Harrison
Professional

CENTRAL F4

MAP F5
(1 COURSE)

PAGES.. 304-305

CEN-CAL MAP...see page 256
adjoining maps
NORTH (E5) ....see page 250
EAST ....no map
SOUTH (G5).......see page 326
WEST (F4).........see page 294

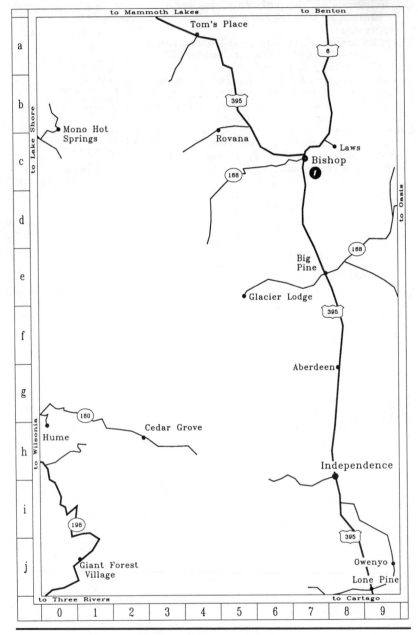

to Mammoth Lakes — to Benton

Tom's Place

6

395

Mono Hot
Springs

Rovana

Laws

Bishop
1

168

168

Big
Pine

Glacier Lodge

395

Aberdeen

180

Cedar Grove

Hume

Independence

198

395

Giant Forest
Village

Owenyo

Lone Pine

to Three Rivers — to Cartago

to Lake Shore

to Wilsonia

to Oasis

0 1 2 3 4 5 6 7 8 9

BISHOP COUNTRY CLUB

1952

Course information: This semi-private course has 18 holes and par is 71. The course is 6,661 yards and rated 70.9 from the championship tees, and 6,138 yards and rated 68.5 from the regular tees. The slope ratings are 122 championship and 118 regular. Women's tees are 5,459 and rated 70.2. The slope rating is 117.

Play policy and fees: Outside play is accepted. Reservations are recommended one week in advance. Green fees are $20 weekdays and $25 weekends. Carts are $18.

Location: Drive one mile south of Bishop on Highway 395.

Course description: The first nine opened for play in 1952, and the second nine opened in 1984. This difficult course has lots of trees and bunkers. Water hazards spice up every hole. Keep the ball out of the rough. This is a course that challenges accuracy.

PO Box 1586
Bishop, CA 93514

Highway 395 South
Bishop, CA 93514

Pro shop   (619) 873-5828

- ■ driving range
- ■ practice greens
- ■ power carts
- ■ pull carts
- ■ golf club rental
- □ locker rooms
- □ showers
- □ executive course
- □ accommodations
- ■ food and beverages
- ■ clubhouse

John Theilade, Jr.
Manager/Professional

CENTRAL F5

MAP G2
(7 COURSES)

PAGES.. 306-311

CEN-CAL MAP ...see page 256
adjoining maps
NORTH (F2) ....see page 282
EAST (G3) ....see page 312
SOUTH (H2) ....see page 332
WEST ....no map

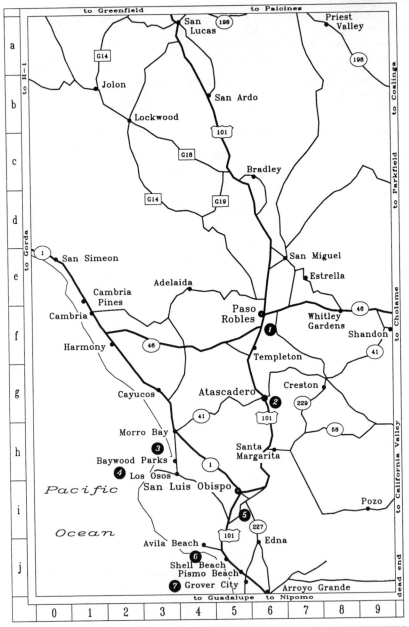

PASO ROBLES GOLF AND COUNTRY CLUB

Course information: This private course has 18 holes and par is 71. The course is 6,195 yards and rated 70.0 from the championship tees, and 6,015 yards and rated 69.2 from the regular tees. The slope ratings are 122 championship, 118 regular and 123 women.

Play policy and fees: Reciprocal play is accepted with members of other private clubs. Guest fees are $20. Carts are $20. Reservations are recommended. This course is available for outside tournaments. Men must wear shirts with collars. No tank tops, cut-offs or short shorts allowed. Bermuda length shorts are permitted.

Location: Travel 27 miles north of San Luis Obispo on Highway 101 to the Spring Street exit in Paso Robles. Turn right onto Niblick Bridge and drive to Country Club Drive.

Course description: Because of the relatively small membership of this club, daily play is light. This short course is very spotty and tight with seven lakes and lots of doglegs. It is a shot-maker's course. It takes a round or two to learn where to lay-up and where to go for it. Among the holes to watch for are number five, which is a sharp dogleg requiring a near perfect tee shot. The green is guarded by trees. The par-4 seventh hole is also a challenge with its huge tree in the center of the fairway. Former baseball great Sandy Koufax was a long-time club member. Annual tournaments include the Jack and Jill Invitational in June and the Member-Guest September Tournament. The Almond Blossom Ladies Invitational is held in February.

PO Box 2120
Paso Robles, CA 93447

1600 Country Club Drive
Paso Robles, CA 93447

Pro shop (805) 238-4722
Clubhouse (805) 238-4710

- ■ driving range
- ■ practice greens
- ■ power carts
- □ pull carts
- □ golf club rental
- □ locker rooms
- □ showers
- □ executive course
- □ accommodations
- ■ food and beverages
- □ clubhouse

Doug Joyner
Professional

Ben H. Swinney
Superintendent

CENTRAL G2

CHALK MOUNTAIN GOLF COURSE

Course information: This public course has 18 holes and par is 72. The course is 6,333 yards and rated 70.6 from the championship tees, and 6,026 yards and rated 68.6 from the regular tees. The slope ratings are 121 championship and 118 regular.

Play policy and fees: Green fees are $8 for nine holes and $12.50 for 18 holes weekdays, and $9.25 for nine holes and $14.50 for 18 holes weekends. Carts are $16. Reservations are recommended one day in advance weekdays, and three days in advance weekends.

Location: Off Highway 101 at the south end of Atascadero, exit at Santa Rosa Avenue heading east. Follow the Heilman Regional Park signs out El Camino Real and El Bordo Road to the course.

Course description: This is a short, narrow course set in the mountains among groves of oak trees. It's the kind of course you have to play before you can actually play it. Don't expect to score well on the first time out. A hole to watch: number four, 404 yards, par-4. Known as "Cardiac Hill," it plays straight up. You can see the green from the tee, which isn't much help. The hole is deceptive in its distance and the tendency is to hit too short. Be straight off the tee or you're in the woods looking for a path through the trees.

10,000 El Bordo Road
Atascadero, CA 93422

Pro shop   (805) 466-8848

- ■ driving range
- ■ practice greens
- ■ power carts
- ■ pull carts
- ■ golf club rental
- ☐ locker rooms
- ☐ showers
- ☐ executive course
- ☐ accommodations
- ■ food and beverages
- ☐ clubhouse

Gary Wishon
Professional
Bob Schneiderhan
Superintendent

MORRO BAY GOLF COURSE

1926

Course information: This public course has 18 holes and par is 71. The course is 6,113 yards and rated 69.1 from the regular tees. Women's tees are 5,727 yards and rated 72.3. The slope ratings are 116 regular and 118 women.

Play policy and fees: Green fees are $11.50 weekdays and $14 weekends. Senior rates are $6.50 Monday through Friday. Junior rates are $6.50 any day. Call for other special rates. Carts are $17. Make reservations one day in advance for weekdays, and three days in advance for weekends and holidays.

Location: North from San Luis Obispo, take Highway 101 and exit on Highway 1 to Morro Bay. Follow the Morro Bay State Park signs to the course.

Course description: This picturesque layout is located in the Morro Bay State Park and has ocean views from almost every hole. It's slightly hilly with tree-lined fairways. It is one of the busiest courses in the state and is referred to as "The Poor Man's Pebble Beach." Tricky greens are compared to Poppy Hills or Spyglass. To speed up play, most of the bunkers were removed in the 1960s. There are only four traps on the course.

State Park Road
Morro Bay, CA 93442

Pro shop   (805) 772-4560
Clubhouse (805) 772-4341

- ■ driving range
- ■ practice greens
- ■ power carts
- ■ pull carts
- ■ golf club rental
- ☐ locker rooms
- ☐ showers
- ☐ executive course
- ☐ accommodations
- ■ food and beverages
- ■ clubhouse

Wendy Hudler
Professional
Ray Festa
Superintendent

BEST WESTERN SEA PINES GOLF RESORT

1954

Course information: This public course has nine holes and par is 56 for 18 holes. The course is 2,728 yards.

Play policy and fees: Green fees are $6 weekdays and $7 weekends.

Location: Off Highway 101 in Los Osos, take the Los Osos Valley Road exit and drive west to the course which is about 11 miles from the highway. Take entrance to Montana de Oro State Park.

Course description: This well-maintained course has more than 200 trees lining the narrow fairways. Most are pine trees over 25 years old. The first fairway has been removed and relocated to make way for a parking lot so watch out for the new row of small connecting ponds along the left side of the fairway.

250 Howard Street
Los Osos, CA 93402

Pro shop   (805) 528-1788

- ■ driving range
- ■ practice greens
- ■ power carts
- ■ pull carts
- ■ golf club rental
- ■ locker rooms
- □ showers
- ■ executive course
- ■ accommodations
- ■ food and beverages
- □ clubhouse

Tauna Matheny
Professional

Ron Morril
Superintendent

CENTRAL G2

SAN LUIS OBISPO GOLF AND COUNTRY CLUB

1957

Course information: This private course has 18 holes and par is 72. The course is 6,858 yards and rated 74.2 from the tournament tees, 6,614 yards and rated 72.3 from the championship tees, and 6,390 yards and rated 70.0 from the regular tees. The slope ratings are 133 tournament, 128 championship and 122 regular. Women's tees are 5,919 yards. The slope rating is 123.

Play policy and fees: Reciprocal play is accepted with members of other private clubs. Members and guests only. Fees for reciprocators are $30 on weekdays and $40 on weekends. Carts are $15. Reservations for morning tee times are recommended.

Location: Take the Marsh Street exit off Highway 101 in San Luis Obispo and turn right. Travel to Broad Street (Highway 227) and turn right. Drive 4.5 miles to Los Ranchos Road, then right to Country Club Drive and right again to the club.

Course description: This rolling course along the central coast plays longer than it looks because of the lush fairways that provide little roll. Thick stands of pine trees line the fairways waiting for errant tee shots. The greens are protected by strategically placed bunkers. The back nine has completely new greens which are much faster and don't hold quite as well as the front nine. Play short onto the green to avoid overrunning. The greens are fairly flat.

255 Country Club Drive
San Luis Obispo, CA 93401

Pro shop   (805) 543-4035
Clubhouse (805) 543-3400

- ■ driving range
- ■ practice greens
- ■ power carts
- ■ pull carts
- ■ golf club rental
- ■ locker rooms
- ■ showers
- □ executive course
- □ accommodations
- ■ food and beverages
- ■ clubhouse

Scott Cartwright
Professional

Ron Thompson
Superintendent

MAP ON PAGE 306

309

SAN LUIS BAY RESORT

Course 6
MAP G2 grid j4

1968
Desmond Muirhead

PO Box 2140
Avila Beach, CA 93424

Pro shop   (805) 595-2307

- ■ driving range
- ■ practice greens
- ■ power carts
- ■ pull carts
- ■ golf club rental
- □ locker rooms
- □ showers
- □ executive course
- □ accommodations
- ■ food and beverages
- □ clubhouse

S. Scott Sickich
Professional

Peter Prentice
Superintendent

Course information: This public course has 18 holes and par is 71. The course is 6,443 yards and rated 70.9 from the championship tees, and 6,048 yards and rated 69.0 from the regular tees. The slope ratings are 122 championship and 116 regular. Women's tees are 5,116 yards and rated 68.2. The slope rating is 121.

Play policy and fees: Green fees are $17 weekdays and $22 weekends. Carts are $20. Reservations are recommended.

Location: Take the Avila Beach exit off Highway 101 north of Pismo Beach, and drive west for three miles to the entrance of the San Luis Bay Inn. Turn right and follow the signs to the club.

Course description: Situated in the heart of California's central coast, this course is both beautiful and challenging. The front nine is nestled in an oak-lined canyon bisected by a gentle flowing creek. Accuracy and club selection are important. The back nine calls for distance and placement as it traverses back and forth across San Luis Creek and a tidal lagoon. Some holes have been reworked, resulting in overall shorter, but insignificantly so, yardage.

PISMO STATE BEACH GOLF COURSE

Course 7
MAP G2 grid j5

1967

9 LeSage Drive
Grover City, CA 93433

Pro shop   (805) 481-5215

- □ driving range
- ■ practice greens
- □ power carts
- ■ pull carts
- ■ golf club rental
- □ locker rooms
- □ showers
- □ executive course
- ■ accommodations
- ■ food and beverages
- ■ clubhouse

Al Carlin
Professional

Course information: This public course has nine holes and par is 54 for 18 holes. The course is 2,795 yards for 18 holes.

Play policy and fees: Green fees are $4.75 weekdays and $5.25 weekends for nine holes. Weekday twilight rates after 4 p.m. are $4.50 and weekend twilight rates are $5. Call for special senior rates.

Location: On Highway 1 in Grover City, turn right on Grand Avenue toward the beach and follow to the course.

Course description: This flat course has water on seven holes, plus excellent ocean views. There are no sand traps. Monterey pines line the fairways, which play tough when the wind blows in March. This is a good course for beginners.

MAP G3
(2 COURSES)

PAGES.. 312-315

CEN-CAL MAP...see page 256
adjoining maps
NORTH (F3) ....see page 288
EAST (G4) ....see page 316
SOUTH (H3) .....see page 338
WEST ((G2) ....see page 306

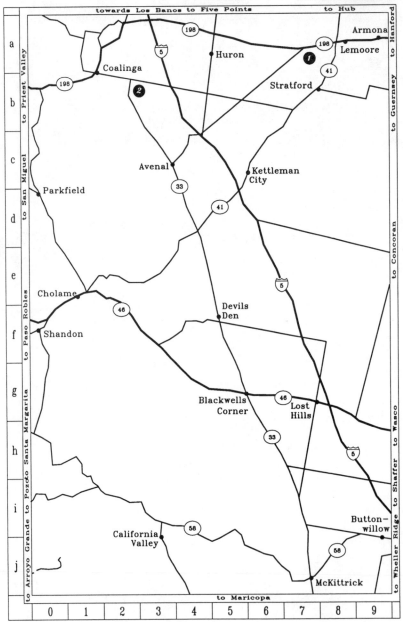

CENTRAL CALIFORNIA

Course information: This public course has nine holes. Par is 72 for 18 holes. The course is 6,134 yards and rated 68.3 from the regular tees (18 holes). The slope rating is 111. Women's tees are 5,180 yards and rated 68.3. The slope rating is 108. The course is expected to expand to a full 18 holes in April, 1992. The yardage will then increase to 6,472 yards and the course will be re-rated.

Play policy and fees: Green fees are $7 weekdays and $8.50 weekends. The twilight rate is $5.50 weekdays and $6 weekends. Carts are $14. Rates are subject to change when the course expands to a full 18 holes.

Location: From Highway 198 in Visalia, drive west to the Lemoore Naval Air Station/Lemoore Airport. The course is on the left.

Course description: This flat course is walkable with lots of trees. There are lakes and four par-5s. With the expansion of the course three new lakes have been added. There will be a new clubhouse and an enlarged pro shop. Note the new address; it's a 9-iron away from the old one on Lemoore Avenue.

350 West Ione
Lemoore, CA 93245

Pro shop   (209) 924-9658

- ■ driving range
- ■ practice greens
- ■ power carts
- ■ pull carts
- ■ golf club rental
- □ locker rooms
- □ showers
- □ executive course
- □ accommodations
- ■ food and beverages
- ■ clubhouse

Bill Holloway
Manager/Professional

Joe Bennitez
Superintendent

CENTRAL G3

POLVADERO GOLF AND COUNTRY CLUB

Course information: This public course has nine holes. Par is 72 for 18 holes. The course is 6,526 yards and rated 70.2 from the regular tees (18 holes). The slope rating is 115. Women's tees are 5,825 yards and rated 72.8. The slope rating is 122.

Play policy and fees: Green fees are $8 for nine holes and $10 for 18 holes weekdays, and $9 and $11 weekends. Carts are $7 for nine holes and $14 for 18 holes. Play is on a first-come first-served basis.

Location: From Interstate 5 by Coalinga, take the Jayne Avenue exit west to Sutter Avenue. Turn left and the course is on the right.

Course description: This hilly course is walkable. There are mature trees and two lakes coming into play on two holes. The course is a good exercise for players of all abilities.

41605 Sutter Avenue
Coalinga, CA 93210

Pro shop   (209) 935-3578

- ■ driving range
- ■ practice greens
- ■ power carts
- ■ pull carts
- ■ golf club rental
- ☐ locker rooms
- ☐ showers
- ☐ executive course
- ☐ accommodations
- ■ food and beverages
- ☐ clubhouse

Charles Hudson
Manager/Professional

MAP G4
(14 COURSES)

PAGES.. 316-325

CEN-CAL MAP...see page 256
adjoining maps
NORTH (F4) ....see page 294
EAST (G5) ....see page 326
SOUTH (H4) ....see page 350
WEST (G3) ....see page 312

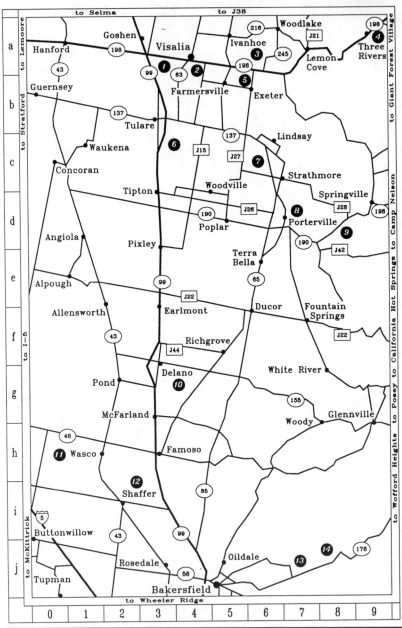

VALLEY OAKS GOLF COURSE

Richard Bigler

1800 South Plaza Drive
Visalia, CA 93277

Pro shop   (209) 651-1441
Clubhouse (209) 651-0840

- ■ driving range
- ■ practice greens
- ■ power carts
- ■ pull carts
- ■ golf club rental
- □ locker rooms
- □ showers
- □ executive course
- □ accommodations
- ■ food and beverages
- ■ clubhouse

Mike Roberson
Professional

Bill Rodriguez
Superintendent

Course information: This public course has 18 holes and par is 72. The course is 6,564 yards and rated 70.7 from the championship tees, and 6,278 yards and rated 69.4 from the regular tees. The slope ratings are 119 championship and 116 regular. Women's tees are 6,269 yards and rated 76.2 from the championship tees, and 5,776 yards and rated 73.0 from the forward tees. The slope ratings are 130 championship and 122 forward.

Play policy and fees: Green fees are $8 for nine holes and $10 for 18 holes weekdays, and $9 for nine holes and $12 for 18 holes weekends. Carts are $10 for nine holes and $16 for 18 holes. Weekday play is on a first-come first-served basis. Weekend reservations are taken the prior Thursday morning. This course is available for outside tournaments.

Location: In Visalia on Highway 99, take the Highway 198 turnoff east. Drive one mile and exit at the Holiday Inn. Continue to the course, located next to the airport.

Course description: Robert Dean Putman re-designed this layout in 1972. It is a flat course with trees and water, and features fast, large, well-maintained greens. Good putting is essential to scoring well. Course records are 61 at the regular tees, 63 (Ted Keanery) at the championship tees and 74 for women.

CENTRAL G4

SIERRA VIEW GOLF COURSE OF VISALIA

1959
Robert Dean Putman

12608 Avenue 264
Visalia, CA 93277

Pro shop   (209) 732-2078

- ■ driving range
- ■ practice greens
- ■ power carts
- ■ pull carts
- □ golf club rental
- ■ locker rooms
- □ showers
- □ executive course
- □ accommodations
- ■ food and beverages
- ■ clubhouse

Darrell Klassen
Professional

Course information: This public course has 18 holes and par is 72. The course is 6,388 yards and rated 68.9 from the championship tees, and 6,169 yards and rated 67.8 from the regular tees. The slope ratings are 107 championship and 105 regular. Women's tees are 5,892 yards and rated 71.6. The slope rating is 114.

Play policy and fees: Green fees are $7.50 for nine holes and $11 for 18 holes weekdays, and $9 and $12 weekends. Carts are $9 for nine holes and $16 for 18 holes. If you want a spot during the weekend, call at least a week in advance. This course is available for tournaments.

Location: On Highway 99 in south Visalia, take the Avenue 264 exit (Tagus exit) east. Continue down four miles to the course.

Course description: Situated in the San Joaquin Valley, this course has fast greens and lots of trees and bunkers. Mostly flat, the four par-5s measure under 500 yards and are easily reachable for long hitters.

VISALIA COUNTRY CLUB

1910

625 Ranch Road
Visalia, CA 93291

Pro shop (209) 734-1458
Clubhouse (209) 734-5871

- ■ driving range
- ■ practice greens
- ■ power carts
- ■ pull carts
- ■ golf club rental
- ■ locker rooms
- ■ showers
- □ executive course
- □ accommodations
- ■ food and beverages
- ■ clubhouse

Brad Stovall
Professional

Rick West
Superintendent

Course information: This private course has 18 holes and par is 72. The course is 6,673 yards and rated 72.0 from the tournament tees, 6,187 yards and rated 69.9 from the championship tees, and 5,438 yards and rated 67.2 from the regular tees. The slope ratings are 122 tournament, 117 championship and 112 regular. Women's tees are 5,824 yards and rated 73.4 from the championship tees, and 5,438 yards and rated 70.8 from the forward tees. The slope ratings are 130 championship and 122 forward.

Play policy and fees: Reciprocal play is accepted with members of other private clubs. Green fees are $15 with a member and $30 without, and $50 if you are from out of the area. Carts are $4 per rider for nine holes and $7 per rider for 18 holes. Reservations are recommended. Closed Mondays.

Location: From Highway 99, take the Visalia exit. Go three stoplights and turn left onto West Main and then left again on Ranch Road and follow it to the end.

Course description: The original nine holes were built in 1910 and Robert Dean Putman redesigned this course in 1960. This flat, open course has lots of trees and bunkers. There's water on eight holes. The greens are large and tricky.

THREE RIVERS GOLF COURSE

1962
Robert Dean Putman

PO Box 202
Three Rivers, CA 93271

41117 Sierra Drive
Three Rivers, CA 93271

Pro shop (209) 561-3133

- □ driving range
- □ practice greens
- ■ power carts
- ■ pull carts
- ■ golf club rental
- □ locker rooms
- □ showers
- □ executive course
- □ accommodations
- ■ food and beverages
- ■ clubhouse

Ken Pilcher
Manager

Kurt Gardiner
Superintendent

Course information: This public course has nine holes. Par is 70 for 18 holes. The course is 5,504 yards and rated 65.7 for 18 holes from the championship tees, and 5,262 yards and rated 64.6 from the regular tees. The slope ratings are 107 championship and 106 regular. Women's tees are 4,082 yards and rated 63.6 for 18 holes. The slope rating is 97.

Play policy and fees: Green fees are $7 for nine holes and $10 for 18 holes weekdays, and $9 for nine holes and $12 for 18 holes weekends and holidays. Carts are $9 for nine holes and $15 for 18 holes.

Location: From Highway 99 in Tulare take Highway 198 east through Visalia to Three Rivers. The course is next to the highway.

Course description: This course is semi-flat with sloping fairways and there are two ponds.

EXETER PUBLIC GOLF COURSE

Course 5
MAP G4 grid b6

1963
R.E. Baldock

510 West Visalia
Exeter, CA 93221

Pro shop   (209) 592-4783

- ■ driving range
- ■ practice greens
- ■ power carts
- ■ pull carts
- ■ golf club rental
- □ locker rooms
- □ showers
- ■ executive course
- □ accommodations
- ■ food and beverages
- ■ clubhouse

Steve Maaske
Professional/Superintendent

Dan Diel
Owner

Course information: This public course has nine holes and par is 60 for 18 holes. The course is 3,286 yards. The course is in the process of being rated.

Play policy and fees: Green fees are $3.50 for nine holes and $6.50 for 18 holes weekdays, and $4.50 and $8 weekends. Pull carts are $1.50. Power carts are $6 for nine holes and $10 for 18 holes. Reservations are recommended. This course is available for outside tournaments.

Location: From Highway 99 in Visalia, drive east on Highway 198 (toward Three Rivers). Turn right on Anderson Road (Highway 180). Follow it to Visalia Road and turn left to the course.

Course description: A lot of water comes into play on this tree-lined, mature course. Three of the holes are par-4s. The course is in excellent condition.

TULARE GOLF COURSE

Course 6
MAP G4 grid c3

1956
R.E. Baldock

5310 South Laspina
Tulare, CA 93274

Pro shop   (209) 686-9839
Clubhouse   (209) 686-0270

- ■ driving range
- ■ practice greens
- ■ power carts
- ■ pull carts
- ■ golf club rental
- ■ locker rooms
- ■ showers
- □ executive course
- □ accommodations
- ■ food and beverages
- ■ clubhouse

Dave Vogt
Professional

Kevin Friesen
Superintendent

Course information: This public course has 18 holes and par is 72. The course is 6,757 yards and rated 71.3 from the championship tees, and 6,557 yards and rated 70.4 from the regular tees. The slope ratings are 118 championship and 116 regular. Women's tees are 6,008 yards and rated 73.7 from the championship tees, and 5,672 yards and rated 71.6 from the forward tees. The slope ratings are 122 championship and 117 forward.

Play policy and fees: Green fees are $8 for nine holes and $12 for 18 holes weekdays, and $10 for nine holes and $15 for 18 holes weekends. Carts are $8 for nine holes and $14 for 18 holes. Weekend reservations are recommended the prior Tuesday morning. This course is available for tournaments.

Location: From Highway 99 in Tulare, head east on Avenue 200. Turn left on South Laspina. The course is on the right.

Course description: This course is mostly flat and open with several lakes. This is a course that plows its money back into the greens, fairways and irrigation system, and it shows in the yearly improvements. An estimated $500,000 was spent in the last two years on improvements.

LINDSAY MUNICIPAL GOLF COURSE

Course 7
MAP G4 grid c6

1961

Course information: This public course has nine holes. Par is 54 for 18 holes. The course is 2,180 yards for 18 holes.

Play policy and fees: Green fees are $2.50 for nine and $4.50 for 18 holes weekdays and $3 for nine holes and $5 for 18 holes weekends. Pull carts are $1.

Location: This course is located in the city park, eight blocks east of Highway 65 between Exeter and Porterville.

Course description: This is a short course that you can play twice. It's located in the Lindsay City Park. It's flat with lots of trees and small greens. It's a good course for beginners, seniors and players wanting to work on their irons.

Tulare and Elmwood
Lindsay, CA 93221

Pro shop   (209) 562-1144

☐ driving range
■ practice greens
☐ power carts
■ pull carts
■ golf club rental
☐ locker rooms
☐ showers
■ executive course
☐ accommodations
■ food and beverages
■ clubhouse

Bill Maaske
Manager/Superintendent

Steve Maaske
Professional

PORTERVILLE GOLF COURSE

Course 8
MAP G4 grid d7

1920

Course information: This public course has nine holes. Par is 70 for 18 holes. The course is 5,650 yards and rated 65.6 from the regular tees (18 holes). The slope rating is 103. Women's tees are 5,472 yards and rated 69.8. The slope rating is 117.

Play policy and fees: Green fees are $7 for nine holes and $11 for 18 holes weekdays, and $8 for nine holes and $12 for 18 holes weekends. Carts are $6 for nine holes and $12 for 18 holes. Play is on a first-come first-served basis. Closed Mondays.

Location: From Highway 99 south of Fresno, take the Highway 196 exit east. Then take Highway 65 into Porterville. Take Olive east and then a right on Piano. Take the first left and continue over the hill to the course.

Course description: This course is mostly flat and narrow with out-of-bounds on every hole. The greens are quite small.

702 East Isham Avenue
Porterville, CA 93257

Pro shop   (209) 784-9468

■ driving range
■ practice greens
■ power carts
■ pull carts
■ golf club rental
☐ locker rooms
☐ showers
☐ executive course
☐ accommodations
■ food and beverages
■ clubhouse

Arlie Morris
Professional

RIVER ISLAND
COUNTRY CLUB

C o u r s e   9
MAP G4 grid d8

1964
Robert Dean Putman

31989 River Island Drive
Porterville, CA 93257

Pro shop   (209) 784-9425
Clubhouse   (209) 781-2917

Course information: This private course has 18 holes and par is 72. The course is 7,027 yards and rated 74.1 from the championship tees, and 6,332 yards and rated 70.3 from the regular tees. The slope ratings are: 124 championship and 116 regular. Women's tees are 5,631 yards and rated 72.5. The slope rating is 128.

Play policy and fees: Reciprocal play is accepted with members of other private clubs. Guest fees are $25 with a member and $40 without. Carts are $8 per person. Reservations are recommended two weeks in advance.

Location: Take Highway 190 and drive past Porterville for 15 minutes. The entrance to this private country club resort course is on the right.

Course description: This long, sprawling course wanders through old oak trees and offers a variety of holes. The Tule River flows through the terrain. You cross the river 11 times, and it comes into play on nine holes. The course is walkable, but there is a lot of distance between holes.

- ■ driving range
- ■ practice greens
- ■ power carts
- □ pull carts
- ■ golf club rental
- ■ locker rooms
- ■ showers
- □ executive course
- ■ accommodations
- ■ food and beverages
- ■ clubhouse

Julius Aquino
Professional

Ruben Longoria
Superintendent

CENTRAL G4

DELANO PUBLIC
GOLF COURSE

C o u r s e   10
MAP G4 grid g4

1962

PO Box 608 Memorial Park
Delano, CA 93216

Pro shop   (805) 725-7527

Course information: This public course has nine holes. Par is 64 for 18 holes. The course is 4,384 yards and rated 58.8. The slope rating is 91.

Play policy and fees: Green fees are $6.50 weekdays and $8.50 weekends.

Location: Take Highway 99 north to Woodlands Avenue exit, head east to Lexington and take a left. Course is on the right.

Course description: This flat course offers undulating fairways. Ponds come into play on the first, eighth and ninth holes. Number three is a 219 yards par-3 with trees on left and right, making for tight play. Number four is a par-5, 501-yard challenge. This traditional course boasts numerous and huge eucalyptus trees along the fairways.

- ■ driving range
- ■ practice greens
- ■ power carts
- ■ pull carts
- ■ golf club rental
- □ locker rooms
- □ showers
- □ executive course
- □ accommodations
- ■ food and beverages
- ■ clubhouse

Jerry Lopez
Professional/Manager

Richard Felix
Superintendent

MAP ON PAGE 316

321

WASCO VALLEY ROSE GOLF COURSE

1991
Robert Dean Putman

301 North Leonard Avenue
Wasco, CA 93280

Pro shop   (805) 758-8301

■ driving range
■ practice greens
■ power carts
■ pull carts
■ golf club rental
□ locker rooms
□ showers
□ executive course
□ accommodations
■ food and beverages
■ clubhouse

Joe Haggerty
Professional

William Stone
Superintendent

Course information: This public course has 18 holes. Par is 72. The course is 6,862 yards and rated 72.5 from the championship tees, and 6,230 yards and rated 69.4 from the regular tees. The slope ratings are 121 championship and 115 regular. Women's tees are 5,356 yards and the rating was unavailable. The slope rating is 115.

Play policy and fees: Green fees are $8.50 weekdays and $10.50 weekends. Carts are $15 with a $5 key deposit. Reservations are recommended. This course is available for outside tournaments.

Location: From Highway 99 take the Highway 46 exit west. Drive two miles west of Wasco and take the Leonard Avenue exit to the course. The course is about 20 miles northwest of Bakersfield.

Course description: Six lakes come into play on this course. There are several undulating fairways and elevated tees and greens. The 18th provides and exciting finish, particularly if you survive the undulating fairway, a large lake and bunker, all of which come into play off the tee.

NORTH KERN GOLF COURSE

1953
Kermit Styber

PO Box 80545
Bakersfield, CA 93380

17412 Quality Road
Bakersfield, CA 93380

Pro shop   (805) 399-0347

■ driving range
■ practice greens
■ power carts
■ pull carts
■ golf club rental
■ locker rooms
■ showers
□ executive course
□ accommodations
■ food and beverages
■ clubhouse

Keith Perkins
Professional

Jack Agar
Professional

Lee Madden
Superintendent

Course information: This public course has 18 holes and par is 72. The course is 6,769 yards and rated 71.4 from the championship tees, and 6,461 yards and rated 69.9 from the regular tees. Women's tees are 6,182 yards and rated 72.7. The slope ratings are 115 championship, 109 regular and 112 women.

Play policy and fees: Green fees are $7.50 weekdays and $10 weekends. Call for special rates. Carts are $15. Reservations are recommended weekends and holidays.

Location: From Bakersfield, travel north on Highway 99 for 12 miles to the Shafter exit. Head east for 2.5 miles to the course.

Course description: This course is packed with trees and bunkers. Nevertheless, the fairways are wide and level, leading to small greens. The sixth hole is a devil. It's a 442-yard, par-4 that plays uphill and into the wind. The green is heavily bunkered in front, leaving only a narrow opening. Pin placement on this hole can add more yardage to an already long hole. The Kern County Amateur Championships are held here each October and the Kern County two-man, Best Ball Tournament is held each April. The course record is 63, set in 1985 by former head pro Bill McKinley.

KERN RIVER GOLF COURSE

1953
William Park Bell

Course information: This public course has 18 holes and par is 70. The course is 6,458 yards and rated 70.3 from the championship tees, and 6,258 yards and rated 68.7 from the regular tees. The slope ratings are 119 championship and 113 regular. Women's tees are 5,971 yards and rated 72.3. The slope rating is 116.

PO Box 6339
Bakersfield, CA 93386

Pro shop   (805) 872-5128

- ■ driving range
- ■ practice greens
- ■ power carts
- ■ pull carts
- ■ golf club rental
- ■ locker rooms
- ■ showers
- □ executive course
- □ accommodations
- ■ food and beverages
- ■ clubhouse

Play policy and fees: Green fees are $7.50 weekdays and $10 weekends. Call for special rates. Carts are $15. Reservations are recommended. Make reservations the prior Wednesday.

Location: From Highway 99 in Bakersfield, take Highway 178 east to Alfred Herrall Highway. Follow the signs to Lake Ming.

Course description: This public facility will test your golf skill. It is one of two courses in the area that is rated over par. It was originally designed in the 1920s as a nine-hole course. Nine more holes were added in the 1950s. The course features rolling terrain and an abundance of mature trees. One word of caution. There are two long par-3 holes on the back nine that can ruin your day. A hole to remember is number 11.

Ruby Foss
President

Jim Foss
Professional

Ron Baker
Superintendent

It is 235 yards from the back. If you miss the green to the right you're stymied behind trees. The green is sharply sloped downhill and difficult to putt. Don't leave the ball above the hole. The course record is 63 for men and 71 for women.

CENTRAL G4

RIO BRAVO GOLF AND TENNIS RESORT

1975
Robert Muir Graves

11200 Lake Ming Road
Bakersfield, CA 93306

Pro shop   (805) 871-4653

- ■ driving range
- ■ practice greens
- ■ power carts
- ▢ pull carts
- ▢ golf club rental
- ■ locker rooms
- ■ showers
- ▢ executive course
- ■ accommodations
- ■ food and beverages
- ■ clubhouse

Gerald Steenerson
Professional
Rick Stone
Superintendent

Course information: This private course has 18 holes and par is 72. The course is 7,018 yards and rated 74.4 from the championship tees, and 6,555 yards and rated 70.9 from the regular tees. The slope ratings are 138 championship and 122 regular. Women's tees are 5,704 yards and rated 72.5. The slope rating is 120.

Play policy and fees: Members and guests only. Rio Bravo Lodge guests are welcome. Green fees are $39 for lodge guests and $50 for reciprocators, including carts. Carts are $16. Reservations are required.

Location: From Highway 99 in Bakersfield, take Highway 178 east and drive about 12 miles to the Rio Bravo Resort area. Continue past the airport and turn right to the course.

Course description: This is a private resort course with a beautiful championship layout set in the foothills of the Tehachapi Mountains. It plays long and has excellent greens. It is the site of the PGA tour qualifying school and the Southern California Open. The hole to watch out for is number 11, affectionately known as Big Bertha. It's par-5 and 616 yards uphill to a difficult green. You never have a flat lie on this hole. The green, the most difficult on the course, is severely sloped left-to-right and tough to read.

CENTRAL G4

MAP G5
(2 COURSES)

PAGES.. 326-327

CEN-CAL MAP ...see page 256
adjoining maps
NORTH (F5) ....see page 304
EAST (G6) ....see page 328
SOUTH (H5) ....see page 362
WEST (G4) ....see page 316

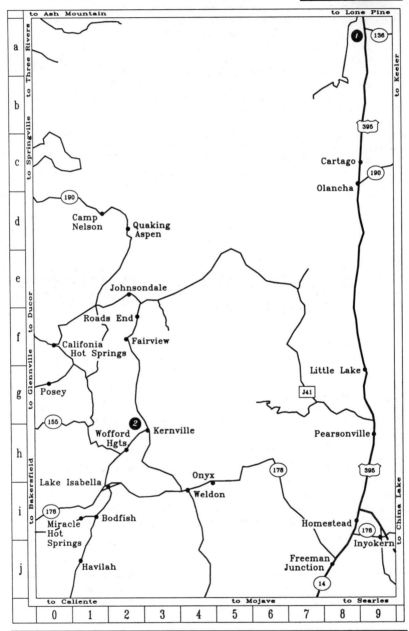

MOUNT WHITNEY GOLF COURSE

Course information: This public course has nine holes. Par is 72 for 18 holes. The course is 6,624 yards and rated 70.1 from the championship tees, and 6,338 yards and rated 69.3 from the regular tees (18 holes). The slope ratings are 116 championship and 114 regular. Women's tees are 5,692 yards and rated 71.0. The slope rating is 112.

Play policy and fees: Green fees are $8 weekdays and $10 weekends. Carts are $8 for nine holes and $16 for 18 holes.

Location: Drive on Highway 395 to Lone Pine.

Course description: This scenic course is situated in the foothills of Mount Whitney. It's flat with some water, bunkers, trees and narrow fairways. Accurate iron play is essential.

PO Box O
Lone Pine, CA 93545

Highway 395
Lone Pine, CA 93545

Pro shop   (619) 876-5795

- ■ driving range
- ■ practice greens
- ■ power carts
- ■ pull carts
- ■ golf club rental
- ■ locker rooms
- □ showers
- □ executive course
- □ accommodations
- ■ food and beverages
- ■ clubhouse

Brad Taylor
Manager/Pro/Superintendent

CENTRAL G5

KERN VALLEY GOLF COURSE COUNTRY CLUB

Course information: This semi-private course has nine holes. Par is 72 for 18 holes. The course is 6,282 yards and rated 68.2 from the regular tees for 18 holes. The slope rating is 101.

Play policy and fees: Outside play is accepted. Green fees are $7 for nine holes and $12 for 18 holes weekdays. On weekends it's $8 for nine holes and $15 for 18. Call for special rates. Carts are $8 for nine and $15 for 18 holes. This course is available for outside tournaments by appointment.

Location: From Bakersfield travel northeast on Highway 178 for 50 miles. The course is located one-half mile south of Kernville on Highway 155.

Course description: This is a well-maintained, fairly flat, short course. Trees line the narrow fairways demanding accuracy off the tees and a good short game.

PO Box 888
Kernville, CA 93238

9472 Burlando Road
Kernville, CA 93238

Pro shop   (619) 376-2828

- □ driving range
- ■ practice greens
- ■ power carts
- ■ pull carts
- ■ golf club rental
- □ locker rooms
- □ showers
- □ executive course
- □ accommodations
- ■ food and beverages
- ■ clubhouse

Rick Eaton
Professional

James Downard
Superintendent

Don Glover
Manager

MAP ON PAGE 326

MAP G6
(1 COURSE)

PAGES.. 328-329

CEN-CAL MAP ...see page 256
adjoining maps
NORTH ....no map
EAST (G7) ....see page 330
SOUTH (H6) ....see page 368
WEST (G5) ....see page 326

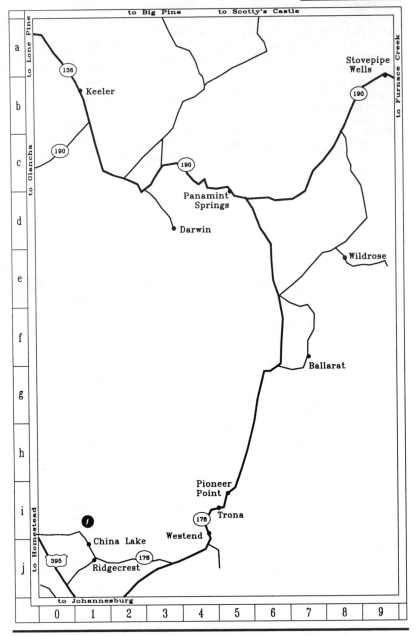

to Big Pine   to Scotty's Castle

to Lone Pine

136

Keeler

Stovepipe
Wells

190

190

190

Panamint
Springs

Darwin

Wildrose

Ballarat

Pioneer
Point

178   Trona

Westend

❶

China Lake

395

178

Ridgecrest

to Olancha

to Homestead

to Furnace Creek

to Johannesburg

0 1 2 3 4 5 6 7 8 9

CHINA LAKE GOLF COURSE

1957
George Bell

PO Box 507
Ridgecrest, CA 93555

411 Midway Drive
Ridgecrest, CA 93555

Pro shop   (619) 939-2990

- ■ driving range
- ■ practice greens
- ■ power carts
- ■ pull carts
- ■ golf club rental
- ■ locker rooms
- ■ showers
- □ executive course
- □ accommodations
- ■ food and beverages
- ■ clubhouse

Keith Holden
Manager

Keith Haywood
Superintendent

CENTRAL G6

Course information: This military course has 18 holes and par is 72. The course is 6,832 yards and rated 72.4 from the championship tees, and 6,533 yards and rated 70.9 from the regular tees. The slope ratings are 119 championship and 114 regular. Women's tees are 5,914 yards and rated 71.2 from the championship tees, and 5,492 yards and rated 68.7 from the forward tees. The slope ratings are 112 championship and 109 forward.

Play policy and fees: Outside play is accepted. Green fees are $13 weekdays and $18 weekends for outside play. Other fees vary according to military or civilian status. Call for special rates. Carts are $14. Reservations are recommended.

Location: From the town of Mojave, travel north on Highway 14 for approximately 40 miles to Highway 178. Turn right and drive east for about 13 miles to the entrance of China Lake Naval Weapons Station. Obtain a pass at the gate and continue to the course on Midway Drive.

Course description: This is a flat, desert course with lots of bunkers and trees. There are no water hazards. Beware of the 10th hole, a 568-yard, par-5. It is an uphill, dogleg right with two fairway traps. The two-tiered green has made more than one military commander wave the white flag and surrender. China Lake hosts a men's and women's club championship each year. Drew Martin and John Hemond share the men's course record with a 65, and Jane Nechero holds the women's record with a 76.

MAP ON PAGE 328

329

MAP G7
(1 COURSE)

PAGES.. 330-331

CEN-CAL MAP...see page 256
adjoining maps
NORTH ....no map
EAST ....no map
SOUTH.........................no map
WEST (G6) ....see page 328

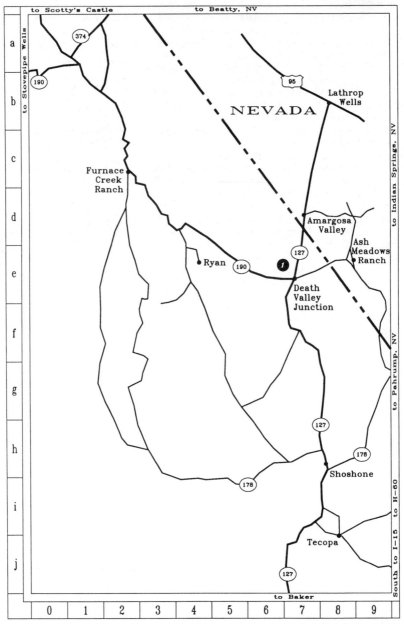

FURNACE CREEK
GOLF COURSE

1930

Course information: This resort course has 18 holes and par is 70. The course is 5,750 yards and rated 65.6 from the regular tees. The slope rating is 96. Women's tees are 5,087 yards and rated 67.1. The slope rating is 99.

Play policy and fees: Green fees are $13 for nine holes and $25 for 18 holes. Outside play is accepted. Carts are $18 for 18 holes. Pro shop closes from May 15 to November 1, but tee times are still sold from the 19th Hole during those months.

Location: Located in Death Valley, west of Highway 127 on Highway 190.

Course description: This is the world's lowest golf course at 214 feet below sea level. Built in 1930, it was one of the first all-grass courses in Southern California, and the bunkers today remain grass rather than sand. There is water on nine holes. Wildlife abounds on this desert course and ranges from coyotes to Canada geese. From the 12th hole there is a spectacular view of the towering Panamint Mountains.

PO Box 187
Death Valley, CA 92328

Furnace Creek Ranch
Death Valley, CA 92328

Pro shop   (619) 786-2301

- driving range
- practice greens
- power carts
- pull carts
- golf club rental
- locker rooms
- showers
- executive course
- accommodations
- food and beverages
- clubhouse

Norm Hedgepeth
Director of Golf

Jay Bruton
Superintendent

CENTRAL G7

MAP H2
(7 COURSES)

PAGES.. 332-337

CEN-CAL MAP...see page 256
adjoining maps
NORTH (G2).......see page 306
EAST (H3) ....see page 338
SOUTH.........................no map
WEST ....no map

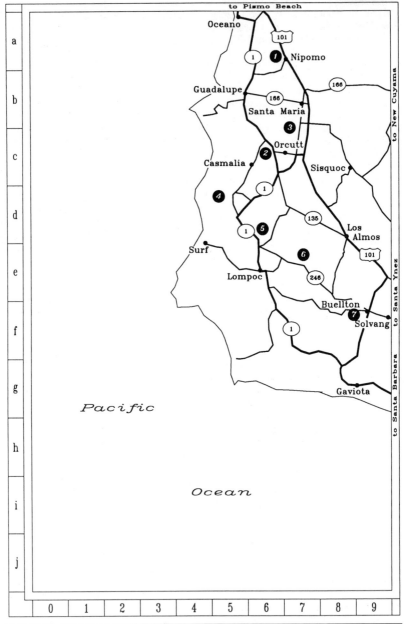

BLACK LAKE GOLF RESORT

1965
Ted Robinson (1986)

Course information: This resort course has 18 holes and par is 72. The course is 6,427 yards and rated 70.7 from the championship tees, and 6,067 yards and rated 68.9 from the regular tees. Women's tees are 5,614 yards and rated 71.8. The slope ratings are 121 championship, 114 regular and 122 women.

Play policy and fees: Green fees are $23 weekdays and $34 on weekends. Call for special rates. Carts are $22 and mandatory until 4 p.m. Reservations are recommended. Give one week lead time for reservations.

Location: Travel north on Highway 101 from Los Angeles past Santa Maria to the Tefft Road exit in Nipomo. Turn left over the highway to Pomeroy, then turn right to Willow and right to the golf course.

Course description: This well-designed course offers tree-lined fairways, several lakes and a rolling terrain. Among the holes to watch for are the par-5 11th, 502 yards with a narrow fairway, left lateral water hazard and bunkered right side. Several annual tournaments are held here including the John Madden Celebrity Golf Classic in June, and the Burton Gilliam Celebrity Golf Classic in March. The course record is 65.

1490 Golf Course Lane
Nipomo, CA 93444

Pro shop   (805) 481-4204
Starter   (805) 343-1214

- ■ driving range
- ■ practice greens
- ■ power carts
- ■ pull carts
- ■ golf club rental
- ☐ locker rooms
- ☐ showers
- ☐ executive course
- ■ accommodations
- ■ food and beverages
- ■ clubhouse

Dan Stills
Professional

Don Utterback
PGA Apprentice

Mike Elwell
PGA Apprentice

CENTRAL H2

RANCHO MARIA GOLF COURSE

1965
R. E. Baldock

Course information: This public course has 18 holes and par is 72. The course is 6,390 yards and rated 70.0 from the championship tees, and 6,148 yards and rated 68.7 from the regular tees. Women's yardage is 5,504 and the rating is 70.3. The slope ratings are 114 championship, 109 regular and 113 women.

Play policy and fees: Green fees are $18 weekdays and $24 weekends. Carts are $16. Reservations are recommended. Make reservations two days in advance during the week and a week in advance for weekends.

Location: Take the Orcutt/Clark Avenue exit off Highway 101 in Santa Maria, and drive west on Clark Avenue for 2.5 miles to Highway 1. Turn right and drive one mile to the course.

Course description: This course is located in the foothills southwest of Santa Maria. There are no parallel fairways and the rolling greens can be very fast. Watch for number 13 in the afternoon. This par-4, 438-yard hole is dangerous in a confronting wind. The wind has been known to blow the ball OB into the trees off the tee, but the real challenge is getting home in two with a long iron from a downhill lie. The green, which slopes to the right, is also well-bunkered on that side. If you miss to the left, it's hard to stop the ball.

1950 Casmalia Road
Santa Maria, CA 93455

Pro shop   (805) 937-2019

- ■ driving range
- ■ practice greens
- ■ power carts
- ■ pull carts
- ■ golf club rental
- ☐ locker rooms
- ☐ showers
- ☐ executive course
- ☐ accommodations
- ■ food and beverages
- ■ clubhouse

Jack O'Keefe
Professional

Don Jones
Superintendant

SANTA MARIA
COUNTRY CLUB

Course information: This private course has 18 holes and par is 72. The course is 6,457 yards and rated 71.2 from the championship tees, and 6,232 yards and rated 69.9 from the regular tees. The slope ratings are 128 championship and 122 regular.

Play policy and fees: Reciprocal play is accepted with members of other private clubs. But aside from that, members and guests only. Guest fees are $20 weekdays and $35 weekends. Carts are $16. Reservations are recommended. Closed Mondays.

Location: Travel south of Santa Maria on Highway 101 to the Betteravia exit. Turn west and drive to Broadway, then south to Waller Lane. From there go right to the club.

Course description: This is a fairly level course, but don't let that fool you. It is heavily wooded and more than one golfer has claimed to have lost a ball to a hungry chipmunk. The original nine holes were built in the 1920s; the second nine were built in the 1950s.

505 West Waller Lane
Santa Maria, CA 93455

Pro shop   (805) 937-7872
Clubhouse (805) 937-2025
Supt.   (805) 937-4945

■ driving range
■ practice greens
■ power carts
■ pull carts
□ golf club rental
■ locker rooms
■ showers
□ executive course
□ accommodations
■ food and beverages
■ clubhouse

Gary Quigley
Professional

VANDENBERG AFB GOLF COURSE

1 9 6 5
Robert Dean Putman

Vandenberg AFB,
CA 93437

Pro shop   (805) 866-6262
Starter   (805) 734-1333

■ driving range
■ practice greens
■ power carts
■ pull carts
■ golf club rental
■ locker rooms
■ showers
□ executive course
□ accommodations
■ food & beverages
■ clubhouse

Rick Vigil
Manager

John Belt
Superintendent

Course information: This military course has 18 holes and par is 72. The course is 6,845 yards and rated 74.1 from the championship tees, and 6,388 yards and rated 71.1 from the regular tees. The slope ratings are 130 championship and 122 regular. Women's tees are 5,404 yards and rated 71.4. The slope rating is 117.

Play policy and fees: Members and guests only. Green fees range from $5 to $20 depending on personnel status. Reservations are recommended.

Location: Highway 101 north to Highway 1 take the Lompoc-Vandenberg exit (just beyond Gaviota coming from the south) north to Vandenberg AFB. Drive past the main gate about four miles to the exit for Marshallia Ranch, left to the course.

Course description: Set three miles from the ocean, this tight and heavily-wooded course becomes increasingly difficult as the prevailing winds pick up. Each hole is separated by dense stands of trees which line the fairways and are behind all the greens. The course is fairly flat and walkable. Number nine and number 16 holes are rated among the best in Santa Barbara County. Number nine is par-4, 434 yards through a chute to a narrow landing area and onto a green with two large bunkers front left and right. Warning: The green is surrounded by ice plant. Number 16 is a par-4 playing 416 yards straight uphill and into the wind. For most golfers it's unreachable in two. Pros play a driver and two iron or a three wood to reach in two. An average of 245 rounds a day are played on this course. First tee time is not until 7 a.m. Morning and evening fog can cut short a day's play. Closed Mondays.

CENTRAL H2

THE VILLAGE
COUNTRY CLUB

Course information: This private course has 18 holes and par is 72. The course is 6,564 yards and rated 71.6 from the championship tees, and 6,269 yards and rated 69.6 from the regular tees. The slope ratings are 125 championship and 115 regular.

Play policy and fees: Reciprocal play is accepted with members of other private clubs. The fees for reciprocators are $30 weekdays and $40 weekends. Carts are $18. Reservations are recommended.

Location: Travel north from Lompoc on Highway 1 to Burton Mesa Boulevard and turn left. At Clubhouse Road, turn right.

Course description: Gently rolling terrain and fairways lined with mature pine and oak trees mark this interesting course. Driving accuracy is rewarded. The par-4 and par-5 holes are doglegs. The greens are mostly contoured and they can be challenging. At par-4 and 370 yards, number 15 is a tough water hazard hole. Water is on the left within the landing zone. Be straight down the fairway: If you get too far to the right you're in the creek. Your second shot should be 130 yards to 140 yards uphill to a two-tiered green. Pin placement makes all the difference here. The green is fast and will hold if you hit the top tier; if you hit the lower tier your ball will roll back.

4300 Clubhouse Road
Lompoc, CA 93436

Pro shop   (805) 733-3537
Clubhouse (805) 733-3535

- ■ driving range
- ■ practice greens
- ■ power carts
- ■ pull carts
- ■ golf club rental
- ■ locker rooms
- ■ showers
- □ executive course
- □ accommodations
- ■ food and beverages
- ■ clubhouse

Dan Unrue
Professional

Phil Brown
Superintendent

LA PURISIMA
GOLF COURSE

C o u r s e   6
MAP H2 grid e7

1 9 8 6
Robert Muir Graves

3455 State Highway 246
Lompoc, CA 93436

Pro shop   (805) 735-8395

- ■ driving range
- ■ practice greens
- ■ power carts
- ■ pull carts
- ■ golf club rental
- □ locker rooms
- □ showers
- □ executive course
- □ accommodations
- ■ food and beverages
- ■ clubhouse

Jim De Laby
Professional

John Canny
Superintendent

Mike McGinnis
Director of Golf

Course information: This long public course has 18 holes and par is 72. The course is 7,105 yards and rated 75.8 from the championship tees, and 6,657 yards and rated 72.8 from the regular tees. Women's tees are 5,763 yards and rated 73.3. The slope ratings are 142 championship, 132 regular and 133 women.

Play policy and fees: Green fees are $40 weekdays and $50 on the weekends. Call for nine-hole rates. Carts are $22. Reservations are recommended especially on weekends and should be made seven days in advance. This course is available for outside tournaments.

Location: The course is 12 miles west of Buellton on Highway 246. It is four miles east of Lompoc.

Course description: This is a highly rated public course. Overlooking Lompoc Valley, this scenic course meanders among the oak groves over rolling terrain. Three lakes come into play here, not to mention the wind, which can pick up in the afternoon. John Mc-Comish holds the course record with a 65. Among the tournaments played here are the Lompoc City Championship in April, the California Stroke Play Championship in July, the La Purisima Invitational in June, and the Santa Barbara County Championship in October.

CENTRAL H2

ZACA CREEK GOLF COURSE

C o u r s e   7
MAP H2 grid f9

223 Shadow Mountain Drive
Buellton, CA 93427

Pro shop   (805) 688-2575

- ■ driving range
- ■ practice greens
- □ power carts
- ■ pull carts
- ■ golf club rental
- □ locker rooms
- □ showers
- □ executive course
- □ accommodations
- ■ food and beverages
- □ clubhouse

Bob Kotowski
Professional

Jeff Young
Superintendent

Course information: This public course has nine holes. Par is 58 for 18 holes. The course is 3,088 yards and rated 50.0 from the regular tees. The slope rating is 76.

Play policy and fees: Green fees are $5 weekdays and $6 weekends for nine holes, and $4 for a replay. Pull carts are $1.50. Reservations are recommended. This course is available for outside tournaments.

Location: Travel 37 miles northwest of Santa Barbara on Highway 101 to the Highway 246 exit and turn west. Drive to the Avenue of Flags and go left. Continue to Shadow Mountain Drive and turn right to the course.

Course description: Nestled in the San Ynez Valley, this flat course offers seven par-3s and two par-4s that will test every club in your bag. The holes range from 90 to 310 yards.

CEN-CAL MAP ...see page 256
adjoining maps
NORTH (G3).......see page 312
EAST (H4) ....see page 350
SOUTH (I3).........see page 378
WEST (H2) ....see page 332

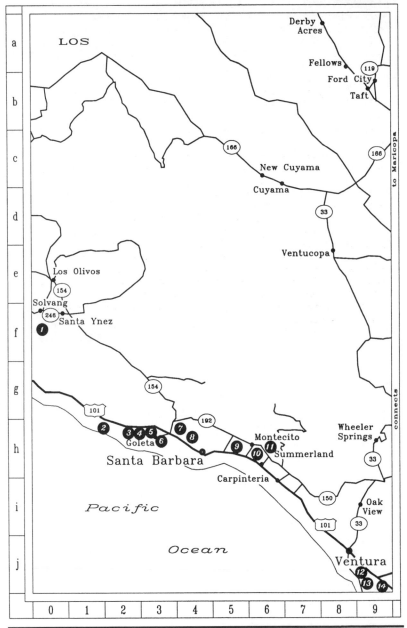

ALISAL GUEST RANCH AND GOLF COURSE

Course information: This resort course has 18 holes and par is 72. The course is 6,396 yards and rated 70.7 from the championship tees, and 6,026 yards and rated 68.5 from the regular tees. The slope ratings are 121 championship and 114 regular. Women's tees are 5,709 yards and rated 72.8. The slope is 123.

Play policy and fees: Reciprocal play is accepted with members of private clubs. Members and guests only. Alisal Guest Ranch guests are welcome. Fee for reciprocators is $65. Play/stay packages can be arranged by Alisal Guest Ranch. Carts are $22. Reservations are recommended.

Location: Off of Highway 101, in Solvang, take Mission Drive (in downtown Solvang) and turn south on Alisal Road and drive 1.75 miles to the course.

Course description: Located on the 10,000-acre Alisal Ranch, a working cattle ranch, the scenic course is set in a valley. When you're not watching for native birds and deer, keep an eye for number five, a par-3 175-yard hole that gives a view of Solvang and the Santa Ynez Valley from its elevated tee. Players hit across Alisal Creek to a green guarded by bunkers on both sides and the creek 60 feet below. The tight fairways of the course are lined with mature oaks and sycamores. The course is well maintained and usually uncrowded. An early morning round offers the chance to see numerous birds and other wildlife on this pleasant and walkable course.

PO Box 26
Solvang, CA 93463

1054 Alisal Road
Solvang, CA 93463

Pro shop   (805) 688-4215
Clubhouse (805) 688-6411

- ■ driving range
- ■ practice greens
- ■ power carts
- ■ pull carts
- ■ golf club rental
- ■ locker rooms
- ■ showers
- □ executive course
- ■ accommodations
- ■ food and beverages
- ■ clubhouse

John Hardy
Professional

Scott Buley
Superintendent

CENTRAL H3

SANDPIPER GOLF COURSE

1971
William Francis Bell

Course information: This public course has 18 holes and par is 72. The course is 7,055 yards and rated 75.0 from the championship tees, and 6,645 yards and rated 72.5 from the regular tees. Women's tees are 5,766 yards and rated 67.5. The slope rating is 126.

Play policy and fees: Green fees are $45 weekdays and $65 weekends. Carts are $22. Reservations are recommended. Collared shirts must be worn on the golf course and golf shoes. Long shorts are permitted.

Location: Travel 12 miles north of Santa Barbara on Highway 101, and turn off at the Winchester Canyon Road/Hollister Avenue exit. Turn left at the stop sign, and drive one-quarter mile on Hollister Avenue to the course.

Course description: This is a wonderful course. It's rated among the top 25 public courses in the nation. It is set along the ocean and offers breathtaking views from just about every hole. It offers rolling fairways and a long, wide-open, links-style layout. The back nine is well bunkered and hilly. The beautiful 510-yard, par-5 13th hole is often used as a backdrop for commercials. For the average golfer, though, it is extremely strategic. The hole is perched on a cliff and there are two chasms to traverse. The first one, off the tee, is unavoidable. The second chasm stands in front of the approach shot and can be avoided by going around it, but it will cost you a stroke. It's a strategic hole because of the choice between a longer, but safer, route or the short way with the most risk involved. The course record of 64 was set in 1977 by Mike McGinnis and tied in 1990 by Don Parsons, former California State Amateur champion.

7925 Hollister Avenue
Goleta, CA 93117

Pro shop   (805) 968-1541

- driving range
- practice greens
- power carts
- pull carts
- golf club rental
- ☐ locker rooms
- ☐ showers
- ☐ executive course
- ☐ accommodations
- food and beverages
- clubhouse

John Hughes
Professional

Mike McGinnis
Director of Golf

Paul Casas
Superintendent

OCEAN MEADOWS GOLF CLUB

Course information: This public course has nine holes. Par is 72 for 18 holes. The course is 6,392 yards and rated 70.0 from the championship tees, and 6,197 yards and rated 69.1 from the regular tees. Women's yards are 5,314 and rated 65.1. The slope ratings are 115 championship, 111 regular and 102 women.

Play policy and fees: Green fees are $11 for nine holes, $15 for 18 weekdays and $12 for nine holes and $20 for 18 holes weekends and holidays. Call for special rates. Carts are $14. This course is available for outside tournaments. Reservations recommended for weekends one week ahead.

Location: Go north of Santa Barbara on Highway 101 to Storke-Glen Annie exit, then drive south one mile to Whittier Drive.

Course description: This relatively flat course has tree-lined fairways and mountain views. It is built within the boundaries of an ecologically rich ocean slough and consequently has numerous lateral water hazards. Bird watchers (not to be confused with birdie watchers) might want to bring binoculars to view the beautiful and abundant wildlife in the area which includes blue herons and white egrets. It'll take more than binoculars to see an eagle.

6925 Whittier Drive
Goleta, CA 93117

Pro shop   (805) 968-6814

■ driving range
■ practice greens
■ power carts
■ pull carts
■ golf club rental
□ locker rooms
□ showers
□ executive course
□ accommodations
■ food and beverages
■ clubhouse

Robin McMann
Professional

Simon Herrera
Superintendent

Herb Wright
General Manager

CENTRAL H3

TWIN LAKES GOLF COURSE

Course information: This public course has nine holes. Par is 58 for 18 holes. The course is 3,008 yards and rated 49.5 from the regular tees for 18 holes. The slope rating is 73.

Play policy and fees: Green fees are $6 weekdays and $6.50 weekends. Replays are $3.25 during the week and $4 on weekends. Ask for senior and junior discounts. Hand carts are $1.50.

Location: Take the Fairview exit off Highway 101 north of Santa Barbara and drive west to the course.

Course description: As its name implies, the course has two lakes, but five years of drought have left them high and dry most of the time. No water hazard here. Players can play out of dry lake bed. This a short, yet tight course that tests iron play. Added attractions: lighted driving range and practice bunkers.

6034 Hollister Avenue
Goleta, CA 93117

Pro shop   (805) 964-1414

■ driving range
■ practice greens
□ power carts
■ pull carts
■ golf club rental
□ locker rooms
□ showers
□ executive course
□ accommodations
□ food and beverages
□ clubhouse

Jim Ley
Professional

Luciano Nungaray
Superintendent

NEW HORIZONS GOLF COURSE

Course information: This private course has nine holes. The course is a pitch and putt.

Play policy and fees: Members and guests only. Open 8 a.m. to 4:30 p.m.

Location: From Santa Barbara on Highway 101, take the Fairview exit and turn right. At the second light, turn right on Encina and drive one block to the course.

Course description: This pitch-and-putt course has no holes over 100 yards. It's situated in a condominium complex in a mountain setting.

250 Moreton Bay Lane
Goleta, CA 93117

Clubhouse (805) 964-4797

□ driving range
□ practice greens
□ power carts
□ pull carts
□ golf club rental
□ locker rooms
□ showers
□ executive course
□ accommodations
□ food and beverages
□ clubhouse

Gary Gruetzmacher
Superintendent

HIDDEN OAKS COUNTRY CLUB

1975

Course information: This public course has nine holes and par is 27. The course is 1,118 yards for nine holes and is not rated.

Play policy and fees: Green fees are $7 weekdays and $9 weekends and holidays.

Location: Off Highway 101 heading south to Santa Barbara, take the Turnpike exit and turn left on Hollister. On Puente turn right, which takes you to Calle Camarade and the course. The course is located on the oceanside.

Course description: This short course is all par-3s. The course has undergone extensive work in the last five years. There are bent greens and lush, narrow fairways. A well on the course provides year-round water and in the drought years the course was the only green spot in the Santa Barbara area. The longest hole is number nine at 175 yards. Number six is tricky shooting down from an elevated tee 122 yards to the green. Don't miss your first shot on any hole or you're in trouble.

4760 Calle Camarade
Santa Barbara, CA 93110

Pro shop (805) 967-3493

□ driving range
□ practice greens
□ power carts
□ pull carts
□ golf club rental
□ locker rooms
□ showers
■ executive course
□ accommodations
□ food and beverages
□ clubhouse

Greg Holland
Owner

LA CUMBRE GOLF
AND COUNTRY CLUB

1957
William Bell

Course information: This private course has 18 holes and par is 71. The course is 6,363 yards and rated 70.8 from the championship tees, and 6,122 yards and rated 69.4 from the regular tees. The slope ratings are 128 championship and 121 regular.

Play policy and fees: Reciprocal play is accepted with members of other private clubs. Members and guests only. Green fees for reciprocators are $85. Carts are $22. Reservations are recommended.

Location: Turn off Hope Avenue/LaCumbre Road, turn left on Frontage Road and then left on LaCumbre Road and continue one-quarter mile past the arched entrance to Hope Ranch Park to Via Laguna, then go left to the club.

Course description: This is a well-maintained flat course with a 30-acre lake coming into play on the back nine. Five holes border the lake. The course pre-dates the surrounding homes of the Hope Ranch residential development.

PO Box 3158
Santa Barbara, CA 93110

4015 Via Laguna
Santa Barbara, CA 93110

Pro shop   (805) 682-3131
Clubhouse (805) 687-2421

■ driving range
■ practice greens
■ power carts
■ pull carts
□ golf club rental
■ locker rooms
■ showers
□ executive course
□ accommodations
■ food and beverages
■ clubhouse

Sam Randolph
Professional

Doug Weddle
Superintendent

CENTRAL H3

SANTA BARBARA
COMMUNITY GOLF COURSE

Course information: This public course has 18 holes and par is 70. The course is 6,009 yards from the championship tees and rated 67.3. It is 5,777 yards from the middle tees and is rated 66.4. From the front tees it is 5,536 yards and rated 64.3. The slope rating is 101.

Play policy and fees: Green fees are $17 weekdays and $19 weekends. Tournament rate is $22 for weekdays and $24 weekends. Carts are $18. Pull carts ar $2.

Location: Turn off Highway 101 at Las Positas Road in Santa Barbara and drive east for three-quarter of a mile to McCaw Avenue. Turn left and continue one-quarter mile to the course.

Course description: This course is set in the foothills above Santa Barbara and offers a nice view of the Channel Islands. Trees border the fairways, which are made up of Kikuyu grass and limit roll. Among the tournaments held here are the Santa Barbara City Championship held over Memorial Day Weekend, the Santa Barbara Classic during the first weekend in August and the Santa Barbara City Seniors held in mid-September. Jeff Hewes holds the men's course record with a 59, and Peggy Hogan's 65 is the women's record. This is a busy golf course, especially when the grass is green following the drought period. Play has returned to more than 300 rounds a day.

PO Box 3033
Santa Barbara, CA 93130

3500 McCaw Avenue
Santa Barbara, CA 93105

Pro shop   (805) 687-7087

- ■ driving range
- ■ practice greens
- ■ power carts
- ■ pull carts
- ■ golf club rental
- ☐ locker rooms
- ☐ showers
- ☐ executive course
- ☐ accommodations
- ■ food and beverages
- ■ clubhouse

Richard Chavez
Professional

David Smoot
Superintendent

MONTECITO
COUNTRY CLUB

1922
Max Behr

PO Box 1170
Santa Barbara, CA 93108

920 Summit Road
Santa Barbara, CA 93108

Pro shop   (805) 969-0800
Clubhouse (805) 969-3216

Course information: This private course has 18 holes and par is 71. The course is 6,184 yards and rated 69.9 from the regular tees. The slope rating is 122. The women's tees are 5,905 yards and rated 73.3 The slope rating is 126.

Play policy and fees: Reciprocal play is accepted with members of other private clubs. The guest fee is $60. Guests should have their club professional make reservations with the Montecito pro shop. Guest rate for carts is $24. Guests of the Santa Barbara Biltmore, San Ysidro Ranch, Red Lion and Montecito Inn may also play the course. Reservations are recommended.

Location: Take Hermosillo exit off Highway 101 south of Santa Barbara. Hermosillo merges with Hot Springs. Turn left on Hot Springs and then take the next left onto Summit Road, which leads into the club.

Course description: Although short, this is a challenging course that emphasizes shot-making. Ocean and mountain views are abundant from the rolling, tree-lined fairways and well-kept, undulating greens. The course plays much longer than yardage indicates. Accuracy and the ability to make good shots from troublesome lies are needed to score well here. Among the holes to watch for are the par-4, 455-yard third hole and the 18th, which is a top-notch 545-yard par-5. On almost every lie the ball is either above or below your feet, which adds to the challenge. There is a practice range under construction.

☐ driving range
■ practice greens
■ power carts
☐ pull carts
■ golf club rental
■ locker rooms
■ showers
☐ executive course
☐ accommodations
■ food and beverages
■ clubhouse

Larry Talkington
Professional

Pete Jaramillo
Superintendent

CENTRAL H3

BIRNAM WOOD GOLF CLUB

Course 10
MAP H3 grid h6

1966
Robert Trent Jones, Sr.

2031 Packing House Road
Santa Barbara, CA 93108

Pro shop   (805) 969-0919
Clubhouse (805) 969-2223

- ■ driving range
- ■ practice greens
- ■ power carts
- ■ pull carts
- □ golf club rental
- ■ locker rooms
- ■ showers
- □ executive course
- ■ accommodations
- ■ food and beverages
- ■ clubhouse

Bob Roux
Professional

Martin Moore
Superintendent

Course information: This private course has 18 holes and par is 70. The course is 5,890 yards and rated 68.7 from the regular tees. The slope rating is 121.

Play policy and fees: Members and guests only. The green fee is $75 or $30 when guest plays with member. Carts are $25.

Location: Take the Sheffield Drive exit off Highway 101 in Santa Barbara and drive to the end. Turn left on East Valley Road and drive up the hill to the club entrance.

Course description: This is a short course that demands accurate shot-making skills. There are numerous out-of-bounds markers to the left and right. Barrancas are found in front of the greens making it impossible to roll the ball on. Sharpen up your iron play before tackling this well-maintained, Robert Trent Jones, Sr. beauty. New placement of the tee on par-4 number seven extends the length of this hole to 375 yards. The hole was proving too easy and to add to the difficulty a tree was planted in the middle of the fairway.

THE VALLEY CLUB OF MONTECITO

Course 11
MAP H3 grid h6

1929
Alister MacKenzie

PO Box 5640
Santa Barbara, CA 93150

1901 East Valley Road
Santa Barbara, CA 93108

Pro shop   (805) 969-4681
Clubhouse (805) 969-2215

- ■ driving range
- ■ practice greens
- ■ power carts
- □ pull carts
- □ golf club rental
- ■ locker rooms
- ■ showers
- □ executive course
- ■ accommodations
- ■ food and beverages
- ■ clubhouse

Scott Puailoa
Professional

Course information: This private course has 18 holes and par is 72. The course is 6,623 yards and rated 71.8 from the championship tees, and 6,341 yards and rated 70.0 from the regular tees. The slope ratings are 125 championship and 117 regular. Women's tees are 5,819 yards and rated 73.3 The slope rating is 124.

Play policy and fees: Members and guests only. Green fees are $100 for guests unaccompanied by a member. With a member it is $30. Carts are $20.

Location: Take the San Ysidro Road exit off Highway 101 and travel north to East Valley Road. Turn right and drive one mile to Valley Club Road, then turn right to the club.

Course description: The course features small greens and a natural setting. A creek runs through about half the holes and the narrow fairways are bordered by large cypress and pine trees. The ocean is visible from many holes. The course is very exclusive. Less than 100 members use it regularly. It is rated among the top 20 courses in the state. There have been no modifications to the course since it opened in 1929.

OLIVAS PARK GOLF COURSE

Course information: This public course has 18 holes and par is 72. The course is 6,750 yards and rated 71.3 from the championship tees, and 6,353 yards and rated 69.5 from the regular tees. The slope ratings are 124 championship and 121 regular. Women's tees are 5,586 yards. The slope rating is 118.

Play policy and fees: Green fees are $13 weekdays and $17 weekends. Call for special rates. Carts are $17. Reservations are recommended.

Location: From Pierpoint Bay in Ventura, take Harbor Boulevard to Olivas Park Drive. Drive three-fourths of a mile to the course.

Course description: This beautiful and flat course is less than one-half mile from Ventura Harbor. Cool ocean breezes can play havoc with shots, but the view is worth the trouble. In about 1969 the Santa Clara River flooded the course and it had to be reconstructed. This is one of the courses that hosts the Ventura County Championships each August. The San Buena Ventura Pro-Am Classic is played here each September.

3750 Olivas Park Drive
Ventura, CA 93003

Pro shop   (805) 485-5712

- ■ driving range
- ■ practice greens
- ■ power carts
- ■ pull carts
- ■ golf club rental
- ▢ locker rooms
- ▢ showers
- ▢ executive course
- ▢ accommodations
- ■ food and beverages
- ▢ clubhouse

Lee Harlow
Professional

Bob Jenkins
Superintendent

CENTRAL H3

BUENA VENTURA GOLF COURSE

Course information: This public course has 18 holes and par is 70.

Play policy and fees: Green fees are $13 weekdays and $16 weekends. Call for special rates. Carts are $17. Reservations are recommended.

Location: From Highway 101 (Ventura Freeway) in Ventura, take Victoria Boulevard to Olivas Park Drive, turn left and go about three miles to the course.

Course description: An excellent course for golfers with a good short game. Tight fairways and quick greens make this a challenge. The number 14 hole is the one to watch on this course. It's a par-3, 130-yard nightmare that requires a straight iron over two legs of a lake that loops through the fairway. (Try saying that fast 10 times in a row.) There is also water on the back side of the medium-sized green. Miss the green to the left and you're in a bunker. A good 7-iron usually does it. Proper clubbing is obviously important on this hole.

5882 Olivas Park Drive
Ventura, CA 93003

Pro shop   (805) 642-2231

- ▢ driving range
- ■ practice greens
- ■ power carts
- ■ pull carts
- ■ golf club rental
- ■ locker rooms
- ■ showers
- ▢ executive course
- ▢ accommodations
- ■ food and beverages
- ▢ clubhouse

Bill Hulbert
Professional

Ed Naylor
Superintendent

RIVER RIDGE GOLF CLUB

Course information: This public course has 18 holes and par is 72. The course is 6,543 yards and rated 70.7 from the championship tees, and 6,111 yards and rated 68.7 from the regular tees. The slope ratings are 114 championship and 109 regular. Women's tees are 5,525 yards and rated 72.0. The slope rating is 116.

Play policy and fees: Green fees are $13 weekdays and $18 weekends. Call for special rates. Carts are $16.

Location: Take the Vineyard exit off Highway 101 in Oxnard and drive west for three miles to the course.

Course description: This is a rolling, links-style course with lots of water. One par-3 features an island green. That's the 191-yard number 14, a pivotal hole in a tight match. If you're in the water on your first effort you still have to make the green from the drop area, which is 70 yards out and that's a tough shot to make if you're trying to close with a bogey. This is another course that hosts the Ventura County Championships each August. The Oxnard City Championships are played here each July. When the SCGA qualifier was played here in 1991, the low qualifier was a 71, which says a lot about the course. You'll need every club in the bag because of the wind and hills and you must pay attention all day. Whew.

2401 West Vineyard Avenue
Oxnard, CA 93030

Pro shop   (805) 983-4653

■ driving range
■ practice greens
■ power carts
■ pull carts
■ golf club rental
□ locker rooms
□ showers
□ executive course
■ accommodations
■ food and beverages
■ clubhouse

Marc Sipes
Professional

Kyle Kanny
Superintendent

MAP H4
(19 COURSES)

PAGES.. 350-361

CEN-CAL MAP...see page 256
adjoining maps
NORTH (G4)......see page 316
EAST (H5) ....see page 362
SOUTH (I4) ....see page 380
WEST (H3) ....see page 338

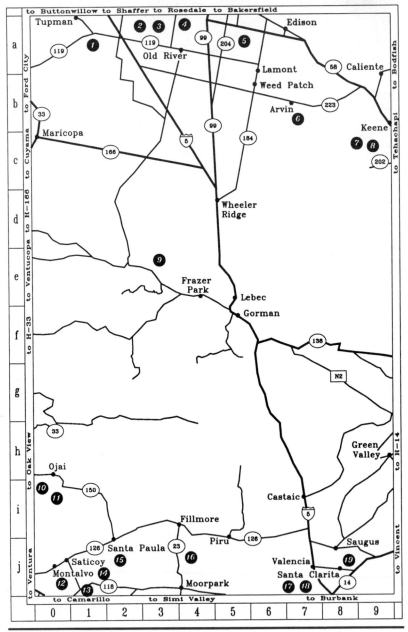

BUENA VISTA GOLF COURSE

1953
George Mifflin

10256 Golf Course Road
Taft, CA 93268

Pro shop   (805) 763-5124

- ■ driving range
- ■ practice greens
- ■ power carts
- ■ pull carts
- ■ golf club rental
- □ locker rooms
- ■ showers
- □ executive course
- □ accommodations
- ■ food and beverages
- ■ clubhouse

David James
Professional

Ray George
Superintendent

Course information: This public course has 18 holes and par is 72. The course is 6,685 yards and rated 69.0 from the championship tees, and 6,292 yards and rated 68.7 from the regular tees. The slope ratings are 124 championship and 118 regular.

Play policy and fees: Green fees are $7.50 weekdays and $10 weekends. Call for special rates. Carts are $15.

Location: Take the Highway 119 exit off Interstate 5 and travel west for about five miles to the golf course.

Course description: Originally a nine-hole layout, this course is the only green spot in the whole desert, thanks to irrigation from an on-site well. An introduction to this course begins with the first hole, a 355-yard par-4. This is not a mirage. The green sits on top of a hill 100 yards in the air and is the highest point on the golf course. Hit your tee shot to the flat area of the fairway in order to avoid an uphill lie, and then go for the large, flat green at the top. Overall, the course offers a rolling layout dotted with many palm trees.

STOCKDALE COUNTRY CLUB

1909
1978
Robert Dean Putman

PO Box 9457
Bakersfield, CA 93309

7001 Stockdale Highway
Bakersfield, CA 93309

Pro shop   (805) 832-0587
Clubhouse   (805) 832-0310

- ■ driving range
- ■ practice greens
- ■ power carts
- ■ pull carts
- □ golf club rental
- ■ locker rooms
- ■ showers
- □ executive course
- □ accommodations
- ■ food and beverages
- ■ clubhouse

Rolly Allen
Professional

Lowell Stone
Superintendent

Course information: This private course has 18 holes and par is 71. The course is 6,327 yards and rated 70.4 from the championship tees, and 6,081 yards and rated 69.2 from the regular tees. The slope ratings are 120 championship and 116 regular. Women's tees are 5,764 yards and rated 73.0. The slope rating is 118.

Play policy and fees: Reciprocal play is accepted with members of other private clubs. Have your club pro call for arrangements. Green fees are $25 when accompanied by a member and $50 for reciprocal play. Call for special rates. Carts are $15. Reservations are recommended.

Location: From the north take the Stockdale exit off Highway 99 in Bakersfield. Travel west to the Stockdale Highway. Turn right and drive one-half mile to the club entrance.

Course description: This 82-year-old course was redesigned in 1978 by Robert Dean Putman. It has numerous trees and few water hazards on a traditional layout. It hosts the Men's Silver Invitational in October and the Mr. and Mrs. Invitational each June.

CENTRAL H4

SUNDALE COUNTRY CLUB

1964

Course information: This private course has 18 holes and par is 72. The course is 6,784 yards and rated 72.3 from the championship tees, and 6,570 yards and rated 70.5 from the regular tees. The slope ratings are 122 championship and 116 regular. Women's yards are 6,166 and rated 74.7. The slope rating is 127.

Play policy and fees: Reciprocal play is accepted with members of other private clubs. Otherwise, members and guests only. Green fees are $30. Carts are $16. This course is available for outside tournaments. Shorts must come to mid-thigh, shirts must have collars and no T-shirts are allowed. Reservations should be made a week in advance.

Location: Take the Ming Avenue exit off Highway 99 in Bakersfield, and travel west to New Stine Road. Turn right and drive one-quarter mile to Sundale Avenue. Turn left and drive one-half mile to the club.

Course description: Formerly a public course known as Kern City, this layout is mostly flat with water and mature trees. The front nine has no parallel holes. Water can be found on six holes and there is one long par-3. The course is deceptively difficult because the par-4 holes are long and the par-3 holes are tough. The course looks extremely simple but it just doesn't play that way. Club pro James Kiger holds the men's course record with a 64. Val Skinner fired a 68 for the women's course record during a mini-tour event. The Bakersfield City Championship has been held at Sundale since 1980. In addition, the Sundale Invitational is held each summer.

6218 Sundale Avenue
Bakersfield, CA 93309

Pro shop   (805) 831-5224
Clubhouse (805) 831-4200

- ■ driving range
- ■ practice greens
- ■ power carts
- ■ pull carts
- □ golf club rental
- ■ locker rooms
- ■ showers
- □ executive course
- □ accommodations
- ■ food and beverages
- ■ clubhouse

James Kiger
Professional

Dave Newman
Superintendent

SEVEN OAKS COUNTRY CLUB

1992
Robert Muir Graves

Course information: This private course has 18 holes. The par is 72. The course is 7,101 yards from the championship tees, and 6,543 yards from the regular tees. The course is in the process of being rated.

Play policy and fees: Reciprocal play is not accepted. Members and guests only.

Location: From Highway 99 in Bakersfield, take the Ming Avenue exit west. The course is on the left.

Course description: There was a limited opening of this course in May, 1991, but the grand opening is scheduled for the summer of 1992 when the clubhouse is completed. The course has mounded flat land. It is well bunkered, with lots of water.

PO Box 1165
Bakersfield, CA 93389

10,000 Ming Avenue
Bakersfield, CA 93311

Pro shop   (805) 665-4653

- ■ driving range
- ■ practice greens
- ■ power carts
- ■ pull carts
- ■ golf club rental
- ■ locker rooms
- ■ showers
- □ executive course
- □ accommodations
- ■ food and beverages
- ■ clubhouse

Steve Jessup
Superintendent

VALLE GRANDE GOLF COURSE

Course information: This public course has 18 holes and par is 72. The course is 6,066 yards and rated 68.4 from the regular tees. The slope rating is 108.

Play policy and fees: Green fees are $9 on weekdays and $12 on weekends. Call for special rates. Carts are $16. Reservations are accepted. This course is available for tournaments.

Location: Travel east on Highway 58 from Bakersfield and turn right on Cottonwood Road and drive 1.25 miles. Turn left on Watts Drive to the club.

Course description: This course is level and appears simple to play, but don't be fooled. Out-of-bound markers and an abundance of trees make this a tight course. There are also two water channels running through the fairways, which add to its charm and difficulty.

1119 Watts Drive
Bakersfield, CA 93307

Pro shop   (805) 832-2259

■ driving range
■ practice greens
■ power carts
■ pull carts
□ golf club rental
□ locker rooms
□ showers
□ executive course
□ accommodations
■ food and beverages
■ clubhouse

Roland Reese
Professional

Henry Chavez
Superintendent

CENTRAL H4

SYCAMORE CANYON GOLF CLUB

Robert Dean Putman

Course information: This public course has 18 holes and par is 72. The course is 7,100 yards and rated 73.0 from the championship tees, and 6,644 yards and rated 70.9 from the regular tees. The slope ratings are 122 championship and 118 regular. Women's tees are 5,744 yards and rated 71.6.

Play policy and fees: Green fees are $8 weekdays and $10 weekends. The twilight rates are $5.50 weekdays and $7.50 weekends. Senior rates are available with a senior card issued by Sycamore Canyon. The card is redeemable at all facilities managed by Golf Corp. The card is $25 for one full year. Carts are $15. Reservations are recommended.

Location: Take Highway 99 south of Bakersfield to Bear Mountain/Arvin exit, then go 10 miles east to South Derby Street, then south 3.5 miles to the course.

Course description: Twenty acres of water come into play on 14 holes. Beware of the 602-yard ninth hole. It doglegs around a lake that runs 300 yards parallel to the hole. This par-5 is the number-one handicap hole on this course. You may not want to see the rest of the back nine after this monster. The course is made up of long par-4 and par-3 holes and every green has at least two bunkers.

500 Kenmar Lane
Arvin, CA 93203

Pro shop   (805) 854-3163

■ driving range
■ practice greens
■ power carts
■ pull carts
■ golf club rental
□ locker rooms
□ showers
□ executive course
□ accommodations
■ food and beverages
■ clubhouse

Don Luttrell
Professional/Manager

Neil Hamman
Professional

Scott Furtak
Superintendent

MAP ON PAGE 350

353

HORSE THIEF GOLF AND COUNTRY CLUB

Course information: This resort course has 18 holes and par is 72. The course is 6,667 yards and rated 72.1 from the championship tees, and 6,327 yards and rated 70.1 from the regular tees. The slope ratings are 129 championship and 121 regular. Women's tees are 5,669 yards and rated 66.9. The slope rating is 106.

Play policy and fees: This course is affiliated with Sky Mountain Lodge at Stallion Springs Resort. Outside play is also accepted. Green fees are $16 weekdays and $26 weekends. Call for special rates. Carts are $19. Reservations are recommended. This course is available for tournaments.

Location: From Bakersfield, travel east on Highway 58 for 38 miles to Tehachapi, and take the Highway 202 exit. Follow the signs for 16 miles to the Stallion Springs Resort.

Course description: This course is set in the mountains, and although not particularly long, it requires accuracy. The most prominent features are the oak trees and rocks that come into play. Water also is a factor on four of the holes.

PO Box 2931
Tehachapi, CA 93561

Star Route 1
Tehachapi, CA 93561

Pro shop   (805) 822-6114

- ■ driving range
- ■ practice greens
- ■ power carts
- ■ pull carts
- ■ golf club rental
- □ locker rooms
- ■ showers
- □ executive course
- ■ accommodations
- ■ food and beverages
- ■ clubhouse

Pete Snider
Professional

Tim Kelly
Superintendent

OAK TREE COUNTRY CLUB

1972

Course information: This private course has nine holes. Par is 72 for 18 holes. The course is 6,298 yards and rated 69.0 from the regular tees for 18 holes. The slope rating is 110.

Play policy and fees: Reciprocal play is accepted with members of other private clubs. Green fees are $10 weekdays and $15 weekends. Call for special rates. Carts are $14 for two people. Reservations are recommended one week in advance.

Location: From Bakersfield, travel east on Highway 58 for 38 miles to the town of Tehachapi and take the Highway 202 exit. Follow the signs for about 14 miles to Bear Valley Springs.

Course description: The course, set at 4,000 feet, is rimmed by mountains. It's a level layout set around a small lake. Trees dot the fairways and jutting rocks add to the mountainous look of the course, but they rarely come into play.

PO Box 4100
Tehachapi, CA 93561

29540 Rolling Oak
Tehachapi, CA 93561

Pro shop   (805) 821-5144
Clubhouse (805) 821-5521

- ■ driving range
- ■ practice greens
- ■ power carts
- ■ pull carts
- ■ golf club rental
- □ locker rooms
- □ showers
- □ executive course
- □ accommodations
- ■ food and beverages
- ■ clubhouse

Don Moulton
Professional

Russ Krok
Superintendent

PINE MOUNTAIN CLUB

Course information: This private course has nine holes. Par is 60 for 18 holes. The course is 3,571 yards and rated 54.8 from the regular tees for 18 holes. The slope rating is 96.

Play policy and fees: Guests may play with members only. Guest fees are $7 for nine holes and $11 for 18 holes weekdays, and $9 for nine holes and $13 for 18 holes weekends and holidays.

Location: Travel 40 miles south of Bakersfield on Interstate 5 and take the Frazier Park exit to Frazier Mountain Road. Drive west five miles and continue west on Cuddly Valley Road for another six miles to the top of the mountain. Turn right on Mill Potrero Road and drive five miles to the course.

Course description: This is an interesting course set at 5,500 feet and nestled among the beautiful pine trees. You may want to pack mountaineering boots. The fifth hole is known as Cardiac Hill, obviously because of its steepness. This hole is one of the reasons why the club now has power carts.

2524 Beechwood Way
Pine Mountain, CA 93222

Pro shop   (805) 242-3734
Clubhouse   (805) 242-3788

■ driving range
■ practice greens
■ power carts
■ pull carts
■ golf club rental
■ locker rooms
□ showers
■ executive course
□ accommodations
■ food and beverages
■ clubhouse

John Nigh
Professional

Jim Furr
Superintendent

CENTRAL H4

OJAI VALLEY INN
AND COUNTRY CLUB

1923
George C. Thomas

Country Club Road
Ojai, CA 93023

Pro shop   (805) 646-5511

- ■ driving range
- ■ practice greens
- ■ power carts
- □ pull carts
- ■ golf club rental
- ■ locker rooms
- ■ showers
- □ executive course
- ■ accommodations
- ■ food and beverages
- ■ clubhouse

Scott Flynn
Director of Golf

Sam Williamson
Superintendent

Course information: This resort course has 18 holes and par is 70. The course is 6,252 yards and rated 70.6 from the championship tees, and 5,909 yards and rated 68.9 from the regular tees. The slope ratings are 123 championship and 117 regular. Women's tees are 5,242 yards and rated 70.0. The slope rating is 121.

Play policy and fees: Outside play is accepted, with starting times arranged one day in advance. The green fees are $90, which includes carts, range balls and club storage. Golf packages are also available. Reservations are recommended.

Location: From Ventura, travel north 13 miles on Highway 33 to Ojai, and turn right on Country Club Drive.

Course description: This beautiful, mountainside course was built in the 1920s by George C. Thomas and was improved by Jay Morrish during 1988. The Ojai Valley Inn has been a long time favorite of the Hollywood set and was once owned by Loretta Young and Hoagy Carmichael. Several films have used the Inn as a setting including *Lost Horizons, Pat and Mike* and *The Two Jakes* with Jack Nicholson. Among the holes to watch for are the par-4, 442-yard fourth, which is a beauty. The drive from the championship tee on this hole must carry up a barranca. Part of the hole is hidden by the barranca and large oak trees. If you're in the fairway you can play the hole; if you're not in the fairway, you're cooked. Number 11 is a 358 yard, par-4 that crosses a barranca not once but twice. The tee shot from the championship tee must carry 200 yards to a safe landing area. Everything kicks toward the barranca so you have to play down the left side. The second shot requires a mid to short iron that has to carry the barranca again. The green is completely surrounded by large oak trees and it's difficult to tell where the pin is. Obviously, distance is difficult to judge on this hole. This course is also the home of the Senior PGA Tour GTE West Classic and numerous Southern California PGA events. Butch Baird set the men's record in the 1989 Senior PGA Tour GTE West Classic with a 63.

SOULE PARK GOLF COURSE

Course 11
MAP H4 grid i0

1962
William Park Bell

PO Box 758
Ojai, CA 93023

1033 East Ojai Avenue
Ojai, CA 93023

Pro shop   (805) 646-5633
Clubhouse (805) 646-5685

■ driving range
■ practice greens
■ power carts
■ pull carts
■ golf club rental
□ locker rooms
■ showers
□ executive course
□ accommodations
■ food and beverages
■ clubhouse

Jim Allen
Professional

Roger Spector
Superintendent

Course information: This public course has 18 holes and par is 72. The course is 6,390 yards and rated 69.1 from the regular tees. The slope rating is 107. Women's tees are 5,901 yards and rated 72.2. The slope rating is 115.

Play policy and fees: Green fees are $15 weekdays and $19 weekends. Senior rates are $10 weekdays. Reservations are recommended. Call for a tee time. The twilight rate is $10 weekdays and $12 weekends.

Location: From Ventura, travel north 16 miles on Highway 33 to the town of Ojai. Turn right on East Ojai Avenue and drive one-half mile to the course.

Course description: This course is set at the base of the mountains in the Ojai Valley and traverses a rolling terrain. A creek runs through the course. Mature trees line the fairways. A hole that will stagger many a golfer is the 568-yard, par-5 fifth. This is a three-shot hole with a creek running in front of the green, requiring a 120-yard carry over the creek for the third shot. The green is partially blocked by a huge oak tree. Number five is definitely a position hole.

SATICOY REGIONAL GOLF COURSE

Course 12
MAP H4 grid j0

1926

1025 South Wells Road
Ventura, CA 93004

Pro shop   (805) 647-6678

■ driving range
■ practice greens
■ power carts
■ pull carts
■ golf club rental
□ locker rooms
□ showers
□ executive course
□ accommodations
■ food and beverages
□ clubhouse

Bob Talbot
Professional

Jan Martinez
Superintendent

Course information: This public course has nine holes and par is 68 for 18 holes. The course is 5,423 yards and rated 64.8 from the regular tees. The slope rating is 97. Women's tees are 5,281 yards and rated 69.3. The slope rating was unavailable.

Play policy and fees: Green fees are $7 for nine holes weekdays and $9 for nine holes weekends, and $9 for 18 holes weekdays and $11 for 18 holes weekends. Call for special rates. Carts are $15. This course is available for outside tournaments.

Location: Take the Central Avenue exit off Highway 101 south of Ventura and continue on Central for 1.5 miles. Turn right on Highway 118 and drive 1.5 miles to Los Angeles Avenue and turn left. Drive four miles to the course.

Course description: This course was built in 1926 as the Saticoy Golf and Country Club. It has narrow fairways, gradual slopes and quick greens.

CENTRAL H4

SATICOY COUNTRY CLUB

1964
William Francis Bell

4450 Clubhouse Drive
Somis, CA 93006

Pro shop   (805) 485-5216
Clubhouse (805) 485-4956

- ■ driving range
- ■ practice greens
- ■ power carts
- □ pull carts
- □ golf club rental
- ■ locker rooms
- □ showers
- □ executive course
- □ accommodations
- ■ food and beverages
- ■ clubhouse

Course information: This private course has 18 holes and par is 72. The course is 6,924 yards and rated 74.4 from the championship tees, and 6,407 yards and rated 71.0 from the regular tees. The slope ratings are 140 championship and 128 regular. Women's tees are 5,855 yards and rated 72.7. The slope rating is 128.

Play policy and fees: Members and guests only. Guests must be accompanied by a member while playing. Green fees are $35 with a member and $75 without a member. Carts are $20. Reservations are recommended.

Location: Take the Central Avenue exit off Highway 101 just south of Ventura and drive north for two miles to Santa Clara Avenue. Turn right and travel 1.25 miles to Los Angeles Avenue and turn left. Drive one-half mile to the club.

Course description: Make sure your tee shots are accurate here or you will be in for a long day. The fairways are tight and demanding. Greens are large and undulating. Many greens are elevated. The par-3 number 10 is 178 yards from the back tees, shooting down about 100 feet, over water to the green. Placed on the side of a mountain, this is the course to play in Ventura County if you're looking for golf and not scenery. Plans call for an additional set of tee boxes to lengthen the course.

LAS POSAS COUNTRY CLUB

955 Fairway Drive
Camarillo, CA 93010

Pro shop   (805) 482-4518
Clubhouse (805) 388-2901

- ■ driving range
- ■ practice greens
- ■ power carts
- ■ pull carts
- ■ golf club rental
- ■ locker rooms
- ■ showers
- □ executive course
- □ accommodations
- ■ food and beverages
- ■ clubhouse

Bruce Hamilton
Professional

Pete Hernandez
Superintendent

Course information: This private course has 18 holes and par is 71. The course is 6,211 yards and rated 70.1 from the regular tees. The slope rating is 124. Women's tees are 5,642 yards and rated 72.1 from the regular tees. The slope rating is 118.

Play policy and fees: Reciprocal play is accepted with members of other private clubs, otherwise members and guests only. Green fees are $35 weekdays and $60 weekends for reciprocators. Carts are $9 per person. Reservations are recommended. This course is available for outside tournaments.

Location: Take the Las Posas Road exit off Highway 101 in Camarillo and drive north for one-half mile to Crestview Avenue. Turn left and drive one-quarter mile to Valley Vista Drive and turn right. Continue one mile to Fairview Drive and turn left to the club.

Course description: The front nine is hilly with narrow fairways. The back nine is flatter, but well bunkered. The greens are soft, but with good speed. You can count on true putts.

MOUNTAIN VIEW GOLF CLUB

Course information: This public course has 18 holes and par is 69. The course is 5,335 yards and rated 64.6 from the regular tees. The slope rating is 103. Women's tees are 5,305 yards and rated 67.9. Slope is 106.

Play policy and fees: Green fees are $10 weekdays and $14 weekends. Call for special rates. Carts are $14 weekdays and $16 weekends. Reservations are recommended.

Location: Take the Highway 126 exit off Highway 101 just south of Ventura and drive east to the 10th Street exit. Turn left under the freeway and drive to Harvard Boulevard and turn right. At 12th Street, turn right and drive one-half mile to South Mountain Road. Turn right to course.

Course description: This is a short course set in a narrow valley at the base of South Mountain. Mature trees border the fairways of this wandering course. Tee boxes have recently been moved back on some holes, adding another 100 yards to its length. The course may seem small, but it's difficult. Keep the ball straight.

16799 S. Mountain Road
Santa Paula, CA 93060

Pro shop   (805) 525-1571

□ driving range
■ practice greens
■ power carts
■ pull carts
■ golf club rental
□ locker rooms
□ showers
□ executive course
□ accommodations
■ food and beverages
■ clubhouse

Debra Burhoe
Manager

Kelly Gratton
Superintendent

CENTRAL H4

ELKINS RANCH GOLF COURSE

1962

Course information: This public course has 18 holes and par is 71. The course is 6,302 yards and rated 70.0 from the championship tees, and 6,010 yards and rated 68.5 from the regular tees. The slope ratings are 115 championship and 110 regular. Women's tees are 5,867 yards and rated 72.7. The slope rating is 110.

Play policy and fees: Green fees are $19 weekdays and $24 weekends. Call for special rates. Carts are $20. This course is available for outside tournaments. Golfers must wear collared shirts. Bermuda shorts are allowed, but no cut-offs. Reservations are recommended and should be made 10 days in advance.

Location: Take Interstate 5 north to Highway 126, turn west and drive 19 miles to Fillmore. At Highway 23, the second stop light, turn left and the course is 1.5 miles on the left.

Course description: This course is set in a canyon in the country. There are lots of water holes and few parallel fairways. It's a very challenging course with five lakes, elevated tees and demanding greens. Fun for all levels of play. It's quiet and scenic; a great getaway course that sees 60,000 rounds a year.

PO Box 695
Fillmore, CA 93016-0695

1386 Chambersburg Road
Fillmore, CA 93015

Pro shop   (805) 524-1440
Clubhouse (805) 524-1121

■ driving range
■ practice greens
■ power carts
■ pull carts
■ golf club rental
□ locker rooms
□ showers
□ executive course
□ accommodations
■ food and beverages
■ clubhouse

Terry Taylor
Professional

Daniel Hodapp
Professional

Robert Shipper
Superintendent

VALENCIA COUNTRY CLUB

1965
Robert Trent Jones, Sr.

Course information: This private course has 18 holes and par is 72. The course is 7,105 yards and rated 76.2 from the tournament tees, 6,723 yards and rated 73.7 from the championship tees, and 6,261 yards and rated 70.8 from the regular tees. The slope ratings are 144, 137 and 126. Women's tees are 5,733 yards and rated 73.6. The slope rating is 130.

Play policy and fees: Members and guests only. Guests must be accompanied by member while playing. Green fees are $45 weekdays and $65 weekends, carts included. Reservations are recommended. Closed Mondays.

Location: From San Fernando, travel north on Interstate 5 for 12 miles to Magic Mountain Parkway and turn east on Tourney Road to the club.

Course description: This Robert Trent Jones, Sr. design offers a scenic, natural layout with lots of trees. Water comes into play on eight holes. It's always a love-hate relationship with Jones, so take your pick on number 3. This hole is 222 yards and par-3 from the back tees. There is no bail out. There's water and bunkers on the right and trees on the left. It's considered one of the toughest par-3 holes in Southern California.

27330 North Tourney Road
Valencia, CA 91355

Pro shop (805) 254-6200

- ■ driving range
- ■ practice greens
- ■ power carts
- ▢ pull carts
- ■ golf club rental
- ■ locker rooms
- ■ showers
- ▢ executive course
- ▢ accommodations
- ■ food and beverages
- ■ clubhouse

Rick Smith
Professional

Wayne Mills
Superintendent

VISTA VALENCIA GOLF CLUB

Course information: This public course has 18 holes and par is 61. There is also a nine hole par-3 course. The course is 4,160 yards and rated 58.0 from the regular tees. The slope rating is 97. Women's tees are 4,021 yards and rated 60.9 from the regular tees. The slope rating is 101.

Play policy and fees: Green fees are $14 weekdays and $22 weekends. Call for special rates. Carts are $18. This course is available for tournaments.

Location: In Valencia, traveling north on Interstate 5, exit at Lyons Avenue. Drive east for one-half mile to Wiley Canyon Road. Turn left and then left again at Tournament Road. Drive one-half mile to Trevino Road, turn left again then drive one-half mile to the club.

Course description: This is a short course that requires good iron play. Five lakes are found on the layout and there is one island green. The course is always in good condition.

24700 West Trevino Drive
Valencia, CA 91355

Pro shop (805) 253-1870
Clubhouse (805) 253-0781

- ■ driving range
- ■ practice greens
- ■ power carts
- ■ pull carts
- ■ golf club rental
- ▢ locker rooms
- ▢ showers
- ■ executive course
- ▢ accommodations
- ■ food and beverages
- ■ clubhouse

Eric Costa
Professional

Bill Phillips
Superintendent

FRIENDLY VALLEY
GOLF COURSE

Course information: This private course is nine holes and par is 27. There is also a pitch-and-putt course. The course is 1,425 yards from the regular tees. Yardage for the women's tees was unavailable.

Play policy and fees: Members and guests only. This is a private residential course.

Location: Take Highway 126 off Interstate 5 and follow to San Fernando Road. From there travel 1.5 miles to Avenue of the Oaks, go left and look for the course.

Course description: This is a good opportunity for members to practice up on their short, short game.

19345 Avenue of the Oaks
Newhall, CA 91321

Pro shop   (805) 252-9859

- ☐ driving range
- ☐ practice greens
- ☐ power carts
- ☐ pull carts
- ☐ golf club rental
- ☐ locker rooms
- ☐ showers
- ☐ executive course
- ☐ accommodations
- ☐ food and beverages
- ☐ clubhouse

CENTRAL H4

MAP H5
(10 COURSES)

PAGES.. 362-367

CEN-CAL MAP ...see page 256
adjoining maps
NORTH (G5).......see page 326
EAST (H6) ....see page 368
SOUTH (I5) ....see page 412
WEST (H4) ....see page 350

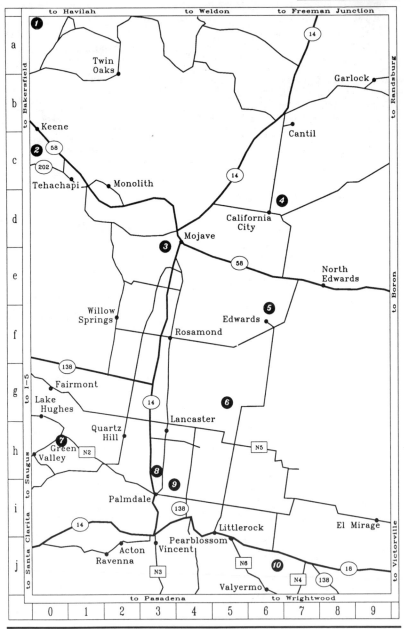

to Havilah   to Weldon   to Freeman Junction

a

to Bakersfield

Twin
Oaks

14

b

Garlock

Keene

Cantil

c

58

202

Monolith

Tehachapi

14

4

d

California
City

Mojave

3

58

e

North
Edwards

to Boron

Willow
Springs

5

Edwards

f

Rosamond

138

g

to I-5

Fairmont

Lake
Hughes

14

6

Lancaster

Quartz
Hill

h

7

Green
Valley

N2

N5

8

9

to Santa Clarita   to Saugus

Palmdale

i

138

14

Littlerock

El Mirage

to Victorville

Acton

Pearblossom
Vincent

j

Ravenna

N3

N6

10

N4   138

18

Valyermo

to Pasadena   to Wrightwood

0   1   2   3   4   5   6   7   8   9

to Randsburg

BAKERSFIELD
COUNTRY CLUB

Course 1
MAP H5 grid a0

1950
William Francis Bell

PO Box 6007
Bakersfield, CA 93306

4200 Country Club Drive
Bakersfield, CA 93306

Pro shop   (805) 871-4121
Clubhouse (805) 871-4000

Course information: This private course has 18 holes and par is 72. The course is 6,819 yards and rated 72.9 from the championship tees, and 6,458 yards and rated 72.9 from the regular tees. The slope ratings are 125 championship and 119 regular. Women's tees are 6,156 yards and rated 75.3. The slope rating is 127.

Play policy and fees: Reciprocal play is accepted with members of other private clubs, otherwise members and guests only. Green fees for guests and reciprocators are $25 with a member and $50 without. Reservations for members only. Carts are $16. Reservations are recommended.

Location: From Highway 99 at Bakersfield go east on Highway 178 about six miles. Take the Oswell Street exit and turn right to Country Club Drive to the club.

Course description: This is a nice, mature course situated on a hill. The layout requires excellent shot-making ability. Every club in the bag comes into play. Several long par-4s highlight the course. The course is the site of the Ben Hogan Tour event each February.

- ■ driving range
- ■ practice greens
- ■ power carts
- □ pull carts
- □ golf club rental
- ■ locker rooms
- ■ showers
- □ executive course
- □ accommodations
- ■ food and beverages
- ■ clubhouse

Dave Barber
Professional

Steve Scarbrough
Superintendent

CENTRAL H5

DEER CREEK COUNTRY CLUB

Course 2
MAP H5 grid c0

1963
Ted Robinson

22630 Woodford-
Tehachapi Road
Tehachapi, CA 93561

Pro shop   (805) 822-9118

Course information: This public course has nine holes. Par is 72 for 18 holes. The course is 6,284 yards and rated 70.6 from the regular tees. The slope rating is 118.

Play policy and fees: Green fees are $7 weekdays and $8 weekends for nine holes, and $12 weekdays and $15 weekends for 18 holes. Call for special rates. Carts are $16.

Location: From Bakersfield, travel east on Highway 58 for 38 miles to the town of Tehachapi, and turn right on Valley Road. Drive to Woodford-Tehachapi Road and turn right. Drive one mile to the course.

Course description: This country course offers a hilly setting with lots of trees and some water. The layout is interesting with few parallel fairways. The addition of a second nine, expected to open in the fall of 1991, will increase the difficulty of this course besides merely making it longer. The new nine is hilly with valleys and big lakes.

- ■ driving range
- ■ practice greens
- ■ power carts
- ■ pull carts
- ■ golf club rental
- □ locker rooms
- □ showers
- □ executive course
- □ accommodations
- ■ food and beverages
- ■ clubhouse

Ken Davis
Professional

Jack Keys
Superintendent

MAP ON PAGE 362

CAMELOT GOLF COURSE

1963

Course information: This public course has nine holes. Par is 72 for 18 holes. The course is 6,331 yards and rated 70.2 from the regular tees. The slope rating is 120.

Play policy and fees: Monthly and yearly memberships available for reduced green fees. Otherwise, green fees are $7.50 for nine holes and $11 for 18 holes weekdays, and $9 for nine holes and $14 for 18 holes weekends. Call for special rates. Carts are $14. Reservations are recommended. This course is available for tournaments. Shirts must be worn at all times on the golf course, as well as golf or tennis shoes.

Location: Drive one mile south of the town of Mojave on Highway 14. Turn west on Camelot Boulevard, and drive 1.5 miles to the course.

Course description: This course features tree-lined, narrow fairways. The greens, which are in excellent shape, are extremely difficult to read and putt. The par-3 fifth hole offers a tough and humbling green. The course record is 63. Among the annual tournaments played here is the PGA sponsored Pro-Am Tournament.

3430 Camelot Boulevard
Mojave, CA 93501

Pro shop   (805) 824-4411

■ driving range
■ practice greens
■ power carts
■ pull carts
■ golf club rental
□ locker rooms
□ showers
□ executive course
□ accommodations
■ food and beverages
■ clubhouse

Don Moulton
Director of Golf

Larry Jost
Professional

Mike Hill
Superintendent

TIERRA DEL SOL

1977
Devlin Von Hagge

Course information: This public course has 18 holes and par is 72. The course is 6,908 yards and rated 74.1 from the championship tees, and 6,300 yards and rated 70.6 from the regular tees. The slope ratings are 125 championship and 112 regular. Women's tees are 5,227 yards and rated 68.4. The slope rating is 122.

Play policy and fees: Green fees are $8 weekdays and $13 weekends. Call for special rates. Carts are $15. Reservations are recommended weekends and holidays one week in advance. Reserve a tee time a week in advance. Shirts must be worn in clubhouse area.

Location: Drive north on Highway 14 from Lancaster to Mojave. Continue on 14 five more miles to California City Boulevard. Drive 8.5 miles to North Loop, turn left and continue two miles to the clubhouse.

Course description: This 10-year-old, links-style course is level, long and open. There is water on 12 holes, there are 146 bunkers, and most of the greens are elevated. Hole five is the stickler: 180-yard carry over water followed by a 240-yard drive leaves a 6-7-8 iron to an elevated green over water. The first Norm Crosby Tournaments were held here. Now the annual tournaments are Gerry Kentner All Events and the High Desert Classic Pro-Am. The course record is 64, set by pro Dave Barber.

10300 North Loop Drive
California City, CA 93505

Clubhouse (619) 373-2384

■ driving range
■ practice greens
■ power carts
■ pull carts
■ golf club rental
■ locker rooms
■ showers
■ executive course
■ accommodations
■ food and beverages
■ clubhouse

Carroll Sharp
Proessional

Buzz Baker
Superintendent

MUROC LAKE GOLF COURSE

Course information: This military course has 18 holes and par is 72. The course is 6,954 yards and rated 73.5 from the championship tees, and 6,540 yards and rated 70.5 from the regular tees. The slope ratings are 128 championship and 120 regular. Women's tees are 5,763 yards and rated 72.3. There is no slope rating.

Play policy and fees: Military personnel and guests only. Outside play accepted. Reciprocal play accepted with members of other Air Forces bases. Green fees are $7 to $15 depending on personnel status. Call for special rates. Carts are $12. Reservations are recommended.

Location: Between the towns of Lancaster and Mojave on Highway 14, take the Rosamond exit and travel northeast for 15 miles to Lancaster Boulevard. Turn left and drive to Fitzgerald Boulevard. Turn left again and drive to Yucca Street and follow the signs.

Course description: This is the greenest place in this part of the Mojave Desert, and it's not because of all the military uniforms. The course is well maintained and features a small lake and numerous mature trees that line the fairways. Tall trees, which offer a welcome relief from the afternoon sun, are spaced every 20 yards on both sides of the fairways. If you hit through the trees, you're at the mercy of the desert. There's very little out-of-bounds on this course.

PO Box 207,
Edwards AFB
Edwards, CA 93523

Pro shop   (805) 277-3469
Clubhouse (805) 277-3467

■ driving range
■ practice greens
■ power carts
■ pull carts
■ golf club rental
□ locker rooms
■ showers
□ executive course
□ accommodations
■ food &beverages
■ clubhouse

Doug Carlton
Professional/Manager
Ralph Connors
Superintendent

CENTRAL H5

RANCHO SIERRA

1963
Jack Roesinger
Sam Fogo

Course information: This public course has nine holes. Par is 70 for 18 holes. The course is 4,904 yards and rated 61.0 from the regular tees. The slope rating is 91.

Play policy and fees: Green fees are $6 for nine holes and $10 for 18 holes weekdays, and $8 for nine holes and $12 for 18 holes weekends. Call for special rates. Pull carts are $1.

Location: Take the I exit off Highway 14 in the town of Lancaster, and travel east for about 10 miles to 60th Street. Turn left and drive 2.5 miles to the course.

Course description: This a flat, short course with narrow fairways. Water comes into play on seven holes. Mature trees line the fairways, and the bunkers are all grass. Jack Roesinger and Sam Fogo designed this course.

47205 60th Street East
Lancaster, CA 93535

Pro shop   (805) 946-1080

□ driving range
■ practice greens
□ power carts
■ pull carts
■ golf club rental
□ locker rooms
□ showers
□ executive course
□ accommodations
■ food and beverages
□ clubhouse

Kevin Kretz
Manager

Kent Kretz
Superintendent

MAP ON PAGE 362

LAKE ELIZABETH GOLF CLUB

Course information: This public course has 18 holes and par is 70. The course is 5,985 yards and rated 68.8 from the championship tees, and 5,658 yards and rated 67.1 from the regular tees. The slope ratings are 118 championship and 114 regular. Women's tees are 5,074 yards and rated 72.9. The slope rating is 115.

Play policy and fees: Green fees are $20 weekdays and $26 weekends. Carts included. Call for special rates. Reservations are recommended. Shirts with collars required. No cut-offs or short shorts. This course is available for tournaments.

Location: Take the Palmdale Boulevard exit off Highway 14 and turn left onto Ranch Club Road. Go about 16 miles to the end of the road, turn left and follow signs to the clubhouse.

Course description: This medium-length course was expanded from nine to 18 holes nearly two years ago. It is fairly hilly with small greens. Seven lakes come into play. The par-4 fifth hole is 434 yards from the championship tees, which doesn't seem significant except for the fact that there is a 200-foot drop from tee to fairway. More than one golfer has been fooled into thinking the drive had more distance than it did.

42532 Ranch Club Road
Lake Elizabeth, CA 93532

Pro shop   (805) 724-1221

- ■ driving range
- ■ practice greens
- ■ power carts
- □ pull carts
- ■ golf club rental
- □ locker rooms
- □ showers
- □ executive course
- □ accommodations
- ■ food and beverages
- ■ clubhouse

John Snabb
Professional

Frank Yorba
Superintendent

ANTELOPE VALLEY COUNTRY CLUB

Course information: This private course has 18 holes and par is 72. The course is 6,740 yards and rated 72.8 from the championship tees, and 6,408 yards and rated 70.6 from the regular tees. The slope ratings are 129 championship and 122 regular. Women's tees are 6,157 yards and rated 74.3 from the forward tees. The slope rating is 118.

Play policy and fees: Reciprocal play is accepted with members of other private clubs; otherwise members and guests only. Guest fees are $25 on weekdays and $35 weekends. Reciprocators are $35 weekdays and $45 weekends. Carts are $16.

Location: Take Avenue P east off Highway 14 in Palmdale and drive east for one block to Country Club Drive. Turn left and drive one-quarter mile to the club.

Course description: Don't forget to bring a sand wedge to this course. It is well bunkered but level, with many trees lining the fairways. Water can be found on several holes of this challenging course. The lake size has been enlarged on the par-3, 163-yard number 11. You must hit over the water to the large green, but don't hit short. The water comes to within five feet of the apron. Winds make every hole on this course different each day.

39800 Country Club Drive
Palmdale, CA 93550

Pro shop   (805) 947-3400
Clubhouse (805) 947-3142

- ■ driving range
- ■ practice greens
- ■ power carts
- ■ pull carts
- □ golf club rental
- ■ locker rooms
- ■ showers
- □ executive course
- □ accommodations
- ■ food and beverages
- ■ clubhouse

Steve Applegate
Professional

Dan McIntyre
Superintendent

DESERT AIRE GOLF COURSE

Course information: This public course has nine holes. Par is 72 for 18 holes. The course is 6,195 yards and rated 68.1 from the regular tees. The slope rating is 102.

Play policy and fees: Green fees are $7 weekdays and $10 weekends. Call for special rates. Carts are $8. This course is available for outside tournaments.

Location: Take Avenue ''P'' east off Highway 14 in Palmdale and drive four miles to the course.

Course description: This level, desert course is well bunkered with one lake. Mature trees line the fairways and offer welcome shade in the afternoon. The toughest hole is the 391-yard, par-4 eighth. It's straight and narrow with out-of-bounds to the right. Accuracy on a windy day is a must on this hole.

3620 East Avenue ''P''
Palmdale, CA 93550

Pro shop   (805) 273-7778
Clubhouse (805) 266-3688

- ■ driving range
- ■ practice greens
- ■ power carts
- ■ pull carts
- ■ golf club rental
- ■ locker rooms
- ☐ showers
- ☐ executive course
- ☐ accommodations
- ■ food and beverages
- ■ clubhouse

Gary Delano
Professional

Bob Chavez
Superintendent

CRYSTALAIRE COUNTRY CLUB

Course information: This private course has 18 holes and par is 72. The course is 6,962 yards and rated 73.8 from the championship tees, and 6,629 yards and rated 71.6 from the regular tees. The slope ratings are 132 championship and 124 regular.

Play policy and fees: Reciprocal play is accepted with members of other private clubs. Green fees are $25 weekdays and $35 weekends. Carts are $16.

Location: South of Lancaster take the Pearblossom exit off Highway 14 and travel about 16 miles east to the town of Llano. Turn south on 165th Street and drive to the club.

Course description: This scenic country course is set in the high desert surrounded by mountains. The terrain is rolling to hilly with lots of mature trees and three lakes. Watch for the par-3, 150-yard sixth. Players must drive over the lake to reach the hole. This hole has been the downfall of many, but it has also recorded more holes-in-one then any other hole on the course. The course is at the 3,500-foot elevation and is usually open in the winter.

15701 Boca Raton
Llano, CA 93544

Pro shop   (805) 944-2111

- ■ driving range
- ■ practice greens
- ■ power carts
- ■ pull carts
- ☐ golf club rental
- ■ locker rooms
- ■ showers
- ☐ executive course
- ■ accommodations
- ■ food and beverages
- ■ clubhouse

Allan Arvesen
Professional

Manuel Delgado
Superintendent

CENTRAL H5

MAP H6
(5 COURSES)

PAGES.. 368-372

CEN-CAL MAP...see page 256
adjoining maps
NORTH (G6).......see page 328
EAST ....no map
SOUTH (I6).........see page 472
WEST (H5) ....see page 362

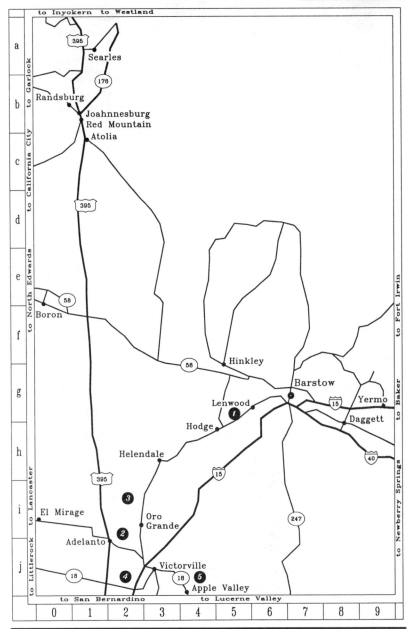

SUN VALLEY COUNTRY CLUB

C o u r s e   1
MAP H6 grid g5

1963
Ted Robinson

2781 Country Club Drive
Barstow, CA 92311

Pro shop   (619) 253-5201

■ driving range
■ practice greens
■ power carts
■ pull carts
■ golf club rental
■ locker rooms
□ executive course
□ accommodations
■ food and beverages
■ clubhouse

Bill Sailors
Manager

Course information: This public course has nine holes. Par is 72 for 18 holes. The course is 6,381 yards and rated 69 for 18 holes from the regular tees. The slope rating is 114. Women's tees are 6,028 yards and rated 71.9. The slope rating is 112.

Play policy and fees: Green fees are $8 for nine holes and $11 for 18 holes weekdays, and $10 for nine holes and $14 for 18 holes weekends. Carts are $8 for nine holes weekdays and $12 for 18 holes weekdays, and $10 for nine holes and $14 for 18 holes weekends. Play is on a first-come, first-served basis. This course is available for outside tournaments.

Location: From Interstate 15, two miles west of Lenwood, take the Lenwood Road exit west. Drive to Main Street and turn west. Drive on Main Street to Country Club Drive and the course.

Course description: Formerly known as the Sun and Sky Country Club, this is a straight and flat, tree-lined course that's perfect for beginners. The greens are small. The course is open year-round.

WEST WINDS GOLF COURSE

C o u r s e   2
MAP H6 grid j2

1964

Building 1140
George AFB, CA 92394

Pro shop   (619) 269-2613

■ driving range
■ practice greens
■ power carts
■ pull carts
■ golf club rental
■ locker rooms
□ showers
□ executive course
□ accommodations
■ food and beverages
■ clubhouse

Don Combs
Manager

Jerry Moore
Superintendent

Course information: This military course has nine holes. Par is 72 for 18 holes. The course is 6,630 yards and rated 72.3 from the regular tees. The slope rating is 130. Women's yardage is 5,558 and rated 71.0.

Play policy and fees: Military personnel and guests only. Green fees vary according to military status.

Location: Take Interstate 15 north from San Bernardino to the "D" Street (Apple Valley-Highway 18) exit north of Victorville. Travel west on Highway 18 for two miles to Air Base Road. Turn left and drive 2.5 miles to the main entrance to George Air Force Base. Go through main gate, travel two blocks, turn right just beyond the medical facility to the course.

Course description: This course is located in the high desert. Upon leaving the tee you are rarely faced with a level lie. Be prepared to use your irons from uphill, downhill and sidehill lies. Just off the fairway you'll find natural, desert terrain. Look out for tumbleweeds. The high desert winds can be cruel to the best of golfers. The greens resemble billiard tables, fast and hard. Don't be surprised to find yourself three- or four-putting. The 506-yard 18th hole is a dogleg left that is out-of-bounds both left and right. The fairway is bunkered on the left side and the green is surrounded by enough sand to replace the Mojave Desert. Once you reach this lightning fast green, the real fun starts.

SILVER LAKES
COUNTRY CLUB

Course information: This private facility has 27 holes and par is 72 for each of the 18-hole combinations. The South-South Course is 6,904 yards and rated 73.4 from the championship tees, and 6,486 yards and rated 70.7 from the regular tees. The slope ratings are 128 championship and 120 regular.

The North-South Course is 6,851 yards and rated 73.0 from the championship tees, and 6,455 yards and rated 70.5 from the regular tees. The slope ratings are 125 championship and 120 regular. Women's tees are 5,564 yards and rated 70.9. The slope rating is 118.

The East-South Course is 6,760 yards and rated 72.3 from the championship tees, and 6,376 yards and rated 69.9 from the regular tees. The slope ratings are 123 championship and 118 regular. Women's tees are 5,635 yards and rated 71.1. The slope rating is 116.

The East-North Course is 6,707 yards and rated 71.8 from the championship tees, and 6,345 yards and rated 69.5 from the regular tees. The slope ratings are 122 championship and 116 regular. Women's tees are 5,467 yards and rated 70.4. The slope rating is 114.

HC Box 2377
Helendale, CA 92342

14814 Club House Drive
Helendale, CA 92342

Pro shop   (619) 245-7435

- ■ driving range
- ■ practice greens
- ■ power carts
- □ pull carts
- ■ golf club rental
- □ locker rooms
- □ showers
- □ executive course
- ■ accommodations
- ■ food and beverages
- ■ clubhouse

Eric Sletten
Professional

Bob Catherwood
Superintendent

The East-East Course is 6,616 yards and rated 71.2 from the championship tees, and 6,266 yards and rated 69.2 from the regular tees. The slope ratings are 121 championship and 116 regular.

Play policy and fees: Reciprocal play is accepted with members of other private clubs. Guests at the Inn at Silver Lakes are welcome. Green fees are $25 weekdays and $30 weekends. Carts are $18. Reservations are recommended three days in advance. This course is available for outside tournaments. Reciprocal players should have their pro call ahead.

Location: Take Interstate 15 north from San Bernardino to the "D" Street/Apple Valley exit in Victorville. Turn left toward George Air Force Base and continue for 14 miles to Vista Road and turn left to the club.

Course description: All combinations are very distinctive. The South Course has lots of water, the East Course has just one hole with water and the North Course has two holes with water. All three courses have good, long holes on them and they also have narrow holes.

VICTORVILLE MUNICIPAL GOLF COURSE

1949

Course information: This public course has 18 holes and par is 72. The course is 6,627 yards and rated 71.2 from the championship tees, and 6,320 yards and rated 69.3 from the regular tees. The slope ratings are 121 championship and 117 regular. Women's tees are 5,731 yards and rated 72.7. The slope rating is 118.

Play policy and fees: Green fees are $12 for nine holes and $14 for 18 holes weekdays and $12 for nine holes and $17 for 18 holes weekends. Carts are $8 for nine holes and $17 for 18 holes. Reservations are recommended. This course is available for tournaments.

Location: From San Bernardino, drive north on Interstate 15 to Victorville. Exit at Palmdale Road and turn right. Drive to Greentree Boulevard and turn right. The course is 100 yards down the road.

Course description: This is a hilly course but it is walkable.

PO Box 1045
Apple Valley, CA 92307

15200 Rancherias Road
Apple Valley, CA 92307

Pro shop   (619) 242-3125
Clubhouse (619) 242-3653

■ driving range
■ practice greens
■ power carts
■ pull carts
■ golf club rental
■ locker rooms
■ showers
□ executive course
□ accommodations
■ food and beverages
■ clubhouse

Clifford Moore
Professional

David Hay
Superintendent

CENTRAL H6

APPLE VALLEY COUNTRY CLUB

Course information: This private course has 18 holes and par is 71. The course is 6,805 yards and rated 73.2 from the championship tees, and 6,477 yards and rated 70.9 from the regular tees. The slope ratings are 129 championship and 123 regular. Women's tees are 5,805 yards and rated 73.1 from the forward tees. The slope rating is 120.

Play policy and fees: Reciprocal play is accepted with members of other private clubs, otherwise members and guests only. Green fees are $35 weekdays and $40 weekends. Carts are $18. Reservations are recommended.

Location: From San Bernardino, drive north on Interstate 15 to the Apple Valley exit. Head east on Highway 18 to Rancherias Road and turn right. The course is on the right.

Course description: This is a fairly level course with wide fairways, mature trees and some water. The greens can be hard and fast. The course plays much more difficult then it looks, espcially when the wind is blowing, which may justify the high rating.

14144 Greentree Boulevard
Victorville, CA 92392

Pro shop   (619) 245-4860

□ driving range
■ practice greens
■ power carts
■ pull carts
■ golf club rental
□ locker rooms
□ showers
□ executive course
□ accommodations
■ food and beverages
□ clubhouse

Ray Echols, Jr.
Professional

Ray Salberg
Superintendent

Southern California Golf Courses

SOUTHERN CALIFORNIA COURSES

The golf urge is clearly present and accounted for in the southland, from the Mexican border to sprawling L.A., from the deserts and the mountains to the ocean. From one corner of the southland to the other, one thing is obvious: Southern California is golf crazy.

With almost half of the courses in the state located in the southern sector, you'll find every type of course imaginable. There are swanky private links with swanky celebrity members, oasis desert tracts, quaint nine-hole courses hidden within trailer parks, and deluxe seaside resort layouts.

In Los Angeles, clubs such as the Bel-Air Country Club, the Riveria Country Club, and the Los Angeles Country Club—all designed by the legendary George C. Thomas in the 1920s—boast some of the finest layouts in the state. If only you could get on them—they're also some of the most private clubs in the state.

Public courses also abound, although they're mostly pretty busy. If you live in Los Angeles, you already know this. But if you're visiting from Weaverville, get ready for some company on the links.

For one thing, the huge population base of Southern California creates greater demand for tee times. Consequently, play can be slower. But look at it this way: The weather is great! That's why everyone is on the golf course, anyway.

If you're looking for a refuge from the Los Angeles area, head to the desert, where some of the state's best resort courses rise out of the sand like brilliant green oases. They offer a unique brand of hazards, these desert tracts-—mind numbing heat in the summer (you'll welcome water hazards, maybe jump in), tumbleweeds, jackrabbits and coyotes and that ubiquitous desert wind.

The San Diego area, too, and the scenic coastline just to its north, is a haven for public and resort golf. And so is the historic Ojai Valley Inn and Country Club just north of Los Angeles. The jury is in: Southern California offers some of the best and most unique golf experiences to be found in the Golden State. Enjoy them!

SOUTHERN

SO-CAL BY AREA
(MAP, COURSES, PAGES)

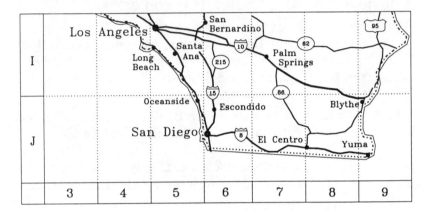

SO-CAL BY CITY
(CITY and MAP PAGE)

SOUTHERN

377

MAP I3
(1 COURSE)

PAGES.. 378-379

SO-CAL MAP .....see page 376
adjoining maps
NORTH (H3).......see page 338
EAST (I4) ....see page 380
SOUTH.........................no map
WEST ....no map

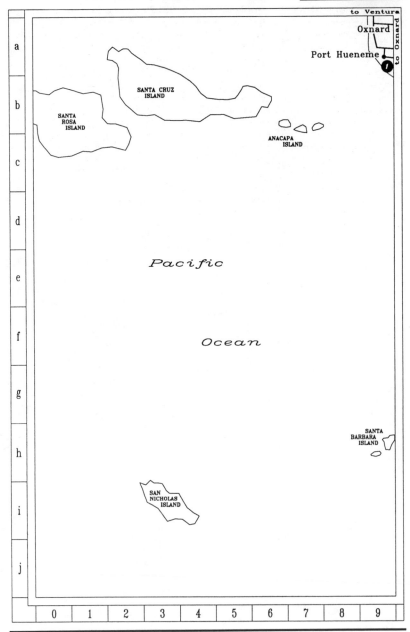

to Ventura

Oxnard

to Oxnard

Port Hueneme

SANTA CRUZ
ISLAND

SANTA
ROSA
ISLAND

ANACAPA
ISLAND

Pacific

Ocean

SANTA
BARBARA
ISLAND

SAN
NICHOLAS
ISLAND

a b c d e f g h i j

0 1 2 3 4 5 6 7 8 9

CBC PORT HUENEME GOLF CLUB

1957
Jack Daray

Course information: This military course has 18 holes and par is 72. The course is 6,298 yards and rated 69.2 from the championship tees, and 6,018 yards and rated 67.8 from the regular tees. The slope ratings are 113 championship and 107 regular. Women's tees are 5,585 yards and rated 72.1. The slope rating is 120.

Play policy and fees: Military personnel and guests only. Green fees vary according to military or civilian status. Reservations are recommended. Carts are $13. Closed Christmas

Location: Take Wagon Wheel Road off Highway 101 in Oxnard and drive south on Ventura Road to Pleasant Valley Road. Turn right and travel to the Port Hueneme Naval Base.

Course description: This is a deceptive course. Although flat, it plays tough because of green and bunker placement. The prevailing west wind off the ocean and numerous trees add to the challenge. Jack Daray built the original nine holes here in 1957. In mid-1990 it was expanded to 18 holes. Give careful study to number 13. It's a par-3, 179 yards from the championship tee. The large green appears to be surrounded by water and it's tough getting there. The green is not only guarded by water, but there are also front bunkers left and right. There is out-of-bounds is to the left and behind the green. Play is usually into a west wind. Aside from that, it's an easy hole!

Recreation Services Code
19–Bldg. 225
Port Hueneme, CA 93043

Pro shop   (805) 982-2620

- ■ driving range
- ■ practice greens
- ■ power carts
- ■ pull carts
- ■ golf club rental
- ■ locker rooms
- □ showers
- □ executive course
- □ accommodations
- ■ food and beverages
- ■ clubhouse

Chuck Green
Professional

George Garcia
Superintendent

MAP ON PAGE 378

379

SOUTHERN 13

MAP I4
(48 COURSES)

PAGES.. 380-411

SO-CAL MAP .....see page 376
adjoining maps
NORTH (H4).......see page 350
EAST (I5) ....see page 412
SOUTH.........................no map
WEST (I3) ....see page 378

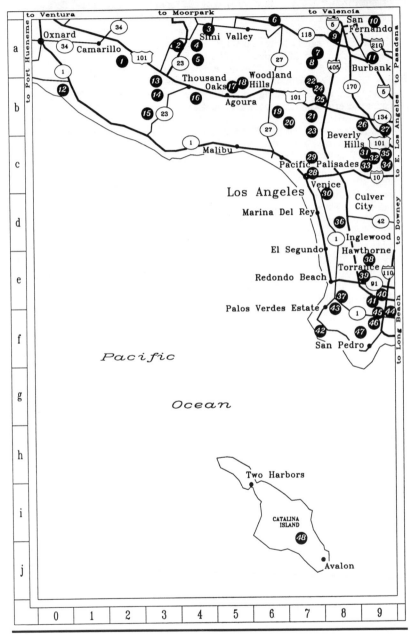

to Ventura · to Moorpark · to Valencia

Oxnard · 34 · Simi Valley · San Fernando

Camarillo · 34 · 101 · Thousand Oaks · Woodland Hills · Burbank

Agoura · Malibu · Pacific Palisades · Beverly Hills

Los Angeles · Venice · Culver City

Marina Del Rey · Inglewood

El Segundo · Hawthorne · Torrance

Redondo Beach

Palos Verdes Estate · San Pedro

Pacific

Ocean

Two Harbors

CATALINA ISLAND

Avalon

CAMARILLO SPRINGS GOLF COURSE

Course information: This public course has 18 holes and par is 71. The course is 6,375 yards and rated 69.9 from the championship tees, and 5,931 yards and rated 67.9 from the regular tees. The slope ratings are 114 championship and 108 regular. Women's tees are 4,975 yards and rated 70.2. The slope rating is 116.

Play policy and fees: Green fees are $20 weekdays and $40 weekends, including mandatory cart. Call for special rates. Reservations are required.

Location: Take the Camarillo Springs Road exit off Highway 101 in Camarillo, and drive south to the course.

Course description: This is a well-maintained, easily walked course with lots of trees. In 1989 the course underwent a complete reconfiguration. Even the hole sequence was changed. Three holes were altered and another two were changed. Water comes into play on 14 holes. Number six is a knockout. This par-5 is 512 yards from the championship tees and hits looking into a beautiful mountain range. Be straight on this hole, if no other. There are two lakes on the left and one is blind. Out-of-bounds is on the right and so are two fairway bunkers. The green is well trapped.

791 Camarillo Springs Road
Camarillo, CA 93012

Pro shop   (805) 484-1075

■ driving range
■ practice greens
■ power carts
■ pull carts
■ golf club rental
■ locker rooms
■ showers
□ executive course
□ accommodations
■ food and beverages
■ clubhouse

Louie Garcia
Professional

Jesse Martinez
Superintendent

SOUTHERN 14

SUNSET HILLS COUNTRY CLUB

Course information: This private course has 18 holes and par is 71. The course is 6,066 yards and rated 68.6 from the championship tees, and 5,769 yards and rated 67.4 from the regular tees. The slope ratings are 110 championship and 107 regular. Women's tees are 5,543 yards and rated 73.5. The slope rating is 124.

Play policy and fees: Reciprocal play is accepted with members of other private clubs. Green fees are $30 weekdays and $40 weekends. Carts are $18. Reservations are recommended. This course is available for outside tournaments Mondays only. Tennis is also available. Golfers must wear collared shirts. No jeans allowed. Shorts must have a six-inch inseam.

Location: From Highway 101 (Ventura Freeway), take the Fillmore exit (Highway 23) and drive north for 4.5 miles to Olsen Road. Turn left and drive one-half mile to Erbes Road. Turn left to the club.

Course description: Narrow fairways, fast greens and blind tee shots are characteristic of this well-maintained course. All the holes are fun, but challenging. The course is consistently one of the best-kept in the area.

4155 Erbes Road North
Thousand Oaks, CA 91360

Pro shop   (805) 495-5407
Clubhouse (805) 495-6484

☐ driving range
■ practice greens
■ power carts
☐ pull carts
☐ golf club rental
■ locker rooms
■ showers
☐ executive course
☐ accommodations
■ food and beverages
■ clubhouse

Michael Pease
Professional/Manager

David L.Foster
Professional

David Reich
Superintendent

SINALOA GOLF COURSE

Course information: This public course has nine holes. Par is 54 for 18 holes. The course is a very short 903 yards.

Play policy and fees: Green fees are $3.25 for nine holes and $6.50 for 18 holes weekdays, and $4 for nine holes and $8 for 18 holes weekends. Call for special rates.

Location: From Simi Valley drive west on Highway 118 to the Madera Road exit, go left and follow the road to the course.

Course description: In the mornings this is where the area teaching pros come to sharpen their short games. Formerly a citrus ranch, this busy course is under the jurisdiction of the Rancho Simi Valley Recreation Park District.

980 Madera Road
Simi, CA 93065

Pro shop   (805)581-2662

■ driving range
■ practice greens
☐ power carts
■ pull carts
■ golf club rental
☐ locker rooms
☐ showers
☐ executive course
☐ accommodations
☐ food and beverages
☐ clubhouse

Angel Lopez
Professional/Manager

WOOD RANCH GOLF CLUB

Course information: This private club has 18 holes and par is 72. The course is 6,972 yards and rated 75.8 from the tournament tees, 6,536 yards and rated 72.1 from the championship tees, and 6,126 yards and rated 69.3 from the regular tees. The slope ratings are 151 tournament, 130 championship and 123 regular. Women's tees are 5,392 yards and rated 72.5. The slope rating is 129.

Play policy and fees: Outside play is accepted. Call for information. Reciprocal play is accepted with members of other private clubs outside of Ventura and Los Angeles County. Guests must be accompanied by a member. Guest fees are $35 weekdays and $75 weekends. Reciprocators are $45 weekdays and $85 weekends. Carts are included. Reservations are recommended. This course is available for outside tournaments on Mondays only.

Location: From Los Angeles, travel north on Highway 101 to Highway 23. Head north to the Olsen Road exit and turn right. At Wood Ranch Parkway, turn right and drive to the club.

Course description: This course is considered one of the toughest in the Los Angeles area. This is an excellent target golf course with water hazards on 11 holes, lots of deep pot bunkers, few trees and deep rough. It's long and demanding with a links-style flavor. The pride of the course is the 464-yard, par-4 16th hole. It drops 120 feet from the tee and requires a testy second shot to a severe, two-tiered green. Designed by Ted Robinson in 1985, the course is rated among the top 20 in the state. The course record from the gold tees is held by Rob Sullivan with a 65. Wood Ranch Golf Club was the site of the 1987 and 1988 GTE West Seniors Classic and the 1986 Pac 10 Golf Championship. A U.S. Amateur qualifier was played here in 1990.

1985
Ted Robinson

PO Box 1749
Simi Valley, CA 93065

301 Wood Ranch Parkway
Simi Valley, CA 93065

Pro shop   (805) 522-7262
Clubhouse (805) 527-9663

■ driving range
■ practice greens
■ power carts
□ pull carts
■ golf club rental
■ locker rooms
■ showers
□ executive course
□ accommodations
■ food and beverages
■ clubhouse

Roger Rockefeller
Professional

Angus MacKenzie
Director

Gary Priday
Superintendent

SOUTHERN 14

NORTH RANCH
COUNTRY CLUB

Course information: This private club has 27 holes which break into three nines. Par is 72 on each of the 18-hole combinations.

The Valley-Oak Course is 6,678 yards and rated 73.0 from the championship tees, and 6,238 yards and rated 70.4 from the regular tees. The slope ratings are 133 championship and 124 regular. Women's tees are 5,447 yards and unrated.

The Valley-Lake Course is 6,879 yards and rated 72.8 from the championship tees, and 6,352 yards and rated 70.1 from the regular tees. The slope ratings are 124 championship and 117 regular. Women's tees are 5,328 yards and rated 73.4. The slope rating is 129.

The Lake-Oak Course is 6,886 yards and rated 72.4 from the championship tees, and 6,363 yards and rated 69.8 from the regular tees. The slope ratings are 124 championship and 117 regular. Women's tees are 5,379 yards and rated 73.5. The slope rating is 125.

4761 Valley Spring Drive
Westlake Village, CA 91362

Pro shop   (818) 889-9421
Clubhouse (818) 889-3531

- ■ driving range
- ■ practice greens
- ■ power carts
- □ pull carts
- ■ golf club rental
- ■ locker rooms
- ■ showers
- □ executive course
- □ accommodations
- ■ food and beverages
- ■ clubhouse

John Shuki
Professional

Duff Shaw
Superintendent

Play policy and fees: Members and guests only. Green fees are $35 weekdays and $60 weekends. Carts are $16. Reservations are recommended. This course is available for outside tournaments on Mondays only.

Location: Travel north on Highway 101 to the Westlake Boulevard exit and drive north for two miles to Valley Spring Drive. Turn right and drive one mile to the club.

Course description: This course is known for its smooth, fast greens and tight fairways. Players who miss the fairway can find themselves in big trouble. The 1988 NCAA Championship was held here. The Southwest Intercollegiate Championships are held here each spring.

SIMI HILLS GOLF COURSE

Course information: This public layout has 18 holes and par is 71. The course is 6,509 yards and rated 70.5 from the championship tees, and 6,133 yards and rated 68.7 from the regular tees. The slope ratings are 115 championship and 110 regular. Women's tees are 5,499 yards and rated 68.9, with a slope rating of 114.

Play policy and fees: Green fees are $13 weekdays and $20 weekends. Call for special rates. Carts are $20. Reservations are recommended and should be made one week in advance. Collared shirts must be worn on the course. Appropriate golf attire required.

Location: From Interstate 5 north of Los Angeles, travel west on Highway 118 for about 15 miles to the Stearns Street exit and turn right. Drive to Alamo Street and turn left to the course.

Course description: This course features both rolling and flat terrain, with some parallel fairways. There are some trees and water comes into play on several holes. The course record is 63. The Simi City Championship is held here in August. Several golf videos have been made at this course including Tom Sharp's *I Hate Golf.*

5031 Alamo Street
Simi Valley, CA 93063

Pro shop   (805) 991-5178
Clubhouse (805) 522-0813

- ■ driving range
- ■ practice greens
- ■ power carts
- ■ pull carts
- ■ golf club rental
- □ locker rooms
- □ showers
- □ executive course
- □ accommodations
- ■ food and beverages
- ■ clubhouse

Tom Szwedzinski
Professional

Kent Alkire
Superintendent

MISSION HILLS LITTLE LEAGUE GOLF COURSE

Course information: This short public course has nine holes. It is 2,254 yards for 18 holes and par is 27.

Play policy and fees: Green fees are $3.25 weekdays and $4 weekends. Students fees are $3 weekdays and $4 weekends. Seniors' Day is Friday and Ladies' Day is Tuesday. Both days allow an additional 25-cent discount to these parties.

Location: Off Interstate 405, take the Nordoff exit west. Turn right on Woodley and you'll see the course on the hill by the Veteran's Administration Hospital.

Course description: This short flat course is good for beginners. A few trees dot the course, but there are no traps.

PO Box 2642
Sepulveda, CA 91343

Pro shop   (818) 892-3019

- □ driving range
- ■ practice greens
- □ power carts
- ■ pull carts
- ■ golf club rental
- □ locker rooms
- □ showers
- □ executive course
- □ accommodations
- □ food and beverages
- □ clubhouse

Mike Mancini
Manager

SOUTHERN 14

PORTER VALLEY COUNTRY CLUB

Course information: This private course has 18 holes and par is 70. The course is 5,971 yards and rated 68.9 from the championship tees, and 5,674 yards and rated 67.6 from the regular tees. The slope ratings are 121 championship and 116 regular. Women's tees are 5,442 yards and rated 71.5. The slope rating is 115.

Play policy and fees: Members and guests only. Green fees are $40 weekdays and $60 weekends. Carts are $19.

Location: Take Interstate 405 to Highway 118 west. In Northridge, get off at Tampa Road and drive to the first light and take Porter Valley Drive to the club.

Course description: This is a short but hilly course offering tight fairways and well-bunkered greens. There are a few water hazards. Golfers enjoy a beautiful view of the entire San Fernando Valley.

19216 Singing Hills Drive
Northridge, CA 91326

Pro shop   (818) 368-2919
Clubhouse (818) 360-1071

- ■ driving range
- ■ practice greens
- ■ power carts
- □ pull carts
- ■ golf club rental
- ■ locker rooms
- ■ showers
- □ executive course
- ■ accommodations
- ■ food and beverages
- ■ clubhouse

Ken Cherry
Professional

Kenneth Mentzer
Superintendent

KNOLLWOOD GOLF COURSE

1956
William Francis Bell

Course information: This public course has 18 holes and par is 72. The course is 6,597 yards and rated 70.7 from the championship tees, and 6,234 yards and rated 69.2 from the regular tees. The slope ratings are 155 championship and 112 regular. Women's tees are 5,838 yards and rated 72.3. The slope rating is 113.

Play policy and fees: Green fees are $11 weekdays and $15 weekends for 18 holes. Carts are $17. Reservations are recommended.

Location: From Los Angeles take Interstate 5 north to Highway 118. Go west and exit at Balboa Boulevard, then go north three-fourths of a mile to the course.

Course description: None of the holes on this course overlap. Instead they run single file through a string of homes. Many fairway shots will be uphill making it tough to judge distance. You might see a celebrity or two on this course. Among the notables who have made an appearance here are Bob Hope, Mickey Rooney, Claude Akins, Joe Don Baker, Omar Bradley and Bret Saberhagen. If you want to swap hole-in-one stories, ask for starter Ron Fitt. The 80-year-old has aced numbers eight, 13 and 17. He might even tell you about Roy Watts who hit his tee shot out-of-bounds at the 306-yard par-4 14th hole, then teed up again and made a hole-in-one, giving him a birdie three on the hole. Dave Berganio holds the men's course record with a 64. Donna Caponi holds the women's record with a 70.

12040 Balboa Boulevard
Granada Hills, CA 91344

Pro shop   (818) 368-5709
Clubhouse (818) 360-2101
Starter   (818) 363-8161

- ■ driving range
- ■ practice greens
- ■ power carts
- ■ pull carts
- ■ golf club rental
- □ locker rooms
- □ showers
- □ executive course
- □ accommodations
- ■ food and beverages
- ■ clubhouse

EL CARISO GOLF COURSE

1975

Course information: This public course has 18 holes and par is 62. The course is 4,483 yards and rated 60.2 from the championship tees, and 4,065 yards and rated 58.3 from the regular tees. The slope ratings are 98 championship and 94 regular. Women's yardage is 3,557 and rated 58.9. The slope rating is 87.

Play policy and fees: Green fees are $9 weekdays and $13 weekends. Call for special twilight and senior rates. Carts are $15. Reservations are recommended.

Location: Take Interstate 210 to Hubbard exit and go east toward the mountains for one mile. At Elridge Avenue turn right and go three blocks to the course.

Course description: A well-placed tee shot is important on this course. Five lakes come into play and each green is well-bunkered. Number five is a tough 389-yard, par-4 that doglegs left and has water to the right.

13100 Elridge Avenue
Sylmar, CA 91342

Pro shop   (818) 367-6157
Clubhouse (818) 367-8742

- ■ driving range
- ■ practice greens
- ■ power carts
- ■ pull carts
- ■ golf club rental
- □ locker rooms
- □ showers
- ■ executive course
- □ accommodations
- ■ food and beverages
- ■ clubhouse

Bob MacLachlan
Professional/Manager

Scott Williams
Superintendent

SOUTHERN 14

HANSEN DAM GOLF COURSE

Course information: This public course has 18 holes and par is 72. The course is 6,591 yards and rated 69.6 from the championship tees, and 6,266 yards and rated 68.1 from the regular tees. The slope ratings are 121 championship and 111 regular. Women's tees are 6,090 yards and rated 75.0. The slope rating is 121.

Play policy and fees: Green fees are $10.50 weekdays and $14.50 weekends. Call for special rates. Carts are $16. Reservations are recommended. This course is available for outside tournaments.

Location: From Interstate 5 take Osborne and go east 1.5 miles to Glen Oaks. Turn right to Montague and turn left to the course.

Course description: This course plays longer than it looks. Big hitters must be careful about staying on the fairways. The greens tend to be small so chipping skills are important. The ninth hole is the number-one handicap hole on this course. It's a par-4, 450-yard stretch from the championship tee that requires the second shot to carry over a little dip and onto an elevated green.

10400 Glen Oaks Boulevard
Pacoima, CA 91331

Pro shop   (818) 899-2200
Clubhouse (818) 899-7456

■ driving range
■ practice greens
■ power carts
■ pull carts
■ golf club rental
□ locker rooms
□ showers
□ executive course
□ accommodations
■ food and beverages
■ clubhouse

Jim Anderson
Professional

Tom Kornkben
Superintendent

POINT MUGU GOLF CLUB

Course information: This military course has nine holes. Par is 70 for 18 holes. The course is 5,908 yards and rated 66.8 from the regular tees. The slope rating is 102.

Play policy and fees: Military personnel and guests only. Green fees vary according to military or civilian status.

Location: Take the Wood Road-USN Point Mugu exit off Highway 1 north of Camarillo Beach. Obtain a guest pass from the Visitor Information Center and enter the base at Mugu Road. Turn right at Third Street and drive to the course.

Course description: This course is wide open and flat for the most part. Four water hazards line the course, but the biggest obstacle is the low-flying aircraft going to and from the nearby airstrip. Bring ear plugs.

PO Box 42287
NAS Point Mugu,
CA 93041

Pro shop   (805) 989-7109

■ driving range
■ practice greens
■ power carts
■ pull carts
■ golf club rental
□ locker rooms
□ showers
□ executive course
□ accommodations
■ food and beverages
■ clubhouse

Gerry Garcia
Professional/Manager/
Superintendent

LOS ROBLES GOLF AND COUNTRY CLUB

Course information: This public course has 18 holes and par is 70. The course is 6,274 yards and rated 69.4 from the championship tees, and 5,868 yards and rated 67.0 from the regular tees. The slope ratings are 118 championship and 110 regular. Women's tees are 5,333 yards and rated 70.1. The slope rating is 117.

Play policy and fees: Green fees are $9 weekdays and $12 weekends. Call for special rates. Carts are $13. Reservations are recommended. Golfers must wear appropriate golf attire.

Location: Travel north on Highway 101 (Ventura Freeway) to the Moorpark Road exit and turn left under the freeway. Drive one block and turn right to the club.

Course description: This is a moderately hilly course with three lakes, and fairways flanked by trees. There are six par-3s. The Thousand Oaks City Championships are played here each August.

299 South Moorpark Road
Thousand Oaks, CA 91361

Pro shop   (805) 495-6421

- ■ driving range
- ■ practice greens
- ■ power carts
- ■ pull carts
- ■ golf club rental
- ■ locker rooms
- ■ showers
- □ executive course
- □ accommodations
- ■ food and beverages
- ■ clubhouse

Bob Meyer
Professional

Alex Alvidrez
Superintendent

SOUTHERN 14

1989
Jack Nicklaus

Course information: This private club has 18 holes and par is 72. The course is 7,025 yards from the tournament tees and rated 75.7, 6,594 yards from the championship tees and rated 72.9, and 6,003 from the regular tees and rated 69.5. The slope ratings are 146 tournament, 136 championship and 127 regular. Women's tees are 5,278 yards and rated at 65.5. The slope rating is 111.

Play policy and fees: Members and guests only. Guests must be accompanied by a member. This club is not reciprocal. Guest fees are $40 weekdays and $60 weekends. Caddies are required. Closed Mondays.

Location: Take Highway 101 to Westlake Boulevard, then drive south two miles to Potrero Road. Turn right and drive three miles to Stafford Road and left to the club.

Course description: With its bent grass fairways and greens, this youngster looks like its been here for years. Huge oak trees more than 100 years old add character. The course is on the west edge of Lake Sherwood. To accommodate national television coverage of some of its events, the course has reverted to its original layout, meaning that once again the front nine has become the back nine. The number six hole, formerly number 15, remains the hole to watch. It is a 186 yard par-3 from the tournament tees. The hole plays over seven different ponds, pools and waterfalls to a fairly narrow green on the edge of the water. Don't be deceived, the green is narrow from front to back, but long from left to right—if that's a help. Arnold Palmer once hit a ball on to an outcropping above this hole, prompting Peter Jacobson to quip, "That's the way Arnie likes it, on the rocks." Number six appears to be a downhill hole, but it is actually going up a mountain and the elevation changes 11 feet. Each November the course hosts the nationally televised Shark Shoot-Out, a benefit for the Ronald McDonald Children's Charities hosted by Greg Norman.

2215 Stafford Road
Thousand Oaks, CA 91361

Pro shop   (805) 496-3036

- ■ driving range
- ■ practice greens
- ■ power carts
- ■ pull carts
- ■ golf club rental
- ■ locker rooms
- ■ showers
- □ executive course
- □ accommodations
- ■ food and beverages
- ■ clubhouse

Ron Rhodes
Professional

Gary Davis
Assistant Professional

Bonnie Kyle
Manager

MALIBU COUNTRY CLUB

Course information: This public course has 18 holes and par is 72. The course is 6,800 yards and rated 72.3 from the championship tees, and 6,282 yards and rated 69.3 from the regular tees. The slope ratings are 130 championship and 121 regular. Women's tees are 5,627 yards. Ratings were unavailable.

Play policy and fees: Green fees are $45 weekdays and $65 weekends, carts included. No jeans or T-shirts.

Location: Off Highway 101 in Malibu, exit on Kanan Road and drive 10 miles toward the beach. After the second tunnel, turn right on Mulholland Highway. The road forks, stay left. You'll see the course in two miles on your right. It's on Encinal Canyon Road.

Course description: Nestled in the Santa Monica Mountains, this hilly course can get so warm you won't mind if your ball lands in one of the two natural lakes. You might want to follow it in!

901 Encinal Canyon Road
Malibu, CA 90265

Pro shop (818) 889-6680

□ driving range
■ practice greens
■ power carts
□ pull carts
■ golf club rental
■ locker rooms
■ showers
□ executive course
□ accommodations
■ food and beverages
■ clubhouse

Ken Domino
Professional

Todd Matsumoto
Superintendent

WESTLAKE VILLAGE GOLF COURSE

Course information: This public facility has 18 holes and par is 67. The course is a shortish 5,109 yards and rated 63.2 from the championship tees, and 4,668 yards and rated 59.9 from the regular tees. The slope ratings are 109 championship and 88 regular. Women's tees are 4,790 yards and rated 66.6. The slope rating is 113.

Play policy and fees: Green fees are $13 weekdays and $20 weekends. Call for special rates. Carts are $16. Reservations are recommended.

Location: Travel north on Highway 101 (Ventura Freeway) and take the Lindero Canyon Road exit. Drive south to Agoura Road and turn right. Continue three-fourths of a mile to Lakeview Canyon Road, and turn right to the course.

Course description: This course offers well-kept greens, three lakes and scenic, tree-lined fairways, but it's the trees that make this course competitive and tough. Slice or hook and you're a dead golfer looking for a way to get back on the course. There are seven par-3s, nine par-4s and two par-5s. The par-5s, thankfully, are straight.

PO Box 4216
Westlake Village, CA 91359

4812 Lakeview Canyon Road
Westlake Village, CA 91361

Pro shop (818) 889-0770
Pro shop (805) 495-8437

■ driving range
■ practice greens
■ power carts
■ pull carts
■ golf club rental
□ locker rooms
□ showers
■ executive course
□ accommodations
■ food and beverages
■ clubhouse

Coleman Gibson
Christine Lehmann
Ron Hinds
Steve Walker
Eric Kjerland
Joe Buttitta
Professionals

Rodolpho Ruiz
Superintendent

SOUTHERN 14

MAP ON PAGE 380

391

LAKE LINDERO GOLF CLUB

Course information: This semi-private course has nine holes. Par is 58 for 18 holes. The course is 3,338 yards and rated 52.9 from the regular tees. The slope rating is 90. Women's tees are 2,770 yards. There is no slope rating.

Play policy and fees: Outside play is accepted. Green fees are $8 weekdays and $10 weekends. Call for special rates. This course is available for outside tournaments.

Location: Travel north on Highway 101 (Ventura Freeway) to the Reyes Adobe exit. Turn right and drive to Thousand Oaks Boulevard. Turn left and continue to Lake Lindero Drive. The course will be on your left.

Course description: This is a tight, but rolling course with lots of trees and relatively small greens. Don't expect to tear this course up with a big game. Accuracy counts. Toughest hole is the par-3, 178-yard number three. You must hit from a slightly elevated tee to a small green guarded on the right by a huge oak and bunker. To the left there is an embankment that leads to a creek that flows through the course. Like all the holes on this course, if you're not where you should be off the drive, which is on or near the green, you're in trouble.

5719 Lake Lindero Drive
Agoura, CA 91301

Pro shop   (818) 889-1158

□ driving range
□ practice greens
□ power carts
■ pull carts
■ golf club rental
□ locker rooms
□ showers
□ executive course
□ accommodations
□ food and beverages
■ clubhouse

Tom Staskus
Professional

Rafael Guillen
Superintendent

CALABASAS PARK COUNTRY CLUB

Course information: This private course has 18 holes and par is 72. The course is 6,323 yards and rated 70.7 from the championship tees, and 6,082 yards and rated 69.6 from the regular tees. The slope ratings are 128 championship and 123 regular. Women's tees are 5,602 yards and rated 72.0. The slope rating is 122.

Play policy and fees: Reciprocal play is accepted with members of other private clubs, otherwise members and guests only. Green fees are $45 weekdays and $60 weekends, cart included. Reservations are recommended. Closed Mondays.

Location: Travel north on Highway 101 (Ventura Freeway) to Parkway Calabasas and turn at the first right and drive to the club.

Course description: This 25-year-old layout is located in a rapidly developing residential area. It is well maintained with many trees, some lakes and rolling terrain.

4515 Park Entrada
Calabasas Park, CA 91302

Pro shop   (818) 222-3222
Clubhouse (818) 222-3200

■ driving range
■ practice greens
■ power carts
■ pull carts
■ golf club rental
■ locker rooms
■ showers
□ executive course
□ accommodations
■ food and beverages
■ clubhouse

Jon Treglown
Professional

Ron Parker
Superintendent

WOODLAND HILLS COUNTRY CLUB

Course 19
MAP 14 grid b6

1924
William Park Bell

21150 Dumetz Road
Woodland Hills, CA 91364

Pro shop (818) 347-1476
Clubhouse: (818) 347-1511

☐ driving range
■ practice greens
■ power carts
☐ pull carts
☐ golf club rental
■ locker rooms
■ showers
☐ executive course
☐ accommodations
■ food and beverages
■ clubhouse

Kerry Hopps
Professional

Vincent Vazquez
Superintendent

Course information: This private club has 18 holes and par is 70. The course is 6,193 yards and rated 70.2 from the championship tees, and 5,954 yards and rated 68.8 from the regular tees. The slope ratings are 123 championship and 119 regular. Women's tees are 5,700 yards and rated 72.7. The slope rating is 124.

Play policy and fees: Members and guests only. Green fees are $30 weekdays and $45 weekends. Carts are $7.50. Closed Mondays.

Location: Travel north on Highway 101 (Ventura Freeway) in Woodland Hills to the DeSoto Avenue exit. Drive south past Ventura Boulevard three-fourths of a mile to Dumetz Road and turn right, then drive one-fourth of a mile to the club.

Course description: This course is located in a park-like setting with rolling hills and oak trees.

BRAEMAR COUNTRY CLUB

Course 20
MAP 14 grid b7

1959
Ted Robinson
(West Course)

PO Box 217
Tarzana, CA 91356

4001 Reseda Boulevard
Tarzana, CA 91356

Pro shop (818) 345-6520

☐ driving range
■ practice greens
■ power carts
☐ pull carts
■ golf club rental
■ locker rooms
■ showers
☐ executive course
☐ accommodations
■ food and beverages
■ clubhouse

Kevin Coombs
Professional

Richard Ray
Superintendent

SOUTHERN 14

Course information: This private club has two 18-hole courses. Par is 70 on the East Course and 71 on the West Course.

The East Course is 6,021 yards and rated 70.1 from the championship tees, and 5,776 yards and rated 68.7 from the regular tees. The slope ratings are 129 championship and 120 regular. Women's tees are 5,386 yards and rated 71.9. The slope rating is 127.

The West Course is 5,857 yards and rated 68.7 from the championship tees, and 5,593 yards and rated 67.3 from the regular tees. The slope ratings are 123 championship and 117 regular. Women's tees are 5,306 yards and rated 69.6, with a slope rating of 111.

Play policy and fees: Members and guests only. Green fees are $35 weekdays and $55 weekends. Carts are $19. This course is available for outside tournaments. No jeans or short shorts are allowed on the course. Men must wear collared shirts.

Location: Travel north on Highway 101 (Ventura Freeway) and take the Reseda Boulevard exit. Drive south for 2.5 miles to the end and turn right.

Course description: Both courses are short, tight and hilly. There are mature trees and a few parallel fairways.

EL CABALLERO COUNTRY CLUB

1926
William Park Bell

Course information: This private course has 18 holes and par is 71. The course is 6,830 yards and rated 73.8 from the championship tees, and 6,418 yards and rated 71.1 from the regular tees. Women's tees are 5,904 yards and rated 74.8. The slope rating is 130.

Play policy and fees: Members and guests only. Guests must be accompanied by a member. Green fees are $30 weekdays and $50 weekends. Carts are $16. Closed Mondays.

Location: Traveling north on Highway 101 (Ventura Freeway) in Tarzana, exit on Reseda Boulevard south (it becomes Mecca Avenue). At Tarzana Drive, turn left to the club.

Course description: This rolling course is challenging with large greens. It is one of the highest slope-rated courses in Southern California.

PO Box 570338
Tarzana, CA 91357-0338

18300 Tarzana Drive
Tarzana, CA 91356

Pro shop   (818) 345-2770

- ■ driving range
- ■ practice greens
- ■ power carts
- ■ pull carts
- □ golf club rental
- ■ locker rooms
- ■ showers
- □ executive course
- □ accommodations
- ■ food and beverages
- ■ clubhouse

Terry Lange
Professional

John M. Pollok
Superintendent

VAN NUYS GOLF COURSE

Course information: This public course has one nine-hole executive course and one 18-hole course. Par is 30 for nine holes and 54 for 18 holes. The 18-hole course is a short 2,181 yards and the nine-hole course is 1,691 yards.

Play policy and fees: Green fees are $4 weekdays for nine holes and $4.25 weekends for nine holes. Pull carts are $1. Call for special rates. Reservations may be made up to seven days in advance.

Location: Off Interstate 405 in Van Nuys, take the Sherman Way exit west. Turn left on Balboa and the course is on your left.

Course description: The executive course is one of the prominent par-3 courses in the area. The longest hole on this pitch and putt is 142 yards. Average playing time is under two hours. The 18-hole course is lined with trees and is relatively flat. There are lakes and ducks. The course is good for beginners.

6550 Odessa Avenue
Van Nuys, CA 91406

Pro shop   (818) 785-8871

- ■ driving range
- ■ practice greens
- □ power carts
- ■ pull carts
- ■ golf club rental
- □ locker rooms
- □ showers
- ■ executive course
- □ accommodations
- ■ food and beverages
- ■ clubhouse

MOUNTAINGATE
COUNTRY CLUB

Course information: This private course has 27 holes and par is 72 for each 18-hole combination.

The South/Lake Course is 6,756 yards and rated 72.9 from the championship tees, and 6,323 yards and rated 70.5 from the regular tees. The slope ratings are 129 championship and 122 regular. Women's tees are 5,715 yards and rated 73.3. The slope rating is 124.

The North/South Course is 6,672 yards and rated 72.0 from the championship tees, and 6,302 yards and rated 70.2 from the regular tees. The slope ratings are 128 championship and 121 regular. Women's tees are 5,744 yards and rated 73.2. The slope rating is 124.

The Lake/North Course is 6,034 yards and rated 70.4 from the championship tees, and 6,057 yards and rated 68.5 from the regular tees. The slope ratings are 118 championship and 110 regular. Women's tees are 5,501 yards and rated 71.8. The slope rating is 122.

Play policy and fees: Reciprocal play is accepted with members of other private clubs (ask your pro to call), otherwise members and guests only. Green fees are $55 weekdays and $95 weekends. Carts are $11. Reservations are recommended. This course is available for outside tournaments on Mondays only.

Location: Travel north on Interstate 405 to the Getty Center exit. Follow the exit to Sepulveda Boulevard and turn left driving 1.5 miles to Mountain Gate Drive. From there, turn left to the club.

Course description: This is a fairly new course with rolling fairways and difficult, undulating greens. The South in general is the most difficult of the courses to play. There are elevated greens and rolling hills. Don't expect to get a flat lie wherever you hit.

12445 Mountain Gate Dr.
Los Angeles, CA 90049

Pro shop   (213) 476-2800
Clubhouse (213) 476-6215

■ driving range
■ practice greens
■ power carts
□ pull carts
■ golf club rental
■ locker rooms
■ showers
□ executive course
□ accommodations
■ food and beverages
■ clubhouse

Mike Miller
Professional

David Bermudez
Superintendent

SOUTHERN 14

MAP ON PAGE 380

395

WOODLEY LAKES
GOLF COURSE

Course information: This public course has 18 holes and par is 72. The course is 6,782 yards and rated 70.9 from the championship tees, and 6,545 yards and rated 69.8 from the regular tees. The slope ratings are 111 championship and 109 regular. Women's tees are 6,242 yards and rated 74.3. The slope is 112.

Play policy and fees: Green fees are $10.50 weekdays and $14.50 weekends. Players must have a Los Angeles Parks and Recreation reservation card.

Location: From Interstate 405 in Van Nuys, exit at Victory Boulevard and drive one-half mile to Woodley Avenue. From there go left and drive to the course.

Course description: This is a relatively long and flat course with large greens. Many of the greens are elevated. The course is not too demanding unless you hit into one or more of its six lakes.

6331 Woodley Avenue
Van Nuys, CA 91406

Pro shop   (818) 787-8163
Starter   (818) 780-6886

- ■ driving range
- ■ practice greens
- ■ power carts
- ■ pull carts
- ■ golf club rental
- □ locker rooms
- □ showers
- □ executive course
- □ accommodations
- ■ food and beverages
- ■ clubhouse

John Perkins
Professional

SEPULVEDA GOLF COURSE

1953
William Park Bell

16821 Burbank Boulevard
Encino, CA 91436

Pro shop　　(818) 986-4560
Starter　　　(818) 995-1170

■ driving range
■ practice greens
■ power carts
■ pull carts
■ golf club rental
□ locker rooms
■ showers
□ executive course
□ accommodations
■ food and beverages
■ clubhouse

Dave Jenkins
Professional

Steve Ball
Superintendent

Course information: This public facility has two 18-hole courses. The Balboa course par is 70. The Encino course par is 72.

The Balboa course is 6,328 yards from the championship tees and rated 68.4, and 6,088 yards from the regular tees and rated 67.3. The slope ratings are 119 championship and 117 regular. Women's tees are 5,890 yards and rated 71.7. The slope rating is 117.

The Encino course is 6,863 yards from the championship tees and rated 70.5, and 6,408 yards from the regular tees and rated 68.4. The slope ratings are 105 championship and 100 regular. Women's tees are 6,185 yards and rated 73.7. The slope rating is 119.

Play policy and fees: Green fees are $11 weekdays and $15 weekends. Carts are $16. Reservations are recommended, but can only be made by holders of a Los Angeles Park and Recreation reservation card.

Location: Take Highway 134 to the Burbank Boulevard exit in Encino, go right about one-half mile and you'll see the course.

Course description: The Balboa course is long and demanding. Shot placement is crucial. The greens are bunkered. There are overhanging trees. It is a good test of golf skill for the intermediate player. The Encino course, although longer, is much easier. It's wide open.

STUDIO CITY GOLF COURSE

4141 Whitsett Avenue
Studio City, CA 91604

Pro shop　　(818) 761-3250

■ driving range
■ practice greens
□ power carts
■ pull carts
■ golf club rental
□ locker rooms
□ showers
□ executive course
□ accommodations
■ food and beverages
■ clubhouse

Course information: This public tract has nine holes. Par is 54 for 18 holes. The course is 975 yards for nine holes.

Play policy and fees: Green fees are $5 weekdays and $6 weekends and holidays.

Location: Take Highway 134 to Whitsett Avenue in Studio City and turn left and drive about two miles to the course.

Course description: This is a nine-hole, par-3 course with no hole longer than 135 yards. The adjoining driving range is open until 11 p.m. For those interested in a quick set of tennis, a tennis club is affiliated with the golf course.

SOUTHERN 14

LAKESIDE GOLF CLUB

1926
Max Behr

Course information: This private course has 18 holes and par is 70. The course is 6,534 yards and rated 71.9 from the championship tees, and 6,272 yards and rated 70.1 from the regular tees. The slope ratings are 129 championship and 121 regular. Women's tees are 5,949 yards and rated 74.3. The slope rating is 123.

Play policy and fees: Members and guests only. Guests must accompany a member. Guests fees are $35.

Location: Travel north on Highway 101 (Hollywood Freeway) to the Barham Boulevard exit, and drive north to Lakeside Drive. From there, turn left and drive to the club. Or, take Ventura Boulevard (Highway 134) to Pass Avenue south, crossing Riverside to Lakeside Drive. Turn right to the club.

Course description: Built in 1926, this rolling course has small undulating greens. It is a short-yardage course, but plays long. These fairways were once a haven for Hollywood's heroes and rogues: Bing Crosby, Dean Martin, Bob Hope and just about anybody else who ever had a golf tournament named for them played a round or two here. The Maury Luxford Pro-Am is held here each August. The Trans-Mississippi Mid-Amateur Championship was held here in 1991.

PO Box 2386
Toluca Lake Station
Toluca Lake, CA 91610

4500 Lakeside Drive
Burbank, CA 91602

Pro shop   (818) 985-3335
Clubhouse (818) 984-0601

- ■ driving range
- ■ practice greens
- ■ power carts
- □ pull carts
- ■ golf club rental
- ■ locker rooms
- ■ showers
- □ executive course
- □ accommodations
- ■ food and beverages
- ■ clubhouse

Dave Allaire
Professional

Brent Weston
Superintendent

THE RIVIERA COUNTRY CLUB

1926
George C. Thomas

Course information: This private course has 18 holes and par is 72. The course is 7,016 yards and rated 75.7 from the championship tees, and 6,522 yards and rated 72.4 from the regular tees. Women's yardage is 5,942 and rated 74.4. The slope ratings are 142 championship, 135 regular and 131 women.

1250 Capri Drive
Pacific Palisades, CA 90272

Operations (213) 454-6591

- driving range
- practice greens
- power carts
- □ pull carts
- golf club rental
- locker rooms
- showers
- □ executive course
- accommodations
- food and beverages
- clubhouse

Play policy and fees: Limited reciprocal play is accepted with members of other private clubs. Hotel guests are welcome. Green fees for unattended guests are $150. The fee for hotel guests is $150. Green fees for guests playing with members is $75 weekdays and $90 weekends. Reservations are essential. This course is available for outside tournaments Mondays only.

Location: Take the Sunset Boulevard exit off Interstate 405 and travel west for three miles to Capri Drive, then turn left to the club.

Peter Oosterhuis
Director of Golf

Jim McPhilomy
Superintendent

Course description: This well-maintained course is more than 60 years old and has been played by scores of Hollywood's rich and famous. George C. Thomas designed the long and tough layout in 1926. The fairways and rough are planted with Kikuyu grass so there's not much roll. The 170-yard-par-3 sixth hole features a bunker in the middle of the green. If that doesn't frighten you maybe the par-4 18th will. It is considered one of the toughest holes in golf. The 1948 U.S. Open was played here and won by the great Ben Hogan, and Hal Sutton captured the 1983 PGA crown here. The Los Angeles Open is played here annually. This course is rated among the top 20 in the state for good reason. The course record of 62 is jointly held by Larry Mize and Fred Couples. The 72-hole tournament record of 264 is held by Lanny Wadkins, set in the 1985 Los Angeles Open.

SOUTHERN 14

BRENTWOOD COUNTRY CLUB

Course information: This private course has 18 holes and par is 72. The course is 6,734 yards and rated 72.3 from the championship tees, and 6,524 yards and rated 70.6 from the regular tees. Women's yardage is 6,035 and rated 68.1. The slope ratings are 124 championship, 117 regular and 110 women.

Play policy and fees: Members and guests only. Green fees are $35 weekdays and $50 weekends. Carts are $18.

Location: Travel west on Wilshire Boulevard to San Vincente Boulevard and bear right. At Burlingame Avenue, turn left to the club.

Course description: Accurate fairway play is important here. The course is fairly tight with lots of trees. The back nine is especially narrow and long. A small lake borders nine holes. The course also gets hilly in spots. What makes this a particularly good course are the greens: they are fast and true. So plan on putting accurately.

590 South Burlingame Avenue
Los Angeles, CA 90049

Pro shop   (213) 451-8011

- ■ driving range
- ■ practice greens
- ■ power carts
- ■ pull carts
- ☐ golf club rental
- ■ locker rooms
- ■ showers
- ☐ executive course
- ☐ accommodations
- ■ food and beverages
- ■ clubhouse

Bob Harrison
Professional
Bob O'Connell
Superintendent

PENMAR GOLF COURSE

Course information: This public course has nine holes. Par is 58 for 18 holes. The yards and rating were unavailable.

Play policy and fees: Green fees are $5.50 for nine holes. Call for special rates.

Location: In Venice, drive north on Lincoln Boulevard (Highway 1) to Rose Avenue, turn right and proceed two blocks to the course.

Course description: This nine-hole course offers an interesting and challenging layout in the heart of wild and wacky Venice.

1233 Rose Avenue
Venice, CA 90291

Pro shop   (213) 396-6228

- ☐ driving range
- ■ practice greens
- ☐ power carts
- ■ pull carts
- ■ golf club rental
- ☐ locker rooms
- ☐ showers
- ☐ executive course
- ☐ accommodations
- ☐ food and beverages
- ☐ clubhouse

BEL-AIR COUNTRY CLUB

1926
George C. Thomas

10768 Bellagio Road
Los Angeles, CA 90077

Pro shop   (213) 440-2423
Clubhouse (213) 476-9563

☐ driving range
■ practice greens
■ power carts
☐ pull carts
■ golf club rental
■ locker rooms
■ showers
☐ executive course
☐ accommodations
■ food and beverages
■ clubhouse

Ed Merrins
Professional

Steve Badger
Superintendent

Course information: This private course has 18 holes and par is 70. The course is 6,483 yards and rated 71.8 from the championship tees, and 6,212 yards and rated 70.3 from the regular tees. Women's yardage is 5,770 and rated 73.2. The slope ratings are 131 championship, 126 regular and 125 women.

Play policy and fees: Green fees are $40 Monday through Thursday and $50 Friday through Sunday with a member. Green fees are $100 without a member. Carts are $18.

Location: Take the Sunset Boulevard exit off Interstate 405 and travel east for three-fourths of a mile to Bellagio Road. Turn left and bear right. You'll shortly find the club entrance on your right.

Course description: This austere, hilly course has narrow fairways and lots of trees. It's well bunkered with small greens and places a premium on accuracy. It was the site of the 1976 U.S. Amateur Championship and is the home course of the UCLA Bruins golf team. Designed by George C. Thomas in 1926, it rates among the top 20 in the state. One of the landmark holes is number 10, a par-3, 210-yard nerve wracker, known as the "Swinging Bridge." You park your cart on one side of a canyon, walk back to the tee box and hope your drive clears the canyon. The green is in sight, but that's no help. Talk about pressure. The tee is next to the club grill where there is always a critical gallery. Some golfers choose to hit from the women's tee which is out of sight from the grill. It's a no-win situation.

SOUTHERN 14

THE LOS ANGELES COUNTRY CLUB

1921
George C. Thomas

10101 Wilshire Boulevard
Los Angeles, CA 90024

Pro shop   (213) 276-6104

- ■ driving range
- ■ practice greens
- ■ power carts
- □ pull carts
- ■ golf club rental
- ■ locker rooms
- ■ showers
- □ executive course
- ■ accommodations
- ■ food and beverages
- ■ clubhouse

Ed Oldfield
Professional

Mike Hathaway
Superintendent

Course information: This private club has two 18-hole courses. Par is 71 on the North Course and 70 on the South Course.

The North Course is 6,895 yards and rated 74.5 from the championship tees, and 6,586 yards and rated 72.5 from the regular tees. The slope ratings are 143 championship and 136 regular. Women's tees are 6,184 yards and rated 76.5. The slope rating is 143.

The South Course is 5,909 yards and rated 68.4 from the championship tees, and 5,638 yards and rated 66.9 from the regular tees. The slope ratings are 120 championship and 112 regular. Women's tees are 5,638 yards and rated 71.6. The slope rating is 112.

Play policy and fees: Members and guests only. Guest fees are $15 Monday, $25 Tuesday through Friday, and $40 on weekends. Carts are $20. There are no tee times. No shorts are allowed on the golf course. Women must wear skirts.

Location: Take the Wilshire Boulevard exit off Interstate 405, and drive east to the club.

Course description: This is a beautiful course designed in 1921 by George C. Thomas. It is ranked the number one course in Southern California and has been the home of five Los Angeles Open championships. The North Course is the more difficult of the two. It features long, tight fairways and small greens with hilly terrain and lots of trees. The South Course is flatter and more open. The greens are tricky. They are small with subtle undulation. There is also a long par-5 at 565 yards. The North Course records are 64 for men and 68 for women.

HILLCREST COUNTRY CLUB

Course information: This private course has 18 holes and par is 71. The course is 6,371 yards and rated 70.5 from the championship tees, and 6,069 yards and rated 68.7 from the regular tees. The slope ratings are: 122 championship and 115 regular. Women's tees are 5,853 yards and rated 73.0. The slope rating is 122.

Play policy and fees: Members and guests only. Green fees were unavailable.

Location: Take the Pico Boulevard exit off Interstate 405 southbound, and travel east to the club. Northbound on Interstate 405 take the Venice Boulevard exit to Motor Street, which turns into Pico Boulevard and drive to the club.

Course description: This is a relatively short and tree-lined course, and it can be testy. The fairways are lush and well-maintained. There is also a pitch and putt, six-hole, par-3 course. The 18-hole course record is 63 and is jointly held by Eric Monty and Greg Starkman. The Los Angeles Open qualifier was formerly held here.

10000 West Pico Boulevard
Los Angeles, CA 90064

Pro shop   (213) 8553-8911

- ■ driving range
- ■ practice greens
- ■ power carts
- □ pull carts
- □ golf club rental
- □ locker rooms
- □ showers
- □ executive course
- □ accommodations
- □ food and beverages
- □ clubhouse

Paul Wise
Professional

David Mastroleo
Superintendent

RANCHO PARK GOLF COURSE

Course information: This public course has 18 holes and par is 71. There is also a nine-hole, par-3 course. The par is 27. The course is 6,585 yards and rated 71.7 from the championship tees, and 6,216 yards and rated 69.4 from the regular tees. The slope ratings are 124 championship and 117 regular. Women's tees are 5,928 and rated 73.4. The slope rating is 121.

Play policy and fees: Green fees are $12 weekdays and $15 weekends. Carts are $18. Reservations are recommended, but can only be made by holders of a Los Angeles Park and Recreation reservation card. Standbys are welcome for non-card holders.

Location: Take the Santa Monica Freeway to Overland exit. Travel north on Overland approximately three-fourths miles to Pico Boulevard. Turn right and drive one-half mile to the course.

Course description: You read about this course in *Vanity Fair* after three paratroopers with smoke flares dropped out of the sky and onto the first hole just to hand L.A.P.D. Chief Daryl Gates a golf ball. It was all for charity, of course. Otherwise, this course was the former site of the Los Angeles Open. It is a championship layout over rolling terrain with small greens. It is now the site of the Ceninela Classic.

10460 West Pico Boulevard.
Los Angeles, CA 90064

Pro shop   (213) 839-4374
Coffee shop(213) 839-7750
Starter   (213) 838-7373

- ■ driving range
- ■ practice greens
- ■ power carts
- ■ pull carts
- ■ golf club rental
- ■ locker rooms
- ■ showers
- ■ executive course
- □ accommodations
- ■ food and beverages
- ■ clubhouse

Ron Weiner
Professional

Ken Novak
Superintendent

SOUTHERN 14

THE WILSHIRE COUNTRY CLUB

1919

Course information: This private club has 18 holes and par is 71. The course is 6,531 yards and rated 71.6 from the championship tees, and 6,295 yards and rated 70.2 from the regular tees. The slope ratings are 126 championship and 121 regular. Women's tees are 6,008 yards and rated 74.2. The slope rating is 127.

Play policy and fees: Members and guests only.

Location: Take the Santa Monica Boulevard exit off Highway 101 (Hollywood Freeway) and travel west for one mile to Vine Street. Turn left and drive one mile (becomes Rossmore Avenue) to the club on the right.

Course description: Built in 1919, this course was used for the Los Angeles Open in 1926. The mostly level fairways are lined with mature trees and the greens are well maintained. A barranca runs through 14 of the 18 fairways.

301 North Rossmore Avenue
Los Angeles, CA 90004

Pro shop   (213) 934-6050
Clubhouse (213) 934-1121

- ■ driving range
- ■ practice greens
- ■ power carts
- ❑ pull carts
- ❑ golf club rental
- ■ locker rooms
- ■ showers
- ❑ executive course
- ❑ accommodations
- ■ food and beverages
- ■ clubhouse

Roland Frenkel
Manager

Patrick Rielly
Junior Professional

Alex Galaviz
Junior Superintendent

WESTCHESTER GOLF COURSE

Course information: This public course has 15 holes and par is 53. The course is 3,470 yards.

Play policy and fees: Green fees are $8 weekdays and $12 weekends. Carts are $15. Pull carts are $2.

Location: Off of Interstate 405 in Westchester (near Inglewood), exit on Manchester Boulevard heading west and drive to the course on your left.

Course description: There aren't many 15-hole executive courses, but this is one of them. The course lost three holes—numbers four, five and six—in 1990 to the Los Angeles International Airport for a road and is still looking for repayment. In the meantime, it has been reconfigured while it waits for overlapping governments to decide its fate. This executive course remains flat with one lake. It offers good practice for the irons.

6900 West Manchester
Los Angeles, CA 90045

Pro shop   (213) 670-5110

- ■ driving range
- ■ practice greens
- ■ power carts
- ■ pull carts
- ■ golf club rental
- ❑ locker rooms
- ❑ showers
- ■ executive course
- ❑ accommodations
- ■ food and beverages
- ❑ clubhouse

Roger Yenny
Professional

Lynn Ralston
Professional

Robert Hall
Manager

Manuel Guttierez
Superintendent

SEA AIRE PARK GOLF COURSE

Course information: This public course has nine holes. Par is 27. The layout runs 618 yards.

Play policy and fees: Green fees are $4 any day. Senior rates are $1 weekdays. Children are $1 any day.

Location: In Torrance, drive west on Sepulveda. Cross Anza and turn left on Reynolds, then left on Lupine to the course.

Course description: This is a short, par-3 course. The longest hole is 90 yards. It is a good practice course for your short iron game. Caters to a good number of beginners and it's cheap!

22730 Lupine Drive
Torrance, CA 90505

Pro shop   (213) 316-9779

- ☐ driving range
- ■ practice greens
- ☐ power carts
- ☐ pull carts
- ■ golf club rental
- ☐ locker rooms
- ☐ showers
- ☐ executive course
- ☐ accommodations
- ☐ food and beverages
- ☐ clubhouse

CHESTER WASHINGTON GOLF COURSE

Course information: This public course has 18 holes and par is 70. The course is 6,348 yards and rated 68.3 from its championship tees, and 6,002 yards and rated 66.7. The slope ratings are 107 championship and 104 regular. Women's tees are 5,646 yards and rated 71.8. The slope rating is 114.

Play policy and fees: Green fees are $11 weekdays and $15 weekends.

Location: From Interstate 405 driving south (near Inglewood and Hawthorne), take the Imperial Highway exit and drive west. You'll see the Hawthorne Municipal Airport on your left. Turn right on Western Avenue to the course.

Course description: This is a wide-open course for free swingers. There are few hazards to worry about.

1930 West 120th Street
Los Angeles, CA 90047

Pro shop   (213) 756-6975

- ■ driving range
- ■ practice greens
- ■ power carts
- ■ pull carts
- ■ golf club rental
- ☐ locker rooms
- ☐ showers
- ☐ executive course
- ☐ accommodations
- ■ food and beverages
- ■ clubhouse

SOUTHERN 14

ALONDRA PARK GOLF COURSE

Course information: This public facility has two 18-hole courses. The main course has a par of 72. The executive course has a par of 54. The main course is 6,500 yards and rated 69.4 from the championship tees, and 6,292 yards and rated 67.7 from the regular tees. The slope ratings are 106 championship and 104 regular. Women's tees are 6,100 yards and rated 73.0. The slope rating is 109. The executive course is 2,356 yards and rated 57.0.

Play policy and fees: The green fees are $11 weekdays and $15 weekends for the main course, and $5.50 weekdays and $6.50 weekends for the executive course. Carts are $17.

Location: Off Interstate 405 in Redondo Beach, take the Redondo Beach exit and drive northeast. The course is located on the corner of Prairie and Redondo Beach Boulevard.

Course description: The main course is flat and open with ocean breezes from two miles away. The executive course is flat also and offers a good practice round.

16400 South Prairie
Lawndale, CA 90260

Pro shop   (213) 217-9915
Starter   (213) 217-9919

■ driving range
■ practice greens
■ power carts
■ pull carts
■ golf club rental
□ locker rooms
■ showers
■ executive course
□ accommodations
■ food and beverages
■ clubhouse

Salvador Flores
Superintendent

VICTORIA GOLF COURSE

1966

Course information: This public course has 18 holes and par is 72. The course is 6,787 yards and rated 70.7 from the championship tees, and 6,558 yards and rated 69.5 from the regular tees. The slope ratings are 111 championship and 109 regular. Women's tees are 6,048 and rated 73.0. The slope rating is 115.

Play policy and fees: Green fees are $11 weekdays and $16 weekends. The twilight rate is $7 weekdays and $9 weekends. Senior citizens play for $5.50 and students are $4.50 during the week. Carts are $16. Reservations are recommended.

Location: Take Interstate 405 to the Avalon exit, then go north on Avalon to 192nd Street, turn left on 192nd Street to the course.

Course description: Most greens are protected by sand at this course. There are no water holes. The 515-yard first hole may put you in a sour mood right off the bat, if you're not aware of the fairway sand traps. The course record is 64.

340 East 192nd Street
Carson, CA 90746

Pro shop   (213) 323-6981

■ driving range
■ practice greens
■ power carts
□ pull carts
■ golf club rental
□ locker rooms
□ showers
□ executive course
□ accommodations
■ food and beverages
□ clubhouse

Eugene Hardy
Professional

JACK THOMPSON PAR-3 GOLF COURSE

Course 41
MAP 14 grid e9

Course information: This public course has nine holes, par 27. The course is 1,008 yards.

Play policy and fees: Green fees are $3.50 weekdays and $4 weekends. Call for special rates.

Location: From Interstate 405 exit at Western Avenue and travel south about one mile to the course.

Course description: This par-3 course offers a good chance to sharpen up your short game. It is a popular course for juniors and beginners.

9637 South Western Avenue
Los Angeles, CA 90047

Pro shop   (213) 757-1650

- ☐ driving range
- ■ practice greens
- ☐ power carts
- ☐ pull carts
- ■ golf club rental
- ☐ locker rooms
- ☐ showers
- ☐ executive course
- ☐ accommodations
- ☐ food and beverages
- ☐ clubhouse

LOS VERDES GOLF AND COUNTRY CLUB

Course 42
MAP 14 grid f7

1964
William Francis Bell

Course information: This public course has 18 holes and par is 71. The course is 6,651 yards and rated 71.1 from the championship tees, and 6,273 yards and rated 69.0 from the regular tees. The slope ratings are 117 championship and 108 regular. Women's tees are 5,689 yards and rated 71.8. No slope rating available.

Play policy and fees: Green fees are $11 weekdays and $15 weekends. Carts are $17. Reservations are recommended. This course is available for outside tournaments.

Location: Travel on Interstate 405 to Rancho Palos Verdes. Exit on Hawthorne Boulevard and turn south and drive 11 miles to the Los Verdes Drive. Turn right and follow it to the club. Or, take Interstate 110 (Harbor Freeway) south to Pacific Coast Highway (Highway 1), then west to Hawthorne Boulevard. Turn south and drive 5.5 miles to Los Verdes Drive. Turn right and follow Los Verdes Drive around to the course.

7000 West Los Verdes Drive
Rancho Palos Verdes, CA 90274

Pro shop   (213) 377-0338
Starter   (213) 377-7370

- ■ driving range
- ■ practice greens
- ■ power carts
- ■ pull carts
- ■ golf club rental
- ■ locker rooms
- ■ showers
- ☐ executive course
- ☐ accommodations
- ■ food and beverages
- ■ clubhouse

Len Kennett
Professional

Paul Rothwell
Superintendent

SOUTHERN 14

Course description: This course offers one of the best golf values in the state. It has views of the Pacific Ocean matched only by Pebble Beach. The course is well maintained with excellent putting surfaces. The course record for men is 63, held by Ben Serns. The course record for women is 71. Numbers 13, 14 and 15 present a tough three-hole sequence, in addition to offering spectacular views of Catalina Island on clear days.

PALOS VERDES GOLF CLUB

1924
C. E. Howard

Course information: This semi-private course has 18 holes and par is 71. The course is 6,221 yards and rated 70.8 from the championship tees, and 5,530 yards and rated 67.5 from the regular tees. The slope ratings are 129 championship and 121 regular. Women's tees are 5,530 yards and rated 76.3. The slope rating is 124.

Play policy and fees: Outside play is accepted. Green fees are $85, carts included. Reservations are recommended.

Location: Travel on Interstate 405 (San Diego Freeway) to Palos Verdes Estates. Exit on Hawthorne Boulevard and go west. Take Palos Verdes Drive north to Via Campesina and go left one-fourth of a mile to the club.

Course description: This is a hilly course noted for its fast greens. Trees line the fairways.

3301 Via Campesina
Palos Verdes Estates
CA 90274

Pro shop   (213) 375-2759
Clubhouse (213) 375-2533

- ☐ driving range
- ■ practice greens
- ■ power carts
- ☐ pull carts
- ■ golf club rental
- ☐ locker rooms
- ☐ showers
- ☐ executive course
- ☐ accommodations
- ■ food and beverages
- ■ clubhouse

Richard Cox
Professional

Reed Carpenter
Superintendent

DOMINGUEZ GOLF COURSE

Course information: This short public course has 18 holes and par is 54. The course is 2,070 yards and rated 51.7 for 18 holes. No slope rating is available.

Play policy and fees: Green fees are $4.75 weekdays for 18 holes and $3.25 weekdays for nine holes. Weekend and holidays green fees are $5.25 for 18 holes. Twilight rate is $5.25 after 5 p.m. for nine holes and $4.50 for 18. The course has lights and is open from 6 a.m. to 10 p.m.

Location: From Interstate 405 north, exit on Main Street in Carson. The course is to the south of the freeway on your left.

Course description: This tight course has a lot of gullies with some bunkers. It's a tough par-3 with undulating greens. It was built on landfill, which may have had some effect on the settling of the greens. It is managed by American Golf Corporation.

19800 South Main Street
Carson, CA 90745

Pro shop   (213) 719-1942

- ■ driving range
- ■ practice greens
- ☐ power carts
- ■ pull carts
- ■ golf club rental
- ☐ locker rooms
- ☐ showers
- ☐ executive course
- ☐ accommodations
- ■ food and beverages
- ■ clubhouse

Don Brown
Professional

NEW HORIZONS GOLF COURSE

Course information: This private course has nine holes and par is 35. The yardage and ratings were unavailable.

Play policy and fees: Current policy and green fees were also unavailable.

Location: Take Interstate 110 north to Torrance Boulevard. Follow Torrance Boulevard about one mile to Maple Avenue. Turn right and go about three-fourths of a mile to the club.

Course description: This is a private course for residents of New Horizons. The course has narrow fairways and undulating greens, making it a difficult layout for anyone with shoddy iron play or an unsteady putting stroke.

22727 Maple Avenue
Torrance, CA 90505

Pro shop   (213) 325-3080

- ■ driving range
- ■ practice greens
- ■ power carts
- ■ pull carts
- ☐ golf club rental
- ☐ locker rooms
- ☐ showers
- ☐ executive course
- ☐ accommodations
- ■ food and beverages
- ■ clubhouse

HARBOR PARK GOLF COURSE

Course information: This public course has nine holes. Par is 72 for 18 holes. The course is 6,302 yards at 18 holes.

Play policy and fees: Green fees are $5.50 weekdays and $7.50 weekends. Reservations are recommended.

Location: Take the Pacific Coast Highway (Highway 1) in Wilmington to Figueroa Street and drive about one-half mile to the course.

Course description: This is a long, nine-hole course. Keep the ball in play and there should be no problem. But when isn't that true? The greens can be difficult, especially in summer when they tend to dry out.

1235 North Figueroa
Wilmington, CA 90744

Pro shop   (213) 549-4953

- ■ driving range
- ■ practice greens
- ■ power carts
- ■ pull carts
- ■ golf club rental
- ☐ locker rooms
- ☐ showers
- ☐ executive course
- ☐ accommodations
- ■ food and beverages
- ☐ clubhouse

Beverly Cox
Manager

SOUTHERN 14

ROLLING HILLS COUNTRY CLUB

1970
Ted Robinson

Course information: This private course has 18 holes and par is 70. The course is 6,081 yards and rated 69.8 from the championship tees, and 5,766 yards and rated 68.2 from the regular tees. The slope ratings are 122 championship and 119 regular. Women's tees are 6,081 yards and rated 73.7 from the championship tees, and 5,309 yards and rated 71.7 from the forward tees. The slope ratings are 130 championship and 126 forward.

Play policy and fees: Members and guests only. Guest fees are $30 weekdays and $45 weekends. Carts are $16. This course is available for outside tournaments when sponsored by a member. No jeans allowed on the course. Tee times are not used.

Location: South of Carson on Interstate 110, turn onto the Pacific Coast Highway west (Highway 1) and drive for 2.25 miles to Narbonne. Turn left and drive one mile to the club.

Course description: This is a well-manicured course that appears short but is tricky because of narrow, tree-lined fairways. Watch out for the 181-yard 11th hole. The green is surrounded by a pond and it's filled with errant golf balls. Many holes feature large double greens and rolling fairways. The men's course record is 63 held by John Cook, and the women's record is 67 held by Mary Enright.

27000 Palos Verdes Dr. East
Rolling Hills Estate,
CA 90274

Pro shop   (213) 326-7731
Clubhouse   (213) 326-4343

☐ driving range
■ practice greens
■ power carts
☐ pull carts
■ golf club rental
■ locker rooms
■ showers
☐ executive course
☐ accommodations
■ food and beverages
■ clubhouse

Jack Hollis
Professional

Pat Chartrand
Director

Jim Neal
Superintendent

CATALINA ISLAND
GOLF COURSE

Course information: This resort course has nine holes. Par is 64 for 18 holes. The course is 4,203 yards and rated 58.0 from the regular tees. The slope rating is 97.

Play policy and fees: Outside play is accepted. Green fees are $10 for each nine holes. Carts are $20 for 18 holes and $10 for nine holes.

Location: Take the boat from San Pedro Bay or Long Beach (Catalina Express of Catalina Cruises) to Catalina Island, 26 miles off the mainland. In the summer boats leave from Redondo and Newport Beaches. Helicopters are available from Long Beach and San Pedro.

Course description: This scenic canyon course was opened in the late 1800s. Although short in length, the holes are narrow and demanding. Greens are small and surrounded by traps offering a challenge to any adventurous golfer. Celebrities have long been attracted to the course and William Wrigley of chewing gum fame sponsored tournaments here in the 1920s. The Catalina Island Junior Championship is held here during Easter week, and the Catalina Island Invitational is held each October.

P.O. Box 1564
Avalon, CA 90704

One Country Club Road
Avalon, CA 90704

Pro shop (213) 510-1530

☐ driving range
■ practice greens
■ power carts
■ pull carts
■ golf club rental
■ locker rooms
☐ showers
■ executive course
☐ accommodations
■ food and beverages
■ clubhouse

Jeff Lake
Manager

Jose Morones
Superintendent

SOUTHERN 14

MAP ON PAGE 380

411

MAP I5
(98 COURSES)

PAGES.. 412-471

SO-CAL MAP .....see page 376
adjoining maps
NORTH (H5).......see page 362
EAST (I6) ....see page 472
SOUTH (J5) ....see page 542
WEST (I4) ....see page 380

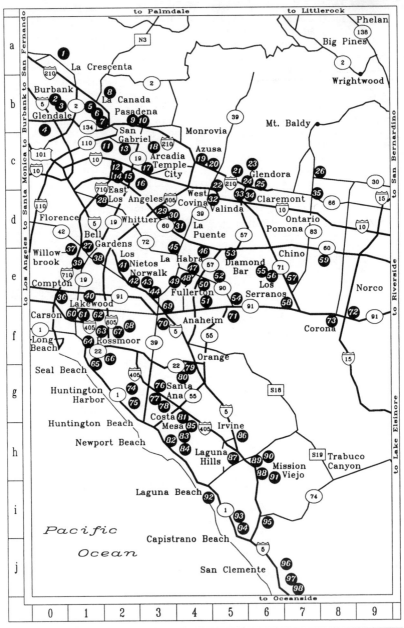

VERDUGO HILLS GOLF COURSE

Course information: This public course has 18 holes and par is 54. The course is 1,805 yards. The course is not rated.

Play policy and fees: Green fees are $7 weekdays and $10 weekends.

Location: On Interstate 210 in Tujunga, take the Lowell Avenue exit. Drive one block and turn left on LaTuna Canyon Road. Veer left to the course, which is located at the junction of LaTuna Canyon Road and Tujunga Canyon Road.

Course description: This hilly, well-kept course has lots of trees. There are no bunkers or water to impede you or your ball. It's walkable. This course is considered to be one of the best conditioned par-3 courses in Southern California. The driving range is open until 10:30 p.m. and the last tee time is 9 p.m.

6433 LaTuna Canyon Road
Tujunga, CA 91042

Pro shop (818) 352-3161

- ■ driving range
- ■ practice greens
- □ power carts
- □ pull carts
- ■ golf club rental
- □ locker rooms
- □ showers
- □ executive course
- □ accommodations
- ■ food and beverages
- ■ clubhouse

John Wells
Manager

DE BELL GOLF COURSE

Course information: This public course has 18 holes and par is 71. The course is 5,813 yards and rated 66.8 from the regular tees. The slope rating is 109. Women's tees are 5,496 yards and rated 70.8. The slope rating is 118.

Play policy and fees: Green fees for Burbank residents are $11 weekdays and $14 weekends. Non-resident green fees are $13 weekdays and $16 weekends. Carts are $9 for nine holes, $16 for 18 holes. Reservations are recommended.

Location: From Interstate 5 take the Olive Avenue exit east about 2.5 miles to Walnut Avenue. Turn right on Walnut and follow it to the course.

Course description: This is a fairly straight course with a minimum of sand traps and no water hazards.

1500 Walnut Avenue
Burbank, CA 91504

Pro shop   (818) 845-5052
Clubhouse (818) 843-8666

- ■ driving range
- ■ practice greens
- ■ power carts
- ■ pull carts
- ■ golf club rental
- ■ locker rooms
- ■ showers
- □ executive course
- □ accommodations
- ■ food and beverages
- ■ clubhouse

Phil Scozzola
Professional

SOUTHERN 15

MAP ON PAGE 412   413

Course information: This private course has 18 holes and par is 72. The course is 6,713 yards and rated 73 from the championship tees, and 6,480 yards and rated 71.3 from the regular tees. The slope ratings are 130 championship, 124 regular. Women's yardage is 6,033 and rated 75. The slope rating is 128.

Play policy and fees: Members and guests only. Green fees are $35 weekdays and $40 Fridays and weekends. Carts are $18.

Location: From the Ventura Freeway take the Glendale Avenue exit and drive north on Verdugo/Canada Road for 3.5 miles to Country Club Drive. Turn left and drive one-half of a mile to the club.

Course description: This mature course has tight fairways and well-maintained, tricky greens. Good ball placement is rewarded.

3100 Country Club Drive
Glendale, CA 91208

Pro shop   (818) 242-2050
Clubhouse (818) 242-3106

- ■ driving range
- ■ practice greens
- ■ power carts
- □ pull carts
- □ golf club rental
- ■ locker rooms
- ■ showers
- □ executive course
- □ accommodations
- ■ food and beverages
- ■ clubhouse

Greg Frederick
Professional

Dave Flaxbeard
Superintendent

GRIFFITH PARK
GOLF COURSE

Course information: This public facility has two 18-hole courses and par is 72 on both. There is also a par-3 course (Los Felix), par 27; and an executive course (Roosevelt), par 33.

The Harding Course is 6,536 yards and rated 70.4 from the championship tees, and 6,317 yards and rated 69.1 from the regular tees. The slope ratings are 112 championship and 108 regular. Women's tees are 6,095 yards and rated 73.1. The slope rating is 118.

The Wilson Course is 6,942 yards and rated 72.7 from the championship tees, and 6,682 yards and rated 70.9 from the regular tees. The slope ratings are 115 championship and 109 regular. Women's tees are 6,483 yards and rated 76.0. The slope rating is 119.

Play policy and fees: Green fees are $10.50 weekdays and $14.50 weekends. Carts are $16. Reservations are recommended. A Los Angeles Park and Recreation reservation card is required.

Location: Take the Los Felix Boulevard West exit off Interstate 5. Turn right on Riverside Drive into Griffith Park and follow the signs for two more miles to the club.

Course description: Both championship courses are fairly open with lots of trees lining the fairways. Water comes into play on both.

4730 Crystal Springs Drive
Los Angeles, CA 90027

Pro shop   (213) 664-2255
Clubhouse (213) 663-2555

- driving range
- practice greens
- power carts
- pull carts
- golf club rental
- locker rooms
- showers
- executive course
- ☐ accommodations
- food and beverages
- clubhouse

Tom Barber
Professional

Randy Haney
Superintendent

SOUTHERN 15

CHEVY CHASE
COUNTRY CLUB

1927

Course information: This private course has nine holes. Par is 66 for 18 holes. The course is 4,895 yards and rated 61.9 from the regular tees. The slope rating is 98.

Play policy and fees: Members and guests only. Green fees are $15 weekdays and $20 weekends. Carts are $14.

Location: From Highway 134 in Glendale, take Harvey exit and travel north for three blocks to Chevy Chase Drive. Turn right and drive two miles to the club.

Course description: This course was built in 1927, and has a variety of holes that traverse the rolling terrain of this area.

3067 E. Chevy Chase Drive
Glendale, CA 91206

Pro shop   (818) 244-8461
Clubhouse   (818) 246-5566

□ driving range
■ practice greens
■ power carts
□ pull carts
□ golf club rental
■ locker rooms
■ showers
■ executive course
□ accommodations
■ food and beverages
■ clubhouse

Derek MacArthur
Professional

Mark Campbell
GM/Superintendent

BROOKSIDE GOLF COURSE

1928
William Park Bell

1133 Rosemont Avenue
Pasadena, CA 91103

Pro shop   (818) 796-8151
Clubhouse (818) 796-0177

- ■ driving range
- ■ practice greens
- ■ power carts
- ☐ pull carts
- ■ golf club rental
- ■ locker rooms
- ■ showers
- ☐ executive course
- ☐ accommodations
- ■ food and beverages
- ■ clubhouse

John Wells
Professional

Dan Dau, Jr.
Superintendent

Course information: This public facility has two 18-hole courses. Par is 72 for the Number One Course, and 70 for the Number Two Course.

The Number One Course is 6,888 yards and rated 73.3 from the championship tees, and 6,661 yards and rated 71.6 from the regular tees. The slope ratings are 125 championship and 117 regular. Women's tees are 6,080 yards and rated 73.7. The slope rating is 117.

The Number Two Course is 5,689 yards and rated 66.3 from the regular tees. The slope rating is 104. Women's tees are 5,408 yards and rated 69.6. slope rating is 108.

Play policy and fees: Green fees for residents playing the Number One Course are $12 weekdays and $16 weekends. Green fees for non-residents playing the Number One Course are $20 weekdays and $25 weekends. Green fees for residents playing the Number Two Course are $11 weekdays and $15 weekends. Green fees for non-residents playing the Number Two Course are $15 weekdays and $20 weekends. Call for cart and special rates. Reservations should be made one week in advance for weekday play. There is a special reservation system for weekends. Call ahead.

Location: From Interstate 210 in Pasadena, take the Seco/Mountain exit. Travel south on Seco to Rosemont; the course is adjacent to the Rose Bowl.

Course description: Number One is long and wide open with mature trees lining the fairways. A lake comes into play. Number Two is short and narrow. Well-placed bunkers guard both courses. The Los Angeles Open was held here in 1968. The Golden State Tour plays this course regularly each year.

SOUTHERN 15

417

ANNANDALE GOLF COURSE

Course information: This private course has 18 holes and par is 70.

The course is 6,418 yards and rated 71.9 from the championship tees, and 6,102 yards and rated 70.1 from the regular tees. The slope ratings are 139 championship and 129 regular. Women's tees are 5,870 yards and rated 75. The slope rating is 132.

Play policy and fees: Members and guests only. Guests must be accompanied by members at time of play. Green fees are $35. Carts are $18.

Location: Take the San Rafael exit off Highway 134 in Pasadena. Turn left and drive one block to the entrance gate.

Course description: This hilly, narrow course is known for its fast, sloping greens. The memorable 14th and 16th holes are set in a canyon with a lake in front of the 16th green.

One N. San Rafael Avenue
Pasadena, CA 91105

Pro shop   (818) 795-8253
Clubhouse (818) 796-6125

- ■ driving range
- ■ practice greens
- ■ power carts
- □ pull carts
- ■ golf club rental
- ■ locker rooms
- ■ showers
- □ executive course
- □ accommodations
- ■ food and beverages
- ■ clubhouse

Patrick Rielly
Professional

David Allec
Superintendent

LA CANADA FLINTRIDGE COUNTRY CLUB

Course information: This private course has 18 holes and par is 70. The course is 5,771 yards and rated 70.1 from the championship tees, and 5,514 yards and rated 69.0 from the regular tees. The slope ratings are 129 championship and 125 regular. Women's tees are 5,230 yards and rated 70. The slope rating is 118.

Play policy and fees: Reciprocal play is accepted with members of other private clubs, otherwise members and guests only. Green fees are $28 weekdays and $35 weekends. Carts are $20. Reservations are recommended. This course is available for outside tournaments.

Location: From Pasadena, drive west on Interstate 210 (Foothill Freeway) and take the Angeles Crest Highway exit. Drive north for 1.5 miles to Starlight Crest Drive. Turn right and drive one-half of a mile to Godbey Drive then turn right to the club.

Course description: This short and narrow course makes up for lack of length with hills and tight fairways. Cart use is recommended for all but the bravest souls. On the back nine watch for the par-5, 462-yard number 12. You tee off from an elevated tee to a narrow landing area, but first you must clear at least 160 yards of brush before you find a safe landing area. The hole then opens up and is a reachable par-5.

5500 Godbey Drive
La Canada, CA 91011

Pro shop   (818) 790-0155
Clubhouse (818) 790-0611

- □ driving range
- ■ practice greens
- ■ power carts
- □ pull carts
- ■ golf club rental
- ■ locker rooms
- ■ showers
- □ executive course
- □ accommodations
- ■ food and beverages
- ■ clubhouse

Mark Saatzer
Professional

Salvador Macias
Superintendent

ALTADENA TOWN AND COUNTRY CLUB

Course information: This public course has nine holes. Par is 72 for 18 holes. The course is 5,990 yards and rated 66.6 from the championship tees, and 5,680 yards and rated 65.2 from the regular tees. The slope ratings are 111 championship and 108 regular. Women's tees are 5,418 yards and rated 68. There is no slope rating.

Play policy and fees: Green fees are $7 weekdays and $9 weekends for nine holes. Carts are $10 for nine holes.

Location: Travel on Interstate 210 to the Lake Avenue exit in Pasadena. Drive 2.5 miles to Mendocino. Turn right and the course is 1.5 miles on the right.

Course description: This is a flat, wide-open golf course with bunkers and some sloping fairways. The San Gabriel Mountains provide a pleasant backdrop when they are not covered with smog.

1456 East Mendocino Drive
Altadena, CA 91001

Pro shop (818) 797-3821
Clubhouse (818) 794-7679

- ■ driving range
- ■ practice greens
- ■ power carts
- ■ pull carts
- ■ golf club rental
- □ locker rooms
- □ showers
- □ executive course
- □ accommodations
- ■ food and beverages
- ■ clubhouse

Billy Gibbs
Professional

Lou Orwig
Superintendent

EATON CANYON GOLF COURSE

Course information: This public course has nine holes. Par is 70 for 18 holes. The course is 2,862 yards and rated 65.8 from the championship tees, and 2,660 yards and rated 64.0 from the regular tees. The slope ratings are 111 championship and 108 regular. Women's tees are 2,453 yards and rated 69.3. The slope rating is 114.

Play policy and fees: Green fees are $7 for nine holes weekdays and $9 for nine holes weekends. Carts are $10.

Location: East of Pasadena on Interstate 210, take the Sierra Madre Boulevard exit. Drive under the freeway and head north on Sierra Madre Boulevard until it becomes Sierra Madre Villa. The course is located at 1150 North Sierra Madre Villa.

Course description: The first four holes are flat and the last five hilly on this tight course. There are lots of trees.

1150 North Sierra
Madre Villa Avenue
Pasadena, CA 91107

Pro shop (818) 794-6773

- ■ driving range
- ■ practice greens
- ■ power carts
- ■ pull carts
- ■ golf club rental
- □ locker rooms
- □ showers
- □ executive course
- □ accommodations
- ■ food and beverages
- ■ clubhouse

David Brown
Professional

SOUTHERN 15

MAP ON PAGE 412

419

ARROYO SECO GOLF COURSE

Course 11
MAP I5 grid c2

Course information: This public course has 18 holes and par is 54. The course is 2,223 yards.

Play policy and fees: Green fees are $3.75 for nine holes and $5.75 for 18 holes weekdays, and $4 for nine holes and $6.50 for 18 holes weekends.

Location: On Highway 110 (Pasadena Freeway) in South Pasadena, exit on Orange Grove Boulevard to the south. Drive one-fourth of a block and turn right on Mission and drive to the end. Look for the course sign.

Course description: This flat course has a small creek wending through the last holes.

1055 Lohman Lane
South Pasadena, CA 91030

Pro shop   (213) 255-1506
Clubhouse (213) 254-5375

■ driving range
■ practice greens
□ power carts
■ pull carts
■ golf club rental
□ locker rooms
□ showers
□ executive course
□ accommodations
■ food and beverages
■ clubhouse

Horace Evans
Professional

John DeLaTorre
Superintendent

ALHAMBRA GOLF COURSE

Course 12
MAP I5 grid c2

1983
William Francis Bell

Course information: This public course has 18 holes and par is 70. The course is 5,206 yards and rated 63.1 from the championship tees, and 4,872 yards and rated 61.6 from the regular tees. The slope ratings are 94 championship and 91 regular. Women's tees are 5,092 yards from the championship tees and rated 68.5, and 4,876 yards and rated 67.3 from the forward tees. The slope ratings are 108 championship and 105 forward.

Play policy and fees: Green fees are $9.50 weekdays and $14 weekends. Seniors and juniors play for $5 on weekdays with a resident card. Carts are $16. Reservations are recommended. Shirts and appropriate shoes required.

Location: From downtown Los Angeles, take Interstate 10 east to the Garfield Avenue exit, turn right on Valley Boulevard and go one-half of a mile to Almansor Street. Turn left on Almansor and go three-fourths of a mile to the club.

Course description: This short course features three par-5s and five par-3s. There are three lakes and 33 bunkers. The front nine is flat but easy to walk, with large groves of eucalyptus and black acacias. The back nine is composed of rolling hills with more sand and water. The two nines are distinctly different, although both have well-maintained greens. The greens are small and quick, requiring a soft touch. One unique feature of this course is the three-tiered driving range. This is a shot-maker's layout.

630 South Almansor Street
Alhambra, CA 91801

Pro shop   (818) 570-5059

■ driving range
■ practice greens
■ power carts
■ pull carts
■ golf club rental
□ locker rooms
□ showers
□ executive course
□ accommodations
■ food and beverages
■ clubhouse

Jerry Wisz
Professional

Zeke Avila, Jr.
Superintendent

SAN GABRIEL COUNTRY CLUB

1904

Course information: This private course has 18 holes and par is 71. The course is 6,544 yards and rated 72.4 from the tournament tees, 6,276 yards and rated 70.6 from the championship tees, and 6,016 yards and rated 68.9 from the regular tees. The slope ratings are 133 tournament, 125 championship and 118 regular. Women's tees are 6,016 yards and rated 75. The slope rating is 129.

Play policy and fees: Members and guests only. Guests must be accompanied by members during play. Green fees are $35 every day. Carts are $18. Reservations are recommended. Golfers must wear collared shirts. No jeans are allowed. Bermuda shorts to the knee are acceptable. Women must wear skirts or culottes.

Location: Travel on Interstate 10 in San Gabriel and take the San Gabriel Boulevard exit. Drive north to Las Tunas Drive, turn left to the club.

Course description: This historic course was built in 1904 and renovated in the mid-1970s by Robert Trent Jones, Jr. It plays longer than it looks because of the bunkers. Lots of mature trees line the fairways and the greens are well maintained. Fairways have been seeded with Kikuyu grass. Among the holes to watch for are the 440-yard seventh, that features a dogleg right. Both sides of the fairway are out-of-bounds. The 433-yard 10th hole, which needs a second shot uphill to a heavily bunkered green, would give Ben Hogan nightmares. The course record of 59 is held by Bruce McCormick. The Cravens Invitational is held here each May and The Mission Bell tournament is played in October.

411 East Las Tunas Drive
San Gabriel, CA 91775

Pro shop   (818) 287-6052
Clubhouse (818) 287-9671
Starter   (818) 287-4235

- ■ driving range
- ■ practice greens
- ■ power carts
- □ pull carts
- ■ golf club rental
- ■ locker rooms
- ■ showers
- □ executive course
- ■ accommodations
- ■ food and beverages
- ■ clubhouse

Michael Jon Kelley
Professional

Tony Cuellar
Superintendent

SOUTHERN 15

MONTEREY PARK GOLF COURSE

Course information: This public course has nine holes. Par is 29. The course is 1,400 yards.

Play policy and fees: Green fees are $4.50 weekdays and $5 weekends. Call for special rates.

Location: From Interstate 710 (Long Beach Freeway) in Monterey Park, take the Ramona Boulevard exit. The course is directly off the freeway on Ramona Boulevard.

Course description: This is an executive course consisting of seven par-3s and two 300-yard par-4s. The course and adjoining driving range are lighted for night play. Last tee time is 9 p.m. weekdays and 8 p.m. Sundays.

3600 Ramona Boulevard
Monterey Park, CA 91754

Pro shop   (213) 266-4632

- ■ driving range
- ■ practice greens
- □ power carts
- ■ pull carts
- ■ golf club rental
- □ locker rooms
- □ showers
- ■ executive course
- □ accommodations
- ■ food and beverages
- □ clubhouse

Bob Mastilski
Professional

WHITTIER NARROWS GOLF COURSE

Course information: This public course has 18 holes and par is 72. The course is 6,490 yards from the regular tees and rated 69.3. The slope is 112. Women's tees are 5,965 yards. The slope rating is 110. There is also a nine-hole course. At 18 holes, the course is 5,050 yards, par-68.

Play policy and fees: Green fees are $11 weekdays and $51 weekends and holidays for the 18-hole course, and $7 weekdays and $9 weekends for the short course. Carts are $8.50 for the nine holes and $16 for 18 holes.

Location: Off Highway 60 in Rosemead, take the San Gabriel Boulevard exit and drive north to Walnut Grove Street. Drive to Rush Street and turn right to the course.

Course description: The main course is flat and narrow with lots of trees and elevated greens. The short course is flat and open.

8640 East Rush Street
Rosemead, CA 91770

Pro shop   (818) 288-1044

- ■ driving range
- ■ practice greens
- ■ power carts
- □ pull carts
- ■ golf club rental
- □ locker rooms
- □ showers
- ■ executive course
- □ accommodations
- ■ food and beverages
- ■ clubhouse

Tupper Russell
Professional

PICO RIVERA MUNICIPAL GOLF COURSE

Course information: This public course has nine holes and par is 29. The course is 1,400 yards.

Play policy and fees: Green fees are $4 weekdays before 6 p.m., and $5 weekends and holidays. Call for special rates.

Location: From Interstate 605 take the Beverly Boulevard exit onto San Gabriel River Parkway to Fairway Drive. The course is off Fairway Drive.

Course description: All the greens are elevated on this nice little course. The longest hole is 270 yards, which is number five. Finishing holes eight and nine are surrounded by lakes.

3260 Fairway Drive
Pico Rivera, CA 90660

Pro shop   (213) 692-9933

- ■ driving range
- ■ practice greens
- □ power carts
- ■ pull carts
- ■ golf club rental
- □ locker rooms
- □ showers
- ■ executive course
- □ accommodations
- ■ food and beverages
- □ clubhouse

Frank Gomez
Professional

ARCADIA PAR-3

Course information: This public course has 18 holes. The course is 1,898 yards.

Play policy and fees: Green fees are $6.50 weekdays and $8 weekends. Call for special evening and senior rates.

Location: Off Interstate 10 in Arcadia, exit on Santa Anita Avenue and drive south for two miles until you reach Live Oak. Follow Live Oak east 1.5 miles to the course on your right.

Course description: This flat course has no bunkers or water. You tee off from mats. The course is lighted for night play. The last tee time is 8 p.m. Good practice for your irons.

620 East Live Oak
Arcadia, CA 91006

Pro shop   (818) 443-9367

- ■ driving range
- ■ practice greens
- □ power carts
- ■ pull carts
- ■ golf club rental
- □ locker rooms
- □ showers
- □ executive course
- □ accommodations
- ■ food and beverages
- □ clubhouse

Greg Castleman
Professional

Jose Castelanos
Superintendent

SOUTHERN I5

SANTA ANITA GOLF COURSE

Course information: This public course has 18 holes and par is 71. The course is 6,823 yards and rated 70.2 from the regular tees. The slope rating is 106. Women's tees are 5,908 yards and rated 73.1. The slope rating is 121.

Play policy and fees: Green fees are $11 weekdays and $15 weekends. Carts are $17. Reservations are recommended one week in advance.

Location: Take Santa Anita Avenue off Interstate 210 and drive south to the course.

Course description: This is a well-maintained course with tight fairways, undulating and smallish greens and several well-placed traps. It is long and challenging.

405 S. Santa Anita Avenue
Arcadia, CA 91006

Pro shop   (818) 447-7156

- ■ driving range
- ■ practice greens
- ■ power carts
- ■ pull carts
- ■ golf club rental
- ☐ locker rooms
- ☐ showers
- ☐ executive course
- ☐ accommodations
- ■ food and beverages
- ■ clubhouse

Bud Merriam
Professional

RANCHO DUARTE GOLF CLUB

Course information: This public course has nine holes. Par is 31. The course is 1,800 yards.

Play policy and fees: Green fees are $6 weekdays and $8 weekends. Reservations are recommended a week in advance.

Location: Driving on Interstate 210 in Duarte, take Mount Olive Drive and go right on Huntington. At the first stop light, turn left on Las Lomas and drive 1/2 block to the course on the right.

Course description: This course offers undulating fairways and greens. It's well bunkered. There are five par-3s and four par-4s.

1000 Las Lomas
Duarte, CA 91010

Pro shop   (818) 357-9981

- ■ driving range
- ■ practice greens
- ☐ power carts
- ■ pull carts
- ■ golf club rental
- ☐ locker rooms
- ☐ showers
- ■ executive course
- ☐ accommodations
- ■ food and beverages
- ■ clubhouse

Doug Ruff
Professional

AZUSA GREENS COUNTRY CLUB

Course information: This public course has 18 holes and par is 70. The course is 6,148 yards and rated 68.9 from the championship tees, and 5,866 yards and rated 67.4 from the regular tees. The slope ratings are 110 championship and 105 regular. Women's tees are 5,484 yards and rated 71.8. The slope rating is 111.

Play policy and fees: Green fees are $16 weekdays and $25 weekends, carts included. Call for special rates. This course is available for outside tournaments.

Location: From Pasadena, travel east on Interstate 210 to the Azusa Avenue exit. Drive north three miles to Sierra Madre Boulevard and turn left to the clubhouse.

Course description: Set at the base of the San Gabriel Valley foothills, this course is fairly level with straight, tree-lined fairways.

919 W. Sierra Madre Blvd.
Azusa, CA 91702

Pro shop (818) 969-1727
Clubhouse (818) 969-1729

- ■ driving range
- ■ practice greens
- ■ power carts
- ☐ pull carts
- ☐ golf club rental
- ☐ locker rooms
- ☐ showers
- ☐ executive course
- ☐ accommodations
- ■ food and beverages
- ■ clubhouse

Jerry Herrera
Professional

Jesus Padilla
Superintendent

SIERRA LA VERNE COUNTRY CLUB

1976
Stan Murray

Course information: This private course has 18 holes and par is 71. The course is 6,276 yards and rated 70.6 from the championship tees, and 5,949 yards and rated 68.9 from the regular tees. The slope ratings are 127 championship and 122 regular. Women's tees are 5,606 yards and rated 72.3. The slope rating is 121.

Play policy and fees: Members and guests only. Guests must be accompanied by a member. Green fees are $30 weekdays and $40 weekends. Carts are $17. Reservations are recommended. This course is available for outside tournaments.

Location: From Pasadena, travel east on Interstate 210. Exit at Foothill Boulevard heading east and drive to Wheeler Road north. At Golden Hills Road turn east and continue to Country Club Road and head south to the club. From Orange County, take Highway 57 north to Foothill Boulevard exit and follow as directed above.

Course description: Set in the foothills of La Verne, this course is both picturesque and challenging. The front nine is more open and not as difficult as the back nine, which requires accuracy with irons and good putting on the well-manicured greens.

6300 Country Club Drive
La Verne, CA 91750

Pro shop (714) 596-2100
Clubhouse (818) 335-0509

- ■ driving range
- ■ practice greens
- ■ power carts
- ☐ pull carts
- ■ golf club rental
- ■ locker rooms
- ■ showers
- ☐ executive course
- ☐ accommodations
- ■ food and beverages
- ■ clubhouse

Harry Sailor
Professional

Charlie Amos
Superintendent

SOUTHERN 15

MAP ON PAGE 412

425

GLENOAKS GOLF COURSE

Course information: This public course has nine holes. Par is 54 for 18 holes. The course is 1,020 yards.

Play policy and fees: Green fees are $3.25 weekdays and $4 weekends. Call for special senior, women and junior day rates.

Location: From Highway 210 exit at Grand Avenue exit. Go one block to Glendora Avenue, turn right and go to Dawson Avenue. Turn right and you're at the course.

Course description: This is a well-maintained par-3 course. The longest hole here is 188 yards, so leave your woods at home. Tennis and racketball courts are nearby.

200 West Dawson
Glendora, CA 91740

Pro shop   (818) 335-7565

- ■ driving range
- ■ practice greens
- □ power carts
- ■ pull carts
- ■ golf club rental
- □ locker rooms
- □ showers
- □ executive course
- □ accommodations
- ■ food and beverages
- □ clubhouse

SAN DIMAS CANYON GOLF CLUB

Murray Dan

Course information: This public course has 18 holes and par is 72. The course is 6,315 yards and rated 70.1 from the championship tees, and 5,943 yards and rated 67.9 from the regular tees. The slope ratings are 119 championship and 108 regular. Women's tees are 5,549 yards and rated 72.3. The slope rating is 117.

Play policy and fees: Green fees are $13 weekdays and $20 weekends. Carts are $19. Reservations are recommended. This course is available for outside tournaments.

Location: Travel east on Interstate 210 (Foothill Freeway) and Highway 30 to the San Dimas Avenue exit. Travel north to Foothill Boulevard and turn right, and drive three-fourths of a mile to San Dimas Canyon Road. Go left and continue one mile to the Terrebonne Avenue entrance to Gray Oaks, then turn left to the club.

Course description: This course offers a distinctive, interesting layout over a relatively level front nine and a hilly back nine. Four water hazards come into play. The 165-yard 16th hole is a real challenge. From an elevated tee, you hit over a lake to a green faced by a rock retaining wall and surrounded by mounds and pot bunkers. The course record is 66 for men and 70 for women.

2100 Terrebonne Avenue
San Dimas, CA 91773

Pro shop   (714) 599-2313
              (818) 966-8547

- ■ driving range
- ■ practice greens
- ■ power carts
- ■ pull carts
- ■ golf club rental
- □ locker rooms
- □ showers
- □ executive course
- □ accommodations
- ■ food and beverages
- ■ clubhouse

GLENDORA COUNTRY CLUB

Course information: This private course has 18 holes and par is 72. The course is 6,597 yards and rated 72.6 from the championship tees, and 6,377 yards and rated 71.2 from the regular tees. The slope ratings are 131 championship and 125 regular. Women's tees are 6,377 yards and rated 76.2 from the championship tees, and 5,992 yards and rated 75.1 from the regular tees. The slope ratings are 131 for both championship and regular.

Play policy and fees: Members and guests only. Green fees are $30. Carts are $16 for two.

Location: Travel east on Interstate 210. (Stay in the middle lane.) At the "End of Freeway/Foothill Boulevard" sign, take the Lone Hill exit and drive north for one-half mile to Alosta Avenue. Turn right and drive one-half mile to Amelia Avenue and turn left to the club.

Course description: This picturesque course is set at the foot of the San Gabriel Mountains. The narrow, tree-lined fairways are fairly level and easy to walk. Plan to spend some time in the trees.

310 South Amelia Avenue
Glendora, CA 91740

Pro shop   (818) 335-3713

- ■ driving range
- ■ practice greens
- ■ power carts
- ■ pull carts
- ■ golf club rental
- ■ locker rooms
- ■ showers
- □ executive course
- □ accommodations
- ■ food and beverages
- ■ clubhouse

Robert Powell
Professional

Condie Lopez
Superintendent

MARSHALL CANYON GOLF CLUB

1966

Course information: This public course has 18 holes and par is 71. The course is 6,115 yards and rated 68.9 from the championship tees, and 5,856 yards and rated 67.7 from the regular tees. The slope ratings are 114 championship and 112 regular. Women's yardage is 5,564 yards and rated 72.3. The slope rating is 117.

Play policy and fees: Green fees are $11 weekdays and $15 weekends. Twilight rates are $7 weekdays and $9 weekends after 4 p.m. Seniors play for $5.50 weekdays. Carts are $16. Reservations are recommended.

Location: Take Interstate 210 east to Wheeler, then go north to Golden Hills. Go east on Golden Hills to Stephens Ranch Road and north to the course.

Course description: This course is located in a canyon at the base of the San Gabriel Mountains. They offer a spectacular backdrop. The greens have a great deal of contour and are extremely tricky. The par-3, 177-yard 11th hole plays over part of the canyon and is particularly scenic. The Pomona Valley Amateur Championship is held over Labor Day weekend. The course record is 59.

6100 North Stephens
Ranch Rd.
La Verne, CA 91750

Pro shop   (714) 593-6914
Clubhouse (714) 593-8211

- ■ driving range
- ■ practice greens
- ■ power carts
- ■ pull carts
- ■ golf club rental
- □ locker rooms
- □ showers
- □ executive course
- □ accommodations
- ■ food and beverages
- ■ clubhouse

Ross Nettles
Professional

A.B. Nunez
Superintendent

SOUTHERN 15

UPLAND HILLS COUNTRY CLUB

Course 26
MAP 15 grid c8

1983
Ted Robinson

1231 East 16th Street
Upland, CA 91786

Pro shop   (714) 946-4711
Clubhouse (714) 946-3057

☐ driving range
■ practice greens
■ power carts
■ pull carts
■ golf club rental
■ locker rooms
■ showers
☐ executive course
☐ accommodations
■ food and beverages
■ clubhouse

Brian Bode
Professional

Jim Janisik
Superintendent

Scott Chaffin
Manager

Course information: This semi-private course has 18 holes and par is 70. The course is 5,827 yards and rated 67.1 from the regular tees. The slope rating is 111. Women's tees are 4,813 yards and rated 66.5. The slope rating is 106.

Play policy and fees: Outside play is accepted. Green fees are $16 weekdays and $23 weekends. Carts are $18. This course is available for outside tournaments.

Location: Travel east on Interstate 10 (San Bernardino Freeway) to Euclid Avenue in Upland. Turn north to 16th Street, then east for one mile to the club on the left.

Course description: Located in the foothills, this relatively young course is fairly flat and easy to walk. Six lakes and fast greens add to the challenge. It is short and tight, causing lots of trouble, but it's always in good condition.

FORD PARK GOLF COURSE

Course 27
MAP 15 grid d1

8000 Park Lane
Bell Gardens, CA 90201

Pro shop   (213) 927-8811

■ driving range
■ practice greens
☐ power carts
■ pull carts
■ golf club rental
☐ locker rooms
☐ showers
☐ executive course
☐ accommodations
■ food and beverages
☐ clubhouse

Course information: This public layout has nine holes, par is 27. The course is 1,017 yards.

Play policy and fees: Green fees are $3.50 weekdays and $4 weekends. Call for special senior rates.

Location: In Bell Gardens, take the Garfield Avenue exit off Interstate 5 and travel west about three miles to Park Lane. From there take a right and you'll see the course.

Course description: This is a short par-3 course.

MONTEBELLO GOLF COURSE

1928

Course information: This public course has 18 holes and par is 71. The course is 6,547 yards and rated 70.5 from the championship tees, and 6,265 yards and rated 68.6 from the regular tees. The slope ratings are 113 championship and 106 regular. Women's tees are 5,883 yards and rated 72.6. The slope rating is 117.

Play policy and fees: Green fees are $11 weekdays and $15 weekends. Carts are $17. Reservations are recommended.

Location: In Montebello, travelling on Highway 60 (Pomona Freeway), exit at Garfield Avenue and drive south for one block. Turn right on Via San Clemente at the club sign.

Course description: Built in 1928, this flat course is one of the better maintained courses in the area.

PO Box 34
Montebello, CA 90640

901 Via San Clemente
Montebello, CA 90640

Pro shop (213) 723-2971
Clubhouse (213) 721-2311

- ■ driving range
- ■ practice greens
- ■ power carts
- □ pull carts
- □ golf club rental
- □ locker rooms
- □ showers
- □ executive course
- □ accommodations
- ■ food and beverages
- ■ clubhouse

Thomas Camacho
Professional/Manager

Henry Aquilar
Superintendent

CALIFORNIA COUNTRY CLUB

Course information: This private course has 18 holes and par is 72. The course is 6,812 yards and rated 72.5 from the championship tees, and 6,522 yards and rated 70.8 from the regular tees. The slope ratings are 126 championship and 120 regular. Women's tees are 6,522 yards and rated 77.3 from the championship tees, and 6,169 yards and rated 75.0 from the forward tees. The slope ratings are 131 championship and 125 forward.

Play policy and fees: Members and guests only. Green fees are $28 weekdays and $50 weekends. Carts are $16. This course is available for outside tournaments on Mondays, Thursday and Fridays.

Location: From Los Angeles, travel on Highway 60 (Pomona Freeway) east to the Crossroads Parkway exit; left over freeway. Then left at the stoplight to Workman Mill Road. Turn right and go to Coleford Avenue, then left to the club.

Course description: This flat course can be deceptively long once the wind picks up. The course record is 66.

PO Box 31
Whittier, CA 90608

1509 S. Workman Mill Road
Whittier, CA 90608

Pro shop (818) 333-4571
Clubhouse (213) 692-0421

- □ driving range
- ■ practice greens
- ■ power carts
- □ pull carts
- ■ golf club rental
- ■ locker rooms
- ■ showers
- □ executive course
- □ accommodations
- ■ food and beverages
- ■ clubhouse

Ric Rodriquez
Professional

Bob Johnson
Superintendent

SOUTHERN 15

WILDWOOD MOBILE COUNTRY CLUB

Course information: This private course has nine holes. Par is 54 for 18 holes. The course is all par-3s.

Play policy and fees: Members and guests only. This is a resident course. Memberships are available at $51 per year. There are no daily fees. No carts are allowed.

Location: This course is located off of Highway 60 in Hacienda Heights. Take the Seventh Avenue exit north. At the first light, turn left on Clark Street, which runs into the course.

Course description: This mostly flat course can be intimidating because it is so narrow. There's a fence on one side and mobile homes on the other.

901 South 6th Avenue
Hacienda Heights, CA 91745

Pro shop   (818) 968-2338

□ driving range
■ practice greens
□ power carts
■ pull carts
□ golf club rental
□ locker rooms
□ showers
□ executive course
□ accommodations
□ food and beverages
□ clubhouse

Herb Middlemiss
Manager

INDUSTRY HILLS GOLF CLUB

Course information: This public club has two 18-hole courses. Par is 72 on the Eisenhower Course and 71 on the Zaharias Course.

The Eisenhower Course is 7,181 yards and rated 76.4 from the championship tees, and 6,735 yards and rated 73.5 from the regular tees. The slope ratings are 149 championship and 138 regular. Women's tees are 5,507 yards and rated 73.0. The slope rating is 126.

The Zaharias Course is 6,830 yards and rated 74.2 from the tournament tees, and 6,600 yards and rated 72.9 from the championship tees, and 6,124 yards and rated 70.3 from the regular tees. The slope ratings are 144 tournament, 137 championship and 130 regular. Women's tees are 5,394 yards and rated 71.8. The slope rating is 123.

Play policy and fees: Green fees are $42 weekdays and $57 weekends. Cart included. Reservations are recommended.

Location: Travel on Highway 60 to the Azusa Avenue exit north. Drive 1.5 miles to the cobblestones and turn left on Industry Hills Parkway and continue to the club. From Interstate 10 (San Bernardino Freeway) take Azusa Avenue exit; drive south on Azusa for three miles to cobblestones and turn right on Industry Hills Parkway to the club.

Course description: Both courses border the Sheraton Hotel complex. The Eisenhower Course has been rated one of the top 25 public courses in the United States by *Golf Digest.* It's not too long, but is a demanding tract. The Zaharias Course is tighter and trickier. A shot-maker will excel here. Both courses cover rolling and hilly terrain and make use of a funicular, imported from Switzerland to transport players.

1 Industry Hills Parkway
City of Industry, CA 91744

Pro shop   (818) 965-0861

■ driving range
■ practice greens
■ power carts
■ pull carts
■ golf club rental
■ locker rooms
■ showers
□ executive course
■ accommodations
■ food and beverages
■ clubhouse

Rick Smith,
Director of Golf/Professional

Richard Stegall
Professional

Kent Davidson
Superintendent

SOUTH HILLS COUNTRY CLUB

1954
William Park Bell

2655 South Citrus Avenue
West Covina, CA 91791

Pro shop   (818) 332-3222
Clubhouse (818) 339-1231

- ■ driving range
- ■ practice greens
- ■ power carts
- ☐ pull carts
- ■ golf club rental
- ■ locker rooms
- ■ showers
- ☐ executive course
- ☐ accommodations
- ■ food and beverages
- ■ clubhouse

Dave Carollo
Professional

Scott McColgan
Superintendent

Course information: This private course has 18 holes and par is 72. The course is 6,384 yards and rated 71.1 from the championship tees, and 5,977 yards and rated 68.8 from the regular tees. The slope ratings are 125 championship and 118 regular. Women's tees are 5,603 yards and rated 72.5. The slope rating is 126.

Play policy and fees: Members and guests only. Guests must be accompanied by member at time of play. Guest fees are $25 weekdays and $35 weekends. Carts are $16. Men must wear collared shirts. Jeans or shorts are not allowed. Women's skirts must be no shorter than four inches above the knee. No halter or tank tops are allowed.

Location: From Los Angeles, travel on Interstate 10 (San Bernardino Freeway) to the Citrus Avenue exit and drive south for one mile to the club at the Lark Hill Drive intersection.

Course description: This is a course for shot-makers. It requires precision iron play and a great imagination on and around the greens. The fairways are medium width over rolling terrain. A fair number of bunkers surround the well-groomed, fast greens. It is a right-to-left course favoring players who hook the ball. The Hustlers Invitational tournament is held here in April, the Mr. and Mrs. Invitational in August, and the Tres Dias in September.

VIA VERDE COUNTRY CLUB

1400 Avenida Entrada
San Dimas, CA 91773

Pro shop   (714) 599-8486
Clubhouse (818) 966-4451

- ■ driving range
- ■ practice greens
- ■ power carts
- ☐ pull carts
- ☐ golf club rental
- ■ locker rooms
- ■ showers
- ☐ executive course
- ☐ accommodations
- ■ food and beverages
- ■ clubhouse

Tim Haas
Professional

Dal Lee
Manager

Rafael Martinez
Superintendent

SOUTHERN 15

Course information: This private course has 18 holes and par is 72. The course is 6,411 yards and rated 69.9 from the championship tees, and 6,129 yards and rated 68.7 from the regular tees. The slope ratings are 126 championship and 121 regular. Women's tees are 5,787 yards and rated 74.5. The slope rating is 116.

Play policy and fees: Members and guests only. Green fees are $25 weekdays and $40 weekends. Carts are $18.

Location: From San Bernardino, drive west on Interstate 10 (San Bernardino Freeway) to the Via Verde exit. Drive north one mile to Avenida Entrada and turn left. Drive three-fourths of a mile to the end and turn left to the club.

Course description: This course is well bunkered with narrow fairways and rolling terrain. It is set within a residential community.

MOUNTAIN MEADOWS
GOLF COURSE

Course information: This public course has 18 holes and par is 72. The course is 6,508 yards and rated 71.5 from the championship tees, and 6,141 yards and rated 68.4 from the regular tees. The slope ratings are 125 championship and 118 regular. Women's tees are 5,637 yards and rated 71.5. The slope rating is 117.

Play policy and fees: Green fees are $11 weekdays and $15 weekends. Carts are $18.

Location: Travel on Interstate 10 (San Bernardino Freeway) to Fairplex Drive exit. Go north on Fairplex to the club.

Course description: This is a hilly course with numerous trees flanking the fairways. For scenery and difficulty, watch out for number 13. It's 226 yards and par-3 over a canyon and overlooking a part of the San Gabriel Valley. It's about as gorgeous as it can get and the most challenging, as well.

1875 Fairplex Drive
Pomona, CA 91768

Pro shop   (714) 623-3704
Starter   (714) 629-1166
Seniors   (714) 623-2953

- ■ driving range
- ■ practice greens
- ■ power carts
- ■ pull carts
- ■ golf club rental
- □ locker rooms
- □ showers
- □ executive course
- □ accommodations
- ■ food and beverages
- ■ clubhouse

Greg Davis
Professional

Joe Lerma
Superintendent

RED HILL COUNTRY CLUB

1921

Course information: This private course has 18 holes and par is 72. The course is 6,621 yards and rated 71.9 from the championship tees, and 6,296 yards and rated 69.7 from the regular tees. The slope ratings are 121 championship and 116 regular. Women's tees are 6,020 yards and rated 75. The slope rating is 130.

Play policy and fees: Members and guests only. Guests must be accompanied by members at time of play. Guest fees are $30. Carts are $17. Golfers must wear collared shirts. Blue jeans and sweats are not allowed.

Location: Take Interstate 10 (San Bernardino Freeway) to the Euclid Avenue exit (west of San Bernardino) and drive north to Foothill Boulevard. Turn right and drive 1.5 miles to Red Hill Country Club Drive and turn left to the club.

Course description: This deceptive course offers a challenging test of golf. There are lots of trees and undulating greens. A point to remember: Two new ponds have been incorporated into holes seven and eight.

8358 Red Hill Country Club
Rancho Cucamonga, CA 91730

Pro shop   (714) 982-4559
Clubhouse (714) 982-1358

- ■ driving range
- ■ practice greens
- ■ power carts
- ■ pull carts
- □ golf club rental
- ■ locker rooms
- ■ showers
- □ executive course
- □ accommodations
- ■ food and beverages
- ■ clubhouse

Jim Porter
Professional

Ernie Pacheco
Superintendent

VIRGINIA COUNTRY CLUB

Course information: This private course has 18 holes and par is 71. The course is 6,518 yards and rated 71.1 from the championship tees, and 6,242 yards and rated 69.6 from the regular tees. The slope ratings are 122 championship and 112 regular. Women's tees are 5,746 yards and rated 73.4. The slope is 123.

Play policy and fees: Members and guests only. Guest fees are $25 weekdays and $35 weekends. Carts are $16.

Location: Travel on Interstate 405 to Long Beach Boulevard north. Turn left on San Antonio Road and right on Virginia Road.

Course description: This is a medium-length, testy course designed in the old traditional style. This is a very private club.

4602 Virginia Road
Long Beach, CA 90807

Pro shop   (213) 424-5211
Clubhouse (213) 427-0924

- ■ driving range
- ■ practice greens
- ■ power carts
- □ pull carts
- ■ golf club rental
- ■ locker rooms
- ■ showers
- □ executive course
- □ accommodations
- ■ food and beverages
- ■ clubhouse

Mike Eacica
Professional

Ray Davies
Superintendent

SOUTH GATE MUNICIPAL GOLF COURSE

Course information: This public course has nine holes. Par is 54 for 18 holes. The yards and rating were unavailable.

Play policy and fees: Green fees are $3.50 weekdays and $4 weekends for nine holes.

Location: From Highway 42 in South Gate, take the Central Avenue exit to Pinehurst, turn right and drive about one-half of a mile to the course.

Course description: This is a par-3 course that requires skilled iron play.

9615 Pinehurst Avenue
South Gate, CA 90280

Pro shop   (213) 564-1434

- □ driving range
- ■ practice greens
- □ power carts
- □ pull carts
- □ golf club rental
- □ locker rooms
- □ showers
- □ executive course
- □ accommodations
- □ food and beverages
- □ clubhouse

SOUTHERN 15

LOS AMIGOS CITY GOLF COURSE

Course information: This public layout has 18 holes and par is 70. The course is 6,006 yards and rated 66.4 from the regular tees. The slope rating is 108. Women's tees are 5,646 yards and rated 71.5. The slope rating is 112.

Play policy and fees: Green fees are $11 weekdays and $15 weekends. Reservations are recommended. This course is available for outside tournaments.

Location: From the Long Beach Freeway (Interstate 710) take the Imperial Highway east to Old River School Road. Turn left to the course on Quill Drive.

Course description: This is a well-maintained public golf facility. It plays long, requiring good distance from fairway shots to reach the greens in regulation. The greens can be quick when baked under the hot summer sun.

7295 Quill Drive
Downey, CA 90242

Pro shop	(213) 862-1717
Starter	(213) 869-0302
Clubhouse	(213) 869-0302

- ■ driving range
- ■ practice greens
- ■ power carts
- ■ pull carts
- ■ golf club rental
- ☐ locker rooms
- ☐ showers
- ☐ executive course
- ☐ accommodations
- ■ food and beverages
- ■ clubhouse

Mark Novorot
Professional

RIO HONDO COUNTRY CLUB

Course information: This public facility has 18 holes and par is 70. The course is 5,921 yards and rated 67.3 from the regular tees. The slope rating is 104. Women's tees are 5,576 and rated 71.3 from the regular tees. The slope rating is 115.

Play policy and fees: Green fees are $12 weekdays and $16 weekends. Carts are $18. Reservations are recommended.

Location: Take Interstate 710 (Long Beach Freeway) in Downey to the Firestone Boulevard exit. Drive east for one mile to Old River Road. Turn left and continue one-half of a mile to the club.

Course description: This is a level course with narrow, tree-lined fairway and small greens. It's in great shape.

10629 Old River School Rd.
Downey, CA 90241

| Pro shop | (213) 927-2329 |
| Starter | (213) 927-2420 |

- ■ driving range
- ■ practice greens
- ■ power carts
- ■ pull carts
- ■ golf club rental
- ■ locker rooms
- ■ showers
- ☐ executive course
- ☐ accommodations
- ■ food and beverages
- ■ clubhouse

Bruce MacDonald
Professional

Bert Spivey
Superintendent

BELLFLOWER MUNICIPAL GOLF COURSE

Course information: This public course has nine holes. Par is 27. The course is 1,335 yards.

Play policy and fees: Green fees are $3.50 for nine holes and $6 for 18 holes weekdays, and $4 per nine holes weekends. Call for special rates. Reservations are recommended.

Location: Take Highway 19 (Lakewood Boulevard) east to Compton Boulevard, turn right and go about one-half of a mile to the course.

Course description: This flat course is all par-3s.

9030 E. Compton Boulevard
Bellflower, CA 90706

Pro shop   (213) 920-8882

■ driving range
■ practice greens
□ power carts
■ pull carts
■ golf club rental
□ locker rooms
□ showers
□ executive course
□ accommodations
■ food and beverages
■ clubhouse

CANDLEWOOD COUNTRY CLUB

Course information: This private course has 18 holes and par is 70. The course is 6,113 yards and rated 68.9 from the championship tees, and 5,889 yards and rated 67.9 from the regular tees. The slope ratings are 122 championship and 119 regular. Women's tees are 5,708 yards and rated 73.3. The slope rating is 126.

Play policy and fees: Reciprocal play is accepted with members of other private clubs (have your pro call to make arrangements), otherwise members and guests only. Green fees are $30 weekdays and $45 weekends and holidays. Carts are $16. Reservations are recommended.

Location: Travel on Interstate 605 (San Gabriel River freeway) to the Telegraph Road exit east and drive about 3.5 miles to the club.

Course description: Lots of mature trees line the narrow fairways and a canal runs through the back nine. This is a walkable course, but beware of number seven, a par-5, 545-yard double dogleg of a devil with water in front. The most difficult shot on this hole is the approach shot, which most likely will require a short iron to the sizeable green. But you're hitting downhill with out-of-bounds to the right and left—so beware.

14000 E. Telegraph Rd.
Whittier, CA 90604

Pro shop   (213) 941-5310
Clubhouse (213) 941-1228

■ driving range
■ practice greens
■ power carts
□ pull carts
■ golf club rental
■ locker rooms
■ showers
□ executive course
□ accommodations
■ food and beverages
■ clubhouse

Greg Johnson
Professional

Mike Caranci
Superintendent

SOUTHERN I5

NORWALK GOLF COURSE

Course information: This public course has nine holes. Par is 27 for nine holes. The course is 960 yards or 1,920 for 18 holes.

Play policy and fees: Green fees are $4 for Norwalk residents and $6 for non-residents.

Location: Off Interstate 5 in Norwalk, exit on Rosecrans. Go east on Rosecrans to Shoemaker Street and left to the course.

Course description: This beginner's course is city owned and operated. The longest hole is 130 yards.

13717 Shoemaker Avenue
Norwalk, CA 90650

Pro shop   (213) 921-6500

☐ driving range
■ practice greens
☐ power carts
■ pull carts
■ golf club rental
☐ locker rooms
☐ showers
☐ executive course
☐ accommodations
☐ food and beverages
☐ clubhouse

Dave Verhaaf
Manager

LA MIRADA GOLF COURSE

Course information: This public course has 18 holes and par is 70. The course is 5,982 yards and rated 67.5 from the championship tees, and 5,770 yards and rated 66.6 from the regular tees. The slope ratings are 114 championship and 112 regular. Women's tees are 5,632 yards and rated 71.7. The slope rating is 115.

Play policy and fees: Green fees are $11 weekdays and $15 weekends. Carts are $17. Reservations are recommended.

Location: From Interstate 5, take Highway 39 east to Norwalk Boulevard. Go left on Norwalk for about one mile to La Mirada and follow it to the course.

Course description: This is a well-maintained course with some trees. The greens are bunkered on most holes.

15501 East Alicante Road
La Mirada, CA 90638

Pro shop   (213) 943-7123

■ driving range
■ practice greens
■ power carts
■ pull carts
■ golf club rental
☐ locker rooms
☐ showers
☐ executive course
☐ accommodations
■ food and beverages
☐ clubhouse

Robert Broga
Professional

BIG TEE GOLF COURSE

Course information: This public course has nine holes. Par is 27. The pitch-and-putt course is 1,098 yards.

Play policy and fees: Green fees are $3.50 weekdays before 5 p.m., $4 weekdays after 5.p.m., and $4 weekends for nine holes.

Location: On Highway 91 heading east in Buena Park, take the Beach Boulevard exit north and drive four miles into La Mirada Boulevard. The course is located on the corner of La Mirada and Beach Boulevard.

Course description: This beginner's course has the eighth hole as its longest at 160 yards. The course is flat and has many trees.

5151 Beach Boulevard
Buena Park, CA 90621

Pro shop   (714) 521-6300

- ■ driving range
- ■ practice greens
- □ power carts
- ■ pull carts
- ■ golf club rental
- □ locker rooms
- □ showers
- □ executive course
- □ accommodations
- ■ food and beverages
- □ clubhouse

John Mahoney
Professional

FRIENDLY HILLS COUNTRY CLUB

Course information: This private course has 18 holes and par is 70. The course is 6,400 yards and rated 72.1 from the championship tees, and 6,141 yards and rated 70.6 from the regular tees. The slope ratings are 135 championship and 128 regular. Women's tees are 5,639 yards and rated 68.4. The slope rating is 128.

Play policy and fees: Members and guests only. Green fees are $40 weekdays and $50 weekends. Guests must be accompanied by a member. Reservations recommended.

Location: From the Pomona Freeway (Highway 60) in Whittier, take Hacienda Boulevard South exit and go south for three miles to Colima Road, turn right and drive 2 1/4 miles to Mar Vista. From there go left to Villaverde Drive and the club.

Course description: This club features rolling terrain, undulating greens and narrow fairways. The course gets off to a tough start at number one, a par-5, 558-yard heavyweight. The hole is straight uphill to a green heavily bunkered on both sides and a creek on the left. Play it straight or it will play you.

8500 Villaverde Drive
Whittier, CA 90605

Pro shop   (213) 698-0331

- ■ driving range
- ■ practice greens
- ■ power carts
- □ pull carts
- □ golf club rental
- ■ locker rooms
- ■ showers
- □ executive course
- □ accommodations
- ■ food and beverages
- ■ clubhouse

Tom Schauppner
Professional

William Martin
Superintendent

SOUTHERN 15

MAP ON PAGE 412

LOS ANGELES ROYAL VISTA GOLF COURSE

1965

Course information: This semi-private course has 27 holes. Par is 71 on the East/North Course. Par is 71 on the North/South Course. Par is 72 on the South/East Course.

The East/North Course is 6,221 yards and rated 69.0 from the championship tees, and 5,828 yards and rated 67.0 from the regular tees. The slope ratings are 115 championship and 108 regular. Women's tees are 5,521 yards and rated 71.4. The slope rating is 114.

The North/South Course is 5,939 yards and rated 67.6 from the championship tees, and 5,597 yards and rated 65.8 from the regular tees. The slope ratings are 110 championship and 105 regular. Women's tees are 5,308 yards and rated 70.4. The slope rating is 112.

The South/East Course is 6,152 yards and rated 68.5 from the championship tees, and 5,797 yards and rated 66.7 from the regular tees. The slope ratings are 112 championship and 105 regular. Women's tees are 5,606 yards and rated 71.6. The slope is rating 114.

20055 East Colima Road
Walnut, CA 91789

Pro shop   (818) 965-1634
(800) 33GOLF3

- ■ driving range
- ■ practice greens
- ■ power carts
- ■ pull carts
- ■ golf club rental
- ■ locker rooms
- ■ showers
- □ executive course
- □ accommodations
- ■ food and beverages
- ■ clubhouse

John Welker
Professional

Dan Hornig
Director

Al Luna
Superintendent

Play policy and fees: Outside play is accepted. Green fees are $12 weekdays and $23 weekends. Carts are $18. Reservations are recommended. No tank tops are allowed on the course.

Location: From Los Angeles, travel on Highway 60 east to the Fairway Drive exit and turn right on the Brea Canyon cutoff. At Colima Road, turn left to the club.

Course description: All the courses are moderately hilly with mature trees and some water. The South Course is the narrowest and moderately short and the East Course plays the longest. On the South Course watch out for the second hole. It's a par-3-199-yard wheeler-dealer that needs a delicate tee shot over a lake to a green tucked between two hills.

HACIENDA GOLF CLUB

1922
Max Behr

Course information: This private course has 18 holes and par is 71. The course is 6,633 yards and rated 73.27 from the championship tees, and 6,352 yards and rated 71.1 from the regular tees. The slope ratings are 132 championship and 127 regular. Women's tees are 5,833 yards and rated 74.2. The slope rating is 129.

Play policy and fees: Members and guests only. Guest fees are $35 weekdays and $45 weekends. Carts are $18. Proper attire for golfers is collared shirts and slacks. Bermuda shorts are acceptable.

Location: Travel on Highway 60 to La Habra Heights and exit on Hacienda Boulevard south. Drive four miles to East Road and turn left. Continue three-fourths of a mile to the club.

Course description: This course was built in 1922, during the golden age of golf. It has a difficult layout with narrow, tree-lined fairways that traverse a rolling terrain. Number 16 is a real beauty. It's 199 yards over a lake to a two-tiered green. The USGA Women's Amateur Championship was held here in 1966. The McGregor Men's Tournament is held each June and the Jewel of the Canyon Invitational is played each August. The course record is 65 for men and 70 for women.

718 East Road
La Habra Heights, CA 90631

Pro shop   (213) 697-3610
Clubhouse   (213) 694-1081

- ■ driving range
- ■ practice greens
- ■ power carts
- □ pull carts
- ■ golf club rental
- ■ locker rooms
- ■ showers
- □ executive course
- □ accommodations
- ■ food and beverages
- ■ clubhouse

Andy Thuney
Professional

Todd Coward
Superintendent

BREA GOLF COURSE

Course information: This public course has nine holes. The course is 1,683 yards at nine holes and not rated.

Play policy and fees: Green fees are $5 weekdays and $6 weekends. Carts are $6. Reservations are recommended a week in advance.

Location: From Highway 57 heading south toward Brea, take the Imperial Highway exit west to Brea Boulevard and turn left. At the second signal, turn right on West Fir, which will dead end at the course.

Course description: This mostly flat course has a storm channel running through its center. There are few trees. The course consists of two par-4s and seven par-3s.

501 West Fir
Brea, CA 92621

Pro shop   (714) 529-3003

- ■ driving range,
- ■ practice greens
- ■ power carts
- □ pull carts
- ■ golf club rental
- □ locker rooms
- □ showers
- ■ executive course
- □ accommodations
- ■ food and beverages
- □ clubhouse

Tony Lopez
Professional

SOUTHERN 15

FULLERTON GOLF CLUB

Course information: This public course has 18 holes and par is 67. The course is 5,242 yards and rated 65.4 from the regular tees. The slope rating is 105. Women's tees are 5,032 yards and rated 70.1. The slope rating is 112.

Play policy and fees: Green fees are $12 weekdays and $16 weekends. Carts are $18. Reservations are recommended.

Location: Exit Highway 91 at Harbor Boulevard in Fullerton. Go north for three miles to the course, just past the condo development Greenview Terrace.

Course description: This pleasant, tight and narrow course is right in town and has excellent greens and a lateral water hazard that comes into play on 14 holes.

2700 N. Harbor Boulevard
Fullerton, CA 92633

Pro shop   (714) 871-5141
Clubhouse (714) 871-5142

- ■ driving range
- ■ practice greens
- ■ power carts
- ■ pull carts
- ■ golf club rental
- □ locker rooms
- □ showers
- □ executive course
- □ accommodations
- ■ food and beverages
- ■ clubhouse

Hank Woodrome
Professional

Tom Ponce
Superintendent

IMPERIAL GOLF COURSE

Course information: This public course has 18 holes and par is 72. The course is 6,376 yards and rated 70.0 from the championship tees, and 5,960 yards and rated 67.6 from the regular tees. The slope ratings are 118 championship and 111 regular. Women's tees are 5,581 yards and rated 71. The slope rating is 114.

Play policy and fees: Green fees are $15 weekdays and $20 weekends. Carts are $20. This course is available for outside tournaments.

Location: From Highway 60 (Pomona Freeway) take Highway 57 south and drive seven miles to the Imperial Highway exit east. From there, drive one-half of a mile to the course.

Course description: This is one of the more challenging courses in the area. The out-of-bounds areas pose problems for some players.

PO Box 1150
Brea, CA 92621

2200 East Imperial Highway
Brea, CA 92621

Pro shop   (714) 529-3923
Clubhouse (714) 524-0923

- ■ driving range
- ■ practice greens
- ■ power carts
- ■ pull carts
- ■ golf club rental
- ■ locker rooms
- ■ showers
- □ executive course
- □ accommodations
- ■ food and beverages
- ■ clubhouse

Bob Breeding
Professional

Bill Mague
Superintendent

ALTA VISTA COUNTRY CLUB

Course information: This private course has 18 holes and par is 72. The course is 6,361 yards and rated 69.8 from the championship tees, and 5,886 yards and rated 67.7 from the regular tees. The slope ratings are 115 championship and 107 regular. Women's tees are 5,851 yards and rated 70.5. The slope rating is 122.

Play policy and fees: Reciprocal play is accepted with members of other private clubs after 12:30 p.m. weekdays and 1 p.m. weekends, otherwise members and guests only. Reciprocator fees are $35 weekdays and $45 weekends. Carts are $18. Reservations are required for reciprocators. This course is available for outside tournaments on Mondays only.

Location: Travel on Highway 91 to Placentia and take the Kraemar Boulevard exit. Drive north two miles to Alta Vista Street and turn right. Turn left on Sue Drive and continue one-half block to the club.

Course description: This is a flat course with mature trees, lots of out-of-bounds and some lakes. Homes line the perimeter.

777 East Alta Vista
Placentia, CA 92670

Pro shop   (714) 528-1103
Clubhouse (714) 524-3319

- ■ driving range
- ■ practice greens
- ■ power carts
- ☐ pull carts
- ■ golf club rental
- ■ locker rooms
- ■ showers
- ☐ executive course
- ☐ accommodations
- ■ food and beverages
- ■ clubhouse

Ted Debus
Professional

Ernie Hernandez
Superintendent

BIRCH HILLS GOLF COURSE

Course information: This public course has 18 holes and par is 59. The course is 3,520 yards and unrated.

Play policy and fees: Green fees are $12 weekdays and $16 weekends for 18 holes. Carts are $14 weekdays and $16 weekends. Reservations are recommended one week in advance. Shirts are required.

Location: Driving south on Highway 57 from Brea, exit at Imperial Highway east. Turn left on Associated Road and right on Birch Street and drive to the course.

Course description: This short, executive course is hilly with good greens.

2250 East Birch Street
Brea, CA 92621

Pro shop   (714) 990-0201

- ■ driving range
- ■ practice greens
- ■ power carts
- ■ pull carts
- ■ golf club rental
- ☐ locker rooms
- ☐ showers
- ■ executive course
- ☐ accommodations
- ■ food and beverages
- ■ clubhouse

Steve LaBarge
Professional

Larry Taylor
Director

Tony Harris
Superintendent

SOUTHERN 15

DIAMOND BAR GOLF COURSE

1962

Course information: This public course has 18 holes and par is 72. The course is 6,819 yards and rated 71.6 from the championship tees, and 6,534 yards and rated 70.4 from the regular tees. The slope ratings are 122 championship and 119 regular. Women's yardage is 5,949 and rated 72.8. The slope rating is 117.

Play policy and fees: Green fees are $11 weekdays and $15 weekends. The weekday twilight rate is $7 and weekend twilight is $9. Los Angeles County senior citizens play for $5.50 for 18 holes and $4.50 for nine holes. Carts are $17 for 18 holes and $11 for nine holes. Reservations are recommended. Shirts must be worn at all times.

Location: From downtown Los Angeles, take Highway 60 east 24 miles to Grand Avenue. Turn right and go one signal, then turn left to the course.

Course description: This is a tree-lined course with water hazards on four holes. It is generally calm in the morning, although the wind can pick up in the after-noon and play havoc with your name brand. Number four is a perfect example. It is a 560-yard par-5 that plays directly into the wind. The course is fairly open so errant tee shots are salvageable. Among the tournaments played here are the Diamond Bar Invitational in September and the Rotary Club Tournament in March. Baseball fans might find a stray Dodger or Angel around the course.

22751 East Golden Springs
Diamond Bar, CA 91765

Pro shop   (714) 861-8282
Clubhouse (714) 861-5757

- ■ driving range
- ■ practice greens
- ■ power carts
- ■ pull carts
- ■ golf club rental
- □ locker rooms
- □ showers
- □ executive course
- □ accommodations
- ■ food and beverages
- ■ clubhouse

Don DiPietro
Professional

Jim Pitmann
Superintendent

YORBA LINDA COUNTRY CLUB

Course 54
MAP 15 grid e5

1957

Course information: This private course has 18 holes and par is 71. The course is 6,810 yards and rated 72.8 from the championship tees, and 6,492 yards and rated 70.5 from the regular tees. The slope ratings are 125 championship and 119 regular. Women's tees are 6,492 yards and rated 77.5 from the championship tees, and 5,918 yards and rated 74 from the forward tees. The slope ratings are 134 championship and 126 forward.

Play policy and fees: Members and guests only. Green fees are $40. Carts are $9 per person. This course is available for outside tournaments on Mondays only.

Location: Take the Riverside Freeway (Highway 91) to the Imperial Highway (Highway 90). Drive north to Kellogg and turn right to Mountain View and the club.

Course description: This old-style course is nestled between numerous homes. There are tree-lined fairways, some hills and bunkers and a little water. It's walkable. In February, 1992 a new clubhouse and locker rooms will be completed.

19400 Mountain View
Yorba Linda, CA 92686

Pro shop   (714) 779-2467
Clubhouse (714) 779-2461

- ■ driving range
- ■ practice greens
- ■ power carts
- □ pull carts
- ■ golf club rental
- ■ locker rooms
- ■ showers
- □ executive course
- □ accommodations
- ■ food and beverages
- ■ clubhouse

Tom Sargent
Professional

Larry Snyder
Superintendent

WESTERN HILLS GOLF AND COUNTRY CLUB

Course 55
MAP 15 grid e6

Course information: This private course has 18 holes and par is 72. The course is 6,669 yards and rated 72.2 from the championship tees, and 6,370 yards and rated 70.6 from the regular tees. The slope ratings are 128 championship and 122 regular. Women's tees are 6,370 yards and rated 77 from the championship tees, and 5,870 yards and rated 73.9 from the forward tees. The slope ratings are 134 championship and 126 forward.

Play policy and fees: Reciprocal play is accepted with members of other private clubs Monday through Friday, otherwise members and guests only. Green fees are $25 weekdays and $40 weekends. Carts are $20. This course is available for outside tournaments on Mondays only.

Location: From Highway 71 take Chino Hills Parkway west to Carbon Canyon Road. Turn left and drive two miles to the club. From Highway 57 take Lambert Road east 11 miles to the club.

Course description: This rolling course has mature trees and is well bunkered. There is a double green that serves two holes, numbers 12 and 14. The U.S. Amateur qualifier is held here each year.

1800 Carbon Canyon Road
Chino, CA 91709

Pro shop   (714) 528-6661
Clubhouse (714) 528-6400

- ■ driving range
- ■ practice greens
- ■ power carts
- □ pull carts
- ■ golf club rental
- ■ locker rooms
- □ showers
- □ executive course
- □ accommodations
- ■ food and beverages
- ■ clubhouse

Brad Stormon
Professional

Jim Fetterly
Superintendent

SOUTHERN 15

LOS SERRANOS LAKES GOLF AND COUNTRY CLUB

Course information: This public club has two 18-hole courses. Par is 74 on the South Course and 72 on the North Course.

The South Course is 7,007 yards and rated 73.6 from the championship tees, and 6,559 yards and rated 70.9 from the regular tees. The slope ratings are 129 championship and 122 regular. Women's tees are 5,935 yards and rated 71.9. The slope rating is 114.

The North Course is 6,292 yards and rated 69.5 from the championship tees, and 6,072 yards and rated 68.5 from the regular tees. The slope ratings are 116 championship and 112 regular. Women's tees are 5,880 yards and rated 71.8. The slope rating is 112.

Play policy and fees: Green fees are $17 weekdays and $22 weekends. Carts are $20. This course is available for outside tournaments.

Location: From Highway 60 (Pomona Freeway), take the Pomona-Corona/Highway 71 exit and travel south on Highway 71 for five miles to Los Serranos Road. Turn right to the club.

Course description: The South Course is long and hilly and gets breezy in the afternoons. The North Course was built in the 1920s and is scenic and rolling.

15656 Yorba Avenue
Chino, CA 91709

Pro shop   (714) 597-1711
Clubhouse (714) 597-1769

- ■ driving range
- ■ practice greens
- ■ power carts
- ■ pull carts
- ■ golf club rental
- ■ locker rooms
- ■ showers
- □ executive course
- □ accommodations
- ■ food and beverages
- ■ clubhouse

John Powell
Professional

Steven Hall
Superintendent

EL PRADO GOLF COURSES

Course information: This public facility has two 18-hole courses. Par is 72 on both.

The Butterfield Stage Course is 6,508 yards and rated 69.7 from the championship tees, and 6,251 yards and rated 68.4 from the regular tees. The slope ratings are 108 championship and 103 regular. Women's tees are 5,503 yards and rated 70. The slope rating is 118.

The Chino Creek Course is 6,671 yards and rated 71.1 from the championship tees, and 6,296 yards and rated 69.1 from the regular tees. The slope ratings are 114 championship and 108 regular. Women's tees are 5,596 yards and rated 70.6. The slope rating is 115.

Play policy and fees: Green fees are $15 weekdays and $20 weekends and holidays. Carts are $20. Reservations are recommended.

Location: From Los Angeles, travel east on Highway 60 (Pomona Freeway) to the Corona Freeway/Highway 71 exit. Turn right and drive six miles to Pomona Rincon Road and turn left and follow the signs.

Course description: The Chino Creek Course is longer and a bit more challenging with water hazards and several out-of-bounds areas. There are rolling hills and the course is very walkable. The Butterfield Stage Course is slightly shorter, flatter and more forgiving, making it receptive to beginning golfers.

6555 Pine Avenue
Chino, CA 91710

Pro shop   (714) 597-1753

- ■ driving range
- ■ practice greens
- ■ power carts
- ■ pull carts
- ☐ golf club rental
- ☐ locker rooms
- ☐ showers
- ☐ executive course
- ☐ accommodations
- ■ food and beverages
- ■ clubhouse

Robert Bickford
Director

Joe McDermott
Professional

Dennis Jobert
Superintendent

SOUTHERN 15

GREEN RIVER GOLF CLUB

Course 58
MAP 15 grid e7

1958
William Francis Bell
Desmond Muirhead

5215 Green River Drive
Corona, CA 91720

Pro shop   (714) 737-7393
Clubhouse (714) 970-8411

Course information: This public facility has two 18-hole courses and par is 71 on both.

The Orange Course is 6,416 yards and rated 70.4 from the championship tees, and 6,167 yards and rated 68.8 from the regular tees. The slope ratings are 119 championship and 110 regular. Women's tees are 5,728 yards and rated 73.2. The slope rating is 120.

The Riverside Course is 6,294 yards and rated 69.0 from the championship tees, and 6,028 yards and rated 67.8 from the regular tees. The slope ratings are 110 championship and 105 regular. Women's tees are 5,573 yards and rated 71.0. The slope rating is 115.

Play policy and fees: Green fees are $15 weekdays, and $20 Fridays and weekends. Carts are $20. Reservations are recommended. This course is available for outside tournaments.

Location: From the Riverside Freeway (Highway 91), take the Green River Drive exit north and travel one mile to the entrance.

Course description: These two courses feature gently rolling slopes with many trees and lakes. An errant tee shot means trouble. The Santa Ana River runs through both courses.

- ■ driving range
- ■ practice greens
- ■ power carts
- ■ pull carts
- ■ golf club rental
- ■ locker rooms
- ■ showers
- □ executive course
- □ accommodations
- ■ food and beverages
- ■ clubhouse

Howard Smith
Professional

Buford Goins
Superintendent

ONTARIO NATIONAL GOLF COURSE

Course information: This public course has 18 holes and par is 72. The course is 6,666 yards and rated 71.4 from the championship tees, and 6,265 yards and rated 69.0 from the regular tees. The slope ratings are 122 championship and 114 regular. Women's tees are 5,987 yards and rated 73.0. The slope rating is 115. There is also a 18-hole, par-3 course.

Play policy and fees: Green fees are $13 weekdays and $17 weekends. Carts are $16 weekdays and $18 weekends. Reservations are recommended.

Location: Travel east of Los Angeles on Highway 60 to the Vineyard exit near Ontario. Turn right on Riverside Drive and travel two blocks and turn left to the club.

Course description: This course has level terrain, mature trees and wide open fairways. It plays long because the ball gets little roll. The driving range has lights.

2525 Riverside Drive
Ontario, CA 91761

Pro shop   (714) 947-3512
Clubhouse   (714) 947-3837

- ■ driving range
- ■ practice greens
- ■ power carts
- ■ pull carts
- ■ golf club rental
- ■ locker rooms
- ■ showers
- □ executive course
- □ accommodations
- ■ food and beverages
- ■ clubhouse

Dave Ferrell
Professional

Jim Noble
Superintendent

LAKEWOOD COUNTY GOLF COURSE

Course information: This public course has 18 holes and par is 72. The course is 7,058 yards and rated 71.6 from the regular tees.

Play policy and fees: Greens fees are $11 weekdays and $15 weekends. Reservations recommended. Be persistent and call early, any day.

Location: Take the Lakewood Boulevard exit off Interstate 405 and head east. At Carson Street turn left and drive about two miles to the club.

Course description: This is a fairly flat course built alongside an 11-acre lake, but the greatest hazard comes from the nearby Long Beach Airport. Bring ear plugs.

3101 Carson Street
Lakewood, CA 90712

Pro shop   (213) 429-9711

- ■ driving range
- ■ practice greens
- ■ power carts
- ■ pull carts
- ■ golf club rental
- □ locker rooms
- ■ showers
- □ executive course
- □ accommodations
- ■ food and beverages
- ■ clubhouse

SOUTHERN 15

SKYLINKS GOLF COURSE

Course information: This public course has 18 holes and par is 72. The course is 6,460 from the championship tees and rated 69.6, and 6,277 yards from the regular tees and rated 68.6. The slope ratings are 113 championship and 108 regular. Women's tees are 5,918 yards and rated 72.0. The slope rating is 113.

Play policy and fees: Green fees are $12.50 weekdays and $15.50 weekends for Long Beach residents, and $16 weekdays and $19 weekends for non-residents. Carts are $17. Pull carts are $3.

Location: Take Interstate 405 south to Long Beach. Exit on Lakewood Boulevard north. The course is located three blocks down on your right. It's across from the Long Beach Airport.

Course description: This course will give you a run of doglegs. It's mostly flat and it is walkable.

4800 Wardlow Road
Long Beach, CA 90808

Pro shop   (213) 429-0030
Starter   (213) 429-0030

- ■ driving range
- ■ practice greens
- ■ power carts
- ■ pull carts
- ■ golf club rental
- ■ locker rooms
- ■ showers
- □ executive course
- □ accommodations
- □ food and beverages
- ■ clubhouse

Jamie Mulligan
Professional

Chris Leavitt
Superintendent

HEARTWELL GOLF PARK

Course information: This public course has 18 holes and par is 54. The course is 2,153 yards. It's all par-3s and rated 50.1.

Play policy and fees: Green fees are $5 weekdays and $5.25 weekends for nine holes for Long Beach residents, and $6.50 weekdays and $6.75 weekends for nine holes for non-residents. Carts are $7 for nine holes and $10 for 18 holes.

Location: Off Interstate 405 in Long Beach, take the Lakewood Boulevard exit north. Follow Lakewood two miles to Carson Street and turn right. The course is 1.5 miles on the right.

Course description: This well-conditioned course has raised greens. The longest hole is the ninth at 140 yards.

6700 East Carson Street
Long Beach, CA 90808

Pro shop   (213) 421-8855

- ■ driving range
- ■ practice greens
- ■ power carts
- ■ pull carts
- ■ golf club rental
- □ locker rooms
- □ showers
- □ executive course
- □ accommodations
- ■ food and beverages
- ■ clubhouse

Roy Eversole
Professional

Kelly Wall
Manager

EL DORADO GOLF COURSE

1955

Course information: This public course has 18 holes and par is 72. The course is 6,695 yards and rated 71.7 from the championship tees, and 6,427 yards and rated 68.9 from the regular tees. The slope ratings are 121 championship and 114 regular. Women's tees are 5,743 yards and rated 73.7. The slope rating is 118.

Play policy and fees: Green fees are $12.50 weekdays and $16 weekends for Long Beach residents, and $15.50 weekdays and $19 weekends for non-residents. Carts are $17.

Location: From Los Angeles, travel south on Interstate 405 (San Diego Freeway) to the Studebaker Road exit. Turn north and drive three-fourths of a mile to the club.

Course description: This course is mostly level with lots of doglegs and mature, tree-lined fairways. Water comes into play on five holes. If the closing holes look reversed since the last time you played this course, don't worry. Be happy. Number 17, formerly a par-5, is now par-3 and 169 yards; and number 18, formerly a par-3, is now a par-5 and 510 yards. Water has been added to the final hole for a finishing touch. The Queen Mary Open was held here until 1983. The Long Beach Open was played here in 1991.

2400 Studebaker Road
Long Beach, CA 90815

Pro shop   (213) 430-5411
Clubhouse   (213) 424-4631
Starter   (213) 498-0977

- ■ driving range
- ■ practice greens
- ■ power carts
- ■ pull carts
- ■ golf club rental
- □ locker rooms
- □ showers
- □ executive course
- □ accommodations
- ■ food and beverages
- ■ clubhouse

Bob Vogel
Professional

Guy Auxer
Superintendent

RECREATION PARK GOLF COURSE

Course information: This public course has nine holes. Par is 64 for 18 holes. The course is 6,337 yards from the championship tees and rated 68.8. The slope is 108.

Play policy and fees: Green fees are $12.50 for 18 holes weekdays and $16 for 18 holes weekends for Long Beach residents, and $15.50 for 18 holes weekdays and $19 for 18 holes weekends for non-residents. Reservations are recommended.

Location: Follow the Pacific Coast Highway (Highway 1) north from Seal Beach and exit at Seventh Street. Drive one-half of a mile on Seventh to the course entrance.

Course description: This course features rolling terrain and undulating greens. The fairways are fairly tight, demanding well-placed tee shots.

5000 East 7th Street
Long Beach, CA 90804

Pro shop   (213) 494-5000
Coffee shop(213) 494-4333

- ■ driving range
- ■ practice greens
- ■ power carts
- ■ pull carts
- ■ golf club rental
- □ locker rooms
- □ showers
- □ executive course
- □ accommodations
- □ food and beverages
- □ clubhouse

SOUTHERN I5

MAP ON PAGE 412

BIXBY VILLAGE GOLF COURSE

Course information: This public course has nine holes. Par is 29. The course is 1,539 yards. It is not rated.

Play policy and fees: Green fees are $5 weekdays and $6 weekends. Replay rate is $3.50 weekdays and $4.50 weekends. Reservations are recommended one week in advance.

Location: On Interstate 405 south in Long Beach exit on Bellflower Boulevard and drive south. Veer left on the Pacific Coast Highway (Highway 1). Turn left on Bixby Village Drive and drive one-eighth of a mile to the course.

Course description: This hilly course has undulating greens and two lakes. The longest hole is the par-4 fifth at 340 yards.

6180 Bixby Village Drive
Long Beach, CA 90803

Pro shop   (213) 498-7003

□ driving range
□ practice greens
□ power carts
□ pull carts
□ golf club rental
□ locker rooms
□ showers
□ executive course
□ accommodations
□ food and beverages
□ clubhouse

Robert Jones
Manager

LEISUREWORLD GOLF COURSE

Course information: This public course has nine holes. Par is 54 for 18 holes. The course is 1,800 yards at 18 holes.

Play policy and fees: Members and guests only. This is a resident course. No reciprocal play is allowed.

Location: On Interstate 405 heading south to Seal Beach, exit on Seal Beach Boulevard east. Turn left (south) and drive two blocks to the course on your right.

Course description: This residential course is flat. A pond offers measurable excitement on four or five of the holes.

13580 Saint Andrews
Seal Beach, CA 90740

Pro shop   (213) 431-6586

□ driving range
□ practice greens
□ power carts
□ pull carts
□ golf club rental
□ locker rooms
□ showers
□ executive course
□ accommodations
□ food and beverages
□ clubhouse

Fred Cooper
Director

OLD RANCH COUNTRY CLUB

1965
Ted Robinson

Course information: This private course has 18 holes and par is 72. The course is 6,581 yards and rated 71.8 from the championship tees, and 6,203 yards and rated 69.4 from the regular tees. The slope ratings are 124 championship and 114 regular. Women's tees are 5,877 yards and rated 72.8 The slope rating is 121.

Play policy and fees: Members and guests only. Guest fees are $35 weekdays and $45 Fridays, weekends and holidays. Carts are $18. Reservations are required. Call the golf pro to arrange reciprocal play.

Location: Near Long Beach, take the Seal Beach exit off Interstate 405 (San Diego Freeway) to the right. Drive one-half of a mile to Lampson Avenue. Turn right again and drive one-half of a mile to the club.

Course description: This course is level, but don't let that fool you. Because of its proximity to the ocean, winds can greatly affect playing conditions. The holes are tight, and the well-maintained greens are protected by water. The USGA Seniors Open qualifying event has been held here.

3901 Lampson Avenue
Seal Beach, CA 90740

Pro shop   (213) 596-4611
Clubhouse (213) 596-4425

■ driving range
■ practice greens
■ power carts
□ pull carts
□ golf club rental
■ locker rooms
■ showers
□ executive course
□ accommodations
■ food and beverages
■ clubhouse

Robert Silver
Professional

Don Parsons
Superintendent

NAVY GOLF COURSES LONG BEACH

1966
Joe Williams

Course information: This military course has 18 holes and par is 72. There is also a par-32, nine-hole executive course.

The Destroyer Course is 6,835 yards and rated 73.5 from the championship tees, and 6,514 yards and rated 71.2 from the regular tees. The slope ratings are 129 championship and 123 regular. Women's tees are 5,905 yards and rated 72.5. The slope rating is 121.

The (executive course) is 4,035 yards and rated 55.8 from the regular tees. The slope rating is 85.

Play policy and fees: Military personnel and guests only. Green fees are $10 for military personnel and $20 for guests. Carts are $15.

Location: South on Interstate 405 (San Diego Freeway) bear right at the intersection with Garden Grove Freeway to Cypress-Valley View exit. Drive north 1.5 miles to Orangewood Avenue, then left to the course.

Course description: Tree-lined fairways, numerous water hazards and offshore breezes add to the character and challenge of this course. Beware of the par-3, 185-yard ninth hole. Tee shots must carry over water to a bunker-lined green. Bring hip boots.

5660 Orangewood Avenue
Cypress, CA 90630

Pro shop   (213) 430-9913
Pro shop   (714) 527-4401
Clubhouse (213) 431-4956

■ driving range
■ practice greens
■ power carts
■ pull carts
■ golf club rental
■ locker rooms
■ showers
■ executive course
□ accommodations
■ food and beverages
■ clubhouse

Dave Smith
Professional

Paul Moreno
Manager

Gilbert Quintero
Superintendent

SOUTHERN 15

MAP ON PAGE 412

LOS COYOTES
COUNTRY CLUB

Course information: This private club has 27 holes. Par is 72 on the Valley-Vista Course and 67 on the Vista-Lake and Lake-Valley courses.

The Valley-Vista Course is 6,965 yards and rated 73.7 from the championship tees, and 6,635 yards and rated 71.5 from the regular tees. The slope ratings are 129 championship and 119 regular. Women's tees are 6,195 yards and rated 75. The slope rating is 125.

The Vista-Lake Course is 5,272 yards and rated 64.6 from the regular tees. The slope rating is 100. Women's tees are 5,085 yards and rated 67. The slope rating is 111.

The Lake-Valley Course is 5,423 yards and rated 65.3 from the regular tees. The slope rating is 101. The women's tees are 5,099 yards and rated 68.4. The slope is 109.

Play policy and fees: Reciprocal play is accepted with members of other private clubs, otherwise members and guests only. Fees for reciprocators are $45 weekdays. No reciprocal play on weekends. Guests on weekends are $60 weekends. Carts are $18 weekdays and $20 weekends. Reservations are required.

Location: Take Highway 91 (Artesia Freeway) or Interstate 5 (Santa Ana Freeway) to the Beach Boulevard exit. Drive north for three miles from Highway 91 or two miles from Interstate 5 to Los Coyotes Drive and turn right, then continue one mile to the club.

Course description: These courses are set around the top of a small hill. The rolling fairways are seeded with Kikuyu grass and the rough is brutal. All three layouts are well bunkered and interesting. Four greens have been re-done in the last year.

8888 Los Coyotes Drive
Buena Park, CA 90621

Pro shop   (714) 523-7780
Clubhouse   (714) 521-6171

- driving range
- practice greens
- power carts
- □ pull carts
- golf club rental
- locker rooms
- showers
- executive course
- □ accommodations
- food and beverages
- clubhouse

Jeff Perkins
Professional

Bill Gallegos
Superintendent

ANAHEIM "DAD" MILLER GOLF COURSE

Course information: This public course has 18 holes and par is 71. The course is 6,060 yards and rated 68.2 from the championship tees, and 5,805 yards and rated 67 from the regular tees. The slope ratings are 107 championship and 103 regular. Women's tees are 5,378 yards and rated 70. The slope rating is 107.

Play policy and fees: Green fees are $15 weekdays and $18 weekends. After 12 noon greens fees are $11 weekdays and $12 weekends. Call for special senior rates. Carts are $15. Reservations are recommended.

Location: Travel on Interstate 5 (Santa Ana Freeway) to the Brookhurst Street exit. Drive south one-half of a mile to Crescent Avenue and turn right. Continue one-half of a mile to Gilbert Street and turn left to the course.

Course description: This course is not long, but it is challenging for the average golfer. The tree-lined fairways are level and well kept for a public course. It's flat and easy to walk, but watch for the irrigation, which makes for a good challenge. It's always in good shape.

PO Box 2366
Anaheim, CA 92804

430 North Gilbert Street
Anaheim, CA 92801

Pro shop   (714) 774-8055
Reservation (714) 748-8900

■ driving range
■ practice greens
■ power carts
■ pull carts
■ golf club rental
□ locker rooms
□ showers
□ executive course
□ accommodations
■ food and beverages
■ clubhouse

Bob Johns
Professional

Gary Wimberly
Superintendent

ANAHEIM HILLS GOLF COURSE

Course information: This public course has 18 holes and par is 71. The course is 6,215 yards and rated 70.0 from the championship tees, and 5,966 yards and rated 68.4 from the regular tees. The slope ratings are 119 championship and 116 regular. Women's tees are 5,356 yards and rated 70. The slope rating is 115.

Play policy and fees: Green fees are $15 weekdays and $18 weekends. Carts are $18. Reservations are recommended. This course is available for outside tournaments.

Location: Take the Riverside Freeway (Highway 91) to the Imperial Highway exit south. Drive one-half of a mile to Nohl Ranch Road and turn left and travel 1.5 miles to the club.

Course description: Most of the fairways are separated on this hilly course (only four are parallel). The greens are undulating and can be fast in the summer.

6501 Nohl Ranch Road
Anaheim, CA 92807

Pro shop   (714) 998-3041
Clubhouse   (714) 748-8900

■ driving range
■ practice greens
■ power carts
□ pull carts
■ golf club rental
□ locker rooms
□ showers
□ executive course
□ accommodations
■ food and beverages
■ clubhouse

Don Poff
Professional

Don Lewis
Superintendent

SOUTHERN 15

CRESTA VERDE GOLF CLUB

1927
Randolph Scott

1295 Cresta Road
Corona, CA 91719

Pro shop   (714) 737-2255

- ■ driving range
- ■ practice greens
- ■ power carts
- ■ pull carts
- ■ golf club rental
- □ locker rooms
- □ showers
- □ executive course
- □ accommodations
- ■ food and beverages
- ■ clubhouse

L.J. Marcuzzo
Professional

Carlos Moreno
Superintendent

Course information: This public course has 18 holes and par is 71. The course is 5,694 yards and rated 66.3 from the championship tees, and 5,390 yards and rated 64.9 from the regular tees. The slope ratings are 101 championship and 98 regular. Women's tees are 5,026 yards and rated 70.0. The slope rating is 119.

Play policy and fees: Green fees are $14 weekdays and $20 weekends. Senior rates are $10 on weekdays. Carts are $20. Carts are mandatory before 12 noon on weekends and holidays. Reservations are recommended one week in advance. This course is available for outside tournaments.

Location: From the Riverside Freeway (Highway 91), take the Main Street North/Norco exit and travel north for one mile to Parkridge Avenue. Turn right and drive 1 1/4 miles to Termino Avenue, and turn left and drive to the club entrance.

Course description: Here's a course with Hollywood history. Henry Fonda, Burt Lancaster and Randolph Scott started this course back in 1927. In fact, Scott, who was a star attraction at the early Bing Crosby National Pro-Am at Pebble Beach, is credited with being the architect. In recent years the course has gone through some renovation. Three new water holes have been added (numbers eight, 15 and 18) for a total of four, and a new clubhouse was built in 1991. Power carts were also added in 1991. The course offers a rolling terrain with some steep slopes, many mature trees and winding fairways. It is not for the casual walker. The 17th hole has an elevated tee of 400 feet. The men's record stands at 61 and the women's at 72.

MOUNTAIN VIEW
COUNTRY CLUB

Course information: This semi-private course has 18 holes and par is 72. The course is 6,308 yards and rated 70.6 from the championship tees, and 6,070 yards and rated 69.0 from the regular tees. The slope ratings are 118 championship and 112 regular. Women's tees are 5,405 yards and rated 70.4. The slope rating is 119.

Play policy and fees: Green fees are $23 weekdays and $33 weekends. There are senior rates of $17 on weekdays with a cart, $9 without a cart. Carts are $23. Reservations are recommended.

Location: From the Riverside Freeway (Highway 91), take the Serfas Club Drive exit and travel east 400 yards to Pinecrest. Turn left and drive to the club entrance at the end of the street.

Course description: This course has tight fairways, tiny greens and lots of trees. The front nine winds through homes, while the back nine is hilly.

2121 Mountain View Drive
Corona, CA 91720

Pro shop   (714) 633-0282
Clubhouse (714) 737-9798

- ■ driving range
- ■ practice greens
- ■ power carts
- ■ pull carts
- ■ golf club rental
- ☐ locker rooms
- ☐ showers
- ☐ executive course
- ☐ accommodations
- ■ food and beverages
- ■ clubhouse

Richard Rush
Professional

MEADOWLARK GOLF COURSE

Course information: This public course has 18 holes and par is 70. The course is 5,761 yards and rated 66.1 from the regular tees. The slope rating is 98. Women's tees are 5,466 yards and rated 71.2. The slope rating is 116.

Play policy and fees: Green fees are $14 weekdays and $19 weekends. Carts are $19. Reservations are recommended.

Location: From South Orange County, travel north on Interstate 405 to the Warner Avenue exit and continue west for about four miles to Graham Street, then turn right to the club.

Course description: Established in the mid-1930s, this is a rolling course with narrow, tree-lined fairways. The greens are small, so shot placement is essential. There are several water hazards on the course.

16782 Graham Street
Huntington Beach
CA 92647

Pro shop   (714) 846-1364

- ■ driving range
- ■ practice greens
- ■ power carts
- ■ pull carts
- ■ golf club rental
- ☐ locker rooms
- ☐ showers
- ☐ executive course
- ☐ accommodations
- ■ food and beverages
- ☐ clubhouse

Jack Henry
Professional

Jody Piconni
Superintendent

SOUTHERN 15

SEACLIFF COUNTRY CLUB

Course information: This private course has 18 holes and par is 72. The course is 6,755 yards and rated 72.8 from the championship tees, and 6,480 yards and rated 70.8 from the regular tees. The slope ratings are 129 championship and 119 regular. Women's tees are 6,125 yards and rated 75.7 from the championship tees, and 5,585 yards and rated 73 from the forward tees. The slope ratings are 130 championship and 123 forward.

Play policy and fees: Members and guests only. Guest fees are $35 weekdays and $50 weekends. Carts are $18. This course is available for outside tournaments on Mondays only.

Location: In Huntington Beach, travel south on Interstate 405 (San Diego Freeway) to the Golden West exit. Turn right and drive seven miles to Palm Avenue. Turn right and drive to the club.

Course description: This course was formerly a public layout under the Huntington Seacliff name, and has been private for eight years. It was remodeled in the late 1980s and is long with undulating greens. It is well maintained.

6501 Palm Avenue
Huntington Beach, CA 92648

Pro shop   (714) 536-7575
Clubhouse (714) 536-8866

- ■ driving range
- ■ practice greens
- ■ power carts
- □ pull carts
- ■ golf club rental
- ■ locker rooms
- ■ showers
- □ executive course
- □ accommodations
- ■ food and beverages
- ■ clubhouse

Terry Ferraro
Professional

Ben McBrien
Superintendent

MILE SQUARE GOLF COURSE

Course information: This public course has 18 holes and par is 72. The course is 6,730 yards and rated 71.3 from the championship tees, and 6,466 yards and rated 69.9 from the regular tees. The slope ratings are 116 championship and 112 regular. Women's tees are 5,532 yards and rated 70.5. The slope rating is 109.

Play policy and fees: Green fees are $16 weekdays and $20 weekends and holidays. Carts are $20. Reservations are recommended. This course is available for outside tournaments.

Location: In Fountain Valley, take the Brookhurst Street/Fountain Valley exit off Interstate 405 (San Diego Freeway) and follow the Brookhurst Street north offramp. Continue north for one mile to Warner Avenue and turn right. Drive one-half of a mile to Ward Street and turn left to the course.

Course description: This is a fairly open and level course. There are numerous mature trees, a small creek and three lakes that add to the course's challenge and scenery. You can find water off the fourth, 15th and 17th tees if you're not careful.

PO Box 8347
Fountain Valley, CA 92708

Pro shop   (714) 545-7106
Clubhouse (714) 968-4556

- ■ driving range
- ■ practice greens
- ■ power carts
- ■ pull carts
- ■ golf club rental
- □ locker rooms
- □ showers
- □ executive course
- □ accommodations
- ■ food and beverages
- ■ clubhouse

Steve Seals
Professional

Marty Bereki
Superintendent

COSTA MESA GOLF AND COUNTRY CLUB

1967
William Francis Bell

PO Box 1829
Costa Mesa, CA 92626

1701 Golf Course Drive
Costa Mesa, CA 92626

Pro shop   (714) 540-7500
Starter   (714) 754-5267

- ■ driving range
- ■ practice greens
- ■ power carts
- ■ pull carts
- ■ golf club rental
- ■ locker rooms
- ■ showers
- □ executive course
- □ accommodations
- ■ food and beverages
- ■ clubhouse

Steve Hookano
Professional

Bob Shipley
Superintendent

Course information: This public facility has 36 holes. Par is 72 on the Los Lagos Course and 70 on the Mesa Linda Course.

The Los Lagos Course is 6,542 yards and rated 70.7 from the championship tees, and 6,233 yards and rated 69.0 from the regular tees. The slope ratings are 116 championship and 110 regular. Women's tees are 5,925 yards and rated 73.3. The slope rating is 118.

The Mesa Linda Course is 5,486 yards and rated 66.0 from the championship tees, and 5,041 yards and rated 63.5 from the regular tees. The slope ratings are 104 championship and 96 regular. Women's tees are 5,925 yards and rated 65.6. The slope rating is 102.

Play policy and fees: Green fees are $16 weekdays and $20 weekends. Carts are $20. Reservations are recommended.

Location: Traveling south on Interstate 405 (near Huntington Beach and Costa Mesa), exit on Harbor Boulevard. Continue south one mile to Adams Avenue and turn right. Drive one-quarter of a mile to Mesa Verde Drive, turn left and then right on Golf Course Drive.

Course description: Los Lagos is the older of the two courses and it features many trees, three lakes and a rolling layout. About five years ago Mesa Linda was upgraded with the addition of bunkers and new undulating greens. The driving range is lighted for night practice.

SOUTHERN 15

MESA VERDE COUNTRY CLUB

1958

Course information: This private course has 18 holes and par is 71. The course is 6,745 yards and rated 72.9 from the championship tees, and 6,285 yards and rated 70.5 from the regular tees. The slope ratings are 132 championship and 124 regular. Women's tees are 5,482 yards and rated 71.7. The slope rating is 124.

Play policy and fees: Members and guests only. Green fees are $45 weekdays and $65 weekends. Carts are $20. This course is available for outside tournaments on Mondays only.

Location: Travel south on Interstate 405 (SanDiego Freeway) to Costa Mesa and take the Harbor Boulevard exit. Drive south and turn right on Baker Street. Continue three-quarters of a mile to Mesa Verde West and turn right on Club House Road.

Course description: This mature course offers a variety of holes and hazards, and is easy walking. Number 18 is a par-3, 200-yard finisher with water in front to the right and out-of-bounds to the left. You must hit into the wind onto a sizeable green that slopes toward the water. Avoid being tight to the right or you're in the drink before you want to be.

3000 Club House Road
Costa Mesa, CA 92626

Pro shop (714) 549-0522
Clubhouse (714) 549-0377

- driving range
- practice greens
- power carts
- pull carts
- golf club rental
- locker rooms
- showers
- ☐ executive course
- ☐ accommodations
- food and beverages
- clubhouse

Art Schilling
Professional

Reed Yenny
Superintendent

RIVER VIEW GOLF COURSE

Course information: This public course has 18 holes and par is 70. The course is 5,554 yards and rated 66.1 from the championship tees, and 5,288 yards and rated 64.4 from the regular tees. The slope ratings are 103 championship and 97 regular. Women's tees are 5,194 yards and rated 70.1. The slope is 112.

Play policy and fees: Green fees are $12 weekdays and $17 weekends. Carts are $16. Reservations are recommended.

Location: Travel south on Interstate 5 (Santa Ana Freeway) to the Bristol exit south to Santa Clara Street, then west to the club.

Course description: This challenging, short course crisscrosses the bed of the Santa Ana River. The front nine requires good ball placement, and the back nine is wide open.

1800 West 22nd Street
Santa Ana, CA 92706

Pro shop   (714) 543-1115

■ driving range
■ practice greens
■ power carts
■ pull carts
■ golf club rental
□ locker rooms
□ showers
□ executive course
□ accommodations
■ food and beverages
□ clubhouse

Vince Lerma
Professional

James Mercer
Superintendent

WILLOWICK GOLF COURSE

Course information: This public course has 18 holes and par is 71. The course is 6,063 yards and rated 67.4 from the regular tees. The slope is 102. Women's tees are 5,742 yards and rated 71.6. The slope rating is 116.

Play policy and fees: Green fees are $12 weekdays and $19 weekends for 18 holes and $7 weekdays and $12 weekends for nine holes. Carts are $20. Reservations are recommended.

Location: In Santa Ana, take the Harbor exit off of Highway 22 (Garden Grove Freeway) and travel one mile south to Fifth Street. Turn left on Fifth Street and drive one-half mile and the course will be on your left.

Course description: This course is wide open and level with many trees and bunkers. It is an established course that has been a favorite of Southern Californians since the 1920s. It is short and walkable, good for exercising the legs. The course record is 61.

3017 West Fifth Street
Santa Ana, CA 92703

Pro shop   (714) 554-0672

■ driving range
■ practice greens
■ power carts
■ pull carts
□ golf club rental
■ locker rooms
■ showers
□ executive course
□ accommodations
■ food and beverages
■ clubhouse

Ken Kobayashi
Professional

Tom Pullium
Professional

Roy Haines
Superintendent

SOUTHERN 15

SANTA ANA COUNTRY CLUB

1929

Course information: This private course has 18 holes and par is 72. The course is 6,564 yards and rated 71.7 from the championship tees, and 6,218 yards and rated 69.6 from the regular tees. The slope ratings are 126 championship and 120 regular.
Play policy and fees: Members and guests only.
Location: Travel south on Interstate 405 to the Newport Freeway (Highway 55). Follow it to the end at Mesa Drive (first signal) turn left and drive 100 yards to Newport Boulevard. Turn left and drive 100 yards to the club.
Course description: This course has many old trees and five lakes. It was built in 1929.

20382 Newport Blvd.
Santa Ana, CA 92707

Pro shop   (714) 545-7260
Clubhouse (714) 556-3000

- ■ driving range
- ■ practice greens
- ■ power carts
- □ pull carts
- ■ golf club rental
- □ locker rooms
- □ showers
- □ executive course
- □ accommodations
- ■ food and beverages
- ■ clubhouse

Mike Reehl
Professional

David Zahrte
Superintendent

THE NEWPORT BEACH COUNTRY CLUB

Course information: This private course has 18 holes and par is 71. The course is 6,587 yards and rated 71.0 from the championship tees, and 6,232 yards and rated 68.9 from the regular tees. Women's yardage is 5,756 and rated 66.6. The slope ratings are 118 championship, 112 regular and 102 women.
Play policy and fees: Reciprocal play is accepted with members of other private clubs. Guest fees are $30 weekdays and $40 weekends. Carts are $18. Reservations are recommended.
Location: Travel north from Laguna Beach on Highway 1 past MacArthur Boulevard one-half mile.
Course description: This older, traditional course is finely manicured and has lots of trees. It's also without the typical damp coastal weather.

1600 East Coast Highway
Newport Beach, CA 92660

Pro shop   (714) 644-9680
Clubhouse (714) 644-9550

- ■ driving range
- ■ practice greens
- ■ power carts
- □ pull carts
- ■ golf club rental
- ■ locker rooms
- ■ showers
- □ executive course
- □ accommodations
- ■ food and beverages
- ■ clubhouse

Monty Blodgett
Professional

Gregory Fox
Superintendent

NEWPORT BEACH GOLF COURSE

Course 83
MAP 15 grid h4

1971
Robert Muir Graves

PO Box 18426
Irvine, CA 92714

3100 Irvine Avenue
Newport Beach, CA 92660

Pro shop   (714) 852-8689
Clubhouse (714) 852-8681

Course information: This public course has 18 holes and par is 59. The course is 3,450 yards and rated 51.5 from the regular tees. The slope rating is 83.

Play policy and fees: Green fees are $8.50 weekdays and $12 weekends.

Location: In Newport Beach from the Newport Freeway (Highway 55), exit at Highway 73/South Corona Del Mar and drive south to Irvine Avenue, turn right and drive one-half mile to the club.

Course description: This executive course offers well-maintained and well-contoured holes with bunkers and water that come into play. Night owls will be happy to know the course is lighted and accepts starting times until 8 p.m.

- ■ driving range
- ■ practice greens
- □ power carts
- ■ pull carts
- ■ golf club rental
- □ locker rooms
- □ showers
- ■ executive course
- □ accommodations
- ■ food and beverages
- ■ clubhouse

John Leonard
Professional

Manuel Mendoza
Superintendent

BIG CANYON COUNTRY CLUB

Course 84
MAP 15 grid h4

1971

One Big Canyon Drive
Newport Beach, CA 92660

Pro shop   (714) 644-5404

Course information: This private course has 18 holes and par is 72. The course is 6,937 yards and rated 73.9 from the championship tees, and 6,672 yards and rated 72.2 from the regular tees. Women's yardage is 5,788 and rated 67.5. The slope ratings are 137 championship and 130 regular.

Play policy and fees: Members and guests only.

Location: From Interstate 405, take the MacArthur Boulevard exit south and drive five miles to San Joaquin Hills Road. Turn right and drive to Big Canyon Drive.

Course description: This course was built in 1971. It has a traditional layout with many trees and bunkers. There are several water hazards as well.

- ■ driving range
- ■ practice greens
- ■ power carts
- ■ pull carts
- ■ golf club rental
- ■ locker rooms
- □ showers
- □ executive course
- □ accommodations
- ■ food and beverages
- ■ clubhouse

Bob Lovejoy
Professional

Ray Layland
Superintendent

SOUTHERN 15

RANCHO SAN JOAQUIN GOLF COURSE

Course information: This public course has 18 holes and par is 72. The course is 6,453 yards and rated 69.8 from the championship tees, and 6,229 yards and rated 68.8 from the regular tees. The slope ratings are 111 championship and 107 regular.

Play policy and fees: Green fees are $15 weekdays without a cart and $30 weekends. Cart is included and mandatory on weekends. Carts are $16. Reservations are recommended. This course is available for outside tournaments.

Location: Travel south on Interstate 405 to the Culver Drive exit west. Turn right on Sandburg Way and follow it to the end.

Course description: This is an interesting and challenging course. It features large, undulating greens, hilly terrain and some water hazards.

One Sandburg Way
Irvine, CA 92715

Pro shop   (714) 786-5522

- ■ driving range
- ■ practice greens
- ■ power carts
- ■ pull carts
- ■ golf club rental
- □ locker rooms
- □ showers
- □ executive course
- □ accommodations
- ■ food and beverages
- ■ clubhouse

Buck Page
Professional

Jack Gallant
Superintendent

EL TORO GOLF COURSE

Course information: This military course has 18 holes and par is 72. The course is 6,750 yards and rated 71.5 from the championship tees, and 6,468 yards and rated 69.7 from the regular tees. The slope ratings are 114 championship and 111 regular. Women's tees are 5,724 yards and rated 71.2. The slope rating is 112.

Play policy and fees: Military personnel and guests only. Green fees vary according to military status. Carts are $15.

Location: Take the Santa Ana Freeway south from Santa Ana to the Sand Canyon exit east. At Trabuco Road turn south to the main gate and take the perimeter road south for 2.5 miles to the course.

Course description: This relatively flat course has mature trees and a few doglegs.

PO Box 7
Irvine, CA 92650

El Toro Marine
Memorial MCAS
El Toro, CA 92650

Pro shop   (714) 726-2577

- ■ driving range
- ■ practice greens
- ■ power carts
- ■ pull carts
- ■ golf club rental
- ■ locker rooms
- ■ showers
- □ executive course
- □ accommodations
- ■ food and beverages
- ■ clubhouse

Wally Bradley
Professional

Paul Moreno, Jr.
Superintendent

Course information: This private facility has 27 holes and par is 71, 69 and 70 respectively for each of the 18-hole combinations listed.

The One and Two Combination is 5,849 yards and rated 66.5 from the regular tees. The slope rating is 100. Women's tees are 5,536 yards and rated 66.5. The slope rating is 113.

The Three and One Combination is 5,559 yards and rated 65.2 from the regular tees. The slope rating is 96. Women's tees are 5,369 yards and rated 65.2. The slope rating is 109.

The Two and Three Combination is 5,454 yards and rated 64.7 from the regular tees. The slope rating is 96. Women's tees are 5,331 yards and rated 64.7. The slope rating is 109.

Play policy and fees: Members and guests only. Green fees are $17 for guests. Carts are $16 for guests. Reservations are recommended.

Location: Take the El Toro Road exit off Interstate 5 and travel west to Moulton Parkway. Turn right and go one-quarter mile to the club.

Course description: Located in a residential community, this rolling course is slightly hilly with mature trees.

PO Box 2307
Laguna Hills, CA 92653

24112 Moulton Parkway
Laguna Hills, CA 92653

Pro shop   (714) 837-7630
Clubhouse (714) 951-2276

- ■ driving range
- ■ practice greens
- ■ power carts
- ■ pull carts
- ■ golf club rental
- □ locker rooms
- □ showers
- □ executive course
- □ accommodations
- ■ food and beverages
- ■ clubhouse

Robert Wilkinson
Professional

Leo Dull
Superintendent

SOUTHERN 15

DOVE CANYON
COUNTRY CLUB

1990
Jack Nicklaus

Course information: This private course has 18 holes. Par is 71. The course is 6,902 yards and rated 75.0 from the tournament tees, 6,489 yards and rated 72.0 from the championship tees, and 5,917 yards and rated 68.0 from the regular tees. The slope ratings are 140 tournament, 133 championship and 120 regular. Women's tees are 5,472 yards and rated 71.2 from the championship tees, and 5,261 yards and rated 69.7 forward tees. The slope ratings are 122 championship and 119 forward.

Play policy and fees: Reciprocal is not accepted. Members and guests only. Guest fees are $60 weekdays and $75 weekends and holidays, including cart and range balls. Reservations are required.

Location: From Interstate 5 south, take the El Toro Road exit east. Drive to Santa Margarita Parkway. Turn south on Santa Margarita Parkway to Plano Trabuco and turn right. Take Plano Trabuco to Dove Canyon and turn left. Follow Dove Canyon to the guard gate and the course.

Course description: This Jack Nicklaus course opened in August, 1990, and the clubhouse followed in March, 1991. This course backs up to the Cleveland National Forest, so count on plenty of wildlife. There are both barrancas and bunnies. The course is rolling, with some water and beautiful old oaks. The most notable water is at the 18th green, which features a waterfall and lake. Because of the high risk of fires, this is a non-smoking course.

22682 Golf Club Drive
Dove Canyon, CA 92679

Pro shop   (714) 858-2888
Clubhouse (714) 858-1800

■ driving range
■ practice greens
■ power carts
□ pull carts
■ golf club rental
■ locker rooms
■ showers
□ executive course
□ accommodations
■ food and beverages
■ clubhouse

Kevin Paluch
Director of Golf

Michael Coopman
Superintendent

CASTA DEL SOL
GOLF COURSE

Course information: This public course has 18 holes and par is 60. The course is 3,868 yards and rated 55.9 from the regular tees. The slope rating is 94. Women's tees are 3,520 yards and rated 58.9. The slope rating is 90.

Play policy and fees: Green fees are $13 weekdays and $17 weekends. Carts are $16. Call for special afternoon rates.

Location: Take the La Paz Road exit off Interstate 5 and travel east for one mile to Marguerite Parkway. Turn left and drive 1.5 miles to Casta del Sol Road and turn right and drive to the course.

Course description: This rolling course has a couple of streams and lakes. It's a testy, short course.

27601 Casta del Sol Road
Mission Viejo, CA 92692

Pro shop   (714) 581-0940
Clubhouse (714) 581-9701

■ driving range
■ practice greens
■ power carts
■ pull carts
□ golf club rental
□ locker rooms
□ showers
□ executive course
□ accommodations
■ food and beverages
■ clubhouse

Mary Rutledge
Professional

Brett Billeadeau
Superintendent

COTO DE CAZA GOLF COURSE

1987
Robert Trent Jones, Jr.

Course information: This private course has 18 holes and par is 72. The course is 7,096 yards and rated 75.8 from the championship tees, and 6,558 yards and rated 72.8 from the regular tees. The slope ratings are 146 championship and 138 regular. Women's tees are 5,369 yards and rated 71.6. The slope rating is 132.

Play policy and fees: Limited reciprocal play is accepted with members of other private clubs (have your pro call for arrangements), otherwise members and guests only. Green fees are $30 weekdays and $40 weekends with a member only. Carts are $17.

Location: Take the El Toro exit off Interstate 5 and drive east to Santa Margarita Road in Coto de Caza. Turn right and drive five miles to Antonio and turn right to the club.

Course description: This spectacular course is set in among the canyons of south Orange County. Designed by Robert Trent Jones, Jr. with the help of Johnny Miller, it's long, tough and scenic.

One Coto de Caza Drive
Coto de Caza, CA 92679

Pro shop   (714) 858-2770

- ■ driving range
- ■ practice greens
- ■ power carts
- ❑ pull carts
- ■ golf club rental
- ■ locker rooms
- ■ showers
- ❑ executive course
- ❑ accommodations
- ■ food and beverages
- ■ clubhouse

Mike Mitzel
Professional

Larry Murphy
Director

Lee Hood
Superintendent

MISSION VIEJO COUNTRY CLUB

1967
Robert Trent Jones, Sr.

Course information: This private course has 18 holes and par is 72. The course is 6,814 yards and rated 73.8 from the championship tees, and 6,456 yards and rated 71.3 from the regular tees. The slope ratings are 138 championship and 126 regular. Women's tees are 5,698 yards and rated 73.2. The slope rating is 126.

Play policy and fees: Members and guests only. Green fees are $30 weekdays and $40 weekends. Carts are $16. This course is available for outside tournaments Mondays only.

Location: Take the Oso Parkway exit off Interstate 5, then travel east one-half mile to Country Club Drive and turn right to the club.

Course description: This is a long and demanding course. The fairways are hilly and parallel. The greens are well maintained and very fast.

26200 Country Club Drive
Mission Viejo, CA 92691

Pro shop   (714) 582-1020
Clubhouse (714) 582-1550

- ■ driving range
- ■ practice greens
- ■ power carts
- ❑ pull carts
- ■ golf club rental
- ■ locker rooms
- ■ showers
- ❑ executive course
- ❑ accommodations
- ■ food and beverages
- ■ clubhouse

Jeremy Dunkason
Professional

Mike Huck
Superintendent

SOUTHERN I5

ALISO CREEK GOLF COURSE

1951

Course information: This resort course has nine holes. Par is 64 for 18 holes. The course is 4,148 yards and rated 57.2 for 18 holes from the regular tees. The slope rating is 104. Women's tees are 4,148 yards and rated 65.4. The slope rating is 109.

Play policy and fees: Green fees are $11 for nine holes weekdays and $12 for nine holes weekends. Reservations are required one week in advance. This course is available for outside tournaments.

Location: Take Interstate 5 or Interstate 405 southbound to Highway 133 (Laguna Freeway). Take Highway 133 (Laguna Freeway) west to Highway 1 (Pacific Coast Highway). Drive south on Highway 1 (Pacific Coast Highway) almost three miles to the green overpass. Take an immediate left turn at Ben Brown's sign. Northbound Interstate 5, take the Beach Cities exit. Drive north on Highway 1 (Pacific Coast Highway) about six miles. Turn right at the sign across from the Aliso State Beach Pier.

Course description: This 40-year-old course is set in a heavily-foliaged canyon, with a meandering creek. There are 19 bunkers and lots of trees. With the ocean just 400 yards away, a sea breeze adds to the quiet atmosphere.

31106 Pacific Coast Highway
Laguna Beach, CA 92677

Pro shop (714) 499-1919
Office (714) 499-2271

- ■ driving range
- ■ practice greens
- ■ power carts
- ■ pull carts
- ■ golf club rental
- ■ locker rooms
- □ showers
- ■ executive course
- □ accommodations
- ■ food and beverages
- ■ clubhouse

Larry Brotherton
Manager/Professional

Severo Mercado
Superintendent

EL NIGUEL COUNTRY CLUB

Course information: This private course has 18 holes and par is 72. The course is 6,909 yards and rated 73.8 from the championship tees, and 6,635 yards and rated 71.8 from the regular tees. The slope ratings are 133 championship and 124 regular. Women's tees are 5,787 yards and rated 72.8. The slope rating is 120.

Play policy and fees: Members and guests only. Guest fees $40 weekdays and $50 weekends. Carts are $16.

Location: Take the Crown Valley Parkway exit off Interstate 5 in Laguna Niguel and drive 4.5 miles to Clubhouse Drive. Turn left to the club.

Course description: This is a challenging course. It is well-bunkered with level fairways and lots of trees. The greens are some of the toughest west of the Rockies. You'll need a fortune teller to help you read them. The par-3 holes are exceptionally fine. Fairways and roughs are Kikuyu grass and play particularly tough in the summer.

23700 Clubhouse Drive
Laguna Niguel, CA 92677

Pro shop (714) 496-2023
Clubhouse (714) 496-5767

- ■ driving range
- ■ practice greens
- ■ power carts
- □ pull carts
- □ golf club rental
- ■ locker rooms
- ■ showers
- □ executive course
- □ accommodations
- ■ food and beverages
- ■ clubhouse

Paul Scodeller
Professional

Leo Renteria
Superintendent

THE LINKS AT
MONARCH BEACH

1983
Robert Trent Jones, Jr.

Course information: This resort course has 18 holes and par is 70. The course is 6,224 yards and rated 69.9 from the championship tees, and 5,655 yards and rated 67.2 from the regular tees. The slope ratings are 127 championship and 117 regular. Women's tees are 4,984 yards and rated 70. The slope rating is 115.

Play policy and fees: Outside play is accepted. Green fees are $50 weekdays and $75 weekends. Carts are included. Reservations are recommended.

Location: Take the Crown Valley Parkway exit off Interstate 5. Drive 3.5 miles to Niguel Road, turn left and travel another three miles to the club.

Course description: Most of the course offers a nice view of the ocean, and two holes run alongside it. The course was built to conform nicely to the terrain. Watch for number 16. It's a par-5, 517-yard twister with a creek intersecting the fairway. To reach the green in regulation it is necessary to clear the creek twice, so if you're successful on the first effort, keep your fingers crossed.

33080 Niguel Road
Dana Point, CA 92629

Pro shop   (714) 240-8247

□ driving range
■ practice greens
■ power carts
□ pull carts
■ golf club rental
□ locker rooms
□ showers
□ executive course
□ accommodations
■ food and beverages
■ clubhouse

Chris Herald
Professional

Brian Sullivan
Superintendent

SAN JUAN HILLS
COUNTRY CLUB

Course information: This public course has 18 holes and par is 71. The course is 6,003 yards and rated 68.3 from the regular tees. The slope rating is 114. Women's tees are 5,513 yards and rated 71.9. The slope rating is 120.

Play policy and fees: Green fees are $16 weekdays and $25 weekends. Special rates are available after 1 p.m. weekdays and 2 p.m. weekends. Carts are $16. Reservations are recommended.

Location: From Interstate 5, turn north on Highway 74 and go one-half mile to San Juan Creek Road.

Course description: The front and back nines are as different as night and day. The front nine is flat with a number of trees lining the fairway. The back nine is hilly with an abundance of trees to get in your way.

32120 San Juan Creek Road
San Juan Capistrano
CA 92675

Pro shop   (714) 493-1167

■ driving range
■ practice greens
■ power carts
■ pull carts
■ golf club rental
□ locker rooms
□ showers
□ executive course
□ accommodations
■ food and beverages
■ clubhouse

Arne Dokka
Professional

Pete Gallardo
Superintendent

SOUTHERN 15

SAN CLEMENTE
GOLF COURSE

1928
William Park Bell

150 East Magdalena
San Clemente, CA 92672

Pro shop   (714) 492-1997
Clubhouse (714) 492-3943

Course information: This public course has 18 holes and par is 72. The course is 6,431 yards and rated 70.1 from the championship tees, and 6,104 yards and rated 68.4 from the regular tees. The slope ratings are 119 championship and 112 regular. Women's tees are 5,727 yards and rated 72.1. The slope rating is 114.

Play policy and fees: Green fees are $14 weekdays and $21 weekends. Twilight rates and resident discounts are available. Carts are $16. Reservations are recommended. This course is available for outside tournaments.

Location: From San Diego, travel north on Interstate 5 and take Avenida Magdalena exit. Turn right on El Camino Real and go one block, then turn left on Magdalena to the course.

Course description: This is a scenic course offering delightful ocean views. Hole 15, a par-3, 197-yarder has an elevated tee with a spectacular view of the Pacific Ocean. The men's course record is 64. The women's record is 69, set in 1989 by Jayne Thobois. The San Clemente City Championship is held here in October.

- ■ driving range
- ■ practice greens
- ■ power carts
- ■ pull carts
- ■ golf club rental
- ☐ locker rooms
- ☐ showers
- ☐ executive course
- ☐ accommodations
- ■ food and beverages
- ■ clubhouse

Dave Cook
Professional

Paul Linden
Superintendent

PACIFIC GOLF CLUB

1988
Gary Player
Carl Litton

200 Avenida La Pata
San Clemente, CA 92672

Pro shop   (714) 498-6604

Course information: This private club has 27 holes and par is 72 for each of the 18-hole combinations.

The Royal Lytham/Muirfield Course is 6,516 yards and rated 73.1 from the tournament tees, 6,082 yards and rated 70.5 from the championship tees, and 5,499 yards and rated 67.4 from the regular tees. The slope ratings are 144 tournament, 134 championship and 125 regular. Women's tees are 5,402 yards and rated 65.8. The slope rating is 107.

The Carnoustie/Royal Lytham Course is 6,489 yards and rated 73.0 from the tournament tees, 5,992 yards and rated 70.1 from the championship tees, and 5,467 yards and rated 67.3 from the regular tees. The slope ratings are 144 tournament, 133 championship and 124 regular. Women's tees are 5,308 yards and rated 67.1. The slope rating is 111.

The Carnoustie/Muirfield Course is 6,759 yards and rated 74.5 from the tournament tees, and 6,272 yards and rated 71.4 from the championship tees, and 5,570 yards and rated 67.7 from the regular tees. The slope ratings are 146 tournament, 136 championship and 125 regular. Women's tees are 5,508 yards and rated 67.5. The slope rating is 114.

- ■ driving range
- ■ practice greens
- ■ power carts
- ☐ pull carts
- ■ golf club rental
- ■ locker rooms
- ■ showers
- ☐ executive course
- ☐ accommodations
- ■ food and beverages
- ■ clubhouse

Bob McCallister
Professional

Jesse Yukon
Superintendent

Play policy and fees: Members and guests only. Reciprocal players must have their golf pro call on Monday through Thursday to arrange starting times. Reservations are recommended. No jeans are allowed. Golfers must wear collared shirts.

Location: Take the Pico exit off Interstate 5 in San Clemente and travel two miles east to Avenida La Pata. Turn right and drive one mile to the club.

Course description: This is a young course offering a traditional links layout that rolls through meadows. The first hole at Carnoustie gives some golfers a scare. It's an uphill par-4 to an undulating, sloping green. To make par, your second shot better be a good one. The course record at Carnoustie/Muirfield is 66, set by Gary Player on opening day.

SOUTHERN 15

SHORECLIFFS GOLF COURSE

Course information: This public course has 18 holes and par is 70. The course is 5,796 yards and rated 67.9 from the championship tees, and 5,577 yards and rated 67.0 from the regular tees. The slope ratings are 113 championship and 109 regular. Women's tees are 5,318 yards and rated 69.4. The slope rating is 112.

Play policy and fees: Green fees are $10 weekdays and $20 weekends. Carts are $16.

Location: Take the Camino de Estrella exit off Interstate 5 and drive east to Avenida Vaquero. Turn right to the course.

Course description: This is a course that demands accuracy. It is short and tight, and meanders in and out of canyons. Hook a tee shot and you might find yourself in a canyon with the coyotes. Now you don't want to do that, do you?

501 Avenida Vaquero
San Clemente, CA 92672

Pro shop   (714) 492-1177

- ■ driving range
- ■ practice greens
- ■ power carts
- ■ pull carts
- ■ golf club rental
- ■ locker rooms
- ■ showers
- □ executive course
- □ accommodations
- ■ food and beverages
- ■ clubhouse

Keith Case
Professional

Fred Pinion
Superintendent

SOUTHERN 15

SOUTHERN 15

MAP I6
(35 COURSES)

PAGES.. 472-495

SO-CAL MAP .....see page 376
adjoining maps
NORTH (H6).......see page 368
EAST (I7) ....see page 496
SOUTH (J6) ....see page 546
WEST (I5) ....see page 412

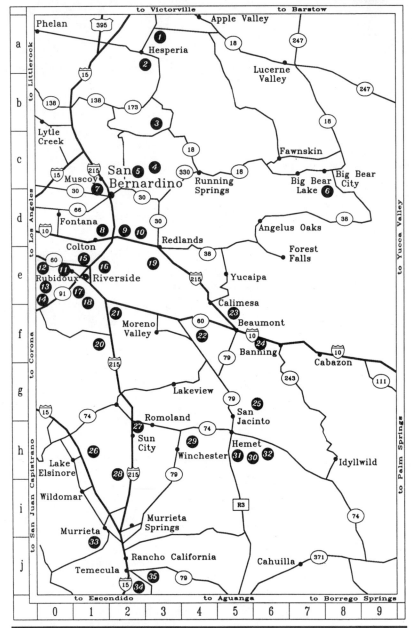

to Victorville • to Barstow

| | 0 | 1 | 2 | 3 | 4 | 5 | 6 | 7 | 8 | 9 |

SPRING VALLEY LAKE COUNTRY CLUB

Course 1
MAP 16 grid a3

1968
Robert Trent Jones, Jr.

13229 Spring Valley Parkway
Victorville, CA 92392

Pro shop   (619) 245-7921
Clubhouse (619) 245-5356

- ■ driving range
- ■ practice greens
- ■ power carts
- ■ pull carts
- ■ golf club rental
- ■ locker rooms
- ■ showers
- □ executive course
- □ accommodations
- ■ food and beverages
- ■ clubhouse

Gregg Combs
Professional

Bob MacBeth
Superintendent

Course information: This private course has 18 holes and par is 72. The course is 6,541 yards and rated 71.2 from the championship tees, and 6,184 yards and rated 69.3 from the regular tees. The slope ratings are 123 championship and 115 regular. Women's tees are 5,572 yards and rated 72.2. The slope rating is 122.

Play policy and fees: Reciprocal play is accepted with members of other private clubs, otherwise members and guests only. Green fees are $40. Carts are included. Reservations are recommended. This course is available for outside tournaments.

Location: From San Bernardino, drive north on Interstate 15 to the Lucerne Valley exit. Turn right and travel east for five miles on Bear Valley Road to Spring Valley Parkway. Turn left through the big archway to Spring Valley Lake and turn left on Country Club Drive.

Course description: The front nine has a number of water holes. The course is mostly level with some hills. It's walkable.

HESPERIA GOLF AND COUNTRY CLUB

Course 2
MAP 16 grid a3

1957
William Francis Bell

17970 Bangor Avenue
Hesperia, CA 92345

Pro shop   (619) 244-9301

- ■ driving range
- ■ practice greens
- ■ power carts
- ■ pull carts
- ■ golf club rental
- □ locker rooms
- ■ showers
- □ executive course
- □ accommodations
- ■ food and beverages
- ■ clubhouse

Alex Rickards
Manager

Dick Renz
Superintendent

Course information: This semi-private course has 18 holes and par is 72. The course is 6,996 yards and rated 74.6 from the championship tees, and 6,695 yards and rated 72.4 from the regular tees. The slope ratings are 133 championship and 127 regular. Women's tees are 6,136 yards and rated 73.9. The slope rating is 124.

Play policy and fees: Reciprocal play is accepted with members of other private clubs. Outside play is also accepted. Green fees are $15 weekdays and $20 weekends. Carts are $18. Reservations are recommended. This course is available for tournaments.

Location: From San Bernardino, travel 33 miles north on Interstate 15 to the Hesperia/Phelan exit. Turn right on Main Street and go 5.5 miles to "I" Avenue and turn right. Go 1.5 miles to Bangor Avenue and turn left.

Course description: This former PGA Tour stop offers a championship layout. It was designed and built 35 years ago and is still a tough test. The fairways are not parallel and are separated by mature trees. It's well bunkered and you'll find three lakes and a rolling terrain. Toughest hole is number 18, a par-4 440-yard stretch from the back tees that's guarded by trees on each side of the fairway. You have to be accurate through the trees. Ask Doug Sanders. Talk around the pro shop is Sanders once took a 12 on this hole. The trees have grown some since Sanders encountered them, so watch out.

SOUTHERN 16

LAKE ARROWHEAD COUNTRY CLUB

Course information: This private course has 18 holes and par is 71. The course is 6,205 yards and rated 70.3 from the championship tees, and 5,957 yards and rated 68.9 from the regular tees. The slope ratings are 126 championship and 123 regular. Women's tees are 5,557 yards and rated 72.1. The slope rating is 128.

Play policy and fees: Members and guests only. Green fees are $30 weekdays and $40 weekends. Carts are $20.

Location: Drive northeast of San Bernardino on Interstate 215 to the Mountain Resorts exit. Continue to Highway 18 (Waterman Avenue) and turn left, following it through the Rimforest to the Blue Jay exit. Bear left to the stop signal, turn left and drive one-half mile to Grass Valley Road. Bear right and continue 1.5 miles to Golf Course Road. Turn left and drive 100 yards to the club.

Course description: Originally a 1930s nine-hole course, it became a full 18 holes in 1959. The front nine is level and open while the back nine is hilly. There is a small lake on the course that comes into play. All the holes are dotted with bunkers.

PO Box 670
Lake Arrowhead, CA 92352

250 Golf Course Road
Lake Arrowhead, CA 92352

Pro shop   (714) 337-3515
Clubhouse (714) 337-2441

■ driving range
■ practice greens
■ power carts
□ pull carts
□ golf club rental
■ locker rooms
■ showers
□ executive course
□ accommodations
■ food and beverages
■ clubhouse

Dennis Murray
Professional

Emilio Castorena
Superintendent

ARROWHEAD COUNTRY CLUB

Course information: This private course has 18 holes and par is 72. The course is 6,573 yards and rated 71.5 from the championship tees, and 6,247 yards and rated 69.6 from the regular tees. The slope ratings are 123 championship and 114 regular. Women's tees are 5,759 yards and rated 72.8. The slope rating is 120.

Play policy and fees: Members and guests only. Green fees are $35. Carts are $15.

Location: From San Bernardino, travel east on Highway 30 to Waterman Avenue north. Drive for one-half mile and turn right on 34th Street. Continue to Parkside Drive and the entrance to the club.

Course description: This course, in one form or another, has been in existence since the 1920s, but became open for memberships in 1944. It has level terrain, young trees and water hazards. It is set at the foot of the mountains in a desert area, so the heat can become unbearable. There is also swimming.

3433 Parkside Drive
San Bernardino, CA 92404

Pro shop   (714) 882-1638
Clubhouse (714) 882-1735

■ driving range
■ practice greens
■ power carts
■ pull carts
■ golf club rental
■ locker rooms
■ showers
□ executive course
□ accommodations
■ food and beverages
■ clubhouse

Tom Miskell
Professional

Don Johnson
Superintendent

SHANDIN HILLS GOLF CLUB

Course information: This public course has 18 holes and par is 72. The course is 6,438 yards and rated 70.4 from the championship tees, and 6,123 yards and rated 68.9 from the regular tees. The slope ratings are 116 championship and 111 regular. Women's tees are 5,652 yards and rated 72.7. The slope rating is 120.

Play policy and fees: Green fees are $15 weekdays and $22 weekends. Carts are $10. Reservations are recommended.

Location: From Los Angeles, travel east on Interstate 10 to Interstate 215. In San Bernardino, take the Mount Vernon/27th Street offramp and turn right on 27th Street, then immediately left on Little Mountain. Travel one mile to the club.

Course description: This is a challenging course with 74 bunkers. The rough is well developed, so fairway placement is optimum. It has some hilly terrain on the front nine, but is walkable.

3380 Little Mountain Drive
San Bernardino, CA 92407

Pro shop   (714) 886-0669

□ driving range
■ practice greens
■ power carts
■ pull carts
■ golf club rental
□ locker rooms
■ showers
□ executive course
□ accommodations
■ food and beverages
■ clubhouse

Leanne Ulmer
Professional

Rick Barnett
Superintendent

BEAR MOUNTAIN GOLF COURSE

Course information: This public course has nine holes. Par is 70 for nine holes. The course is 5,528 yards from the championship tees for 18 holes (unrated). It is 5,218 yards and rated 65 from the regular tees. The slope rating is 107. Women's tees are 4,398 yards and unrated.

Play policy and fees: Green fees are $10 for nine holes and $14 for 18 holes weekdays, and $13 for nine holes and $19 for 18 holes weekends. Carts are $11 for nine holes and $16 for 18 holes.

Location: In San Bernardino, take Highway 30 east to Highland Avenue. Drive north on Highway 330 to Highway 18, then east to Moonridge Road. Drive 1.25 miles to Club View Drive. Turn left on Goldmine Drive and left into the parking lot. It is about 40 miles from San Bernardino.

Course description: The elevation here is 7,200 feet and the course closes when it snows. It offers long par-3s and gently rolling hills. In 1988, a lake was added in addition to tees for women. New clubhouse facilities are planned for summer of 1992. This course, now under new ownership, was formerly known as Goldmine Golf Course.

43100 Goldmine Drive
Big Bear Lake, CA 92315

Pro shop   (714) 585-8002

■ driving range
■ practice greens
■ power carts
■ pull carts
■ golf club rental
■ locker rooms
□ showers
□ executive course
□ accommodations
■ food and beverages
■ clubhouse

Mack Provart
Professional

Brad Wilson
Superintendent

SOUTHERN 16

EL RANCHO VERDE
COUNTRY CLUB

Course information: This public course has 18 holes and par is 72. The course is 6,844 yards and rated 71.8 from the championship tees, and 6,615 yards and rated 70.3 from the regular tees. The slope ratings are 112 championship and 106 regular. Women's tees are 5,589 yards and rated 70.2. The slope rating is 116.

Play policy and fees: Green fees are $11 weekdays and $21 weekends. Carts are $16. Reservations are recommended. This course is available for tournaments.

Location: From Los Angeles, drive east on Interstate 10 (San Bernardino Freeway) to Riverside Avenue in the town of Rialto. Then travel north six miles to Country Club Drive.

Course description: This course offers gentle rolling hills with many pine and eucalyptus trees on the front nine and orange groves on the back nine. It boasts tough par-3s and a view of the San Bernardino Mountains.

PO Box 1234
Rialto, CA 92376

Foot of Country Club Drive
Rialto, CA 92376

Pro shop   (714) 875-5346

- ■ driving range
- ■ practice greens
- ■ power carts
- ☐ pull carts
- ☐ golf club rental
- ☐ locker rooms
- ☐ showers
- ☐ executive course
- ☐ accommodations
- ■ food and beverages
- ■ clubhouse

Troy Burton
Professional

Pete Laws
Superintendent

SUNSET DUNES GOLF CLUB

Course information: This short public course has 18 holes and par is 57. It is 3,095 yards long.

Play policy and fees: Green fees are $6 weekdays and $6.50 weekends for nine holes, and $11 weekdays and $12 weekends for 18 holes. Carts are $6 for nine holes and $10 for 18 holes weekdays, and $7 for nine holes and $12 for 18 holes weekends.

Location: Take Interstate 10 to Colton and exit at Riverside Avenue. Follow Riverside to Valley Boulevard, turn left and go about one mile to the course. You can take the Pepper exit off Interstate 10 and proceed to Valley Boulevard also.

Course description: This is an executive course, designed for those who want to test almost every club in the bag. There are three par-4s and 15 par-3s of varying length. When Sam Snead is in the area, this is where he plays.

1901 Valley Boulevard
Colton, CA 92324

Pro shop   (714) 877-1712

- ■ driving range
- ■ practice greens
- ■ power carts
- ■ pull carts
- ■ golf club rental
- ☐ locker rooms
- ☐ showers
- ■ executive course
- ☐ accommodations
- ■ food and beverages
- ■ clubhouse

Bill Brode
Owner/Professional

SAN BERNARDINO GOLF COURSE

1969
Mike Murphy

1494 South Waterman Avenue
San Bernardino, CA 92408

Pro shop   (714) 825-1670
Clubhouse (714) 885-2414

- ■ driving range
- ■ practice greens
- ■ power carts
- ■ pull carts
- ■ golf club rental
- ☐ locker rooms
- ■ showers
- ☐ executive course
- ☐ accommodations
- ■ food and beverages
- ■ clubhouse

Cheryl Thomas
Professional

Abel Moreno
Superintendent

Course information: This public course has 18 holes and par is 70. The course is 5,771 yards and rated 67.2 from the championship tees, and 5,571 yards and rated 66.3 from the regular tees. The slope ratings are 107 championship and 104 regular. Women's tees are 5,080 yards and rated 68.7. The slope rating is 109.

Play policy and fees: Green fees are $11 weekdays and $19 weekends. Senior rates are $9 weekdays. Carts are $16. Reservations are recommended.

Location: In San Bernardino, take Interstate 10 (San Bernardino Freeway) to the Waterman Avenue exit north and travel three-fourths of a mile to the course.

Course description: This course has only two bunkers but five holes with water. Don't be fooled by the apparent short length of this course. Typically, scores here are higher on the average than on neighboring courses. Stay in the fairways or you're in tall rough. This is a thinking player's course. The men's course record is 60 and is held by Walt "Sonny" Hammond, set in 1985. The women's course record is 64 held by Kathy Dougherty. The San Bernardino County Men's Amateur Championships are held here each Labor Day Weekend.

SOUTHERN 16

MAP ON PAGE 472

477

PALM MEADOWS
GOLF COURSE

1958

Course information: This military course has 18 holes and par is 72. The course is 6,659 yards and rated 71.6 from the championship tees, and 6,372 yards and rated 69.9 from the regular tees. The slope ratings are 115 championship and 111 regular. Women's tees are 5,794 yards and rated 72.5. The slope rating is 118.

Play policy and fees: Military personnel and guests only. Green fees are $7 weekdays and $11 weekends for military. Guest green fees are $14 weekdays and $20 weekends. Carts are $12. Reservations are recommended. Golfers must wear appropriate attire.

Location: Drive southeast of San Bernardino on Interstate 10 for about two miles to the Tippecanoe exit. Travel north for two miles to the main gate, and then go north one block to "A" Street and turn right. Drive to Fifth Street and turn right again. At the next stop sign, go right, then bear left to the course. Too complicated? Ask for instructions at the main gate.

Course description: This course was carved out by civil engineers and the hard work of its early members. It's a scenic course with an easy, flat front nine and a tough back nine that gives players lots of trouble. The tee box and fairway at hole six run along the flight line of this Air Force base, causing unique hazards: Beware of low-flying F-4s. And try not to tee off while a plane is landing. The sheer noise might throw your swing off. The course records are 69 for men and 73 for the women.

Building 818, Norton AFB
San Bernardino, CA 92409

Pro shop   (714) 382-2500
Clubhouse   (714) 382-3421

- driving range
- practice greens
- power carts
- pull carts
- golf club rental
- locker rooms
- showers
- ☐ executive course
- ☐ accommodations
- food and beverages
- clubhouse

"Sonny" Ryan
Professional

Sam Zeigler
Superintendent

FAIRMOUNT PARK GOLF CLUB

Course information: This public course has nine holes. Par is 72 for 18 holes. The course is 6,326 yards and rated 68.6 from the regular tees (18 holes). The slope rating is 103. Women's yardage and ratings were unavailable.

Play policy and fees: Green fees are $6 for nine holes and $8 for 18 holes weekdays, and $8 for nine holes and $10 for 18 holes weekends. Carts are $12 for 18 holes.

Location: From Los Angeles, travel east on Highway 60 (Pomona Freeway) to the city of Riverside. Take the Market Street exit to the course.

Course description: This is an older course but it has character. Numerous mature palm and cypress trees line the level fairways. It's a fader's course with mean doglegs and more trees. Fortunately, there is a nice finishing hole because the first hole can be a rough start, thanks to a large tree in the middle of the fariway that requires your tee shot to either go over it or around it. Either way, have a nice day.

2681 Dexter Drive
Riverside, CA 92501

Pro shop   (714) 683-9030

- ■ driving range
- ■ practice greens
- ■ power carts
- ■ pull carts
- ■ golf club rental
- ☐ locker rooms
- ☐ showers
- ☐ executive course
- ☐ accommodations
- ■ food and beverages
- ■ clubhouse

Jim DeRosa
Professional

Mike Bush
Superintendent

INDIAN HILLS COUNTRY CLUB

Course information: This public course has 18 holes and par is 70. The course is 6,173 yards and rated 70.0 from the championship tees, and 5,880 yards and rated 68.1 from the regular tees. The slope ratings are 123 championship and 117 regular. Women's tees are 5,562 yards and rated 70.5. The slope rating is 118 regular.

Play policy and fees: Green fees are $16 weekdays and $23 weekends. Carts are $20 weekdays and $22 weekends. Reservations are recommended. This course is available for tournaments.

Location: From Los Angeles, take Highway 60 (Pomona Freeway) east to the Van Buren/Etiwanda Avenue exit in Riverside. Travel south on Van Buren Boulevard for 4.5 miles to Limonite Avenue and turn left. Drive to Clay Street and turn left, then right on Lakeside Drive. Follow the signs to the club on top of the hill.

Course description: This is a rolling course with numerous mature trees and no parallel fairways. The greens are undulating and can be tough. Walking on this hilly course is for the adventurous.

5700 Clubhouse Drive
Riverside, CA 92509

Pro shop   (714) 685-7443
Clubhouse (714) 685-6424

- ☐ driving range
- ■ practice greens
- ■ power carts
- ☐ pull carts
- ■ golf club rental
- ■ locker rooms
- ■ showers
- ☐ executive course
- ☐ accommodations
- ■ food and beverages
- ■ clubhouse

Don Willis
Professional

Scot Vlahos
Superintendent

SOUTHERN I6

JURUPA HILLS COUNTRY CLUB

Course 13
MAP 16 grid e0

1960
William Francis Bell

6161 Moraga Avenue
Riverside, CA 92509

Pro shop   (714) 685-7214

■ driving range
■ practice greens
■ power carts
■ pull carts
■ golf club rental
□ locker rooms
■ showers
□ executive course
□ accommodations
■ food and beverages
■ clubhouse

Ron Robinson
Professional/Manager

Jason Taylor
Professional

Jim Fareio
Superintendent

Course information: This public course has 18 holes and par is 70. The course is 6,017 yards and rated 68.1 from the regular tees. The slope rating is 109 regular. Women's tees are 5,773 and rated 71.9. The slope rating is 117.

Play policy and fees: Green fees are $14 weekdays and $21 weekends. Carts are $20. Reservations are recommended. This course is available for tournaments.

Location: From Los Angeles, take Highway 60 (Pomona Freeway) east to the Van Buren/Etiwanda Avenue exit in Riverside. Travel east on Van Buren Boulevard for 4.5 miles and turn left on Limonite Avenue. Drive 1.5 miles to Camino Real. Turn right and drive to Linares. Then left one-half mile to the club.

Course description: Trees of all sizes outline this fairly level course. Locally, the course is known for its well-kept, fast greens. It's a favorite spot for local tournaments. The SCPGA Senior's Championship is held here. Olin Dutra, the club's first pro, was a former U.S. Open champ.

PARADISE KNOLLS

Course 14
MAP 16 grid e0

9330 Limonite Avenue
Riverside, CA 92509

Pro shop   (714) 685-7034

□ driving range
■ practice greens
■ power carts
■ pull carts
■ golf club rental
□ locker rooms
□ showers
□ executive course
□ accommodations
■ food and beverages
■ clubhouse

Margaret Wood
Owner/Manager

Jeff Jackson
Superintendent

Course information: This public course has 18 holes and par is 72. The course is 6,191 yards and rated 68.3 from the regular tees. The slope rating is 104. Women's tees are 5,865 yards and rated 72.5. The slope rating is 117.

Play policy and fees: Green fees are $11.50 weekdays and $19 weekends. Call for senior weekdays rates. Carts are $19 weekdays and $21 weekends. Reservations are recommended. This course is available for outside tournaments.

Location: Travel east on Highway 60 (Pomona Freeway) to the Van Buren/Etiwanda Avenue exit and turn right onto Etiwanda. Drive about three miles to Limonite Avenue, turn left and proceed three miles to the course.

Course description: This is a pretty course with an interesting mix of mature eucalyptus, palm and pepper trees that act as natural dividers between fairways. Another 1,000 baby eucalyptus trees were planted in early 1991 along holes three, four and 14. The trees are only three inches tall, so now's a good time to play this course before they mature. The course is fairly level with parallel fairways and small greens.

EL RIVINO COUNTRY CLUB

1956

Course information: This public course has 18 holes and par is 72. The course is 6,422 yards and rated 69.5 from the championship tees, and 6,195 yards and rated 68.2 from the regular tees. The slope ratings are 109 championship and 102 regular. Women's tees are 5,848 yards and rated 72.0. The slope rating is 113.

Play policy and fees: Green fees are $20 weekdays and $26 weekends. Carts are $22. Reservations are recommended. This course is available for outside tournaments. Golfers must wear sleeved shirts. Short shorts and bathing suits are not allowed.

Location: From Los Angeles, travel east on Interstate 10 (San Bernardino Freeway) to the Cedar Avenue exit in Bloomington. Head south on Cedar Avenue for three miles to El Rivino Road and then turn east on El Rivino Road to the club.

Course description: Built in 1956, this wide open course has five lakes, level terrain and mature trees. The first hole is a long, 626-yard par-6 designed to scare off the fainthearted. If number one doesn't send you packing, wait until the fourth hole. The green is surrounded on three sides by water.

Box 3369
Riverside, CA 92519

5530 El Rivino Road
Riverside, CA 92519

Pro shop   (714) 684-8905

- ☐ driving range
- ■ practice greens
- ☐ power carts
- ☐ pull carts
- ☐ golf club rental
- ☐ locker rooms
- ☐ showers
- ☐ executive course
- ☐ accommodations
- ☐ food and beverages
- ■ clubhouse

Dennis Burdo
Professional

William Anderson
Superintendent

RIVERSIDE GOLF CLUB

Course information: This public course has 18 holes and par is 72. The course is 6,760 yards and rated 72.0 from the championship tees, and 6,494 yards and rated 70.0 from the regular tees. The slope ratings are 122 championship and 116 regular. Women's tees are 6,200 yards and rated 73.0. The slope rating is 115 regular.

Play policy and fees: Green fees are $9 weekdays and $14 weekends. Call for special senior rates. Carts are $16. Reservations are recommended.

Location: Take the Columbia Avenue exit off the Riverside Freeway (Highway 91) and travel north on Orange Street to the club.

Course description: This course is long, but fairly level. It is lined with pine and mulberry trees.

1011 Orange Street
Riverside, CA 92517

Pro shop   (714) 682-3748

- ■ driving range
- ■ practice greens
- ■ power carts
- ■ pull carts
- ■ golf club rental
- ☐ locker rooms
- ☐ showers
- ☐ executive course
- ☐ accommodations
- ■ food and beverages
- ■ clubhouse

Dennis Kahn
Manager

Maurilio Briseno
Superintendent

SOUTHERN 16

VICTORIA GOLF CLUB

1903

Course information: This private course has 18 holes and par is 72. The course is 6,483 yards and rated 71.3 from the championship tees, and 6,256 yards and rated 69.8 from the regular tees. The slope ratings are 125 championship and 121 regular. Women's tees are 5,849 and rated 73.3. The slope rating is 122.

Play policy and fees: Reciprocal play is accepted with members of other private clubs on Tuesdays, Thursdays and Fridays, otherwise members and guests only. Green fees are $35 with a member. Carts are $16. Reservations are required.

Location: In Riverside, take the Central Avenue exit off Highway 91 (Riverside Freeway) and travel east for one mile to the first traffic light (Victoria) and turn left. From there, go one-half mile to Arroyo Drive and turn right into the club entrance.

Course description: Roughly 90 years old, this course has that old-world look to it. There are many interesting holes. There is a lake on the first hole and a large creek bed meanders through the course. Accurate placement is crucial. Accurate tee shots will ruin your day.

2521 Arroyo Drive
Riverside, CA 92506

Pro shop   (714) 684-5035
Clubhouse (714) 683-5323

- ■ driving range
- ■ practice greens
- ■ power carts
- ■ pull carts
- □ golf club rental
- ■ locker rooms
- ■ showers
- □ executive course
- □ accommodations
- ■ food and beverages
- ■ clubhouse

Jeff Cross
Professional

Lionel Guzman
Superintendent

CANYON CREST COUNTRY CLUB

Course information: This private course has 18 holes and par is 72. The course is 6,588 yards and rated 71.6 from the championship tees, and 6,331 yards and rated 70.1 from the regular tees. The slope ratings are 126 championship and 121 regular. Women's tees are 5,863 yards and rated 73.4. The slope rating is 122.

Play policy and fees: Members and guests only. Green fees are $35 weekdays and $45 weekends. Carts are $9. Reservations are recommended.

Location: In Riverside, take the Pennsylvania Avenue exit off Highway 60 (Pomona Freeway) and travel west for about one-quarter mile to Canyon Crest Drive. Turn left to the club.

Course description: This course is very hilly with lots of mature trees and numerous bunkers. Accurate shot placement is critical or your round could become a nightmare. Carts are advisable because the hills make for strenuous walking.

975 Country Club Drive
Riverside, CA 92506

Pro shop   (714) 274-7906
Clubhouse (714) 274-7900

- ■ driving range
- ■ practice greens
- ■ power carts
- ■ pull carts
- ■ golf club rental
- ■ locker rooms
- ■ showers
- □ executive course
- □ accommodations
- ■ food and beverages
- ■ clubhouse

Paul Hjulberg
Professional

Chris Seliga
Superintendent

REDLANDS COUNTRY CLUB

1897
A.E. Sterling
J.H. Fisher

Course information: This private course has 18 holes and par is 70. The course is 6,276 yards and rated 70.0 from the championship tees, and 6,061 yards and rated 69.0 from the regular tees. The slope ratings are 123 championship and 118 regular. Women's tees are 6,061 yards and rated 74.8 from the championship tees, and 5,730 yards and rated 73.0 from the forward tees. The slope ratings are 134 championship and 121 forward.

*Play policy and fees:*Reciprocal play accepted. Otherwise, members and guests only. Guests must be accompanied by a member. Green fees are $20 weekdays and $25 weekends. Carts are $14. Reservations are recommended.

Location: Take the Ford exit off Interstate 10 east of San Bernardino and travel south for 1.5 miles. Bear right at the fork on Garden Hill and turn left on Garden Street to the club.

Course description: This course was originally built as a nine-hole layout by old money during the old days. In 1927 it was expanded to an 18-hole course under the direction of club member Raven Hornby and the consultation of Alister MacKenzie, according to club records. It has similar characteristics to the Lake Course at the Olympic Club and Cherry Hills. There are lots of oaks and many tall cypress and pine trees.

1749 Garden Street
Redlands, CA 92373

Pro shop   (714) 793-1295
Clubhouse (714) 793-2661

- driving range
- practice greens
- power carts
- pull carts
- ☐ golf club rental
- locker rooms
- showers
- ☐ executive course
- ☐ accommodations
- food and beverages
- clubhouse

Norman Bernard
Professional

Ray Navarro
Superintendent

SOUTHERN 16

GENERAL OLD GOLF COURSE

1957

Course information: This military course has 18 holes and par is 72. The course is 6,757 yards and rated 72.6 from the championship tees, and 6,482 yards and rated 70.6 from the regular tees. The slope ratings are 125 championship and 119 regular. Women's tees are 5,882 yards and rated 72.9. The slope is 118.

Play policy and fees: Military personnel and guests only: active duty, retired military, Department of Defense employees and dependents.

Location: From Riverside drive southeast on Interstate 215 four miles to Van Buren Boulevard. That's the first exit past the main gate to March AFB. Turn right and drive one mile to Village West Drive and turn left to the golf course.

Course description: General Peyton C. March, who was Chief of Staff during WW I, was once confronted with the logistical question of how the military was going to transport its troops across the Atlantic to the European front. "You can march them over there," he suggested in exasperation. Well, this Air Force Base boasts a course with just about as many logistical problems as the general faced more than 70 years ago. He didn't live long enough to see this course open for play, but chances are he would have appreciated its championship layout. There are numerous doglegs and bunkers, and although the water hazards don't match crossing the Atlantic on foot, there are seven holes that must be reached over or around water. The front nine is relatively flat and the back nine is up and down.

March AFB
Village West Drive
Riverside, CA 92518

Pro shop   (714) 653-7913

■ driving range
■ practice greens
■ power carts
■ pull carts
■ golf club rental
■ locker rooms
■ showers
□ executive course
□ accommodations
■ food and beverages
■ clubhouse

Dick Couts
Professional

Jerry Zigan
Superintendent

MORENO VALLEY RANCH
GOLF CLUB

Course information: This public facility has 27 holes and par is 36 on each nine.

The Lake/Valley Course is 6,930 yards and rated 74.4 from the tournament tees, 6,497 yards and rated 71.5 from the championship tees, and 5,933 yards and rated 68.9 from the regular tees. The slope ratings are 138 tournament, 126 championship and 119 regular. Women's tees are 5,246 yards and rated 69.8. The slope rating is 114.

The Valley/Mountain Course is 6,875 yards and rated 74.2 from the tournament tees, 6,372 yards and rated 70.9 from the championship tees, and 5,847 yards and rated 68.5 from the regular tees. The slope ratings are 137 tournament, 125 championship and 118 regular. Women's tees are 5,196 yards and rated 69.7. The slope rating is 113.

The Mountain/Lake Course is 6,697 yards and rated 73.1 from the tournament tees, 6,389 yards and rated 70.9 from the championship tees, and 5,854 yards and rated 68.5 from the regular tees. The slope ratings are 135 tournament, 125 championship and 118 regular. Women's tees are 5,108 yards and rated 69.1. The slope rating is 112.

Play policy and fees: Green fees are $35 Monday through Thursday, and $50 Fridays and weekends. Carts are included. Reservations are recommended.

Location: From Highway 60, exit south on Moreno Beach Drive. Travel two miles to John F. Kennedy Avenue, then turn left and follow it to the course.

Course description: This is a well-maintained course with fast sloping greens. The fairways are tight in some places, demanding accurate tee shots.

28095 John F. Kennedy Avenue
Moreno Valley, CA 92555

Pro shop   (714) 924-4444

- ■ driving range
- ■ practice greens
- ■ power carts
- □ pull carts
- ■ golf club rental
- □ locker rooms
- ■ showers
- □ executive course
- □ accommodations
- ■ food and beverages
- ■ clubhouse

Ken Winn
Professional

Murray Nonhoff
Superintendent

SOUTHERN 16

PALM CREST RESORT
AND COUNTRY CLUB

1 9 6 9
Desmond Muirhead

Course information: This course is under new owner-
ship. Current status of the course is unknown. It has
18 holes and par is 72. Course yardage and ratings
were unavailable.

Play policy and fees: Green fees were unavailable. Club
management asks guests to call for current information.

Location: From Highway 91 take Highway 60 east about
14 miles to the Gilman Springs exit. Drive four miles
south to the club.

Course description: This course was formerly known as
Quail Ranch Resort and Country Club, but changed its
name to Palm Crest—and for good reason, too. The
course was renovated in mid-1991 and 1,000 full-
grown palm trees were planted in clusters around the
greens and along the fairways. The Southern California Golf Association rated this course as one of its top
10 public golf facilities in 1988. It's a Scottish, links
style course with rolling terrain and undulating
greens. The PGA Tour School qualifier and the U.S. Open qualifier have been
held here. Craig Stadler impressed the locals once when he finished a round in
the dark and asked the pro staff if they would park their cars around the 18th
green with their headlights on so he could finish his game. Gary McCord holds
the course record with a 64.

15960 Gilman Springs Road
Moreno Valley, CA 923555

Pro shop   (714) 654-2631
Clubhouse (714) 654-2727

- ■ driving range
- ■ practice greens
- ■ power carts
- ■ pull carts
- ■ golf club rental
- ■ locker rooms
- ■ showers
- □ executive course
- □ accommodations
- ■ food and beverages
- ■ clubhouse

Claude Waymire
Professional

Brian Smithling
Superintendent

CALIMESA GOLF
AND COUNTRY CLUB

Course information: This public course has 18 holes and par is 70. The course is 5,914 yards and rated 67.9 from the championship tees, and 5,571 yards and rated 66.0 from the regular tees. The slope ratings are 111 championship and 103 regular. Women's tees are 5,214 yards and rated 69.2. The slope rating is 112.

Play policy and fees: Green fees are $11 weekdays and $18.50 weekends. Carts are $18. Reservations are recommended one week in advance. This course is available for tournaments.

Location: Travel eight miles east of Redlands on Interstate 10 to Calimesa. Turn east on County Line Road to Third Street and travel south to the club.

Course description: This scenic little course is set in a canyon. It's up and down with mature trees and shows lots of character. You can have fun on this course. The entryway, lounge and dining facilities have all been recently remodeled.

1300 South Third Street
Calimesa, CA 92320

Pro shop   (714) 795-2488

- ■ driving range
- ■ practice greens
- ■ power carts
- ■ pull carts
- ■ golf club rental
- □ locker rooms
- □ showers
- □ executive course
- □ accommodations
- ■ food and beverages
- ■ clubhouse

Mark Wotherspoon
Professional

Richard Hamilton
Superintendent

SUN LAKES COUNTRY CLUB

Course information: This semi-private course has 18 holes and par is 72. The course is 6,997 yards and rated 74.3 from the championship tees, and 6,617 yards and rated 72.0 from the regular tees. The slope ratings are 132 championship and 128 regular. Women's tees are 5,497 yards and rated 72.7. The slope rating is 118.

Play policy and fees: Outside play is accepted after 12 noon. Green fees are $30 weekdays and $40 weekends and holidays, carts included. Reservations are recommended.

Location: Take the Highlands Springs Avenue exit off Interstate 10 in Banning (east of San Bernardino) and travel south to Sun Lakes Boulevard. Head east and turn on Country Club Drive south and continue to the club.

Course description: This is a long course with a traditional layout. Bring sand-moving equipment: There are 104 bunkers. There are also seven lakes and microscopic greens to make this challenging course even more difficult. The only green enlarged recently, with an added tier, is number four, a par-4 349-yard toughy. Depending on the pin placement and the wind, the hole is one of the more difficult on the course. Also, remember to keep the ball on the fairway or you'll have a miserable day. It helps to shoot long and accurately, but when doesn't it?.

850 South Country Club Drive
Banning, CA 92220

Pro shop   (714) 845-2135

- ■ driving range
- ■ practice greens
- ■ power carts
- □ pull carts
- ■ golf club rental
- ■ locker rooms
- □ showers
- □ executive course
- □ accommodations
- ■ food and beverages
- ■ clubhouse

Buddy Allin
Professional

Jess Padilla
Superintendent

SOUTHERN 16

SOBOBA SPRINGS COUNTRY CLUB

1967
Desmond Muirhead

Course information: This semi-private course has 18 holes and par is 73. The course is 6,826 yards and rated 73.5 from the championship tees, and 6,352 yards and rated 70.5 from the regular tees. The slope ratings are 134 championship and 123 regular. Women's tees are 5,829 yards and rated 73.1. The slope rating is 123.

Play policy and fees: Reciprocal play is accepted with members of other private clubs. Outside play is accepted. Green fees are $34 for non-members weekdays and $40 for non-members weekends, carts included. Reservations are recommended one week in advance. No reservations prior to 10 a.m. on Tuesdays, Wednesdays and Saturdays.

Location: Travel east of San Bernardino on Interstate 10 to the town of Beaumont. Then take Highway 60 to the San Jacinto-Hemet exit south to Soboba Road and head east to the club.

Course description: This is a fairly flat course but it plays long. There are lots of trees and six holes with water hazards. This course is a rare par-73.

1020 Soboba Road
San Jacinto, CA 92383

Pro shop (714) 654-9354
Clubhouse (714) 654-9357

- ■ driving range
- ■ practice greens
- ■ power carts
- ■ pull carts
- ■ golf club rental
- ■ locker rooms
- ■ showers
- □ executive course
- □ accommodations
- ■ food and beverages
- ■ clubhouse

David Bartholomew
Professional

Jaime Barrera
Superintendent

CANYON LAKE COUNTRY CLUB

1968
Ted Robinson

Course information: This private course has 18 holes and par is 71. The course is 5,867 yards and rated 68.2 from the championship tees, and 5,613 yards and rated 66.7 from the regular tees. The slope ratings are 109 championship and 105 regular. Women's tees are 5,391 yards and rated 70.7. The slope rating is 121.

Play policy and fees: Reciprocal play is accepted with members of other private clubs. Have your club pro call for arrangements. Green fees are $14 for members and $24 for guests. Carts are $16. Reservations are recommended. Golfers must wear collared shirts.

Location: From Riverside, travel south on Interstate 215 to Newport Road, and turn right, heading west to the last stop and turn left. The club entrance is 300 yards past the traffic light.

Course description: This hilly course is short and tight with many hidden greens. Watch for number 15. It is a par-3 185 yard hole with a drop of 200 feet off the tee to a green that's thankfully in sight. The green has trees and bunkers around it, so be straight.

Box 4251
Canyon Lake, CA 92587

32001 Railroad Canyon Road
Canyon Lake, CA 92380

Pro shop (714) 244-2853

- ■ driving range
- ■ practice greens
- ■ power carts
- □ pull carts
- ■ golf club rental
- ■ locker rooms
- ■ showers
- □ executive course
- □ accommodations
- ■ food and beverages
- ■ clubhouse

Gabe Hrab
Professional

MENIFEE LAKES COUNTRY CLUB

Course 27
MAP I6 grid h2

1989
Ted Robinson

29875 Menifee Lakes Drive
Menifee, CA 92355

Pro shop   (714) 672-3090
Clubhouse (714) 672-4824

- ■ driving range
- ■ practice greens
- ■ power carts
- ☐ pull carts
- ■ golf club rental
- ☐ locker rooms
- ☐ showers
- ☐ executive course
- ☐ accommodations
- ■ food and beverages
- ■ clubhouse

Rick Bartlett
Professional

Mark Livingston
Superintendent

Course information: This semi-private course has 18 holes and par is 72. The course is 6,472 yards and rated 71.2 from the championship tees, and 6,075 yards and rated 69.0 from the regular tees. The slope ratings are 128 championship and 119 regular. Women's tees are 5,390 yards and rated 71.3. The slope rating is 119.

Play policy and fees: Green fees are $30 weekdays and $45 weekends. Carts are included. Reservations are recommended.

Location: From Perris, take the Newport Road exit off Interstate 215, follow it about one-half mile to Menifee Lakes Drive turn left and follow the road to the course.

Course description: This Ted Robinson-designed course features tight fairways, plenty of signature water and sand. There are two practice holes reserved for club members in need of pre-round tune-ups and a marvelous driving range.

CHERRY HILLS GOLF CLUB

Course 28
MAP I6 grid h2

26583 Cherry Hills Boulevard
Sun City, CA 92586

Pro shop   (714) 679-1182

- ■ driving range
- ■ practice greens
- ■ power carts
- ☐ pull carts
- ■ golf club rental
- ☐ locker rooms
- ☐ showers
- ☐ executive course
- ☐ accommodations
- ■ food and beverages
- ■ clubhouse

Bill Lytle
Professional

Antolin Coria
Superintendent

SOUTHERN I6

Course information: This semi-private course has 18 holes and par is 72. The course is 6,900 yards and rated 71.8 from the championship tees, and 6,465 yards and rated 69.4 from the regular tees. The slope ratings are 111 championship and 105 regular. Women's tees are 5,925 yards and rated 73.3 from the forward tees. The slope rating is 118.

Play policy and fees: Outside play is accepted. Green fees are $20. Carts are $16. Reservations are recommended.

Location: In Sun City, take the McCall Boulevard/Sun City exit off Interstate 215 and travel west on McCall for one-quarter mile to Sun City Boulevard. Turn left and drive one-quarter mile to Cherry Hills Boulevard. Turn right and go one block to the club.

Course description: This is a flat, open course with numerous doglegs and a desert-like rough. Bring sun screen.

COLONIAL COUNTRY CLUB

Course information: This private course has 18 holes and par is 60. The course is a short 3,200 yards from the regular tees.

Play policy and fees: Members and guests only. Green fees are $3 for nine holes.

Location: In Hemet, take Florida Avenue (Highway 74) to Warren Avenue, turn left and continue about three-fourths of a mile to Kirby Street, then turn right and follow Kirby to the course.

Course description: This is a small executive course with a pair of par-4s. It is reserved for residents and guests of the adjoining mobile home park.

25115 Kirby Street
Hemet, CA 92545

Clubhouse (714) 925-2664

☐ driving range
☐ practice greens
☐ power carts
☐ pull carts
☐ golf club rental
☐ locker rooms
☐ showers
■ executive course
☐ accommodations
■ food and beverages
■ clubhouse

SEVEN HILLS GOLF CLUB

Course information: This public course has 18 holes and par is 72. The course is 6,618 yards and rated 70.7 from the championship tees, and 6,305 yards and rated 69.0 from the regular tees. The slope ratings are 118 championship and 114 regular. Women's tees are 5,771 yards and rated 70.5. The slope rating is 106.

Play policy and fees: Green fees are $16 weekdays and $20 weekends. Carts are $9 per player for 18 holes. Reservations are recommended one week in advance. This course is available for outside tournaments on contractual basis.

Location: Take the Highway 79 exit off Interstate 10 east of San Bernardino and travel south to Highway 74 in Hemet. Turn left and drive to Lyon Avenue and then right to the club.

Course description: This is a flat course with trees and water. It is medium short with four water hazards and not an excess of bunkers. The greens are small, which makes the shots semi-demanding.

1537 South Lyon Avenue
Hemet, CA 93545

Pro shop (714) 925-4815

■ driving range
■ practice greens
■ power carts
■ pull carts
■ golf club rental
☐ locker rooms
☐ showers
☐ executive course
☐ accommodations
■ food and beverages
■ clubhouse

Jerry Preuss
Professional

Roger Mueller
Superintendent

ECHO HILLS GOLF CLUB

Course information: This public course has nine holes. Par is 70 for 18 holes. The course is 4,458 yards and rated 60.2 from the regular tees. The slope rating is 87.

Play policy and fees: Green fees are $7 for nine holes. Carts are $8 for two people for nine holes.

Location: From Interstate 215, take the Highway 74 exit to the town of Hemet and drive through town. Turn right on Buena Vista Street and drive 1.5 miles to Thorton Avenue then go left to the club.

Course description: This well-maintained, short course has narrow fairways and many mature trees.

545 East Thornton Avenue
Hemet, CA 92543

Pro shop   (714) 652-2203

☐ driving range
■ practice greens
■ power carts
■ pull carts
■ golf club rental
☐ locker rooms
☐ showers
☐ executive course
☐ accommodations
■ food and beverages
☐ clubhouse

William Bennington
Owner

Moon Park
Manager

ARROYO FAIRWAYS GOLF COURSE

Course information: This private course has 11 holes. The Lower Course is 1,834 yards for nine holes. The Upper Course, which is the same layout as the lower course with exeption of two holes—creating the odd number of 11 for the course—is 2,054 yards for its nine holes.

Play policy and fees: Members and guests only. Green fees are $2 for nine holes and $3 for 18 holes any day.

Location: In Hemet, follow Florida Avenue (Highway 74) east to the course.

Course description: This is a pitch-and-putt layout reserved for residents and their guests staying at the adjoining mobile home park. It is well maintained with lots of trees and bunkers.

42751 East Florida
Hemet, CA 92544

Pro shop   (714) 927-1610

☐ driving range
■ practice greens
☐ power carts
☐ pull carts
☐ golf club rental
☐ locker rooms
☐ showers
☐ executive course
☐ accommodations
☐ food and beverages
☐ clubhouse

SOUTHERN 16

BEAR CREEK GOLF
AND COUNTRY CLUB

1983
Jack Nicklaus

Course information: This private course has 18 holes and par is 72. The course is 6,992 yards and rated 75.2 from the championship tees, and 6,422 yards and rated 71.9 from the regular tees. The slope ratings are 144 championship and 133 regular. Women's tees are 5,566 yards and rated 70.4. The slope rating is 121.

Play policy and fees: Limited reciprocal play is accepted with members of other private clubs, otherwise members and guests only. Green fees are $42 escorted and $77 unescorted, carts included. This course is available for outside tournaments.

Location: Take Interstate 15 to the Clinton Keith exit in Murrieta then travel west to Bear Creek and turn north to the club.

Course description: This championship course is aptly named because it is a bear. It was designed by Jack Nicklaus in 1983. It features a natural rolling terrain with pot bunkers, mounds and creeks. Water guards half the course and the greens are large and tricky. Nicklaus' favorite hole is the 435-yard, par-4 fourth hole. It has a split-level fairway divided by grass bunkers. The course was the site of the 1985 Skins Game and is used regularly for PGA Tour qualifying. It rates among the top 20 courses in the state.

22640 Bear Creek Drive North
Murrieta, CA 92362

Pro shop   (714) 677-8631
Clubhouse   (714) 677-8621

■ driving range
■ practice greens
■ power carts
□ pull carts
■ golf club rental
■ locker rooms
■ showers
□ executive course
□ accommodations
■ food and beverages
■ clubhouse

Eddie Brown
Professional

John Martinez
Superintendent

TEMECULA CREEK INN GOLF COURSE

Course information: This resort facility has 27 holes and par is 72 for each 18-hole combination.

The Creek/Oaks Course is 6,757 yards and rated 72.6 from the championship tees, and 6,344 yards and rated 69.8 from the regular tees. The slope ratings are 125 championship and 115 regular. Women's tees are 5,737 yards and rated 72.8. The slope rating is 123.

The Oaks/Stone House Course is 6,649 yards and rated 72.6 from the championship tees, and 6,252 yards and rated 70.1 from the regular tees. The slope ratings are 131 championship and 117 regular. Women's tees are 5,683 yards and rated 72.4. The slope rating is 125.

The Creek/Stone House Course is 6,580 yards and rated 71.8 from the championship tees, and 6,262 yards and rated 69.7 from the regular tees. The slope ratings are 123 championship and 113 regular. Women's tees are 5,686 yards and rated 71.9. The slope rating is 120.

Play policy and fees: Outside play is accepted. Hotel guests welcome. Green fees are $44 weekdays and $55 weekends, including cart. Reservations are recommended. This course is available for outside tournaments.

Location: From the intersection of Highways 15 and Highway 79, travel east one-half mile to Pala Road and turn right. Drive to Rainbow Canyon Road and the course.

Course description: A Ted Robinson-designed nine-hole course opened on April Fool's Day 1990, bringing to 27 the number of holes on this course. Each of the nines are distinctly different. They range in character from flat and rolling to hilly with lots of trees to more hills and more trees. A restful resort, Temecula is known for its sunny clime.

PO Box 129
Temecula, CA 92390

44-501 Rainbow Canyon Road
Temecula, CA 92390

Pro shop   (714) 676-2405
Clubhouse   (714) 676-5631
            (619) 728-9100

- ■ driving range
- ■ practice greens
- ■ power carts
- ■ pull carts
- ■ golf club rental
- □ locker rooms
- □ showers
- □ executive course
- ■ accommodations
- ■ food and beverages
- ■ clubhouse

Michael Bratschi
Professional

Tim Ketterer
Superintendent

SOUTHERN 16

RED HAWK GOLF CLUB

1991
Ron Fream

Course information: This public course has 18 holes. Par is 72. The course is 7,070 yards and rated 75.3 from the tournament tees, 6,655 yards and rated 72.4 from the championship tees, and 6,130 yards and rated 69.6 from the regular tees. The slope ratings are 142 tournament, 133 championship and 125 regular. Women's tees are 5,460 yards and rated 72.4. The slope rating is 135.

Play policy and fees: Green fees are $45 weekdays and $65 weekends. Carts are included. Reservations are required. This course is available for tournaments weekdays or after 12 p.m. weekends.

Location: From Highway 15 in Temecula, take the Highway 79 South exit. Travel east on Highway 79 for 2.5 miles, then turn right on Red Hawk Parkway and drive straight to the course.

Course description: This is a rolling course with narrow, tree-lined fairways. The greens are undulating and deceptive.

45100 Red Hawk Parkway
Temecula, CA 92592

Pro shop   (714) 695-1424

- ■ driving range
- ■ practice greens
- ■ power carts
- ☐ pull carts
- ■ golf club rental
- ☐ locker rooms
- ☐ showers
- ☐ executive course
- ☐ accommodations
- ■ food and beverages
- ☐ clubhouse

Robin Kohlhaas
Professional

Bob Hall
Superintendent

MAP I7
(65 COURSES)

PAGES.. 496-539

SO-CAL MAP .....see page 376
adjoining maps
NORTH ....no map
EAST (I8) ....see page 540
SOUTH (J7) ....see page 578
WEST (I6) ....see page 472

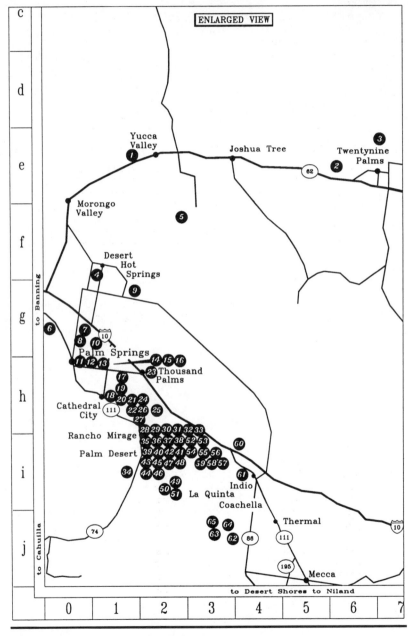

ENLARGED VIEW

BLUE SKIES COUNTRY CLUB

Course information: This semi-private course has 18 holes and par is 71. The course is 6,380 yards and rated 70.1 from the championship tees, and 6,162 yards and rated 68.4 from the regular tees. The slope ratings are 117 championship and 109 regular. Women's tees are 5,769 yards and rated 70.9. The slope rating is 115 regular.

Play policy and fees: Reciprocal play is accepted with members of other private clubs. Outside play is accepted. Green fees are $15 weekdays and $17 weekends and holidays. Seniors and active military rates are $10 weekdays and $12 weekends. Carts are $16 weekdays and $18 weekends for 18 holes. Reservations are recommended.

Location: Take the Twenty Nine Palms/Yucca Valley exit off Interstate 10 and drive about 18 miles north on Highway 62. Turn left at the Yucca Inn sign and continue to the club.

Course description: This upgraded course has tree-lined fairways and two lakes. The fairways are fairly open. Number three is a scenic lake hole. It is par-3 164 yards from an elevated tee hitting over the lake. The green is bunkered in the front and the way the trees are located makes for a tight shot.

55-100 Martinez Trail
Yucca Valley, CA 92284

Pro shop   (619) 365-0111

- ■ driving range
- ■ practice greens
- ■ power carts
- ■ pull carts
- ■ golf club rental
- □ locker rooms
- □ showers
- □ executive course
- □ accommodations
- ■ food and beverages
- ■ clubhouse

John Neubauer
Professional

Winston Bullock
Assistant Professional

Rusty Scott
Superintendent

COMBAT CENTER GOLF COURSE

Course information: This military course has nine holes. Par is 72 for 18 holes. The course is 6,627 yards and rated 71.1 from the regular tees (18 holes). The slope rating is 119 regular. Women's tees are 5,691 yards.

Play policy and fees: Military personnel and guests only.

Location: Take the Twenty Nine Palms/Yucca Valley exit off Interstate 10 and drive about 40 miles to the town of Twenty Nine Palms. Turn left at Adobe Road and drive five miles to the main gate at the Marine Combat Center. Continue through the main gate for three miles to the flashing light. Turn left and drive one-half mile to first paved road, then right to the course.

Course description: If you like toying with the elements, this course is for you. It is built on the side of a hill in the middle of the desert. It is wide open but challenging with out-of-bounds areas, desert-style rough, and seasonal winds. Four ponds come into play, but during the summer, the water will be a welcome sight. Plans call for this course to expand to 18 holes.

Box 337
Twenty Nine Palms
CA 92277

Pro shop   (619) 368-6132
Clubhouse   (619) 368-7253

- ■ driving range
- ■ practice greens
- ■ power carts
- ■ pull carts
- ■ golf club rental
- □ locker rooms
- ■ showers
- □ executive course
- □ accommodations
- ■ food and beverages
- ■ clubhouse

George Fisher
Manager

SOUTHERN 17

ROADRUNNER DUNES GOLF CLUB

Course 3
MAP 17 grid e7

Course information: This public course has nine holes. Par is 72 for 18 holes. The course is 6,305 yards and rated 69.3 from the regular tees. The slope rating is 115. Women's tees are 5,604 yards and rated 70.2. The slope rating is 112.

Play policy and fees: During the week, green fees are $6 for nine holes and $9.50 for 18 holes. Weekends are $8 for nine holes and $10 for 18 holes. The junior rate is $4.50 for nine holes and $7.50 for 18 holes. Senior rates are $5 for nine holes and $8 for 18. Carts are $6 for nine holes and $11 for 18 holes.

Location: Take the Twenty Nine Palms/Yucca Valley exit off Interstate 10 and drive about 40 miles to the town of Twenty Nine Palms. Turn left on Adobe Road and drive two miles. Turn right on Amboy and then left on Desert Knoll Avenue.

Course description: This challenging and short course has narrow fairways, small greens, grass bunkers and a frightening number of out-of-bounds areas. There is water on two holes.

PO Box 204
Twenty Nine Palms
CA 92277

4733 Desert Knoll Ave.
Twenty Nine Palms
CA 92277

Pro shop   (619) 367-7610

- ■ driving range
- ■ practice greens
- ■ power carts
- ■ pull carts
- ■ golf club rental
- ☐ locker rooms
- ☐ showers
- ☐ executive course
- ☐ accommodations
- ■ food and beverages
- ■ clubhouse

Steve Barron
Professional

Randy Councell
Superintendent

MISSION LAKES COUNTRY CLUB

Course 4
MAP 17 grid f1

1971
Ted Robinson

Course information: This semi-private course has 18 holes and par is 71. The course is 6,737 yards and rated 72.1 from the championship tees, and 6,396 yards and rated 70.2 from the regular tees. The slope ratings are 122 championship and 115 regular. Women's tees are 5,390 yards and rated 69.9. The slope rating is 109.

Play policy and fees: Outside play is accepted. Green fees are $55 weekdays and $60 weekends, carts included. During the summer, from June 1 to September 30, fees are $30 weekdays and $35 weekends. Reservations are recommended. Proper attire required on the course.

Location: Take the Indian Avenue exit off Interstate 10. Drive north to Mission Lakes Avenue east and turn north on Clubhouse Drive.

Course description: This is a high desert course which means you can expect searing sun and wicked wind. The greens are modern speed and there are three mountain holes. Long par-3s also make this a demanding course. Five par-3s are 200 yards or longer.

8484 Clubhouse Drive
Desert Hot Springs
CA 92240

Pro shop   (619) 329-8061
Clubhouse (619) 329-6481

- ■ driving range
- ■ practice greens
- ■ power carts
- ☐ pull carts
- ■ golf club rental
- ■ locker rooms
- ■ showers
- ☐ executive course
- ■ accommodations
- ■ food and beverages
- ■ clubhouse

David Sarricks
Professional

Bob Kennedy
Superintendent

DESERT DUNES GOLF CLUB

Course 5
MAP 17 grid f2

1989
Robert Trent Jones, Jr.

19300 Palm Drive
Desert Hot Springs
CA 92240

Pro shop   (619) 329-2941

- ■ driving range
- ■ practice greens
- ■ power carts
- □ pull carts
- ■ golf club rental
- ■ locker rooms
- ■ showers
- □ executive course
- □ accommodations
- ■ food and beverages
- ■ clubhouse

R.H. Sikes
Professional

Jim Timke
Superintendent

Course information: This semi-private course has 18 holes and par is 72. The course is 6,876 yards and rated 74.1 from the championship tees, and 6,614 yards and rated 72.1 from the regular tees. The slope ratings are 135 championship and 129 regular. Women's tees are 5,359 yards and rated is 70.7. The slope rating is 119.

Play policy and fees: Green fees are $80 weekdays and $90 weekends during peak season. Call for special seasonal rates. Reservations are recommended.

Location: From Palm Springs, take Gene Autry Trail and cross over the freeway. When you cross the freeway, the name changes to Palm Drive. Continue on Palm Drive two miles to the course.

Course description: This has a unique Scottish-links design. Natural sand dunes and mesquite brush line the fairways. There is also an abundance of wildlife including jack rabbits, roadrunners, and coyotes in the surrounding desert. The par-3 fifth hole requires a long tee shot over a desert setting with a very undulating green and a mesquite backdrop. Good luck.

O'DONNELL GOLF CLUB

Course 6
MAP 17 grid g0

301 North Belardo Road
Palm Springs, CA 92262

Pro shop   (619)325-2259

- □ driving range
- ■ practice greens
- ■ power carts
- □ pull carts
- ■ golf club rental
- ■ locker rooms
- □ showers
- □ executive course
- □ accommodations
- ■ food and beverages
- ■ clubhouse

John DeSantis
Professional

Remedios Munoz
Superintendent

Course information: This private course has nine holes. Par is 70 for 18 holes. The course is 5,370 yards and rated 64.8 from the regular tees. The slope rating is 99. Women's tees are 5,350 yards and rated 66.0. The slope rating is 110.

Play policy and fees: Members and guests only. Guest fees are $30, cart included.

Location: Take Highway 111 into the town of Palm Springs. Turn west on Amado Road and drive one block to the club.

Course description: This is a tranquil course in downtown Palm Springs set against the base of the mountains. It is a peaceful spot for some mellow golfing.

SOUTHERN 17

MAP ON PAGE 496

499

PALM SPRINGS COUNTRY CLUB

Course information: This resort layout has 18 holes and par is 72. The course is 6,396 yards and rated 70 from the championship tees, and 5,885 yards and rated 67 from the regular tees. The slope ratings are 110 championship and 102 regular. Women's tees are 5,885 yards and rated 67. The slope rating is 102.

Play policy and fees: Reciprocal play is accepted with members of private clubs. Outside play is also accepted. Green fees are $20 weekdays and $30 weekends. Carts are included. Reservations are recommended. Call for seasonal rates.

Location: Take the Palm Drive exit off Interstate 10 and drive south to Vista Chino. Turn right and drive one-half mile to the club entrance.

Course description: This is a mature desert course with lots of trees. The well-conditioned greens are also well protected. Tee boxes have recently been enlarged.

2500 Whitewater Club Drive
Palm Springs, CA 92262

Pro shop   (619) 323-8625
Clubhouse (619) 323-2626

- ■ driving range
- ■ practice greens
- ■ power carts
- □ pull carts
- ■ golf club rental
- ■ locker rooms
- ■ showers
- □ executive course
- ■ accommodations
- ■ food and beverages
- ■ clubhouse

Pete Bonestrell
Profesional

Ramon Rubio
Superintendent

CANYON COUNTRY CLUB

Course information: This private course has 18 holes and par is 72. The course is 6,819 yards and rated 73.5 from the tournament tees, 6,468 yards and rated 71.1. from the championship tees, and 6,041 yards and rated 68.8 from the regular tees. The slope ratings are 129 tournament, 122 championship and 114 regular. Women's tees are 5,862 yards and rated 72.9. The slope rating is 117.

Play policy and fees: Members and guests only. Green fees are $55. Carts are $10. Reservations are recommended one day in advance. Call for special seasonal rates.

Location: Take the Indian Avenue exit off Interstate 10 in Palm Springs and drive south to Murray Canyon. Turn left and drive six blocks to the club.

Course description: This mature course is beautifully maintained. It's set among million-dollar homes with out-of-bounds markers on all but one hole.

1100 Murray Canyon Drive
Palm Springs, CA 92264

Pro shop   (619) 323-3921
Clubhouse (619) 327-1321
Starter   (619) 327-5831

- ■ driving range
- ■ practice greens
- ■ power carts
- □ pull carts
- □ golf club rental
- ■ locker rooms
- ■ showers
- □ executive course
- □ accommodations
- ■ food and beverages
- ■ clubhouse

David Reardon
Professional

Brian Smithling
Superintendent

SANDS RV COUNTRY CLUB

1983

Course information: This public course has nine holes. Par is 64 for 18 holes. The course is 5,254 yards and rated 57.5 from the regular tees (18 holes).

Play policy and fees: Green fees are $12 for non-residents.

Location: Take the Palm Drive exit north off Interstate 10. Turn right on Dillon Road and drive three-fourths of a mile to Bubbling Wells Road. The entrance to the motor home park and the course is on the corner.

Course description: This is an executive course adjoining a motor home park. It is short and wide open with a few trees and no bunkers. It's a hacker's paradise. One little lake on number seven offers some relief.

16400 Bubbling Wells Road
Desert Hot Springs
CA 92240

Pro shop   (619) 251-1173

- ■ driving range
- ■ practice greens
- □ power carts
- ■ pull carts
- ■ golf club rental
- □ locker rooms
- □ showers
- ■ executive course
- □ accommodations
- □ food and beverages
- □ clubhouse

Bruce Rogers
Superintendent

SOUTHERN 17

DESERT PRINCESS
COUNTRY CLUB

1985
David Rainville

28-555 Landau Boulevard
Cathedral City, CA 92234

Pro shop   (619) 322-2280
Clubhouse (619) 322-1655

■ driving range
■ practice greens
■ power carts
□ pull carts
■ golf club rental
■ locker rooms
■ showers
□ executive course
■ accommodations
■ food and beverages
■ clubhouse

David McKeating
Professional

Mike Kocour
Superintendent

Course information: This resort facility has 27 holes and par is 72 for each 18-hole combination.

Vista/Cielo Course is 6,764 yards and rated 72.5 from the tournament tees, 6,319 yards and rated 70 from the championship tees, and 5,912 yards and rated 67.6 from the regular tees. The slope ratings are 126 tournament, 121 championship and 114 regular. Women's tees are 5,217 yards and rated 69.1. The slope rating is 118.

Cielo/Lagos Course is 6,587 yards and rated 71.2 from the tournament tees, 6,111 yards and rated 68.8 from the championship tees, and 5,663 yards and rated 66.2 from the regular tees. The slope ratings are 121 tournament, 117 championship and 110 regular. Women's tees are 5,394 yards and rated 70.1. The slope rating is 119.

Vista/Lagos Course is 6,687 yards and rated 71.8 from the tournament tees, 6,224 yards and rated 69.4 from the championship tees, and 5,805 yards and rated 67.2 from the regular tees. The slope ratings are 123 tournament, 118 championship and 113 regular. Women's tees are 5,313 yards and rated 65.8. The slope rating is 118.

Play policy and fees: Reciprocal play is accepted with members of other private clubs. Hotel guests welcome. Guest fees from October 1 through December 25, 1991 are $50 Monday through Thursday and $60 Fridays and weekends. Guest fees from December 26, 1991 through May 31, 1992 are $60 Monday through Thursday and $75 Fridays and weekends. Guest fees from June 1 through September 30, 1992 are $30 Monday through Thursday and $40 Fridays and weekends. Carts included. Reservations are recommended. A dress code does apply.

Location: Take the Date Palm exit off Interstate 10 in Cathedral City and turn right and drive 100 yards to Vista Chino. Turn right and drive 1.25 miles to Landau Boulevard. Go left to the club.

Course description: Another nine holes have been added to this maturing course, bringing a wide variety of fairways and water holes into play. The course is well maintained and mostly flat. Water comes into play on 17 holes. The new nine is placed in a wash and features six holes with a Scottish-links flair and three new water holes. Four sets of tees make the course playable for golfers at all levels. The well-bunkered greens and bent grass make the course a challenge. Former course records have been thrown out with the new mix-and-match configuration of the layout. The USO Bob Hope Charity Golf Event has been held here, and the SCPGA Entenmann's Pro-Lady Tournament is held here each year.

CANYON SOUTH
GOLF COURSE

Course information: This public course has 18 holes and par is 71. The course is 6,536 yards and rated 70.8 from the championship tees, and 6,205 yards and rated 68.6 from the regular tees. The slope ratings are 119 championship and 109 regular. Women's tees are 6,205 yards and rated 72.0. The slope rating is 109.

Play policy and fees: Green fees are $50 weekdays and $60 weekends during peak season. The rate is $30 after 2 p.m. Carts are included. Reservations are recommended one week in advance.

Location: Take the Indian Avenue exit off Interstate 10 in Palm Springs and drive south to Murray Canyon. Turn left and drive three blocks to the club.

Course description: Set in the Indian Canyons, this is one of the most scenic courses in the area. It's a good test of golf with some tough par-3s.

1097 Murray Canyon Drive
Palm Springs, CA 92264

Pro shop   (619) 327-2019

- ■ driving range
- ■ practice greens
- ■ power carts
- □ pull carts
- ■ golf club rental
- ■ locker rooms
- □ showers
- □ executive course
- □ accommodations
- ■ food and beverages
- ■ clubhouse

Brian Morrison
Professional

Duke January
Superintendent

MESQUITE GOLF
AND COUNTRY CLUB

1984
Bert Stamps

Course information: This public course has 18 holes and par is 72. The course is 6,328 yards and rated 69.8 from the championship tees, and 5,944 yards and rated 67.9 from the regular tees. The slope ratings are 117 championship and 111 regular. Women's tees are 5,244 yards and rated 69.2. There is no slope rating.

Play policy and fees: Green fees are $45 weekdays and $55 weekends during peak season. Carts are included. Call for seasonal rates. Reservations are recommended two days in advance. This course is available for tournaments. No cut-offs or tank tops are allowed on the course. Golfers must wear collared shirts.

Location: Take the Palm Drive exit off Interstate 10 and drive south to Ramon Road and turn west. At Farrell, turn south and drive to the course at Mesquite Avenue.

Course description: This is a flat course with beautiful mountain scenery. It is well bunkered with eight small lakes and many palm trees. Mac O'Grady holds the course record with a 62.

2700 East Mesquite Avenue
Palm Springs, CA 92264

Pro shop   (619) 323-1502
Clubhouse   (619) 323-9377

- ■ driving range
- ■ practice greens
- ■ power carts
- □ pull carts
- ■ golf club rental
- ■ locker rooms
- ■ showers
- □ executive course
- □ accommodations
- ■ food and beverages
- ■ clubhouse

Bruce Conroy
Professional

Susumu Kubota
Director of Golf

FAIRCHILD'S BEL AIR GREENS

Course information: This public course has nine holes. Par is 32 for nine holes. The course is 1,675 yards for nine holes.

Play policy and fees: Green fees are $10 any day during the summer season. Winter fees are $20 for nine holes and $25 for 18 holes (October through May). Pull carts are $2. Reservations are recommended.

Location: In Palm Springs, take Highway 111 (East Palm Canyon Drive) to Escoba Drive. Follow Escoba about one-third of a mile to El Cielo and turn left, then go one-half mile to the course.

Course description: This is a well-maintained, nine-hole course with small, quick greens and narrow fairways. It is one of the most scenic courses in the desert with mature trees and a lot of water. One of its main attractions is the air-conditioned driving range. Yes, it's true. Go give the micro-mister a try.

1001 South El Cielo Road
Palm Springs, CA 92264

Pro shop   (619) 327-0332

- ■ driving range
- ■ practice greens
- □ power carts
- ■ pull carts
- ■ golf club rental
- □ locker rooms
- □ showers
- ■ executive course
- □ accommodations
- ■ food and beverages
- ■ clubhouse

Bill Roberts
Professional

Anne Richardson
Superintendent

PALM SPRINGS MUNICIPAL GOLF COURSE

Course information: This public course has 18 holes and par is 72. The course is 6,551 yards and rated 69.4 from the regular tees. The slope rating is 102. Women's tees are 6,044 yards and rated 71.9. The slope rating is 105.

Play policy and fees: Green fees are $14 during the summer. Call for other seasonal rates. Carts are $18. Reservations are recommended.

Location: In Palm Springs, take Palm Drive off Interstate 10 and drive south 4.5 miles to Ramon Road and turn left. Drive one-half mile to Crosley Road and turn right and then drive one mile to the club.

Course description: This well-maintained course is treelined, providing some much needed shade in the summer. It is fairly level with no bunkers. Leave your sandie at home. The Palm Springs City Seniors tournament is held here in November.

1885 Golf Club Drive
Palm Springs, CA 92264

Pro shop   (619) 328-1005
Clubhouse   (619) 328-1956

- ■ driving range
- ■ practice greens
- ■ power carts
- ■ pull carts
- ■ golf club rental
- ■ locker rooms
- □ showers
- □ executive course
- □ accommodations
- ■ food and beverages
- ■ clubhouse

Mike Carroll
Professional

Terry Lortz
Superintendent

LAWRENCE WELK'S DESERT OASIS GOLF AND TENNIS RESORT

Course information: This semi-private course has 27 holes and par is 72 for each of three 18-hole combinations.

The Lakeview/Mountainview Course is 6,510 yards and rated 71.6 from the championship tees, and 6,177 yards and rated 69.5 from the regular tees. The slope ratings are 128 championship and 117 regular. Women's tees are 5,346 yards and rated 70.2. The slope rating is 118.

The Mountainview/Resort Course is 6,482 yards and rated 70.9 from the championship tees, and 6,072 yards and rated 68.7 from the regular tees. The slope ratings are 119 championship and 111 regular. Women's tees are 5,182 yards and rated 70.2. The slope rating is 117.

The Lakeview/Resort Course is 6,366 yards and rated 70.3 from the championship tees, and 6,021 yards and rated 68.5 from the regular tees. The slope ratings are 118 championship and 110 regular. Women's tees are 5,106 and rated 68.8. The slope rating is 116.

34567 Cathedral Canyon Drive
Cathedral City, CA 92234

Pro shop   (619) 328-6571

- ■ driving range
- ■ practice greens
- ■ power carts
- □ pull carts
- ■ golf club rental
- ■ locker rooms
- □ showers
- □ executive course
- □ accommodations
- ■ food and beverages
- ■ clubhouse

J.B. Kemp
Professional

Pete Isidoro
Superintendent

Play policy and fees: Outside play is accepted. Green fees are $30 during the summer and $60 during peak season. Call for seasonal rates. Carts are included in fees. Reservations are recommended. This course is available for outside tournaments.

Location: Take the Date Palm exit off Interstate 10 and drive south to Dinah Shore Drive and turn right. Drive one mile to Cathedral Canyon Road and turn left, then continue south one mile to the club.

Course description: Formerly known as Cathedral Canyon Country Club, this is a beautiful, tree-lined course which plays fairly tight and requires a variety of shot-making skills to score well. Refreshingly, water comes into play on almost every hole.

SOUTHERN 17

WESTIN MISSION HILLS RESORT

1986
Pete Dye

1991
Gary Player

71-501 Dinah Shore Drive
Rancho Mirage, CA 92270

Pro shop   (619) 328-3198

- ■ driving range
- ■ practice greens
- ■ power carts
- □ pull carts
- ■ golf club rental
- ■ locker rooms
- ■ showers
- □ executive course
- ■ accommodations
- ■ food and beverages
- ■ clubhouse

John Herndon
Professional

Course information: This resort facility has 36 holes. Par is 70 on the Pete Dye Course and par is 72 on the Gary Player Course.

The Pete Dye Course is 6,706 yards and rated 73.5 from the tournament tees, 6,196 yards and rated 70.3 from the championship tees, and 5,629 yards and rated 67.5 from the regular tees. The slope ratings are 137 tournament, 126 championship and 117 regular. Women's tees are 4,841 yards and rated 67.4. The slope rating is 107.

The Gary Player Course is 7,062 yards from the tournament tees, 6,643 yards from the championship tees, and 6,044 yards from the regular tees. Women's tees are 4,907 yards. The course has not been rated.

Play policy and fees: Guests of the Westin Mission Hills Resort have priority on tees times. Public play is welcome. Green fees are seasonal. Call for rates. Reservations are recommended. These courses are available for outside tournaments for groups of 12 or more. Advance deposit required.

Location: Take the Bob Hope Drive/Ramon Road exit off Interstate 10 and drive south on Bob Hope Drive to Dinah Shore Drive. Then turn right and drive one-half mile to the resort entrance.

Course description: The Pete Dye Course is a links-style layout with rolling fairways and large, undulating greens. There are also numerous pot bunkers and railroad ties. The Gary Player Course, which opened in October, 1991, is a championship course featuring nine lakes and four waterfalls on 12 of its holes. Expected to open very mature, it will be as challenging as the Pete Dye Course, but thankfully forgiving because the greens are not as severe or difficult and the wide fairways encourage the ball to roll greenward. Typical of a Player-designed course, each hole presents a different type of challenge.

OUTDOOR RESORT
AND COUNTRY CLUB

Course 17
MAP I7 grid h1

1986

69-411 Ramon Road
Cathedral City, CA 92234

Pro shop   (619) 324-4005

Course information: This private course has 18 holes
and par is 54. The course is 1,801 from the championship tees, and 1,771 yards from the regular tees. A
nine-hole executive course is also available.

Play policy and fees: Members and guests only. The
guest fee is $7.50 for nine holes and $15 for 18 holes.

Location: Take Interstate 10 to Date Palm Drive and turn
left to Ramon Road. Go left and drive one-half mile
to the course.

Course description: This is a very short par-3 course
with no hole over 145 yards. The greens are small and
well protected.

□ driving range
■ practice greens
□ power carts
■ pull carts
■ golf club rental
□ locker rooms
□ showers
□ executive course
□ accommodations
■ food and beverages
■ clubhouse

Kerry Johnston
Professional

DE ANZA PALM SPRINGS
COUNTRY CLUB

Course 18
MAP I7 grid h1

1971
Ted Robinson

36-200 Date Palm Drive
Cathedral City, CA 92234

Pro shop   (619) 324-7575
Clubhouse (619) 328-1315

Course information: This semi-private layout has 18
holes and par is 58. The course is a short 3,083 yards
and rated 50.8 from the regular tees. The slope rating
is 82. Women's tees are 2,517 yards and rated 50.8.

Play policy and fees: Reciprocal play is accepted with
members of other private clubs. Outside play is also
accepted. Green fees are seasonal and range from $9
to $20. Carts are from $9 to $18. Reservations are
recommended. No tank tops allowed on the course.

Location: Take the Date Palm exit off Interstate 10 in
Cathedral City and drive south for four miles to the
club entrance on the left.

Course description: This course is set in a retirement
area, so it is quiet, private and walkable. Seven lakes
dot the course and many trees line the fairways, including eucalyptus, olive and pine trees, some as old
as 300 years. The 175-yard eighth hole is a standout.
It takes an accurate tee shot over a beautiful lake. The
green is guarded by trees on two sides. The Phil Harris
Classic has been held here, and a tournament benefitting special and handicapped
children is held annually. The course is closed for three weeks in late October.

□ driving range
■ practice greens
■ power carts
■ pull carts
■ golf club rental
■ locker rooms
■ showers
■ executive course
□ accommodations
■ food and beverages
■ clubhouse

Grant Kinman
Manager

Bobbie Reyes
Superintendent

SOUTHERN I7

MISSION HILLS
COUNTRY CLUB

1978
Arnold Palmer
Ed Seay

1988
Pete Dye

1970
Desmond Muirhead

34-600 Mission Hills Drive
Rancho Mirage, CA 92270

Pro shop   (619) 328-2153
Clubhouse (619) 321-8484

■ driving range
■ practice greens
■ power carts
□ pull carts
■ golf club rental
■ locker rooms
■ showers
□ executive course
□ accommodations
■ food and beverages
■ clubhouse

Chipper Cecil
Professional

Dave Johnson
Superintendent

Course information: This private facility has three 18-hole courses. Par is 72 on all of them.

The Arnold Palmer Course is 6,753 yards and rated 73.0 from the championship tees, and 6,218 yards and rated 70.0 from the regular tees. The slope ratings are 129 championship and 121 regular. Women's tees are 6,218 yards and rated 75.8 from the championship tees, and 5,482 yards and rated 71.6 from the forward tees. The slope ratings are 128 championship and 117 forward.

The Dinah Shore Course is 6,919 yards and rated 74.4 from the tournament tees, 6,582 yards and rated 72.2 from the championship tees, and 6,060 yards and rated 69.4 from the regular tees. The slope ratings are 141 tournament, 130 championship and 122 regular. Women's tees are 6,060 yards and rated 71.5 from the championship tees, and 5,079 yards and rated 68.5 from the forward tees. The slope ratings are 121 championship and 113 forward.

The Old Course is 7,246 yards and rated 75.5 from the tournament tees, and 6,880 yards and rated 73.4 from the championship tees, and 6,369 yards and rated 70.5 from the regular tees. The slope ratings are 137 tournament, 129 championship and 121 regular.

Play policy and fees: Reciprocal play is accepted with members of other private clubs from June through September, otherwise members and guests only. Guest fees range from $35 to $150 depending on season. Fees for reciprocators range from $40 to $45. Carts are included. Reservations are recommended one day in advance.

Location: Take the Date Palm Drive/Cathedral City exit off Interstate 10 and drive south for four miles to Gerald Ford Road. Turn left and drive 1.5 miles to the entrance.

Course description: This is golf at its finest. The Arnold Palmer Course was designed by Arnie himself along with Ed Seay and opened in 1978. It's a links-style course that is relatively flat and heavily bunkered with bent grass greens. It's immaculate. The Dinah Shore Course was designed by Pete Dye and opened in 1988. It's a stadium-type course with big rolling hills and deep bunkers. The greens are small but undulating with bent grass. The rough and surrounding area consists of natural desert. The Old Course opened in 1970 and was designed by Desmond Muirhead. It is the home of the LPGA Nabisco Dinah Shore Tournament. It has rolling terrain, mature trees, undulating bermuda greens and is quite challenging. Amy Alcott owns a piece of this course and the pond at the 18th. (She jumped in after a victory!)

TAMARISK COUNTRY CLUB

1952
William Park Bell

70-240 Frank Sinatra Drive
Rancho Mirage, CA 92270

Pro shop   (619) 328-2141

- ■ driving range
- ■ practice greens
- ■ power carts
- □ pull carts
- □ golf club rental
- ■ locker rooms
- ■ showers
- □ executive course
- □ accommodations
- ■ food and beverages
- ■ clubhouse

Dave Albrecht
Professional

Richard Sall
Superintendent

Course information: This private course has 18 holes and par is 72. The course is 6,818 yards and rated 72.8 from the championship tees, and 6,435 yards and rated 70.2 from the regular tees. The slope ratings are 125 championship and 115 regular. Women's tees are 6,044 yards and rated 73.8. The slope rating is 118.

Play policy and fees: Members and guests only. Green fees are $30 with a member and $50 if sponsored. Carts are $20. This course closes for a portion of the summer. Call ahead.

Location: Take the Bob Hope Drive/Ramon Road exit off Interstate 10 in Rancho Mirage, and drive south on Bob Hope Drive, and then turn right on Frank Sinatra Drive and travel one mile to the club on the right.

Course description: This is one of the Bob Hope Classic tournament courses, and it's the second oldest course in the desert. It's a very challenging, mature course with lots of trees. The club's first golf pro was Ben Hogan.

THE SPRINGS COUNTRY CLUB

1975
Desmond Muirhead

One Duke Drive
Rancho Mirage, CA 92270

Pro shop   (619) 328-0590
Clubhouse (619) 324-8292

- ■ driving range
- ■ practice greens
- ■ power carts
- □ pull carts
- ■ golf club rental
- ■ locker rooms
- ■ showers
- □ executive course
- □ accommodations
- ■ food and beverages
- ■ clubhouse

Doug Hart
Professional

Ross O'Fee
Superintendent

Course information: This private course has 18 holes and par is 72. The course is 6,637 yards and rated 72.3 from the championship tees, and 6,279 yards and rated 70.1 from the regular tees. The slope rating is 128. Women's tees are 5,607 yards and rated 71.6. The slope rating is 118.

Play policy and fees: Members and guests only. The guest fees are $25 June through October and $50 the rest of the year. Carts are $20. Reservations are recommended.

Location: Take the Bob Hope Drive/Ramon Road exit off Interstate 10 in Rancho Mirage and drive south on Bob Hope Drive four miles to the club entrance on the right.

Course description: Water comes into play on 11 of the holes. The greens are well bunkered and undulating. The tree-lined fairways are well maintained.

THE CLUB AT MORNINGSIDE

Jack Nicklaus

Course information: This private course has 18 holes and par is 72. The course is 6,776 yards and rated 73.6 from the tournament tees, 6,237 yards and rated 70.3 from the championship tees, and 5,530 yards and rated 66.5 from the regular tees. Women's tees are 6,237 yards and rated 75.6 from the championship tees, and 5,530 yards and rated 71.7 from the forward tees. The slope ratings are 132 championship and 123 forward.

Play policy and fees: Members and guests only. Green fees for guests are $40 with a member and $100 without a member. Carts are $12 per person. Pro shop closes at 11:30 a.m. during summer season.

Location: Take the Bob Hope Drive/Ramon Road exit off Interstate 10, and drive south on Bob Hope Drive. Turn right on Frank Sinatra Drive and travel one-half mile to Morningside Drive. Turn left and travel one-quarter mile to the club entrance on the right.

Course description: Jack Nicklaus designed this links-style course. It's immaculate and scenic. The golfer has the option to gamble or play it safe from every tee.

Morningside Drive
Rancho Mirage, CA 92270

Pro shop   (619) 321-1555
Clubhouse (619)324-1234
Starter   (619) 321-1556

- ■ driving range
- ■ practice greens
- ■ power carts
- ▢ pull carts
- ■ golf club rental
- ■ locker rooms
- ■ showers
- ▢ executive course
- ▢ accommodations
- ■ food and beverages
- ■ clubhouse

Vernon Fraser
Professional

Cal Hardin
Superintendent

IVEY RANCH COUNTRY CLUB

Course information: This semi-private course has nine holes. Par is 70 for 18 holes. The course is 5,080 yards and rated 68.0 from the regular tees (18 holes). The slope rating is 100. Women's tees are 4,796 yards and rated 64.0. The slope rating is 114.

Play policy and fees: Outside play is accepted. Green fees are $20 summer season and $30 winter season. Carts are included. Reservations are recommended one week in advance.

Location: Take the Monterey Avenue exit off Interstate 10 and drive east to Varner Road and then turn north and drive along the frontage road 1.5 miles to the club.

Course description: This well-maintained course has bent grass greens, some trees and fairly narrow fairways. It's a regulation nine-hole course, and an enjoyable course to play.

74-580 Varner Road
Thousand Palms, CA 92276

Pro shop   (619) 343-2013

- ■ driving range
- ■ practice greens
- ■ power carts
- ▢ pull carts
- ■ golf club rental
- ▢ locker rooms
- ▢ showers
- ▢ executive course
- ▢ accommodations
- ■ food and beverages
- ■ clubhouse

Dennis Foster
Professional

Jesse Troche
Superintendent

RANCHO MIRAGE COUNTRY CLUB

1984
Harold Heers

Course information: This private course has 18 holes and par is 70. The course is 6,111 yards and rated 69.5 from the championship tees, and 5,823 yards and rated 67.7 from the regular tees. The slope ratings are 119 championship and 111 regular. Women's tees are 5,309 yards and rated 67.8. The slope rating is 113.

Play policy and fees: Reciprocal play is accepted with members of other private clubs. Green fees for guests range from $25 to $70. Carts are included. Reservations are recommended. Golfers are expected to wear appropriate golf attire.

Location: Take the Bob Hope Drive/Ramon Road exit off Interstate 10 in Rancho Mirage, head south on Bob Hope Drive and drive four miles to the club entrance on the left.

Course description: This gently rolling, sporty course has narrow fairways and small greens. Water comes into play on nine holes. And, because it's located centrally in the valley, there are views of the Santa Rosa and San Jacinto Mountains. It's a good test of golf for both the advanced and the beginning golfer.

38-500 Bob Hope Drive
Rancho Mirage, CA 92270

Pro shop   (619) 324-4711
Clubhouse (619) 328-1444

■ driving range
■ practice greens
■ power carts
□ pull carts
■ golf club rental
■ locker rooms
■ showers
□ executive course
□ accommodations
■ food and beverages
■ clubhouse

Steve Wickliffe
Professional

Jim Garrett
Superintendent

EMERALD DESERT COUNTRY CLUB

1990
J. Laier, Jr.

Course information: This semi-private course has nine holes. Par is 62 for 18 holes. The course is 3,507 yards and rated 53.0. The slope rating is 92.

Play policy and fees: Green fees are $15 for nine holes and $20 for 18 holes weekdays, and $20 for nine holes and $25 for 18 holes weekends. Carts are $15. Reservations are recommended.

Location: From Interstate 10, take Monterey Avenue exit in Palm Desert to Frank Sinatra Drive, go east on Frank Sinatra approximately four miles to the course.

Course description: This new course features lakes, bent grass greens protected by numerous sand traps and narrow fairways. The par-4, 301-yard sixth hole demands good shot placement. The steeply elevated green is protected front and left by water.

76-000 Frank Sinatra Drive
Palm Desert, CA 92260

Pro shop   (619) 345-4770

□ driving range
■ practice greens
■ power carts
■ pull carts
■ golf club rental
□ locker rooms
■ showers
■ executive course
□ accommodations
■ food and beverages
□ clubhouse

Clem Hernandez
Superintendent

SOUTHERN I7

RANCHO LAS PALMAS
COUNTRY CLUB

Course information: This semi-private facility has 27 holes and par is 71, 69 or 70 depending on the 18-hole combination played.

The North/South Course is 5,779 yards and rated 67.2 from the championship tees, and 5,569 yards and rated 65.7 from the regular tees. The slope ratings are 115 championship and 103 regular. Women's tees are 5,270 yards and rated 69.7 from the forward tees. The slope rating is 113.

The South/West Course is 5,427 yards and rated 65.6 from the championship tees, and 5,160 yards and rated 63.9 from the regular tees. The slope ratings are 106 championship and 97 regular. Women's tees are 4,782 yards and rated 66.8 from the forward tees. The slope rating is 110.

The West/North Course is 5,360 yards and rated 65.3 from the championship tees, and 5,129 yards and rated 63.7 from the regular tees. The slope ratings are 105 championship and 100 forward. Women's tees are 4,824 yards and rated 66.9 from the forward tees. The slope rating is 105.

42-000 Bob Hope Drive
Rancho Mirage, CA 92270

Pro shop   (619) 568-0955
Clubhouse   (619) 568-2727

- ■ driving range
- ■ practice greens
- ■ power carts
- □ pull carts
- ■ golf club rental
- ■ locker rooms
- ■ showers
- □ executive course
- ■ accommodations
- ■ food and beverages
- ■ clubhouse

Tom Gees
Manager/Professional

Ray Metz
Professional

Play policy and fees: Reciprocal play is accepted with members of other private clubs. A Marriott hotel is affiliated with this course, and hotel guests welcome. Guest fees range from $70 to $80, including cart. Reservations are recommended three days in advance, one day in advance for reciprocators.

Location: Take the Bob Hope/Ramon Road exit off Interstate 10 and drive five miles south to the resort entrance on the left.

Course description: The North nine is the longest and has the most hills. The South nine is the narrowest and threads through condominiums. The West nine is the shortest and most scenic. It also has the most water. Numerous palm trees are spread throughout this well-maintained course.

DESERT ISLAND GOLF AND COUNTRY CLUB

Course information: This private course has 18 holes and par is 72. The course is 6,684 yards and rated 71.6 from the championship tees, and 6,310 yards and rated 69.6 from the regular tees. The slope ratings are 121 championship and 114 regular. Women's tees are 5,604 yards and rated 66.4. The slope rating is 116.

Play policy and fees: Members and guests only. Guest fees in-season are $55 with a member and $75 without a member. Guest fees out-of-season (June-October) are $45 with a member and $65 without a member. Carts are included. Closed in October. Reservations are recommended.

Location: Take the Bob Hope Drive/Ramon Road exit off Interstate 10 and drive south on Bob Hope Drive to Frank Sinatra Drive. Turn right and drive one block to the entrance on the left.

Course description: This is a well-maintained course set around a lake with an island. It is challenging with narrow fairways and numerous bunkers surrounding the greens. There are also some panoramic views of the mountains.

71-777 Frank Sinatra Drive
Rancho Mirage, CA 92270

Pro shop   (619) 328-0841
Clubhouse   (619) 328-2111

■ driving range
■ practice greens
■ power carts
□ pull carts
■ golf club rental
■ locker rooms
■ showers
□ executive course
□ accommodations
■ food and beverages
■ clubhouse

Dennis Callahan
Professional

Keith Rogers
Superintendent

PALM DESERT GREENS COUNTRY CLUB

Course information: This private course has 18 holes and par is 63. The course is 4,088 yards and rated 59.6 from the regular tees. The slope rating is 90. Women's tees are 3,682 yards and rated 59.4 from the forward tees. The slope rating is 88.

Play policy and fees: Members and guests only. Guests must be accompanied by members at time of play. Guest fees are seasonal and range from $15 to $30. Closed in October. Carts are $15. Reservations are recommended.

Location: Take the Monterey Drive exit off Interstate 10 and drive south to Country Club Drive. Turn left to the club entrance.

Course description: This 18-hole executive course is level with several lakes and mature trees. It's a sporty layout and in great shape.

73-750 Country Club Drive
Palm Desert, CA 92260

Pro shop   (619) 346-2941
Clubhouse   (619) 346-8005

□ driving range
■ practice greens
■ power carts
■ pull carts
■ golf club rental
■ locker rooms
■ showers
■ executive course
□ accommodations
■ food and beverages
■ clubhouse

Joe Casey
Professional

SOUTHERN 17

SUNCREST COUNTRY CLUB

Course information: This semi-private course has nine holes. Par is 66 for 18 holes. The course is 4,683 yards and rated 60.0 from the regular tees. The slope rating is 93. Women's tees are 3,930 yards and rated 63.2. The slope rating is 99.

Play policy and fees: Green fees are $21. Carts are $18. Reservations are recommended.

Location: Take the Monterey Drive exit off Interstate 10 and drive south to Country Club Drive. Turn left and travel one-half mile to the club on the left.

Course description: Set in Suncrest Park, this nicely-maintained course is flat with trees and two lakes. The elevation here is slightly higher than the surrounding courses and provides a nice view. The course record is 57. It is closed during September and October.

73-450 Country Club Drive
Palm Desert, CA 92260

Pro shop   (619) 340-2467
Clubhouse (619) 346-5866

- ■ driving range
- ■ practice greens
- ■ power carts
- ■ pull carts
- ■ golf club rental
- ■ locker rooms
- ■ showers
- ■ executive course
- ☐ accommodations
- ■ food and beverages
- ■ clubhouse

Gary Stevenson
Professional

Robert Sanchez
Superintendent

SANTA ROSA COUNTRY CLUB

Course information: This private course has 18 holes and par is 67. The course is 5,443 yards and rated 65.6 from the regular tees. The slope rating is 103. Women's tees are 5,161 yards and rated 68.7 from the forward tees. The slope rating is 107.

Play policy and fees: Reciprocal play is accepted with members of other private clubs. Members and guests only. Guest fees are $15 in summer and $30 the rest of the year. Carts are $20 and mandatory for guests. Reservations are recommended two days in advance.

Location: Take the Monterey exit off Interstate 10 and drive south to Country Club Drive. Turn left and travel to Portola Avenue and turn left.

Course description: This desert course has tree-lined fairways and two large lakes. It's challenging and offers a view of the Santa Rosa Mountains. New tee boxes were the latest in a program to upgrade the course.

PO Box 87
Palm Desert, CA 92260

38-105 Portola Avenue
Palm Desert, CA 92260

Pro shop   (619) 568-5717

- ■ driving range
- ■ practice greens
- ■ power carts
- ☐ pull carts
- ■ golf club rental
- ☐ locker rooms
- ☐ showers
- ☐ executive course
- ☐ accommodations
- ■ food and beverages
- ■ clubhouse

Dennis Pogue
Professional

Scott Szydloski
Superintendent

DESERT FALLS
COUNTRY CLUB

Course information: This semi-private course has 18 holes and par is 72. The course is 7,017 yards and rated 75.0 from the championship tees, and 6,565 yards and rated 72.2 from the regular tees. The slope ratings are 145 championship and 133 regular. Women's tees are 5,288 yards and rated 71.0. The slope rating is 119.

Play policy and fees: Outside play is accepted. Green fees are seasonal, ranging from $40 during the off-season (summer) to $110 during the high season (winter). Call for rates. Carts are included. Reservations are recommended. This course closes in October.

Location: Take the Monterey Avenue exit off Interstate 10 and drive south to Country Club Drive. From there, turn left and travel two miles to the club.

Course description: This course will really test your ability. It is long, and one of the few desert courses with a Scottish layout. The greens sport bent grass and are big enough to play football on. This course serves as a tour qualifying school.

1111 Desert Falls Parkway
Palm Desert, CA 92260

Pro Shop   (619) 341-4020
Clubhouse (619) 340-5646

■ driving range
■ practice greens
■ power carts
□ pull carts
■ golf club rental
■ locker rooms
■ showers
□ executive course
□ accommodations
■ food and beverages
■ clubhouse

Luanne Costello
Professional

Phil Villalobos
Superintendent

AVONDALE GOLF CLUB

Course information: This private course has 18 holes and par is 72. The course is 6,771 yards and rated 73.1 from the championship tees, and 6,386 yards and rated 70.6 from the regular tees. The slope ratings are 128 championship and 122 regular. Women's tees are 5,766 yards and rated 73.3. The slope rating is 122.

Play policy and fees: Members and guests only. Green fees are $45 June 1 through mid-September, and $65 November 1 through May 31, 1992. The course is closed from mid-September to early November. Carts are included.

Location: Take the Washington Street exit off Interstate 10 and drive south. Turn right on Country Club Drive and travel 2.5 miles to El Dorado. From there turn right to the course.

Course description: This is not a typical desert course. There are water hazards and lots of trees dispersed on rolling terrain. This was formerly a semi-private course that went private in 1991.

75-800 Avondale Drive
Palm Desert, CA 92260

Pro shop   (619) 345-3712
Clubhouse   (619) 345-2727

■ driving range
■ practice greens
■ power carts
□ pull carts
■ golf club rental
■ locker rooms
■ showers
□ executive course
□ accommodations
■ food and beverages
■ clubhouse

Fred Scherzer
Professional

Carlos Lopez
Superintendent

SOUTHERN 17

PALM VALLEY
COUNTRY CLUB

Course information: This private course has two 18-hole courses. Par is 72 on the South Course and 63 on the North Course.

The South Course is 6,436 yards and rated 71.1 from the championship tees, and 6,040 yards and rated 69.2 from the regular tees. The slope ratings are 125 championship and 119 regular. Women's tees are 5,295 yards and rated 70.7 from the forward tees. The slope rating is 125.

The North Course is 4,151 yards and rated 58.0 from the championship tees, and 3,850 yards and rated 56.2 from the regular tees. The slope ratings are 96 championship and 93 regular. Women's tees are 3,565 yards and rated 61.0. The slope rating is 99.

Play policy and fees: Reciprocal play is accepted with members of other private clubs. During the summer, fees are $45 for the South Course and $35 for the North Course. During the peak winter season, fees are $85 for the South Course and $50 for the North course. Carts are included. Reservations are recommended one day in advance.

Location: Take the Washington Street exit off Interstate 10 and drive south to Country Club Drive. Turn right and travel one mile to the club on the right.

Course description: The South Course has quite a bit of undulation for a desert course and offers beautiful panoramic views of the area. The North Course is difficult for a short course with water hazards that come into play on 15 holes. It's a tough challenge for mid- to low-handicap players.

76-200 Country Club Drive
Palm Desert, CA 92260

Pro shop   (619) 345-2742

- ■ driving range
- ■ practice greens
- ■ power carts
- □ pull carts
- ■ golf club rental
- ■ locker rooms
- ■ showers
- ■ executive course
- □ accommodations
- ■ food and beverages
- ■ clubhouse

Scott Walter
Professional

Collier Miller
Superintendent

BIGHORN GOLF CLUB

1991
Arthur Hills

215 Kiva Drive
Palm Desert, CA 92260

Pro shop   (619) 773-2468

- ■ driving range
- ■ practice greens
- ■ power carts
- □ pull carts
- ■ golf club rental
- □ locker rooms
- □ showers
- □ executive course
- □ accommodations
- ■ food and beverages
- ■ clubhouse

Donnie Cude
Professional

Ruben Ramirez
Superintendent

Course information: This new private course has 18 holes. Par is 72. The course is in the process of being measured and rated.

Play policy and fees: Reciprocal play is not accepted. Members and guests only. Guests must be sponsored by a member. Guest fees are $100, including cart. Tees times are not necessary.

Location: From Highway 10 in Palm Desert exit on Monterey Avenue. Drive south until Monterey Avenue becomes Highway 74. The club is 3.5 miles south on Highway 74.

Course description: This dramatic desert course is part of a private residential community. Its official opening was scheduled for November 1, 1991. Carved into the Santa Rosa Mountains, with elevation changes ranging up to 400 yards, the course provides spectacular views of the mountains and the Coachella Valley. A clubhouse is scheduled to open in the fall of 1992.

THUNDERBIRD COUNTRY CLUB

1952
Johnny Dawson

Box 5005
Rancho Mirage, CA 92270

70-612 Highway 111
Rancho Mirage, CA 92270

Pro shop   (619) 328-2161

- ■ driving range
- ■ practice greens
- ■ power carts
- □ pull carts
- □ golf club rental
- ■ locker rooms
- ■ showers
- □ executive course
- ■ accommodations
- ■ food and beverages
- ■ clubhouse

Don Callahan
Professional

Bruce Duenow
Superintendent

Course information: This private course has 18 holes and par is 71. The course is 6,460 yards and rated 71.5 from the championship tees, and 6,185 yards and rated 69.6 from the regular tees. The slope ratings are 126 championship and 119 regular. Women's tees are 5,854 yards and rated 73.9. The slope rating is 124.

Play policy and fees: Members and guests only. Guests must be accompanied by members at time of play. Green fees for guests are $35 from June to October and $100 the rest of the year. Carts are $22.

Location: Take the Bob Hope Drive/Ramon exit off Interstate 10, and drive south on Bob Hope Drive. Turn right on Country Club Drive and travel 1.5 miles to the club entrance on the left.

Course description: This exclusive course was designed by Johnny Dawson in 1952. The gently rolling fairways are lined with mature trees. It's a well-maintained tract, which gives older players a fair chance.

SOUTHERN 17

MAP ON PAGE 496

SUNRISE COUNTRY CLUB

Course information: This private course has 18 holes and par is 64. The course is 3,828 yards and rated 54.9 from the regular tees. The slope rating is 84. Women's tees are 3,828 yards and rated 60.4 from the forward tees. The slope rating is 90.0 .

Play policy and fees: Reciprocal play is accepted with members of other private clubs, otherwise members and guests only. Green fees are $26 for guests and $40 for reciprocators. Carts are $10 per player anytime. Reservations are recommended. Summer season hours are 6 a.m. to 1 p.m. Closed Mondays.

Location: Take the Bob Hope Drive/Ramon Road exit off Interstate 10 and drive about six miles south on Bob Hope Drive. Then turn right on Country Club Drive and travel several yards to the entrance on the left.

Course description: This is a mature, 18-hole executive course with water and lots of sand. It boasts 10 par-4s and eight par-3s.

71-601 Country Club Drive
Rancho Mirage, CA 92270

Pro shop   (619) 328-1139
Clubhouse (619) 328-6549

- ■ driving range
- ■ practice greens
- ■ power carts
- ❑ pull carts
- ■ golf club rental
- ■ locker rooms
- ■ showers
- ■ executive course
- ❑ accommodations
- ■ food and beverages
- ■ clubhouse

Jim Dayton
Professional

John Hernandez
Superintendent

CHAPARRAL COUNTRY CLUB

Course information: This private course has 18 holes and par is 60. The course is 3,920 yards and rated 56.4 from the championship tees, and 3,664 yards and rated 54.7 from the regular tees. The slope ratings are 108 championship and 100 regular. Women's tees are 3,103 yards and rated 55.9. The slope rating is 80.

Play policy and fees: Reciprocal play is accepted with members of other private clubs. The guest fees are $50. Carts are included. Reservations are recommended.

Location: Take the Monterey Drive exit off Interstate 10 and drive south to Country Club Drive. Turn left and drive to Portola Road then turn right and drive to the club.

Course description: Known as the "Little Monster," this tough executive course is well bunkered with water on 13 holes. It's a shot-maker's course.

100 Chaparral Dr.
Palm Desert, CA 92260

Pro shop   (619) 340-1501
Clubhouse (619) 340-1893

- ■ driving range
- ■ practice greens
- ■ power carts
- ❑ pull carts
- ■ golf club rental
- ❑ locker rooms
- ❑ showers
- ■ executive course
- ■ accommodations
- ■ food and beverages
- ■ clubhouse

David M. James
Professional

John Rodriquez
Superintendent

THE LAKES COUNTRY CLUB

1982
Ted Robinson

161 Old Ranch Road
Palm Desert, CA 92260

Pro shop   (619) 568-5674
Clubhouse (619) 568-4321

- ■ driving range
- ■ practice greens
- ■ power carts
- □ pull carts
- ■ golf club rental
- ■ locker rooms
- ■ showers
- □ executive course
- □ accommodations
- ■ food and beverages
- ■ clubhouse

Mike Clifford
Professional

Ty Broadhead
Superintendent

Course information: This private facility has 27 holes and par is 72 for each of the 18-hole combinations.

The North/East Course is 6,414 yards and rated 70.6 from the championship tees, and 6,027 yards and rated 68.3 from the regular tees. The slope ratings are 122 championship and 109 regular. Women's tees are 5,396 yards and rated 70.8 from the forward tees. The slope rating is 123.

The South/North Course is 6,683 yards and rated 72.1 from the championship tees, and 6,278 yards and rated 69.4 from the regular tees. The slope ratings are 127 championship and 111 regular. Women's tees are 5,707 yards and rated 72.6 from the forward tees. The slope rating is 122.

The East/South Course is 6,607 yards and rated 71.6 from the championship tees, and 6,215 yards and rated 69.2 from the regular tees. The slope ratings are 125 championship and 110 regular. Women's tees are 5,697 yards and rated 72.6 from the forward tees. The slope rating is 123.

Play policy and fees: Limited reciprocal play is accepted with members of other private clubs from June through September, otherwise members and guests only. Guest fees are $45 with a member and $86 without, including cart. Unaccompanied guests are allowed Monday through Thursday. Fees for reciprocators are $55. Carts are $11. Reservations are recommended.

Location: Take the Monterey Drive exit off Interstate 10 and drive south to Country Club Drive. Turn left and go three miles to the course.

Course description: These well-bunkered courses have lots of water and spectacular views of the Santa Rosa Mountains. Two of the nines are set among the condos.

SOUTHERN 17

MONTEREY COUNTRY CLUB

1979
Ted Robinson

41-500 Monterey Avenue
Palm Desert, CA 92260

Pro shop   (619) 340-3885
Clubhouse (619) 568-9311

Course information: This private facility has 27 holes and par is 72 or 71 for the 18-hole combinations.

The South/West Course is 6,185 yards and rated 69.2 from the championship tees, and 5,898 yards and rated 67.7 from the regular tees. The slope ratings are 116 championship and 108 regular. Women's tees are 5,417 yards and rated 71.6 from the forward tees. The slope rating is 123.

The East/West Course is 6,108 yards and rated 68.9 from the championship tees, and 5,790 yards and rated 67.2 from the regular tees. The slope ratings are 115 championship and 107 regular. Women's tees are 5,259 yards and rated 70.8 from the forward tees. The slope rating is 123.

The East/South Course is 6,005 yards and rated 68.3 from the championship tees, and 5,720 yards and rated 66.9 from the regular tees. The slope ratings are 114 championship and 106 regular. Women's tees are 5,226 yards and rated 70.4 from the forward tees. The slope rating is 124.

- ■ driving range
- ■ practice greens
- ■ power carts
- ☐ pull carts
- ■ golf club rental
- ■ locker rooms
- ■ showers
- ☐ executive course
- ☐ accommodations
- ■ food and beverages
- ■ clubhouse

Terry Naughton
Professional

Shannon Cook
Superintendent

Play policy and fees: Reciprocal play is accepted with members of other private clubs. Green fees are $65 for guests unaccompanied by a member and $60 with a member. Green fees for reciprocators are $75. Carts are included. Reservations are required. Reciprocators call one day in advance.

Location: Take the Monterey Avenue exit off Interstate 10, and drive south four miles to the club.

Course description: This tight, target golf course has strategically placed bunkers and water hazards. The narrow fairways are lined with condos on both sides.

PORTOLA COUNTRY CLUB

42-500 Portola Avenue
Palm Desert, CA 92260

Pro shop   (619) 568-1592

Course information: This short private course has 18 holes and par is 54. The course is 2,167 yards. Women's tees are 1,913 yards.

Play policy and fees: Members and guests only. Green fees are $10 weekdays and $15 weekends.

Location: From Interstate 10 take Country Club Drive to Portola Avenue. Go left on Portola and follow it about one mile to the club.

Course description: Situated on 27 acres, this par-3 course is flat, but somewhat rolling with many lakes and water hazards. It is situated in a mobile home park.

- ☐ driving range
- ■ practice greens
- ☐ power carts
- ■ pull carts
- ■ golf club rental
- ☐ locker rooms
- ☐ showers
- ■ executive course
- ☐ accommodations
- ☐ food and beverages
- ■ clubhouse

Rusty Uhly
Professional

INDIAN WELLS GOLF RESORT

1986
Ted Robinson

44-500 Indian Wells
Indian Wells, CA 92210

Pro shop   (619) 346-4653

- ■ driving range
- ■ practice greens
- ■ power carts
- □ pull carts
- ■ golf club rental
- ■ locker rooms
- □ showers
- □ executive course
- ■ accommodations
- ■ food and beverages
- ■ clubhouse

Ron Cleveland
Professional

Glenn Miller
Superintendent

Course information: This resort facility has two 18-hole courses with a par of 72 on both.

The East Course is 6,662 yards and rated 71.6 from the championship tees, and 6,227 yards and rated 69.4 from the regular tees. The slope ratings are 118 championship and 110 regular. Women's tees are 6,227 yards and rated 74.7 from the championship tees, and 5,521 yards and rated 70.7 from the forward tees. The slope ratings are 122 championship and 113 forward.

The West Course is 6,478 yards and rated 70.3 from the championship tees, and 6,115 yards and rated 68.7 from the regular tees. The slope ratings are 116 championship and 109 regular. Women's tees are 6,115 and rated 74.0 from the championship tees, and 5,387 yards and rated 70.0 from the forward tees. The slope ratings are 120 championship and 110 forward.

Play policy and fees: Green fees are $80 weekdays and $90 weekends from January through April, carts included. Prices vary during other months. Twilight rates are $30. Reservations are recommended. This course is available for outside tournaments.

Location: From Interstate 10 take the Washington Street exit about one-half mile to Highway 111, turn right and follow Highway 111 to Indian Wells Lane and you'll see the course.

Course description: Both courses were designed by Ted Robinson and feature beautiful greens, rolling fairways and a natural desert setting. Vice President Dan Quayle has been spotted on this course at least once.

SOUTHERN 17

DESERT HORIZONS COUNTRY CLUB

Course 42
MAP 17 grid I2

1979
Ted Robinson

44-900 Desert Horizons Drive
Indian Wells, CA 92210

Clubhouse (619) 340-4646
Pro shop   ext. 221 or 222
Starter   (619) 340-4652

- ■ driving range
- ■ practice greens
- ■ power carts
- ☐ pull carts
- ■ golf club rental
- ■ locker rooms
- ■ showers
- ☐ executive course
- ☐ accommodations
- ■ food and beverages
- ■ clubhouse

Paul Lemcke
Director of Golf

Rick Ruppert
Professional

Mark Smith
Superintendent

Course information: This private course has 18 holes and par is 72. The course is 6,614 yards and rated 71.7 from the championship tees, and 6,117 yards and rated 68.9 from the regular tees. The slope ratings are 123 championship and 115 regular. Women's tees are 5,498 yards and rated 71.6. The slope rating is 121.

Play policy and fees: Members and guests only. Green fees are $50 for guests accompanied by a member and $100 for guests unaccompanied by a member. This course is closed in October.

Location: Travel one mile west of Indian Wells on Highway 111. At Desert Horizons Drive turn north and drive to the club.

Course description: This championship course has more sand than Iwo Jima and lots of water. In other words, it is very challenging. Beware of number nine. It's a par-3, 210-yard brute that demands an 180-yard carry over water to a two-tiered, hour-glass green. The green is bunkered on the left, with water on the right.

SHADOW MOUNTAIN GOLF CLUB

Course 43
MAP 17 grid I2

1959
Gene Sarazan

PO Box 667
Palm Desert, CA 92260

45-700 San Luis Rey Avenue
Palm Desert, CA 92260

Pro shop   (619) 346-8242

- ■ driving range
- ■ practice greens
- ■ power carts
- ■ pull carts
- ■ golf club rental
- ■ locker rooms
- ☐ showers
- ☐ executive course
- ☐ accommodations
- ■ food and beverages
- ■ clubhouse

Sherry Wilder
General Manager/
Professional

Gaylord Moller
Superintendent

Course information: This private course has 18 holes and par is 70. The course is 5,418 yards and rated 65.5 from the regular tees. The slope rating is 108. Women's tees are 5,418 yards and rated 70.7. The slope rating is 115.

Play policy and fees: Reciprocal play is accepted with members of other private clubs. Green fees are $50 during the winter season and $25 during the summer season. Carts are included. Reservations are mandatory. Appropriate attire required. The course is closed during October.

Location: Take the Monterey Avenue exit off Interstate 10 and drive south to Highway 111 in Palm Desert and turn left. At San Luis Rey Avenue turn right and drive to the end of the road. Turn left into the club.

Course description: This course is well bunkered with some water and lots of palm trees. It's a challenging course for the average player. The men's course record is held by Fred Hawkins with a 55. Sherry Wilder holds the women's record with a 65. The 17th hole is a new 415-yard par-4. It features a beautifully landscaped rock garden.

EL DORADO COUNTRY CLUB

Course information: This private course has 18 holes and par is 72. The course is 6,702 yards and rated 72.6 from the championship tees, and 6,317 yards and rated 70.0 from the regular tees. The slope ratings are 123 championship and 116 regular. Women's tees are 5,942 yards and rated 76.2. The slope rating is 130.

Play policy and fees: Members and guests only. The guest fees are $40 weekdays and $50 weekends. Carts are $20. This course is formally open from November 1 to May 31.

Location: Take the Monterey Avenue exit off Interstate 10 and drive south to Highway 111 in Palm Desert and turn left. At El Dorado Drive turn right and drive one-half mile to Fairway Drive. Turn right and drive one-half block to the club on the left.

Course description: This is a mature course that is fairly level and with out-of-bounds areas on every hole. A fairway returns to the clubhouse every four to five holes for those in need of refreshments.

Fairway Drive
Indian Wells, CA 92210

Pro shop   (619) 346-8081

■ driving range
■ practice greens
■ power carts
□ pull carts
□ golf club rental
■ locker rooms
■ showers
□ executive course
□ accommodations
■ food and beverages
■ clubhouse

Don Fairfield
Professional

Mike Mongiello
Superintendent

MARRAKESH COUNTRY CLUB

Course information: This short, semi-private course has 18 holes and par is 60. The course is 3,595 yards and rated 53.9 from the regular tees. The slope rating is 87. Women's yardage and ratings were unavailable.

Play policy and fees: Reciprocal play is accepted with members of other private clubs. Green fees are $20 weekday and $25 weekends. Reservations are recommended. The course is closed in October.

Location: Take the Monterey Avenue exit off Interstate 10 and drive south to Country Club Drive. Turn left at Portola Avenue turn south to the club.

Course description: This is a flat course with four lakes and many trees.

47-000 Marrakesh Drive
Palm Desert, CA 92260

Pro shop   (619) 568-2660

■ driving range
■ practice greens
■ power carts
□ pull carts
■ golf club rental
□ locker rooms
□ showers
□ executive course
□ accommodations
■ food and beverages
□ clubhouse

Chris Egan
Professional

John Figgen
Superintendent

IRONWOOD COUNTRY CLUB

Ted Robinson
North Course

Dsemond Muirhead
Ted Robinson
South Course

Course information: This private facility has two 18-hole courses. Par is 72 on the South Course and 70 on the North Course.

The South Course is 7,404 yards and rated 76.7 from the tournament tees, 6,741 yards and rated 73.0 from the championship tees, and 6,514 yards and rated 71.3 from the regular tees. The slope ratings are 136 tournament, 128 championship and 122 regular. Women's tees are 5,909 yards and rated 73.0 from the forward tees. The slope rating is 120.

The North Course is 6,093 yards and rated 68.9 from the regular tees. The slope rating is 117. Women's tees are 5,980 yards and rated 69.6 from the forward tees. The slope rating is 113.

Play policy and fees: Members and guests only. Guest fees are $75 with a member and $95 without during the winter season, and $55 with a member and $75 without during the summer season. Carts are included. Reservations are required. The course closes at 1 p.m. during the summer season. It is open all year.

Location: Take the Monterey Drive exit off Interstate 10 and drive south to Highway 111. Turn left and drive to Portola Avenue, then turn right and drive about two miles to the club.

Course description: Situated above the desert floor, the South Course is very scenic. It's long and winds through the desert. Arnold Palmer was the original designer of the course, but after the great flood of the early 1970s it was reconstructed by Muirhead and Robinson. There are several tough holes from the back tees. The North Course is also very scenic with mountain and desert valley views. There are some water hazards and the fairways are lined with condos and homes, but it isn't as tough as the South Course.

49-200 Mariposa Drive
Palm Desert, CA 92260

Pro shop　(619) 568-4884
Clubhouse　(619) 346-0551

- ■ driving range
- ■ practice greens
- ■ power carts
- ☐ pull carts
- ■ golf club rental
- ■ locker rooms
- ■ showers
- ☐ executive course
- ■ accommodations
- ■ food and beverages
- ■ clubhouse

Ed Montgomery
Professional

Robert Stuczynski
Superintendent

THE VINTAGE CLUB

1980
Tom Fazio

Course information: This private facility has two 18-hole courses and par is 72 on both.

The Desert Course is 6,279 yards and rated 70.6 from the regular tees. The slope rating is 126. Women's tees are 5,718 yards and rated 68.4. The slope rating is 119.

The Mountain Course is 6,871 yards and rated 73.6 from the tournament tees, 6,456 yards and rated 70.8 from the championship tees, and 6,084 yards and rated 68.6 from the regular tees. The slope ratings are 129 tournament, 123 championship and 109 regular. Women's tees are 5,694 yards and rated 68.7. The slope rating is 118.

Play policy and fees: Members and guests only. Guest fees are $50 with a member and $150 sponsored. Carts are $12.50 per rider.

Location: Take the Monterey Avenue exit off Interstate 10 and drive south to Highway 111 in Palm Desert and turn left. At Cook Street, turn right and drive one-half mile to the club at the end of the road.

Course description: The Desert Course is short but deceptive, requiring precise shot-making to the very small greens. It has a Scottish touch with deep pot bunkers, sand and shrubbery. The Mountain Course is a wide-open, easy-driving course with a British accent. It features deep pot bunkers, sprawling fairways, natural rock formations, citrus groves, indigenous shrubs, colorful flowers and waterfalls. The 379-yard, par-4 16th hole is flanked by three lakes and two greenside waterfalls, while the scenic 158-yard, par-3 17th is fronted by a lake and affords a panoramic view. This exclusive club is used annually for the Senior PGA Tour's Vintage Invitational. The seniors rated it the best groomed course on the senior tour and it is rated among the top 20 courses in the state.

75-001 Vintage Drive West
Indian Wells, CA 92210

Pro shop   (619) 568-0865
Clubhouse (619) 340-0500

- ■ driving range
- ■ practice greens
- ■ power carts
- □ pull carts
- ■ golf club rental
- ■ locker rooms
- ■ showers
- □ executive course
- □ accommodations
- ■ food and beverages
- ■ clubhouse

Buddy Cook
Professional

Jeff Markow
Superintendent

SOUTHERN 17

INDIAN WELLS COUNTRY CLUB

Course 48
MAP 17 grid 12

1955
Eddie Susella

46-000 Club Drive
Indian Wells, CA 92210

Pro shop   (619) 345-9774
Clubhouse (619) 345-2561

■ driving range
■ practice greens
■ power carts
□ pull carts
■ golf club rental
■ locker rooms
■ showers
□ executive course
□ accommodations
■ food and beverages
■ clubhouse

Frank Rector
Professional

Doug Anderson
Superintendent

Course information: This private course has 27 holes and par is 72 on each of the five 18-hole combinations.

The Bob Hope Classic Course is 6,512 yards and rated 71.6 from the championship tees, and 6,153 yards and rated 69.4 from the regular tees. The slope ratings are 126 championship and 117 regular. Women's tees are 5,665 yards and rated 71.7. The slope rating is 117.

The Cove Course is 6,521 yards and rated 71.7 from the championship tees, and 6,245 yards and rated 69.6 from the regular tees. The slope ratings are 127 championship and 118 regular. Women's tees are 5,763 yards and rated 72.4. The slope rating is 118.

The North/Cove Course is 6,654 yards and rated 72.4 from the championship tees, and 6,285 yards and rated 70.0 from the regular tees. The slope ratings are 128 championship and 118 regular. Women's tees are 5,755 yards and rated 72.2. The slope rating is 117.

The West/Cove Course is 6,485 yards and rated 71.6 from the championship tees, and 6,108 yards and rated 69.3 from the regular tees. The slope ratings are 126 championship and 117 regular. Women's tees are 5,600 yards and rated 71.3. The slope rating is 116.

The North Course is 6,373 yards and rated 70.4 from the regular tees. The slope rating is 119. Women's tees are 5,841 yards and rated 72.6. The slope rating is 118.

Play policy and fees: Members and guests only. The green fee is $150 without a member and $75 with a member, include cart and range fee. Regular dress code applies.

Location: From Interstate 10 take the Monterey Avenue exit, go south to Highway 111, then east to Club Drive.

Course description: The five layouts are distinctly different. The North/Cove nine is the oldest and has tree-lined fairways. The West/Cove nine has a desert layout. The Cove nine is set at the base of the mountains. The Classic Course is contrived from a selection of holes from all three nines. Choose your poison. Bert Yancey holds the course record with a 61. The Bob Hope Classic is held here each year.

LA QUINTA HOTEL GOLF CLUB—DUNES COURSE

1982
Pete Dye

Course information: This semi-private course has 18 holes and par is 72. The course is 6,805 yards and rated 73.8 from the tournament tees, 6,251 yards and rated 70.6 from the championship tees, and 5,697 yards and rated 67.0 from the regular tees. The slope ratings are 139 tournament, 129 championship and 113 regular. Women's tees are 5,024 yards and rated 68.0. The slope rating is 114.

Play policy and fees: Outside play is accepted. Members and guests have priority. There are reduced fees for hotel guests. Green fees range from $40 to $100 depending on time of year. Fees include cart and range fees. Reservations are recommended. Shorts are permitted on the course, although cut-offs are not allowed. Dress code enforced. Collared shirts are preferred.

Location: Take the Washington Street exit off Interstate 10 and drive south past Highway 111 to Avenue 50 and turn right. Continue past Eisenhower Drive to the gate and follow the road to the club.

Course description: This a traditional Pete Dye course. It is well bunkered with railroad ties and lots of water. PGA of America rated the 416-yard, par-4 17th one of country's toughest holes. The PGA Tour Qualifying School was held here in 1990. The California State Open was played here in 1990.

PO Box 29
La Quinta, CA 92253

50-200 Avenue Vista Bonita
La Quinta, CA 92253

Pro shop   (619) 564-7610
Clubhouse (619) 564-3672

- ■ driving range
- ■ practice greens
- ■ power carts
- □ pull carts
- ■ golf club rental
- ■ locker rooms
- ■ showers
- □ executive course
- ■ accommodations
- ■ food and beverages
- ■ clubhouse

Greg Abadie
Professional

Ken Williams
Superintendent

SOUTHERN 17

LA QUINTA HOTEL GOLF CLUB—MOUNTAIN COURSE

1980
Pete Dye

Course information: This private course has 18 holes and par is 72. The course is 6,735 yards and rated 74.3 from the tournament tees, 6,303 yards and rated 71.4 from the championship tees, and 5,451 yards and rated 66.7 from the regular tees. The slope ratings are 146 tournament, 136 championship and 117 regular. Women's tees are 5,217 yards and rated 69.7. The slope rating is 115.

Play policy and fees: Members and guests only. Guests must be accompanied by members. Guest fees vary according to time of year, but include cart and range fees. Reservations are recommended.

Location: Take the Washington Street exit off Interstate 10 and drive south past Highway 111 to Avenue 50 and turn right. Drive past Eisenhower Drive to the gate and follow the road to the club.

Course description: This is a challenging desert course noted for pot bunkers, rock formations, sand and water. The large, undulating greens are set naturally against the mountains. Accuracy is the key. Watch for the par-3 16th hole. The green is surrounded by mountain rocks. This has been the home of the World Cup and the PGA National Club Pro Championships and the California State Open. Golf pros and superintendents rate it the top course in the desert and it rates among the top 20 in the state. The Senior Skins Game was held here in 1989 featuring Arnold Palmer, Billy Casper, Chi Chi Rodriquez and Gary Player. Fred Couples holds the course record with a 63.

PO Box 29
La Quinta, CA 92253

50-200 Avenue Vista Bonita
La Quinta, CA 92253

Pro shop   (619) 564-7610
Clubhouse   (619) 564-3672

- driving range
- practice greens
- power carts
- ☐ pull carts
- golf club rental
- locker rooms
- showers
- ☐ executive course
- accommodations
- food and beverages
- clubhouse

Greg Abadie
Director of Golf

Ken Williams
Superintendent

LA QUINTA HOTEL GOLF CLUB—CITRUS COURSE

1987
Pete Dye

Course information: This semi-private course has 18 holes and par is 72. The Citrus Course is 7,135 yards and rated 75.0 from the tournament tees, 6,477 yards and rated 70.9 from the championship tees, and 5,932 yards and rated 68.0 from the regular tees. The slope ratings are 135 tournament, 123 championship and 110 regular. Women's tees are 5,106 yards and rated 68.3 from the forward tees. The slope a rating is 112.

Play policy and fees: Outside play is accepted after 11 a.m. during the season and subject to availability, otherwise members and guests only. Men only until 10 a.m. Guests must be accompanied by a member before 11 a.m. Hotel guest play is subject to availability after 11 a.m., although they have priority over outside play. Guest fees range from $40 to $100 depending on time of year. Cart and range fee are included. Reservations are recommended.

Location: Take the Jefferson Street exit off Interstate 10 and drive south for three miles to the course.

Course description: This is a level course carved out of a citrus orchard and it is anything but a lemon. In fact, this is one of the more scenic courses in the area. It was designed by Pete Dye. A typically challenging Pete Dye design, the course features rolling contours, bent grass greens, scenic views of the Santa Rosa Mountains. This layout has plenty of character with a mix of sand and water. It's a forgiving course if you don't try to outplay it.

PO Box 942
La Quinta, CA 92253

50-503 Jefferson
La Quinta, CA 92253

Pro shop   (619) 564-7620
Clubhouse (619) 345-8430

- ■ driving range
- ■ practice greens
- ■ power carts
- ☐ pull carts
- ■ golf club rental
- ☐ locker rooms
- ☐ showers
- ☐ executive course
- ■ accommodations
- ■ food and beverages
- ■ clubhouse

Greg Abadie
Director of Golf

Rick Neal
Professional

Jerry Dearie
Superintendent

SOUTHERN 17

MAP ON PAGE 496

529

PALM DESERT RESORT COUNTRY CLUB

1980
Joe Holleneaux

Course information: This semi-private course has 18 holes and par is 72. The course is 6,571 yards and rated 70.7 from the championship tees, and 6,288 yards and rated 69.2 from the regular tees. The slope ratings are 112 championship and 107 regular. Women's tees are 5,464 yards and rated 70.6 from the forward tees. The slope rating is 112.

Play policy and fees: Outside play is accepted. Green fees range from $42 to $60 weekdays and $50 to $80 weekends. Carts are included. Reservations are recommended. This course is available for outside tournaments. Golfers are not allowed to wear tank tops or cut-off pants. The course is open daily, however the pro shop is closed Mondays and Tuesdays during the summer season.

Location: Take the Washington Street exit off Interstate 10, and drive south to Country Club Drive. Turn right and travel three-fourths of a mile to the club on the left.

Course description: This course has fairly wide fairways, bent grass greens and nine lakes that come into play. It's well bunkered and in excellent condition. It challenges the good golfer as well as the average golfer.

77-333 Country Club Drive
Palm Desert, CA 92260

Pro shop   (619) 345-2791
Clubhouse (619) 345-2781

- ■ driving range
- ■ practice greens
- ■ power carts
- □ pull carts
- ■ golf club rental
- ■ locker rooms
- ■ showers
- □ executive course
- ■ accommodations
- ■ food and beverages
- ■ clubhouse

Tom Bienek
Professional

Ray Cymbalisty
Superintendent

WOODHAVEN COUNTRY CLUB

1985

Course information: This private course has 18 holes and par is 70. The course is 5,609 yards and rated 66.6 from the championship tees, and 5,257 yards and rated 64.6 from the regular tees. The slope ratings are 111 championship and 107 regular. Women's tees are 5,243 yards and rated 68.8. The slope rating is 109.

Play policy and fees: Reciprocal play is accepted with members of other private clubs. The fees for reciprocators are $42 in the fall and spring and $52 in winter. Green fees for guests accompanied by a member are $42 in the fall and spring and $46 in winter. Carts are included. Reservations are recommended. Bermuda shorts are acceptable. The course is closed in October.

Location: Take the Washington Street exit off Interstate 10 and drive south three-fourths of a mile to the club on the right.

Course description: This is a well-maintained, challenging course that offers narrow fairways, trees, bunkers, small greens and some water. It's set among numerous condominiums.

41-555 Woodhaven Dr. East
Palm Desert, CA 92260

Pro shop   (619) 345-7513
Clubhouse (619) 345-7636

- ■ driving range
- ■ practice greens
- ■ power carts
- □ pull carts
- ■ golf club rental
- ■ locker rooms
- ■ showers
- □ executive course
- □ accommodations
- ■ food and beverages
- ■ clubhouse

Mark Range
Professional

Jim Holub
Superintendent

PALM DESERT COUNTRY CLUB

William Park Bell

77-200 California Drive
Palm Desert, CA 92260

Pro shop   (619) 345-2525

- ■ driving range
- ■ practice greens
- ■ power carts
- ■ pull carts
- ■ golf club rental
- ■ locker rooms
- ■ showers
- ■ executive course
- ☐ accommodations
- ■ food and beverages
- ■ clubhouse

Nancy Little
Professional

Larry Dean Holt
Superintendent

Course information: This semi-private course has 27 holes and par is 72 for 18 holes.

The First and Second Nine is 6,678 yards and rated 70.8 from the championship tees, and 6,375 yards and rated 69.5 from the regular tees. The slope ratings are 117 championship and 111 regular. Women's tees are 5,899 yards and rated 72.5 from the forward tees. The slope rating is 117.

The First and Third Nine is 5,435 yards and rated 65.0 from the championship tees, and 5,288 yards and rated 63.8 from the regular tees. The slope ratings are 99 championship and 94 regular. Women's tees are 4,987 yards from the forward tees.

The Second and Third Nine is 5,329 yards and rated 64.6 from the championship tees, and 5,257 yards and rated 63.6 from the regular tees. The slope ratings are 98 championship and 94 regular. Women's tees are 4,914 yards from the forward tees.

Play policy and fees: Outside play is accepted. Hotel guests welcome. Green fees are $10 for the nine-hole course, and $45 weekdays and $50 weekends for 18 holes. Carts are included. Reservations are recommended three days in advance. This course is available for outside tournaments. The course closes in October.

Location: Take the Washington Street exit off Interstate 10 and turn right and drive 1.5 miles to Avenue of the Stars. Turn right and merge into California Drive and continue one mile to the club entrance.

Course description: These are mature courses designed by Billy Bell. The wide, tree-lined fairways are well laid out and challenging.

SOUTHERN 17

THE OASIS COUNTRY CLUB

Course information: This semi-private course has 18 holes and par is 60. The course is short at 3,617 yards and rated 54.0 from the championship tees, and 3,201 yards and rated 51.5 from the regular tees. The slope ratings are 90 championship and 84 regular. Women's tees are 3,201 yards and rated 57.6 from the championship tees, and 2,800 yards and rated 52.1 from the forward tees. The slope rating is 89 championship.

Play policy and fees: Outside play is accepted. Green fees are $39 weekdays and $45 weekends. Carts are included. Reservations are recommended. This course is available for outside tournaments. The course is closed in October. During the summer months the pro shop closes at 2 p.m.

Location: Take the Washington Street exit off Interstate 10 and drive south to Avenue 42. Turn right and drive one mile to the club.

Course description: This is a fun and challenging executive course with some of the finest greens to be found in the desert. There are 22 lakes guarding six par-4s and 12 par-3s. Good luck.

42-330 Casbah
Palm Desert, CA 92260

Pro shop   (619) 345-2715
Clubhouse (619) 345-5661

- ■ driving range
- ■ practice greens
- ■ power carts
- ■ pull carts
- ■ golf club rental
- □ locker rooms
- □ showers
- ■ executive course
- □ accommodations
- ■ food and beverages
- ■ clubhouse

Daryl Boone
Manager/Director of Golf

Les Holt
Superintendent

BERMUDA DUNES
COUNTRY CLUB

Course information: This private course has 27 holes and par is 72 for each 18-hole combinations.

The One and Two Course is 6,927 yards and rated 73.5 from the championship tees, and 6,542 yards and rated 70.8 from the regular tees. The slope ratings are 126 championship and 118 regular. Women's tees are 6,081 yards and rated 74.4. The slope rating is 123.

The One and Three Course is 6,716 yards and rated 72.2 from the championship tees, and 6,360 yards and rated 69.8 from the regular tees. The slope ratings are 123 championship and 115 regular. Women's tees are 5,857 yards and rated 73.1. The slope rating is 120.

The Two and Three Course is 6,749 yards and rated 72.4 from the championship tees, and 6,434 yards and rated 70.1 from the regular tees. The slope ratings are 124 championship and 116 regular. Women's tees are 6,016 yards and rated 74.3. The slope rating is 124.

Play policy and fees: Members and guests only. Guest fees are $50 summer season and $65 during the winter. Carts are $24. This course closes at noon on Mondays and 2 p.m. other days during the summer. It is closed in October.

Location: Take the Washington Street exit off Interstate 10 and drive south to Avenue 42. Turn left and drive one mile to the club.

Course description: This is not a typical desert course. It offers rolling hills with an assortment of trees guarding the fairways. There is some water. You can expect a lot of variation from hole to hole.

42-360 Adams Street
Bermuda Dunes, CA 92201

Pro shop   (619) 345-2232
Clubhouse (619) 345-2771

- ■ driving range
- ■ practice greens
- ■ power carts
- □ pull carts
- □ golf club rental
- □ locker rooms
- □ showers
- □ executive course
- □ accommodations
- ■ food and beverages
- ■ clubhouse

Bill Ogden
Director of Golf

Ron Hostick
Superintendent

SOUTHERN 17

MAP ON PAGE 496   533

INDIAN SPRINGS COUNTRY CLUB

Course information: This public course has 18 holes and par is 72. The course is 6,438 yards and rated 69.5 from the championship tees, and 6,223 yards and rated 68.5 from the regular tees. The slope ratings are 109 championship and 104 regular. Women's tees are 6,023 yards and rated 72.4 from the forward tees. The slope rating is 113.

Play policy and fees: Green fees are $30 weekdays and $35 weekends. Carts are included. Reservations are recommended. This course is available for outside tournaments. The course is closed during the summer season.

Location: Take the Jefferson Street exit off Interstate 10 and drive south on Jefferson for about a mile to the course entrance on the left.

Course description: This older course has some trees and a few bunkers. There is a lot of sand off the fairway.

46-080 Jefferson Street
La Quinta, CA 92253

Pro shop   (619) 347-0651
Clubhouse (619) 347-8583

■ driving range
■ practice greens
■ power carts
□ pull carts
■ golf club rental
□ locker rooms
□ showers
□ executive course
□ accommodations
■ food and beverages
■ clubhouse

Bette Pardo
Director of Golf

Ben Gonzalez
Superintendent

PALM ROYALE COUNTRY CLUB

1985
Ted Robinson

Course information: This public course has 18 holes and par is 54. The course is 2,118 yards and rated 54.0 from the regular tees. Women's tees are 1,861. The rating was unavailable.

Play policy and fees: Green fees are $12 any day during the summer, and $19.50 before 3 p.m. and $15 after 3 p.m. during the winter season.

Location: Take Interstate 10 and exit at Washington Street in La Quinta. Follow Washington to the club.

Course description: This is a short par-3 course with water on nine holes.

78-259 Indigo Drive
La Quinta, CA 92253

Pro shop   (619) 345-9701
Clubhouse (619) 345-9703

□ driving range
□ practice greens
□ power carts
■ pull carts
■ golf club rental
■ locker rooms
■ showers
□ executive course
□ accommodations
■ food and beverages
■ clubhouse

Tom Marcuzzo
Professional

LA QUINTA COUNTRY CLUB

1959
Larry Hughes

Course information: This private course has 18 holes and par is 72. The course is 6,837 yards and rated 73.8 from the championship tees, and 6,533 yards and rated 72.0 from the regular tees. The slope ratings are 133 championship and 129 regular. Women's tees are 6,136 yards and rated 74.5. The slope rating is 122.

Play policy and fees: Members and guests only. Guests must be accompanied by members at time of play. Guest fee is $50. Carts are $20. The course is closed in October.

Location: Take the Washington Street exit off Interstate 10 and drive south for six miles to Avenue 50 and turn right. Drive one mile to the club on the right.

Course description: Larry Hughes designed this mature course. It has tree-lined fairways, lakes, bunkers and undulating greens. The emphasis is on driving accuracy.

PO Box 99
La Quinta, CA 92253

77-750 Avenue 50
La Quinta, CA 92253

Pro shop   (619) 564-4151

- ■ driving range
- ■ practice greens
- ■ power carts
- □ pull carts
- □ golf club rental
- ■ locker rooms
- ■ showers
- □ executive course
- □ accommodations
- ■ food and beverages
- ■ clubhouse

Jeff Jackson
Professional

William Baker
Superintendent

INDIO GOLF COURSE

Course information: This public course has 18 holes and par is 54. The course is 3,004 yards and rated 49.1 from the regular tees. The slope rating is 71. Women's tees are 2,662 yards and unrated.

Play policy and fees: Green fees are $8 winter and $7 summer for 18 holes. Carts are $8 for 18 holes. Junior rate is $2 for nine holes. Reservations are recommended weekend mornings only. The course closes at 6 p.m. weekends.

Location: Take the Jackson Street exit off Interstate 10 and drive north to Avenue 42 and turn right.

Course description: This is a great little course. It is one of the longest par-3 courses in the country. The holes range from 110 to 240 yards, so bring your irons. There is one lake that intersects three holes, or four, depending on your shot. The course is night-lighted and the last weekday tee time is 7:30 p.m. for 18 holes.

PO Box X
Indio, CA 92202

83-040 Avenue 42
Indio, CA 92202

Pro shop   (619) 347-9156

- ■ driving range
- ■ practice greens
- ■ power carts
- ■ pull carts
- ■ golf club rental
- □ locker rooms
- □ showers
- □ executive course
- □ accommodations
- ■ food and beverages
- ■ clubhouse

Scott Daniels
Professional

SOUTHERN 17

INDIAN PALMS
COUNTRY CLUB

Course information: This semi-private course has 27 holes and par is 72 on each of the 18-hole combinations.

The Indian/Mountain Course is 6,807 yards and rated 72.0 from the championship tees, and 6,403 yards and rated 70.0 from the regular tees. The slope rating is 119. Women's tees are 5,858 yards and rated 72.4. The slope rating is 119.

The Mountain/Royal Course is 6,749 yards and rated 70.4 from the championship tees, and 6,284 yards and rated 69.5 from the regular tees. The slope rating is 115. Women's tees are 5,622 yards and rated 70.0. The slope rating is 116.

The Royal/Indian Course is 6,766 yards and rated 70.1 from the championship tees, and 6,279 yards and rated 69.4 from the regular tees. The slope rating is 115. Women's tees are 5,547 yards and rated 70.0. The slope rating is 116.

48-630 Monroe Street
Indio, CA 92201

Pro shop   (619) 347-2326
Clubhouse (619) 347-0941

- ■ driving range
- ■ practice greens
- ■ power carts
- □ pull carts
- ■ golf club rental
- ■ locker rooms
- □ showers
- □ executive course
- ■ accommodations
- ■ food and beverages
- ■ clubhouse

Homer Smith
Director of Golf

Toby Skeen
Superintendent

Play policy and fees: Outside play is accepted. Green fees are $40 weekdays and $45 weekends during the winter season, and $30 weekdays and $35 weekends during the summer. There is a summer twilight rate of $25 any day after 1 p.m. Carts are included. Reservations are recommended.

Location: Take the Monroe Street/Central Indio exit off Interstate 10 and drive south on Monroe for 2.5 miles to the club entrance.

Course description: The original nine-hole course, called Indian Palms, was built in 1948 by world famous female aviatrix Jackie Cochran. It was built upon a ranch that once served as a retreat for the rich and famous of the 1940s and 1950s. Dwight Eisenhower wrote his memoirs here. The Mountain and the Royal nines were built around 1980. The Royal has eight holes on which water comes into play. All the courses have trees and natural growth along gently rolling terrain.

PGA WEST
NICKLAUS RESORT

1987
Jack Nicklaus

56-150 PGA Boulevard
La Quinta, CA 92253

Pro shop   (619) 564-7170
Clubhouse (619) 564-7429

- ■ driving range
- ■ practice greens
- ■ power carts
- □ pull carts
- ■ golf club rental
- ■ locker rooms
- ■ showers
- □ executive course
- □ accommodations
- ■ food and beverages
- ■ clubhouse

Course information: This semi-private course has 18 holes and par is 72. The course is 7,126 yards and rated 75.5 from the tournament tees, 6,541 yards and rated 72.0 from the championship tees, and 6,001 yards and rated 69.2 from the regular tees. The slope ratings are 138 tournament, 129 championship and 122 regular. Women's tees are 5,043 yards and rated 69.0. The slope rating is 116.

Play policy and fees: Outside play is accepted. Green fees June 1 through September 30 are $75. Carts are included. Reservations are recommended one day in advance. This course is available for outside tournaments.

Location: Take the Indio Boulevard/Jefferson Street exit off Interstate 10 and drive south to the end of Jefferson Street.

Course description: If you want to test your golf skills, this is the place. It is a long, challenging course designed by Jack Nicklaus. It has lots of mounds, bunkers and water. There are sharp drops off the fairway.

Steve Walser
Director of Golf

Jeff Walser
Professional

Scott Mendenhall
Superintendent

PGA WEST
NICKLAUS PRIVATE

1987
Jack Nicklaus

55-955 PGA Boulevard
La Quinta, CA 92253

Pro shop   (619) 564-7100
Clubhouse (619) 564-7429

- ■ driving range
- ■ practice greens
- ■ power carts
- □ pull carts
- ■ golf club rental
- ■ locker rooms
- ■ showers
- □ executive course
- □ accommodations
- ■ food and beverages
- ■ clubhouse

Course information: This private course has 18 holes and par is 72. The course is 6,933 yards and rated 75.1 from the tournament tees, 6,418 yards and rated 71.8 from the championship tees, and 5,709 yards and rated 67.9 from the regular tees. The slope ratings are 142 tournament, 132 championship and 119 regular. Women's tees are 5,233 yards and rated 67.8. The slope rating is 116.

Play policy and fees: Members and guests only. Guests must be accompanied by members at time of play.

Location: Take the Indio Boulevard/Jefferson Street exit off Interstate 10 or Highway 111 and drive south to the end of Jefferson Street to PGA Boulevard.

Course description: This is a very unique course with flowers, tall desert grasses and water off the fairways. There are huge desert bunkers throughout the course. You may need a dune buggy to get in and out of these traps. Many fairways are defined with large mounds of grass.

Steve Walser
Director of Golf

Steve Bruton
Superintendent

SOUTHERN 17

PGA WEST—THE TPC STADIUM GOLF COURSE

1986
Pete Dye

56-150 PGA Boulevard
La Quinta, CA 92253

Information (619) 564-7170

- ■ driving range
- ■ practice greens
- ■ power carts
- ☐ pull carts
- ■ golf club rental
- ■ locker rooms
- ■ showers
- ☐ executive course
- ■ accommodations
- ■ food and beverages
- ■ clubhouse

Jeff Walser
Professional

Steve Walser
Director of Golf

Scott Mendenhall
Superintendent

Course information: This semi-private course has 18 holes and par is 72. The course is 7,265 yards and rated 77.3 from the tournament tees, 6,836 yards and rated 74.4 from the championship tees, and 6,331 yards and rated 71.2 from the regular tees. The slope ratings are 151 tournament, 139 championship and 130 regular. Women's tees are 5,675 yards and rated 72.3 from the championship tees, and 5,087 yards and rated 69.0 from the forward tees. The slope ratings are 126 championship and 119 forward.

Play policy and fees: Outside play is accepted. Green fees are $85. Carts and range balls are included. Reservations are recommended. Call Tee Time Central at (619) 564-6666 for reservations from May 31 to October 31. Men must wear collared shirts on the golf course. No blue jeans are allowed.

Location: Take the Indio Boulevard/Jefferson Street exit off Interstate 10 or Highway 111 and drive south to the end of Jefferson Street to PGA Boulevard. Continue on PGA Boulevard to the Resort Golf House.

Course description: This course opened in 1986 and immediately made its place in golf lore. It is packed with pot bunkers, sand, water and sidehill lies. Large, undulating greens with several tiers make putting a chore. Among the course highlights is a 19-foot-deep, greenside bunker that flanks the par-5 16th hole. The annual Skins Game has been played here since 1986. Lee Trevino holed out an eagle on number seven during the 1986 Skins Game and followed that with a hole-in-one on number 17 in 1987. The 1987 Bob Hope Chrysler Classic was held here. Former House Speaker Thomas "Tip" O'Neill made a spectacle of himself when he could not recover from the 19-foot bunker at number 16. The course is considered one of the 100 greatest in the world.

PGA WEST
ARNOLD PALMER COURSE

1986
Arnold Palmer

Course information: This private course has 18 holes and par is 72. The course is 6,894 yards and rated 73.7 from the tournament tees, 6,334 yards and rated 70.7 from the championship tees, and 5,749 yards and rated 68.0 from the regular tees. The slope ratings are 133 tournament, 125 championship and 117 regular. Women's tees are 5,530 yards and rated 68.5 from the forward tees. The slope rating is 113.

Play policy and fees: Members and guests only. Guests must be accompanied by members at time of play.

Location: Take the Indio Boulevard/Jefferson Street exit off Interstate 10 or Highway 111 and drive south to the end of Jefferson Street to PGA Boulevard.

Course description: This demanding course is a tough track. It plays as long as any of the courses in this group, except perhaps the TPC Stadium Course. Bunkers distinguish the front nine, and hills the back nine. The last four holes are tight against the Santa Rosa Mountains. The tees are elevated above the large greens, just the way Arnie likes them. The greens are backed by boulders.

55-955 PGA Boulevard
La Quinta, CA 92253

Pro shop   (619) 564-7100
Clubhouse (619) 564-7429

■ driving range
■ practice greens
■ power carts
□ pull carts
■ golf club rental
■ locker rooms
□ showers
□ executive course
□ accommodations
■ food and beverages
■ clubhouse

Steve Walser
Director of Golf

Dave Bergstrom
Superintendent

SOUTHERN 17

MAP I8
(1 COURSE)

PAGES.. 540-541

SO-CAL MAP .....see page 376
adjoining maps
NORTH ....no map
EAST ....no map
SOUTH (J8) ....see page 580
WEST (I7) ....see page 496

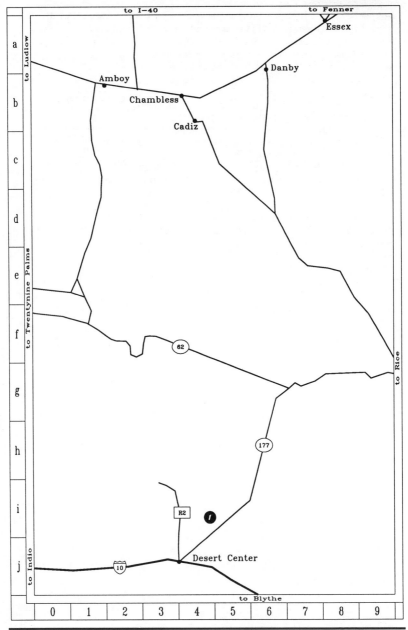

to I-40

to Fenner

Essex

a

to Ludlow

Danby

Amboy

b

Chambless

Cadiz

c

d

e

to Twentynine Palms

f

62

g

h

177

i

R2

1

to Indio

j

10

Desert Center

to Blythe

| 0 | 1 | 2 | 3 | 4 | 5 | 6 | 7 | 8 | 9 |

to Rice

LAKE TAMARISK GOLF CLUB

Course information: This public course has nine holes. Par is 70 for 18 holes. The course is 5,932 yards and rated 67.1 from the regular tees for 18 holes. The slope rating is 100. Women's tees are 5,606 yards and rated 69.9. The slope rating is 104.

Play policy and fees: Green fees are $12 for 18 holes. Carts are $9 for nine holes and $12 for 18 holes. Reservations are recommended January through April.

Location: Travel east from Indio on Interstate 10 for about 50 miles and take the Desert Center Road exit north. Bear left onto Kaiser Road and drive 1.5 miles to the entrance.

Course description: This is literally an oasis in the middle of the desert. Refreshing lakes line the course and palm trees and oleanders line the fairways. The course is fairly level and the tees and greens are elevated.

PO Box 315
Desert Center, CA 92239

26-251 Parkview Drive
Desert Center, CA 92239

Pro shop   (619) 227-3203

- ■ driving range
- ■ practice greens
- ■ power carts
- ■ pull carts
- ■ golf club rental
- ☐ locker rooms
- ■ showers
- ☐ executive course
- ☐ accommodations
- ☐ food and beverages
- ■ clubhouse

Steve Jones
Manager

SOUTHERN 18

MAP J5
(5 COURSES)

PAGES.. 542-545

SO-CAL MAP .....see page 376
adjoining maps
NORTH (I5).........see page 412
EAST (J6) ....see page 546
SOUTH..........................no map
WEST ....no map

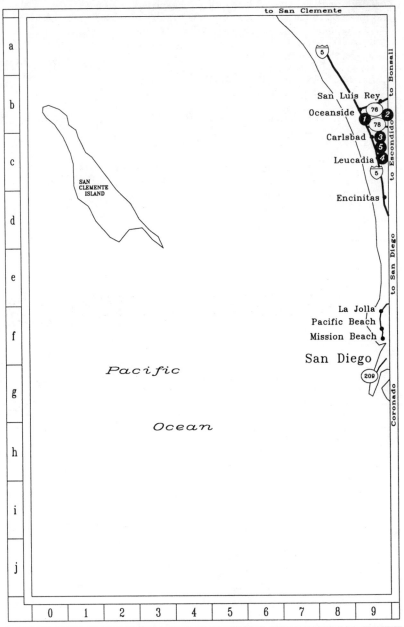

to San Clemente

5

to Bonsall

San Luis Rey

Oceanside 76 2
1 78

Carlsbad 3
5

Leucadia 4
5

Encinitas

to Escondido

to San Diego

La Jolla
Pacific Beach
Mission Beach

San Diego

209

Coronado

SAN
CLEMENTE
ISLAND

Pacific

Ocean

| 0 | 1 | 2 | 3 | 4 | 5 | 6 | 7 | 8 | 9 |

CENTER CITY GOLF COURSE

Course information: This public course has nine holes. Par is 72 for 18 holes. The course is 3,020 yards and unrated from the championship tees, and 2,724 yards and rated 34.6 from the regular tees. The slope rating is 104 regular (18 holes). Women's tees are 2,450 yards and rated 33.3. There is no slope rating.

Play policy and fees: Green fees are $5 for nine holes and $9 for 18 holes.

Location: In Oceanside, exit off Interstate 5 on Oceanside Boulevard. Drive inland. Stay in the left lane and turn left on Greenbrier. The course is one-quarter mile from the freeway.

Course description: This is a regulation nine-hole course with long and open fairways.

PO Box 1088
Oceanside, CA 92054

2323 Greenbrier Street
Oceanside, CA 92054

Pro shop   (619) 433-8590

- ■ driving range
- ■ practice greens
- ■ power carts
- ■ pull carts
- ■ golf club rental
- □ locker rooms
- □ showers
- □ executive course
- □ accommodations
- ■ food and beverages
- □ clubhouse

Ludwig Keehn
Professional

EL CAMINO COUNTRY CLUB

Course information: This private course has 18 holes and par is 72. The course is 6,774 yards and rated 72.6 from the championship tees, and 6,439 yards and rated 70.2 from the regular tees. The slope ratings are: 125 championship and 115 regular. Women's tees are 5,802 yards and rated 73.5. The slope rating is 120.

Play policy and fees: Reciprocal play is accepted with members of other private clubs. Hotel guests welcome. Green fees are $30 weekdays and $35 weekends. Carts are $19. Reservations are recommended.

Location: Take Interstate 5 to the Highway 78 exit in Oceanside, drive to the El Camino Real exit north and cross the overpass to Vista Way and turn right. Drive a one-quarter mile to the club.

Course description: This course offers a flat layout with plenty of trees and narrow fairways that offer little trouble. The course plays long, so be prepared.

3202 Vista Way
Oceanside, CA 92056

Clubhouse (619) 757-2100
Pro shop   (619) 757-0321

- □ driving range
- ■ practice greens
- ■ power carts
- ■ pull carts
- ■ golf club rental
- ■ locker rooms
- ■ showers
- □ executive course
- ■ accommodations
- ■ food and beverages
- ■ clubhouse

Tommy Jackson
Professional

Chris Bridge
Superintendent

SOUTHERN J5

MAP ON PAGE 542

543

LA COSTA RESORT AND SPA

Dick Wilson
Joe Lee

Course information: This private facility has two 18-hole courses and par is 72 on both.

Costa del Mar Road
Carlsbad, CA 92009

Pro shop   (619) 438-9111

The North Course is 6,987 yards and rated 74.8 from the tournament tees, 6,608 yards and rated 72.1 from the championship tees, and 6,269 yards and rated 69.9 from the regular tees. The slope ratings are 137 tournament, 128 championship and 121 regular. Women's tees are 5,939 yards and rated 74.7. The slope rating is 127.

- driving range
- practice greens
- power carts
- pull carts
- golf club rental
- locker rooms
- showers
- executive course
- accommodations
- food and beverages
- clubhouse

The South Course is 6,894 yards and rated 74.4 from the tournament tees, 6,524 yards and rated 72.0 from the championship tees, and 6,198 yards and rated 69.8 from the regular tees. The slope ratings are 138 tournament, 129 championship and 121 regular. Women's tees are 5,612 yards and rated 72.1. The slope rating is 123.

John Spiroplaus
Professional

Harold Vaubel
Superintendent

Play policy and fees: Members and guests only. Hotel guests welcome. Green fees are $65. Carts are $30. Reservations are required.

Location: Travel 20 miles north of San Diego on Interstate 5 to the La Costa Avenue exit east. Drive 1.5 miles to El Camino Real and turn left to the club.

Course description: The North Course is wide open and rolling while the South Course is tighter and more demanding. This is the site of the PGA Tour's Tournament of Champions. Parts of both courses are used to create the tournament layout.

RANCHO CARLSBAD GOLF COURSE

Course information: This public executive course has 18 holes and par is 56. The course is 2,068 yards and rated 54.0 from the regular tees.

5200 El Camino Real
Carlsbad, CA 92008

Pro shop   (619) 438-1772
              (619) 438-9926

Play policy and fees: Green fees are $4.50 for nine holes and $8 for 18 holes any day before 2 p.m. After 2 p.m. the green fee is $4.50 for nine or 18 holes.

Location: From Interstate 5, take Highway 78 east to El Camino Real (County Road S-11). Then drive south to Rancho Carlsbad Drive and turn left to the course.

- driving range
- practice greens
- power carts
- pull carts
- golf club rental
- locker rooms
- showers
- executive course
- accommodations
- food and beverages
- clubhouse

Course description: This is a well-maintained course with flat terrain. It's challenging for any caliber golfer. It's a tight, tree-lined course. If you hit a bad shot it costs, but a good shot is rewarded. The greens tend to be fast and for this reason they can be difficult to putt.

Craig Hunt
Professional

FOUR SEASONS RESORT AVIARA

1991
Arnold Palmer

Course information: This resort course has 18 holes. Par is 72. The course is 7,007 yards and rated 74.4 from the tournament tees, 6,591 yards and rated 71.6 from the championship tees, and 6,054 yards and rated 68.4 from the regular tees. The slope ratings are 131 tournament, 123 championship and 115 regular. Women's tees are 5,007 yards and are in the process of being rated.

Play policy and fees: Outside play is accepted. Green fees are $65 weekdays and $80 weekends, cart included. Reservations are recommended seven days in advance. This course is available for tournaments.

Location: From Interstate 5, take Poinsettia Avenue exit east to Batiquitos Drive. Drive south to the club.

Course description: This is a challenging new layout bordered by the Batiquitos Lagoon. It is sculpted around natural topography and there are several water features.

7447 Batiquitos Drive
Carlsbad, CA 92009

Pro shop   (619) 929-0077

- ■ driving range
- ■ practice greens
- ■ power carts
- □ pull carts
- ■ golf club rental
- ■ locker rooms
- ■ showers
- □ executive course
- □ accommodations
- ■ food and beverages
- ■ clubhouse

Jim Bellington
Director of Golf

Bill Crist
Professional

Dick Rudolph
Superintendent

SOUTHERN J5

MAP J6
(53 COURSES)

PAGES.. 546-577

SO-CAL MAP .....see page 376
adjoining maps
NORTH (I6).........see page 472
EAST (J7) ....see page 578
SOUTH.........................no map
WEST (J5) ....see page 542

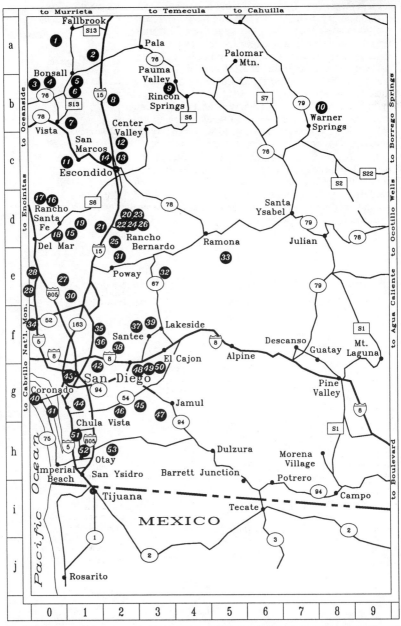

PALA MESA RESORT

1964
Dick Rossen

2001 South Highway 395
Fallbrook, CA 92028

Pro shop   (619) 728-5881

- ■ driving range
- ■ practice greens
- ■ power carts
- □ pull carts
- ■ golf club rental
- □ locker rooms
- □ showers
- □ executive course
- ■ accommodations
- ■ food and beverages
- ■ clubhouse

Chris Starkjohann
Professional

Dale Hahn
Superintendent

Course information: This resort course has 18 holes and par is 72. The course is 6,461 yards and rated 72.0 from the championship tees, and 6,172 yards and rated 70.1 from the regular tees. The slope ratings are 131 championship and 125 regular. Women's tees are 5,814 yards and rated 74.5. The slope rating is 128 regular.

Play policy and fees: Outside play is accepted. Hotel guests welcome. Green fees are $45 Mondays through Thursdays, and $60 Fridays and weekends. Carts are included. Reservations are recommended one week in advance.

Location: From San Diego, drive north on Interstate 15 to the Highway 76. Turn left and drive to Old Highway 395. Turn right and drive two miles to the course.

Course description: This scenic, mature course rolls through oak woodlands with tight fairways and fast greens. The course record is 62, set by host pro Chris Starkjohann in 1988.

FALLBROOK GOLF CLUB

PO Box 746
Fallbrook, CA 92028

2757 Gird Road
Fallbrook, CA 92028

Pro shop   (619) 728-8334

- ■ driving range
- ■ practice greens
- ■ power carts
- ■ pull carts
- □ golf club rental
- □ locker rooms
- □ showers
- □ executive course
- □ accommodations
- ■ food and beverages
- ■ clubhouse

Barry McDonnell
Professional

Blair Cooke
General Manager

Ken Holloway
Superintendent

SOUTHERN J6

Course information: This public course has 18 holes and par is 72. The course is 6,223 yards and rated 69.8 from the regular tees. The slope rating is 117. Women's tees are 5,597 yards and rated 69.8. The slope rating is 119.

Play policy and fees: Green fees are $18 weekdays and $22 weekends. Carts are $16. Reservations are recommended 10 days in advance. This course is available for outside tournaments.

Location: From Interstate 15, take Highway 76 west two miles to Gird Road, drive north two miles to the course.

Course description: This course features greens tightly guarded by sand. Shot-makers will score well here, especially those with a good short game.

MARINE MEMORIAL GOLF COURSE

Course information: This military course has 18 holes and par is 72. The course is 6,770 yards and rated 71.5 from the championship tees, and 6,379 yards and rated 69.5 from the regular tees. The slope ratings are 124 championship and 112 regular. Women's tees are 5,570 yards and rated 71.0. The slope rating is 113.

Play policy and fees: Military personnel and guests only. Fees vary according to military personnel status.

Location: From Highway 76 east of Oceanside, travel north on Douglas Drive 1.25 miles. Turn right on North River Road and drive 3.5 miles to the San Luis Rey entrance. From the Camp Pendleton main gate go one mile and turn left at the course sign.

Course description: This is a relatively level course set in a peaceful valley. Some holes are strategically placed along the hills and slopes of the fairway. The fairways are tight and sand protects the greens.

PO Box 486
San Luis Rey, CA 92068

Marine Memorial Course
Camp Pendleton, CA 92055

Pro shop   (619) 725-4756
Clubhouse   (619) 725-4704

- ■ driving range
- ■ practice greens
- ■ power carts
- ■ pull carts
- ■ golf club rental
- ☐ locker rooms
- ☐ showers
- ☐ executive course
- ☐ accommodations
- ■ food and beverages
- ■ clubhouse

Doug Blanchard
Professional

OCEANSIDE MUNICIPAL GOLF COURSE

Course information: This public course has 18 holes and par is 72. The course is 6,403 yards and rated 70.8 from the championship tees, and 6,043 yards and rated 68.7 from the regular tees. The slope ratings are 118 championship and 109 regular. Women's tees are 5,398 yards and rated 70.6. The slope rating is 116.

Play policy and fees: Green fees are $10 weekdays and $15 weekends. Carts are $16. Reservations are recommended. This course is available for outside tournaments.

Location: From Interstate 15 travel west on Highway 76 and turn right on Douglas Drive and go two miles to the course.

Course description: This course has level terrain, but water comes into play on 13 holes. The greens are fairly large. Mature trees line the fairways. The course offers a practice sand bunker for those in need.

825 Douglas Drive
Oceanside, CA 92056

Pro shop   (619) 433-1360

- ■ driving range
- ■ practice greens
- ■ power carts
- ■ pull carts
- ■ golf club rental
- ☐ locker rooms
- ☐ showers
- ☐ executive course
- ☐ accommodations
- ■ food and beverages
- ■ clubhouse

Fred Wood
Professional

Bill Houlihan
Superintendent

SAN LUIS REY DOWNS GOLF AND COUNTRY CLUB

Course information: This resort course has 18 holes and par is 72. The course is 6,650 yards and rated 72.6 from the championship tees, and 6,365 yards and rated 70.5 from the regular tees. The slope ratings are 128 championship and 122 regular. Women's tees are 5,493 yards and rated 71.4. The slope rating is 118.

Play policy and fees: Outside play is accepted. Hotel guests are welcome. Green fees are $28 weekdays and $35 weekends. Carts included. Reservations are recommended. This course is available for outside tournaments.

Location: From Interstate I5, travel 4.5 miles west on Highway 76 to West Lilac Road in the town of Bonsall. Turn left over the bridge and bear left at the sign for San Luis Rey Downs. Continue for three-fourths of a mile to the golf resort.

Course description: The San Luis Rey River snakes through this level course. There are narrow fairways, several lakes and lots of trees.

31474 Golf Club Drive
Bonsall, CA 92003

Pro shop   (619) 758-9699
Clubhouse: (619) 758-3762

- ■ driving range
- ■ practice greens
- ■ power carts
- ■ pull carts
- ■ golf club rental
- □ locker rooms
- □ showers
- □ executive course
- ■ accommodations
- ■ food and beverages
- ■ clubhouse

Pinky Stevenson
Professional

Joe Ponce
Superintendent

VISTA VALLEY COUNTRY CLUB

1 9 7 8
Ted Robinson

Course information: This private course has 18 holes and par is 71. The course is 6,411 yards and rated 71.3 from the championship tees, and 6,090 yards and rated 69.8 from the regular tees. The slope ratings are 128 championship and 122 regular. Women's tees are 5,630 yards and rated 72.4. The slope is 123.

Play policy and fees: Reciprocal play is accepted with members of other private clubs. Members and guests only. Guest fees are $40 with a member and $60 without a member. Carts and range balls are included. Reservations are recommended.

Location: From Interstate 15 take the Gopher Canyon Road exit and travel west for 2.5 miles to Vista Valley Drive. Turn left and drive one-half mile to the club.

Course description: This course is nestled in a valley with a creek meandering through the hills. There are scenic mountain views. This is a good, challenging golf course for the low- and high-handicapper.

29354 Vista Valley Drive
Vista, CA 92084

Pro shop   (619)758-5275
Clubhouse (619) 758-2800

- ■ driving range
- ■ practice greens
- ■ power carts
- ■ pull carts
- □ golf club rental
- ■ locker rooms
- ■ showers
- □ executive course
- □ accommodations
- ■ food and beverages
- ■ clubhouse

Phillip Machamer
Professional

Ronald Nolf
Superintendent

SOUTHERN J6

SHADOW RIDGE COUNTRY CLUB

1981
Ted Robinson

1980 Gateway Drive
Vista, CA 92083

Pro shop   (619) 727-7706
Clubhouse: (619) 727-7700

Course information: This private course has 18 holes and par is 72. The course is 6,859 yards and rated 73.3 from the championship tees, and 6,374 yards and rated 70.2 from the regular tees. The slope ratings are 128 championship and 118 regular. Women's tees are 5,355 yards and rated 73.3. The slope rating is 127.

Play policy and fees: Members and guests only. Green fees are $44 including cart.

Location: Travel north from San Diego on Interstate 5 or Interstate 15 to Highway 78. Take the Sycamore exit off Highway 78 and go south to Shadowridge Drive. Turn right and continue to Gateway Drive.

Course description: This is a rolling layout with eucalyptus-lined fairways, several picturesque lakes and a beautiful finishing hole with a stone-edged lake set in front of the green.

■ driving range
■ practice greens
■ power carts
□ pull carts
■ golf club rental
■ locker rooms
■ showers
□ executive course
□ accommodations
■ food and beverages
■ clubhouse

Hank George
Professional

Ed Mena
Superintendent

CASTLE CREEK COUNTRY CLUB

Route 2 Box 301
Escondido, CA 92026

8797 Circle "R" Drive
Escondido, CA 92026

Pro shop   (619) 749-2422
Clubhouse (619) 749-2877

Course information: This semi-private course has 18 holes and par is 72. The course is 6,254 yards and rated 70.4 from the championship tees, and 5,899 yards and rated 68.3 from the regular tees. The slope ratings are 124 championship and 117 regular. Women's tees are 5,476 yards and rated 70.3. The slope rating is 114.

Play policy and fees: Outside play is accepted. Green fees are $18 weekdays and $25 weekends. Carts are $20.

Location: From Interstate 15, take the Old Castle Road/Gopher Canyon Road exit and travel east. Turn left and drive one-half mile to the club.

Course description: Castle Creek meanders through this well-maintained course. The front nine is flat and the back nine is hilly. There are numerous trees lining the fairways.

□ driving range
■ practice greens
■ power carts
■ pull carts
■ golf club rental
■ locker rooms
■ showers
□ executive course
■ accommodations
■ food and beverages
■ clubhouse

John Urner
Professional

Henry Hashimoto
Superintendent

PAUMA VALLEY COUNTRY CLUB

Course 9
MAP J6 grid b3

Robert Trent Jones, Sr.

PO Box 206
Pauma Valley, CA 92061

Pauma Valley Drive
Pauma Valley, CA 92061

Pro shop   (619) 742-1230
Clubhouse (619) 742-3721

■ driving range
■ practice greens
■ power carts
□ pull carts
□ golf club rental
■ locker rooms
■ showers
□ executive course
□ accommodations
■ food and beverages
■ clubhouse

Bill Stutzer
Professional

Wayne Graf
Superintendent

Course information: This private course has 18 holes and par is 71. The course is 7,077 yards and rated 75.5 from the championship tees, and 6,468 yards and rated 71.4 from the regular tees. The slope ratings are 137 championship and 126 regular. Women's tees are 5,891 yards and rated 73.5. The slope rating is 122.

Play policy and fees: Members and guests only. Green fees are $50. Carts are $20.

Location: From Interstate 15 travel east on Highway 76 for 14 miles to the town of Pauma Valley. Turn right on Pauma Valley Drive and continue three-fourths of a mile to the club.

Course description: Pick your trap; they are everywhere. This is a difficult course with more than 120 bunkers and is considered a ball striker's course. It's an original Robert Trent Jones, Sr. layout and plays very long.

WARNER SPRINGS RANCH

Course 10
MAP J6 grid b8

1984
Ted Robinson

Box 10
Warner Springs, CA 92086

31652 Highway 79
Warner Springs, CA 92086

Pro shop   (619) 782-3555

■ driving range
■ practice greens
■ power carts
■ pull carts
□ golf club rental
■ locker rooms
■ showers
□ executive course
□ accommodations
■ food and beverages
■ clubhouse

Rex Pietz
Professional

David Waymire
Superintendent

Course information: This private course has 18 holes and par is 72. The course is 6,701 yards and rated 71.7 from the championship tees, and 6,252 yards and rated 69.1 from the regular tees. The slope ratings are 121 championship and 116 regular. Women's tees are 5,468 yards and rated 70.2. The slope rating is 119.

Play policy and fees: Reciprocal play is accepted with members of other clubs. Green fees are $35 weekdays and $45 weekends for reciprocators. Carts are included. Reservations are a must. This course is available for outside tournaments. Proper golf attire required.

Location: From Interstate 15 at Temecula, drive 38 miles south on Highway 79.

Course description: This mature course traverses rolling, desert-mountain terrain and is fairly open. Three lakes come into play.

SOUTHERN J6

LAKE SAN MARCOS COUNTRY CLUB

Course information: This resort course has 18 holes and par is 72. There is also an executive course. The course is 6,474 yards and rated 70.2 from the championship tees, and 6,280 yards and rated 69.2 from the regular tees. The slope ratings are 116 championship and 110 regular. Women's tees are 5,959 yards and rated 72.2. The slope rating is 117. The executive course is 2,700 yards. Women's tees are 2,226 yards.

Play policy and fees: Reciprocal play is accepted with members of other private clubs, otherwise members and guests only. Hotel guests welcome. Green fees are $40 for hotel guests and $45 for all others. Carts are included. Reservations are recommended. Greens fees for the executive course are $10 before 3 p.m. and $6 after 3 p.m. For juniors 17-and-under the green fee is $5.

Location: From Los Angeles, take Interstate 5 to Palomar Airport Road. Travel seven miles east to Rancho Santa Fe Road and turn right. Continue to Lake San Marcos. To reach the executive course, continue to Camino del Arroyo. Turn left to the course.

Course description: This is a well-maintained course that meanders through a housing development at Lake San Marcos. The narrow fairways and small greens make this a challenging course.

1750 San Pablo Drive
Lake San Marcos, CA 92069

Pro shop   (619) 744-1310
Executive   (619) 744-9092

- ■ driving range
- ■ practice greens
- ■ power carts
- ■ pull carts
- ■ golf club rental
- ☐ locker rooms
- ☐ showers
- ■ executive course
- ■ accommodations
- ■ food and beverages
- ■ clubhouse

Bob Hitzel
Professional

Ed Kelly
Superintendent

MEADOW LAKE COUNTRY CLUB

Course information: This semi-private course has 18 holes and par is 72. The course is 6,536 yards and rated 72.5 from the championship tees, and 6,327 yards and rated 71.0 from the regular tees. The slope ratings are 131 championship and 124 regular. Women's tees are 5,758 yards and rated 72.8. The slope rating is 123.

Play policy and fees: Outside play is accepted. Green fees are $32 weekdays and $36 weekends, including carts. Green fees without golf carts are $22 weekdays and $26 weekends. Reservations are recommended seven days in advance.

Location: Take the Mountain Meadows exit off Interstate 15 and travel east 1.5 miles to the club located on Meadow Glen Way.

Course description: This is a mountainous course with lots of doglegs. You will be making numerous blind shots. But, hey, that's what makes this course fun!

10333 Meadow Glen East
Escondido, CA 92026

Pro shop   (619) 749-1620
Clubhouse   (619) 749-0983

- ■ driving range
- ■ practice greens
- ■ power carts
- ☐ pull carts
- ■ golf club rental
- ■ locker rooms
- ☐ showers
- ☐ executive course
- ☐ accommodations
- ■ food and beverages
- ■ clubhouse

Jim Gilbert
Professional

Mike Shaw
Superintendent

LAWRENCE WELK RESORT

1986
David Rainville

Course information: This resort has two 18-hole courses. Par is 62 on the Fountain Executive Course and 54 on the par-3 Oaks Course.

The Fountain Executive Course is 4,002 yards and rated 57.3 from the championship tees, and 3,581 yards and rated 54.6 from the regular tees. The slope ratings are 95 championship and 89 regular. Women's tees are 3,099 yards and rated 58.1. The slope rating is 84.0.

The par-3 Oaks Course is 1,837 yards. Women's tees are 1,652 yards.

Play policy and fees: Outside play is accepted. Green fees are $28 weekdays and $32 weekends for the Fountain Executive Course, including cart. Twilight rate for the Fountains Executive Course is $20 after 2 p.m. summers, and 1 p.m. winters. Green fees are $12 any day for the Oaks Course. A cart is not required for the Oaks Course. Reservations are recommended. This course is available for outside tournaments.

8860 Lawrence Welk Drive
Escondido, CA 92026

Pro shop   (619) 749-3225

☐ driving range
■ practice greens
■ power carts
■ pull carts
■ golf club rental
☐ locker rooms
☐ showers
■ executive course
■ accommodations
■ food and beverages
■ clubhouse

Cachi Trejo
Professional

Jim Brown
Superintendent

Location: Travel 33 miles north of San Diego on Interstate 15 to the Mountain Meadow Road exit. Turn north on Champagne Boulevard and drive to the course entrance.

Course description: The Fountains Executive Course is short and well maintained with narrow fairways. The men's course record is 57, held by Jim Robbyn. The Oaks Course is a challenging par-3 with century-old California oak trees lining the fairway and undulating greens.

ESCONDIDO COUNTRY CLUB

Course information: This private course has 18 holes and par is 70. The course is 6,177 yards and rated 69.1 from the championship tees, and 5,925 yards and rated 67.7 from the regular tees. The slope ratings are 111 championship and 107 regular. Women's tees are 5,536 yards and rated 71.1. The slope rating is 116.

Play policy and fees: Members and guests only. Green fees are $30 weekdays and $40 weekends. Carts are $20.

Location: Take the Centre City Parkway off Interstate 15 two miles north of Escondido. Turn left on Country Club Lane and drive one mile to the club.

Course description: This course has level terrain with tight, eucalyptus-lined fairways. There are undulating greens and water comes into play on five holes.

1800 West Country Club Lane
Escondido, CA 92026

Pro shop   (619) 746-4212
Clubhouse (619) 743-3301

■ driving range
■ practice greens
■ power carts
☐ pull carts
■ golf club rental
■ locker rooms
■ showers
☐ executive course
☐ accommodations
■ food and beverages
■ clubhouse

Tom Sims
Professional

Jose Canedo
Senior Superintendent

SOUTHERN J6

HERITAGE HILLS COUNTRY CLUB

Course 15
MAP J6 grid d0

1991
Joseph Lee

6001 Camino Santa Fe
Rancho Santa Fe, CA 92067

Pro shop   (619) 759-5900

■ driving range
■ practice greens
■ power carts
□ pull carts
□ golf club rental
■ locker rooms
■ showers
□ executive course
□ accommodations
■ food and beverages
■ clubhouse

Jim Moher
Professional

David Major
Superintendent

Jim Robson
General Manager

Course information: This private course has 18 holes. Par is 72. The course is 6,950 yards from the tournament tees, and 6,508 yards from the championship tees, and 5,972 yards from the regular tees. Women's tees are 5,381 yards. The course is in the process of being rated.

Play policy and fees: Members and guests only. Reciprocal play is not accepted. Green fees were not available.

Location: Take the Via de la Valle exit off Interstate 5 and drive east to El Camino Real south. At San Dieguito Road, travel one mile and turn east. The course is about 600 yards east of the entrance to the Fairbanks Country Club.

Course description: This course opened in December, 1991. It features bent grass from tee to green and four lakes coming into play on four holes. The course is situated in a natural valley. There is a riparian of natural timbers and stands of old eucalyptus, plus new plantings. Last but not least, there are 80 bunkers with which to contend.

RANCHO SANTA FE GOLF CLUB

Course 16
MAP J6 grid d0

PO Box 598
Rancho Santa Fe, CA 92067

Via de la Cumbre
Rancho Santa Fe, CA 92067

Pro shop   (619) 756-3094
Clubhouse (619) 756-1174

■ driving range
■ practice greens
■ power carts
■ pull carts
■ golf club rental
■ locker rooms
■ showers
□ executive course
■ accommodations
■ food and beverages
■ clubhouse

Chuck Courtney
Professional

Tony Guerra
Superintendent

Course information: This private course has 18 holes and par is 72. The course is 6,797 yards and rated 73.0 from the championship tees, and 6,497 yards and rated 71.3 from the regular tees. The slope ratings are 132 championship and 126 regular. Women's tees are 5,950 yards and rated 73.8. The slope rating is 123.

Play policy and fees: Members and guests only. Hotel guests welcome. Current green fees were unavailable. Carts are $17 weekdays and $30 weekends. Reservations are recommended.

Location: Take Interstate 5 to Lomas Santa Fe Drive and travel east for four miles on Highway 8 to the inn. Turn left on Avenida de Acacias and drive one-half mile to Via de la Cumbre, then go left one-half mile to the club.

Course description: This course has some history. It was the original site of the Bing Crosby National Pro-Am and was the hangout of many Hollywood types during the 1940s and 50s. It has a rolling layout among mature trees with very little water.

LOMAS SANTA FE COUNTRY CLUB

Course information: This private course has 18 holes and par is 72. There is also an executive course. The main course is 6,558 yards and rated 71.2 from the championship tees, and 6,158 yards and rated 69.6 from the regular tees. The slope ratings are 127 championship and 119 regular. Women's tees are 5,796 and rated 72.7. The slope rating is 120. The executive course is 2,380 yards. Women's tees are 2,119 yards.

Play policy and fees: Members and guests only. Green fees are $30 weekdays and $40 weekends. Carts are $19. Executive green fees are $12 weekdays and $15 weekends for 18 holes. Carts are $14. Call for other special rates.

Location: Take the Lomas Santa Fe Drive exit off Interstate 5 and drive east one mile to the club. The executive course is on the north side.

Course description: This is a well-maintained course in a beautiful setting. The course offers rolling terrain with tight fairways.

PO Box 1007
Solana Beach, CA 92075

Lomas Santa Fe Drive
at Highland
Solana Beach, CA 92075

Pro shop   (619) 755-1547
Clubhouse   (619) 755-6768
Executive   (619) 755-0195

■ driving range
■ practice greens
■ power carts
■ pull carts
□ golf club rental
□ locker rooms
□ showers
■ executive course
□ accommodations
■ food and beverages
■ clubhouse

Robert Bellesi
Professional

Chris Lemke
Superintendent

FAIRBANKS RANCH COUNTRY CLUB

1984
Ted Robinson

Course information: This private course has 18 holes and par is 72. The course is 7,200 yards and rated 75.0 from the tournament tees, 6,922 yards and rated 73.4 from its championship tees, and 6,656 yards and rated 71.8 from the regular tees. The slope ratings are 135 tournament, and 132 championship and 123 regular. Women's tees are 5,724 yards and rated 73.9. The slope rating is 127.

Play policy and fees: Members and guests only.

Location: Take the Via de la Valle exit off Interstate 5 and drive east to El Camino Real south. At San Dieguito Road, travel one mile and turn east 1.5 miles.

Course description: Ted Robinson designed this challenging course, which bears his trademarks: The greens are surrounded by mounds and palm trees, and there is quite a bit of water.

PO Box 8055
Rancho Santa Fe, CA 92067

15150 San Dieguito Road
Rancho Santa Fe, CA 92067

Pro shop   (619) 259-8819
Clubhouse   (619) 259-8811

■ driving range
■ practice greens
■ power carts
□ pull carts
■ golf club rental
■ locker rooms
■ showers
□ executive course
□ accommodations
■ food and beverages
■ clubhouse

Richard "Tag" Merritt
Professional

Brian Darrock
Superintendent

SOUTHERN J6

WHISPERING PALMS
COUNTRY CLUB

Course information: This resort club has 27 holes. Par is 72 for East/South and 71 for the South/North and North East courses.

The South/North Course is 6,346 yards and rated 69.7 from the championship tees, and 6,051 yards and rated 67.9 from the regular tees. The slope ratings are 112 championship and 105 regular. Women's tees are 5,603 yards and rated 71.7. The slope rating is 117.

The East/South Course is 6,443 yards and rated 70.2 from the championship tees, and 6,131 yards and rated 68.3 from the regular tees. The slope ratings are 112 championship and 105 regular. Women's tees are 5,705 yards and rated 72.6. The slope rating is 120.

The North/East Course is 6,141 yards and rated 68.8 from the championship tees, and 5,860 yards and rated 67.0 from the regular tees. The slope ratings are 110 championship and 103 regular. Women's tees are 5,514 yards and rated 71.7. The slope rating is 117.

Play policy and fees: Outside play is accepted. Green fees are $23 weekdays and $28 weekends and holidays. Carts are $22. Reservations are recommended three days in advance. This course is available for outside tournaments.

Location: Take the Valley Parkway (S-6) off Interstate 15 in Escondido and drive 10 miles west and turn left at Concha de Golf.

Course description: This flat course is easy to walk, but the narrow fairways and long rough make it challenging. A river snakes through two of the nines.

PO Box 3209
Rancho Santa Fe, CA 92067

4000 Concha de Golf
Rancho Santa Fe, CA 92067

Pro shop   (619) 756-3255
Clubhouse (619) 756-2471

□ driving range
■ practice greens
■ power carts
■ pull carts
■ golf club rental
□ locker rooms
□ showers
□ executive course
■ accommodations
■ food and beverages
■ clubhouse

John Combs
Professional

Larry Jones
Superintendent

MIRAMAR MEMORIAL GOLF CLUB

Course information: This military course has 18 holes and par is 72. The course is 6,678 yards and rated 72.1 from the championship tees, and 6,370 yards and rated 69.9 from the regular tees. The slope ratings are 122 championship and 114 regular. Women's tees are 5,958 yards and rated 73.1. The slope rating is 118.

Play policy and fees: Military personnel and guests only. Green fees are based on military status.

Location: From Los Angeles, travel south on Interstate 15 to the Miramar Way exit and drive west to the main gate.

Course description: This course was reputedly built by stockade labor back in the 1960s. While the military prisoners removed the rocks, the retirement community waited patiently for the course to open. But that's only rumor. Fact is the course is a flat but challenging layout that is loaded with bunkers and trees. If you don't keep the ball in the fairway you're in deep trouble with trees, not water. There are only three holes where water comes into play. The trees are the big problem.

PO Box 45312
San Diego, CA 92145

NAS Miramar
San Diego, CA 92145

Pro shop   (619) 537-4155

- ■ driving range
- ■ practice greens
- ■ power carts
- ■ pull carts
- ■ golf club rental
- ■ locker rooms
- □ showers
- □ executive course
- □ accommodations
- ■ food and beverages
- ■ clubhouse

Neal Patton
Professional

Gene Stoddard
Superintendent

SOUTHERN J6

CARMEL HIGHLAND
GOLF AND TENNIS RESORT

1986
Jack Duray

Course information: This resort course has 18 holes and par is 72. The course is 6,501 yards and rated 71.1 from the championship tees, and 6,112 yards and rated 68.9 from the regular tees. The slope ratings are 122 championship and 115 regular. Women's tees are 5,488 yards and rated 71.4. The slope rating is 119.

Play policy and fees: Green fees are $30 weekdays plus cart. Carts are $10. Walking is optional on weekdays. Green fees are $50 weekends, including mandatory cart. Senior rate during the week is $30, cart included. Reservations are recommended five days in advance. Proper golf attire is required.

Location: Travel 20 miles north of San Diego on Interstate 15 to the Carmel Mountain Road exit. Drive west for one-quarter mile to Penasquitos Drive and turn right to the club entrance.

Course description: This course is well groomed with exceptional greens. Water comes into play on four holes. The par-5 sixth hole has a lateral water hazard running alongside the fairway and a pond in front of the green. Hole eight is a long par-4 up a hill to a sloped green. The Gatlin Brothers and several members of the San Diego Padres and Chargers frequent this course. Some annual tournaments that are held here include: County Women's Championship, Qualifying Two-man Better Ball, Oldsmobile Scramble Qualifier and the Padres Press Box Classic. The course record is 62, held by Caesar Sanudo.

PO Box 28565
San Diego, CA 92128

14455 Penasquitos Drive
San Diego, CA 92129

Pro shop   (619) 672-2200

- ■ driving range
- ■ practice greens
- ■ power carts
- □ pull carts
- ■ golf club rental
- ■ locker rooms
- ■ showers
- □ executive course
- ■ accommodations
- ■ food and beverages
- ■ clubhouse

Michael Flanagan
Director of Golf

Mike Magnani
Superintendent

RANCHO BERNARDO INN AND COUNTRY CLUB

1962
William Francis Bell

Box 28074
San Diego, CA 92128

17550 Bernardo Oaks Drive
San Diego, CA 92128

Pro shop   (619) 487-0700
Clubhouse   (619) 487-1611
Executive   (619) 487-3021

Course information: This resort course has 18 holes and par is 72. There is also a 27-hole executive course. The course is 6,430 yards and rated 70.6 from the championship tees, and 6,182 yards and rated 69.3 from the regular tees. The slope ratings are 122 championship and 118 regular. Women's tees are 5,448 yards and rated 71.0. The slope rating is 119. The executive course averages 1,800 yards for each nine-hole combination.

Play policy and fees: Outside play is accepted and hotel guests are welcome. The green fee is $44. Mandatory carts are $11. Reservations are recommended one week in advance. No jeans or running shorts allowed. Shirts must have collars and sleeves. Green fees for the executive course $12 for nine holes and $18 for 18 holes weekdays, $15 for nine holes and $29 for 18 holes weekends.

Location: Travel eight miles south of the town of Escondido on Interstate 15 to Rancho Bernardo Road east. Drive one mile to Bernardo Oaks Drive, and turn left to the inn and golf course.

Course description: Set in a small valley and enclosed by homes, this course offers sloping fairways, a meandering creek and two lakes.

- ■ driving range
- ■ practice greens
- ■ power carts
- ■ pull carts
- ■ golf club rental
- ☐ locker rooms
- ☐ showers
- ■ executive course
- ■ accommodations
- ■ food and beverages
- ■ clubhouse

Tom Wilson
Director of Golf

Bill Nolde
Superintendent

STONERIDGE COUNTRY CLUB

17166 Stoneridge Country
Club Lane
Poway, CA 92064

Pro shop   (619) 487-2117
Clubhouse   (619) 487-2138

Course information: This private course has 18 holes and par is 72. The course is 6,286 yards and rated 69.9 from the championship tees, and 6,042 yards and rated 68.5 from the regular tees. The slope ratings are 118 championship and 111 regular. Women's tees are 5,679 yards and rated 72.0. The slope rating is 119.

Play policy and fees: Reciprocal play is accepted with members of other private clubs weekdays only. Green fees are $70 for reciprocators, including cart. Green fees are $60 for guests with members, including cart. Reservations are recommended.

Location: From Interstate 15 take the Rancho Bernardo Road exit and travel east for 2.5 miles to Stoneridge Country Club Lane.

Course description: The front nine is level and the back nine is sloping on this well-maintained course. It is set in the hills and is the site of the annual LPGA Inamori Classic.

- ■ driving range
- ■ practice greens
- ■ power carts
- ☐ pull carts
- ☐ golf club rental
- ■ locker rooms
- ■ showers
- ☐ executive course
- ☐ accommodations
- ☐ food and beverages
- ■ clubhouse

Ben Stewart
Professional

Delfino Cano
Superintendent

SOUTHERN J6

MAP ON PAGE 546

RANCHO BERNARDO
GOLF CLUB

Course information: This private course has 18 holes and par is 72. The course is 6,468 yards and rated 70.3 from the tournament tees, 6,186 yards and rated 68.6 from the championship tees, and 5,663 yards and rated 65.9 from the regular tees. The slope ratings are 116 tournament, 109 championship and 103 regular. Women's tees are 5,525 yards and rated 70.5. The slope rating is 113.

Play policy and fees: Members and guests only. Guests must be accompanied by a member.

Location: Travel eight miles south of the town of Escondido on Interstate 15 to Rancho Bernardo Road east. Drive one mile to Bernardo Oaks Drive and turn left to the club.

Course description: The terrain is slightly rolling on this course. There are many hole-in-one opportunities on the short, par-3 holes. The course is in the top 10 in the nation for aces scored. There has been an average of 35 holes-in-one scored each year for the last eight years on this course. That's a remarkable number, considering that the par-3s range in length from 150 to 190 yards and some players crank up a four iron to reach the greens.

PO Box 28074
San Diego, CA 92128

12280 Greens East Road
San Diego, CA 92128

Pro shop   (619) 487-1212
Clubhouse   (619) 487-1134

☐ driving range
■ practice greens
■ power carts
■ pull carts
☐ golf club rental
☐ locker rooms
☐ showers
☐ executive course
☐ accommodations
■ food and beverages
■ clubhouse

Richard Carmody
Professional

CARMEL MOUNTAIN RANCH
GOLF COURSE

Course information: This semi-private course has 18 holes and par is 72. The course is 6,615 yards and rated 72.9 from the championship tees, and 6,217 yards and rated 70.5 from the regular tees. The slope ratings are 136 championship and 128 regular. Women's tees are 5,372 yards and rated 70.2. The slope rating is 118.

Play policy and fees: Outside play is accepted. Green fees are $45 weekdays and $60 weekends. Carts are included. Reservations are recommended. This course is available for outside tournaments.

Location: Take Interstate 15 to Carmel Mountain Road exit then take Highway 60 east to Highland Ranch Road and follow the signs to the clubhouse.

Course description: The holes on this rolling, narrow course follow the contours of the hills. There are no parallel fairways. The greens are well kept and fast.

14050 Carmel Ridge Road
San Diego, CA 92128

Pro shop   (619) 487-9224

■ driving range
■ practice greens
■ power carts
☐ pull carts
■ golf club rental
■ locker rooms
■ showers
☐ executive course
☐ accommodations
■ food and beverages
■ clubhouse

Gary Glaser
Professional

Charles Reider
Superintendent

BERNARDO HEIGHTS COUNTRY CLUB

Course information: This private course has 18 holes and par is 72. The course is 6,699 yards and rated 72.5 from the championship tees, and 6,325 yards and rated 70.0 from the regular tees. The slope ratings are 125 championship and 118 regular. Women's tees are 5,608 yards and rated 71.9. The slope rating is 116.

Play policy and fees: Reciprocal play is accepted with members of other private clubs. Green fees for guests are $25 weekdays and $40 weekends. Green fees for reciprocators are $50. Carts are $18. Reservations are recommended.

Location: Take the Bernardo Center Drive exit off Interstate 15 and drive east to Bernardo Heights Parkway, then turn right to the club.

Course description: This well-maintained course is hilly with a few trees, some water and fast greens. It is set in a beautiful location surrounded by mountains.

16066 Bernardo Heights Prky.
San Diego, CA 92128

Pro shop   (619) 487-3440
Clubhouse (619) 487-4022

- ■ driving range
- ■ practice greens
- ■ power carts
- □ pull carts
- ■ golf club rental
- ■ locker rooms
- ■ showers
- □ executive course
- □ accommodations
- ■ food and beverages
- ■ clubhouse

Russ Bloom
Professional

Robert Steele
Superintendent

RANCHO SANTA FE FARMS GOLF CLUB

1988
Pete Dye

Course information: This private course has 18 holes and par is 72.

Play policy and fees: Members and guests only.

Location: From Interstate 5, take the Carmel Valley Road exit and drive east four to five miles. Turn left on Rancho Santa Fe Road. At the dead end, turn right, the course is one-quarter mile.

Course description: Members consider this maturing course a very private retreat. Michael Jordon and Janet Jackson are members. This very hilly course has three man-made lakes that come into play on five holes. You'll want to keep the ball in the fairway on this links-style course. The rough is a foot high.

PO Box 5025
Rancho Santa Fe, CA 92067

8500 Saint Andrews Road
Rancho Santa Fe, CA 92067

Pro shop   (619) 756-5585

- ■ driving range
- ■ practice greens
- ■ power carts
- □ pull carts
- ■ golf club rental
- ■ locker rooms
- ■ showers
- □ executive course
- □ accommodations
- ■ food and beverages
- ■ clubhouse

John Schroeder
Director of Golf

Tommy Jacobs
Senior Tour Representative

Patrick Holden
Superintendent

SOUTHERN J6

TORREY PINES GOLF COURSE

1955
William Francis Bell

PO Box 9223
San Diego, CA 92109

11480 N. Torrey Pines Road
La Jolla, CA 92037

Pro shop   (619) 452-3226
Clubhouse   (619) 453-8148
Starter   (619) 552-1784
Reservation (619) 570-1234

Course information: This public facility has two 18-hole courses and par is 72 on both.

The South Course is 7,027 yards and rated 74.4 from the championship tees, and 6,706 yards and rated 72.2 from the regular tees. The slope ratings are 131 championship and 124 regular. Women's tees are 6,447 yards and rated 73.5. The slope rating is 121.

The North Course is 6,636 yards and rated 72.0 from the championship tees, and 6,375 yards and rated 70.0 from the regular tees. The slope ratings are 124 championship and 116 regular. Women's tees are 6,104 yards and rated 74.9. The slope rating is 125.

Play policy and fees: Green fees are $38 weekdays and $44 weekends. Carts are $22. Reservations are recommended seven days in advance. This course is available for outside tournaments.

Location: From San Diego, drive north on Interstate 5 to Genesse and turn west to North Torrey Pines Road and turn north into the club.

Course description: This is an excellent public facility. The South Course is wide open but it can be tough when the wind is blowing off the ocean. The North Course is shorter and more scenic. Both courses are used for the PGA Tour's San Diego Open. There are spectacular views of the coastline throughout the course. After playing 18 you might want to break out your surfboard and hang 10.

- ■ driving range
- ■ practice greens
- ■ power carts
- ■ pull carts
- ■ golf club rental
- ☐ locker rooms
- ☐ showers
- ☐ executive course
- ☐ accommodations
- ■ food and beverages
- ■ clubhouse

Joe DeBock
Professional

John Walter
Superintendent

LA JOLLA COUNTRY CLUB

Course information: This private course has 18 holes and par is 72. The course is 6,695 yards and rated 72.9 from the championship tees, and 6,262 yards and rated 70.2 from the regular tees. The slope ratings are 133 championship and 125 regular. Women's tees are 5,979 yards and rated 65.8. The slope rating is 134.

Play policy and fees: Members and guests only. Green fees are $40 weekdays and $60 weekends. Carts are $14.

Location: Take the Ardath Road exit (becomes Torrey Pines Road) off Interstate 5 north of San Diego and drive 3.25 miles. Turn left on Girard Street and the left on Pearl Street. Drive two blocks to High Street and turn right, then continue one block to the club.

Course description: This is an older traditional course perched on a bluff overlooking the Pacific. It's not unusual to see dolphins frolicking in the surf below. It is well maintained and relatively hilly with lots of trees and bunkers. When the wind picks up, it can be a tough course.

PO Box 1760
La Jolla, CA 92037

7301 High Avenue Extension
La Jolla, CA 92038

Pro shop   (619) 454-2505
Clubhouse (619) 454-9601

- ■ driving range
- ■ practice greens
- ■ power carts
- □ pull carts
- ■ golf club rental
- ■ locker rooms
- ■ showers
- □ executive course
- □ accommodations
- ■ food and beverages
- ■ clubhouse

Pete Coe
Professional

Carlos Gaines
Superintendent

SAN DIEGO NAVAL STATION GOLF COURSE

Course information: This military course has nine holes. Par is 54 for 18 holes. The course is 2,500 yards.

Play policy and fees: Green fees are according to military status.

Location: Going south on Interstate 5 take the Main Street exit. Cross Main Street and drive directly to the gate.

Course description: This is a short course with open fairways and small greens.

MWR Code 10, NSGC
San Diego, CA 92136

Clubhouse (619) 556-7502

- ■ driving range
- ■ practice greens
- □ power carts
- ■ pull carts
- ■ golf club rental
- □ locker rooms
- □ showers
- □ executive course
- □ accommodations
- □ food and beverages
- □ clubhouse

SOUTHERN J6

MAP ON PAGE 546

OAKS NORTH
EXECUTIVE COURSE

Course information: This public facility has 27 holes. There are three nines and each 18-hole combination is par 60.

The North/South course is 3,565 yards and rated 57.8. The slope rating is 88. Women's tees are 3,253 yards and rated 57.8. The slope rating is 87.

The South/East Course is 3,495 yards and rated 53.0. The slope rating is 87. Women's tees are 3,220 yards and rated 57.6. The slope rating is 85.

The North/East Course is 3,342 yards and rated 52.2. The slope rating is 86. Women's tees are 3,041 yards and rated 57.0. The slope rating is 86.

Play policy and fees: Green fees are $12 for nine holes and $18 for 18 holes weekdays, and $15 for nine holes and $20 for 18 holes weekends. Carts are $11 for nine holes and $16 for 18 holes. Dress code requires collared shirts, Bermuda-length shorts or slacks for men. No tank tops or short shorts for women.

Location: Off Interstate 15 in Rancho Bernardo, take the Highland Valley Road/Pomerado exit and take it to Oaks North Drive. Turn left to the course.

Course description: These executive courses have tight fairways and undulating greens. There are three nines for mix-and-match lunch hours.

12602 Oaks North Drive
Rancho Bernardo, CA 92128

Pro shop   (619) 487-3021
Clubhouse   (619) 487-9148

- ■ driving range
- ■ practice greens
- ■ power carts
- ■ pull carts
- ■ golf club rental
- □ locker rooms
- □ showers
- ■ executive course
- □ accommodations
- ■ food and beverages
- □ clubhouse

Alice Herzog
Manager

Tom Wilson
Professional

Bob Dobeck
Superintendent

MOUNT WOODSON
COUNTRY CLUB

1991
Landmark Signature
Lee Schmidt

16302 North Woodson Drive
Ramona, CA 92065

Pro shop   (619) 788-6255

☐ driving range
■ practice greens
■ power carts
☐ pull carts
■ golf club rental
☐ locker rooms
☐ showers
☐ executive course
☐ accommodations
■ food and beverages
■ clubhouse

Scott Bentley
Professional

Jon Marzolf
Superintendent

Course information: This semi-private course has 18 holes. Par is 71. This course is 6,180 yards and rated 67.7 from the championship tees, and 5,830 yards and unrated from the regular tees. The slope rating is 116 championship. Women's tees are 4,441 yards and rated 64.7. The slope rating is 108.

Play policy and fees: Outside play is accepted. Green fees are $38 weekdays and $50 weekends. Carts are included. Twilight rates are $25 weekdays after 3 p.m., and $35 weekends after 3 p.m. Reservations recommended five days in advance. This course is available for outside tournaments.

Location: From Interstate 5, take Poway Road east to Highway 67. Turn right on Highway 67 and drive for three miles to Archie Moore Road. Turn left to the club entrance.

Course description: This course opened for play in late August, 1991. Tucked away in the mountains of Romona at the base of Mount Woodson, this course is spectacular in its natural setting. There are huge boulders, lakes and mature trees that pre-existed the construction of the course. There are numerous elevation changes. Soon to be a landmark is the 50-foot bridge that links the second green to the third tee. Holes 13, 15 and 17 offer superb views of the valley below. Six lakes come into play. Both the fairways and the undulating greens are well bunkered. Bunkers at the greens are especially nice with white sand layered over a hard undersurface. There are no parallel fairways.

SOUTHERN J6

MAP ON PAGE 546   **565**

SAN VICENTE INN AND GOLF CLUB

Course 33
MAP J6 grid e5

1973
Ted Robinson

24157 San Vicente Road
Ramona, CA 92065

Pro shop   (619) 789-3477

- ■ driving range
- ■ practice greens
- ■ power carts
- □ pull carts
- ■ golf club rental
- □ locker rooms
- □ showers
- □ executive course
- ■ accommodations
- ■ food and beverages
- ■ clubhouse

Course information: This semi-private resort course has 18 holes and par is 72. The course is 6,585 yards and rated 71.4 from the championship tees, and 6,180 yards and rated 69.2 from the regular tees. The slope ratings are 121 championship and 111 regular. Women's tees are 5,595 yards and rated 71.2. The slope rating is 125.

Play policy and fees: Outside play is accepted. Green fees are $35 weekdays and $45 weekends, including cart. Reservations are recommended five days in advance. This course is available for outside tournaments.

Location: From Main Street in downtown Ramona, drive south on 10th Street and continue for six miles to the San Diego Country Estates.

Course description: This picturesque course is set in a valley and follows the topography of the land. There are lots of trees.

Terry Horn
Professional

Ken Sommermeyer
Superintendent

DE ANZA—MISSION BAY GOLF COURSE

Course 34
MAP J6 grid f0

2702 North Mission Bay Drive
San Diego, CA 92109

Pro shop   (619) 490-3370

- ■ driving range
- ■ practice greens
- ■ power carts
- ■ pull carts
- ■ golf club rental
- □ locker rooms
- □ showers
- ■ executive course
- □ accommodations
- ■ food and beverages
- ■ clubhouse

Course information: This public course has 18 holes and par is 58. The course is 3,175 yards from the regular tees.

Play policy and fees: Green fees are $12 weekdays and $14 weekends. Senior rates are $10 weekdays and $12 weekends. Carts are $14. Reservations are recommended.

Location: Take Interstate 5 from San Diego and go west on Clairmont Drive and north on Mission Bay Drive to the course.

Course description: This executive course features four par-4s. It is fairly wide open, but there are several lakes and some sand. The course record is 48.

Al Starr
Professional

Mark Mucerino
Superintendent

NAVY GOLF COURSES
MISSION GORGE

1957
Jack Daray

Course information: This military facility has two 18-hole courses. Par is 72 on the North Course and 70 on the South Course.

The North Course is 6,685 yards and rated 73.1 from the championship tees, and 6,553 yards and rated 70.9 from the regular tees. The slope ratings are 124 championship and 116 regular. Women's tees are 5,951 yards and rated 70.2. The slope rating is 115.

The South Course is 5,774 yards and rated 66.6 from the regular tees. The slope rating is 103. Women's yardage and ratings were unavailable.

Play policy and fees: Military personnel and guests only. Green fees are $10 for military personnel. Guests are $15 weekdays and $20 weekends. Carts are $14.

Location: Take the Interstate 5 off ramp off Interstate 8, and drive north for one-quarter mile to the Friars Road East exit. Drive east to Admiral Baker Road and turn left past the security gate to the club.

Course description: The North Course is the more interesting of the two and offers a variety of holes traversing rather hilly terrain. The South course is shorter and more level, but there are plans to extend this course to a par-72.

Friars Road
and Admiral Baker Road
San Diego, CA 92021

Pro shop   (619) 556-5520
Clubhouse   (619) 556-5502
Starter   (619) 556-5521

- driving range
- practice greens
- power carts
- pull carts
- golf club rental
- locker rooms
- showers
- executive course
- ☐ accommodations
- food and beverages
- clubhouse

Tim Bigham
Operations Manager

Howard Fisher
Superintendent

SOUTHERN J6

MAP ON PAGE 546

STARDUST COUNTRY CLUB

Course information: This semi-private course has 27 holes and par is 72 for each 18-hole combination.

The Valley/Lake Course is 6,686 yards and rated 72.4 from the championship tees, and 6,383 yards and rated 70.2 from the regular tees. The slope ratings are 126 championship and 119 regular. Women's tees are 5,797 yards and rated 72.1. The slope rating is 115.

The River/Valley Course is 6,687 yards and rated 72.4 from the championship tees, and 6,384 yards and rated 70.2 from the regular tees. The slope ratings are 126 championship and 118 regular. Women's tees are 5,871 yards and rated 72.6. The slope rating is 117.

The Lake/River Course is 6,599 yards and rated 71.6 from the championship tees, and 6,303 yards and rated 69.8 from the regular tees. The slope ratings are 123 championship and 117 regular. Women's tees are 5,734 yards and rated 72.0. The slope rating is 115.

Play policy and fees: Reciprocal play is accepted with members of other private clubs. Hotel guests welcome. Green fees are $40 with cart for hotel guests and $60 for non-hotel guests. Reservations are recommended.

Location: In Mission Valley, turn off Highway 8 at the Stardust Hotel and Country Club sign.

Course description: These courses date back to the 1940s. They are flat with well-bunkered greens. The fairways tend to be narrow and demand good shot placement. The game starts on the greens, which are very quick. Water comes into play on four holes.

950 Hotel Circle
San Diego, CA 92108

Pro shop   (619) 297-4796
Clubhouse (619) 298-0511

- ■ driving range
- ■ practice greens
- ■ power carts
- ■ pull carts
- ■ golf club rental
- ■ locker rooms
- ■ showers
- □ executive course
- ■ accommodations
- ■ food and beverages
- ■ clubhouse

Cliff Crandall
Director of Golf

K.C. Crandall
Professional

Steve Parker
Superintendent

CARLTON OAKS LODGE AND COUNTRY CLUB

1989
Perry Dye

Course information: This resort course has 18 holes and par is 72.

The course is 7,088 yards and rated 75.4 from the tournament tees, 6,534 yards and rated 72.2 from the championship tees, and 6,024 yards and rated 69.0 from the regular tees. The slope ratings are 143 tournament, 133 championship and 117 regular. Women's tees are 5,611 yards and rated 73.1 from the executive tees, and 4,548 yards and rated 67.1 from the forward tees. The slope ratings are 128 executive and 114 regular.

Play policy and fees: Outside play is accepted and hotel guests are welcome. Green fees are $65 any day. Carts are included. Reservations are recommended three days in advance. Collared shirts are required and shorts must be Bermuda length.

Location: Take the Mission Gorge exit off Interstate 8, and drive north for 6.5 miles. Turn left at Mast Boulevard. Drive one-half mile and turn right on Carlton Oaks Drive. Continue one mile and turn right on Inwood Drive.

Course description: This course reopened two years ago after being closed for renovations. It has the highest course rating in San Diego County from the back tees. Perry Dye of Dye Designs was the renovating architect.

9200 Inwood Drive
Santee, CA 92071

Pro shop   (619) 448-8500
Clubhouse (619) 448-4242

■ driving range
■ practice greens
■ power carts
□ pull carts
■ golf club rental
□ locker rooms
□ showers
□ executive course
■ accommodations
■ food and beverages
■ clubhouse

Rex Cole
Professional

Craig Zellers
Superintendent

SOUTHERN J6

MISSION TRAILS GOLF COURSE

Course information: This public course has 18 holes and par is 71. The course is 5,989 yards and rated 68.6 from the championship tees, and 5,601 yards and rated 66.4 from the regular tees. The slope ratings are 113 championship and 104 regular. Women's tees are 5,175 yards and rated 64.4. The slope rating is 101.

Play policy and fees: Green fees are $16 weekdays and $22 on weekends. Senior rates $12 on weekdays only. Carts are $19. Shirts are required at all times. Reservations recommended one week in advance for the general public, and 10 days in advance for American Golf members.

Location: In San Diego, drive on Interstate 8 to College Avenue, and turn north and drive one mile to Navajo Road. Turn right and drive two miles to Golfcrest Drive. Turn right and continue one-quarter mile to Golfcrest Place. Turn left into the club.

Course description: Set in a little valley, the layout of this scenic course follows the contours of the land with two of the holes running alongside Lake Murray. Mature trees separate the fairways.

Box 19402
San Diego, CA 92219

7380 Golfcrest Place
San Diego, CA 92219

Pro shop   (619) 460-5400

- ■ driving range
- ■ practice greens
- ■ power carts
- ■ pull carts
- ■ golf club rental
- □ locker rooms
- □ showers
- □ executive course
- □ accommodations
- ■ food and beverages
- ■ clubhouse

WILLOWBROOK COUNTRY CLUB

1955

Course information: This public course has nine holes. Par is 72 for 18 holes. The course is 5,891 yards and rated 67.3 from the regular tees. The slope rating is 107. Women's tees are 5,272 yards and rated 70.5. The slope rating is 116.

Play policy and fees: Green fees are $13 weekdays and $17 weekends for 18 holes. Carts are $17. Reservations are recommended. This course is available for outside tournaments.

Location: Take Interstate 8 east from San Diego to the Highway 67 exit in El Cajon. Travel north to the Riverford Road exit (bear left). Make a left onto Riverford Road and then turn right onto Riverside Drive. The club is on the right hand side about one-half mile.

Course description: This course is fairly level, with three lakes. Mature cypress and oak trees line the fairways and add to the scenic mountain surroundings.

11905 Riverside Drive
Lakeside, CA 92040

Pro shop   (619) 561-1061

- □ driving range
- ■ practice greens
- ■ power carts
- ■ pull carts
- ■ golf club rental
- □ locker rooms
- □ showers
- □ executive course
- □ accommodations
- ■ food and beverages
- ■ clubhouse

Spero Tzathas
Manager

Howard Fisher III
Superintendent

CORONADO GOLF COURSE

Course information: This public course has 18 holes and par is 72. The course is 6,446 yards and rated 69.9 from the regular tees. The slope rating is 120. Women's tees are 5,917 yards and rated 72.7. The slope rating is 120.

Play policy and fees: Green fees are $16. After 4 p.m. the green fees are $9. Carts are $18. Reservations are recommended.

Location: From Interstate 5, take the Coronado Bridge west and turn left at the end of the bridge. Go left on Fifth Street to Glorietta Boulevard. Turn right to the club.

Course description: Open fairways and large greens typify this course.

PO Box 18055
Coronado, CA 92178

2000 Visalia Way
Coronado, CA 92118

Pro shop   (619) 435-3121

- ■ driving range
- ■ practice greens
- ■ power carts
- ■ pull carts
- ■ golf club rental
- □ locker rooms
- □ showers
- □ executive course
- □ accommodations
- ■ food and beverages
- ■ clubhouse

SEA 'N' AIR

Course information: This military course has 18 holes and par is 72. There is also a seven-hole, par-3 executive course. The course is 6,336 yards and rated 69.9 from the championship tees, and 6,134 yards and rated 68.8 from the regular tees. The slope ratings are 113 championship and 109 regular. Women's tees are 5,539 yards and rated 70.8. The slope rating is 113.

Play policy and fees: Military personnel guests only. Green fees are $9 for military personnel with a rank of E-5 and above, and $5 for E-4 and below any day. Green fees for guests and Department of Defense employees are $12 weekdays and $15 weekends. Carts are $12 for 18 holes and $6 for nine holes. Reservations are recommended. This course is available for outside tournaments on a limited basis. Call for information.

Location: Take the Coronado exit off Interstate 5 in San Diego and drive across the Coronado Bay Bridge through the toll gate. Continue on Third Avenue and turn left on Alameda Street. At Fourth Avenue, turn right through the main gate and drive one-quarter mile to Rogers Road and then left to the club.

Course description: This is a fairly level course with a nice view of the ocean. Locally it used to be known as the Poor Man's Pebble Beach because the seventh, eighth and ninth holes border the ocean, but that's all changed. In December, 1988, the course was turned around and the seventh, eighth and ninth holes are now numbers 13, 14 and 15.

PO Box 180751
Coronado, CA 92178

Building 800, NAS North Is.
San Diego, CA 92135

Pro shop   (619) 545-9659

- ■ driving range
- ■ practice greens
- ■ power carts
- ■ pull carts
- ■ golf club rental
- ■ locker rooms
- ■ showers
- ■ executive course
- □ accommodations
- ■ food and beverages
- ■ clubhouse

John Shipley
Professional

Kelly Wolf
Superintendent

SOUTHERN J6

COLINA PARK GOLF COURSE

Course information: This is a par-3 public course. The par is 54 for 18 holes. The course is 1,252 yards.

Play policy and fees: Green fees are $4. Juniors and seniors are $3 any day.

Location: Take Interstate 805 to University Avenue and go east about 3.5 miles. At 52nd Street go left to the course. The course is on the right.

Course description: This course has rolling fairways and undulating greens.

4085 52nd Street
San Diego, CA 92105

Pro shop   (619) 582-4704

☐ driving range
■ practice greens
☐ power carts
☐ pull carts
■ golf club rental
☐ locker rooms
☐ showers
☐ executive course
■ accommodations
☐ food and beverages
■ clubhouse

PRESIDIO HILLS PITCH AND PUTT

1932

Course information: This public course has 18 holes. Par is 54. The course is 1,426 yards.

Play policy and fees: Green fees are $6.

Location: From Interstate 8 in San Diego, take the Taylor Street exit. Drive to Juan Street, turn left and drive one block to the course. The course is on the left.

Course description: This is the oldest course of its kind in the San Diego area. It's been a family operation for many years. The grandfather of Donna Abrego was the first pro. This is a fun little pitch-and-putt course for tuning up the short game. There are full-grown sycamore trees keeping the course in welcome shade.

PO Box 10532
San Diego, CA 92210

4136 Wallace Street
San Diego, CA 92210

Clubhouse (619) 295-9476

☐ driving range
■ practice greens
☐ power carts
☐ pull carts
■ golf club rental
☐ locker rooms
☐ showers
☐ executive course
☐ accommodations
■ food and beverages
■ clubhouse

Donna Abrego
Manager

BALBOA PARK GOLF CLUB

William Park Bell

2600 Golf Course Drive
San Diego, CA 92102

Pro shop   (619) 239-1632
Starter   (619) 232-2470
Reservations (619) 570-1234

- ■ driving range
- ■ practice greens
- ■ power carts
- ■ pull carts
- ■ golf club rental
- ■ locker rooms
- ■ showers
- ■ executive course
- □ accommodations
- ■ food and beverages
- ■ clubhouse

Jim Hillsbery
Professional

Gene Bianchi
Superintendent

Course information: This public course has 27 holes. Par is 72 on the 18-hole course and 32 on the nine-hole course. The 18-hole course is 6,058 yards and rated 68.2 from the regular tees. The slope rating is 110. Women's tees are 5,391 yards and rated 69.8. The slope rating is 112.

Play policy and fees: Green fees are $12 weekdays and $14 weekends for residents of San Diego. Green fees for non-residents are $33 weekdays and $38 weekends and holidays. Green fees for San Diego County residents are $17 weekdays and $21 for weekends and holidays. Carts are $18. Reservations are recommended.

Location: Take the Pershing Drive exit off Interstate 5 and drive east to 26th Street then turn right to Golf Course Drive and the club.

Course description: Both courses play tight with small greens. The 18-hole course is a traditional links course.

BONITA GOLF CLUB

Box 455
Bonita, CA 91902

5540 Sweetwater Road
Bonita, CA 91902

Pro shop   (619) 267-1103

- ■ driving range
- ■ practice greens
- ■ power carts
- ■ pull carts
- ■ golf club rental
- □ locker rooms
- □ showers
- □ executive course
- □ accommodations
- ■ food and beverages
- ■ clubhouse

Bill Nary
Professional

Charles N. Hamilton III
Manager

Robert Scribner
Superintendent

SOUTHERN J6

Course information: This semi-private course has 18 holes and par is 71. The course is 6,248 yards and rated 68.3 from the championship tees, and 5,916 yards and rated 67.8 from the regular tees. The slope ratings are 110 championship and 104 regular. Women's tees are 5,542 yards and rated 69.6. The slope rating is 112.

Play policy and fees: Outside play is accepted. Green fees are $15 weekdays and $22 weekends. Carts are $18. Reservations are recommended one week in advance. This course is available for outside tournaments.

Location: Drive on Interstate 805 to the South Freeway East for 4.5 miles. At Sweetwater Road, turn right and drive three-fourths of a mile to the course.

Course description: This flat course is set in a river valley and has a few doglegs. The friendly greens do not have any bunkers set directly in front of them. The trees are maturing, and there are two lakes on the course.

MAP ON PAGE 546

CHULA VISTA GOLF CLUB

Course information: This public course has 18 holes and par is 73. The course is 6,776 yards and rated 72.7 from the championship tees, and 6,529 yards and rated 70.8 from the regular tees. The slope ratings are 125 championship and 116 regular. Women's tees are 5,859 and rated 72.7. The slope rating is 113.

Play policy and fees: Green fees are $13 weekdays and $17 weekends. Carts are $19. Reservations are recommended.

Location: Take the E Street exit off Interstate 805 in Chula Vista and travel east two miles to the club.

Course description: This is a walkable, level course with five par-5s. It has large greens and wide open, rolling terrain. Water is everywhere on the front nine, but if you survive that, the back nine is shorter and easier...sort of.

PO Box 403
Bonita, CA 92002

4475 Bonita Road
Bonita, CA 92002

Pro shop   (619) 479-4141
Clubhouse   (619) 427-9634

■ driving range
■ practice greens
■ power carts
■ pull carts
■ golf club rental
□ locker rooms
□ showers
□ executive course
□ accommodations
■ food and beverages
■ clubhouse

John Gonzales
Professional

Steve Schroeder
Regional Superintendent

STEELE CANYON GOLF COURSE

1991
Gary Player

Course information: This semi-private course has 18 holes. Par is 71. The course is 6,670 yards and rated 72.2 from the championship tees, and 6,200 yards and rated 69.1 from the regular tees. The slope ratings are 125 championship and 116 regular. Women's tees are 5,657 yards and rated 65.5 from the championship tees, and 4,656 yards and rated 66.6 from the forward tees. The slope ratings are 110 championship and 107 forward.

Play policy and fees: Green fees are $35 weekdays and $45 weekdays, including cart. Twilight rates are $20 weekdays and $25 weekends after 3 p.m. Reservations are recommended seven days in advance. No tee times for singles. This course is available for tournaments.

Location: From Interstate 5 in San Diego, exit east on Interstate 94/Jamacha Road. Drive to Willow Glen Drive. Turn right and drive to Steele Canyon Drive. Turn right on Steele Canyon Drive to travel to Jamul Drive (the first traffic light). Turn left and drive one mile to the club.

Course description: This course opened for play July 13, 1991. It covers rolling countryside terrain. There are various elevation changes. Another nine holes, bringing the total to 27, are scheduled to open in June, 1992.

3199 Stonefield Drive
Jamul, CA 91935

Pro shop   (619) 441-6900

■ driving range
■ practice greens
■ power carts
□ pull carts
■ golf club rental
□ locker rooms
□ showers
□ executive course
□ accommodations
■ food and beverages
■ clubhouse

Art Noehren
Manager

Jeffrey Johnson
Professional

David Buckles
Superintendent

SUN VALLEY GOLF COURSE

Course information: This public course has nine holes and par is 27. The course is 1,080 yards.

Play policy and fees: Green fees are $3.50 for nine holes and $6 for 18 holes any day.

Location: Take Interstate 8 east of San Diego to El Cajon Boulevard, go left to La Mesa Boulevard and follow it to Memorial Drive and the course.

Course description: This course has open fairways and it's hilly.

5080 Memorial Drive
La Mesa, CA 92041

Pro shop   (619) 466-6102

☐ driving range
■ practice greens
☐ power carts
■ pull carts
■ golf club rental
☐ locker rooms
☐ showers
☐ executive course
☐ accommodations
■ food and beverages
☐ clubhouse

SINGING HILLS COUNTRY CLUB AND LODGE

1956
Ted Robinson

Course information: This semi-private club has two 18-hole courses. Par is 71 on the Oak Glen Course and 72 on the Willow Glen Course. A par-3 executive course is also available. This is also a resort.

The Oak Glen Course is 6,132 yards and rated 69.0 from the championship tees, and 5,749 yards and rated 66.9 from the regular tees. The slope ratings are 111 championship and 107 regular. Women's tees are 5,308 yards and rated 69.3. The slope rating is 112.

The Willow Glen Course is 6,608 yards and rated 71.9 from the championship tees, and 6,247 yards and rated 69.4 from the regular tees. The slope ratings are 124 championship and 114 regular. Women's tees are 5,585 yards and rated 71.4. The slope rating is 122.

Play policy and fees: Reciprocal play is accepted with members of other private clubs. Outside play is accepted. Hotel guests welcome. Green fees are $23 weekdays and $27 weekends. Carts are $18. Reservations are recommended. This course is available for outside tournaments.

Location: From Interstate 5 or Interstate 805, take Interstate 8 east to the Second Street exit in El Cajon. Turn right and bear left on Washington Street. Turn right immediately on Dehesa Road and drive three miles to the club.

Course description: *Golf Digest* ranks this course in the top 100 in the country. Mature trees line the flat straight fairways on the Oak Glen Course. The Willow Glen Course offers a rolling layout and is known for its elevated tee on the fourth hole. Overall, there are lots of trees and bunkers.

3007 Dehesa Road
El Cajon, CA 92019

Pro shop   (619) 442-3425

■ driving range
■ practice greens
■ power carts
■ pull carts
■ golf club rental
■ locker rooms
■ showers
■ executive course
■ accommodations
■ food and beverages
■ clubhouse

Tom Addis III
Professional

Tamo Maldanado
Superintendent

SOUTHERN J6

RANCHO SAN DIEGO GOLF COURSE

Course information: This public facility has two 18-hole courses. The Ivanhoe Course is 7,089 yards and rated 74.4 from the championship tees, and 6,728 yards and rated 71.9 from the regular tees. The slope ratings are 129 championship and 115 regular. Women's tees are 5,624 yards and rated 72.0. The slope rating is 116.

The Monte Vista Course is 6,036 yards and rated 68.3 from the championship tees. The slope rating is 108. Women's tees are 5,407 yards and rated 73.1. The slope rating is 118.

Play policy and fees: Green fees are $25 for Ivanhoe and $22 for Monte Vista weekdays, and $30 for Ivanhoe and $26 for Monte Vista weekends. Senior rates are $19 for Ivanhoe and $17 for Monte Vista Mondays through Thursdays. Carts are $19. Reservations are recommended two weeks in advance.

Location: From Interstate 5 or Interstate 805, take Interstate 8 east to the Second Street exit in El Cajon. Drive south on Second Street for about four miles to Willow Glen Road and turn left to the club.

Course description: These courses have a lot of trees, ponds and lakes, and even a river runs through in the winter. The Ivanhoe Course has a lot of doglegs and is one of the best maintained public courses in the area. The Monte Vista Course has tight fairways and is shorter.

3121 Willow Glen Road
El Cajon, CA 92019

Pro shop   (619) 442-9891

- ■ driving range
- ■ practice greens
- ■ power carts
- ■ pull carts
- ■ golf club rental
- □ locker rooms
- □ showers
- □ executive course
- □ accommodations
- ■ food and beverages
- ■ clubhouse

Rick Sprouse
Professional

Javier Ruiz
Superintendent

NATIONAL CITY GOLF COURSE

Course information: This public course has nine holes and par is 34. The course is 4,810 yards and rated 60.5 from the championship tees, and 4,440 yards and rated 59.9 from the regular tees. Women's tees are 4,000 yards and rated 60.5.

Play policy and fees: Green fees are $7.50 for nine holes weekdays and $9.50 for nine holes weekends. The twilight rate after 5 p.m. is $5. The senior rate is $6 weekdays and $8 weekends. Reservations are recommended.

Location: Follow Interstate 805 south to Sweetwater Road west which leads to the course.

Course description: This course is extremely tight with out-of-bounds markers on almost every hole. The 525-yard second hole is very narrow and needs pinpoint placement for success. The course record is 55. Beware of the cat that hangs out near the first fairway. He steals balls.

1439 Sweetwater Road
National City, CA 92050

Pro shop   (619) 474-1400

- ■ driving range
- ■ practice greens
- ■ power carts
- ■ pull carts
- ■ golf club rental
- □ locker rooms
- □ showers
- □ executive course
- □ accommodations
- ■ food and beverages
- ■ clubhouse

Jack Sands
Manager

Bobby Canedo
Superintendent

SAN DIEGO COUNTRY CLUB

Course information: This private course has 18 holes and par is 72. The course is 6,887 yards and rated 74.2 from the championship tees, and 6,564 yards and rated 71.9 from the regular tees. The slope ratings are 133 championship and 126 regular. Women's tees are 6,137 and rated 75.5. The slope rating is 131.

Play policy and fees: Members and guests only.

Location: Take the L Street exit off Interstate 5 and drive 1.5 miles east to the club or take Telegraph Canyon/"L" Street exit off Interstate 805 and drive one mile west.

Course description: This course is the last golf op before reaching the Mexican border. It was built in the 1920s, making it the oldest private course in San Diego County. It is a mature course with undulating greens and fairways.

88 "L" Street
Chula Vista, CA 91911

Pro shop   (619) 422-0108
Clubhouse (619) 422-8895

■ driving range
■ practice greens
■ power carts
■ pull carts
■ golf club rental
■ locker rooms
■ showers
□ executive course
□ accommodations
□ food and beverages
■ clubhouse

Thomas Hust
Professional

Gary Dalton
Superintendent

EASTLAKE COUNTRY CLUB

1991
Ted Robinson

Course information: This public layout has 18 holes. Par is 72. The course is 6,608 yards and temporarily rated 70.7 from the championship tees, and 6,225 yards and rated 68.7 from the regular tees. The slope ratings are 122 championship and 116 regular. Women's tees are 5,834 yards and rated 72.5 from the championship tees, and 5,118 yards and rated 68.8 from the forward tees. The slope ratings are 122 and 114.

Play policy and fees: Green fees $25 weekdays and $40 weekends. Weekday twilight rates after 3 p.m. are $18 without a cart and $15 with a cart. Weekend twilight rates after 2 p.m are $26 without a cart and $33 with a cart. No pull carts allowed. Carts are $10 per person. Reservations are recommended. This course is available for tournaments.

Location: Take Interstate 805 south to the Telegraph Canyon Road exit in Chula Vista. Drive east four miles to EastLake Greens Community/EastLake Parkway. Turn right and drive one-quarter mile to Clubhouse Drive. The club is on the right.

Course description: There are four sets of tees on this course. There are undulating fairways, bent grass greens, six lakes and trees all the way to the greens.

2375 Clubhouse Drive
Chula Vista, CA 91914

Pro shop   (619) 482-5757

■ driving range
■ practice greens
■ power carts
□ pull carts
■ golf club rental
□ locker rooms
□ showers
□ executive course
□ accommodations
■ food and beverages
■ clubhouse

Mike Marcum
General Manager/
Professional

Sandy Clark
Superintendent

SOUTHERN J6

MAP J7
(2 COURSES)

PAGES.. 578-579

SO-CAL MAP .....see page 376
adjoining maps
NORTH (I7).........see page 496
EAST (J8) ....see page 580
SOUTH.........................no map
WEST (J6) ....see page 546

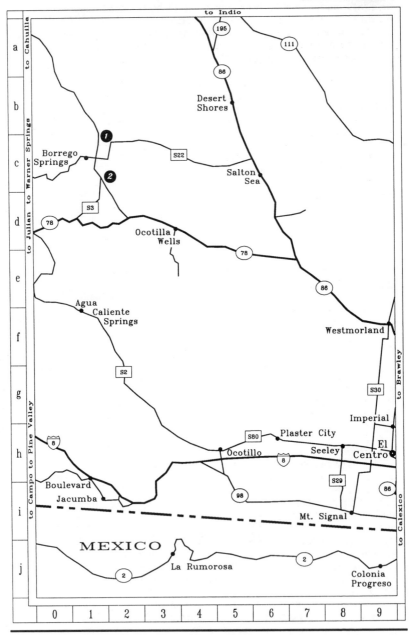

to Indio

195

111

86

Desert
Shores

a

to Cahuilla

b

Borrego
Springs

S22

Salton
Sea

c

to Warner Springs

1

2

S3

78

Ocotilla
Wells

78

86

d

to Julian

e

Agua
Caliente
Springs

Westmorland

f

to Brawley

S2

g

S30

Imperial

to Pine Valley

8

S80

Plaster City

El
Centro

h

to Campo

Ocotillo

8

Seeley

S29

86

Boulevard
Jacumba

98

Mt. Signal

i

to Calexico

MEXICO

2

j

2

La Rumorosa

2

Colonia
Progreso

0 1 2 3 4 5 6 7 8 9

DE ANZA DESERT COUNTRY CLUB

1958
Tige Stanley

PO Box 120
Borrego Springs, CA 92004

509 Catarina Drive
Borrego Springs, CA 92004

Pro shop (619)767-5577
Clubhouse (619)767-5105

Course information: This private course has 18 holes and par is 72. The course is 6,819 yards and rated 73 from the tournament tees, 6,450 yards and rated 70.5 from the championship tees, and 6,021 yards and rated 68.3 from the regular tees. The slope ratings are 131 tournament, 119 championship and 111 regular. Women's tees are 5,601 yards and rated 71.5. The slope rating is 71.5.

Play policy and fees: Members and guests only. Fees for sponsored guests are $40. Carts are $16. Reservations are recommended. Course is open daily.

Location: From Palm Canyon Drive in Borrego Springs, turn north on Ocotillo Circle and drive one-half mile to Lazy "S" Drive. Turn right and travel 1.5 miles to Pointing Rock Drive and turn right.

Course description: This flat course has plenty of mature trees and two lakes. It's surrounded by homes. One of the toughest challenges of the course is number three, a 211-yard, par-3. You must hit over a lake and bunker to reach the green. There is a big eucalyptus on the left, but you can bail out to the right with some luck. Regulars consider themselves fortunate to land anywhere on the green, so don't be picky.

- ■ driving range
- ■ practice greens
- ■ power carts
- ■ pull carts
- □ golf club rental
- ■ locker rooms
- □ showers
- □ executive course
- □ accommodations
- ■ food and beverages
- ■ clubhouse

Andy Gorton
Manager

Denny Mays
Professional

Tom Baty
Superintendent

RAMS HILL COUNTRY CLUB

PO Box 664
Borrego Springs, CA 92004

1881 Rams Hill Road
Borrego Springs, CA 92004

Pro shop (619)767-5125

Course information: This semi-private course has 18 holes and par is 72. The course is 6,852 yards and rated 74.0 from the championship tees, and 6,329 yards and rated 70.7 from the regular tees. The slope ratings are 133 championship and 125 regular. Women's tees are 5,694 yards and rated 71.9. The slope rating is 119.

Play policy and fees: Outside play is accepted. Green fees are $65. Carts are included. Reservations are recommended seven days in advance. This course is available for outside tournaments. The course is open from 6:30 a.m. to 6:30 p.m. during the summer season. Closed in September.

Location: Travel on Interstate 10 or Highway 111 to Indio. Turn on Highway 86 to Salton City. Turn right on County Road S-22 to Borrego Valley Road, go left and drive six miles to the club.

Course description: This is a long, well-maintained course with sloping, palm-lined fairways and seven scenic water holes. The course closes in September for fairway re-seeding.

- ■ driving range
- ■ practice greens
- ■ power carts
- ■ pull carts
- ■ golf club rental
- ■ locker rooms
- ■ showers
- □ executive course
- □ accommodations
- ■ food and beverages
- ■ clubhouse

John Bell, Jr.
Professional

Bill Nestle
Superintendent

SOUTHERN J7

MAP J8
(2 COURSES)

PAGES.. 580-581

SO-CAL MAP .....see page 376
adjoining maps
NORTH (I8)........see page 540
EAST (J9) ....see page 582
SOUTH.........................no map
WEST (J7) ....see page 578

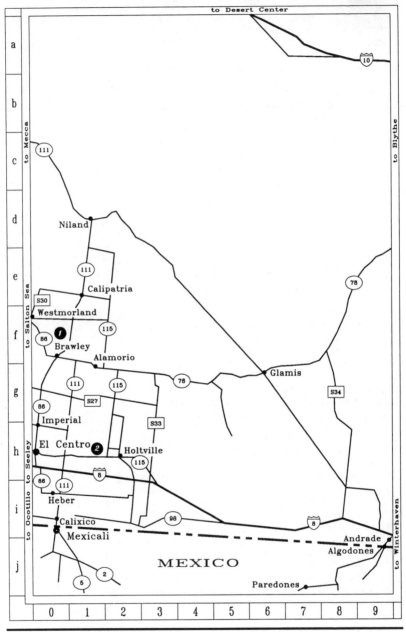

to Desert Center

10

to Mecca

111

Niland

111

Calipatria

S30

Westmorland

115

86 1
Brawley

Alamorio

to Salton Sea

111 115 78

Glamis

g

86 S27

Imperial

S33

S34

El Centro 2
Holtville

115

8

to Ocotillo to Seeley

86 111

Heber

98

8

to Winterhaven

Calixico
Mexicali

Andrade
Algodones

MEXICO

2

5

Paredones

to Blythe

78

0 1 2 3 4 5 6 7 8 9

DEL RIO COUNTRY CLUB

Course information: This semi-private course has 18 holes and par is 70. The course is 5,958 yards and rated 67.9 from the regular tees. The slope rating is 105. Women's tees are 5,738 yards and rated 72.8. The slope rating is 118.

Play policy and fees: Reciprocal play is accepted with members of other private clubs. Outside play is also accepted. Green fees are $25 weekdays and $30 weekends, carts included. Reservations are recommended.

Location: Travel east on Interstate 10 to the town of Indio and take Highway 86 south to Brawley. Take Highway 111 north and drive two miles to the course.

Course description: This course is short and tight, demanding strategic shot placement. It has fairly level terrain, tree-lined fairways, many doglegs and small greens.

102 East Del Rio Road
Brawley, CA 92227

Pro shop   (619) 344-0085

- ■ driving range
- ■ practice greens
- ■ power carts
- ■ pull carts
- ■ golf club rental
- □ locker rooms
- □ showers
- □ executive course
- □ accommodations
- ■ food and beverages
- ■ clubhouse

William Kissick
Superintendent

BARBARA WORTH COUNTRY CLUB

1 9 2 0
Lawrence Hughes

Course information: This semi-private course has 18 holes and par is 71. The course is 6,302 yards and rated 70.0 from the regular tees. The slope rating is 115. Women's tees are 5,879 yards and rated 72.6. The slope rating is 120.

Play policy and fees: Reciprocal play is accepted with members of other private clubs. Outside play is accepted. Green fees are $14 weekdays and $18 weekends during the summer season, and $18 weekdays and $22 weekends during the winter season. Carts are $16. Reservations are recommended. This course is available for tournaments.

Location: For reference, the club is 110 miles south of Palm Springs and 120 miles east of San Diego. Travel east from San Diego on Interstate 8 for about 125 miles to Bowker Road and turn left. At Highway 80, turn right and drive to the club.

Course description: This older, desert course has tree-lined fairways, good putting greens and several ponds. It's nicely maintained. It's quite a course for being out in the middle of essentially nowhere. This is a stay-and-play course, with more than a 104 motel rooms, three apartments and four executive suites.

2050 Country Club Drive
Holtville, CA 92250

Pro shop   (619) 356-5842
Clubhouse (619) 356-2806

- ■ driving range
- ■ practice greens
- ■ power carts
- ■ pull carts
- ■ golf club rental
- □ locker rooms
- □ showers
- □ executive course
- ■ accommodations
- ■ food and beverages
- ■ clubhouse

John Hildreth
Professional

Randy Heasley
Superintendent

SOUTHERN J8

SO-CAL MAP .....see page 376
adjoining maps
NORTH ....no map
EAST ....no map
SOUTH.........................no map
WEST (J8) ....see page 580

to Rice   to Vidal

95

Blythe

to Desert Center

10   Quartzsite

10   95

Ehrenberg

Ripley

78

Palo
Verde

to Glamis

ARIZONA

95

to Andrade

Winterhaven   Dome

Yuma

95   8

| 0 | 1 | 2 | 3 | 4 | 5 | 6 | 7 | 8 | 9 |

BLYTHE GOLF COURSE

Course information: This public course has 18 holes and par is 72. The course is 6,567 yards and rated 70.7 from the regular tees. The slope rating is 109. Women's tees are 6,567 yards and rated 75.8 from the championship tees, and 5,684 yards and rated 70.6 from the forward tees. The slope ratings are 121 championship and 110 forward.

Play policy and fees: Green fees are $12. Carts are $12. Reservations are recommended.

Location: Travel east of Palm Springs on Interstate 10 for 120 miles and take the Lovekin Boulevard exit north. Travel three miles to Sixth Avenue and turn left. At Defrain Boulevard turn right to the course.

Course description: This nicely maintained course sits on top of a mesa overlooking the Palo Verde Valley. A moderate number of eucalyptus and pine trees line the fairways that go up and down the mesa.

PO Box 329
Blythe, CA 92226

Defrain Street
Blythe, CA 92226

Pro shop   (619) 922-7272
Clubhouse (619) 922-8737

- ■ driving range
- ■ practice greens
- ■ power carts
- ■ pull carts
- ■ golf club rental
- ☐ locker rooms
- ☐ showers
- ☐ executive course
- ☐ accommodations
- ■ food and beverages
- ■ clubhouse

Willie Getchell
Professional

Frank Uyemura
Superintendent

SOUTHERN J9

MAP ON PAGE 582

APPENDICES

CALIFORNIA'S TOP 20 COURSES

Normally a poll such as this is subjective. However, in 1986, Mark Soltau instituted a yearly feature in the *San Francisco Examiner* called "The Top 20 Golf Courses in Northern California."

A 45-member panel of golfing experts and enthusiasts contribute to the selection process. Participants have included professional golfers George Archer, Dan Forsman, Roger Maltbie, Johnny Miller, Nathaniel Crosby and Julie Inkster; golf course architects Robert Trent Jones, Jr. and Ronald Fream; former United States Golf Association president Frank "Sandy" Tatum and current USGA president Grant Spaeth.

With help from several Southern California colleagues, including Fred Robledo of the *Los Angeles Times* and T.R. Reinman of the *San Diego Tribune*, here are the state's top 20 courses:

1. PEBBLE BEACH GOLF LINKS - page 267
2. CYPRESS POINT CLUB - page 269
3. OLYMPIC CLUB (Lake Course) - page 483
4. LOS ANGELES COUNTRY CLUB - page 402
5. RIVIERA COUNTRY CLUB - page 399
6. SAN FRANCISCO GOLF CLUB - page 171
7. PGA WEST (Stadium Course) - page 538
8. PASATIEMPO GOLF COURSE - page 260
9. VALLEY CLUB OF MONTECITO - page 346
10. SPYGLASS HILL - page 270
11. BEAR CREEK GOLF AND COUNTRY CLUB - page 492
12. STANFORD GOLF COURSE - page 199
13. THE VINTAGE CLUB (Mountain Course) - page 525
14. LAKE MERCED COUNTRY CLUB - page 172
15. BEL-AIR COUNTRY CLUB - page 401
16. SILVERADO COUNTRY CLUB (North Course) - page 101
17. WOOD RANCH GOLF CLUB - page 383
18. LA QUINTA GOLF CLUB (Mountain Course) - page 528
19. THE LINKS AT SPANISH BAY - page 265
20. SANDPIPER GOLF COURSE - page 340

(Courtesy of Mark Soltau)

CALIFORNIA'S TOP 20 PUBLIC COURSES

The courses selected were rated by a panel of golf officials, golf writers and golf enthusiasts. The criteria used in selecting the "Top 25" included: the degree of difficulty, playability according to personal preference, attitude of shop staff and the treatment the golfer receives at the course, and finally the architecture and number of demanding holes.

1. PEBBLE BEACH GOLF LINKS - page 267
2. SPYGLASS HILL GOLF COURSE - page 270
3. PGA WEST (Stadium Course) - page 538
4. PASATIEMPO GOLF COURSE - page 260
5. SANDPIPER GOLF COURSE - page 340
6. POPPY HILLS GOLF COURSE - page 271
7. LA PURISIMA GOLF COURSE - page 337
8. TORREY PINES GOLF COURSE (South Course) - page 562
9. INDUSTRY HILLS GOLF COURSE (Eisenhower Course) - page 430
10. HALF MOON BAY GOLF LINKS - page 191
11. MORENO VALLEY RANCH GOLF COURSE - page 485
12. RANCHO MURIETA COUNTRY CLUB (North Course) - page 142
13. LA QUINTA HOTEL GOLF COURSE (Dune Course) - page 527
14. THE LINKS AT SPANISH BAY - page 265
15. CHARDONNAY GOLF CLUB - page 108
16. RANCHO CANADA GOLF COURSE (West Course) - page 277
17. BROOKSIDE GOLF COURSE (North Course) - page 417
18. LOS SERRANOS GOLF COURSE (South Course) - page 444
19. RECREATION PARK GOLF COURSE - page 449
20. ANCIL HOFFMAN GOLF COURSE - page 123

(Courtesy of California GOLF Journal)

POPULIST POLL

AND THE WINNERS ARE.... Professional golfers and those within the golfing industry are generally the people who vote for the best courses, the most difficult courses, and so forth. We thought it would prove interesting to find out what you, the folks who play the courses and pay the fees, have to say on the same subject. So, in the previous edition of this book, we asked you to send in *your* votes for your favorite courses in California. The results matched the pros in some cases, but we think a few others will surprise you. The populist vote:

1. SPYGLASS HILL GOLF COURSE - page 270
2. PASATIEMPO GOLF COURSE - page 260
3. POPPY HILLS GOLF COURSE - page 271
4. PEBBLE BEACH GOLF LINKS - page 267
5. EDGEWOOD TAHOE GOLF COURSE - page 148
6. BODEGA HARBOUR GOLF LINKS - page 84
7. OLYMPIC CLUB - page 173
8. CHARDONNAY GOLF CLUB - page 108
9. OJAI VALLEY INN & COUNTRY CLUB - page 356
10. Three tied for 10th:
    SANDPIPER GOLF COURSE - page 350
    LA PURISIMA GOLF COURSE - page 337
    SAN FRANCISCO GOLF CLUB - page 171

INDEX

Szody, June (Manager/Pro) 75
Szwedzinski, Tom (Pro) 385
Szydloski, Scott (Supt.) 514

T

TABLE MOUNTAIN GOLF
   COURSE 71
Taft 351
Tahoe City 148
TAHOE CITY GOLF AND COUN-
   TRY CLUB 148
TAHOE DONNER GOLF AND
   COUNTRY CLUB 145
TAHOE PARADISE GOLF
   COURSE 149
TAK Ladies Invitational 195
Talbot, Bob (Pro) 357
Talkington, Larry (Pro) 345
TALL PINES GOLF COURSE 70
Tall Tree Invitational Tournament 208
Talley, Doug (Pro) 151
TAMARISK COUNTRY CLUB 509
Tarzana 393, 394
Tatum, Frank "Sandy" 265
Taylor, Brad (Manager/Pro/Supt.) 327
Taylor, Jason (Pro) 480
Taylor, Larry (Director) 441
Taylor, Terry (Pro) 359
Taylorsville 76
TAYMAN PARK GOLF COURSE
   90
Tehachapi 354, 363
Temecula 493, 494, 551
TEMECULA CREEK INN GOLF
   COURSE 493
Thanksgiving Tournament 195
Theilade, Jr. John (Manager/Pro) 305
Theis, Leonard (Supt.) 314
Thigpin, Jim (Manager) 162
Thobois, Jayne 468
Thomas, Alan (Pro) 231
Thomas, Cheryl (Pro) 477
Thomas, George C. 356, 399, 400,
   401, 402
Thomas, Harrie (Manager) 100
Thomas, Randy (Pro) 141
Thompson, Grant (Supt.) 280
Thompson, Ron (Supt.) 309
Thormann, Jerry (Pro) 196
Thousand Oaks 382, 389, 390
Thousand Oaks City Championships
   390
Thousand Palms 510
Thrasher, Rex (Supt.) 87
Three Rivers 318, 319
THREE RIVERS GOLF COURSE
   318
THUNDERBIRD COUNTRY CLUB
   517
THUNDERBIRD GOLF COURSE
   212
Thuney, Andy (Pro) 439
Thurman, Kim (Pro) 54
Thurston, Eric (Pro) 300
Tiedeman, Steve (Supt.) 95
TIERRA DEL SOL 364
Tilden Park 163
TILDEN PARK GOLF COURSE 163
Tillema, Robert (Supt.) 301
Tillinghast, A.W. 171
Times-Tribune Junior Tournament
   200
Timke, Jim (Supt.) 499
Toledo, Estaban 204
Tompkins, Joe (Supt.) 299
Tonelli, Lou (Supt.) 172
TONY LEMA GOLF COURSE 187
Tor, Pete (Co-Manager) 115

Torrance 405
TORREY PINES GOLF COURSE
   562
Toschi, Tom (Pro) 192
Toulumne River 236
Towle, Bruce (Pro) 145
Town & Country Women's Golf Tour-
   nament 200
Tracy 235
TRACY GOLF AND COUNTRY
   CLUB 235
Tracy, Daniel R. (Supt.) 274
Trans-Mississippi Mid-Amateur
   Championship (1991) 398
Transamerica Open 101
Travis AFB 110
Treasure Island 270
Treece, Terry (Pro) 292
Treglown, Jon (Pro) 392
Trejo, Cachi (Pro) 553
Trent Jones, Jr., Robert 193
Tres Dias 431
Tres Pinos 286
Trevino, Bob (Manager) 286
Trevino, Lee 538
Trinity Alps 50
TRINITY ALPS GOLF AND COUN-
   TRY CLUB 50
Trinity River 49
Triplett, Foy "Cotton" (Supt.) 116
Troche, Jesse (Supt.) 510
Truckee 76, 78, 145, 146, 147
Truckee River 149
Tucker, Darien 39
Tuhn, Dennis (Assist. Pro) 64
Tujunga 413
Tulare 318, 319
TULARE GOLF COURSE 319
Tule River 321
Tulelake 43
Tuolumne River 235
Turlock 245
TURLOCK GOLF AND COUNTRY
   CLUB 245
Turner, Campbell (Supt.) 259
Twain Harte 242
TWAIN HARTE GOLF AND COUN-
   TRY CLUB 242
Twenty Nine Palms 497, 498
TWIN LAKES GOLF COURSE 341
Tyler, Bobby (Supt.) 50
Tzathas, Spero (Manager) 570

U

U.S. Amateur 383, (qualifier) 444
U.S. Amateur Championship (1976)
   401
U.S. Golf Association 278
U.S. NAVY GOLF COURSE 274
U.S. Open 104, 171, 173, 267,
   (1948) 399, 486
U.S. Senior Open 148
U.S. Senior Women's Amateur Cham-
   pionship 234
U.S. Women's Amateur 260
U.S. Women's Open 129
UCLA Bruins 401
Uhl, Rusty (Pro) 520
Ukiah 64
Ukiah Junior Open 64
UKIAH MUNICIPAL GOLF
   COURSE 64
Ulmer, Leanne (Pro) 475
United Express Pro-Scratch 299
University of California, Los Angeles
   401
Unrue, Dan (Pro) 336
Unruh, Tom (Supt.) 129

Upland 428
UPLAND HILLS COUNTRY CLUB
   428
Urner, John (Pro) 550
U.S. Open (sectional qualifying,
   1981) 197
USGA Boys' National Championship
   172
USGA Junior Championship 199, 299
USGA Publinx 121
USGA Senior Women's Amateur 129
USGA Seniors Open (qualifying) 451
USGA Women's Amateur Champion-
   ship 129, 439
USO Bob Hope Charity Golf Event
   502
Utterback, Don (PGA Appr.) 333
Uyemura, Frank (Supt.) 583

V

Vacaville 106
Vaccaro, Al (Pro) 185
Valencia 360
VALENCIA COUNTRY CLUB 360
VALLE GRANDE GOLF COURSE
   353
Vallejo 109, 111, 153, 154
Vallejo City Open 154
VALLEJO GOLF COURSE 154
VALLEY CLUB OF MONTECITO,
   THE 346
VALLEY GARDENS GOLF
   COURSE 259
VALLEY HI COUNTRY CLUB 132
VALLEY OAKS GOLF COURSE
   317
Valley Springs 240
VAN BUSKIRK GOLF COURSE
   229
Van Lienden, Mark (Supt.) 47
Van Nuys 394, 396
VAN NUYS GOLF COURSE 394
Vandenberg AFB 335
VANDENBERG AFB GOLF
   COURSE 335
Vaubel, Harold (Supt.) 544
Vazquez, Vincent (Supt.) 393
Venetian Gardens 223
VENETIAN GARDENS GOLF
   COURSE 223
Venice 400
Ventura 347, 357, 358, 359
Ventura County Championships 348
Ver Brugge, Maurice (Pro) 185
VERDUGO HILLS GOLF COURSE
   413
Verhunce, Val (Pro) 94
Veteran's Administration Hospital
   385
VIA VERDE COUNTRY CLUB 431
VICTORIA GOLF CLUB 482
VICTORIA GOLF COURSE 406
Victorville 371, 473
VICTORVILLE MUNICIPAL GOLF
   COURSE 371
Videtta, Steve (Pro) 177
Vigil, Rick (Manager) 335
VILLAGE COUNTRY CLUB, THE
   336
VILLAGE GREEN GOLF COURSE
   298
VILLAGES GOLF AND COUNTRY
   CLUB, THE 216
Villalobos, Phil (Supt.) 515
VINTAGE CLUB, THE 525
VIRGINIA COUNTRY CLUB 433
Visalia 302, 303, 313, 317, 318
VISALIA COUNTRY CLUB 318

Ray A. March has been a been a sports journalist since a
teenager, and recalls that his first interview question of a golfer
came at the 1949 Bing Crosby National Pro-Am when his
father introduced him to Ben Hogan. As March shook hands
with Hogan, who would go on to win the tournament that year,
March astutely asked: "How do you do?" He grew up on the
Monterey Peninsula, and since those formative years his arti-
cles on golf have appeared in magazines and newspapers
nationally and internationally, including *Time, Palm Springs
Life, Robb Report,* Associated Press, and the *San Francisco
Chronicle.* He is considered an authority on the history of
Pebble Beach, and is currently writing a book on Pebble Beach
for *GolfDigest,* in addition to being a consulting editor for that
publication for the 1992 U.S. Open.

RECREATION TITLES AVAILABLE FROM FOGHORN PRESS

■ **The Complete Guide, Golf Series**

California Golf by Ray A. March describing more than 700 golf courses. $16.95

Hawaii Golf by George Fuller describing every golf course in the golfer's paradise of Hawaii. $16.95

■ **The Complete Guide, Camping Series**

California Camping by Tom Stienstra describing 1500 campgrounds. $16.95

Pacific Northwest Camping by Tom Stienstra describing 1400 campgrounds in Washington and Oregon. $16.95

Rocky Mountain Camping by Tom Stienstra describing 1200 campgrounds in Colorado, Wyoming and Montana. $14.95

PLUS *The Camper's Companion* by Hal Kahn & Rick Greenspan, a pack-along guide to better outdoor trips for hikers, campers, cyclists, canoeists. $12.95

■ **Outdoor Adventure and Getaway Guides**

Great Outdoor Getaways to the Bay Area and Beyond by Tom Stienstra describing secret and little known camping, hiking and fishing spots. $16.95

Great Outdoor Adventures of Hawaii by Rick Carroll describing more than 120 unusual outdoor adventures. $14.95

■ **For a complete catalog, call or write Foghorn Press.**

ORDER INFORMATION

To order by phone, call toll free **(800)842-7477 or (415)241-9550.** We accept Visa or Mastercard. To order by mail, enclose your name, street address and phone number along with a check or money order or Visa/Mastercard number (include exp. date) for the total book amount plus $3.50 shipping.

Mail to:

Foghorn Press
555 De Haro Street
The Boiler Room, #220
San Francisco, CA 94107

(*Books are shipped via UPS within 48 hours of receipt of your order)

Courtesy Discount: If you currently own an old edition of a Foghorn Press title, you may mail in the copyright page from that edition with an order for a new edition of the same book and take a $3 courtesy discount off the price. Call or write for more information. Only redeemable through Foghorn Press.

TRADE DISTRIBUTION

Book trade: Distributor: Publishers Group West, 4065 Hollis Street, Emeryville, CA 94608. (415)658-3453; (800)365-3453. Wholesalers: Ingram Book Co., Baker & Taylor, Pacific Pipeline, Bookpeople, L-S Distributors and Inland Book Company

Golf trade: Distributor: The Booklegger, 13100 Grass Valley Avenue, Grass Valley, CA 95945. (916)272-1556; U.S. (800)262-1556; Canada(800)235-1556

Libraries: Quality Books, Unique Books or Foghorn direct

Outdoor wholesalers: Sunbelt, Alpenbooks, Mountain 'N Air, Universal Telescopic, Maverick Distributors, Falcon Press and Menasha Ridge

Canada: Raincoast Books

UK and Europe: World Leisure Marketing

GROUP SALES

Please call the publisher directly to arrange tee prizes, corporate gifts, amenities and other group sales. (800)842-7477